THE POLITICAL ETHICS OF JEAN-FRANÇOIS LYOTARD
AND JACQUES DERRIDA

BIBLIOTHECA
EPHEMERIDUM THEOLOGICARUM LOVANIENSIUM

UNIVERSITÉ CATHOLIQUE DE LOUVAIN   KATHOLIEKE UNIVERSITEIT LEUVEN
LOUVAIN-LA-NEUVE   LEUVEN

BIBLIOTHECA EPHEMERIDUM THEOLOGICARUM LOVANIENSIUM

CCXXXVI

THE POLITICAL ETHICS
OF JEAN-FRANÇOIS LYOTARD
AND JACQUES DERRIDA

BY

GEORGES DE SCHRIJVER

UITGEVERIJ PEETERS
LEUVEN – PARIS – WALPOLE, MA
2010

A catalogue record for this book is available from the Library of Congress.

ISBN 978-90-429-2327-0
D/2010/0602/66

© 2010 – Peeters, Bondgenotenlaan 153, B-3000 Leuven (Belgium)

PREFACE

It is almost a truism to say that every book has a history. This is also
true for this book. My acquaintance with Lyotard and Derrida dates back
to the mid 1980s. At that moment I was busy teaching Habermas' *Theory of Communicative Action* in my courses of foundational theology
at the Theological Faculty of the Catholic University Leuven. I tried to
apply this theory to a renewed understanding of ecclesial life in the midst
of a world that was rapidly becoming detached from its religious roots.
But I soon discovered that this attempt at transposing basic elements of
the Christian faith to the key of secular existence had its limits. For the
means on which this transposition rested was a consensus formation
whose procedures of accountability remained within the boundaries of
Europe's hegemonic thinking vis-à-vis other cultures. Habermas' consensus theory was thoroughly modern and utterly European. Confronted
with this difficulty I was fortunate to familiarize myself with Lyotard's
epoch making publication *The Postmodern Condition* (1979). I was
struck by its claim that only daring moves that depart from general consensus are capable of ushering in real innovations. Because of its leap
outside modernity, Lyotard's book was an eye-opener for me, so much
so that I also began to study Derrida's deconstructionism which, in its
own way, was undoing uniform (European) patterns of thought. It was
also a period in which Nietzsche, the harsh critic of modernity, came to
be more in vogue than Marx, soon followed by the implosion of the
Eastern Bloc (1989): an event that Lyotard seemed to have predicted
with his battle-cry of the end of the grand stories – of political regimes
that were able to rally people around the same ideal only by establishing a reign of terror.

Parallel to my study of the postmodern criticism of modernity I had
also been examining the newest developments in Latin American Theologies of Liberation. In 1996 I organized a symposium around this topic
with a discussion paper 'Paradigm Shift in Third-World Theologies of
Liberation: From Socio-Economic Analysis to Cultural Analysis?'[1]
In this paper I touched upon the breakdown of the European communist
regimes in which I saw with Zygmunt Bauman "the end of modernity,

---

1. Later published in *Liberation Theologies on Shifting Grounds*, ed. G. De Schrijver,
BETL, 134 (Leuven: Leuven University Press/Peeters, 1998) 1-83.

for communism had desperately attempted to make modernity work"[2] But clearly had failed. I also pointed to the dissipation of the unitary dream of liberation that till now had animated the Latin American liberation theologians. This unitary dream had been replaced with diversified movements of liberation, such as native theology (*teología India*), feminist and ecological theologies, and local activist groups organized around gaining greater respect for human rights. The landscape of liberation had undergone the metamorphosis of diversification, something that the rigid schemes of a Marxist-inspired socio-economic analysis had obstructed for so long. I opined that this release of 'local' energies could only benefit the struggle for human dignity in the 'South'.

In order to corroborate the postmodern claim for diversification I had, in the same paper, given a succinct presentation of Lyotard's notion of the sublime. I select two points from it: 1. In the wake of Kant, Lyotard underlines the fact that the sublime relates to an Idea of Reason whose content cannot be made present in empirical reality. This unpresentability is crucial to Lyotard because it gives the lie to the claim of encompassing, totalitarian systems: "The experience of the sublime, in terms of the majestic void, throws one off balance because of its entirely unpresentable character; it forbids any attempt at establishing a totalizing discourse, one disrespectful of alterity."[3] 2. Yet, going beyond Kant, Lyotard honors this majestic void as the amazing cradle of pluralization, so much so that from now onward respect for the different becomes part of one's experience of the sublime: "Lyotard's dealing with Kant has not only encouraged him to acknowledge the existence of an unfathomable noumenal ground beyond empirical reality; it also had led him to suggest that, instead of qualifying this ground as ungraspable 'ultimate unity' (as Kant did), one would do better to refer to it in terms of 'ultimate heterogeneity'."[4] The enlargement, in Lyotard, of the experience of the sublime to include the tenacious expectation of the break-through of respect for plurality was an issue that kept on intriguing me.

I have already mentioned my growing interest in Derrida. In my courses of the early 1990s I had shown that he espoused, to be sure, Nietzsche's theory of interpretation, but that he omitted any treatment of the latter's vital affirmation of life. Nietzsche succeeded in giving an aesthetic justification to life in spite of the inevitability of having to live with an avalanche of fragmental interpretations with which to decipher a

---

2. *Ibid.*, 32; with reference to Z. Bauman, *Intimations of Postmodernity* (New York/London: Routledge, 1992) 222.
3. *Liberation Theologies on Shifting Grounds*, 38.
4. *Ibid.*, 39.

world bereft of proper consistency. Yet, this absence of metaphysical anchorage also prompted him to rely on the vital impulses of his life-force; he had experienced that this life-force was to increase in intensity when daring to face up to the hardships of sickness and decay. This straining of the 'will to power' recedes to the background in Derrida's assimilation of Nietzsche. Derrida only retains from Nietzsche the fact that we live in the house of language: "Our concepts are designed to linguistically organize our human life-world. We must content ourselves with this linguistic construct – it is our house to live in – and give up the illusion that this construct is grounded in a reality prior to it."[5] The whole focus is on the erring from fragment to fragment, away from the alleged center that an age-long tradition of metaphysics had constructed, and which must now allow itself to be deconstructed.

In 2001 Prof. Jacques Haers and some promotees of mine organized a symposium in my honor, on the occasion of my retirement from Catholic University Leuven. In the keynote I delivered, I focused on a possible abuse that could be made of the postmodern recognition of diversity: using it merely as a launching pad for the retrieval of pre-modern religious thought forms. This is what, in my opinion, happened in John Milbank's neo-orthodox theology. Milbank welcomed the breakdown of unitary centers; for it allowed him to highlight the particular narrative of Christianity: "In postmodernity there are infinitely many possible versions of truth, inseparable from particular narratives."[6] But it did not take long before Milbank presented his neo-Augustianism as the sole truth from which to condemn all other narratives for their nascent nihilism: only those dwelling in the 'city of God' are able to lead a peaceful existence, whereas the outsiders tend to spread waves of violence. I pointed out that Milbank, in spite of paying lip-service to postmodern fragmentation, opted in fact "for a ghettoizing type of church," one that no longer believed, as modern theology had done, that "the most deeply secular concerns are also the most deeply religious concerns."[7] A fine example of modern theology is Karl Rahner's theology of the universal offer of God's grace, a theology that had no place in Milbank's ghettoizing theology. But is genuine theology possible without fostering a universal

5. G. De Schrijver, "Postmodernity and Theology," *Philippiniana Sacra* 27, n. 81 (1992) 446.
6. G. De Schrijver, "Mediations in Theology," *Mediations in Theology. Georges De Schrijver's Wager and Liberation Theologies*, ed. J. Haers, et al. (Leuven, Paris and Dudley, MA: Peeters 2003) 25; citing from J. Milbank, "Postmodern Critical Augustianism," *Modern Theology* 7 (April 1991) 225.
7. De Schrijver, "Mediations in Theology," 63

perspective? This is the question I tackled in my book *Theological Debates in Europe: Their Impact on Interreligious Dialogue*.[8] The same question must be raised, when it comes to working out a genuine philosophical ethics.

Having become emeritus professor, I began to accept regular annual teaching stints in Ateneo de Manila University, The Philippines, Saint Joseph's Major Seminary in Ikot Ekpene, Nigeria, and Dharmaram College, Bangalore, India. In 2005 I got an invitation from Dharmaram College to give a series of lectures on Derrida's postmodern ethics. It is only with great hesitancy that I accepted the invitation. Up to that time, I had been reading various Derridean texts, those in which he deconstructed the revered products of western systematic philosophy. So, I wondered, how could a genuine ethics possibly come out of such a negativistic approach? Nonetheless I told my contact person in Dharmaram College that I was willing to do further reading of Derrida's later writings to see whether and at which juncture a turn towards a positive ethics might have taken place. I felt encouraged to do so because, on three different occasions – in 1997, 1999, and 2001 –, I had seen Derrida act 'live' during his interventions at the *Conferences on Religion and Postmodernism*, organized by Villanova University, Philadelphia, U.S.A. From these interventions I could still recall the radical ethical stand he took in matters of unconditional hospitality and forgiveness. So, in February 2006 I gave the lectures on Derrida that I had been asked to give at Dharmaram College. They became the foundation of a book that gradually began to take shape.

That the book would become a diptych was from the outset clear to me. Parallel to my further reading of Derrida's later writings, I had also reassumed the examination of Lyotard's distinctive interpretation of Kant's notion of the sublime. I discovered that both Derrida and Lyotard placed a heavy accent on things that can and must be thought but whose full realization could never present itself in empirical reality. I began to understand that what both of them had in mind was a new type of universality: a universality that can hardly be imagined but the lure of which takes one to an open, cosmopolitan space beyond the Eurocentrism of the grand stories of modernity (Lyotard), at the other side of the self-referential definitions obtained by a phenomenological analysis of presence-to-oneself (Derrida). This new, worldwide universality is basically a universality without exclusion (Lyotard), rendered thematic by Derrida in terms of hospitality without reserve, without limiting conditions. Lyotard's

---

8. G. De Schrijver, *Theological Debates in Europe: Their Impact on Interreligious Dialogue* (Bangalore: Dharmaram Publications, 2004) 347.

fascination with the unpresentable (the mysterious cradle of pluralization) is definitely intertwined with Derrida's aphanology and its evocation of the excess of the 'impossible thing to come' (impossible democracy, justice etc.).

I cannot conclude this preface without expressing some words of thanks. Thanks to my former students and promotees, especially Prof. Daniel Franklin Pilario (Manila), who encouraged me to pursue a line of thought in postmodern reflection that would not lead to a provincial retrieval of pre-modern thought forms, as is often the case in so-called postmodern theologies. Thanks to the Reading Committee that decided on the publication of this book in the prestigious BETL Series. Thanks to the libraries of the Theological Faculty and the Philosophical Institute of the Catholic University Leuven. A special thanks to Prof. David Gentry-Akin (Moraga, California) who has been so generous as to edit the whole bulk of this work.

Prof. Emeritus Georges De Schrijver s.j.
Faculty of Theology
Catholic University Leuven

TABLE OF CONTENTS

PART TWO
JACQUES DERRIDA

CHAPTER SIX
THE NIETZSCHEAN INFLUENCE 175

CHAPTER SEVEN
DERRIDA AND PHENOMENOLOGY 207

INTRODUCTION

Some thirty years ago Jean-François Lyotard announced the end of the grand narratives. No wonder that his name is associated with postmodernity. Postmodern features also surface in Jacques Derrida's relentless deconstruction of monolithic centers. It is evident then that a study like this which aims at bringing into focus the political ethics of Lyotard and Derrida cannot abstain from delving into the phenomenon of postmodernity. 'Postmodernity' as a cultural milieu is not exactly the same as 'postmodernism' in architecture and literature, where the qualification postmodern is linked to a daring novelty in style and expression. Rather postmodernity is best understood as a protest movement that – from within the evolving construct of modern civilization – voices its dissatisfaction with certain key-dogmas of modernity that have lost their credibility. To these key-dogmas belong the belief in a single truth and sense of reality, the superiority of Western, European civilization, and a philosophy of history that sees in the European social and political organization of life the goal to which all other civilizations should aspire. Postmodern people, on the contrary, value plurality, respect for otherness, and liberation from the constraints of the unilateralism of modern, logical planning.

Various attempts have been made at explaining the emergence of the postmodern mind. In 1989 the Italian philosopher Gianni Vattimo published a work, translated three years later as *The Transparent Society*, in which he attempted to pinpoint the main factors that played a decisive role in the birth of the postmodern society. He singled out two of them: the spread of the mass media and the crisis of European colonialism. The mass media creates a consumer market in which a plurality of world views are available; it is up to consumers to make choices from amongst the often conflicting messages: "Newspapers, radio, television, what is now called telematics have been decisive in bringing about the dissolution of centralized perspectives [...] The increase in possible information of the myriad forms of reality makes it increasingly difficult to conceive of a single reality."[1] Another fact that, for Vattimo,

1. G. Vattimo, *The Transparent Society*, trans. D. Webb (Baltimore, MD: The Johns Hopkins University Press, 1992) 5-7.

also accounts for postmodernity's decentering was the crisis in European colonialism after the Second World War. Asian and African colonized countries shook off the yoke of foreign dominance; this enfranchisement dealt a serious blow to the European self-image. Europeans used to regard themselves as the champions of a superior civilization they felt they had to export to other parts of the world. But revolts in the colonies showed that their civilizing mission rested on the use of force and coercion: "The so-called 'primitive' peoples colonized by Europe in the good and rightful name of 'superior' and more evolved civilization have rebelled, making a unilinear and centralized history *de facto* problematic. The European ideal of humanity has been revealed as one ideal amongst others, not necessarily worse, but unable, without violence, to obtain as the true essence of man, of all men."[2] The new situation put an end to the unquestioned Western dream of molding the whole world after the pattern of its own center. The right to 'otherness' – of alien peoples with their own traditions and ways of life – posed a serious challenge to a great many intellectuals, including those of France, the homeland of Lyotard and to a certain extent also of Derrida.

As incomplete as Vattimo's analysis might be, it does shed a light on the mindset of Lyotard and Derrida in their early period of philosophizing, for both had in their own way a colonial experience. Born in 1924, Jean-François Lyotard, was 26 years old when he got a teaching job in the lycée of Constantine in the then French colony Algeria. He would stay there from 1950 to 1952, enough time to get first hand information about the dire plight of the peasants who were preparing a war of revolt against their colonizers. When looking at this period in retrospect, he wrote: "I owe Constantine a picture of what it was for me then, when I arrived from the Sorbonne to teach in its high school. But with what colors should I paint what astonished me, that is, the immensity of the injustice? An entire people, from a great civilization, wronged, humiliated, denied their identity."[3] Indeed, for him it was a real scandal that France denied Algeria its freedom in the name of the Rights of Man. Once back in France, where he taught for seven years at a school for the sons of military personnel at La Flèche, he engaged in critical reflection with the leftist group *Socialisme ou barbarie*, and

2. *Ibid.*, 4.
3. J.-F. Lyotard, *Political Writings*, trans. B. Readings and K. Geiman (Minneapolis, MN: University of Minnesota Press, 1993) 170. The chapter referred to was originally published in idem, *La guerre des Algériens* (Paris: Galilée, 1989).

contributed various articles to the group's journal on the Algerian war of independence that was launched in 1954. In these articles, later published in his *Political Writings*, he conducted a meticulous economic and political analysis of the social classes that were engaged in the war of independence, pondering which chance Algeria stood of becoming a real socialist state after independence. This analysis brought him into conflict with the French communist party which Lyotard had blamed for taking an overly cautious position regarding Algerian independence throughout the eight years of the Algerian war. Following the directives of Moscow, the communist party, – instead of siding with the Algerian Front of National Liberation (FNL) whose leaders came from the Muslim proletariat – rather wagered on the Marxist dialectics of history. According to this dialectical understanding, the new post-colonial independent states must first be ruled by a bourgeois government before the proletariat, turned in the meantime into industrial proletariat, would be in a position to seize power. Lyotard's involvement in this battle with communism laid the foundation of his later skepticism about the value of grand narratives.

Jacques Derrida was born in 1930 in El-Biar, Algeria, into a Jewish family which had lived in Algeria for five generations (a great many Jews settled in North Africa after their expulsion from Spain in 1492). Under the French occupation, the Algerian Jews developed a favorable penchant toward France. The reason for this is that the Crémieux decrees of 1870 made the Algerian Jews automatically French citizens. The same privilege was offered to the Algerian Muslims – the large majority of the population – under the condition, however, that they renounce the customary Islamic laws, which included the establishment of shariah courts to regulate marriages, divorces, and hereditary rights, and to punish offenders. So, few Muslims were willing to apply for French citizenship, since this step for them boiled down to apostasy. The French colonizers had not only imposed French as the official language; they had also shut down Koranic schools. As a member of a privileged group, the young Derrida could thus hardly be considered a full-blood Algerian, although the Algerian Jews had good relations with their Muslim neighbors. During the Second World War, under the German-controlled Vichy regime of General Henri Pétain in France, the situation was to change dramatically. Pétain revoked the Crémieux decrees and at once the Algerian Jews lost the privilege of French citizenship. Derrida was then twelve years old. In his later biographical accounts he writes: "they expelled from the lycée de Ben Aknoun in 1942 a little black and very Arab Jew who understood nothing about it."[4] The little boy had overnight become a Jew and was no longer French. A teacher said that day: "French culture is not made for little Jews,"[5] a remark that made the young Derrida feel like an outsider: "thus expelled, I became the outside."[6] From now on he had to attend an informal school for Jewish children and wait until 1947 to again join French intellectual life with his studies at the Sorbonne in Paris. In an 1992 interview he summarizes his Algerian experience in terms of "Vichy, official anti-semitism, The Allied landing [in North Africa] at the end of 1942, [and] the terrible colonial repression of Algerian resistance in 1945 at the time of the first serious outbursts heralding the Algerian war."[7]

True, Lyotard's and Derrida's colonial experience was not anchored deeply enough to turn them into proponents of post-colonialism, as heralded, e.g., by the Martiniquian psychiatrist Frantz Fanon. When Fanon wrote in 1961 his book *Les damnés de la terre* (*The Wretched of the Earth*), the classic of post-colonial studies, he had taken part in the armed resistance of the Algerian FNL, until he was expelled from the country. In most of his publications Fanon reflects on the dynamics of 'indigenous consciousness' from the perspective of the subjective awareness of people of color. Lyotard's and Derrida's itinerary will be different. They will, each in their own way, examine the epochal dissolution of centralizing world views, the aspect which Vattimo brought to the fore.

For Lyotard, this honoring of the fragmentary already surfaces in his early works. In *Libidinal Economy* (1975)[8] he shows the importance of the singular and distinct events that emerge from libidinal impulses; in their felt presence they have the power to renew structures which without them would become sterile. In terms of styles his means: there is no overall dominant structure in the text; the text is open to several competing modes of reading, and multiple interpretations. *Lessons on Paganism* (1977),[9] in turn, inaugurates a revisiting of polytheism; it celebrates the healthiness of a civilization in which various gods are allowed to act

---

4. J. Derrida and G. Bennington, *Jacques Derrida*, trans. G. Bennington (Chicago, IL: University of Chicago Press, 1999) 58.

5. *Ibid.*, 326.

6. *Ibid.*, 289.

7. J. Derrida and D. Attridge, "This Strange Institution Called Literature: An Interview with Jacques Derrida," *Acts of Literature*, ed. D. Attridge, trans. G. Bennington and R. Bowlby (New York; Routledge, 1992) 38-39.

8. J.-F. Lyotard, *Économie libidinale* (Paris: Les Éditions de Minuit, 1975).

9. J.-F. Lyotard, *Instructions païennes* (Paris: Galilée, 1977).

in competition upon the scene, thus removing to the background the pallid face of one single deity. Reality is constituted by the happenings of singular events: there is no universal judgment that can do justice to all of them in their particularity. Paganism is the abandonment of one universal judgment in order to give room to a multiplicity of judgments regarding particular events. Justice of multiplicities requires a multiplicity of justices. In the work that made him famous, *The Postmodern Condition: A Report on Human Knowledge* (1979),[10] Lyotard deepens this insight to include the domain of knowledge production. With the dawn of a computerized society he foresees that new branches of knowledge are going to shake off the yoke of an encompassing scientific system that used to give them their legitimacy. The success of these branched-off specialties rests on their performative inventiveness, which no longer stands in need of an overall justification: "The diminished tasks of research have become compartmentalized and no one masters them all [...] This is what the postmodern world is all about. Most people have lost the nostalgia for the lost [grand] narrative. It in no way follows that they are reduced to barbarity. What saves them from it is their knowledge that legitimation can only spring from their own linguistic practice and communicational interaction."[11]

With his deconstruction Derrida pursues the same goal: the dismantling of self-sufficient overarching systems. In *Of Grammatology* (1967)[12] he draws the consequences of de Saussure's semiology which posits that signs (words) refer to other signs: they are part of a (sometimes) hidden web of significations: "Writing is not a sign of a sign, except if one says it of all signs, which would be more profoundly true."[13] This leads him to doubt the hierarchies and subordinations set up by systems that deem themselves immune from the influence of their surrounding. The classical superiority of speech over writing is an example in case. Speech is more highly valued than writing because it mirrors the 'presence to oneself' of the speaking subject, a resonance that is not to be found in writing. Yet, Derrida asks, why should this assurance of self-presence, which underlies the whole tradition of Western metaphysics, be taken for granted? Measured against the interconnected web of significations, of

---

10. J.-F. Lyotard, *La condition postmoderne: Rapport sur le savoir* (Paris: Les Éditions de Minuit, 1979).

11. J.-F. Lyotard, *The Postmodern Condition: A Report on Knowledge*, trans. G. Bennington and B. Marsuni (Manchester: Manchester University Press, 1984) 41.

12. J. Derrida, *De la grammatologie* (Paris: Les Éditions de Minuit, 1967).

13. J. Derrida, *Of Grammatology*, trans. G. Spivak et al. (Baltimore, MD: The Johns Hopkins University Press, 1976) 43.

which one becomes aware in distanced writing, this exaltation of full presence is sheer illusion. Full presence can only be a floating moment against a hidden background of absence. On closer inspection, philosophies of presence deconstruct themselves in that an attentive reading discovers in them elements that contradict their own position. In a 1997 Round Table discussion, Derrida states: "What is the law of this self-deconstruction, this 'auto-deconstruction'? Deconstruction is not a method or some tool that you apply to something from the outside. Deconstruction is something which happens and which happens inside: there is a deconstruction at work within Plato's work, for instance. As my colleagues know, each time I study Plato, I try to find some heterogeneity in his own corpus [... something] that is incompatible with this supposed system of Plato."[14] With his deconstructive reading of classics – also the classics of modernity – Derrida seeks to demonstrate their non-avowed limitations, or what is worse: their hidden mechanism of subordination and exclusion. For him, the practice of deconstruction is, first of all, a matter of justice, justice done to the outcasts and unjustifiably downgraded.

On the merit of their academic qualifications and their critical publications Lyotard and Derrida both earned academic positions in Paris. From 1968 to 1970 Lyotard was *chargé de recherches* at the Centre National de la Recherche Scientifique. In the early 1970s he was appointed to the University of Paris VIII, Vincennes; in 1972 he was made *maître de conférences*, and in 1987 he became Professor Emeritus at Vincennes. In the 1980s and 90s, because of the success of his work *The Postmodern Condition*, he lectured widely outside of France: at the University of California at Irvine; at Emory University in Atlanta, and was a visiting professor at Johns Hopkins, the University of California at Berkeley and San Diego, the University of Minnesota, and the Université de Montréal, Canada. He died in 1998. Derrida (1930-2004), on the other hand, had a less stable position in Paris. From 1964 to 1984 he taught the History of Philosophy at the *École normale supérieure*, which he would soon combine with a teaching post at Johns Hopkins University, U.S.A, and with visiting professor stints at Yale, Cornell and New York University. Having defended his *thèse d'état* at the University of Paris in 1980 through presentation of a selection of his published works, he was appointed in 1982 the chairman of the non-conventional institution *Collège International de Philosophie*, followed in 1983 by his election to a new position in the *École pratique des hautes études* (social

---

14. "The Villanova Round Table: A Conversation with Jacques Derrida," *Deconstruction in a Nutshell*, ed. J. Caputo (New York: Fordham University Press, 1997) 9.

sciences) in Paris, whereas in the USA he became Professor of the Humanities at the University of California at Irvine in 1986.

Until now I have sketched 'the postmodern' from the standpoint of Europe, of a Europe divided into East and West. How will this picture look after the fall of the Berlin Wall (1989), that is: in the era of globalization? The sociologist Zygmunt Bauman, who includes globalization in his analysis of postmodernity, lists in this respect the growing gap worldwide between the wealthy and the poor, whereby the 'Third World' stands as symbol for dire poverty. For him, the versatility extolled by the postmodern mind eventually led to a parting of the ways: on the one hand are the 'tourists' who joyously travel throughout the whole world (cosmopolitan businessmen feel at home in whichever Hilton Hotel they happen to find themselves anywhere on the globe); on the other hand are the 'vagabonds' who have no stable place to live and are not welcome in the place in which they would like to settle down.[15] In the age of globalization these two aspects are part of the postmodern condition. With globalization Bauman mainly has in view two aspects: the communication of information that stretches across borders and communities, and international financial transactions that are no longer effectively regulated by the nation states. Did Lyotard and Derrida face up to this new situation? How did they assess the triumph of global capitalism?

For Lyotard, the answer to these questions is not straightforward, for his book *The Postmodern Condition* can be read as a plea for the liberal market. In it he sketched the future of an inventive, computerized society that is constantly on the move thanks to a techno-science freed of the burden of centralizing bureaucracies. So, some of his adversaries have wondered whether this was not exactly the blueprint that facilitated the globalization of international capital: of a liberalized economy that is no longer hindered by state regulations? Moreover, this suspicion seems to be corroborated by the fact that Lyotard ventured to say that "there is something of the sublime in capitalistic economy."[16] However, it is crucial to understand what he means by the sublime (as we will see a central notion in his political ethics) when applied to capitalism. In his *Political Writings* Lyotard relates capitalism to the desire for infinity: "In capitalism, infinity is posed as that which is not yet determined, as that

15. See D. Smith, *Zygmunt Bauman: Prophet of Postmodernity* (Oxford: Polity Press,1988) 162.
16. J.-F. Lyotard, *The Inhuman: Reflections on Time*, trans. G. Bennington and R. Bowlby (Cambridge: Polity Press, 1991) 105. Originally published as idem, *L'inhumain: Causeries sur le temps* (Paris: Galilée, 1988).

which the will must indefinitely dominate and appropriate. It bears the names of cosmos and energy, it gives rise to research and development. It has to be conquered."[17] Capitalism is, in other words, boosted by the will and the idea of absolute mastery. In that sense there is something sublime in it, that is: it is geared towards an Idea of mastery that is so high and uplifting that there can be no example of such a power empirically demonstrable. There is always a gulf between the Idea and its realization, and this brings the capitalistic economy close to the sphere of the sublime. Yet, this gulf, and this is Lyotard's point, always entails the danger of an uncertainty: "[Capitalism] only succeeds [...] in making reality ungraspable, subject to doubt, unsteady."[18] Capitalism harbors thus also an element of unsettlement and anxiety.

This neutral description, however, is abandoned when Lyotard begins to look at capitalism as a closed system. From that moment his judgment carries an undertone of moral indignation. In his work *The Inhuman* (1988) he compares the self-totalizing logic of late capitalism with Leibniz' monads and their capacity of infinite expansion. The ultimate consequence of this logic is the exclusion or annihilation of all that which does not serve this aim. He writes: "When the point is to extend the capacities of the monad [of late capitalism], it seems reasonable to abandon, or even actually destroy, those parts of the human race which appear superfluous, useless for that goal. For example, the populations of the Third World."[19] It is this tone that dominates also Derrida's late considerations on the liberal economy and its global expansion. After the fall of the Berlin wall Derrida explores, in his *Specters of Marx* (1993), the contours of the emergence of a New International, made up of people from various races and nations and united on the basis of their discontent with the New World Order – with an international law system and jurisprudence that safeguard the interests of the rich countries. More particularly, he contests the thesis of Fukuyama's book *The End of History* according to which no alternative is left to the triumph of capitalism in its conjunction with liberal democracy. For him, this thesis is fraudulent, because liberal democracy does not care at all about those who are falling out of the boat. When assessing the era of globalization he exclaims: "Never have violence, inequality, exclusion, famine, and thus economic oppression affected as many human beings in the history of the earth and

17. J.-F. Lyotard, *Political Writings*, trans. B. Readings and K. Geiman (Minneapolis, MN: University of Minnesota Press, 1993) 25. The chapter referred to was originally published in idem, *Tombeau de l'intellectuel et autres papiers* (Paris: Galilée, 1984).
18. J.-F. Lyotard, *The Inhuman*, 105.
19. *Ibid.*, 76-77.

of humanity [...] Never have so many men, women, and children been subjugated, starved, or exterminated on the earth."[20]

Compared with Lyotard, Derrida's engagement in political ethics comes rather late. As early as the late 1970s and early 1980s, Lyotard began to wage a war on totalitarian regimes and their reign of terror. Auschwitz under Hitler, and Kolyma, the most dehumanizing concentration camp in Stalin's Gulag Archipelago, are, for him, the tragic symbols of the atrocities of such regimes. Totalitarian systems are renowned for mixing up the 'ought' and the 'is'; they impose their grand narratives – their speculative phrases in the parlance of Lyotard's language pragmatics – on the reality they want to transform, without questioning the legitimacy of this procedure. In doing so they decide on the logic that is bound to rule the linkage of phrases, so that no novelty or surprise is allowed to see the light of day. The way in which phrases are linked to each other is determined in advance. In order to tear down the constraints of this ironclad logic, Lyotard will pay heed to the required differentiation of regimes of phrases. It is only on this basis that an awareness of the unexpected can arise, an awareness which prompts one to ask the excruciating question: '*Is it happening?*' 'Is it happening that respect is being paid to the heterogeneous?' 'Is it happening that losers are no longer silenced?'

The emotional tone of the '*Is it happening?*' can hardly be explained from the background of language pragmatics. For Lyotard, language pragmatics is an apt instrument for drawing neat distinctions, but it cannot account for the feeling of the sublime that accompanies one's longing for the unexpected, for the quasi-unattainable. It is at this juncture that Lyotard revisits Kant's Third Critique, the *Critique of Judgment*, and this for a double motive. The *Critique of Judgment* deals, first of all, with the difficulty of judging particular events (the judgment of taste) without any recourse to universal rules. This is, for Lyotard, the essence of political judgment, which – in the wake of Kant's reflective judgment – is still in search of its rules, guided by some strong feelings of what is right and what is not. Second, the *Critique of Judgment* also offers a detailed analysis of the uplifting feeling of the sublime. This feeling arises when the reflective person comes in touch with the supersensible reality, which makes itself felt through the collapse of the creative imagination in its attempt at visualizing the domain of unpresentable Ideas of

---

20. J. Derrida, *Specters of Marx: The State of Debt, the Work of Mourning, and the New International*, trans. P. Kamuf and B. Magnus (New York and London: Routledge, 1994) 85. Originally published as idem, *Spectres de Marx: L'état de la dette, le travail du deuil et la nouvelle internationale* (Paris: Galilée, 1993).

totality and majesty. As an antidote to the misuse that modern grand narratives make of speculative phrases as instruments of domination, Lyotard opts for the Kantian unpresentability of the speculative Ideas. These Ideas can and must be thought, but their reality cannot be found in empirical reality. As such, however, they create a restlessness in the human mind, which feels itself taken hostage by the grandeur of the unpresentable.

It is my contention that Lyotard's deepest concern cannot be grasped without a serious study of his appropriation of Kant. This study will be the focus of the first part of this book. Yet, appropriation does not mean slavish dependence. A detailed analysis will show that, especially in his comments on the Kantian sublime, Lyotard replaces Kant's vision of an ultimately united world with the ideal of respect for plurality and heterogeneity. In doing so, however, he remains faithful to the centrality of emotions in Kant's ethics and reflections on politics. More explicitly than Kant perhaps, he links these emotions to the Jewish background of the Covenant: to listen to the commanding voice is more essential than deducing rules from principles. Lyotard acknowledges that this return to Jewishness is inspired by what he learned from Emmanuel Levinas.

The influence of Kant is also to be found in Derrida. In his later works he refers to the unpresentable that can and must be thought but which cannot be found in empirical reality, and which for that reason awakens a strong desire for an 'impossible' justice to come. On the whole, however, he reaches this insight through a lifelong critical reflection on Husserl's phenomenology. This reflection thrives from the outset on Nietzsche's joyous demolition of metaphysical constructs (Plato!). However, while Derrida will not tire of falling back on this Nietzschean humus, his real intellectual achievement lies in his unremitting exploration of the limits of phenomenology. When deconstructing Husserl's project of the immediate perception of the *eidos* (*Wesensschau*), Derrida discovers that this immediate grasp – when placed in a larger context – is always deferred, an accent that resonates in his notion of *différance*. Just as the Kantian Idea of totality and completeness recedes into unknowability, overall knowledge is an ideal the contours of which escape our understanding. The second part of this book will examine at length Derrida's deconstruction of Husserl. This deconstruction hinges on new insights from semiotics but also on the 'aphanology' Derrida associates with Levinas' 'naked face of the other': the 'other' issues commands from a realm that is beyond the immediately graspable; it addresses us from the other side of that which immediately appears to consciousness.

'Aphanology' lies at the basis of Derrida's concept of messianicity, that is: of his unwavering commitment to 'impossible' things to come. In a first movement, Derrida fills in these 'things impossible' with an 'impossible' democracy to come, based on the requirement that justice be done to each and every body worldwide, beyond the narrow restrictions of legal justice. Whenever Derrida uses the notion 'impossible' he has in mind an excess that shatters existing notions of justice and democracy. It does not take long, though, before he fills in this excess of the 'impossible' with examples taken from the religions of the book, from Judaism in particular. Unconditional hospitality to the stranger, the undesired immigrant, combined with the exuberance of giving and forgiving without expecting any reward or counter-gift constitutes the basic attitude of a civilization worthy of this name. Unconditional hospitality becomes, for him, the benchmark against which to judge the extent to which persons and nations have come to embrace a genuine cosmopolitan ethics.

Lyotard's and Derrida's turn towards the excess of 'things impossible', finally, prompts us to revisit the notion of universality. Lyotard's announcement of the 'end of the grand stories', as well as Derrida's passion for deconstruction may, on prima facie consideration, suggest that for them the death knell of a universal ethics has sounded. This is, however, absolutely not the case. It is my contention that with their focus on the unpresentable – in Derrida's parlance: on the 'things impossible' that because of their excessive purity and 'strangeness' cannot be rendered phenomenologically present – they launch a much broader notion of universality than is currently en vogue. They profess their firm belief in a universality 'without any exclusion', impossible as such an outlook may appear. As long as this excessive universality has not been reached, they will continue to combat the mindset of 'might makes right', whether in the order of jurisprudence, or in that of political arrangements.

PART ONE

JEAN-FRANÇOIS LYOTARD

CHAPTER ONE

FIRST ACQUAINTANCE WITH LYOTARD

In 1979 Jean-François Lyotard wrote a study on the production of postmodern knowledge which he submitted "to the *Conseil des universités* of
the government of Quebec at the request of its president."[1] This study,
The Postmodern Condition: A Report on Knowledge became in no time
a best seller and a 'classic' in the study of postmodern societies. It gives
a good picture of how postmodern societies diverge from modern ones,
especially with respect to the procedures of scientific research and how
these changes effect the structures of social life. I will start this chapter
with Lyotard's analysis, in *The Postmodern Condition*, of the major shifts
that took place in the second half of the 20th century. These major shifts
are: increased pragmatism that no longer stands in need of an overall-
justification by grand narratives; the important role played by innovative
performances in subsystems, at the expense of the authority of central
planning in megasystems; the emergence of an indefinite number of
meaning generating agencies, all disconnected from one another; and the
replacement of modernity's notion of truth, understood as objective validity, with a growing appreciation of the utility of daring moves to increase
one's performativity and saleability in the marketplace.

The analysis of these major shifts is followed by an intermezzo: 'Personal Enjoyment and Technological Innovations', features of an aesthetic
postmodernity (enjoyment, easygoingness) which some of Lyotard's readers perceived in his programmatic book. Indeed, when performativity
becomes the norm, playfulness will never be far away. The game is being
played. Performativity and personal enjoyment go hand in hand. No wonder that some critics blame Lyotard for giving a legitimization to the
deadly game of late-modernity's high technology which was already
engaged in a 'Star Wars' program. This intermezzo thus deals with the
effect that *The Postmodern Condition* had on some of its readers. It is

1. J.-F. Lyotard, *The Postmodern Condition: A Report on Knowledge*, trans. G. Ben-
nington and B. Massumi (Minneapolis, MN: University of Minnesota Press, 1984) xxv.
Originally published as idem, *La condition postmoderne: Rapport sur le savoir* (Paris: Les
Éditions de Minuit, 1979).

important to keep in mind that the book was written at the request of the Canadian Council of Universities with the goal of improving knowledge production so as to bring it to the market. Lyotard's text gives the impression of being only descriptive, without passing an ethical judgment on the attractive and newly emerging phenomena. Thus one might conclude that Lyotard's report on knowledge is itself under the spell of the newly discovered innovations, and thus an example of the very phenomena the book purports to explore.

Ethical concern, however, definitely appears in Lyotard's 'language pragmatics' which I will examine in the second part of this chapter. Language pragmatics takes its point of departure in postmodern versatility, but at the same time calls attention to the crude injustices that can be perpetrated through the strategic use of language games. In the explanation of his basic vocabulary, Lyotard makes it clear that language pragmatics places us in a certain speech situation, based on three elements whose relation to one another can change: the sender (addressor), the receiver (addressee), and the subject matter (referent). At a certain instant the addressee can take on the role of addressor, with the result that the referent may change or be viewed from a different perspective. One's place in the speech situation, moreover, depends on the regimes of sentences that are being used: descriptive, prescriptive, interrogative regimes etc, as well as on the genres of discourses (exposition, discussion, assessment). Crucial for Lyotard is that, in the speech situation, the next sentence in the discourse is never decided in advance. The linkage of sentences one to another is not planned; it is contingent. Without such a 'contingency' of linkage no room is left for surprise.

A new event becomes impossible in situations in which a totalitarian logic dictates the varied linkage of sentences. In *The Postmodern Explained* Lyotard reconstructs the various phases of a typically modern deliberation the end result of which will be the elimination of the enemy. He shows that when a deliberation starts with an interrogative prescriptive 'What ought we to be?' (e.g. 'Germans of the pure Arian race', or 'the vanguard of the proletariat') this interrogative prescriptive, from the onset of the discourse, is determinative of the other sentences that are going to be linked. Possible alternatives are not taken into consideration. 'What ought we to be?' is followed by a hypothetical imperative 'What ought we to do to be so?', which in turn is linked to the enumeration of possible strategies' (descriptive regime). Then comes the discussion as to which strategy will be most effective (the discussion genre), followed by the verdict and the decree that infractions will be punished. In terms of language pragmatics this means that, although 'heterogeneous' regimes of sentences and genres of discourse are used in the deliberation, they are all subsumed under one universal principle that imposes its iron constraint. No justice can be done to the particularity of each of the genres. Illicit bridges are built in order to reconcile language games that are separated from each other by an abyss.

In his foreword to the English edition of *The Postmodern Condition* Frederic James writes: "Lyotard is, after all, writing in the wake of a certain French 'post-Marxism', that is, an enormous reaction on all levels against various Marxist and Communist traditions in France, whose prime target on the philosophical level is the Hegel/Lukács concept of 'totality' (often overhastily assimilated to Stalinism or even to the Leninist party on the political level)."[2] As a French post-Marxist Lyotard is horrified by the regimes of terror that seek to legitimate their actions with the help of a speculative concept of totality. As we will see, Lyotard is convinced, with Kant, that such a speculative concept of totality can never be accounted for with empirical proofs. The Idea of the vanguard of the proletariat, or of the universal history of humankind, can never be found in empirical reality. The same is true for the modern European dream of spearheading the universal history of humanity. There always remains a chasm between what one thinks one ought to be and what one is. In Lyotard's words: "The narrative of the universal history of humanity [...] remains suspended from an Ideal of practical reason (freedom, emancipation). It cannot be verified by empirical proofs but only by indirect signs [...] So any discussion of this history is 'dialectical' in the Kantian sense, which is to say, without conclusion. The ideal is not presentable to the sensibility [...] There will always be a profound tension between what one ought to be and what one is."[3]

Lyotard's language pragmatics seeks to do justice to the multiplicity of alternative options that have been eliminated in the 'totalitarian' linkage of sentences. It also seeks to do justice to the victims of terror whom the system regards as redundant or inimical to the goals of the totalitarian world view. When commemorating the victims of terror Lyotard becomes emotional. In the third part of this chapter, 'The Transition Towards the Sublime', I will explain the origin of this emotional undertone. This origin is to be found in the way in which Lyotard connects his language pragmatics with some basic Kantian concepts: respect for heterogeneous discourses (in Kantian terms: faculties), the importance in

---

2. F. Jameson, "Foreword," J.-F. Lyotard, *The Postmodern Condition*, x.
3. J.-F. Lyotard. *The Postmodern Explained*, trans. D. Barry et al. (Minneapolis, MN and London: University of Minnesota Press, 1992) 50. Originally published as idem, *Le postmoderne expliqué aux enfants* (Paris: Galilée, 1988).

politics of a reflective judgment that is still in search of its rules, instead of starting from a universal principle under which the particular is to be subsumed; and, most importantly, the sublime feeling of testifying to the unpresentable Idea of human grandeur at the other side of concepts of 'totality' that conflate this Idea with a totalitarian project that seeks to make this Idea visible, if needed by force, in empirical reality.

I. The Postmodern Condition: The End of the Grand Narratives

In his book *The Postmodern Condition* Lyotard describes the foreseeable development of human knowledge in a society of computers and databanks, a society that has become completely pragmatic. Insofar as pragmatism has become the hallmark, the need to legitimate what one is doing is no longer felt. We are thereby ushered into a new realm in which the great legitimating stories are no longer needed, in contrast to modernity which worked towards the promotion of the 'life of the spirit' (Hegel) and the 'emancipation of humankind' (Fichte, Marx). Postmodernity has taken leave of these great narratives: "I will use the term modern to designate any science that legitimates itself with reference to a metadiscourse of this kind making an explicit appeal to some grand narrative, such as the dialectics of Spirit, the hermeneutics of meaning, the emancipation of the rational or working subject, or the creation of wealth." Lyotard is quick to note, however, that these metanarratives have never functioned independently, since they are linked to theories of consensus formation, as well as affiliated to institutions which they are expected to legitimate: "For example, the rule of consensus between the sender and addressee of a statement with truth-value is deemed acceptable if it is cast in terms of a possible unanimity between rational minds: this is the Enlightenment narrative, in which the hero of knowledge works towards a good ethico-political end – universal peace. As can be seen from this example, if a metanarrative implying a philosophy of history is used to legitimate knowledge, questions are raised concerning the validity of the institutions governing the social bond: these must be legitimated as well. Thus justice is consigned to grand narratives in the same way as truth." And he concludes: "Simplifying to the extreme, I define postmodern as incredulity toward metanarratives [...] To the obsolescence of the metanarrative apparatus of legitimation corresponds, most notably, the crisis of metaphysical philosophy and of the university institution which in the past relied on it."[4]

4. J.-F. Lyotard, *The Postmodern Condition*, xxiii-xxiv.

Postmodernity, thus, is characterized by the decline of an encompassing metalanguage or metanarrative which might shed a universal, normative light on humankind's search for truth, veracity, and beauty. Because they threaten to curtail one's pragmatic and inventive dealings with truth, the pretensions of a universal metalanguage are no longer generally accepted in a 'high technology' age.

1. *The Limits of Systems Theory*

To portray the late modern society, Lyotard makes use of the systems theory developed by Parsons and Luhmann. These authors optimistically hold the view that subsystems (the development of subspecialties in industries and institutions of knowledge, leading industrial complexes to develop distinct entities within the social fabric) admit and promote novelty and creativity, whereas this locally produced creativity, on the other hand, is seen as prompting the self-regulating 'total system' to enter into new, unexpected phases of flexible improvement. A new and creative education system, for example, is bound to heighten the level of education but also that of marketing, technology, macroeconomics, etc. In other words, the relationship of the sub-systems to the comprehensive total system is cybernetic and self-regulative. Partial innovations fortify the creative self-regulating potential of the total system, which is never thrown off its balance. The underlying vision is this: the differentiated, creative language games in the subsystem (in technological specialties and localized sectors) will eventually serve the dynamic self-unfolding of the total system.

In assessing Niklas Luhmann's description of an optimal modern self-regulative system and its ability to profitably integrate local innovations (and to come to grips with local crises), Lyotard adopts a twofold stance. (i) First, he appreciates the fact that this systems theory highlights the importance of 'performativity', which is defined in terms of creating a surplus value: "The true goal of the system, the reason it programs itself like a computer, is the optimization of the global relationship between input and output – in other words performativity."[5] In plain English: the output or the surplus value created by a scientific or cognitive performance should outweigh the costs invested in the research program (or more generally, the expenditures on the infrastructure). Performativity, as the production of an additional 'surplus value', is one of the key concepts in Lyotard's vocabulary. He cherishes this concept because it aims

5. *Ibid.*, 11.

at the increase of productivity, be it in the realm of knowledge (knowledge production) or in the realm of enhanced profit-making in the commodity circulation on the market. (ii) But in spite of this positive appreciation, Lyotard feels that Luhmann's systems theory still pays a heavy tribute to the 'system as a whole' at the expense of singular performative innovations. Systems theory, as well as its mechanisms of 'internal readjustments', are, in Lyotard's assessment, outdated. The reason is simple: it gives too much credit to the self-regulating capability of the overarching system, to which the multiple, atomized subspecialties are supposed to be subserviently subordinated. Yet this subordination will eventually thwart the spontaneity of local inventive moves.

The overarching system and the blockages it creates can take on many faces. It can be the compact entity of a big enterprise whose top managers want to be in control of every separate 'performative action' that is taking place in one of its local subsections. Or it can designate the 'whole of the social fabric', insofar as the system claims to be the ultimate arbiter for deciding which local innovations (the flourishing of entire enterprises and industries) are going to be legitimated as genuine factors promotive of the self-regulative readjustments of the social fabric. Lyotard is skeptical about the predominance of centralizing systems, even when some of them establish mutual cooperation. Particularly, he blames the classical social systems theoreticians for debasing themselves as the handmaids of program managers: "'Traditional' theory is always in danger of being incorporated into the programming of the social whole as a simple tool for the optimization of its performance; this is because its desire for a unitary and totalizing truth lends itself to the unitary and the totalizing practice of the system's managers."[6] In short, Lyotard voices a strong apprehension that the preponderance of the 'totality' or 'the whole', whatever it may be, may end up putting limits on the free game of innovative performative practices.

As a Parisian intellectual, Lyotard has recourse to post-structuralist insights about the ever changing, criss-crossing webs of language games. He is convinced that this criss-crossing both guarantees a certain self-regulation of the system and allows for eruptive moves of creativity at nodal points where various language games intersect: "One is always located at a post through which various kinds of messages pass. No one, not even the least privileged among us, is ever entirely powerless over the messages that traverse and position him at the post of sender, addressee,

6. *Ibid.*, 12.

or referent."[7] So, why not take full advantage of this ability to creatively react to messages? Such an asset can only lead to the enhanced performativity of the system. Even system theoreticians will have to admit that no system will be able to overcome its own entropy, unless it allows new, unexpected moves to take place within its own fabric. Indeed, "one's mobility in relation to these language game effects (language games, of course, are what this is all about) is tolerable, at least within certain limits (and the limits are vague); it is even solicited by regulatory mechanisms, and in particular by the self-adjustments the system undertakes in order to improve its performance. It may even be said that the system can and must encourage such movement to the extent that it combats its own entropy; the novelty of an unexpected 'move', with its correlative displacement of a partner or group of partners, can supply the system with that increased performativity it forever demands and consumes."[8]

Lyotard not only advocates a differentiation of language games but also realizes that language utterances have a strategic effect. Thus, he wants these strategies to be as versatile as possible. He calls attention to the fact that we are living in an 'agonistic society' (a term that evokes Nietzsche's exaltation of the *Agoon*[9]), in which each creative move elicits a reaction from its environment. This reaction, however, should not result in a countermove whose essential features can already be predicted by the opponent. In this case, the actors would be reduced to just being a link in the chain of some self-regulating, cybernetic system. No, the new skills postmodern people should acquire, within the parameters of an agonistic society, are those which allow them to regard every 'move' that is made as an occasion for them to deploy their own strategy in making unpredictable, 'heterogeneous' moves: "The atoms are placed at the crossroads of pragmatic relationships, but they are also displaced by the messages that traverse them, in perpetual motion. Each language partner, when a 'move' pertaining to him is made, undergoes a 'displacement', an alteration of some kind that not only affects him in his capacity as addressee and referent, but also as sender. These 'moves' necessarily provoke 'countermoves' – and everyone knows that a countermove that is merely reactional is not a 'good' move."[10]

---

7. *Ibid.*, 15.
8. *Ibid.*, 15.
9. For John Milbank, Lyotard "had made the most sustained attempt to articulate the ethics of an agonistic politics." See idem, *Theology & Social Science: Beyond Secular Reason* (Oxford and Cambridge, MA: Blackwell, 1990 [1995]) 316.
10. J.-F. Lyotard, *The Postmodern Condition*, 16.

At this juncture, Lyotard questions Habermas' 'theory of communicative action', which is geared towards attaining a consensus among provisionally disagreeing communication partners. In his eyes, this 'communication theory' is still too close to the 'modern' ideal of commonly shared grand narratives, and must therefore be replaced by "a theory of games which accepts agonistics as a founding principle."[11] If this procedure were to be accepted, then 'deviation from the normal or habitual' would become something desirable, a condition for novelty (new statements with enhanced circulation value) to happen eventfully. In other words, a certain flexibility and 'tolerance' (absence from constraints) in institutions of knowledge production should become the rule. The game players should be allowed to play the game the way they would like to play it creatively so that their countermoves would be appreciated for their originality within the fluctuation of message waves: "The 'atomization of the social into flexible networks of language games may seem far removed from the modern reality, which is depicted, on the contrary, as afflicted with bureaucratic paralysis."[12]

2. *Science, Technology, and Performativity*

According to postmodern pragmatism, truth should simply be efficient, a situation which allows for an unending multiplication of disparate, different language games designed to promote an ever greater efficiency. This differentiating multiplication of knowledge grows through the use of creative imagination, competition, and daring combinations of new telecommunicated data. What counts are only the answers to the following questions: What is the use of this or that novel (computer) language – what is it good for? What is its unprecedented effect? Accordingly, 'grounding' questions can only take the form of a reduplication: What is the use of this particular research designed to produce utility? – a tautological formula, indeed, that only fortifies the awareness that science must be efficient and competitive in the market: "The question (overt or implied) now asked by the professionalist student, the State, or institutions of higher education is no longer: 'is it true?', but 'What use is it?' In the context of the mercantilization of knowledge, more often than not this question is equivalent to: 'Is it saleable?' And in the context of power growth: 'Is it efficient?'"[13]

11. *Ibid.*, 16.
12. *Ibid.*, 17.
13. *Ibid.*, 51.

To authors who were educated at classically modern universities, this replacement of truth with efficiency is rather disturbing. Not only is the scientific question of truth receding to the background, but also the persuasion that true statements are beneficial to the human life community (without truth the human community has no firm basis on which to rest) begins to vanish. Zygmunt Bauman describes this uneasiness as follows: "The postmodern world-view entails the dissipation of objectivity. The element most conspicuously absent is a reference to the supracommunal, 'extraterritorial' grounds of truth and meaning. Instead, the postmodern perspective reveals the world as composed of an indefinite number of meaning-generating agencies, all relatively self-sustained and autonomous, all subject to their own respective logics and armed with their own facilities of truth-validation. Their relative superiority may be argued solely, if at all, in pragmatic and overtly self-referential mode, with no claim made to supracommunal authority."[14]

Bauman traces this change back to the collapse of the dominant position of the West on the world scene (after World War II the European countries lost their colonies). But the change results also from an endemic disintegration: (i) The notion of science has changed; it has given up its denotative function, which is replaced now by performative language. In modernity, and this in spite of the turn towards the ordering subject, the aim of knowledge was to shed a light of understanding on the phenomena. The cognitive apparatus had, in other words, the pretension to possess and to 'represent' the truth extracted from the subject-matter under investigation. Science was in this sense geared towards 'objective validity'. In each field of knowledge, something ought to be true or not true, with nothing wavering hesitantly in between. This scientific mind created a coherence among the various communities of research, even when they examined different problem fields – be it in the realm of economics, law, or medicine. With postmodernity, however, modern universalistic science is replaced by "an indefinite number of meaning-generating agencies" that are pragmatic and self-referential. People begin to put up with the idea that meaning is generated according to the rules of the specific field, and thus an encompassing legitimating structure of these divergent truth generators is no longer possible.

To underpin this argument, Bauman summarizes Lyotard's thought as follows: "Drawing on Wittgenstein's metaphor of language as a maze of little streets surrounded by solitary islands of orderly and planned suburbs,

---

14. Z. Bauman, *Intimations of Postmodernity* (London and New York: Routledge, 1992) 35.

Lyotard questions the centredness of the emerging conurbation. But he also points to the autarky of the suburban subcenters – they do not need to communicate with other suburbs, or for that matter with the 'old city' in the centre, to maintain a reasonably complete life. Visits between them are rare, and no resident of the city has visited them all: 'Nobody speaks all of those languages, they have no universal metalanguage, the project of the system-subject is a failure, the goal of emancipation has nothing to do with science, we are all stuck in the positivism of this or that discipline of learning, the learned scholars have turned into scientists, the diminished tasks of research have become compartmentalized and no one can master them all [...] That is what the postmodern world is all about. Most people have lost nostalgia for the lost [grand] narrative. It in no way follows that they are reduced to barbarity. What saves them from it is their knowledge that legitimation can only spring from their own linguistic practice and communicational interaction'."[15]

This description – the impossibility of mastering all the language games – is only the beginning of a more serious questioning that Lyotard undertakes in his book. He notably asks the question as to why the idea of encompassing standardized scientificity has been 'delegitimated' in the course of the discussions on scientific validity. To answer this question, he first points out that, in recent decades, scientists have become aware of the fact that the rules for providing proofs rest on a tacit agreement among colleagues about the procedures they are going to use within their sector of the scientific community. But then, the question must be asked, as a second step, from where do these agreed-upon procedures draw their validity? In mathematics for example, Goedel has pointed out that the closed system of mathematics allows for deviations that can neither be demonstrated nor refuted within the rules of the system: "Goedel has effectively established the existence in the arithmetic system of a proposition that is neither demonstrable nor refutable within that system; this entails that the arithmetic system fails to satisfy the condition of completeness."[16] This paradox also applies to other sciences, for all of them, in fact, have recourse to some form of conclusive logic, similar to that of mathematics. From this, Lyotard concludes that what is at stake is precisely that "the question of proof [within a particular specialty] is problematic, since proof needs to be proven."[17]

---

15. Z. Bauman, *Intimations of Postmodernity*, 38, citing J.-F. Lyotard, *The Postmodern Condition*, 41.

16. J.-F. Lyotard, *The Postmodern Condition*, 42.

17. *Ibid.*, 44.

In a next step, however, Lyotard moves from considerations on pure, disinterested science – and the paradoxes and paralogisms arising there – to focus on the modern and postmodern alliance of science and technology. And here he perceives that the procedural practice of providing proofs is closely linked to perfomativity, which boils down to the profit calculation of input/output. Laboratories that specialize in providing proofs are expensive. This means pragmatically: "No money no proof – and that means no verification of statements and no truth. The games of scientific language become the games of the rich, in which whoever is wealthier has the best chance of being right. An equation between wealth, efficiency, and truth is thus established."[18] To set up a scientific program, a lot of money is required – money which should pay off. So only programs that have been granted subsidies by universities or industrial research units can really come off the ground, and this under the restriction that they promise to link knowledge and truth (the validation of truth) to increased performance.

I quote some of Lyotard's daring statements in this respect: (i) "The 'organic' connection between technology and profit preceded its union with science. Technology became important to contemporary knowledge only through the mediation of a generalized spirit of performativity."[19] And (ii) "The production of proof, which is in principle only part of an argumentation process designed to win agreement from the addressees of scientific messages, thus falls under the control of another language game, in which the goal is no longer truth, but performativity – that is, the best possible input/output equation. The State and/or company must abandon the idealist and humanist narratives of legitimation in order to justify the new goal: in the discourse of today's financial backers of research, the only credible goal is power. Scientists, technicians, and instruments are purchased not to find truth, but to augment power."[20]

3. *Intermezzo: Personal Enjoyment and Technological Innovations*

Lyotard, at least in this period of his writing, seems to welcome aesthetic postmodernity. He seems to feel at home in the new easygoing culture, with its expressive individualism, its boom of technological media innovations, and its exaltation of the creative 'now'. He seems to think that it is good for postmodern people to appreciate living in the Nietzschean 'innocence of becoming': erring away from fixed norms and liberated from the coercion of controlling 'origins'. He is convinced that

18. *Ibid.*, 45.
19. *Ibid.*, 45.
20. *Ibid.*, 46.

postmodern people no longer care about the death of legitimating meta-narratives: 'Even the nostalgia', he says, 'for the lost story is gone for most of us'. Every individual lives out his/her own existence aesthetically, enjoying it to the full in private life and in the attractive work situation typical of highly technological (mediatized) societies. Why not make the research activities of the computer and telecommunication industries as rewarding and pleasurable as one's home life used to be? After all, these industries will flourish and be even more profitable when staffed by pleasant people who take delight in working on innovative programs.

His critics are especially quick to point out that Lyotard wagers on the postmodern persons' aesthetic justification of life. To live in the eternal now-moment of joy, without having to ask universal questions of ethical responsibility, is for postmodern people a sufficient motive to 'justify their lives as a beautiful phenomenon' (Nietzsche). Indeed, what is more exciting about life than to be allowed to creatively perform what one really likes to do, having experiences that are really 'different' from present and past ones? The act of innovation amounts to the liberation from the terror of 'the same'.

In some passages of his book, Lyotard criticizes Habermas for persistence in continuing to assert the value of a universal discourse of communicative action, however much that discourse may follow qualified rules of reasoning when one endeavors to account for actions related either to truth (science), rightness (ethics), or authenticity/beauty (aesthetics). For Lyotard, this anti-fragmental, universally binding approach to truth, justice, and enjoyment is in fact desperately *passé*. As he sees it, postmodern people feel perfectly at home in a pragmatic setting that merely invites our engagement in discussions of immediate, practical interest (in family life and the work situation). Rarely will they begin to discuss things that transcend their immediate (aestheticized/privatized) interest. At this stage of his writing, Lyotard seems to regard this easygoing carelessness as a blessing. Why shouldn't an individualistic bohemian life style and professional efficiency go hand in hand to fortify each other? Playfulness has an affinity to game, to the game to be played in the work situation. Easygoingness is, indeed, the major asset in the renewed 'social systems theory' (beyond Parsons), for it is under the impulse of the joyous inventiveness (the 'moves') in the subsystems that the 'total system' (i.e., the late capitalistic economy and industry) will playfully move to its next stage of pragmatic consolidation. The system always comes right side up even when it is pushed to move under the pressure of effervescent subsystems. That is the reason why some of his

critics[21] blame Lyotard for justifying, in terms of arts, play, and easygoingness, the mortal game of late-capitalistic high technology, which produces nuclear weapons and already plans the 'Star Wars' anti-missile
defense program.

II. LYOTARD'S LANGUAGE PRAGMATICS

Apart from *The Postmodern Condition*, the work Lyotard wrote on the
question of how Canadian Universities might better function, Lyotard
also published some works in which he began to elucidate the postmodern condition with the help of language pragmatics. The relevant works
here are *Just Gaming* (1979) and *The Differend* (1983).[22] In these works,
he proposes a language theory which studies the functioning of language
in a society that has lost or abandoned its unifying metaphysical language
(hereafter referred to as 'metalanguage'). This does not mean that the
interest in a sort of metadiscourse is gone. On the contrary, Lyotard sets
out to depict a new metadiscourse that must, so to speak, legitimate the
heterogeneity of language games without one of them being allowed to
establish a hegemonic position.[23]

1. Basic Vocabulary: Phrase, Regimes of Phrases, Discourse Genres

In *The Postmodern Explained* Lyotard gives a good summary of his
language pragmatics. While Wittgenstein remains a basic inspiration for
Lyotard, he refocuses the former's description of the existence of various,
irreconcilable language games (language games are like isolated islands,
which denote a specialty) by arguing that these language games are, in
fact, caught up in situations of war and competition. Not only are there
various language games, but by their very nature they engage in ongoing
and interminable conflict with each other. So, if one acknowledges this
conflict, then the question cannot be avoided as to whether or not justice

21. F. Jameson, "Postmodernism or the Cultural Logic of Late Capitalism," *New Left Review* 146 (1984) 53-92.

22. J.-F. Lyotard and J.-L. Thébaud, *Just Gaming*, trans. W. Godzich and S. Weber (Minneapolis, MN: The University of Minnesota Press, 1985). Originally published as iidem, *Au Juste: Conversations* (Paris: Christian Bourgeois, 1979). J.-F. Lyotard, *The Differend: Phrases in Dispute*, trans G. Van Den Abbeele (Manchester: Manchester University Press, 1988). Originally published as idem, *Le Différend* (Paris: Minuit, 1983).

23. R. Beardsworth, "Lyotard's Agitated Judgment," *Judging Lyotard*, ed. A. Benjamin (London and New York: Routledge, 1992) 73-77.

can be done to the 'losers' in the competition (see next point: The Question of Justice).

Lyotard takes it for granted that our linguistic utterances (and also the unexpected 'moves') take place within an evolving web of criss-crossing language games – or, as he is going to specify – within changing genres of discourse.

(a) To get an insight into the impact of the genres of discourse, one must know something about the essential building blocks of which they are made up. Therefore Lyotard starts his examination with a study of the 'sentence' or the 'phrase'. In the introduction to this chapter I used, for simplicity's sake, the term 'sentence' to render the French noun 'la phrase'. But this must be nuanced. Whereas 'phrase' in English denotes a group of words that forms part of a sentence ('on Friday morning' e.g.), the French word 'phrase' indicates a grammatical sentence. Yet, Lyotard, in his language pragmatics, gives a specific meaning to the French word 'phrase'. For him, it not just designates a grammatical sentence or semantic unit, but also indicates a particular situation in which one is placed through the speech act. Phrase, in his understanding, is not only a text; it also includes the context or the particular constellation in which the discussion partners find themselves with respect to one another. The 'Glossary of French Terms' at the end of the book *The Differend* puts it as follows: "A phrase is defined by – as it, in fact, defines – the situation of its instances (addressor, addressee, referent) with regard to one another. Rather than defining a grammatical or semantic unit, a *phrase* designates a particular constellation of instances, which is as contextual as it is textual – if it is not indeed precisely what renders the 'opposition' between text and context impertinent." [24] Whenever the term phrase is used in the pages that follow, it is this meaning that is intended. English translations of Lyotard's works also use the term 'phrase' with this special connotation. In *The Postmodern Explained* Lyotard himself gives the following definition: "[T]he only *givens* [we have at our disposal] are phrases, in their hundreds and thousands. We see that these phrases do not simply convey meanings: however unassuming and ephemeral (or silent) they may be, they situate, within the universe of the present, an addressor [a speaker], an addressee [a listener], and a referent [a subject matter]." [25] Phrases, thus, create a speech situation in which something happens.

(b) But apparently, the way in which addressor, addressee, and referent (that which the speech act is about) relate to each other, is subject to

---

24. "Glossary of French Terms," J.-F. Lyotard, *The Differend*, 194.
25. J.-F. Lyotard. *The Postmodern Explained*, 42.

change, depending on the regime of phrases one wants to use. So one ought to distinguish, for example, between phrases which are predicated on the regime of denotative or descriptive language (the observation that the 'door is closed'), and others that are predicated on the regime of pre-scriptive language ('close the door'), or on that of performative language ('I declare the university open'), just to mention three categories of phrase regimes. Lyotard explains as follows: "We see that we can distinguish different families or regimes of phrases from one another, since it is impossible to convert one phrase into another without modifying what I will simply call the pragmatic situation of the instances I have just men-tioned (referent, addressee, addressor). *The door is closed* is a descriptive phrase. In the universe it presents, the question is whether or not the door is closed: it is therefore governed by the criterion of truth or falsity. *Close the door* is a prescriptive phrase, and the question it raises hinges on the justice of the order given to the addressee and on the execution of the act it prescribes. As we can see, the regime governing a normative [descrip-tive in terms of being true or false] phrase is completely different from the regime governing a prescriptive phrase. The same is true of interrog-ative, performative (in the strict sense), and exclamatory phrases."[26]

In studying this procedure, one ought to realize that a phrase is always followed by another phrase, but that it is not decided in advance which new phrase is going to be linked to the opening phrase. Normally, a phrase is followed by another phrase, but *what* the content or the regime of this new phrase will be, is – from the standpoint of the linkage of phrases – not determined in advance. This non-determination causes every new phrase to be an 'event', a 'happening'. The phrase 'the door is closed' can be followed by the utterance 'this is so, because it is cold outside', but also by the utterance 'of course, for the key has been lost', and also by 'today there is no class; it is a banking holiday' – linkages which give us a clear idea of the situation that prompts the speakers to intervene. Lyotard has this to say about the event character of the linkages: "The other point underlying my argument, and one that is essential for an understanding of [my criticism of] totalitarianism, is that each phrase, no matter how ordinary, arrives as an event. I am not saying that each phrase is exceptional, sensational, or unprecedented, but that what it con-tains is never necessary. It is necessary *that* something happens (the event); but *what* happens (the phrase, its meaning, object, interlocutors) is never necessary – the necessity of contingency or, if you like, the being

26. *Ibid.*, 42.

of nonbeing. The linkage between phrase and phrase is not, as a rule, predetermined."[27]

(c) This brings us to the notion of 'discourse genres'. Indeed, the direction an eventful flow of 'the linkage of phrases' takes depends on a particular genre of discourse. The discourse genre, thus, sets a particular 'rule' to the linkage of phrases, though this 'rule' is hardly applicable, in an identical way, to all possible arrangements within a discourse genre. The 'rule' is rather 'dictated' or 'inspired' by the end or objective one pursues within a particular genre. Lyotard characterizes the importance of this (flexible) rule system as follows: "Genres of discourse clearly exist: exposition (like the present one), the genre of dialectics (which we call discussion), the genre of comedy, the genre of tragedy, satire (the genre of genres), the essay, the diary, and so forth. These genres of discourse set rules for the linking of phrases to ensure that the discourse proceeds towards its generically assigned end: to convince, to persuade, to inspire laughter or tears, and so forth."[28] And he is quick to add that, depending on the genre of discourse, one will have a stricter or less strict observance of the way in which descriptive phrases can be followed by prescriptive or performative phrases – transition from one phrase regime to another. At any rate, what one observes is that rules of linkage (even in the flexible way they are allowed to occur in a particular genre of discourse) are not always followed, especially not in postmodern texts: "But, as you would know, these rules of linking are seldom (if ever) respected outside of classical poetics and rhetoric. Modern writers and artists continually break these rules, precisely because they set a greater value on questioning the event than on worrying about imitation or conformity [....] What is interesting about these modern infractions is not that they are transgressive, as Bataille thought, but that they constantly open the question of nothingness, the question of the event."[29] Rules can be interrupted on behalf of the event one wants to save.

2. The Question of Justice

Infraction of the rules of the genre of discourse, thus, seems to confirm again Lyotard's preference for 'unexpected moves' from the part of postmodern inventive scientists. But there is more to it. On the level of a political philosophy, the ethicist/philosopher must also see to it that the occurrence of the 'event' be salvaged ('is there still something happening? Is there still an echo of expectancy left after the linkage of a new

27. *Ibid.*, 42-43.
28. *Ibid.*, 43.
29. *Ibid.*, 43.

phrase to a previous one?). This concern makes the ethicist alert for the possible abuses that can be made of regimes of phrases, in terms of establishing an oppressive hegemonic regime (as it occurs when statements with a limited range are made *as if* they had universal validity). In this respect, Lyotard is critical of any attempt at claiming a universally binding validity for what one is doing when regimes of phrases are combined with each other. What is at stake is, again, the indefensible pretension of lending a totalizing authority to a particular 'legitimating narrative'. These legitimating narratives lack instruments of their own with which to analyze to what extent they are causing damage to those who are excluded from the narrative. On the other hand it is easy to dismantle the arrangements of genres of discourse and regimes of phrases and to debunk their often hidden totalizing agenda. To give an idea of such a strategy of dismantling, Lyotard analytically lists the moments of a 'modern deliberation' to show that, in them, only heterogeneous regimes of phrases are presented, which taken all together, do not properly allow us to jump to a totalizing prescription.

He lists seven moments of such a deliberation: 1. The leaders of the community formulate their highest end in the mode of an interrogative prescriptive: "'What ought we to be?' The phrase is full of possible meanings: happy, wise, free, equal, rich, powerful, artistic, American?" 2. Then one sees that to this 'What ought we to be?' a new phrase is linked which takes on the form of a 'hypothetical imperative': 'What ought we to do in order to be that?' 3. This leads to an enumeration of the "means to attain this end: an analysis of the situation, a description of the resources available to both allies and adversaries, and a definition of their respective interests." This is a purely cognitive, descriptive genre within the deliberative discourse, a matter of specialists, experts, advisers, and consultants. 4. Then comes the moment of the montage of scenarios: 'What might we do?' (an intuition without clear conceptual cognition). 5. Each party in the deliberation comes up with a possible scenario, and here the dispute starts; steps of persuasion are undertaken in order not only to refute the other party but also to persuade a third party (a judge, a president, or the electoral body in a democracy). 6. Then comes the judgment or final verdict, which can take the form of ballots or arbitrations: 'This is what we ought to do'. 7. And finally "The judgment must be legitimated. This is the role of normative discourse ('does one have the right to decide in this way?')." If the answer is 'Yes', then decrees are issued and, accordingly, infractions must be punished.[30]

30. *Ibid.*, 48-49.

Lyotard gives this example to show that all these stages, in fact, function as heterogeneous elements, which are then put in a certain flow of arrangement. These elements are heterogeneous, for how can a prescriptive phrase 'We ought to do this' (stage 6) possibly be deduced from a descriptive phrase 'This is what we can do' (stage 5)? Yet, if the heterogeneous elements are nonetheless perceived as having a sequential unity, then this can only mean that a certain option already taken in stage 1 ('What ought we to be?') is setting the tone to all that is going to follow. But precisely, this option relates to the 'grand narrative' one believes or thinks one ought to believe: the project that is directed toward a goal (the attainment of progress, of a socialist state etc.). Now, Lyotard argues, this sort of option cannot be discussed in terms of conclusive proofs since the option is not verifiable in the empirical world (he refers to Kant): "[T]he narrative of the universal history of humanity [...] must remain suspended from an Ideal of practical reason (freedom, emancipation). It cannot be verified by empirical proofs but only by indirect signs, *analoga*, which signal in experience that this ideal is present in people's minds. So any discussion of this history is 'dialectical' in the Kantian sense, which is to say, without conclusion. The ideal is not presentable to the sensibility; the free society is no more demonstrable than the free act. And in the same way, there will always be a profound tension between what one ought to be and what one is."[31]

What has all this to do with linguistic pragmatics? For Lyotard, it is evident that, in the flow of linguistic arrangements, "many types of linkages are possible, and one has to decide. Deciding nothing is still deciding. Remaining silent is still speaking. Politics always rests on the way one phrase, the present phrase, is linked to another phrase. It is not about the volume of discourse or the importance of the speaker or addressee. From the different phrases that are actually possible, one will be actualized, and the actual question is, which one?"[32] Now in the deliberation process carried out under the aegis of one of modernity's metanarratives, such as 'We must do something to create social democracy, or progressive welfare', all the steps in the deliberation are linked according to a strategy that is already dictated, from the onset, by the starting point. This dictate is totalizing, and does not leave any open space for phrases in which one may expect something to happen that had not yet been decided in advance. This process ends with the consequence that the totalizing concept with which one started the discourse is bound to result in terror.

31. *Ibid.*, 50.
32. *Ibid.*, 30.

The reason why terror is the end-result is clear: The judgment about the means one is going to use collectively is from the onset a judgment that rules out all other alternatives, whereby those who would like to experiment with an alternative strategy have been – with the means of political coercion – branded as 'outlaws' from the inception of the discourse. All this shows that, in this type of deliberation, no justice is done or can be done to a plurality of alternative possibilities that nonetheless are virtually present in a democratic society. Or to state it in a still cruder way: no justice at all is done or can be done to those who are doomed to be oppressed and killed in the name of an Idea (or shall one say: an ideology?) whose validity cannot possibly be verified in empirical reality. Auschwitz is the example. For here, the opponents (the Jews who 'had' to be sent to the extermination camps) were given no voice at all to defend their alternative standpoint, when brought to the tribunal of 'reason', a tribunal which was clearly already biased from the onset because of the exclusive claim contained in the Nazis' grand story that what 'ought to be done' was the propagation and exaltation of the German race, as the authentic bearers of emancipatory ideals, against all those who still clung to remnants of obscurantism.

At this juncture, Lyotard's comes to his provisional and personal conclusion. He is convinced that a critical mind that sees through this despotic linkage of the phrases will perhaps not be able to reach a conclusion as to which linkage might be correct. But also that what he, at any rate, must do is to voice a protest against the totalizing/totalitarian style which is bound to give a particular preconceived direction to the linkage of phrases. By voicing this protest, Lyotard maintains, the postmodern intellectual will, at least, have 'borne witness' to the unduly repressed possibilities. All of these possibilities exemplify the wealth of human language considered in its essential diversity.

III. Transition Towards the Sublime

In the course of his studies on language pragmatics, Lyotard increasingly refers to Kant's *Critique of Judgment*. If one knows a little bit of the history of philosophy, then this interest becomes understandable. For in this work, Immanuel Kant (1724-1804) tackled the intricate question as to whether and under which respect two distinct and heterogeneous language games, such as the scientific discourse which studies the general laws of nature (examined in the *Critique of Pure Reason*), and the ethical discourse which studies the universal obligation of the categorical imperative (examined in the *Critique of Practical Reason*), might be brought to a certain rapprochement with one another. On a basic level, these two discourses are separated by a chasm, since the former deals with the examination of the mechanical determination inherent in the laws of nature (the Newtonian universal laws of nature allow of no exception), whereas the latter delves into the realm of human freedom (those persons act responsibly who live up to the maxim that their behavior ought to be such that it reflects a universal standard of morality, a standard which everybody would accept as a matter of moral obligation). Because of the discrepancy between mechanical determination (in nature) and freely assumed obligation (in ethics), Kant reaches the conclusion that one is dealing with two non-connected islands which, so to speak, make up different life-worlds. Nevertheless, it must be possible for human persons to travel back and forth from one island to the other, which at least suggests that eventually a way must be found to construct a bridge over the deep waters.

This succinct description may suffice to situate the problem dealt with in the *Critique of Judgment*, though this does not mean that the problem is already resolved. For apparently, the bridging of the gap cannot be obtained by having recourse to a higher meta-language under which the two heterogeneous discourses would be subsumed. Such a subsumption could not possibility do justice to the heterogeneous character of the two discourses. A different approach is needed, one which does not proceed with fixed rules at hand, but which proceeds with a pondering attitude. For only in this reflective mood will one be able to perceive an analogy between the realm of nature and that of human freedom. To characterize this rather subjective, aesthetic approach, Kant draws the distinction between a determinant and a reflective judgment; he says: "If the universal (the rule, principle, law) is given, then judgment, which subsumes the particular under it, is *determinative* [...] But if only the particular is given and judgment has to find the universal for it, then this power is merely *reflective*."[33] The reflective judgment starts thus from the particular thing or event, to venture itself on the search for a not yet known universal scheme which is expected to shed a light of appreciation on the particular case.

As to the question of how a certain analogy could be ascertained between the realm of necessity (nature) and the realm of freedom (human responsibility), Kant – after many pages of philosophical meditation – proposes that we should look at the particular products of nature (a beautiful rose-garden, animals, mountains, stellar constellations) *as if* they

---

33. I. Kant, *Critique of Judgment*, *Akademie* edition, 179, trans. W. Pluhar (Indianapolis, IN: Hackett Publishing Company, 1987) 18.

were produced purposively by Providence. The 'as if'-formula is important, for Kant has shown that we are not able to prove (with the help of cosmological arguments that start from the alleged order of nature[34]) *that* Providence has, indeed, endowed things in nature with a specific purposefulness. The repudiation of the 'that' is part of Kant's agnosticism; the 'as if' reveals his own concern about aesthetically perceiving analogies between the behavior of things in the realm of nature and the purposive actions of the ethical human agents. Or as Richard Beardsworth puts it: "[In the *Critique of Judgment*] nature is reflected upon *as if* its ultimate end (and the end of all the physical ends of nature, reflected upon *analogically*) were man, whose end is 'culture' (the setting of ends independent of nature in its mechanical sense)."[35] It is clear that this 'as if' (as if there was an analogy) has something aesthetic about it. At any rate, it honors the role of 'productive imagination', which for Kant functions as an intermediate power between the senses and the mind.

As we will see in later chapters, Lyotard is particularly interested in Kant's procedures developed in the *Critique of Judgment*, although he skirts around the very problematic Kant wanted to clarify, namely whether we can look at nature as if things in it were purposefully ordered? For Lyotard, Kant's *procedures* are important, rather than the subject matter of the possible affinity between nature and humans. Lyotard therefore highlights the fact that Kant, in building a bridge between two heterogeneous domains, says repeatedly that this 'bridge' is *only aesthetically valid*. To take the 'as if' view as a real bridge between the two heterogeneous domains will land one in a 'transcendental illusion'. Lyotard says: "[We should] not expect the slightest reconciliation between 'language games'. Kant, in naming them the faculties, knew that they are separated by an abyss and that only a transcendental illusion (Hegel's) can hope to totalize them into a real unity. But he also knew that the price of this illusion is terror."[36]

A second procedure Lyotard appreciates in the *Critique of Judgment* is Kant's new approach of engaging in a search for the 'rule' (Kant's definition of the 'reflective judgment'), rather than relying on some already pre-established rule or principle under which the particular data are to be subsumed. This appreciation comes to the fore in his definition of the postmodern artist or writer: "The postmodern artist or writer is in the

34. Newtonian science is only able to examine the mechanical functioning of nature, and not the purposefulness or finality of the same.

35. R. Beardsworth, "Lyotard's Agitated Judgment," *Judging Lyotard*, ed. A. Benjamin, 66.

36. J.-F. Lyotard, *The Postmodern Explained*, 15-16.

position of a philosopher: the text he writes or the work he creates is not in principle governed by pre-established rules and cannot be judged according to a determinant judgment, by the application of given categories to this text or work. Such rules and categories are what the work or text is investigating. The artist and the writer therefore work without rules and in order to establish the rules for *what will have been made*. This is why the work and the text can take on the properties of an event."[37] Yet it is not only the writer and the artist that are in search of the rules of the game: the same is true for postmodern scientists: with their daring moves they try to escape from the grip of the system. Hegemonic systems 'know' from the onset what the – mandatory – rules of the game are.

As will become evident in the next chapters, Lyotard attaches enormous importance to feelings that lie at the basis of judgments. It is exactly this rootedness in feelings that account for the reflective judgment's engagement in a search for the rules, at the other side of (hegemonic) deductive systems that start from first principles. In this context one has also to place the special feeling of the sublime, which consists of a mixture of horror and delight. This special feeling arises in one's contact with the supersensible Ideas of Reason whose unfathomable content cannot be exhausted by empirical presentations. As we will see, Lyotard is under the spell of the supersensible which he wants to shield from profanation. For him, the grand narratives of modernity have taken possession of the reality of the supersensible; they deemed it possible to give a sensible presentation of the Kantian 'Ideas of Reason' (*Vernunftidee*) – the supersensible notions of grandeur and majesty. But as Kant in his analysis of the sublime shows: these ideas are conceivable and, indeed, must be conceived, but ultimately they escape every presentation.

This allows us to understand Lyotard's statement: "[I]t should be made clear that it is not up to us to *provide reality*, but to invent allusions to what is conceivable but not presentable [...] The nineteenth and twentieth centuries have given us our fill of terror. We have paid dearly for our nostalgia for the all and the one, for a reconciliation of the concept [*Vernunftidee*] and the sensible [...] Beneath the general demand for relaxation and appeasement, we hear murmurings of the desire to reinstitute terror and fulfill the phantasm of taking possession of reality. The answer is this: war on totality. Let us attest to the unpresentable; let us activate the 'differends' and save the honor of the name."[38] Lyotard wants to safeguard the purity of the supersensible Ideas against every attempt at putting

37. *Ibid.*, 15.
38. *Ibid.*, 16.

them in the service of pseudo-universal narratives which in the end turn into oppressive ideologies. For him, his task as a philosopher consists in bearing witness to the unpresentable, even if this would bring him into conflict with hegemonic powers.

CHAPTER TWO

KANT'S NOTION OF THE SUBLIME AND ITS APPROPRIATION BY LYOTARD

Lyotard is renowned for his skill in language pragmatics. This skill helps him to lay bare objectionable confusion of regimes of phrases (especially descriptive and prescriptive phrases). Such confusion usually betrays a hidden strategy for establishing a monopolistic empire. Heterogeneous regimes of phrases must never be lumped together. This he has learned from Wittgenstein (1989-1951). In addition to this Wittgensteinian influence, however, Lyotard is heavily indebted to the insights of Immanuel Kant. Pivotal in this respect is his appropriation of Kant's notion of the feeling of the sublime. As rational as Lyotard's language pragmatics are, the Kantian elements he employs are full of emotion. One might even say, while language pragmatics provide Lyotard with tools of analysis, Kant makes him speak from his heart (*Gemüt*). Bearing witness to the unpresentable is a question of strong, motivating feelings – the 'place' of contact with the absolute.

In this chapter I will, first, explain the distinction Kant draws between experiences of the beautiful and experiences of the sublime. Whereas the experience of the beautiful presupposes a harmonious interplay between the imagination and an indeterminate concept of human understanding (*Verstand*), this harmony is broken in the feeling of the sublime. Here too, an interplay occurs: between the imagination and the Ideas of Reason (*Vernunft*), but this interplay is characterized by a rupture. Ideas of Reason come into play as soon as one is confronted with objects that are limitless, such as vast magnitudes or chaotic elements in nature. At that moment the imagination is no longer able to synthesize the excessive impressions and has recourse to Ideas of Reason, which by definition relate to vastness, immensity, and the moral grandeur of humankind. When exposed to a hurricane, for example, it may dawn upon the spectator that, compared to the Idea of human grandeur, this terrifying menace is insignificant. In this awareness one tries to expand the power of one's imagination in order to visualize the Idea of human grandeur. Yet one must finally admit that even the greatest power of one's imagination is still inadequate to present the whole content of this Idea of Reason. The

painful but also uplifting experience of this inadequacy, and the resonance it produces in one's heart (*Gemüt*), form the core of the feeling of
the sublime.

A second notion that will be examined is that of enthusiasm, which for
Kant is a modality of the feeling of the sublime. Enthusiasm consists in
the straining of our forces by Ideas that impart to the *Gemüt* a momentum
whose effects are mightier than those coming from the senses. Enthusiasm is the might of the *Gemüt* to rise above obstacles of sensibility under
the spell of the unpresentable Idea. Kant illustrates this with the help of
the commandment of the Jewish Law: 'Thou shall not make unto thee any
graven image, or any likeness of anything that is in heaven or on earth'.
This commandment fills the Jewish community with a spirited emotion.
At the same time Kant warns against the illusion of wanting to *see* something beyond all bounds of sensibility, since this will unavoidably lead
to fanaticism. Another important field in which enthusiasm comes to the
fore is in the realm of politics. Such a political enthusiasm arose, for
example, among the European nations when watching the events of the
French revolution. For Kant, such a unanimously shared enthusiasm testifies to humankind's moral capacity.

It is at this juncture that Lyotard begins his appropriation of Kant. He
starts by pointing out that, unlike in Kant's days, people at present have
little reason for political enthusiasm. On the contrary, the scene of history abounds with atrocities committed by regimes that initially were
hailed with enthusiasm: one ought only to think of the abomination of
Auschwitz under Hitler and of the Gulag Archipelago under Stalin. So,
it is imperative that we examine what went wrong with this enthusiasm.
A case in point is the enthusiasm which Karl Marx saw at work in the
new universal class of the proletariat as it stood up against the bourgeoisie. For Lyotard, Marx does not interpret this enthusiasm in the same
manner as Kant did. Kant saw in the enthusiasm that arose among the
spectators of the French revolution only a 'sign' that humankind had
made a step forward towards its moral end, whereas Marx understands
feelings of enthusiasm as a request emanating from a speculative philosophy that, with visionary precision, already *sees* how the proletariat is to
attain its unity under the guidance of the party. The linkage between
enthusiasm and the logically conceived unfolding of history in the style
of Hegel accounts for Marxism's lapse into fanaticism, a lapse against
which Kant had warned. The same linkage corrupts and spoils the genuine feeling of the sublime, of which enthusiasm is a modality. Speculative philosophies of history want to steer the course of history by themselves, thus taking hold, with their imagination, of the supersensible

domain that escapes all visual presentation. As far as Lyotard himself is concerned, he wants to bear witness to the power of the unpresentable, even when this witness will take the form of a deep sense of melancholy.

I. Kant on the Difference between the Beautiful and the Sublime

1. *The Beautiful*

Kant defines the artistic experience of the beautiful in terms of a 'pure pleasure without any interest'. The focus here is on the effect that a work of art has on us when we are taking delight in it. This delight is pure pleasure. As a result, an artistic experience does not pay attention to the market-value of the work of art (e.g. a painting by Van Gogh that is brought to the hammer in Sotheby's), nor is it induced by one's histori-cal knowledge of the provenance of this or that Greek vase (scientific interest), nor has it anything to do with ethical purposes (although the performance of a Greek drama may induce a certain catharsis of our feel-ings). The experience of the beautiful gives us pleasure because our judg-ment of taste makes us appreciate a harmonious configuration on display. This judgment differs both from scientific knowledge (which results from the application of conceptual categories) and ethical knowledge (which results from one's dealing with ethical standards). It is rather a reflective judgment which, at the occasion of one's exposure to a thing of beauty which induces delight, launches one on a search for the rules that might explain the authentic quality of this delight. [This search for the rules – rules that are not given in advance – is the aspect that Lyotard will bor-row from Kant, and which he also will apply to other domains, such as the art of writing, or the process of creative, artistic invention. See the next chapters].[1]

Central to artistic experience, thus, are (i) the subjective feelings occa-sioned by the presence of a work of art, and (ii) feelings which cannot be subsumed under any precise or determinate concept. This makes the expe-rience of the beautiful less clear and more indeterminate than conceptual knowledge. Nonetheless, some purposiveness comes to mind in the act

---

1. Recall again Kant's definitions: "If the universal (the rule, principle, law) is given, then judgment, which subsumes the particular under it, is *determinative* [...] But if only the particular is given and judgment has to find the universal for it, then this power is merely *reflective*:" I. Kant, *Critique of Judgment, Akademie* edition, 179, trans. W. Pluhar (Indianapolis, IN: Hackett Publishing Company, 1987) 18.

of artistic contemplation. Thus, Kant defines beauty as "an object's form of purposiveness insofar as it is perceived in the object without the presentation of a purpose."[2] Or in a shorter formulation: beauty is 'purposiveness without purpose'. Indeed, if the perceived purposiveness of the beautiful object would be accompanied by the presentation of a clear-cut instrumental purpose, one would have to do with a scientific assessment of the matter in question: "There are 'purposive' wholes which cannot, without being mis-described, be referred to any determinate purpose or subsumed under any determinate concept. The harmonious interplay and interdependence of sounds in a musical composition or of colours in a landscape are cases in point. Indeed the art of many modern painters, and of non-representational artists, in general, seems to be directed to the creation of 'purposive' wholes which cannot, even by the most insensitive public, be referred to any purpose or any determinate concept."[3] In short, there are beautiful harmonious configurations in which we take pleasure, though they cannot be used for any practical purpose and are also not meant to fulfill that need. Take for example a flower, a rose garden, a sun-lit landscape, or the paintings representing them. They arouse an unspecified pleasure simply because they are a thing of beauty. We might, of course, look at the rose garden or at a landscape from a different perspective – what is its use as an eco-system for the environment? – but then we are no longer experiencing the flower, landscape, etc. in a purely artistic contemplation.

The absence of a concise conceptual understanding is crucial for Kant. What matters in the judgment of taste is rather the free play of imagination (*Einbildungskraft*) in conjunction with an imprecise notional understanding. A comparison with the procedures of scientific knowledge makes this point clear: "In the *Critique of Pure Reason* Kant distinguishes between (i) the given manifold of presentations; (ii) their collection by the imagination; (iii) the application of a Category [of understanding] which confers objective empirical reference. The unity of an aesthetic, purposive whole does not involve the third feature. What is collected by the imagination has unity. It is a unity consisting in the reference to 'indeterminate concepts'; it is conferred on what has been collected by the imagination through a vague understanding but not through determinate or specific concepts."[4]

The fact that no clear concepts are being used does not, however, entail a blockage of communication. For everyone certainly realizes what a

2. Kant, *Critique of Judgment*, *Akademie* edition, 236, trans. W. Pluhar, 84.
3. S. Körner, *Kant* (London: Penguin Books, 1945 [1974]) 184.
4. *Ibid.*, 185.

judgment of taste is about, viz., that it results from the 'free play of imagination' in conjunction with 'indeterminate concepts'. Whoever utters judgments of taste, then, can rely on the basic agreement of others whose judgments of taste are operating along the same line. There will, of course, always be some variety in taste, but this is no reason to doubt the basic common structure in aesthetical experience. Artists are able to understand each other without much ado, even if they disagree on particular details. Interesting in all of this is Kant's underlying argument. Just as he is convinced that the perception of a specific purpose ('we ought to do this') is able to unite people around a common goal, so too the perception of a 'purposive whole without practical purpose', must have the force of making people agree on the fact that one has to do with a thing of beauty: "In judging of anything that is beautiful, we 'assume agreement' on the part of everybody who perceives it. This 'ascription' (*Ansinnen*) to everybody, of agreement, presupposes a sense common to all human beings" – a common sense "which is, however, no external sense, but merely the effect of the free interplay of our cognitive powers".[5]

2. *The Sublime*

Kant set for himself the goal of conveying, in the terms of his own philosophical method, the widespread interest in aesthetics in 18th-century Europe (especially England). This method consists in revealing how the human faculties (imagination, conceptual and ideational knowledge) relate to each other when forming a judgment on a particular domain of human existence. We have already seen how this method was applied to the study of the experience of the beautiful. But in 18th-century Britain, there was also a vivid interest in the sublime as distinct from the beautiful (Edmund Burke). This notion was borrowed from pseudo-Longinus (*Peri hypsous*), a first-century rhetorician. While Longinus studied the sublime effects inherent in the use of particular literary styles, Burke's attention was drawn to the feelings of 'horror' and 'delight' stirred by the encounter with grandeur and majesty in the brute forces of nature (tempests, impressive mountains, etc.): "Awe, compounded of mingled terror and exultation, once reserved for God, passed over in the 17th century first to an expanded cosmos, then from the macrocosm to the greatest objects in the geocosm – mountains, oceans, deserts ... Scientifically minded Platonists, reading their ideas of infinity into a God of Plenitude, then reading them out again, transferred from God to Space to Nature

5. *Ibid.*, 87.

conceptions of majesty, grandeur, vastness in which both admiration and awe were combined. The 17th century discovered 'the Aesthetics of the Infinite'."[6]

Kant meets, thus, the challenge of transposing the 'Aesthetics of the Infinite' (the sublime) into the patterns of his transcendental method of philosophizing. For he is somewhat dissatisfied with Anglo-Saxon empiricism in so far as it tends to leave out the role of Reason in engendering bright Ideas. He seeks to understand how, in the case of the sublime, imagination (*Einbildungskraft*), which is sensuous, relates to speculative Reason (*Vernunft*), which deals with noumenal Ideas[7] of the infinite (vastness, grandeur). Note that 'Reason' as the faculty that generates noumenal Ideas differs from mere 'understanding' (*Verstand*), which provides conceptual knowledge. Whereas 'understanding' operates with concepts deduced from empirical data, 'Reason' is totally super-empirical in that it explores Ideas that are objects of pure thought – ideational contents that cannot be met or exhausted by empirical experience, such as the ideational content of absolute vastness, or of absolute, total freedom or human grandeur.

Within this framework, Kant finds out that the experience of the sublime results from the clashing interaction between productive imagination (*Einbildungskraft*) and the ungraspable content of the noumenal Idea of grandeur produced by Reason (*Vernunft*) – a clash that takes place at the very moment when one is being overwhelmed, e.g., by the tremendous force of natural events such as tempests or hurricanes. Strictly speaking, it is not so much the sweeping tempest that must be called sublime but rather the unsettling experience of awe compounded with mingled horror and exultation. Horror and exultation are the effects of the aforementioned clash between the two cognitive powers. This allows us to see not only the common ground but also the difference between the experience of the beautiful and that of the sublime.

The main difference between the sublime and the beautiful lies according to Kant in the following features. First, "the beautiful in nature concerns the form of the object, which consists in [the object's] being bounded. But the sublime can also be found in a formless object insofar as we present *unboundedness*, either [as] in the object or because the object prompts us to present it, while yet we add to this unboundedness

---

6. M. Nicholson, *Mountain Gloom and Mountain Glory; the Development of the Aesthetics of the Infinite* (Ithaca, NY: Cornell University Press, 1959) 143.

7. Noumenon is "an object of pure thought not connected with sense perception" (Webster's Dictionary).

the thought of its totality."[8] Secondly, "the intrinsic and most important distinction between the sublime and the beautiful is presumably the following: [...] (Independent) natural beauty carries with it a purposiveness in its form, by which the object seems as it were predetermined for our power of judgment, so that this beauty constitutes in itself an object of our liking. On the other hand, if something arouses in us, merely in apprehension and without any reasoning on our part, a feeling of the sublime, then it may indeed appear, in its form, contrapurposive for our power of judgment (*zweckwidrig für unsre Urteilskraft*), incommensurate with our power of exhibition, and as it were violent to our imagination (*Einbildungskraft*), and yet we judge it all the more sublime for that."[9]

The common feature between the experiences of the beautiful and the sublime is that in both instances the faculty of judgment has recourse to a reflective judgment which is in search of its rule. This search of the rule expresses itself in the oscillating interplay between the productive imagination and an indeterminate notional element. Yet the difference comes to the fore when the exposure to vastness and majesty is given its due. At that moment the productive imagination is confronted with a totally unusual unboundedness, which makes it turn not to indeterminate concepts (related to understanding) but to supersensible Ideas of Reason (as the highest faculty). The ideational content of the latter, however, does violence to the imagination to the point of making it clear to the imagination that what happens to be 'revealed' painfully surpasses its power of presentation.

II. THE SUBLIME AS CONTRAST EXPERIENCE

In what follows I will mainly limit myself to what Kant calls the 'dynamic sublime', which he distinguishes from the 'mathematical sublime'. The mathematical sublime is experienced when one compares various big objects with one another, extrapolating the measure of their magnitudes to the very big. For example, compare the size of a tree with that of a mountain, and this again with the diameter of the earth, and this again with the diameter of the solar system, the Milky Way, etc. This cosmic panorama brings us into a state of disarray: we feel lost in the vastness of the cosmos till we are rescued by realizing – through widened imagination and its felt inadequacy of presentation – how incommensurably superior human intellectual and moral powers are to the rest of the

8. I. Kant, *Critique of Judgment*, *Akademie* edition, 244, trans. W. Pluhar, 98.
9. *Ibid.*, 245, trans. W. Pluhar, 98-99.

universe. The same is true for the dynamical sublime; but here, the focus is on the perception of the chaotic elements in nature, so much so that one even begins to reckon with the absence of purposiveness in nature. Here, too, the dismay before the chaotic elements recedes, in that the soul (viz. imagination) – however inadequate its vision might be – suddenly beholds the majestic purposiveness of the sublime destiny of human beings on earth.

1. *The Various Phases of the Contrast Experience*

One should not lose sight of the fact that Kant refuses to locate the sublime in nature itself, as premodern societies had done. Indeed, for premodern people, the stormy sea or an impressive waterfall was considered a phenomenon that contained sublimity within itself - the core of which is referred, then, to the fascinating and tremendous glory of the Creator. While Kant is not ignorant of this ancient habit of perceiving the '*fascinans et tremendum*' in nature, he deems that it does not fulfill the requirements of his own method. Confronted with the same chaotic natural phenomena, he instead sought to introspectively examine what happens, at this occasion, as an uplifting within the cognitive faculties of the human subjects: through the free play of imagination in conjunction with ideational unpresentability.

In her study of the sublime Christine Pries explains the contrast-experience of the sublime as follows. She distinguishes two phases: (1) Confronted with natural phenomena of excessive magnitude and power, imagination as a sensuous faculty fails to come to grips with the crushing impressions by which it is overpowered. The imagination no longer succeeds in synthesizing this excessive, measureless object into a purposive whole. The imagination collapses; nature appears to be bereft of purposiveness, which causes dismay. (2) In spite of all this, delight adds itself to dismay, for it dawns upon the person that even natural phenomena of such an excessive magnitude and power are, in fact, infinitesimally small, when gauged by the power of Reason (*Vernunft*): nature's forces may, to be sure, defeat the human being's sensuousness, but not his/her intellectual faculty. The human being is saved in virtue of his/her intellectual faculty which makes one superior to nature. The fact that eventually delight emerges proves, for Kant, the existence of supersensible Ideas and their corresponding faculty, 'Reason' (*Vernunft*). The noumenal sphere ('Reason') succors the collapsing sensuous imagination by showing that the lack of purposiveness in nature points to a higher purposiveness, namely the purposiveness of the emotional uplifting of the human person. This purposiveness proves the existence and the majesty of Reason. A 'negative' presentation of the infinite – of the Idea of Reason – is given.[10]

A more detailed analysis shows that Kant is constructing an oscillating bridge or passage between the sensuous imagination and the ideational (noumenal) realm of Reason (*Vernunft*). On the one hand, Kant maintains that, under the pressure of Reason and its noumenal Ideas, the sensuous imagination begins, in a contrast effect, to behold visions and images of the human being's sovereignty and moral superiority over nature. In this activity the imagination is 'stretched' beyond its current capacity. Yet, this 'stretching' (*Erweiterung*) of the imagination is kept within limits, for that which the widened imagination is tentatively bringing into picture can never exhaust the whole content of the Ideas of Reason (*Vernunft*), since these Ideas are 'unpresentable'. It is because of this inadequacy that creative imagination must do violence unto itself up to the point of plunging into an abyss in which it is both lost and pays respect (*Achtung*) to the supersensible Idea of human grandeur. The stretching of imagination is both painful and delightful. Painful, because the awful coercion to embark on an expansion of imagination's view adds itself to the dismay before the chaotic phenomena of nature. Delightful, because this expansion engenders an emotional uplifting of the soul (*Gemüt*), when finding all the might of the imagination still inadequate to the Ideas of Reason.[11]

More convincingly than Burke, Kant has succeeded in showing how, in the experience of the sublime, 'delight' relates to 'horor', and also how these alternating feelings flow from the violence imagination must do unto itself in order to broaden its view and to engender images and representations that point to the noumenal realm, however painfully inadequate these images must remain. This shows that true sublimity must be sought in the mind and emotions of the judging subject, and not in the objects of nature – which only occasion this feeling. About this focus on interiority Kant has this to say: "Who would want to call sublime such things as shapeless mountain masses piled on one another in wild disarray; with their pyramids of ice, or to the gloomy raging sea? But the mind (*das Gemüt*) feels elevated in its own judgment of itself when it contemplates these without concern for their form and abandons itself to the imagination and to a Reason that has come to be connected with it – though quite

---

10. See C. Pries, "Einleitung," *Das Erhabene: Zwischen Grenzerfahrung und Grössenwahn*, ed. idem (Weinheim: Acta Humaniora, 1989) 8-9.
11. See H. Böhme "Das Steinerne: Anmerkungen zur Theorie des Erhabenen aus dem Blick des Menschenfremdesten," *Das Erhabene*, ed. C. Pries, 120.

without a determinate purpose, and merely expanding it – and finds all the might of the imagination still inadequate to Reason's Ideas."[12]

Lyotard interprets Kant as follows: "The faculty of presentation, the imagination fails in its attempt at presenting a vision commensurate to the Idea. This failure in presenting causes displeasure, a scission within the person between that which he can comprehend but is unable to present in images. But this displeasure again generates pleasure, even a double one: firstly, the powerlessness of imagination testifies *e contrario* that it seeks to make visible things that cannot be made visible; that it endeavors to make its object correspond to that of Reason. Secondly, the dismay at the inadequacy of presentation negatively signals the incommensurability of the power of the Ideas."[13]

2. The Clash between Mind and Nature as the Core Experience of the Sublime

In its essence, the experience of the sublime is the elevation of the mind above nature. This elevation takes place with respect to both outer nature (mountains, seas) and inner nature (senses, imagination). In this process, the productive imagination must broaden itself beyond its natural capacities, attracted by the lure of noumenal Ideas. This shows that Kant admits a certain affinity between the experience of the sublime and ethics. Already in his *Critique of Practical Reason* he had ventured to say: "Two things fill the mind with ever new and increasing admiration and awe [...]: the starry heavens above me and the moral law within me."[14]

Indeed, also at the level of ethics (practical reason), Kant depicts a tension between chaotic elements and a superior calling: between one's unbridled sensuality and one's ethical duty. Here, too, he underlines the need for an elevation: the ethical person must do violence unto him or herself in order to pass from sensual habits to a moral option. In this passage the moral superiority of human beings over brute nature is affirmed. But, unlike the case of aesthetics, this superiority is established in the proper domain of ethical decisions: to the extent that the moral person lives up to the summons of the categorical imperative s/he is brought into

---

12. I. Kant, *Critique of Judgment*, Akademie edition, 256, trans. W. Pluhar, 113.
13. J.-F. Lyotard, "Das Erhabene und die Avantgarde," *Verabschiedung der (Post)Moderne? Eine interdisziplinäre Debatte*, ed. J. Le Rider and G. Raulet (Tübingen: publisher, 1987) 260 [translation mine].
14. I. Kant, *Critique of Practical Reason*, A 288/289, trans. L. Beck (Indianapolis, IN: Bobbs-Merrill Educational Publishing, 1956) 166.

immediate contact with the supersensible, noumenal world. This contact takes place without any sensuous mediation, for the simple reason that sensuous considerations must be eliminated as detrimental to the ethical enterprise. The universal obligation of the categorical imperative is incompatible with the sensuous feelings of the human person.

In aesthetics, however, this elevation of the mind above nature takes place in the medium of a sensitive faculty: in the broadening of imagination's view under the shock and the spell of noumenal Ideas. Although this elevation is basically spiritual,[15] it is effected in the medium of a widened imagination, which as such is a sensuous faculty. The imagination embarks on visualizing the noumenal ideas, whose total content it is unable to adequately present. This *sensuous mediation and its felt inadequacy* make up the difference between the aesthetics of the sublime and the realm of ethics. True, in the experience of the sublime the expanded imagination must finally bow its head before the superior might of the noumenal world. Yet, in doing so, the soul (*Gemüt*) "feels elevated in its own judgment of itself [...on finding] all the might of imagination still unequal to Reason's Ideas."[16]

If 'sensuous mediation' is important in the aesthetics of the sublime, this raises the question as to how imagination exactly relates to Reason. Here it is said that, in the aesthetic judgment of the sublime, the creative imagination acts in conjunction with the Ideas of Reason. What does this mean? It means that even if there is a disparity between the creative imagination (as a sensible power) and Reason (as purely intellectual power), and even if this disparity would eventually lead to a subjugation of the former by the latter, the role of imagination remains too important to be neglected. When comparing morality and the aesthetic judgment of the sublime, Kant makes it clear that in morality "Reason must exert its dominance over sensibility" in order to keep one's respect for the categorical imperative intact. But he is quick to add that, in the aesthetic judgment of the sublime, things are slightly different: Here "we present this dominance as being exerted by imagination itself, as an instrument of Reason."[17] Compared with the experience of the beautiful, which results in pure delight, the experience of the sublime is characterized by a delight that is 'only negative', that is: a delight that is based on sacrifice: not a sacrifice to alien powers, but to a power – to Reason as the source of

---

15. "Spiritual" means "not just sensuous," since one has to do with a widening of imagination under the coercion of the supra-empirical idea of grandeur.

16. I. Kant, *Critique of Judgment*, *Akademie* edition, 256, trans. W. Pluhar, 113.

17. *Ibid.*, 268-269, trans. W. Pluhar, 128.

noumenal Ideas – of which imagination consents to become the instrument. Imagination agrees to function as the handmaid of Reason, putting
its talents in the service of this higher power (so as to be determined by
a law that is different from its own) and hereby feels both a deprivation
of its own freedom and an expansion of its might, an expansion that is
more potent than the felt sacrifice, although the felt sacrifice adds a negative connotation to the jubilation of imagination's expanded might.

Kant puts this as follows: "A liking for the sublime in nature is only
negative (whereas a liking for the beautiful is *positive*); it is a feeling
that the imagination by its own action is depriving itself of its freedom,
in being determined purposively according to a law different from that of
its empirical use. The imagination thereby acquires an expansion
[*Erweiterung*] and a might that surpasses the one it sacrifices: but the
basis of this might is concealed from it; instead the imagination *feels* the
sacrifice or depravation and at the same time the cause to which it is
being subjugated."[18]

In his analysis of the sublime, Kant is undoubtedly endeavoring to
build a 'passage' between two heterogeneous (to use Lyotard's parlance)
faculties – creative imagination and Reason as the seat of supersensible
Ideas, without merging them. That is the reason why he, on the one hand,
ventures to speak about a potent expansion of creative imagination, which
does violence unto itself under the lure of the unpresentable Ideas of Reason, and, on the other hand, seeks to show that the unpresentable Ideas
exhibit their might by making the creative imagination feel its painful
inadequacy in rendering visual these unpresentable Ideas. As far as the
latter is concerned, he even speaks about a conflict (*Widerstreit*) between
the two mental powers, whose subjective play nonetheless gives rise to
a subjectively felt purposiveness: namely the feeling that only through the
inadequacy of an imagination that has become itself unbounded can the
superiority of the supersensible ideas of totality and greatness be made
intuitable. He writes: "The judgment itself, however, always remains
only aesthetic here. For it is not based on a determinate concept of the
object, and presents merely the subjective play of the mental powers
themselves [imagination and reason] as harmonious by virtue of their
contrast. For just as, when we judge the beautiful, imagination and *understanding* give rise to a subjective purposiveness of the mental powers by
their *accordance*, so do imagination and *reason* here give rise to such a
purposiveness by their *conflict*, namely to a feeling that we have a pure
and independent Reason, or a power for estimating magnitude, whose

18. *Ibid.*, 269, trans. W. Pluhar, 129.

superiority cannot be made intuitable [*anschaulich*] by anything other than the inadequacy of that power which in exhibiting magnitudes [of sensible objects] is itself unbounded."[19]

Here is underlined again what is essential to aesthetic judgment: this judgment never relates to a determinate concept, but only deals with the subjective interplay of imagination with understanding (for the beautiful) and of imagination with Reason (for the sublime). This interplay results in a harmony without which one cannot call their interplay purposeful. This harmony is evident in the case of the beautiful because here harmony is reached on the basis of a concurrence of the two contrasting powers. In the case of the sublime this harmony is a bit more difficult to grasp, for what takes place is a harmony on the basis of a conflict between two powers. The conflict comes to the fore (i) in the violence the imagination must do unto itself to broaden its capacities (so as to operate according to a different regime) and (ii) in the feeling that even the most intensive expansion of imagination must fail in exhibiting the power of the unpresentable Ideas. But the conflict is also overcome with the realization that the might of Reason (the seat of supersensible Ideas) cannot be made intuitable (*anschaulich*) by anything else than by the felt inadequacy of imagination at the moment that it became itself unbounded.

In this conflictive relationship, imagination, even if it has to recede before the might of Reason, plays an irreplaceable role in evoking the feeling of the sublime. This role is not properly valued by simply stating that imagination is incapable of exhibiting noumenal Ideas – which therefore are unpresentable. Forgotten in this statement is the emotional component, i.e., Reason lures the imagination into an expansion, whose felt incapacity is then grasped as a sign or a proof of our supersensible vocation: "If we speak literally and consider the matter logically, Ideas cannot be exhibited. But when in intuiting nature we expand our empirical power of presentation (mathematically or dynamically), then reason, the ability to [think] an independent and absolute totality, never fails to step in and arouse the mind [*Gemüt*] to an effort, although a futile one, to make the presentation of the senses adequate to this [idea of] totality. This effort, as well as the feeling that the imagination (as it synthesizes empirical nature) is unable to attain to that idea, is itself an exhibition of the subjective purposiveness of our mind [*Gemüt*], in the use of our imagination, for the mind's [*Gemüt*] supersensible vocation."[20]

19. *Ibid.,* 258, trans. W. Pluhar, 115-116.
20. *Ibid.,* 268-269, trans. W. Pluhar, 127-128.

In this text Kant uses affective language. The aesthetically judging person speaks 'from his heart', 'from his soul' – in German: from his *Gemüt*. *Gemüt* – which in English is generally rendered as 'Mind' – "is the moral and emotional nature of man" (Webster's Dictionary). Now, it is to this moral and emotional nature of the humans that reason appeals for making an effort to find an adequate presentation of the unpresentable Idea. It is also this moral and emotional nature that recognizes a purposiveness in the imagination's inadequacy for presenting the Idea: *Gemüt* feels that this inadequacy, in spite of all the efforts invested in the expansion of productive imagination, truly manifests our supersensible vocation – *Gemüt* feels the import and the impact of our sublime destiny.

As we will see in detail in later chapters, this use of affective language is specifically honored in Lyotard's analysis of Kant's notion of the sublime in his *Lessons on the Analytic of the Sublime*.[21]

3. *Enthusiasm as a Modality of the Feeling of the Sublime*

Towards the end of his analysis of the sublime, Kant asks the question as to how enthusiasm, which is a modality of the feeling of the sublime, relates to the Idea of the good. He first of all says that enthusiasm is an affect and that an affect is an agitation of the *Gemüt* that makes it unable to engage in a free deliberation about the principles that must steer our actions. As far as that is concerned, this agitation cannot merit the esteem of reason. Yet, he continues, "enthusiasm is sublime aesthetically, because it is a straining of our forces by Ideas that impart to the mind (*Gemüt*) a momentum whose effects are mightier and more permanent than are those of an impulse produced by presentations of sense."[22]

Enthusiasm is thus a 'spirited' (*mutig*) emotion unleashed by the lure of supersensible Ideas and not by a sensible presentation. Therefore "we present it as a might of the mind (*Gemüt*) to rise above *certain* obstacles of sensibility by means of moral principles."[23] It is this connection with moral principles that makes this special agitation of the *Gemüt* sublime. The agitations of the *Gemüt* can have as their object a religious interest or a social interest, but "no matter how much they may strain the imagination, unless they leave us with a mental attunement (*Gemütsstimmung*) that influences, at least indirectly, our consciousness of our fortitude and

---

21. J.-F. Lyotard, *Lessons on the Analytic of the Sublime*, trans. E. Rottenberg (Stanford, CA: Stanford University Press, 1994). Originally published as idem, *Leçons sur l'analytique du sublime* (Paris: Galilée, 1991).

22. I. Kant, *Critique of Judgment*, Akademie edition, 272, trans. W. Pluhar, 132.

23. *Ibid.*, 271, trans. W. Pluhar, 132.

resolution concerning what carries with it pure intellectual purposiveness (namely the supersensible),"[24] they cannot be called sublime feelings. And, he concludes: "Hence the sublime must always have reference to our *way of thinking*, i.e. to providing the intellectual [side in us] and our rational ideas with supremacy over sensibility."[25]

At this juncture Kant brings up an objection which he immediately refutes. Could it not be, he asks himself, that such an abstract approach to the sublime may definitely frustrate the courageous impetus of enthusiasm? Is there still a place left for emotional uplifting, once such an emphasis has been placed on the supremacy of our intellectual side over sensibility? His answer is: 'no worry': "For though the imagination finds nothing beyond the sensible that could support it, this very removal of its barriers also makes it feel unbounded, so that its separation [from the sensible] is an exhibition of the infinite; and though an exhibition of the infinite can as such never be more than merely negative, it still expands the soul [*die aber doch die Seele erweitert*]. Perhaps the most sublime passage in the Jewish Law is the commandment: Thou shalt not make unto thee any graven image, or any likeness of anything that is in heaven or on earth, or under the earth etc. This commandment alone can explain the enthusiasm that the Jewish people in their civilized era felt for its religion when it compared itself with other peoples, or that can explain the pride that Islam inspires. The same holds also for our presentation of the moral law, and for the predisposition within us for morality. It is indeed a mistake to worry that depriving this presentation of whatever could commend it to the senses will result in its carrying with it no more than a cold and lifeless approval without any moving force or emotion. It is exactly the other way round. For once the senses no longer see anything before them, while yet the unmistakable and indelible Idea of morality remains, one would sooner need to temper the momentum of an unbounded imagination so as to keep it from rising to the level of enthusiasm, than to seek to support these ideas with images and childish devices for fear that they would otherwise be powerless."[26]

The removal from the senses makes the imagination feel unbounded, and this expansion becomes the medium in which the infinite is exhibited – in a merely negative presentation, which has nevertheless the power to expand the soul. For Kant this merely negative presentation is crucial, for it prevents one from falling prey to fanaticism "which is the *delusion*

24. *Ibid.*, 273, trans. W. Pluhar, 134.
25. *Ibid.*, 274, trans. W. Pluhar, 134-135.
26. *Ibid.*, 274, trans. W. Pluhar, 135.

[*Wahn*] *of wanting to SEE something beyond all bounds of sensibility.*"[27]
If enthusiasm is "comparable to *madness* [*Wahnsinn*]," fanaticism "is
comparable to *mania* [*Wahnwitz*];" "in enthusiasm, an affect, the imagination is unbridled, but in fanaticism, a deep-seated and brooding passion, it is ruleless. Madness is a passing accident that presumably strikes
even the soundest understanding on occasion; mania is a disease that
deranges it."[28]

To complete his treatment of enthusiasm, Kant still lists various modes
of sublime feelings; he even includes what one might call an enthusiasm
e contrario: sadness (*Traurigkeit*) and grief (*Betrübnis*) on moral grounds
and not just as a sympathy for people who are hit by misfortune: "This
sadness, which does not concern evils that fate imposes on other people
(in which case it would be caused by sympathy), but those that they inflict
on themselves (a sadness that rests on an antipathy involving principles),
is sublime because it rests on ideas, whereas the sadness caused by sympathy can at most count as beautiful [...];even grief (but not a dejected
kind of sadness) may be included among the *vigorous* affects, if it has its
basis in moral ideas."[29] I mention this type of sublime feeling because it
will become central in Lyotard's understanding of the sublime.

The experience of the sublime also appears in Kant's political essays.
There he brings up the Idea of a 'sublime war': a war can be horrible and
terrifying; yet it can also be sublime insofar as from it the breakthrough
of a more just and humane society is expected. In other words, a war can
unleash an enthusiasm in those who allow their *Gemüt* to be grasped by
the uplifting Idea of 'a morally improved humanity to come'. In this context, he mentions the 'political enthusiasm' that took possession of most
of the European peoples when contemplating the achievements of the
French revolution in 1789. Kant, certainly, knew of the terror that accompanied this revolution, but this did not prevent him from interpreting that
political enthusiasm as a 'sign' that, through this event, humankind had
come closer to its true moral vocation. These and other 'signs' in history
can be read as an anticipation of the hoped-for breakthrough of the reign
of freedom: The enthusiasm which the spectators of the French revolution experience "testifies to mankind's moral capacity,"[30] and can thus
be called sublime.

27. *Ibid.*, 275, trans. W. Pluhar, 136.
28. *Ibid.*, 275, trans. W. Pluhar, 136.
29. *Ibid.*, 276, trans. W. Pluhar, 137.
30. I. Kant, *Streit der Fakultäten*, zweiter Abschnitt: *Der Streit der philosophischen Fakultät mit der juristischen* (Hamburg: Meiner, 1975) 84 [translation mine].

III. Lyotard's Revised Reading of the Sublime

While Kant gives a lot of consideration to the contrast-experience of human superiority over nature precisely in the confrontation with the brute forces of nature, this confrontation with nature hardly plays a role in Lyotard's study of the sublime (he rather focuses on Kant's explanation of the mathematical sublime[31]). Indeed, Kant's analysis of the sublime must be seen in the light of the achievements of early industrialization. At that moment, human conquest of nature was within reach, although not to the extent we know today. When Kant wrote about the sublime (1790), he was still haunted by the memory of the earthquake in Lisbon (1755), and welcomed the moral as well as the nascent techno-scientific elevation of the human over nature. To liberate humankind from its tremendous exposure to natural catastrophes was part of his program: "Here the pathos of the Enlightenment philosopher becomes palpable: to liberate the human being from the brute forces of nature which mainly reach him through the gate of fear and divest him of intellectual and practical self-determination."[32]

As far as Lyotard is concerned, he already belongs to a different type of culture. He self-evidently breathes the air of technological innovations and, therefore, sees the chaotic elements emerge in historical disasters. To call attention to these atrocities so that they never may happen again, becomes, for him, a gesture of testifying to the sublime. He accounts for this transition from nature to history by pointing out that Kant's *Critique of Judgment* should logically have been followed by a *Critique of Political Reason* which Kant intimated but never wrote: "Kant's historico-critical texts," he writes, "are, *grosso modo*, scattered through the three *Critiques* and a dozen or so opuscules. The *Critique of Political Reason* was not written."[33] From the *Critique of Judgment* he mainly borrows, in addition to Kant's interest in the sublime, the method of searching for a rule that is not given in advance. As to the *Critique of Political Reason* which he proposes to write himself, this work will attempt to lay bare the deceptive pretensions – the 'transcendental illusions', to use Kantian vocabulary – of modernity's grand narratives about humankind's steady progress. For him, these grand narratives have made havoc of human history; far from contributing to the advance of civilization they are, rather,

---

31. See J.-F. Lyotard, *Lessons on the Analytic of the Sublime*, 77-122.
32. H. Böhme "Das Steinerne," *Das Erhabene*, ed. C. Pries, 121 [translation mine].
33. J.-F. Lyotard, "The Sign of History," *The Lyotard Reader*, ed. A. Benjamin (Oxford: Blackwell, 1989) 396.

responsible for ever-greater historical calamities. His new quest will consist then in looking for signs of the sublime in the ashes of history.
Although he avidly makes use of Kantian categories, he wants to present
a revised view of Kant's notion of the sublime, one adapted to our time.
Lyotard's most serious attempt at writing a *Critique of Political Reason*
is without doubt his work *The Differend: Phrases in Dispute*.

1. *Signs of the Sublime in History?*

Lyotard aims at transposing Kant's analysis of political enthusiasm
into the key of the late 20th century mode of looking at history. His point
is this: granted that Kant must have had good reasons to regard particular historical events as anticipations of the breakthrough of the reign
of freedom and morality, people today are no longer in the mood for
sharing his visionary enthusiasm. More than two centuries after the
French Revolution, we are mostly confronted with anti-signs of, and anti-
testimonies to, the 'victorious' breakthrough of the *humanum*. One can
no longer expect one to be swept up by enthusiasm when observing the
horrible facts of human rights violations. Auschwitz and other holocausts
simply forbid us from believing in the progress of history. Lyotard's
account of history is rather distressing. In a lecture delivered in 1982 at
the Center for Twentieth-Century Studies in Milwaukee he said the following: "Adorno pointed out that Auschwitz is an abyss in which the
philosophical genre of Hegelian speculative discourse seems to disappear, because the name 'Auschwitz' invalidates the presuppositions of
that genre, namely that all that is real is rational, and that all that is rational is real. Budapest 1956 is another abyss in which the genre of [Marxist]
historical materialist discourse seems to disappear, because this name
invalidates the presupposition of that genre, namely that all that is proletarian is communist, and that all that is communist is proletarian. 1968 is
an abyss in which the genre of democratic liberal discourse seems to disappear, because this name invalidates the presupposition of that genre,
namely that all that concerns the political community can be said within
the rules of the game of parliamentary representation."[34]

In an earlier work *Enthusiasm, the Kantian Critique of History* (1986)
Lyotard also mentioned "Kolyma, an abyss in which the speculative
notion of the dictatorship of the proletariat seems to disappear."[35]

---

34. J.-F. Lyotard, "The Sign of History," 393.
35. J.-F. Lyotard, *L'enthousiasme: La critique Kantienne de l'histoire* (Paris: Galilée, 1986) 109 [translation mine].

Kolyma, located in the far northeastern part of Siberia, has perhaps the most severe icy climate in the world. It became the most notorious region of Stalin's GULAG (the Russian acronym for the Main Administration of the Corrective Labor Camps). "According to research done by Robert Conquest more than three million people may have died en route to the area or in the mount Kolyma's series of gold mining, lumbering, road building and other camps between 1932 and 1954. It was Kolyma's fearsome reputation that caused Alexandr Solzhenitsyn to characterize it as 'the pole of cold cruelty' in the GULAG system."[36] For Lyotard, Kolyma unmasks the speculative (and illusory) notion of the dictatorship of the proletariat. Just as members of the proletariat that dared to revolt against their masters were sent to the labor camps, so the intervention of the Russian troops to crush the insurrection in Budapest in 1956 unmasks the Marxist discourse of the basic identity between the proletariat and communism. In his eyes it is clear that the Marxist ideology, like all ideologies with a universal claim, uses a language game (or an idiom, as he says) whose totalizing pretension is purely speculative, that is: it cannot be validated in empirical reality.

In *The Differend: Phrases in Dispute* (1983) he critically examines the use Karl Marx makes of speculative language when solemnly announcing that the proletariat is the new universal class that is going to determine the course of history. He hereby quotes Karl Marx, who describes it as "a class with radical chains, a class of bourgeois society which is not a class of bourgeois society, a sphere which has a universal character by its universal suffering and claims no particular right because no particular wrong but wrong generally (*ein Unrecht schlechtin*) is perpetrated against it."[37] Lyotard admits that what surfaces in this statement is a serious conflict or disagreement (a 'differend' as he calls it). The disagreement flows from the way in which the capitalistic system imposes its hegemony and practically dictates how (to use language pragmatics) phrases must be linked to other phrases, thus causing frustration among those who have no voice in the discourse: the subordinate workers are supposed to carry out orders without grumbling. Apparently complaints there are and grievances about their dire plight abound. For Lyotard, the philosopher cannot keep him/herself aloof from this 'differend' but has

36. Art. Kolyma http://en.wikipedia.org/wiki/Kolyma.
37. K. Marx, *Contribution to the Critique of Hegel's Philosophy of Law, Collected Works of Marx and Engels* (New York: International Publishers, 1975) 186, cited in J.-F. Lyotard, *The Differend: Phrases in Dispute*, trans G. Van Den Abbeele (Manchester: Manchester University Press, 1988) no. 236, p. 171. Originally published as idem, *Le Différend* (Paris: Minuit, 1983).

the duty to listen to these grievances and to reflectively ponder what is at stake. This is something a philosopher today, he says, can still learn from Marx. But then he is quick to remark that Marx, having listened to these grievances, begins to build on them a speculative system with its typically all-inclusive jargon: the class that is part of the bourgeois society without being really part of it merits the name of a universal class, for its suffering is universal; it claims more than just a particular right since the wrong perpetrated against it is not a particular wrong but wrong generally. Were these statements intended as pure rhetoric, Lyotard would have tolerated it. But seeing that this all-inclusive language is really meant to convey a message of speculative philosophy, he feels compelled to protest.

He therefore carefully examines Marx's description of the enthusiasm felt by the workers who are engaged in shaking off the yoke of their exploitation. Marx says: "No class of the bourgeois society can play this role [of emancipation] without arousing a moment of enthusiasm in itself and in the masses, a moment in which it fraternalizes and merges with society in general, becomes confused with it and is perceived and acknowledged as its general representative."[38] The proletariat stands up to emancipate itself; this gesture arouses enthusiasm in the proletariat as well as in the larger masses who witness this event. It is not at random that Marx brings up the notion of political enthusiasm – which in earlier days the contemporaries of Kant experienced at the occasion of the French revolution; for him, a wave of enthusiasm sweeps over the proletarian workers as they realize that they are the protagonists of a new social history. This enthusiasm allows them to perceive themselves as the (recognized) general representatives of the true self (*das gemeine Wesen*) of society.

In spite of the allusion to Kant, Marx's text is definitely Hegelian. We are no longer working in Kantian categories, which entail a forced withdrawal of the widening imagination before the supersensible Idea of human freedom (a withdrawal that was required to keep the unpresentable Idea unpresentable). No, Hegel is a visionary who definitely beholds how the Idea (for him: initially empty) dialectically develops into a fully realized Idea. The same is true with Marx. Marx beholds the essence of an emancipated class; right from the outset this essence squarely demands its realization in history, whereas the enthusiasm he describes is nothing else but the effect of the triumphant deployment of

38. K. Marx, *Contribution to the Critique of Hegel's Philosophy of Law*, 186, cited in J.-F. Lyotard, *The Differend*, no. 237, pp. 171-172.

this essence: "A prisoner of the logic of the [indispensable] result and its presupposition of a self [that right from the outset already beholds the successful outcome of its actions], Marx understands the feeling of enthusiasm as a request emanating from an (ideal, emancipated) self. The referent of the Idea of communism is transcribed as a subject (addressor) who prescribes communism. The common being wants it." And Lyotard concludes: "This can be formulated only within the speculative genre."[39]

This speculative genre resulted in the constitution of an ideally emancipated self; this is followed by a next step: the attempt to endow this ideal self with a historical political reality. In 1864 Marx founded in London the 'International Working Men's Association' (IWMA), abbreviated: the International, at the occasion of which he launched the *Communist Manifesto*. Later in 1871 he interpreted the enthusiasm aroused among the civil rights movement of the Paris Commune "as if it signaled the political project of the real class and as if it realized the organization of a real party." For Lyotard, however, these 'as if' constructions betray a double illusory 'passage' between two heterogeneous phrase regimes: "the first passes from the sign that is solidarity enthusiasm to the ideal of a revolutionary subject, the proletariat; the second passes from this ideal to the real political organization of the working class."[40]

Lyotard calls attention to this double illicit 'passage' because in the end it will eventually lead to the erection under Stalin of labor camps like Kolyma, an abyss that gives the lie to the speculative construct of the dictatorship of the proletariat. As a matter of fact, in order to legitimate itself, the communist party "must supply the proof that the proletariat is real;" if not, its actions would be pointless. "But it cannot [supply this proof], not more than one can supply the proof for an ideal of Reason,"[41] and this for the simple reason that an Idea of Reason is never to be found in empirical reality. The party apparently knows of this dilemma, and therefore decides "to give itself as proof and to undertake a realist politics," one in which it "assumes [itself] a monopoly over the procedures for establishing historical-political reality."[42] In line with this logic, the party sets out to determine for each historical epoch the norms and criteria to which the proletarian masses (that are brought under its control)

39. J.-F. Lyotard, *The Differend*, no. 237, p. 172.
40. *Ibid.*, no. 238, p. 172.
41. *Ibid.*, no. 239, p. 172.
42. *Ibid.*, no. 239, p. 172.

will be held accountable in order to deserve the name 'communists'. The imposition of this monopoly, Lyotard predicts, will inevitably call forth serious disagreements ('differends') up to the point of breeding dissidents. The party arrogates to itself the right to tell what is ideologically correct and what is not, and, in so doing, mixes up the 'ought' and the 'is'. The party presumes to know the aspirations of the working class, without having to consult the working class. This inevitably leads to category mistakes. Or as Lyotard puts it: "The party is constraint to mistake the proletariat – a referent of the dialectic genre, namely the ideal object (and perhaps subject) of the Idea of emancipated working humanity – for the real working classes, the multiple referents of 'positive' cognitive phrases."[43]

In practice, this way of proceeding will result in the party presenting as homogenous what, in fact, is diversified. But this endeavor is doomed to failure. The proletariat is an Idea of Reason the embodiment of which cannot be proven to exist in reality, whereas the workers, as they concretely exist in history, do not at all form a homogeneous bloc. Historical and sociological research show that the life conditions of the workers (salaried laborers, low middle class, people engaged in informal economy) are too varied to be lumped together. What has been erroneously called the proletariat is, in fact, made up of various types of the working class which all have their own specificity. On this account they cannot be subsumed under one homogeneous category, as Marxists would like to have it.

2. *The Solely Indicative Function of 'as if' Presentations: No Guidelines for Political Action*

At this juncture Lyotard has recourse to the Kantian notion of 'enthusiasm' in order to show what went wrong with Marxism. For him, Kant's notion of enthusiasm is far more modest than that of Marx; it is not meant to provide an incentive for political action, but *only signals* through the commonly shared strong emotions aroused by political events that humanity is undeniably on its way to further ethical progress. Kant regards political enthusiasm as a 'sign of history' and he uses this sign for reflectively musing over the ethical capability of humankind, not, however, for 'proving' that this or that political fraction is going to inaugurate a new era (the latter would be a determinative judgment – in Lyotard's jargon: a positive cognitive phrase).

43. *Ibid.*, no. 239, p. 172.

This difference in approach comes, first of all, to the fore in the specificity of the actors who are said to be overwhelmed by feelings of enthusiasm. In Marx's analysis these actors are the workers who want to shake off the yoke of their alienating work conditions: a wave of enthusiasm sweeps over them and makes them look for the cooperation of other companions in solidarity with them. In Kant's analysis, on the contrary, those experiencing enthusiasms are the spectators outside of France who emotionally welcome the felt humanitarian achievements of the French revolution. Kant's reflective judgment examines the feelings of the foreign spectators and comes to the conclusion that these act *as if* their 'sublime' feelings of approval had a universal validity, but – he adds – they continue to behave as distant spectators that watch the events in France "without the least intention of cooperating with them (ohne *die mindeste Absicht der Mitwirkung*)."[44] That is the reason why Lyotard says that what these 'supporters' feel has only an aesthetic value: "If these signs have a universal value, they are on the side of the audience, they have an aesthetic and not a 'practical' value. They are awaited, they come at any time, they are evaluations, not actions."[45] The Kantian stress on 'without the least intention of cooperating' with the revolutionary movement is important and in line with one of the basic rules of his aesthetics: the aesthetic emotions are disinterested: they cannot be used for a practical purpose. Or as Lyotard says: "they are evaluations" based on strong emotions of the *Gemüt*, but they cannot serve as guidelines for political action, not even for ethical decisions.[46]

This does, of course, not mean that these strong emotions would have no rapport with ethics. They certainly do, but only in the way of a *Wunsch*; they contain the strong volition and the enthusiastic wish that human history may ever more make progress toward the better. This enthusiastic wish results, so to speak, from the interplay between creative imagination and the inexhaustible Idea of human freedom examined in the previous section. In his political writings Kant specified this Idea of freedom in terms of 'self-determination of the peoples' and 'cosmopolitan world citizenship'. This explains why he is so interested in the enthusiastic reaction of the spectators on the various European scenes. These apparently welcome the positive achievements of the French Revolution because they see it as the beginning of a larger movement that is going

44. I. Kant, *Conflict of the Faculties*, §6, cited in J.-F. Lyotard, *The Differend*, Kant 4 §5, p. 167.

45. J.-F. Lyotard, *The Differend*, no. 238, p. 172.

46. *Ibid.*, no. 238, p. 172.

to spread out unto the rest of the European countries, so that Europe may get a step closer to the cosmopolitan idea of world citizenship. Lyotard puts it as follows: "It may be that the revolutionaries' activity [in France] is directed not only toward a French political constitution under the authority of the sole legitimate sovereign *de jure* (the people, that is) but also toward a federation of States in a peace project, which then concerns all of humanity [...] The participation (*Teilnehmung*) through desire is not a participation in the act [of revolution]. But it is worth more because the feeling of the sublime, for its sake, is in fact spread out unto all the national stages. Potentially, at least, it is universal."[47]

A crucial question to be asked is: how does it happen that distant spectators experience a political enthusiasm before the brute facts of a revolution that is repulsive and frightening? A comparison with the experience of the dynamic sublime suggests an answer. Here too, as we have seen, the observed facts – a vehement natural scene devoid of purposiveness – led to the visionary contrast-experience of humankind's elevation above the forces of nature. Under the pressure of the Idea of human freedom the creative imagination was forced to 'widen itself' to the point of having to admit that even in this largest expansion it was unable to present the whole Idea of freedom. Something similar happens in political enthusiasm. Here, the spectators are confronted with historical events that, at a first glance, are formless and without purposiveness; but, in a second moment, they are rescued from their fear of being lost by having recourse to the Idea of freedom which reveals to them their true destiny: "Great changes, like the French Revolution, are not, in principle, sublime by themselves. Qua objects they are similar to those spectacles of (physical) nature on whose occasion the viewer experiences the sublime. 'Nature excites the idea of the sublime in its chaos or in its wildest and most irregular disorder and desolation, provided size and might are perceived'. 'The sublime is best determined by the indeterminate, by the *Formlosigkeit*'. The sublime in nature [...] may be regarded as 'quite formless and devoid of figure'. The same ought to apply for a revolution, and for all great historical upheavals: they are what is formless and without figure in historical human nature. Ethically they are nothing validatable. They fall, on the contrary, under the sway of the critical [reflective] judgment."[48]

47. J.-F. Lyotard, *The Differend*, Kant 4 §5, p. 167.
48. *Ibid.*, Kant 4 §5, p. 167, citing from I. Kant, *Critique of Judgment* §23, *Akademie* edition, 246.

Precisely this reflective judgment strengthens the spectators in the awareness that the formless upheavals they are observing are, in fact, infinitesimally small, compared to the huge potential of the Idea of freedom. Yet, this message can only be properly understood by cultivated people who are "susceptible to Ideas."[49] Translated into the language of strong emotions, this means that the spectators feel that "something which is 'formless' alludes to a beyond of experience" – to the supersensible realm of human grandeur. This contact with the supersensible unleashes an enthusiasm in the spectators' *Gemüt*. This enthusiasm, however, does not allow them to see or to validate the already present form of civil society as is should be or of cosmopolitan society as it should be (this would be *Schwärmerei* or fanaticism); the enthusiasm only provides them with "an 'as-if presentation' of civil society, and even of cosmopolitan society, and thus an 'as-if presentation' of the Idea of morality; precisely where that Idea nevertheless cannot be presented within experience. It is in this way that the sublime is a sign" – an emotional anticipation of a hoped-for reality. The 'as-if' presentation' is only indicative: it points to a progress of humanity towards the better, "even though civil societies are nowhere near republican in their regimes nor States anywhere near world federation (far from it!)."[50]

On the other hand, this 'as-if presentation' must be regarded as a proof in its own right. Not in the sense that in virtue of it one would be able to ascertain through facts that the human community has effectively made progress towards republican regimes or to a world federation. But rather in the sense that those who are emotionally lifted up by this vision are proof that a higher degree of culture has taken roots in their lives. Relying on their new 'mode of thinking' they will without hesitation proclaim that humankind has a capability to live up to higher values, for the simple reason that they themselves have experienced this: "Their enthusiasm by itself 'not only permits people to hope for progress towards the better, but is already itself progress insofar as its capacity is sufficient for the present'."[51] In other words, those who are swept over by political enthusiasm when confronted with the upheavals in France must already have acquired a level of culture "that has civil and perhaps international peace as its horizon."[52] This acquisition validates their enthusiasm and renders it authentic.

---

49. J.-F. Lyotard, *The Differend*, Kant 4 §6, p. 169.
50. *Ibid.*, Kant 4 §6, p. 170.
51. *Ibid.*, Kant 4 §6, p. 170, citing from I. Kant, *Conflict of the Faculties*, §6.
52. *Ibid.*, Kant 4 §6, p. 170.

Lyotard concludes his analysis of Kant's political enthusiasm by sum-marizing what was exactly Kant's real concern: to explain the specta-tor's 'mode of thinking' when confronting the facts of the French Revo-lution. This 'mode of thinking' is reflective and in search of a rule with is not given advance –in consonance with the basic presuppositions of the *Critique of Aesthetic Judgment*; it has no intention at all to make prog-noses about the concrete historical facts that might be conducive to the attainment of a republican regime or a peaceful federation of States. This, however, does not prevent Kant from solemnly predicting something irre-versible: "Now I claim to be able to predict (*vorhersagen*) to humankind – even without prophetic insight – according to the aspects and omens (*Vorzeichen*) of our day the attainment (*Erreichung*) of this end. That is, I predict its progress toward the better which, from now on, turns out to be no longer completely reversible. For such a phenomenon in history [like the general enthusiasm aroused by the French Revolution] can no longer be forgotten (*vergisst sich nicht mehr*)."[53]

Kant has apparently found a fragile 'passage' between the occurrences in nature (including the historical facts of the French Revolution) and the enthusiastic consciousness-raising toward humanity's moral destination. This 'passage', however, only allows him to make indeterminate state-ments (the aesthetic judgment being in search of its rule); it strictly for-bids the lumping together of two heterogeneous domains, nature and mind (*Geist*), or the intermingling of their respective laws. Occurrences in his-tory belong to the realm of facts, accessible to historical and sociologi-cal research, whereas the conviction that humankind is progressing for the better can only be gained from signs of enthusiasm in history. To inves-tigate facts is the task of the historian. To reflect on the felt ethical res-onance these facts provoke is the task of the philosopher. It is up to the philosopher to call attention to the 'signs of history' whenever these pre-sent themselves, but s/he will never be able to tell when exactly these signs will surface in humankind's historical consciousness; not even the historian who provides facts can help the philosopher in this respect: "'There is progress' – the critical watchman can legitimate this phrase every time he is able to present a sign which serves as a referent for that assertion. But he cannot say when such 'objects' will present themselves; the historical sequences that form series give the historian only data (which are, at best, statistically regular), but not signs."[54] To perceive 'signs' of progress presupposes a high degree of cultural awareness to be

53. *Ibid.*, Kant 4 §6, p. 170, citing from I. Kant, *Conflict of the Faculties*, §7.
54. *Ibid.*, Kant 4 §6, p. 171.

shared, in principle, by all alert contemporaries. This cultural awareness must, moreover, espouse an aesthetic 'disinterestedness' without which no real uplifting admiration for the ethico-practical achievements of humankind is possible.

Such a 'disinterestedness' is hardly compatible with an engagement in *Realpolitik* and its inherent calculations of means and ends. This calculation comes to the fore in the philosophy of history of Hegel and Marx, where the Kantian 'as-if presentation' (to look at human history *as if* humanity were progressing toward the better, and to take this as a guiding principle) has been pressed into the straight-jacket of a self-moving logic of history. As a result, the fragile 'passage' which Kant had built between history and the realm of Ideas has been hardened to become a stable bridge through which the two domains dialectically interact, whereby this inter-action results in the single, dominant construct of a philosophy of history whose logic of deployment is given in advance. In this construct, Kant's reflective aesthetic judgment (which is in search of its rule) has been replaced with a series of determinant judgments. To recap, the difference between both can be formulated as follows: If the universal (the rule, prin-ciple, law) is given, then judgment, which subsumes the particular under it, is *determinative* [...] But if only the particular is given and judgment has to find the universal for it, then this power is merely *reflective.*"[55]

We have seen that Marx, when interpreting the enthusiasm of the work-ers in their struggle for emancipation, immediately jumped to a universal statement with ostensive power: 'When you look for a new universal class, here it is: the proletariat whose suffering is universal'. In his stringent logic of history this new universal class must of necessity assume the hege-monic position which the bourgeoisie has been holding until now. In order to guarantee this dominant position the communist party will see to it that the real existing proletariat will live up to the ideal of the new universal class to which it has been promoted. The party apparently knows the rules and norms of this ideal class, and imposes them on the existing proletariat, if necessary by force and coercion. The end of the story is Kolyma, and other repressive intrusions which have been noted. But, Lyotard laments, all these mechanisms of repression are the awful outcome of a 'transcen-dental illusion' (to use this Kantian expression): "confusing what can be presented as an object for a cognitive phrase and what can be presented as an object for a speculative and/or ethical phrase."[56]

---

55. I. Kant, *Critique of Judgment, Akademie* edition, 179, trans. W. Pluhar, 18.
56. J.-F. Lyotard, "The Sign of History," *The Lyotard Reader*, ed. A. Benjamin (Oxford: Blackwell, 1989) 399.

This confusion of 'phrase regimes' – taking 'what ought to be' (the object of a speculative phrase) for 'what really is the case in reality' (the object of a cognitive phrase) – not only leads to a 'transcendental illusion' with all the horrors flowing from it; it also casts upon Lyotard a mood of melancholy, a sadness which we have already seen in Kant, an enthusiasm '*e contrario*'. In his reflection on enthusiasm, Kant ventured to speak about a sublime sadness over evils brought forth by human beings, contrary to their true vocation. He specified that this sadness "does not concern evils that fate imposes on other people" (which would be a ground for commiseration). Rather, this sadness results from considering the evils "that humans inflict on themselves." And he adds: it is a "sadness that rests on an antipathy involving principles." Such a sadness "is sublime because it rests on ideas; even grief [...] may be included among the *vigorous* affects, if it has its basis in moral ideas."[57] This sadness is in its own manner 'uplifting', for it keeps alive the lure emanating from the Ideas of Reason (*Vernunft*), in spite of the presence of so many self-incurred evils in the world. It keeps these ideas alive against the grain of those whose disrespect for moral principles one can but emotionally disallow.

Kant's meditation on sublime sadness struck a chord in Lyotard. In an interview, Christine Pries asked him whether, upon facing up to Auschwitz, Budapest 1956, etc. he could still allow himself to speak honestly about 'signs' that point to humanity's moral progress. His answer was: 'Yes, today there are still these historically meaningful signs, but they are all negative. Just as in Kant's analysis of the political enthusiasm that after the French revolution swept over the whole of Europe, these 'signs' do not arise from the catastrophic events themselves; they are generated by the unanimous feelings of the spectators who engage in a reflective judgment on them. In this reflection they become overwhelmed by a sublime sadness, in the style of Kant'. And he concludes: Political enthusiasm today shows itself in the mode of melancholy. "A deep melancholy can be a feeling of the sublime. Can we say that some of the historical events alluded to at the end of my book may have the effect of unanimously arousing feelings of melancholy? Some of them, and especially Auschwitz, will certainly do, yes... Why should this not mean a step forward [in humanity's moral progress]? Each sublime feeling testifies to an Idea of Reason. Melancholy testifies to an Idea of Reason and to its absence in empirical reality. This is a way to testify to things relegated to oblivion. It is a feeling that can point to the sublime,

---

57. I. Kant, *Critique of Judgment*, *Akademie* edition, 276, trans. W. Pluhar, 137.

and thus 'prove', signify, and bear witness to the fact that this Idea is not lost. Grief over politics, provided this feeling is unanimous and not geared towards a particular interest, can be regarded as an historically meaningful sign."[58]

58. C. Pries, "Das Undarstellbare – Gegen das Vergessen: Ein Gespräch zwischen Jean-François Lyotard und Christine Pries," *Das Erhabene: Zwischen Grenzerfahrung und Grössenwahn*, ed. idem (Weinheim: Acta Humaniora, 1989) 332 [translation mine].

CHAPTER THREE

TRANSPOSING KANT TO THE KEY OF THE POSTMODERN

Lyotard had already developed a vivid interest in Kant before writing *the Postmodern Condition*. This raises the question: Why this interest in Kant? And, more importantly, which Kant? In *Les Instructions païennes* (1977) Lyotard's answer is clear: not the Kant of the concepts and the moral law, but the Kant of the *Critique of Judgment*, who rediscovered the role of imagination and the importance of a reflective judgment in search of its rules. The Kant of the *Third Critique*, thus, serves as a guide for Lyotard. Yet, how can a classic of modernity possibly provide answers to postmodern questions? Will it not be the case that in following Kant's method this method will be used to transpose Kant to the key of the post-modern? This is the question I will tackle in the first part of the chapter.

Lyotard's use of Kant's regulative Idea is a case in point. Postmodernity is often characterized as an epoch of opinions and undecidability. In order to overcome this situation Lyotard has recourse to the Kantian regulative Idea of a 'society of free citizens'. For him, such a regulative Idea does not tell what one must do in the concrete, but offers nonetheless a perspective or guideline against which to gauge one's concrete decisions: 'Is what I am deciding to do in line with the regulative Idea of a society in which the citizens are free from oppression?'. In *Just Gaming* (French edition 1979) Lyotard discusses this insight with Jean-Loup Thébaut. They reflect on the need for a *Critique of Political Reason* which Kant envisioned writing, but never wrote. If Kant had written a *Critique of Political Reason*, Thébaut opines, it would have been based on the dictates of the categorical imperative. Lyotard disagrees. As he sees it, Kant's *Critique of Political Reason* would have been based on the notion of reflective judgment and its use of regulative Ideas, so that a purely legislative reason is out of the question. Thébaut, in turn, objects that Kant's regulative Idea has a universal range and that, for that reason, it imposes a stricter obligation upon the moral agent than Lyotard would like to admit. At that moment Lyotard puts his cards on the table; he acknowledges that he is not certain that he can locate himself in the strictly Kantian tradition, and explains why this is the case: Kant is still beholden to a metaphysics that pivots around the 'Idea of totality'. So, Kant reflects on what is just and unjust against the horizon of a social totality, whereas Lyotard wishes to focus on what is just and unjust against the horizon of a multiplicity and of a diversity.

In a later article Lyotard further elucidates his deviation from Kant. Kant could still see the political enthusiasm that swept over the spectators of the French revolution as a 'sign' that humanity had come a step closer to the ideal of what it means to be human. But he still conceives this ideal as a uniform pattern to be adopted by everyone. Lyotard takes leave of this uniformity. For him, the 'enthusiasm *e contrario*' people experience when being confronted with historical catastrophes (Kolyma, Budapest) can be seen as a 'sign' that, with the implosion of the grand political stories, humanity has moved a step closer to a civilization that honors diversity and heterogeneity. With respect to the feeling of the sublime this means: one should not only feel the irremediable gap between the Idea and what presents itself to realize that Idea, but also the gap between the various families of phrases and their respective legitimate presentations. Kant was still thinking in terms of a big transcendental subject with its schemes of totality, all aimed at the attainment of a single purpose. This grand transcendental subject must be dissolved so that room will be given to the exploration of Ideas in the plural, as well as to the emergence of an infinity of heterogeneous finalities.

The second part of this chapter will examine 'Lyotard's distinctive reading of Kant's *Critique of Judgment*'. The conventional reading focuses on the rapprochement Kant sought to establish between the realm of necessity (examined in the *Critique of Pure Reason*) and the realm of freedom (examined in the *Critique of Practical Reason*). In his *Lessons on the Analytic of the Sublime*, Lyotard follows a different line of thought which can also be found in the *Critique of Judgment*: the psychological approach to the 'unification' of the faculties of the soul: the theoretical, the ethical and the aesthetic faculty. Here, too, he will in a subtle way adjust Kant's thought to the postmodern sensibility.

Lyotard's approach highlights the psychological resonance of the reflective judgment: feelings of pleasure and/or displeasure lay at the basis of the reflective judgment that is in search of its rule, for this search is stimulated by the felt presence of thought to itself. Thought feels itself thinking, and takes delight in it. Pure thought is the ability of thought to be informed about its state without any other means than feeling itself. From this it follows that the thinking/feeling subject must already be able to judge before knowing what judging properly is. This insight, developed in the *Third Critique*, is crucial for Lyotard. Kant, to be sure, also requires the objective validation of the judgment. But this validation comes at the end. First comes the formation of fuzzy assemblages of representations by the 'thought that feels itself thinking'. Only in a second step, these pre-logical assemblages are submitted to the faculty's logical processes in order to obtain objective validation. In this way a floating 'unison' of imagination and concept is achieved.

On the basis of this approach Lyotard will demonstrate that a grand transcendental subject is redundant. In aesthetic judgment the stable subject which Kant presupposes elsewhere in his philosophy is dissolved in the successive sensations that 'thought that feels itself thinking' has of itself. The 'subject' is always in a state of infancy: it finds itself in this state each time pleasure arises from the beautiful. Taste, as pure pleasure, cannot be grounded in any pre-existing unity. In recurrent experiences of pleasure, this unity is rather felt as being constantly in the making. A similar dissolution must be acknowledged for the *sensus communis*. This sense 'common to all' is not, as it is often believed, the element that unites an assignable community of feeling. For Lyotard, as well as for Kant, the *sensus communis* must not be understood as an already existing consensus. Such would lead to the dictatorship of the community of taste. The universal communicability made possible by the *sensus communis* is rather a promise. This promise arises whenever a particular judgment of taste (and its timbre of inner proportion between imagination and conceptual understanding) serves as an *example* that carries with it the fascinating power of seducing everyone towards a similar state of mind: the example is such that it necessarily stirs in everyone the desire for awakening to a similar capacity of aesthetic judgment. The singular judgment of taste is enjoined (*ansinnen*) on everyone. But then comes the important nuance. In each single case one has to do with an *example, always singular, for a rule* to which everybody should give their consent. But this rule always remains elusive; it is never found. Having stressed with Kant the irreplaceable particularity of each example, Lyotard jumps to the conclusion that examples in the plural, and even totally heterogeneous examples, are needed, to stir in the aesthetic community an ongoing search for the rule or norm of the aesthetic judgment of taste.

Here again we see how Lyotard, faithful to Kant insofar as possible, interprets the author of the *Third Critique* in light of postmodern sensitivity. What remains basically Kantian – although not always sufficiently articulated in studies on Kant – is the insight that contact with the supersensible is only possible on the basis of feeling. Lyotard is particularly interested in the sign-function of feelings. At the level of the aesthetic judgment the feeling that the singular judgment of taste is enjoined (*ansinnen*) on everyone is the signal or the sign of an Idea of Reason. The content of this Idea is the 'transcendental proportionality or euphony of the faculties'. This Idea of Reason is unpresentable but makes its presence felt. Something similar happens in ethics (practical reason). Here contact with the supersensible leads to a feeling of respect. Respect is the presence of the law regarded subjectively, its sign. Respect is the specific way in which 'feeling thought' reacts to the summons of the categorical imperative. The feeling of respect reappears in the experience of the sublime, where it alternates with delight. The feeling one has when one's imagination is inadequate to present an Idea is a feeling of respect. From the moment a person realizes that her true vocation consists in hearkening to the voice of Reason (which speaks to her from the supersensible realm), a soul-stirring delight arises. At the level of theoretical reason, finally, contact with the supersensible is intimated at the very moment at which theoretical reason is carried to its limits. There it feels that the absolute is never given, but is always present as a call to think beyond the 'there', toward the ungraspable but unforgettable.

This insight paves the way for a 'unification' of the three faculties: the theoretical, the ethical, and the aesthetic. Indeed, the three faculties seek to discover the supreme condition of the specific conditions of possibility that allow them to be operative in their respective domain. In this quest they are brought to the 'limit of their power'; they realize that grasping this supreme condition (which is the supersensible realm) is beyond their reach. This supersensible realm, however, signals its presence in the specific feelings it arouses in the distinct faculties. For the judgment of taste, the aroused feeling is that of a demand for universal communicability. In the domain of ethics the unpresentable Idea of freedom makes its presence felt by the feeling of respect, whereas in theoretical reason the Idea of completeness is intimated in a call to think beyond the 'there'. Moreover, when the three faculties, each in their own heterogeneous way, are carried to the limit of their power, this limit has a different name. At first glance, it looks as if the faculties culminate in the same Idea of Reason: But on closer inspection this threefold striving is guided by different Ideas of Reason: the Idea of an unlimited freedom to imagine presentations in aesthetics; the Idea of an unlimited freedom to desire the highest good in ethics, and the Idea of an unlimited freedom to conceive Ideas in theoretical knowledge.

These Ideas form an ever receding horizon. Any attempt at trying to grasp this horizon will end up in antinomies or irresolvable contradictions. With the means reflection has at its disposal in each of these territories, reflection cannot determine the absolutes upon which these means depend. The unconditioned of knowledge cannot be known in theoretical reason. The absolute law of the faculty of desire cannot be desired.

The supersensible principle that founds the demand for the universal communication of taste cannot be the object of an aesthetic pleasure. Each faculty is seized with the impossibility of thinking its limit with the means it has at its disposal, but that it must try to think this limit is the sign of the supersensible. Since each of the faculties strives for reaching out to this receding horizon in its own way, Lyotard prefers to speak of horizons in the plural, or of absolutes in the plural. This preference is consistent with his endeavor to safeguard heterogeneity. On the other hand he is faithful to Kant when affirming that the three horizons of unknowability have an affinity or analogy to each other and that this affinity is the decisive reason for accepting a 'unification' of the faculties. One could even speak of an analogy regarding the feeling of the sublime. In a central passage of his analysis Lyotard brings up the following consideration: The sublime feeling is the subjective state critical thought must feel in its being carried to its limits (therefore beyond them) and its resistance to this impetus. According to this statement the sublime feeling is each time diversified in the three faculties, the theoretical, the ethical and the aesthetic.

The third part of the chapter will take stock of the 'postmodern features' in Lyotard's analysis of the *Critique of Judgment*. It starts with clearing up a possible misunderstanding, namely that Lyotard's psychological reading of Kant's *Third Critique* forms his only methodological approach to the study of the subject. In his work *The Differend*, for example, he follows the conventional reading of the *Third Critique* and jumps to a different conclusion. Whereas the psychological reading understands a 'unification' of the faculties to be possible on the basis of an affinity between the three horizons of unknowability, his appropriation of the widely accepted reading primarily stresses the 'as if' character of the analogy between the realm of mechanical causation (science) and that of freedom (ethics): aesthetically nature can be viewed *as if* it had a finality – a finality analogous to the finality of human freedom. Under the influence of Wittgenstein's exploding of language into families of heterogeneous language games, Lyotard warns against taking this aesthetic view literally, under penalty of falling prey to a transcendental illusion. He compares the two heterogeneous domains to isolated islands in an archipelago. To establish some contact the faculty of judgment navigates between the islands and offers them 'as if' intuitions about what they might have in common. At the same time, however, that selfsame faculty of judgment makes it clear that no bridge can be built between them. The islands will always remain separated on the basis of their heterogeneity. The two faculties must remain heterogeneous. Their possible (aesthetically perceived) commonalities cannot lead to the construction of a grand unifying subject at which Kant hinted with his 'as-if' schemas (looking at them 'as if' they had something in common). Language pragmatics gets precedence over the emotional language of the psychological reading.

This comparison allows us to appreciate the distinctly postmodern features in Lyotard's psychological reading of the *Third Critique*. Basic to this reading is his stress on feelings. This can already be seen in the way in which he anchors the reflective judgment in the 'presence of thought to itself'. The reflective judgment relies on feelings and emotions as sources of estimation. This emotional undertone persists in his dissolution of the unifying subject. Such a substantial subject is replaced with a succession of sensations that always arrive 'for the first time' and keep the subject in a state of infancy. The same is true for the dissolution of the *sensus communis* understood in terms of consensus. Here again is the emergence of irreplaceable 'examples' of experienced harmonious proportion, in the plural, that lure the community of taste to engage in a search for the rule or norm of the aesthetic judgment of taste. Typically postmodern also is Lyotard's stress on the particular feelings that point to the faculties' – diversified – contact with the supersensible: feelings of respect, feelings of awe, feelings of jubilation. This is also true for the strong feeling of surrender (the disturbing/delightful feeling of the sublime) that each faculty experiences when being carried to its limit: the sublime feeling is the subjective state critical thought must feel in its being carried to its limits (therefore beyond them) and its resistance to this impetus.

This chapter will end with some methodological considerations which I can briefly summarize as follows. Lyotard's emotional language in the evocation of the feeling of the sublime originates in his psychological approach to Kant's *Third Critique*. On the other hand, Lyotard also uses this emotional language in his language pragmatics, when asking the question 'Does it happen?' 'Does it happen that justice is done to the loser in the debate?' and he associates this with a feeling of melancholy that is, at the bottom, sublime. My contention is that in his language pragmatics he borrows the feeling of the sublime from elsewhere, from the context of the faculties' limit-experience in their felt contact with the supersensible. In other words, it is not his critical dialogue, in a Wittgensteinian style, with the standard interpretation but his psychological reading of Kant's *Critique of Judgment* that gives him access to the notion of the sublime. This clarification is important, since a great many of Lyotard's commentators focus primarily on Lyotard's work *The Differend* and on the language pragmatics developed in it. Within this framework they employ the idiom of the sublime. Whenever they observe an interruption in the concatenation of sentences they call this hiatus a sign of something higher. But because they are working from what I would call the Wittgensteinian side of Lyotard, they fail to properly understand the language they are using.

I. WHY THIS INTEREST IN KANT? AND WHICH KANT?

In his early publications, Jean-François Lyotard engaged the topic of Freud and psychoanalysis. Starting in 1977, however, we see the development of a vivid interest in Kant. In *Les instructions païennes*[1] he pleads for engaging in an array of 'little stories' (taken from real social life) to counter the hegemony of grand mobilizing narratives. He does so as a leftist author disillusioned with the rigid party line of communism. As a matter of fact, he had been for years a member of the left-wing group *Socialisme ou barbarie* that "was responsible for an analysis of the Soviet Union as bureaucratic totalitarianism."[2] After having taught philosophy in then-French Algeria, he sided in Paris with the Algerian freedom fighters and with the French working class whose concerns were not addressed by the communist party. In *Les instructions païennes*, which were written in the form of a dialogue, the question is brought up as to why the spread of little stories is so important. The answer is: "[C]apitalism affects everything. So everything provides a basis for stories. You can see it as a finality without end, and that, to paraphrase Kant, is the interest we can pursue without becoming pathological cases." At that juncture the interlocutor remarks: "So, you are supporting Kant now, are you?" Lyotard's answer: "If you like, but only the Kant who wrote the *Third Critique*. Not the Kant of the concepts and the moral law, but the Kant of the imagination, the one who recovered from the sickness of knowledge and rules and converted to the paganism of art and nature."[3]

Detailed analyses of Kant, especially of the *Third Critique*, can be found in his *Just Gaming* (1979),[4] *The Differend: Phrases in Dispute*

---

1. J.-F. Lyotard, *Les instructions païennes* (Paris: Galilée, 1977).
2. W. Godzich, "Afterword," in J.-F. Lyotard, *The Postmodern Explained*, trans. W. Godzich (Minneapolis, MN: The University of Minnesota Press, 1992) 111. Originally published as idem, *Le postmoderne expliqué aux enfants* (Paris: Galilée, 1988).
3. J.-F. Lyotard, "Lessons in Paganism," *The Lyotard Reader*, ed. A. Benjamin (Oxford: Basil Blackwell, 1989) 133.
4. J.-F. Lyotard and J.-L. Thébaud, *Just Gaming*, trans. W. Godzich and S. Weber (Minneapolis, MN: The University of Minnesota Press, 1985). Originally published as idem, *Au Juste: Conversations* (Paris: Christian Bourgeois, 1979).

(1983)[5] and in the article 'Judiciousness in Dispute, or Kant after Marx' (1985).[6] Later to be followed by two books on Kant: *L'enthousiasme: La critique Kantienne de l'histoire* (1986)[7] and *Lessons on the Analytic of the Sublime* (1991),[8] which is a publication of earlier course notes. Looking back at all these publications one has to admit that Lyotard can pride himself on having become a specialist in Kant. The question, however, remains: did he assimilate the whole Kant of the third *Critique*, or did he rather present a reading of Kant adapted to the contemporary outlook, and in harmony with his own critical philosophy? Indeed, given the fact that Kant is one of the classics of modernity (Lyotard will say: of pre-Hegelian modernity), the question can be raised as to how he possibly could serve as a mentor for Lyotard's exploration of the postmodern condition?

In his article 'Lyotard Before and After the Sublime' Serge Trottein tackles this question. He points out that Lyotard's interest in Kant is linked to his interest in political theory, but he is also quick to add that if Kant had written a *Critique of the Political* (which he never did) he would most probably have made it an appendix of his *Critique of Practical Reason* with its plainly legislative character. What Lyotard, however, wants to develop is a *Critique of Political Reason* that draws its inspiration from the reflective judgment in the *Critique of Judgment*, the *Third Critique*, a reflective judgment that is not at all determinant or legislative.

For Trottein, this shift in emphasis points to the postmodern context in which Lyotard would like to function as a critical thinker. He therefore asks the following illuminating question: "Under what conditions is a political or even ethical practice possible after deconstruction, that is, in a postmodern world of particular relations, forces, values, quantities, and qualities to be evaluated without criteria? In lieu of such criteria, one is left with opinions. This realm of opinions is what Lyotard calls the 'pagan'." He then points out that Lyotard wants to bring some clarity to

---

5. J.-F. Lyotard, *The Differend: Phrases in Dispute*, trans. G. Van Den Abbeele (Manchester: Manchester University Press, 1988). Originally published as idem, *Le Différend* (Paris: Minuit, 1983).

6. J.-F. Lyotard, "Judiciousness in Dispute, or Kant after Marx," *The Arms of Representation: Subject/Text/History*, ed. M. Krieger (New York: Colombia University Press,1987) 23-67. Originally published as idem, "Justicieux dans le différend," *La faculté de juger*, ed. J.-F. Lyotard (Paris: Minuit, 1985) 195-236.

7. J.-F. Lyotard, *La critique Kantienne de l'histoire* (Paris: Galilée, 1986).

8. J.-F. Lyotard, *Lessons on the Analytic of the Sublime*, trans. E. Rottenberg (Stanford, CA: Stanford University Press, 1994). Originally published as idem, *Leçons sur l'analytique du sublime* (Paris: Galilée, 1991).

this situation, by looking for guidelines as to how to eliminate the possibility of decisions that in no case can be tolerated. He writes: "we need something (and here he quotes Lyotard) 'that allows us, if not to decide in every specific instance, at least to eliminate in all cases (and independently of the convention of positive law) decisions, or to put it in Kant's language, maxims of the will, that cannot be moral'.[9] That which allows us to escape the indecidability of opinions is 'a regulating Idea' (in Kant's terminology)."[10] And, Trottein concludes, the challenge is, indeed, "to articulate this philosophy of opinions with the Kantian notion of Idea."[11] But how is one going to succeed in this enterprise?

In *Just Gaming* Lyotard attempts to answer this question in conversation with Jean-Loup Thébaud. At a certain moment Thébaud asserts that if Kant would have developed a *Critique of Political Reason* he would have come up with determinant judgments to regulate the political. He argues that, for Kant, the very notion of freedom is determinant because it legislates: it tells us, in concrete circumstances, what we ought to do and not to do. As we might have foreseen, Lyotard disagrees with this view. For him, freedom does not act upon our decisions like a cause determines its effect. Freedom must rather be seen as a horizon or a teleological Idea that regulates our actions without determining in the concrete what we ought to do. He says: "Freedom is regulatory; it appears in the assertion of the law only as that which must be respected; but one must always reflect in order to know if in repaying a loan or in refusing to betray a friend, etc. one is actually acting, in every single instance, in such a way as to maintain the Idea of a society of free citizens."[12] With this answer Lyotard gives evidence of his profound knowledge of Kant. He points out that Kant, in his considerations about the categorical imperative, demonstrated that by obeying this imperative one becomes, to be sure, aware of one's freedom, but that this awareness does not yet disclose the whole content of freedom, since the latter is an Idea of Reason. He thus correctly refers to this Idea as a regulative Idea that must guide our actions, namely the 'Idea of a society of free citizens'. And he adds that this idea puts us in a position that requires us to make use of our reflective judgment. It will be up to us to make out what – and what not – furthers, in the concrete circumstances, the cause of upholding this noble Idea. Thébaud has

9. J.-F. Lyotard and J.-L. Thébaud, *Just Gaming*, 74.
10. S. Trottein, "Lyotard Before and After the Sublime," *Lyotard: Philosophy, Politics and the Sublime*, ed. H. Silverman (New York: Routledge, 2002) 194.
11. J.-F. Lyotard and J.-L. Thébaud, *Just Gaming*, 75.
12. *Ibid.*, 85.

grasped the reasoning and uses it to clarify his own position. He remarks that Lyotard, in his reply, had rightly stressed the importance of entrusting oneself to the guidance of the supersensible realm of Ideas, but that his – Thébaud's – view presupposes that selfsame realm of the supersensible, since what he had said earlier about the legislative character of freedom only makes sense if freedom is seen as rooted in the supersensible realm of morality, which is, in the last resort, purely normative.

At this juncture Lyotard replies that what he has in view is the 'Idea of a society of free citizens', and not some legislative norm one would be tempted to deduce from the supersensible realm of morality (as Thébaud would like to have it). The Idea of a society of free citizens "is not a concept that determines, it is a concept in its reflective, and only in its reflective use [...] Supersensible nature *does not* determine *what* I have to do. It regulates me, but without telling me *what* there is to be done. This is what Kant calls formalism (a very poor term, as far as I am concerned)."[13] Thébaud, in turn, zooms in on the notion of formalism to bring his point home to Lyotard. He counters that, for Kant, the formal character of the categorical imperative gives a specific content to the obligation: a content with a universal range, which, in turn, is based on the supersensible Idea of totality. So then, given this comprehensive obligation, one can no longer make plausible that the supersensible realm is absolutely undetermined. When pushed to the point of having to acknowledge that the notion of 'totality' lays the foundation of the categorical imperative's universal obligation, Lyotard brings the discussion to an end and concedes that he may not be a Kantian in the manner of Kant. He says: "[Indeed], the Kantian Idea is not absolutely undetermined [...] it is presupposed that this Idea is the Idea of a totality. Whereas the problem that faces us, even if it is put in terms of Idea and reflective judgment, is that it is no longer a matter, for us, of reflecting upon what is just or unjust against the horizon of a social totality, but, on the contrary, against the horizon of a multiplicity or of a diversity. This is both where practical reason and political reason are still beholden, in Kant, to metaphysics, because of this Idea of totality. [...] This is where I would insert a divide, at my own risk, because I am not certain that I am in the strict Kantian tradition."[14]

Elsewhere, too, Lyotard admits that he professes a Kantianism of a special kind, one that has dropped the notions of totality and of a single purpose that were so vital for Kant and the modern era. At the end of his

---

13. *Ibid.*, 85.
14. *Ibid.*, 87-88.

essay 'The Sign of History' (1982) he reflects on the signs of history that may awaken again contemporary people's awareness of the sublime. These signs are, more exactly, countersigns, occasioned by the falling apart of the great discursive nuclei in the terrible events of Auschwitz, Kolyma, Budapest and May 1968 – events that invalidate the grand legitimating narratives of modernity. For Kant, as we have seen, the impressive event (*Begebenheit*) he had to reflect upon was occasioned by the French Revolution. Yet, Lyotard stresses, "the *Begebenheit* we shall have to think through as philosophers and moral politicians, and which is in no way homologous to the enthusiasm of 1789 (since it is not aroused by the Idea of one purpose but by the Idea of several purposes or even by Ideas of heterogeneous purposes) – this *Begebenheit* for our time, then, would induce a new type of the sublime in which we would feel not only the irremediable gap between an Idea and what presents itself to 'realize' that Idea, but also the gap between the various families of phrases and their respective legitimate presentations."[15]

This statement makes tt clear that Lyotard's appropriation of Kant is, in the last resort, a transposition of some basic insights of Kant to the postmodern frame of mind. In this transposition the accent is sometimes placed on what seems to be a reversal of the Kantian terms. In point of fact, Lyotard speaks of a new type of the experience of the sublime, one that is aroused by the historical catastrophes with which one is confronted. For him, such an experience liberates, because it transfers one to a sphere in which fixed criteria of judgment can no longer be used. The reflective judgment is left without rules and the excitement it provokes derives from a special feeling that tells one that in spite of – or perhaps as a result of – these terrible events humanity is on its way to moral improvement. He says: "But however negative the signs to which most of the proper names of our political history give rise, we should nevertheless have to judge them *as if* they proved that this history had moved on a step in its progress, i.e. in the culture of skill and of will."[16] From the classical Kantian standpoint such an utterance would be hard to stomach, for how could a local historical setback possibly be seen as a sign that we have come closer to a cosmopolitan world community? The occurrence of such an event would rather smash the dream of cultural progress. Not so, however, for Lyotard. For him, the implosion of the *modern* dream of a universal brotherhood can be seen as the 'sign' that a new 'world' is being

---

15. J.-F. Lyotard, "The Sign of History," *The Lyotard Reader*, ed. A. Benjamin (Oxford: Blackwell, 1989) 409.
   16. *Ibid.*, 409.

born in which heterogeneity is respected and recognized: "This step [for-ward] would consist in the fact that it is not only the Idea of a single pur-pose which would be pointed to in our feeling, but already the Idea that this purpose consists in the formation and free exploration of Ideas in the plural, the Idea that this end is the beginning of the infinity of heteroge-neous finalities. Everything that fails to satisfy this fission of the single purpose, everything that presents itself as the 'realization' of a single pur-pose, as is the case with the phrase of politics, of the 'political moralist', is felt not to be up to (*angemessen*), not to be akin to (*abgezielt*) the infi-nite capacity of phrases aroused by this fission."[17]

In this passage Lyotard has invested the maximum of enthusiasm of which he is capable – by expressing the feeling that it makes sense to look at the historical setbacks as if they were the beginning of an infinity of heterogeneous finalities. With regard to this prospective view his thought is consistent with Kant's, for whom the signs of history allow one to make the prognosis that humanity has moved forward in a step to moral improvement. He also has appropriated Kant's insight that the proof of this prognosis lies in the spectator's attainment of a higher degree of cul-ture. But he definitely deviates from Kant, as far as the content of this prognosis is concerned. For Kant, 'to look at humanity *as if* it had moved on a step in its progress' was sustained by the expectation of humankind's growth towards a commonly shared autonomy – an autonomy which was still conceived in terms of a uniform pattern without any diversification. Lyotard, on the contrary, regards diversification – the infinity of hetero-geneous finalities – as the real objective of human progress.

Lyotard makes this option clear by questioning the reason as to why Kant thought it necessary to build 'passages' between the heterogeneous human faculties – for fear namely that without them the human intellect would be bereft of its sense of unity. If this sense of unity were to be lost, the transcendental subject would be weakened in carrying out its task as the chief legislator. For Lyotard, the difficulty does not lie in the fact that Kant is in search of passages and 'as if phrases', a method which Lyotard also practices. The problem lies in Kant's motive for doing this. Kant's motive is clear: he builds passages between the het-erogeneous faculties in order to safeguard the unbroken unity of the tran-scendental subject. Lyotard writes: "Kant pulls the Idea of this drive to commerce between [heterogeneous] phrases – [in Kant's terminology: between heterogeneous faculties] – down onto that of a subject which otherwise would fall to pieces, and of a rationality which otherwise

17. *Ibid.*, 409.

would be in conflict with itself and no longer worthy of its name. We today – and this is part of the *Begebenheit* of our time – feel that the fission given in this *Begebenheit* attacks that subject and that rationality too."[18]

Lyotard's style has been characterized as "a deft admixture of Kant and Wittgenstein."[19] In the above reasoning, however, Wittgenstein gets the upper hand. It was Wittgenstein, after all, who radicalized Kant's division of the faculties and replaced it with "the exploding of language into families of heterogeneous languages games"[20] which, however, continuously interact with each other in their heterogeneity. This is the favorite model Lyotard uses, in contradistinction to Kant. His dealing with passages is modeled after Wittgenstein's interaction of heterogeneous language-games. This interaction does not eliminate conflicts; on the contrary, it often increases them, depending on the type of interaction that takes place. It is from this background that Lyotard questions, in the end, the Kantian judge, who tends to reduce the differends (serious disagreements) to litigations (court cases) in an attempt at pacifying the quarrelling parties. To be sure, Lyotard does not reject tribunals en block. He is of the opinion that we need critical reason and critical tribunals, especially to challenge the "blindly calculating rationality, called Capital, [that] lays hold on [all other] phrases[21] in order to commercialize them and make surplus value out of them in the new condition of the *Gemeinwesen* [generic being] called 'computerized society'."[22] So, in the face of this commodification of our life world critical judges and tribunals are needed. Yet, he adds, this tribunal "will not be the same as the tribunal of Kant's critical philosophy. For we cannot judge [the pretension and the imposture of Capital's phrase] according to the Idea of man and within a philosophy of the subject but only according to the 'transitions' between heterogeneous phrases, and respecting their heterogeneity."[23]

Above I mentioned that Lyotard was swept by a certain enthusiasm when looking at the historical setbacks 'as if' they were the beginning

---

18. *Ibid.*, 410.
19. W. Godzich, "Afterword," in J.-F. Lyotard, *The Postmodern Explained*, 125.
20. J.-F. Lyotard, "The Sign of History," 410.
21. To recap: "A phrase is defined by – as it, in fact, defines – the situation of its instances (addressor, addressee, referent, sense) with regard to one another. Rather than defining a grammatical or semantic unit, a *phrase* designates a particular constellation of instances, which is as contextual as it is textual – if it is not indeed precisely what renders the 'opposition' between text and context impertinent:" Glossary of French Terms in J.-F. Lyotard, *The Differend*, 194.
22. J.-F. Lyotard, "The Sign of History," 410.
23. *Ibid.*, 410.

of an infinity of heterogeneous finalities. But he is not always that optimistic in his writings. A great many of his analyses of the political ends with the question: 'Is it happening?'[24] 'Is there still a free linkage of phrases not being forced upon by a previous regime of phrases that lays a claim to monopoly?'. In *The Differend* he even muses over the possible loss of the high degree of culture (an aptitude for Ideas) that is required to pass a critical judgment on the dealings of capitalism. Capitalism can be defined as a rigid system of calculation that uses time as economically as possible. A faster fabrication of high quality products significantly enhances the rate of profit. The same is true for the circulation of information in the era of 'space-time contraction', where instantaneous communication with other parts of the world through e-mails and internet has become essential. From this Lyotard concludes that the rapid pace with which capitalism urges its employees to work has also infected our dealings in every day life. The hectic rhythm imposed by the capitalistic mentality threatens to suffocate our human potential for reflection – for reflection always requires time. In this context he asks himself the following question: "But what assurance is there that humans will become more cultivated than they are? If culture (culture of the mind, at least) requires work and thus takes time, and if the economic genre imposes its stakes of gaining time on the greater part of phrase regimes and genres of discourse, then culture, as a consumer of time, ought to be eliminated. Humans will thereby no longer feel even sorrow before the incommensurability between realities and ideas, since they will lose their capacity to have Ideas. They will become more and more competent at strategies of exchange, but exclusively so."[25]

This situation makes the work of intellectuals (of those having a culture of the mind) not easy, for that matter. They will have to go on bearing witness to the Idea of Reason (or rather to the Idea of the infinity of heterogeneous finalities – see above), even when the majority of the people will no longer understand them. For most of them, the Idea is lost – is no longer part of their universe. Yet, the alert intellectual must continue to signal, through silences, gestures, and words, that this Idea is not lost. That is the right moment, for Lyotard, to bring up the notion of melancholy: "Each sublime feeling testifies to an Idea of Reason. Melancholy testifies to an Idea of Reason and to its absence in empirical reality. This is a way to testify to things relegated to oblivion. It is a feeling that can

24. See e.g. J.-F. Lyotard, *The Differend*, no. 263, p. 172.
25. *Ibid.*, no. 260, p. 181.

point to the sublime, and thus 'prove', signify, and bear witness to the fact that this Idea is not lost."[26]

II. LYOTARD'S DISTINCTIVE READING OF KANT'S *CRITIQUE OF JUDGMENT*

Lyotard is an expert in the exegesis of Kant, which does not prevent him from giving a distinctive reading of the *Critique of Judgment*. In 1991 he published his course notes on Kant, '*Lessons on the Analytic of the Sublime*'. In this work of 240 pages he offers a comment on some 40 pages of Kant's text, and spares no effort in doing so. He regularly elucidates the topics under discussion by comparing them with similar 'headings' in the *Critique of Pure Reason* and in the *Critique of Practical Reason*. He looks, for example, for similarities between the antinomies of pure reason and those arising in reflective judgment to find out that some of them are resolved in the latter. So, too, he meticulously examines why the aesthetic experience of the sublime differs from the feeling of respect for the law.

His close reading of Kant's texts has a clear purpose: to identify the elements that decidedly go beyond Kant as the system-builder and moralist witnessed in the *Critique of Pure Reason* and the *Critique of Practical Reason*. The reflective judgment Kant develops in his *Critique of Judgment* is something special: it is a judgment in search of its rules, operating without pre-established norms. This is an ideal Lyotard, as a matter of fact, wants to put into practice himself.

From the outset he makes it clear that the line of thought he is going to pursue has hardly been explored. Most of the interpreters follow the standard interpretation. This interpretation argues that what Kant wanted to achieve in the *Critique of Judgment* was a rapprochement between theoretical reason and practical reason. Research in the scientific study of nature uses concepts that are determined by the law of causality, whereas ethics focuses on the exercise of human freedom. The two methods apparently cannot be reconciled: the iron law of mechanical causality clashes with the free decisions taken in ethics, and vice versa. Or as Kant himself says: "The concept of freedom determines nothing with regard to our theoretical cognition of nature, just as the concept of nature

---

26. C. Pries, "Das Undarstellbare: Gegen das Vergessen: Ein Gespräch zwischen Jean-François Lyotard und Christine Pries," *Das Erhabene: Zwischen Grenzerfahrung und Grössenwahn*, ed. idem (Weinheim: Acta Humaniora, 1989) 332 [translation mine].

determines nothing with regard to the practical laws of freedom."[27] The appropriate means to build bridges or transitions (*Übergänge*) between the two heterogeneous language games is the faculty of judgment. This faculty judges particular occurrences as pleasing or repulsive under the guidance of a subjective teleology. Under this guidance it is able to project an 'as if' scheme of finality on the mechanical workings of nature: Aesthetically nature can be viewed *as if* it had a finality – a finality analogous to the finality of human freedom.

Lyotard has no objection against the standard reading. Yet, he wants to call attention to a second area of investigation which Kant deems at least as important, namely to bring about a certain rapprochement between the theoretical, the ethical and the aesthetic. This area is that of 'the faculties of the soul', studied in the discipline of rational psychology that was en vogue in Kant's days. In this area the focus is on the felt resonance of reflection: "For 'logically' reflection is called judgment, but 'psychologically', if we may be permitted the improper use of this term for a moment, it is nothing but the feeling of pleasure and displeasure. Pleasure and displeasure are at once both a 'state of the soul' and the 'information' collected by the soul relative to its state."[28]

In order to present this alternative approach I will start with dwelling on the import of the psychological resonance ('the felt presence of thought to itself', for which Lyotard coins the term: the tautegorical). In a second step I will examine the notion of the thinking/feeling 'subject' that flows from it ('erasure of the substantial subject'). In a third step I will explain Lyotard's specific understanding of '*sensus communis*', hereby relying on a special article he wrote on this topic. Finally I will tackle the question of the 'unification' of the faculties, as explained in *Lessons on the Analytic of the Sublime*, after having explained the importance of feelings in the faculties' contact with the supersensible.

1. The 'Tautegorical': The Felt Presence of Thought to Itself

Lyotard is intrigued by Kant's notion of reflective judgment, and grounds it as follows: "Pure reflection is first and foremost the ability of thought to be immediately informed of its state by its state and without other means of measure than feeling itself."[29] There is thus a coincidence between the 'state' in which the soul (or thought) finds itself

---

27. I. Kant, *Critique of Judgment*, Akademie edition, 195, trans. W. Pluhar (Indianapolis, IN: Hackett Publishing Company, 1987) 35.
28. J.-F. Lyotard, *Lessons on the Analytic of the Sublime*, 4.
29. *Ibid.*, 11.

and the 'information' it gains from it. Lyotard calls this the tautegorical disposition of the soul, which lies at the basis of a reflection that is in search of its rule, in order to extract something vaguely universal from one's aesthetic dealing with the particular. For Lyotard, this tautegorical disposition is given in its purest form in the aesthetic reflective judgment, although traces of it are also to be found in the mental operations of theoretical and practical reason: thought *feels itself* on each and every occasion.

This emphasis on feeling can already be found in Lyotard's work *Libidinal Economy* (1974),[30] in which he gave a libidinal reading – in terms of *jouissance* (enjoyment) and pain – of the capitalistic economy and Marx's critique of it. He came to the conclusion that labor is both enjoyable and painful, and not just alienating as Marx would have it. So, too, the 'aesthetic judgment' (*ästhetische Urteilskraft*) is based on a pleasant and/or unpleasant feeling. In this quality it has the capacity to pass a judgment before being able to account for its proper use of the rules (technically: the conditions of possibility of the judgment). He writes: "The power to critique must have the enigmatic capacity to judge the proper conditions of judgment 'before' being able to make use of, before having the right to make use of these conditions in judging whether they are the proper ones. Yet, reflection is, as we have said, tautegorical in that it is nothing but the feeling, pleasant and/or unpleasant, that thinking has about itself while it thinks, that is: judges or synthesizes."[31]

This is a baffling statement. Indeed, why is it that the thinking/feeling 'subject' is already able to judge before properly knowing the rules of the game of judging? Lyotard is very well aware of this difficulty, which he resolves by having recourse to a felt 'pre-logic'. He writes: "How, in short, can [the thinker] judge properly 'before' knowing what judging properly is, and in order to know what it might be? The answer is that critical thinking has at its disposal in its reflection, in the state in which a certain synthesis not yet assigned places it, a kind of transcendental pre-logic."[32] This kind of transcendental pre-logic must, in fact, be purely aesthetic. It consists in "the sensation that affects all actual thought insofar as it is merely thought –thought feeling itself *thinking* and feeling [feeling] itself [engaged in a process of] *thought*." And, he goes on,

---

30. J.-F. Lyotard, *Libidinal Economy*, trans. I. Gant (Bloomington, IN and Indianapolis, IN: Indiana University Press, 1993). Originally published as idem, *Économie libidinale* (Paris: Éditions de Minuit, 1974).

31. J.-F. Lyotard, *Lessons on the Analytic of the Sublime*, 31.

32. *Ibid.*, 32.

"because thinking is judging, feeling itself judging and judged at the same time."[33]

Lyotard stresses the importance of the subjective dimension of thinking. This dimension boils down to a 'pre-logical' exercise in which thinking learns how to judge in the ambience of thought that is merely thought (without any precise object); that is: at a level where thinking reflects upon itself with the help of feelings, pleasant and/or unpleasant – feelings that thinking has about itself as it thinks. Let us call this a 'private' exercise in judging. Although it starts with non being fixed on anything concrete, it nevertheless prepares the thinking/feeling 'subject' to develop the ability to give a certain direction to the further logical operations that are required for reaching a valid judgment. This ability initiates the transition from the 'private' exercise in judging to its 'public' use.

Kant is very detailed about these further logical operations. Lyotard faithfully renders this as follows: First, the 'pre-logical' reflection starts producing elementary syntheses or spontaneous assemblages of 'representations'. These are still fuzzy, having only a subjective value. To determine their objective use, the 'thinking that feels itself thinking' ought to assign them to a controlling faculty, which it does on the basis of insights gained in its 'private' exercise in judging. Or, as Lyotard writes: 'The thinking that feels itself thinking' "*guides itself* in determining the dwelling place or places of the faculties that authorize each of the syntheses. Only in a certain realm can a particular synthesis legitimately take 'place' because it will have been localized and circumscribed by the conditions of possibility of its tutelary faculty."[34] In other words, the lessons learned from its 'private' exercise in judging enable thinking to 'domicile' its elementary, pre-conceptual syntheses, that is: to allocate them to the faculty with which they are felt to have an affinity – where they will be submitted to the rules and working procedures of that faculty.

For Lyotard, it is vital that the 'thinking that feels itself thinking' *guides itself* in choosing the tutelary faculty that must validate the fuzzy syntheses. For the rest he admits with Kant that once under the control of the tutelary faculty, these syntheses will receive a limitation but also an objective recognition. He writes: "In this subjective presence of thought to itself there is the domiciling gesture that sends the spontaneous syntheses [...] to their tutelary faculties, thus limiting their use and establishing their legitimacy."[35] Lyotard emphasizes this subjective input. Only such

33. *Ibid.*, 32.
34. *Ibid.*, 31 [italics mine].
35. *Ibid.*, 32.

an input makes it plausible that the aesthetic judgment of taste is 'in search of its rules', by obeying an *a priori* principle that has only a *guiding function*, in contradistinction to science and ethics where the *a priori* principles result in determinant, 'legislative' judgments. The aesthetic judgment is basically guided by the pleasure or displeasure which 'thinking that feels itself thinking' experiences in its reflections. For this reason it is able to distance itself from intellectualism, and to "resist the unwarranted assimilation [of its intuitions] into the [strict] categories of understanding."[36]

2. *Erasure of the Substantial Subject*

The above analysis shows the importance that must be given to the initial stage of a 'thought that feels itself thinking, that feels itself judging and judged'. This initial stage is, for Lyotard, so crucial that he raises it to the rank of the true 'actor'. In *Lessons on the Analytic of the Sublime* he various times broaches the question of the transcendental subject, or the *I think*. Kant takes this *I think* as the point of departure for establishing objective scientific knowledge. Yet, in his study of the reflective judgment, Lyotard explains, this *I think* is, so to speak, dissolved in the successive sensations that 'thought that feels' has of itself. The focus on successive sensations is in line with the view he took in his early work *Phenomenology* (1954). There he showed that the mature Husserl replaced the transcendental Ego that was initially central to him with a more empirical Ego that realizes its 'thrownness' into the world of temporality. Temporality undoes the allegedly central unity of the subject.[37]

In the section *Aesthetic Temporality* he points out that the experience of the beautiful is characterized by a floating 'unison' between imagination and concept. But the experience of this floating 'unison' is not static. It is "singular and recurrent and always as if it were occurring anew, as something that appeared every time for the first time, like the outlines of a 'subject'. Each time a form provides the pure pleasure that is the feeling of the beautiful, it is as if the dissonances that divide thought, those of the imagination and the concept, were on the wane and left the

---

36. *Ibid.*, 38.
37. "History cannot be given to the subject as the object, the subject must be historical in herself – not accidentally but originarily. How then is the historicity of the subject compatible with its unity and totality?": J.-F. Lyotard, *Phenomenology*, trans. B. Beakley and G. Ormiston (Albany, NY: State University of New York Press, 1991) 112. Originally published as idem, *La Phénoménologie* (Paris: Presses Universitaires de France, 1954).

way open, if not to a perfect agreement, then to a peaceful conjugality or at least to a benevolent and gentle emulation resembling the one uniting fiancés."[38] In his earlier *Critiques* Kant defined the transcendental subject as the perfect unity of the faculties. But taste, as pure pleasure, cannot be grounded in any pre-existing unity. In the recurrent experiences of pleasure, this unity is rather felt as being constantly in the making. The subject is not pre-given; it "results from the 'engagement' of the two faculties and thus announces the hoped-for birth of a united couple. There is no one subjectivity (the couple) that experiences pure feelings; rather, it is the pure feeling that promises a subject. In the aesthetic of the beautiful the subject is in a state of infancy. It finds itself in this state each time pleasure arises from the beautiful."[39]

In his article on *sensus communis* he repeats the same insight: "If we try to keep the level of the pleasure in the beautiful, when describing it, then we must not say that it is experienced by the subject; it is an uncertain and unstable sketch of the subject ... There simply is no aesthetic transcendental '*I*'. At the most there is a pre-'*I*', a pre-cogito, some sort of floating synthesis between the faculties [of imagination and conceptual understanding]."[40] This starting point in a pre-cogito, however, raises the question as to its further development and final orientation. This question is not easy to answer, for there always lurks the temptation of affirming a substantial transcendental Ego. Therefore Lyotard starts again with the pre-cogito, in order to point from there to the ever-receding horizon of the pre-ego's final orientation: "For Kant, what one calls the subject is either the subjective aspect of thinking, and as such consists entirely in the tautegory that makes feeling the sign, for thought, of its state, thus the sign of a feeling itself because the 'state' of thinking is feeling; or else the subject is only a ground zero where the synthesis of concepts is suspended (in the first *Critique*) or is the ever receding horizon of the faculty's synthesis (in the *Third Critique*)."[41] This ever receding horizon – the final stage of the pre-cogito – will occupy a central place in Lyotard's account of the unification of the faculties (see below). One thing, however, becomes clear: the 'subject' cannot be properly understood, in its inception or in its final orientation, unless one takes seriously the sign-function of its feelings.

---

38. J.-F. Lyotard, *Lessons on the Analytic of the Sublime*, 19-20.
39. *Ibid.*, 20.
40. J.-F. Lyotard, "Sensus Communis," *Judging Lyotard*, ed. A. Benjamin (London and New York: Routledge, 1992) 19-20.
41. J.-F. Lyotard, *Lessons on the Analytic of the Sublime*, 25.

3. *Sensus Communis Does Not Imply Unanimity*

Equally distinctive is Lyotard's explanation of the *sensus communis* in Kant's *Critique of Judgment*, especially when compared with Hannah Arendt's treatment of the same. The notions of judgment and *sensus communis* became pivotal in her attempt at overcoming totalitarianism. For Arendt, totalitarianism is the forced imposition of a consensus among the citizens. The only factor with which it can be countered is a politically reflective judgment that starts from particular cases of resistance. Hannah Arendt is one of the first late modern thinkers to return to Kant and his method of assessing political events from the standpoint of the spectator.

In her analysis, Arendt examines the basic condition for arriving at an 'unbiased' reflective judgment: it must be disinterested. Feelings of political resistance arise from the creative imagination's project of a new beginning in the history of freedom. But in order to make sure that these feelings are authentic, one has to judge them on their disinterestedness. Only those will pass the test who are capable of adopting a universal standpoint, that of the *sensus communis*: A person of 'enlarged mind' (Arendt's term for creative imagination) "detaches himself from subjective personal conditions of his judgment, which cramp the minds of so many others, and reflects upon his judgment from a universal standpoint (which he can only determine by shifting his ground to the standpoint of others)."[42]

To corroborate her argument, Arendt refers to Kant's insistence that a truly universal standpoint can only be reached by putting oneself in the place of any other person. Or as Kant puts it himself: "Under the *sensus communis* we must include the Idea of a sense common to all, i.e. of a faculty of judgment which, in its reflection, takes into account (*a priori*) the mode of representation of all other men in thought, in order, as it were, to compare its judgment with the collective reason of humanity [...] This is done by comparing our judgment with the possible rather than the actual judgments of others, and by putting ourselves in the place of any other man, by abstracting from the limitations which contingently attach to our own judgment."[43] From this text she deduces the real possibility of a community of taste whose members share with each other their aesthetic experience of the beautiful. The purer and the more disinterested this community of taste becomes, the more also will its members

---

42. D. Inram, "The Kantianism of Arendt and Lyotard," *Judging Lyotard*, 131.
43. I. Kant, *Critique of Judgment*, trans. J.H. Bernard (London: Macmillan, 1951) 130, cited by D. Inram, "The Kantianism of Arendt and Lyotard," 132.

be united by a common concern about starting something new in the history of freedom.

Lyotard disagrees with this explanation, just as he disagrees with Habermas' theory of communicative action, which – in a typically modern fashion – is geared towards creating a consensus among the discussion partners. He is afraid that Kant's advice of 'comparing our judgment with the collective reason of humanity' – even when this comparison is carried out by putting oneself in the place of any other man – may be read along the lines of modern consensus formation. For him, such a reading is doomed to give rise again to some form of totalitarian collectivism. He writes: "This operation of comparison apparently occurs over a collectivity of individuals. Interpreted like this, this operation induces a realist empirical anthropological definition of the said *sensus*. How many illusions or political crimes have been able to nourish themselves with pretended, immediate sharing of feelings?"[44] He, therefore, focuses on the clause in Kant's definition – often glossed over by commentators – which excludes such an empirical interpretation: "This [reflection] is done by comparing our judgment with the *possible* rather than the *actual* judgments of others."[45] He highlights this specification 'of the *possible*' judgments of others', since it leaves room for a multiplicity of judgments, taken in their irreducible singularity – which all of them, in spite of their heterogeneity, can lay claim to a basic communicability, that of the *sensus communis*.

Not contenting himself, however, with the more faithful rendering of the above text of Kant, Lyotard also delves into the latter's psychological approach to the *sensus communis*.[46] The deepest motive for the communicability of the aesthetic judgment lies in the psychological resonance of the act of reflection. This resonance is a 'state of the mind' in which pleasure is experienced in the exercise of reflective judgment. It is this pleasure that lends itself to communication. Therefore it is important to stress the emotional undertone of the aesthetic judgment of taste. He writes: "The faculty of judgment acts reflexively, according to the Kantian vocabulary [...] Its effect on the mind, is the feeling of pleasure [...] One judges everywhere, in every domain, and in all of them there is some *sensus* at work, a state of mind, even if it knows and wills."[47]

44. J.-F. Lyotard, "Sensus Communis," 23.
45. *Ibid.*, 23.
46. See I. Kant, *Critique of Judgment, Akademie* edition, 238-239, trans. W. Pluhar, 87-88.
47. J.-F. Lyotard, "Sensus Communis," 7.

This emotional undertone is not restricted to the aesthetic judgment of taste. It is also present in the communication of knowledge and of ethical persuasions. The 'thing' to be communicated in knowledge is not just a set of enunciations; it also comprises a state of mind in virtue of which these enunciations deserve to be communicated to the community of scientists. Something similar happens in ethics. What is communicated here is a feeling of respect for the law – for a law that includes in its definition the ethical community and its commitment to the Idea of freedom. In both cases the message and the feeling to be communicated have also an objective referent: (a) a newly discovered piece of knowledge that is offered to the scientific community for evaluation; (b) deep respect for a moral law that regulates the behavior of the ethical community. The aesthetic judgment of taste, however, cannot boast of such an objective referent that directly connects to a community. It is, therefore, instructive to see how Kant accounts for the communicability of the judgment of taste. In paragraph 21 of the *Critique of Judgment* he points to the experience of an inner proportion or *euphony* (harmony, *Stimmigkeit*) between 'imagination' and 'conceptual understanding', and calls it the core of the judgment of taste. This inner proportion is not the result of a reasoning – scientific or ethical –, but manifests itself as the timbre of "an interior music,"[48] always diversified according to the particularity of the aesthetic judgment of taste.

Kant presents the communication of this timbre of an 'interior music' as universally possible and even necessary, but not without specifying these terms. It is universally communicable, in the sense that "the singular judgment of taste is enjoined (*ansinnen*) on everyone;" it is intimated to everyone without exception that such a judgment of taste with its timbre of 'interior music' is also within their reach. The same is true for the aspect of necessity. The communication of this timbre of an 'interior music' is not accidental, it is necessary; but this necessity "is not given apodictically, as the conclusion of a piece of reasoning, but as an *example*, always singular, for a rule or norm of aesthetic feeling to which everyone should give their consent, but which always remains to be found; which is never found."[49] In other words, the communication of this *particular* judgment of taste is necessary, because the aesthetic community needs models and examples in its search for the rule or norm of aesthetic feelings. A particular judgment of taste (and a particular experience of a timbre of 'inner music') serves as an *example* that carries with

48. *Ibid.*, 13.
49. *Ibid.*, 10-11.

it the fascinating power of seducing everyone towards a similar state of mind: the example is such that it necessarily stirs in everyone the desire for awakening to a similar capacity of aesthetic judgment.

Or, as Lyotard says more clearly in his *Lessons*: As far as the communicability of the aesthetic judgment of taste is concerned, "universality and necessity are promised but are promised singularly every time, and are only just promised. There could be no greater misunderstanding of the judgments of taste than to declare them simply universal and necessary."[50] Part of the promise is, as stated above, that in each single case one has to do with an example *for a rule* which always remains to be found, and which is never found. So far Lyotard is faithful to Kant's text, which he explains with an admirable perspicacity; at the same time, however, he seems to suggest –in conformity with his own thinking –that examples in the plural, and even totally heterogeneous examples, are needed, to stir in the aesthetic community a search for the rule or norm of the aesthetic judgment of taste that is always still to be found. This pluralization of 'examples' sheds a clarifying light on his statement above that the *sensus communis* must not be understood as something unanimously shared *in actuality*. For him, this *sensus* "is not common but only *in principle* communicable. There is no assignable community of feeling, no affective consensus in fact. And if we claim to have recourse to one, or *a fortiori* to create one, we are victims of a transcendental illusion and we are encouraging impostures."[51]

4. *The Importance of Feelings in the Faculties' Contact with the Supersensible*

Lyotard is particularly interested in the sign-function of feelings. This already comes to the fore in his article on *sensus communis*, in the section in which he discusses Kant's transcendental deduction of the judgment of taste. Such a deduction "establishes the legitimacy of a claim," to see whether "a synthesis [judgment] is well founded when it claims truth, goodness or beauty."[52] Compared with the deduction in the *Critique of Pure Reason* and of *Practical Reason*, the deduction in the *Critique of Judgment* is relatively simple. "What makes the deduction so easy is that it is spared the necessity of having to justify the objective reality of a concept."[53] The legitimacy of the claim to universal communicability must thus be established starting from aesthetic feelings.

---

50. J.-F. Lyotard, *Lessons on the Analytic of the Sublime*, 19.
51. J.-F. Lyotard, "Sensus Communis," 24.
52. *Ibid.,* 20.
53. I. Kant, *Critique of Judgment, Akademie* edition, 290, trans. W. Pluhar, 156.

In this context of deduction Lyotard asks himself the question: Is the *sensus communis* itself a transcendental Idea, just as in the *Critique of Pure Reason* the Idea of totality and completeness is an Idea of Reason (an Idea which can be thought but not be intuited or presented in empirical reality)? The answer is 'no': "No, the *sensus communis*, as unanimity about the beautiful, unanimity required and promised in each singular aesthetic judgment, is the witness or the sign (and not the proof) 'lying in' [...] subjectivity, the witness or sign of an Idea [of Reason] which relates itself to this subjectivity and which legitimates this requirement and this promise."[54]

Why is the requirement and promise of unanimity (*sensus communis*) only a sign, a sign that witnesses to something else? Because the requirement and the promise let themselves be guided by the Idea of Reason 'that there must be an affinity between the faculties', in this case: between imagination and conceptual understanding. The felt promise of the universal communicability of the aesthetic judgment can, therefore, only be the *sensible medium* in which this Idea of Reason manifests itself. He writes: "The *sensus communis* is still therefore [...] the sensible *analogon* of the transcendental euphony of the faculties, which can only be the object of an Idea [of Reason] and not of an intuition."[55]

The Idea of Reason implies "that it is in the nature of the subject [to admit] that all his faculties agree to make possible knowledge in general [...] so that even the freest form in the imagination keeps an affinity with the power of understanding."[56] Therefore, whenever in empirical reality a singular judgment of taste experiences a charming proportion between imagination and conceptual understanding, this experience must be seen as the sign and the signal of the 'transcendental' truth of the Idea of Reason. It is in its quality of 'sign' and 'witness' that the experienced euphony keeps alive the promise of unanimity. Whoever mistakes the promise for the 'real thing', falls prey to a transcendental illusion. That's why Lyotard is skeptical about every self-styled community of taste.

In *Lessons on the Analytic of the Sublime* he broadens this perspective by examining the specific feelings that arise in the three faculties – intellect, will, and judgment of taste – in their contact with supersensible Ideas. At the level of the judgment of taste the feeling of inner harmony or euphony, as we have seen, is the sign of the faculty's contact with the supersensible, whereas at the level of practical reason this contact leads to a feeling of 'respect': Respect is "not the incentive to morality, it is

54. J.-F. Lyotard, "Sensus Communis," 18.
55. *Ibid.*, 24.
56. *Ibid.*, 18.

the 'presence' of the law regarded subjectively, its 'sign'."[57] Respect is, thus, the specific way in which 'feeling thought' reacts to the summons of the categorical imperative. The sign-function of the feeling of respect is even more explicit in the ethical person's contact with the Idea of freedom. This Idea of Reason remains incomprehensible, and as such lures the person into her commitment to freedom: "Even the pure feeling of respect, which is tautegorical, is only pure insofar as it 'says' at once a state of thought and the *other* of thought, the transcendence of freedom with its 'complete incomprehensibility'. The pure feeling is the ethical 'manner' in which transcendence can be 'present' in immanence."[58]

Something similar happens in the feeling of the sublime. Yet, here, we have to do with a double response, respect and delight. When confronted with chaotic elements in nature, the imagination is thrown out of gear because it is unable to synthesize excessive magnitudes with its proper means. This incapacity makes it look for the Idea of 'an absolute whole', which however it cannot intuit or make visible: this awakens in the 'soul' awe and respect: "The feeling, namely, that our imagination is inadequate (*unangemessen*) to attain to an Idea that is a law for us –this feeling is respect (*Achtung*)."[59] But in addition to respect, a soul-stirring delight arises from the moment the person realizes that her true vocation consists in harking to the voice of Reason (which speaks to her from the supersensible realm). Lyotard puts it as follows: "Thus in sublime feeling thought feels sensation as an 'appeal' made to a 'force' in it that is not 'one of nature'. This sensation is a soul-stirring delight, a sharp pleasure. Why is this? Because this appeal actualizes the *destination* (*Bestimmung*) of our *Geistesvermögen*, of our spiritual faculty – of the power of thought at its strongest –as it discovers this destination [...] The mind *(das Gemüt)* harkens now to the voice of Reason [...] Thought is destined for the absolute."[60] And he adds: "For thought to feel called on or requisitioned by the voice of Reason is an absolute delight, because it is the absolute vocation of thought to think the absolute;"[61] "[this] intransigent, inevitable (*unvermeidliche*) requisition is reflexively felt as a soul-stirring delight."[62]

The specific manner in which the aesthetic of the beautiful and of the sublime, and the ethical respond to the 'irruption' of the supersensible, reveals a family relationship between them – a certain convergence that

57. J.-F. Lyotard, *Lessons on the Analytic of the Sublime*, 227.
58. *Ibid.*, 45.
59. *Ibid.*, 117, citing from I. Kant, *Critique of Judgment*, §27, *Akademie* edition, 257.
60. J.-F. Lyotard, *Lessons on the Analytic of the Sublime*, 119-120.
61. *Ibid.*, 121.
62. *Ibid.*, 120.

does not obliterate their specific difference: euphony (for the beautiful); respect (for the ethical) and respect and delight (for the feeling of the sublime). To establish a similar family relationship with theoretical reason – in terms of feelings – is a bit more difficult, since Kant's *First Critique* mainly deals with shattering the illusion that theoretical reason would be able to go beyond the empirical realm and to grasp, with its own means of thinking, the supersensible Ideas. When, however, bringing up the topic of the supersensible Ideas, Kant makes it clear that, deceptive as they are when trying to get at them speculatively, these Ideas nonetheless play an important role when taken in their practical use.[63] We have seen this practical use at work in the domains of ethics and aesthetics, where the contact with supersensible Ideas had a bearing on the emergence of specific feelings.

There is, however, a passage in Lyotard's *Lessons* which reveals something about the practice of thinking when it is carried to its limits and feels, at the same time, constrained from taking this step. The passage starts with a consideration on the feeling of the sublime (which is the central theme of the *Lessons*). It says: "The sublime feeling [...] is the subjective state critical thought must feel in its being carried to its limits (and therefore beyond them) and its resistance to this impetus, or, conversely, what it must feel in its passion to determine and in its resistance to this passion. One might consider this a philosophical neurosis. Rather it is a faithfulness par excellence to the philosophical feeling, 'brooding melancholy', as Kant suggested in *Observations on the Feeling of the Beautiful and the Sublime*."[64] But then he jumps to a more general statement that equally could apply to theoretical reason at the moment it is carried to its limits: "The absolute is never there, never given in a presentation, but it is always 'present' as a call to think beyond the 'there'. Ungraspable but unforgettable. Never restored, never abandoned."[65]

5. 'Unification' of the Faculties through Their Affinity in the Felt Contact with the Supersensible

Kant's three critiques, especially when attempting to resolve the speculative antinomies that arise in their respective domains, wrestle with the

---

63. "Consequently, if there be any correct employment of pure reason, in which case there must be a canon of its employment, the canon will deal not with the speculative but with the *practical employment of reason*." I. Kant, *Critique of Pure Reason*, A 825/B 797, trans. N. Smith (London and Basingstoke: The Macmillan Press, 1929 [1982]) 630.
64. J.-F. Lyotard, *Lessons on the Analytic of the Sublime*, 150.
65. *Ibid.*, 150.

notion of the supersensible. In the *Critique of Pure Reason* Kant already stated that "the transcendent concept (*transzendenter Begriff*) [the supersensible Idea, thus] exceeds all sensible intuition and escapes all means of proof".[66] The same insight comes back in the *Critique of Practical Reason*: the "concept of transcendental freedom: it is indemonstrable."[67] This, however, does not at all mean that there may be any doubt about the real existence of these concepts (or better: Ideas). To the extent that the faculties set out to establish the legitimacy of their operations and claims – in the case of the judgment of taste: the claim to universal communicability – they simply presuppose such an ultimate unifying Idea.

Yet that which this Idea is in itself cannot be known with the means the faculty in question has at its disposal. For this reason Kant distinguishes between a *transcendental* Idea, and its purely *transcendent* character. Lyotard puts this as follows: "So long as an Idea regulates the legitimate use of a faculty in its realm or territory, it is transcendental. It is transcendent when it makes for itself 'objects' for which experience supplies no material, either in the realm or the territory. It is not determinable by the means that govern judgment in that field. It is a 'mere thought entity' [...] it is transcendent in that its object remains unknown."[68]

This unknown 'mere thought entity', however, signals its presence in the specific feelings it arouses in the distinct branches of thought and judgment. For the judgment of taste, the aroused feeling is that of a demand for universal communicability, whereby "this demand is but the 'presence' or the sign of this [mere thought entity] that is absolutely absent, insensible, in the strictest sense of the word 'knowledge'."[69] The same is true in ethics for the Idea of freedom. Insofar as this Idea acts as transcendental Idea, it makes possible morality in the realm of practical reason. But insofar as it is transcendent "its 'presence' is only signaled by the feeling of respect, which also implies the obligation to be universally communicated."[70] In both cases there is a feeling, related to universal communicability, that testifies to the felt presence of the 'unpresentable'.

In a further step, Lyotard makes it clear that each of the faculties testifies to this presence in a unique way (or in his terminology: in a heterogeneous manner). That which is signaled in aesthetics and in ethics is in each case an unpresentable Idea, but "[t]his is not to say that both

66. *Ibid.*, 211.
67. *Ibid.*, 211.
68. *Ibid.*, 211.
69. *Ibid.*, 211.
70. *Ibid.*, 212.

Ideas, the one governing the aesthetic, and the one governing the ethical, are the same. They are not identical but are in a relation of 'analogy'."[71]

Analogy implies commonality or affinity and difference. (a) What the three faculties have in common – and which constitutes their affinity – is a passion for legitimating their function. They "seek to discover the supreme condition of the specific conditions of possibility of their respective territories or realms."[72] This means that they seek to ground, at a still deeper level, the specific conditions of possibility that allow them to be operative in their respective domain. In so doing, they try to grasp the supreme condition on which their own structuring power depends. In this quest for the absolute, they are brought to the 'limit of their power'; they realize that to grasp this supreme condition (which is the supersensible realm) is definitely beyond their reach. This frustration prepares them to acknowledge the might of the supersensible.

But then (b) comes the differentiation. Lyotard observes that the three faculties are, each in their own, heterogeneous way, carried to the limit of their power when trying to grasp the supreme condition of their proper function. In each case, this limit has a different name. At first glance, it looks as if the faculties culminate in the same Idea of Reason: "The faculty of desire culminates in the Idea of a transcendental freedom [or absolute completeness] for the ethical realm, and the faculty of [aesthetic] presentation culminates in the Idea of a transcendental freedom [or absolute completeness] for the territory of the aesthetic. But they are not alone. Understanding also cannot avoid maximizing its concepts (that condition the possibility of a knowledge of experience) to the Idea of 'absolute completeness'."[73] But on closer inspection this threefold striving for absolute completeness culminates in different Ideas of Reason: the Idea of a transcendental freedom of the imagination in aesthetics – unrestricted freedom to imagine presentations – is not the same as the Idea of a transcendental freedom of the will in ethics –unrestricted freedom to desire the highest good –; and so too for knowledge where the Idea of a transcendental freedom takes on the form of an unrestricted "freedom to conceive ideas."[74]

A similar differentiation takes place in the respective antinomies of the three faculties. To the extent that each of the faculties attempts to fathom their limit-Ideas (an urge that drives them), they are unavoidably caught

71. *Ibid.*, 212.
72. *Ibid.*, 213.
73. *Ibid.*, 213.
74. *Ibid.*, 214.

up in antinomies, antinomies being the markers of the contradictions that arise when the faculties attempt to go beyond their limits. Here, again a parallelism crops up. Antinomies arise in the cognitive faculty (theoretical reason) when understanding is carried to the point of seeking to understand the 'unconditioned of knowledge': they arise in the practical reason (ethics) when the faculty of desire is carried to the point of desiring the 'absolute law'; they occur in aesthetics when the aesthetic judgment is carried to the point of 'demanding universal communicability'. The three faculties are, thus, each in their own way, carried to the point at which they reach their limit, from which the respective sets of antinomies arise. This limit is, in fact, the unthinkable and ever-receding horizon towards which the faculties are moving in their passion to legitimate their proper function.

Each of the faculties strives for reaching out to this receding horizon in its own way. Therefore, Lyotard insists, it would be more accurate to speak of horizons in the plural, or of absolutes in the plural: "It is a question of horizons because the unconditioned of the conditions of thought in each of its capacities is always deferred and its search has no end [...] With the means reflection has at its disposal in each of the realms or territories mentioned, reflection cannot determine the absolutes upon which these means depend. The unconditioned of knowledge cannot be known [in theoretical reason]. The absolute law of the faculty of desire cannot be desired. The supersensible principle that founds the demand for the universal communication of taste cannot be the object of an aesthetic pleasure." And then he concludes: "However, the horizon is 'present' everywhere. What we are calling 'presence' in contradistinction to presentation is the effect of this transcendence, its sign, on theoretical, practical and aesthetic thought."[75]

The fact that the three horizons of unknowability have an affinity or analogy to each other – without loosing their specific heterogeneity – is for Lyotard the decisive reason for accepting a 'unification' of the faculties. Yet, this 'unification' can never result in a monolithic system, in the style of Fichte's or Hegel' s idealism. The unification is and remains an open unification that honors the specific (Lyotard would say: heterogeneous) manner in which the faculties, each in their own way, experience their limit before the ever-receding horizon of the absolute. On the other hand, it is precisely the affinity in experiencing their limit that brings them into an analogous situation before the absolute or the supersensible. In that sense they are united 'in the supersensible': "The supersensible

75. *Ibid.*, 214.

guarantees that these profoundly heterogeneous capacities of thinking – theoretical, practical and aesthetic – nonetheless share an affinity with each other. This affinity is revealed by way of the similarity of their respective inconsistencies [read: antinomies]. Each faculty is seized with the impossibility of thinking its limit with the means it has at its disposal, but that it must try to think this limit is the sign of the supersensible. And he adds: "This sign is transitive in relation to the heterogeneity of the faculties,"[76] which means that the sign is always specific to the heterogeneous context from which it arises.

Is this not a strange manner of bringing the *Lessons on the Analytic of the Sublime* to an end? The answer is 'yes' and 'no'. Yes, because in this conclusion no mention at all is made of the Sublime. No, because in the elaboration of the above analogies the very core of the sublime has been presupposed. As Lyotard stated earlier: "The sublime feeling [...] is the subjective state critical thought must feel in its being carried to its limits (therefore beyond them) and its resistance to this impetus, or, conversely, what it must feel in its passion to determine and in its resistance to this passion."[77]

III. POSTMODERN FEATURES IN LYOTARD'S READING OF KANT

In his analysis of the *Critique of Judgment* Lyotard gives a fairly reliable reading of Kant. When commenting on it, however, he allows some postmodern features to creep in, mostly without identifying them. In this section I will bring them out more explicitly. Before tackling the postmodern features, however, I must first warn against a possible misunderstanding.

1. *Clearing Up a Possible Misunderstanding*

Earlier I mentioned that Lyotard, in deliberate divergence from the standard interpretation, opted for a 'psychological' reading of Kant's *Critique of Judgment*. This line of thought turned out to be very productive. From this, however, it does not follow that Lyotard's dealing with Kant would be limited to this sole line of thought. In his *Lessons on the Analytic of the Sublime*, with its emphasis on the felt contact with the unpresentable, the psychological reading forms the backbone of his exposé.

76. *Ibid.*, 215.
77. *Ibid.*, 150.

Yet, in other works he explicitly enters into conversation with the standard reading of the *Critique of Judgment*. This interest in the standard reading was occasioned by his study of Wittgenstein's language-games through which Kant's separation of the faculties is undeniably radicalized. Lyotard appropriates this radicalization. This leads him to re-read Kant's attempts at bridging the gap between mechanical causation (science) and freedom (ethics) through the lens of Wittgenstein's "exploding of language into families of heterogeneous languages-games."[78] This inevitably must end up in a parting of the ways with Kant's meticulously differentiated but ultimately unitary program.

To recap: For Kant the language game of mechanical causation practiced in scientific research (*Critique of Pure Reason*) cannot possibly be taken as a rule for studying human beings' reactions to ethical obligations, as analyzed in the *Critique of Practical Reason*. Also the reverse is true: the language-game of ethical reflection is of no use for the study of nature. Precisely at this point, Kant – and that is what the standard interpretation highlights – wanted to build bridges or transitions (*Übergänge*) between the two heterogeneous language games. The appropriate instrument through which to achieve this is the faculty of judgment. This faculty judges particular occurrences as pleasing or repulsive under the guidance of a subjective teleology. Under this guidance it is able to project an 'as-if' scheme of finality on the mechanical workings of nature: aesthetically nature can be viewed *as if* it had a finality –a finality analogous to the finality of human freedom. In spite of realizing the incompatibility between theoretical and practical reason, Kant succeeds, thus, in upholding the unbroken unity of the thinking subject on the basis of the aesthetic judgment's power to poetically invent analogies between them. This creative invention of affinities (of 'as-if schemes') does not, however, obliterate the difference between the theoretical and the ethical approach. If one would obliterate the difference, one would fall prey to transcendental illusion. One would say 'this is objectively the case', whereas in reality it is not. 'This is the case' has only an aesthetic value for the feeling subject and their valuations.

The 'as if-schemes' build 'passages' in a special way. The reflective judgment of taste only judges on the basis of a particular mood it deems trustworthy. It has no universal rules or norms at its disposal, as is the case with theoretical and practical reason. Even so it succeeds in bringing

---

78. J.-F. Lyotard, "The Sign of History," 410.

about 'passages' by navigating between the two domains, with the purpose – that is Kant's rationale – of evoking a unity within the thinking subject. As already said, the 'passage' is only aesthetically valid. To take it literally, and to assert that through it the two domains are really bonded, would be devastating. Such a stand would lead to the emergence of a monolithic world without diversification.

In order to describe the mediating role of the aesthetic judgment of taste, Lyotard has recourse to the metaphor of the archipelago. This metaphor, however, already slightly distorts Kant's view. Lyotard writes: "Each genre of discourse would be like an island; the faculty of judgment would be, at least in part, like an admiral or like a provisioner of ships who would launch expeditions from one island to the next, intended to present to one island what was found (or invented, in the archaic sense of the word) in the other, and which might serve the former as an 'as-if intuition' with which to validate it. Whether war or commerce, this interventionist force has no object, and does not have its own island, but it requires a milieu – this would be the sea– the *Archipelagos* or primary sea as the Aegean was once called."[79]

In this metaphor Lyotard makes it clear that the faculty of judgment does not have its own island – it has no proper cognitive object of its own, and is therefore not a faculty in the strict sense of the word; it only navigates and mediates between islands or genres of discourse. Genres of discourse or regimes of phrases are so specific that they are not convertible the one into the other: they are isolated islands, each with their proper regime: "the regime governing a normative (i.e., descriptive in terms of being true or false) phrase is completely different from the regime of a prescriptive phrase. The same is true of interrogative, performative (in the strict sense), and exclamatory phrases."[80] Lyotard makes use of the vocabulary of 'language pragmatics' to elucidate Kant's concern. Yet, the question can be raised as to whether this method is not going to press Kant into a straightjacket.

In line with his language pragmatics Lyotard perceives a parallel between descriptive phrases and what Kant examined in the *Critique of Pure Reason*, namely objective knowledge; he also takes it for granted that prescriptive sentences have an affinity with the ethical obligation in the *Critique of Practical Reason* (Ethics). But on closer inspection this latter parallel can be questioned. For him, the prescriptive phrase reads as follows: "*Close the door* is a prescriptive phrase, and the question it

79. J.-F. Lyotard, *The Differend*, 131.
80. J.-F. Lyotard, *The Postmodern Explained*, 42.

raises hinges on the justice of the order given to the addressee and on the execution of the act it prescribes."[81] But it is questionable as to whether this definition can be applied to Kant's categorical imperative. There the prescription is perceived internally in one's conscience; it does not come from an external addressor who, in a next step, would be able to verify whether the prescribed act is properly executed (so that between addressee and addressor a discussion can start as to whether or not the prescription is justified). This change in perspective indicates that we are miles away from Kant's concern as to how to build a rapprochement between a world of facts and the domain of ethics, a rapprochement in which the exercise of human freedom is to be found. It goes without saying that a reading of Kant through the lens of Wittgenstein is a risky enterprise.

The deviation from Kant becomes fully evident in Lyotard's description of the 'milieu' (of the sea in which the navigating fleet carries out its commerce or its war-activities). This 'milieu' is that of judgment. But instead of acting as the mediator *between* the islands (genres, regimes of phrases), judgment seems already to be at work *before* navigating between them, in that it assigns to each of them their zone of influence and their legitimate authority. Lyotard states: "[The faculty of judgment] is the faculty of the milieu, within which every circumscription of legitimacy is secured. Furthermore, it is this faculty which enabled the territories and realms to be delimited, which has established the authority of each genre [i.e. of each family of sentences] on its island. And this it was only able to do thanks to the commerce or to the war it fosters between genres."[82] Commenting on this statement, Richard Beardsworth remarks: "It is clear from the above that Lyotard has made the reflective judgment of the *Third Critique* the faculty of the 'milieu'. In a sense it is not a faculty because it does not constitute in Lyotard's terms 'a family of sentences'. It is rather the operation of formation and presentation of all the other families."[83] And he concludes: "Lyotard is implicitly arguing behind his description of judgment that the law of reflective judgment, its 'meta-prescription', is heterogeneity and that heterogeneity is therefore its 'ultimate end'."[84]

With the information they get from the navigating fleet about the other (heterogeneous) islands, each of the islands is, to be sure, given the opportunity to look at the other islands 'as if' something common existed

81. *Ibid.*, 42.

82. J.-F. Lyotard, *The Differend*, 131.

83. R. Beardsworth, "Lyotard's Agitated Judgment," *Judging Lyotard*, ed. A. Benjamin (London and New York: Routledge, 1992) 70.

84. *Ibid.*, 70.

between them. Yet, the meta-prescription of judgment – 'judge in terms of heterogeneity!' – forbids each of the islands to take such a commonality seriously. 'To stretch the "as if" too far', the islanders seem to say, 'would land us in the trouble waters of transcendental illusion. Let us stress the heterogeneity'. No wonder thus that Lyotard, in the end, finds himself asking: "What are we doing here other than navigate between islands in order paradoxically to declare that their regimens or genres are incommensurable?"[85] This makes it clear again that, for him, heterogeneity is the ultimate end of reflective judgment, whereas Kant was still in search of a reflective judgment that would be able to evoke a frail unity of the respective faculties. In the words of Richard Beardsworth: "In Kant, the way in which judgment judges, beyond its immediate 'practicality', is to anticipate the unity, be it reflective, of the faculties – the very thing [...] that Lyotard considers to be Kant's humanism and to be 'unjust' to the social fabric [of contemporary society]."[86]

2. *Five Postmodern Features*

We are in a position now to list the 'postmodern' features in Lyotard's psychological reading of the *Critique of Judgment*. This psychological reading is, to be sure, more faithful to Kant than the above considerations on the archipelago in which the influence of Wittgenstein's exploding of language into families of heterogeneous languages games is palpable. But here, too, Lyotard aims at dissolving unanimity and the (monolithic) substantial subject, so as to replace them with plurality and difference. This dissolution is in line with classic topics of postmodern thinking: the 'death' of the subject and the 'end' of straightforward finalities. Besides these deconstructive themes, some positive ones which are linked to the psychological approach must also be mentioned, such as the importance of feelings in the act of judgment and the way in which specific, diversified feelings testify to the limit-experience of the supersensible. I start by reviewing the deconstructive themes.

1. Although Lyotard still uses the classic notion of *sensus communis*, he definitively departs from its modern understanding of unanimous agreement. He disallows the existence of a community of taste whose members would share an agreed-upon aesthetic judgment of taste. For him, such a consensus-model is frightening, because it tends to silence

85. J.-F. Lyotard, *The Differend*, 135.
86. R. Beardsworth, "Lyotard's Agitated Judgment," 67.

alternative views and opinions. He therefore holds that the *sensus communis* "is not common but only *in principle* communicable. There is no assignable community of feeling, no affective consensus in fact. And if we claim to have recourse to one, or *a fortiori* to create one, we are victims of a transcendental illusion and we are encouraging impostures".[87] Kant's rule of thumb, that we should place ourselves in the place of others must be specified: we should not compare our judgment with the *actual* judgment of others, but with their *possible* judgment; only then will room for plurality and difference be created.

2. In line with the deconstruction of a 'collectivity of persons' is also his erasure of the substantial subject. Reacting against features of intellectualism so prominent in modern thinking, Lyotard opts for highlighting the 'tautegorical'. By this he means that thinking can never be disconnected from feelings: thinking feels itself thinking, judging feels itself judging, and whoever is in search of a rule or guiding principle, feels themselves passionately engaged in the stakes of this search. This stress on feelings honors the importance of desires and emotions as the cradle for critical thinking in the perspective of plurality and heterogeneity; yet, there is also an aspect of temporality involved. From the late Husserl, Lyotard has learned that our human activities take place in the dispersal of time. This makes us understand his eagerness for obliterating even the vestiges of a substantial subject –of the Cogito, of the organizing transcendental Ego. For him, the subject is always in the making; it is never ready made. It 'comes into being' again and again under the impulse of feelings – of feelings that prompt one to think. That is why Lyotard prefers to speak not of a subject, but of the 'sketch' of a subject that arises from experiences of pleasure and/or displeasure. In this experience, the floating unison between imagination and concept is "singular and recurrent and always as if it were occurring anew, as something that appeared every time for the first time, like the outlines of a 'subject'."[88] Instead of being deduced from a stable transcendental Ego, the subject is always reborn to itself, enriched with, and challenged by new experiences that keep it in a state of infancy.

3. Typically postmodern is the way in which Lyotard anchors the reflective judgment in the 'presence of thought to itself' – which implies a channeling of the reflective judgment into the vivid awareness of feelings and emotions as sources of estimation. To this aspect Lyotard has devoted many reflections – already in his work *Libidinal Economy* – up

---

87. J.-F. Lyotard, "Sensus Communis," 24.
88. J.-F. Lyotard, *Lessons on the Analytic of the Sublime*, 19-20.

to the point of coining the term the 'tautegorical' (which seems to con-
note the opposite of the unemotional, clear-cut 'categorical'). For him,
just as for Kant, the aesthetic judgment's power emerges from pleasant
and/or unpleasant feelings. But more perhaps than Kant he stresses that
in this quality it has the surprising capacity to judge the proper conditions
of judgment, even before being capable of rationally accounting for their
appropriateness. This is in line with what he says elsewhere: that the
artist does not know in advance the rules s/he is going to use in describing a certain state of affairs. The artist is, like the postmodern philosopher, in search of the rules s/he is supposed to follow: "The texts he produces are not in principle governed by pre-established rules, and they
cannot be judged according to a determinant judgment, by applying familiar categories to the text or the work. Those rules or categories are what
the work of art itself is looking for."[89] This search is specified now, as
taking its lead from the pleasant and/or unpleasant feelings that thought
experiences when engaged in thinking.

4. Lyotard's insistence on the specific way in which the three faculties 'signal' their felt contact with the supersensible must also be termed
postmodern. The roots of this thinking are, to be sure, to be found in
Kant. But there must be a reason as to why this aspect of Kant's thought
has become fashionable again in the postmodern condition. Postmodern
authors – Jacques Derrida is among them – strongly react against the new
'absolutes' of modernity, such as the substantial subject and the straightforward finality of history; but precisely by toppling these new 'absolutes'
they again open the perspective on some 'supersensible reality' which
they are only able to name and to evoke – but not to understand. In this
context one must place the importance Lyotard attaches to the specific
feelings that arise in the contact with the 'supersensible' in ethics, in the
experience of the sublime, and in the experience of scientific research.
The description of these feelings can be found in Kant; yet a special sensitivity is required to become aware of them, even in a close reading of
Kant's texts. In ethics, respect is the sign of the presence of the law; in
the experience of the sublime, respect in conjunction with a soul-stirring
delight signals our supersensible vocation; whereas in theoretical reason,
the absolute – which is never given in presentation – is felt to be present
as a incessant call to think beyond the 'there'.

5. Lyotard's analysis of the 'unification' of the three faculties also
reveals some affinity with the postmodern interest in aesthetics, especially the feeling of the sublime. He points out that the faculties of pure

89. J.-F. Lyotard, *The Postmodern Explained*, 15.

reason, practical reason, and aesthetic judgment are analogously structured but nonetheless obey the same 'meta-prescript': they are all forced
to embark on a search for the supreme condition that regulates their functioning, in spite of the fact that they will never succeed in grasping this
supreme condition: "Each faculty is seized with the impossibility of
thinking its limit with the means it has at its disposal, but that it must try
to think this limit is the sign of the supersensible."[90] The force of the
supersensible is signaled, and testified to, in the very moment in which
the faculty in question collapses in its attempt at presenting the supersensible as the supreme condition of its inner working. In this collapse it
experiences a mixture of pain and delight: pain because of the felt failure to make visible this supreme condition; delight because "the dismay
at the inadequacy of presentation negatively 'signals' the incommensurability of the power of the Ideas."[91] This mixture of pain and delight is
typical of the experience of the sublime. The three faculties are 'united'
(by analogy) in their respective way of experiencing the sublime, a theme
that runs through Lyotard's whole œuvre.

IV. SOME METHODOLOGICAL CONSIDERATIONS

Having listed five areas in which postmodern features surface, some
methodological considerations are still in order.

1. Jean-François Lyotard is renowned for his emphasis on heterogeneity. His metaphor of the archipelago made it clear that all the islands (faculties) in it are incommensurate, so that no bridge can be built between
them. As explained above, he came to this insight through a dialogue with
the standard interpretation, which focuses on the way in which Kant tried
to construct a rapprochement between the mechanical causation in nature
and the realm of human freedom. In order to bring about this rapprochement, Kant made use of the judgment of taste, which allowed him to look
at nature 'as if' it had a finality analogous to that of human freedom. This
'as-if' scheme is purely aesthetic, but nonetheless bridges in a special way
the gap between the two heterogeneous domains. Lyotard, too, realizes
that the 'passage' is only aesthetically valid. Yet, in order to thwart any
objectifying understanding that would see the two domains as really
bonded in actual fact, he makes use of Wittgenstein's distinction between

---

90. J.-F. Lyotard, *Lessons on the Analytic of the Sublime*, 215.
91. J.-F. Lyotard, "Das Erhabene und die Avantgarde," *Verabschiedung der
(Post)Moderne? Eine interdisziplinäre Debatte*, ed. J. Le Ridier and G. Raulet (Tübingen,
1987) 260 [translation mine].

language games. As a result the analogies Kant wanted to establish are dissolved. What remains is the affirmation of heterogeneity. For Lyotard, the reflective judgment keeps things apart. It must do so to call attention to 'differends', that is: to give a voice to those who are silenced. They have been silenced through the use of a particular linguistic strategy that denies them the right to use their own idiom in the conversation. This is accomplished by the more powerful discussion partners when they insist that their idiom alone must be used in the debate.

Can one call this 'keeping apart' of domains a sublime gesture of doing justice to the silenced voice? Lyotard would say 'yes'. At various times, he asks the question 'Does it happen?' 'Does it happen that justice is done to the loser in the debate?', and he associates this with a feeling of melancholy that is, at the bottom, sublime. Yet, what is the logic behind it? On what grounds does he associate the gesture of separation with sublimity? These grounds are not explained and are also far from evident. Apparently he borrows the feeling of the sublime from elsewhere, from the context of the faculties' limit-experience in their felt contact with the supersensible. In other words, it is not his critical dialogue with the standard interpretation but his psychological reading of Kant's *Critique of Judgment* that gives him access to the notion of the sublime. True, in the case of the faculties' limit-experience, we are also concerned with the bridging of a gap. Yet, this gap is no longer that which occurs between mechanical causality and freedom. The gap that arises is that between the faculties' search for completeness and their respective ungraspable supreme condition. Each faculty is forced to think its supreme condition of possibility – which is also its limit – and is seized with the impossibility of thinking that limit, and this clash results in the experience of the sublime. As Lyotard says: "The sublime feeling is the subjective state critical thought must feel in its being carried to its limits (therefore beyond them) and its resistance to this impetus, or, conversely, what it must feel in its passion to determine and in its resistance to this passion."[92]

Now, typical of the experience of the sublime is the reality that, at one and the same time, a bridge is being destroyed and a new type of bridge is being built. Destroyed is the illusion that the faculties would ever be able to grasp and present the supreme condition of possibility of their respective functioning. What comes into existence, however, is the contact with the supersensible whose powerful presence is felt, and to whose tremendous majesty the collapsing faculty testifies. The following text makes this double move of 'destruction' and 'new beginning' clear: "The

---

92. J.-F. Lyotard, *Lessons on the Analytic of the Sublime*, 150.

absolute law of the faculty of desire cannot be desired. The supersensible principle that founds the demand for the universal communication of taste cannot be the object of an aesthetic pleasure. However, the horizon is 'present' everywhere. What we are calling 'presence' in contradistinction to presentation is the effect of this transcendence, its sign, on theoretical, practical and aesthetic thought."[93] This consideration shows that the real location of the sublime is to be found in the awareness of the faculties' disturbing contact with the supersensible, at the very moment at which they are carried to their limits. If Lyotard mentions the feeling of the sublime in other contexts, such as the 'keeping apart' of heterogeneous language games, then that notion of the sublime must be derivative. The discussion with that follows will clarify this point.

2. Lyotard's proper understanding of the supersensible Idea is more diversified than was possible with Kant. For Lyotard, there exist supersensible Ideas in the plural, not only because there are three heterogeneous faculties (scientific knowledge, ethics and esthetics), but because pluralization is part and parcel of the supersensible. The supersensible is the cradle of heterogeneity. It offers, on that account, the prospect of a genuine advance in civilization. Beyond Kant, Lyotard speaks up for a supersensible realm that would allow for "the formation and free exploration of Ideas in the plural," and for an "infinity of heterogeneous finalities."[94] Also in this broadened perspective the double move of 'destruction' and 'new beginning' remains in place. Destroyed is, again, the illusion that the faculties would ever be able to grasp and present their supreme condition of possibility. What emerges is the contact with the supersensible whose presence is felt, and to whose majesty the collapsing faculty testifies: the collapsing faculty emotionally honors the power of the receding horizon of unknowability that lies at the origin of pluralization

In his comments on Lyotard, James Williams seems to hint at this double move when he states: "The sublime is a 'sign' that any structure of signifieds and overarching meaning is an illusory bridge between absolute differences. So, there is nothing to be decoded in the sublime due to the absence of a possible code or set of underlying relations; there is only a differend, an absolute difference that cannot be read and understood. Thus we have the paradox of a sign that indicates an impossible passage, or better makes us understand that impossibility."[95] Williams focuses on the 'differend', and defines it as "a sign that indicates an impossible passage

93. *Ibid.*, 214.
94. J.-F. Lyotard, "The Sign of History," 409.
95. J. Williams, *Lyotard & the Political* (London and New York: Routledge, 2000) 95.

and makes us understand that impossibility," thus alluding to the disturbing contact with the absolute in which the collapse of the passage-from-
below signals the felt presence of the transcendent 'absolute' (as the supersensible is also called). At the same time he gives a horizontal turn to this
disturbing contact; for him, the sublime is a sign that any overarching
structure in the horizontal plane of existence is an illusory bridge between
absolute differences (or heterogeneous islands in the archipelago of language). A critical reading, however, shows that he tacitly borrows the
emotional intonation of the 'sign' that denounces an illusory bridge in the
horizontal plane of the Wittgensteinian language games from a different
area with which he seems to have less familiarity, namely from the sublime feeling experienced in the faculties' surrender to the absolute which
makes its presence felt in the collapse and limit-experience of these faculties. Such a mix-up is unfortunate; it robs the basic notions of 'sublime'
and 'sign' of the emotional undertone that should resonate with them.

Methodologically, therefore, I would prefer to make explicit what
Williams tacitly presupposes (or copies as a fashionable presupposition).
I would distinguish between two sorts of uplifting experiences, of which
the first is decisive:

(a) The real core of the sublime lies in the encounter with the absolute
    or the Idea of absolute vastness and completeness (a vastness and
    completeness that is also the cradle of heterogeneous pluralization).
    The feeling of the sublime arises when the faculties' passage to the
    supersensible collapses and this collapse is experienced as the sign of
    the felt presence of the unpresentable. This feeling makes one under-
    stand the impossibility of reaching the absolute with the means one
    has at one's disposal, but precisely this insight necessitates that the
    person emotionally testify to the unsettling presence of the absolute.
    Or as Lyotard himself says in a text already partially quoted: "It is a
    question of horizons because the unconditioned of the conditions of
    thought [...] is always deferred and its search has no end [...] With
    the means reflection has at its disposal [...], reflection cannot deter-
    mine the absolutes upon which these means depend [...] However, the
    horizon [of the supersensible] is 'present' everywhere. What we are
    calling 'presence' in contradistinction to presentation is the effect of
    this transcendence, its 'sign', on theoretical, practical and aesthetic
    thought."[96] One might call this experience an 'initiation' into the felt
    contact with the supersensible.

96. J.-F. Lyotard, *Lessons on the Analytic of the Sublime*, 214.

(b) The shock of this experience is so radical and overwhelming that from now on the 'initiated' will be alert to the illusory passages or illusory bridges that, in the horizontal plane of history, are being built between things that must not be fused together, under penalty of silencing the voice of the weaker partner. The 'initiated' will protest against these usurpations and illegitimate passages in the name of the absolute – the cradle of heterogeneity – whose voice remains unforgettable. To account for this protest the 'initiated 'will, if necessary, delve into the details of language pragmatics to lay her finger on the precise spot where the usurpation takes place. But she does so, in the first, place because she has been initiated in the emotional uplifting of the sublime.

3. I took Williams as a example of what a great many of Lyotard's commentators are doing. They mainly focus on Lyotard's work *The Differend* and on the language pragmatics developed in it.[97] Within this framework they use (or copy) the idiom of the sublime, without realizing its provenance from Kant. Whenever they observe an interruption in the concatenation of sentences (technically: linkage of phrases) they call this hiatus a sign of something higher. But because they remain on what I would call the Wittgensteinian side of Lyotard, they fail to properly understand the language they are using. With Lyotard himself, of course, things are different. He perfectly understands that the 'element' that allows him to introduce sublimity into the interruptions of the sentences is his appropriation, sometimes in the key of melancholy, of Kant's notion of the sublime. Unlike his commentators who think along the lines of language pragmatics, he also perfectly realizes that this notion cannot be understood except by going back to the emotional language that Kant used in his psychological approach to the 'unification' of the faculties. It is this psychological approach that gives one access to the wealth of feelings that comes into play, as an inner music, in one's felt contact with the overwhelming presence of the supersensible.

---

97. This becomes evident, for example, in Lieven Boeve's methodological considerations: "Whoever wants to investigate the relevance of Lyotard's 'postmodern' thinking for theology will do better by proceeding the other way round [i.e. not to start with his aesthetics] and read Lyotard from his language pragmatics." L. Boeve, "Method in Postmodern Theology," *The Presence of Transcendence*, ed. idem and J. Ries (Leuven, Paris, Sterling, VA: Peeters, 2001) 35.

CHAPTER FOUR

THE ROLE OF FEELINGS IN LYOTARD'S POLITICAL JUDGMENT

For Lyotard, the political judgment is a judgment about particular facts. Thus it ought to proceed with a search for its rules on the basis of feelings, as Kant expounded in his *Critique of Judgment*. The first part of the present chapter will deal with Lyotard's analysis of Kant's *Critique of Practical Reason*. In this analysis he demonstrates that Kant's notion of obligation cannot be derived from theoretical knowledge; it comes from listening to the commanding voice of the law and the feeling of respect that is born from it. Since the obligation cannot be deduced from theoretical knowledge, the person who feels obligated has to judge without criteria. Something similar is true for the categorical imperative. This imperative imposes the obligation 'that the maxim of my action be universalizable'. Yet, this insistence on universalization does not tell us what has to be done in the concrete; it primarily urges us to reflect on what we feel we are obliged to do in the light of the Idea of 'a republic of reasonable beings'. Lyotard apparently gives a reading of Kant's ethics 'in retrospect': based on what he has learned earlier from Kant's *Critique of Judgment*: the importance of feelings as the source of further reflection.

The second part of the chapter will examine the shift that took place in Lyotard's thought from *Just Gaming* (1979) to *The Differend* (1983). In *Just Gaming* Lyotard still sympathizes with liberationist movements, like the Red Army Fraction (RAF) in Germany that was engaged in terrorist acts. The RAF destroyed the US computer that was used in Germany to program the bombing of Hanoi during the Vietnam war. For Lyotard, this is a justified act of rebellion born from the felt obligation to combat the forces that obstruct a people's striving for self-determination, a self-determination that is promised and required by the regulative Idea of a 'republic of reasonable beings'. In *The Differend* this combative tone has changed: the basic conviction that the judge is still in search of the rules is upheld, but this conviction is now linked to a notion of justice that honors heterogeneity and refuses to stifle 'differends'. Lyotard now sides with the 'silenced' party. He defines the differend as follows: "The differend is the unstable state and instant of language wherein something which must be able to be put into phrases cannot yet be [...] This state is signaled by what one ordinarily calls a feeling: 'One cannot find the words', etc."[1]

The third part of the chapter will deal with the 'feeling left by Auschwitz', also analyzed in *The Differend*. It begins with the case of a 'negationist' who maintained that the gas chambers in Auschwitz were never used. This leads Lyotard to criticize the 'objective' language (the 'cognitive regimen of phrases') of the historians, who often forget to lend an ear to other linguistic utterances (in Lyotard's jargon: phrases), such as silence. The Jewish survivors are wrapped in a silence that is difficult to decipher. The silence can be seen as a sign of protest against the fact that the survivors have to prove something that is called into question, or it can be seen as speechlessness before the atrocities: ('What can possibly be the meaning of the Shoah!'). Lyotard mainly focuses on the latter aspect – meaninglessness – by asking the question as to whether the death toll in the extermination camps can be regarded as a 'beautiful death', the honorable death of heroes who gave up their lives for their people. The answer is negative: the Jews were not even treated as human beings; they were looked upon as specimens who had no right to live. This inquiry renders one speechless. It suggests that something more foundational was at stake: Nazism wanted to eliminate a people with a tradition of 'listening' to a commanding voice that held them hostage. This tradition does no longer fit in the European culture of Nazi Germany.

The fourth part of the chapter will discuss the question as to why Heidegger kept silent in the face of the Shoah, a question which Lyotard addresses in his book *Heidegger and the "jews"* : Why did Heidegger, the philosopher who protested against the forgetfulness of Being, 'forget' to pass a political judgment on the holocaust? Lyotard's answer: because, in his retrieval of the Pre-Socratics, he was still too indebted to Greek thought. Heidegger, to be sure, deconstructed the notion of temporality, but not the notion of place and soil. His aesthetics is an aesthetic of the beautiful but not an aesthetic of the sublime, which presupposes an utter 'passibility' that leaves the soul open to a shock. In order to describe this receptivity, Lyotard analyzes at length the effects of the shock of the covenant on the Jewish soul. He does so with the help of some insights developed by Freud in his *Moses and Monotheism*: the Jewish soul is taken hostage by a strange voice that commands 'remember', 'be just'.

---

1. J.-F. Lyotard, *The Differend*, trans. G. Van Den Abbeele (Manchester: University of Manchester Press, 1988) no. 22, p. 13. Originally published as idem, *Le Différend* (Paris: Minuit, 1983).

The Jews (and also those who follow their lead) are dazed by the shock of a covenant, of an immemorial encounter whose affection they try to reserve against all compromise.

The fifth part of the chapter will present Lyotard's analysis of the avant-garde painters whose non-figurative canvasses try to convey the shock of their encounter with a commanding voice. Central in this analysis are the works and the testimonies of the Jewish American painter Barnett Newman. In his paintings one can perceive the influence of Kant – of one's contact with the supersensible only a negative presentation can be given – but also of Edmund Burke. For Burke, the feelings of the sublime consists in the momentary suspense of overwhelming threats of darkness, a suspension one is afraid it will not last for long. Hence the question 'Is it happening?' 'Is it happening that a new moment of creation pierces the void?' 'Is it happening' is also a recurrent theme in Lyotard's linguistic pragmatics. There, time and again, he comes up with the vexing question: 'Is it happening that an unexpected, disturbing phrase disrupts the quasi-automatic linkage of phrases?' In Lyotard's analysis of the avant-garde painters one encounters the emotional undertone of this question, an undertone that can hardly be conveyed with the analytic tools of language pragmatics.

The sixth and final part of this chapter will bring out what runs as a golden thread through the whole chapter: the Jewish roots of the feeling of the sublime. This section will collect and systematize the various passages through which Lyotard characterized the Jewish soul; it will call attention to the Jewish background of Kant's categorical imperative; and will highlight the Jewish roots of the feeling of the sublime, both in Kant and in Burke – and in Barnett Newman.

I. *JUST GAMING*: THE FELT OBLIGATION: JUDGING WITHOUT CRITERIA

In his language pragmatics, Lyotard proves to have a razor-sharp analytical mind, relentlessly distinguishing between genres of discourse and regimes of phrases: a constative is not an interrogative (or a hypothetical interrogative), just as a descriptive phrase lacks the quality of a prescriptive. These neat distinctions enable him to pass a judgment on the purity or impurity of texts. In the end, the philosopher as 'watchman', seeing to it that no alien elements slip in and contaminate the proper language regime. Such infiltrations – especially where prescriptives are concerned – reveal a lust for dominance. The language regime in question then tends to turn hegemonic; in the name of justice this tendency must be denounced. At the end of the long dialogue with Jean-Loup Thébaut in *Just Gaming* (1979), Lyotard states: "[The idea of justice] intervenes inasmuch as these games are impure. By this I mean something very specific: inasmuch as these games are infiltrated by prescriptions. If a narrative masquerades as a prescriptive, that is, if it claims to prescribe or if it appears to legitimate prescriptions, or if a denotative discourse presenting itself as scientific contains or implies prescriptions as well – something that happens frequently in the case of 'experts' in modern capitalistic society – then, in such case, one can say that the game is impure, and it is clear that, at that moment, its effects must be regulated by the Idea of justice. Here the Idea of justice will consist in preserving the purity of each game."[2]

Language pragmatics, thus, becomes an instrument in Lyotard's hands for identifying hidden hegemonic strategies that cannot possibly be tolerated. Yet, if one asks from where the motivation comes for this verdict on things intolerable, the answer is: from feelings about what is just or unjust. The reader will not be surprised to hear that it is precisely here that feelings come into play, since they form the undercurrent of Lyotard's assimilation of Kant. Not by accident does he refer, in the above text, to the 'Idea of justice'. This Idea is, as he explains in another passage, the supersensible Idea "of a society of free and responsible beings" which serves as a "regulator for the determination of actions by means of reflection."[3] This supersensible Idea cannot adequately be presented by any of the classical faculties – dealing with science, ethics, or aesthetics – it emotionally signals its presence through particular feelings: through the feeling of encouragement to pursue one's research (science), through the feeling of respect for the law (ethics), and through the clashing feeling of dismay and delight when confronted with the imagination's inadequacy to render the Idea of totality visible (aesthetics of the sublime).

Judgments about justice – Lyotard calls them political judgments – fall, in Kantian parlance, under the class of aesthetics, since they have to judge particular facts and unforeseeable events for which no universal rules of assessment are given in advance: they must be judged case by case on the basis of feelings of pleasure and/or displeasure which, in turn, initiate a reflection that is in search of its rules. Lyotard is frank in this

    2. J.-F. Lyotard and J.-L. Thébaut, *Just Gaming*, trans. W. Godzich and S. Weber (Minneapolis, MN: The University of Minnesota Press, 1985) 96. Originally published as iidem, *Au Juste: Conversations* (Paris: Christian Bourgeois, 1979).
    3. *Ibid.*, 86.

matter: "There cannot be a *sensus communis* [to judge human praxis]. We judge without criteria. We are in the position of Aristotle's prudent individual, who makes judgments about the just and the unjust without the least criterion."[4] Lyotard goes to some lengths to stress Aristotle's penchant for assimilating the view of the Sophists that an unalterable rule for assessing human behavior does not exist, and that Plato had reacted to this by conceiving of the realm of unchangeable, intelligible ideas, from which stable norms for human behavior can and must be deduced. As a postmodern author, who is alert to the unforeseeable, Lyotard rejects the theoretical superstructure Plato erected to account for the validity of ethical and political decisions. For the same reason, he distances himself from the Marxist dogma that genuine praxis must be in conformity with theory, the revolutionary theory of dialectical materialism in this case. When assessing the organization of the Paris Commune, Marx was convinced "that they make sense only insofar as they verify, if not apply, the description that is implied in the theoretical analysis of capital."[5]

1. *Obligation Cannot Be Derived from Theoretical Knowledge; it Comes from Listening*

For Lyotard, political judgments cannot possibly be based in or derived from an ontology or a theoretical construct. To jump from the language game of theoretical *description* to that of *prescription* is illegitimate. One cannot judge what is good or bad on the grounds of theoretical knowledge because it is not equipped for this task. This is also true for modern political theories. They all begin with the premise of the collective autonomy of the citizens, from which they infer "that the set of prescriptions produced by the whole of a social body to which the prescriptions apply, will be just,"[6] and compulsory. But language pragmatics forbids the deduction of ethico-political prescriptions from elaborated bodies of knowledge. Such a deduction is illusory and dangerous. Oppression is always lurking around the corner. This is not to say that Lyotard himself would be insensitive to obligations (in the jargon of language pragmatics: prescriptions). Quite the contrary. But for him, it is crucial that one feels obliged to act in a particular way because of the voice of conscience.

---

4. *Ibid.*, 14.
5. *Ibid.*, 21.
6. *Ibid.*, 25.

From various sides Lyotard attempts to elucidate this kind of 'felt' obligation. He first of all refers to the narrative practice of a so-called primitive clan, that of the Cashinahua Indians in the upper Amazon whose traditional habits have been studied by André Marcel d'Ans. From this study it becomes evident that whenever a chief or shaman tells a story that narrates the origins of the behavioral codes of the community, the narrator starts by saying: 'This is the story that was told to me', so that it is understood that the story which is told is one that has been handed down from a previous generation, who in turn heard it from still more distant ancestors. From this Lyotard concludes that in ancient cultures the element of 'listening' is central, something Western thought has virtually forgotten. Ever since Descartes, Western philosophers have become accustomed to constructing their worldviews in a purely theoretical way, without lending an ear to what is being told to them (through a pre-given residue of wisdom or by the environment in which they happen to live). This remark implies a plea for the rediscovery of a certain heteronomy or sense of 'transcendence' – notions which Lyotard borrows from Emmanuel Levinas' philosophy of 'the commanding voice of the other' as well as from the latter's reflections on Talmudic texts.

Secondly, Lyotard reflects on the Jewish law as a tradition that sheds light on the notion of a 'felt' obligation. Judaism is renowned for its neglect, or better, avoidance of ontology; it never developed an overarching theoretical construct, for the absence of which it incurred the contempt of Hegel. Judaism only knows the commanding voice of YHWH, the unpronounceable name of God. The result is "a whole slew of small, unbelievable things: how to cook lamb, and so on" ascribed to the will of a God, who, in spite of his concern with such trivia, remains shrouded in absolute mystery. The same is true for the law: "We merely say: There is a law. And when we say 'law', it does not mean that the law is defined and that it suffices to abide by it. There is a law, but we do not know what this law says."[7] Lyotard's comments on JHWH and the Jewish law sound, on the surface, quite irreverent, but this is, in fact, not the case. What he wants to stress is that, behind the law, there is "a kind of law of the laws, a meta-law that says: 'Be just'. That is all that matters in Judaism." Here again, he remarks, one does not know in advance what it means to be just; the only thing one really comprehends is the seriousness of the command addressed to each of us in concrete circumstances. For the rest, it will be up to us to judge what must be done: "Every time it will be necessary to decide, to commit oneself, to judge, and then to reflect on whether the

7. *Ibid.*, 52.

decision made was just. It implies that this community thinks the problem of the prescriptive in terms of the future."[8]

Here again the issue of heteronomy and 'listening' comes to the fore. One must listen to God's command, just as one must listen to what the neighbor in need is requesting. One is never able simply to speak from one's own authority. Always reference has to be made to the 'other' who spoke first, and who says 'be just'. This orientation towards 'listening' also characterizes the Talmudic commentator: it is a matter for him "of taking up speech again from a text that one has heard, and that at the same time one has not heard,"[9] since earlier commentators have already reflected on it at length. The subtle point, however, to be grasped is that the framework of heteronomy and listening by no means encourages a dreary, pharisaic or 'legalistic' adherence to the law. The 'passivity' of listening to the imperative 'be just' urges one, on the contrary, to be persistent in reflecting on one's commitments in the face of ever changing circumstances. The listener cannot shake off the responsibility of judging one's actions in light of their consequences in history. History in Judaism, Lyotard underlines, is "what is to be done. That is all that is important. It is a game of the history of the human community in as much as it is held by prescriptions and only by that."[10] To ponder the consequences of one's actions also involves that one makes use of one's creative imagination in view of letting one's decisions be steered by a guiding finality: "To be just [in Judaism] is to venture to formulate a hypothesis on what is to be done, and that is where one gets back to this idea of 'Idea': one regulates oneself upon the imagining of effects, upon a sort of finality. It is the imagining of the effects of what one will decide that will guide the judgment."[11]

Thirdly, Lyotard reflects on Kant as a source for elucidating the notion of the 'felt' obligation. Lyotard prefers to highlight the 'Jewish' side of Kant. This 'Jewish' side consists in the fact that Kant disconnected the categorical imperative as well as the aesthetic reflective judgment from the rational body of knowledge he previously examined in the *Critique of Pure Reason*. This amazing decision makes Lyotard exclaim: "What seems to me so strong in Kant's position, of course, as well as in Levinas' is that they reject in principle [...] a derivation or [...] a deduction"[12] of the 'you must' from an intellectual construct or from a metaphysical superstructure in the style of Plato. The 'you must' abruptly

8. *Ibid.*, 52-53.
9. *Ibid.*, 39.
10. *Ibid.*, 53.
11. *Ibid.*, 65.
12. *Ibid.*, 45.

interrupts the logic of the system builder: its exigency goes beyond calculating planning. The 'you must' is not even part of what is called an experience, "because experience, by itself, always supposes its description, and thus the privilege granted to the play of the descriptive,"[13] namely that it has an 'author' engaged in describing states of affairs but who, in actuality, does not listen. These two characteristics – absence of intellectual superstructure and absence of experience in the above mentioned sense, is totally in agreement with what Kant tells us in the *Critique of Practical Reason*: "The objective reality of the moral law can be proved through no deduction, through no exertion of the theoretical, speculative, or empirically supported reason; and, even if one were willing to renounce its apodictic certainty, it could not be confirmed by any experience and thus proved a posteriori. Nevertheless it [the reality of the moral law] is firmly established in itself."[14] The obligation of the moral law cannot be deduced from theoretical considerations; it can also not be proved *a posteriori* by empirical experience, and this for the simple reason that it is received, not by the senses, as the source of experiences but by the will and its feeling of respect for the law. Only this respectful reception proves the objective reality of the moral law.

Again the whole focus is on receptivity. Explained in term of language pragmatics this means that in order to understand what an obligation means, the pole of the sender or the author (the one who describes states of affairs) must be neutralized: "Only if [this pole] is neutralized, will one become sensitive, not to what it [the obligation] is, but to the fact that it prescribes and obligates ... [In the game of the just] one speaks as a listener, and not as an author. It is a game without an author. In the same way as the speculative game of the West is a game without a listener."[15] In his comment on this crucial insight David Carroll remarks that nowhere in his interpretation of Kant is Lyotard so close to Emmanuel Levinas' receptivity than here, and also that what most attracts him in Kant's *Critique of Practical Reason* is what Hegel found so objectionable in it, namely that Kant massively stresses the obligation without specifying what has to be done in the concrete.[16] In the context of what I am examining here, I would like to emphasize, in addition, that for Lyotard the felt obligation basically consists in a strong 'feeling'. It is not enough to say

13. *Ibid.*, 46.
14. I. Kant, *Critique of Practical Reason, Original* edition, 82, trans. L.W. Beck (Indianapolis, IN, 1956) 48, cited in J.-F. Lyotard, *The Differend*, 119.
15. J.-F. Lyotard and J.-L. Thébaud, *Just Gaming*, 71-72.
16. D. Carroll, "Rephrasing the Political with Kant and Lyotard: From Aesthetics to Political Judgment," *Diacritics* 14,3 (1984) 80.

that the moral law can only be perceived by a receptive listener; one ought also to state that the response given to the demand of the law is the feeling of being obligated. As Lyotard says in *The Differend*: "In the phrase of obligation, dependence upon the law is presented as a feeling, at the same time independence from the regimen of cognition is presented as a mysterious presupposition. The law remains undeduced."[17]

2. *Kant's Categorical Imperative: The Role of Reflection*

Kant's categorical imperative is empty; it is without any concrete content, since it enjoins pure obligation. This does, however, not mean that it would not proffer a certain rule. The categorical imperative insists on universalization. It imposes "the obligation that the maxim of my action be universalizable:" "To be just is to act in such a way that (*so dass*; says the German) the maxim of the will may serve as a principle of universal legislation;" or framed in a prohibitive way: "Never act in such a way that your action be incompatible with a republic of reasonable beings," that is, with a republic of reasonable beings "that may themselves be obligated precisely because they are free."[18]

From these definitions it becomes clear that the insistence on universalization does not tell us what we have to do in the concrete; it primarily urges us to reflect on what we feel we are obliged to do in the light of the Idea of 'a republic of reasonable beings'. But what the whole content of this Idea is, we do not know; we are even unable to grasp its full extent and scope precisely because it is an Idea of Reason. An Idea of Reason can only be thought, but not properly presented in empirical reality. In order to shed light on this Kantian notion, Lyotard offers a handy tip; he invites the reader to focus on a concept and to maximize it beyond its usual meaning: The Idea of Reason is "the maximization of the concept; one follows the concept beyond what reality can give it as sensible to subsume and one sees then what can be thought by extending thus the scope of the concept."[19] If we take the notion of 'freedom' as it appears in our empirical reality, we do not yet know what 'freedom' is in its maximum deployment, not only in our personal life histories but also with respect of the whole of humanity. To get at this ungraspable Idea we must stretch the concept in such a way that it can no longer be

17. J.-F. Lyotard, *The Differend*, Kant, 2, p. 122.
18. J.-F. Lyotard and J.-L. Thébaud, *Just Gaming*, 47.
19. *Ibid.*, 58.

presented with sensible images, and merges with a broader supersensible reality that carries with itself the connotation of entirety.

With this explanation Lyotard has moved far beyond the popularized understanding of Kant's categorical imperative: 'Do not do unto somebody else what you would not wish this person to do unto you', the so-called 'golden rule' enjoined by the categorical imperative. Lyotard's deepened understanding of this golden rule has brought us in the sphere of the reflective judgment of taste, at the very moment that this judgment allows itself to be guided by an Idea of totality. Understood in this manner the golden rule forms the transition to the *Critique of Judgment* and to the reflective mood that constitutes the backbone of this work. Yet Kant, as Lyotard correctly underlines, not only had recourse to this reflective judgment in the aesthetics of the beautiful and of the sublime; he also made use of it in his political wirings on 'cosmopolitanism' as the new world order.

For Lyotard, too, reflective judgment is the instrument for judging political facts, especially insofar as this reflection allows itself to be guided by the horizon of an ungraspable Idea of totality: the totality or the republic of reasonable beings. In order to explain this guidance he comes back again to the dictum "To be just is to act in such a way that (*so dass*, says the German) the maxim of your will may serve as a principle of universal legislation."[20] He comments on it as follows: "The famous *so dass* [so that] of the imperative does not say: 'if you want to be this, then do that'. [...] The *so dass* marks the properly reflective use of judgment. It says: Do whatever, not on condition that, but *in such a way as* that which you do, the maxim of what you do, can always be valid as, etc. We are not dealing here with a determinant synthesis but with an Idea of human society [This supersensible Idea] *does not* determine *what* I have to do. It regulates me, but without telling me *what* there is to be done."[21]

The result is again a feeling; no longer just a moral feeling of respect for the law that obligates, but a feeling that already borders on a feeling of the sublime: the felt contact with the supersensible Idea of totality that smashes all our attempts at presenting it in empirical reality. That is why the feeling of the sublime is a compounded feeling of terror and delight. Such a feeling is born from the awareness of the immense task that befalls us: to act in such a way that one's decisions may help steer the course of human history. It is up to us to take steps that bring humanity closer to its final ethical vocation.

20. *Ibid.*, 47.
21. *Ibid.*, 85.

II. LYOTARD'S POLITICAL JUDGMENT: FROM *JUST GAMING* TO *THE DIFFEREND*. THE REFUSAL TO STIFLE THE DIFFEREND

At a certain moment in the conversation, Jean-Loup Thébaud pushed Lyotard to reveal where he stood in judging the 'terrorist' acts of the Red Army Fraction (RAF) that started with the Baader-Meinhof group. The RAF was a city guerilla group that was active in the late 1970s in Germany. They were responsible for various bombings, of US barracks, of German police stations, and of the *Axel Springer Verlag* in Hamburg. They also kidnapped Hans-Martin Schleyer, the chairman of the German Employer's Organization, whom they held hostage and threatened to kill unless a ransom was paid. To the German population they addressed the message: 'We will make you aware of the collusion between Schleyer and the State's police terror'. Finally they shot Schleyer. Prior to that they had made an incursion into, and destroyed the computer of, the American garrison in Heidelberg, because evidence was found that this computer was used to program the bombing in Hanoi.

In order to disentangle these facts, Lyotard, starts by drawing a distinction: all these 'terrorist' acts cannot be placed on the same footing. For him, holding Schleyer hostage is a terrorist act because it jeopardized the life of a citizen who was not directly involved in the armed struggle between the RAF and the German state. With the kidnapping, the RAF wanted to influence public opinion in Germany. To use Schleyer as a pawn in this propaganda stunt can never be justified, according to Lyotard. It is an injustice done to a person whose kidnapping is strategically used as a means to an end. Things are different, however, with the attack on military targets. In a situation of war, an attack on the enemy is justified; it belongs to the rules of the game. Judged from that standpoint and taking the RAF for what it claims to be, 'an army', the destruction of the American computer in Heidelberg cannot strictly be called a 'terrorist act', it is simply an act of warfare. In warfare one is allowed to weaken the enemy. This is what the RAF did at that moment.

Focusing then on the sole fact of the destruction of the American computer, Lyotard points to what he later will call a 'differend', a clash of irreconcilable opinions. He says: "It is difficult to decide [whether that act is just or unjust]. For example, is it just that there be an American computer in Heidelberg that, among other things, is used to program the bombing of Hanoi? In the final analysis, Schleyer thinks so. In the final analysis, the 'Baader-Meinhof' group thinks not. Who is right? It is up to everyone to decide."[22] At that juncture Thébaut bluntly asks him about his personal opinion in this matter: "But you think it is unjust that there be an American computer in Heidelberg?" The answer is without hesitancy: "Yes, absolutely. I can say that such is my opinion. I feel committed in this respect." When further asked 'why' he is committed in that direction, Lyotard says: "If you asked me why I am on that side, I think that I would answer that I do not have an answer to the question 'why?' and that this is of the order of ... 'transcendence'. That is: here I feel a prescription to oppose a given thing, and I think that it is a just one. This is where I feel that I am playing the game of the just."[23]

To avoid misapprehension, Lyotard explains what he means by 'transcendence'. He took this notion from Levinas, for whom transcendence is experienced as a prescription one hears and whose obligation cannot be derived from criteria used in the descriptive language regime: 'Transcendence' means "that there is an obligation that comes, if you will, to me under the form of a ... prescription. Yes, I feel obliged with respect to the prescription that Americans should [get] out of Vietnam, or the French out of Algeria." In a further elucidation he, finally, has recourse to the Kantian Idea of the 'republic of reasonable beings'; "If I were to be pushed, I would answer that what regulates this feeling of obligation is the Kantian Idea. The Americans in Vietnam, the French in Algeria, were doing something that prohibited that the whole of reasonable beings could continue to exist. In other words, the Vietnamese or the Algerians saw themselves placed in a position where the pragmatics of obligation was forbidden to them. They had the right to rebel."[24]

This is clearly a leftist employment of Kant's Idea of a 'republic of reasonable beings', for Kant himself disallowed rebellion, which in his eyes is a self-defeating concept: rebellion can never lay the foundation of a rationally organized state. Lyotard's justification of the 'right to rebel' apparently feeds on the reflective mood he developed during his stay in Algeria as a young teacher. There he had come to understand the motives of the population in fighting for their independence from colonial rule: colonization by world powers cannot possibly be in accordance with the demands of justice. From this background he criticizes the presence of the American armed forces in Vietnam, and finds it legitimate that the RAF destroyed the computer that was used in Germany to program the bombing of Hanoi. He overtly approves this 'terrorist' act. For him, it is a

22. *Ibid.*, 68.
23. *Ibid.*, 69.
24. *Ibid.*, 70.

justified act of rebellion born from the felt obligation to combat the forces that obstruct the Vietnamese people's striving for self-determination, a self-determination that is promised and required by the regulative Idea of a 'republic of reasonable beings'.

This stand must have scandalized a many great readers, perhaps less because it reveals a remnant of Lyotard's Marxist past, but more because of the 'paganism' (see his work: *Les instructions païennes*) it displays. 'Paganism' rejects the possibility of deriving just prescriptions and obligations from general rules that are commonly used in the genre of descriptives. It starts from particular cases, and consequently from particular 'felt obligations'; it repudiates all systems that perpetuate the injustice of a 'universal' judgment. For some, this program must have sounded like sheer anarchism. Their objection is that when the 'correctness' of judgments is founded on feelings, even if these allow themselves to be guided by an Idea of 'justice for everyone', then terrorist attacks are of necessity going to lurk around the corner – then (to use contemporary examples) there will be no longer any reason for not hailing as champions of the cause of justice all those who in Islamic countries engage in suicide bombings; then the Al-Qaeda suicide hijackers who on September 11th crashed American Airlines Flight 11 and United Airlines Flight 175 into the twin towers of the World Trade Center in New York must be logically declared heroes.

Did Lyotard foresee such reactions? The question is difficult to answer. At any rate, he must have felt the insufficiency of his approach which at that period of time was, unconsciously perhaps, still framed in a 'liberation paradigm' that he wanted to eliminate. Violent liberators might, after their victory, turn into violent oppressors. With his work *The Differend* (1983) a new perspective is opened. David Carroll defines this shift as follows: "In *Au juste* [*Just Gaming*] and other works related to this period justice and the associated issue of critical judgment are still considered to be the problem at the heart of the political, but now by recasting the political in terms of a 'philosophy of phrases' Lyotard hopes to undermine and destroy all myths or narratives of liberation which he would claim have served to enslave more than to free."[25] In *The Differend* "Lyotard's goal is to clear the historical-political ground of all speculative, dialectical totalizations," in which a succession of hegemonic systems is taken for granted, "so that a radical critical politics of heterogeneity can be practiced and differends affirmed rather than suppressed or resolved."[26]

25. D. Carroll, "Rephrasing the Political with Kant and Lyotard," 75.
26. *Ibid.*, 75.

In *The Differend* the basic conviction that the judge is still in search of the rules is upheld, but this conviction is now linked to a notion of justice that honors heterogeneity and refuses to stifle 'differends'.

In fact, the dialogue with Thébaud ends with this turn to heterogeneity. At a certain moment Thébaud points out that the Idea of 'a republic of reasonable beings' is, in the Kantian perspective, organically linked to a notion of totality, and that on this account it is not completely undetermined, as Lyotard would like to have it. In his reply Lyotard makes it clear that indeed, he partly deviates from Kant. In his reading of Kant he follows the basic logic and coherence of Kant's argumentation, but at the same time he departs from Kant in that for him 'totality' must be replaced with a multiplicity of heterogeneous perspectives. He says: "[Indeed], the Kantian Idea is not completely undetermined ... it is presupposed that this Idea is the Idea of a totality. Whereas the problem that faces us, even if it is put in terms of Idea and reflective judgment is that it is no longer a matter, for us, of reflecting upon what is just or unjust against the horizon of a social totality, but, on the contrary, against the horizon of a multiplicity or of a diversity. This is both where practical reason and political reason are still beholden, in Kant, to metaphysics, because of this Idea of totality. [...] This is where I would operate a divide, at my own risk, because I am not certain that I am in the strict Kantian tradition,"[27] a crucial text I have already quoted earlier.

By giving a new content to 'totality' as a total release of heterogeneous perspectives, Lyotard changes the whole orientation of his reflection on justice. The ethical obligation that befalls one is, in this new understanding, oriented towards the guiding Idea of a 'sacrosanct plurality'. This guiding Idea will, as much as in Kant's 'unitary reading', call forth a strong feeling of commitment to an 'impossible' task (hence the resonances of terror and delight). In the meantime, however, the whole orientation has been changed. Whereas in Kant the 'reflective judgment in search of its rules', singular and particular as it is, was still geared towards creatively thinking the unity of all our intellectual faculties, symbolized by the substantial 'transcendental subject', Lyotard's version of the 'reflective judgment in search of its rules' is geared towards creatively thinking a point X where the total release of heterogeneous perspectives takes place. In more simple terms: no perspective is allowed to assume a dominant position, not even that of the party who feels wronged (for this would fuel a revengeful 'liberation' struggle). All perspectives must submit to the higher demand that only the emergence of heterogeneous

27. J.-F. Lyotard and J.-L. Thébaud, *Just Gaming*, 87-88.

perspectives can guarantee a brighter future for humankind (for 'the republic of reasonable beings'). This is the new guiding Idea that will, from this point forward, steer Lyotard's understanding of justice.

In this new understanding of justice, Lyotard sides with the 'silenced party' by calling attention to the persistence of a differend that must not be stifled. A differend arises when a party feels wronged and is unable to express its grievance in the idiom of the other party. A case in point is the claim of the indigenous peoples to land ownership in colonized countries. Take, for example, the issue of Aboriginal land rights in Australia. The descendents of European colonists claim that, according to government law, the land they owe is theirs; they bought it from the state who is the owner of derelict land. To this the Aboriginals counter that, prior to government law, their own tribal law gave them the title to the land. The court of appeal will have to settle this dispute using its own rules of jurisprudence. Strictly speaking, however, one cannot say that the two parties are in litigation, since they cannot agree on the principles by which their dispute might be settled. That's why Lyotard speaks of a differend and not of a litigation. However much the Aboriginals come up with titles that are recognized in their community, the court of appeals, acting on the basis of government law, cannot possibly regard them as valid. The Aboriginals are thereby injured and have no means by which to redress their grievance; two different 'language games' are in operation, and the entity having more power in the situation will win. Thus, in this case, the descendents of European colonists will win the litigation, much to the dismay of the silenced party. By calling attention to the silenced party – and to their inability to make their voice heard – Lyotard testifies to the Idea of justice and its absence in empirical reality.

The issue of Aboriginal land rights is a concrete illustration of Lyotard's definitions of the differend. I quote some of them: "Litigation takes place. I would call a differend the case where a plaintiff is divested of the means to argue and becomes a victim."[28] "A case of differend between two parties takes place when the 'regulation' of the conflict that opposes them is done in the idiom of one of the parties while the wrong suffered by the other is not signified in that idiom."[29] "The differend is signaled by this inability to prove. The one who lodges a complaint is heard, but the one who is a victim and who is perhaps the same one, is reduced to silence."[30] "The differend is the unstable state and instant of

28. J.-F. Lyotard, *The Differend*, no.12, p. 9.
29. *Ibid.*, no. 12, p. 9.
30. *Ibid.*, no. 13, p. 10.

language wherein something which must be able to be put into phrases cannot yet be ... This state is signaled by what one ordinarily calls a feeling: 'One cannot find the words', etc."[31] Having given these definitions of the differend, Lyotard then moves on to invite artists, philosophers and even politicians to invent new idioms that do not yet exist in order to put into words what otherwise painfully remains unsaid. "A lot of searching must be done to find new rules for forming and linking phrases that are able to express the differend disclosed by the feeling ... What is at stake in a literature, in a philosophy, in a politics perhaps, is to bear witness to differends by finding idioms for them."[32] "In the Differend something 'asks' to be put into phrases and suffers from the wrong of not being able to be put into phrases right away. This is when human beings who thought they could use language as an instrument of communication learn through the feeling of pain which accompanies silence (and of pleasure which accompanies the invention of a new idiom) that they are summoned by language, not to augment to their profit the quantity of information communicable through existing idioms, but to recognize that what remains to be phrased exceeds what they can presently phrase, and that they must be allowed to institute idioms which do not yet exist."[33]

III. THE FEELING LEFT BY AUSCHWITZ

The above definitions of the differend show the crucial role played by feelings: the incapacity of putting events into phrases is signaled by a feeling: 'I cannot find words for it'. The instant of language in which communication collapses is a feeling that borders on that of the sublime: a feeling of pain that accompanies the silence to which one is reduced, and a feeling of pleasure when one succeeds in tentatively finding a new idiom by which to make oneself heard. Feelings of anguish and pain come to the fore in the paradigmatic differend that Lyotard examines in *The Differend*: the denial of the existence of gas chambers in Auschwitz. Famous in this respect is the assertion of Robert Faurisson: "I have analyzed thousands of documents. I have tirelessly pursued specialists and historians with my questions. I have tried in vain to find a single former deportee capable of proving to me that he had really seen, with his own eyes,

31. *Ibid.*, no. 22, p. 13.
32. *Ibid.*, no. 22, p. 13.
33. *Ibid.*, no. 23, p. 13.

a gas chamber."[34] Between December 1978 and February 1979 Faurisson had published in the French newspaper *Le Monde* three letters in which he maintained that the gas chambers at the death camps were never used, thus denying the systematic extermination of Jews.

For Lyoard, a statement like this prompts one to doubt the 'objectivity' of the historians. These are wont to carry out their examination within the framework of a purely cognitive regimen of phrases in order to validate historical truth. But this positivistic approach easily leads to a situation in which the victims are unable to prove, in the idiom of the dominant 'language', the wrong that has been done to them. In order to convince Faurisson of the fact that the gas chambers were used, one would, ironically, need dead eye-witnesses, Jews who died in the gas chambers and whose corpses were cremated in the crematoria. In line with this positivistic approach to the construction of history, only those who underwent the verdict of being gassed and cremated are credible witnesses, whereas all the others might be accused of fantasizing about the extermination and how it took place. Lyotard is rather sarcastic about this sort of historicism: "[Faurisson] complains that he has been fooled about the existence of gas chambers, fooled, that is, about the so-called Final Solution. His argument is: in order for a place to be identified as a gas chamber, the only eyewitness I will accept would be a victim of the gas chamber: now according to my opponent, there is no victim that is not dead: otherwise, this gas chamber would not be what he or she claims it to be. There is therefore no gas chamber."[35]

In the style of language pragmatics, Lyotard makes it clear that the language universe of a cognitive regimen of phrases is not the same as that of a prescriptive or a logical regime of phrases, and that these are still different from a phrase that simply consists of silence (a silence that can take on various modalities). One of the major aims of his book, however, is to show the shortcomings of regimens of phrases that stifle the differend by reducing it to a litigation, a reduction in which the (impotent, but protesting) silence of the victims is ignored. In a litigation the dispute is settled with the help of procedures that are (or are supposed to be) generally recognized. Reality is defined in term of a particular referent whose existence and characteristics are beyond discussion, just as this is the case in historical positivism: "Reality is not what is 'given' to this or that 'subject'; it is a state of the referent (that about which one speaks) which

34. *Ibid.*, no. 2, p. 3; with reference to P. Vidal-Naquet, "A Paper Eichmann," *Democracy* I, 2 (1983) 81.
35. J.-F. Lyotard, *The Differend*, no. 2, p. 4 [translation modified].

results from the effectuation of establishment procedures defined by a unanimously agreed-upon protocol, and from the possibility offered to anyone to recommence this effectuation as often as he or she wants."[36] "Positivism confuses reality and referent."[37] In these definitions one recognizes the Newtonian scientific ideal that has shaped modern legislation and jurisprudence, and also modern historiography. In this modern approach no place is given to the differend and to the feelings that are involved in it.

'Silence' as a phrase – the silence of the survivors of the Shoah – can take on various modalities. It can be a refusal to recognize the authority of the addressor (the one who requests proofs); it can be a protest against those who negate the existence of the gas chambers (Faurisson); it can be an expression of speechlessness before the atrocities of the Final Solution; it can be a manifestation of the fact that one feels unworthy to testify to the atrocities. The last two categories are the most difficult to interpret, because they relate to the vexing question as to how attribute meaning to the Holocaust. As to the crime itself, Lyotard admits that it is difficult to establish its quantity, because "the documents necessary for the validation were themselves destroyed [by the Nazis] in quantity. That at least can be established [...] But the silence imposed on knowledge does not impose the silence of forgetting; it imposes a feeling."[38] This feeling shared by so many survivors acts as a sign of history: "The silence that surrounds the phrase *Auschwitz was the extermination camp* is not a state of mind (*état d'âme*), it is the sign that something remains to be phrased which is not, something which is not determined. This sign affects a linking of phrases."[39] With this remark, Lyotard invites the historians to abandon their positivism, and to look for a new idiom that does justice to the victims: "The historian must break with the monopoly over history granted to the cognitive regimen of phrases, and he or she must venture forth by lending his or her ear to what is not presentable under the rules of knowledge."[40]

As to the meaning or lack of meaning of the Holocaust, Lyotard devotes a lengthy analysis to the reasons as to why death in the extermination camps can never be called a 'beautiful death'. A 'beautiful death' is a honorable death, one that is freely accepted for a noble cause, and in virtue of which the deceased will be commemorated by the community

36. *Ibid.*, no. 3, p. 4.
37. *Ibid.*, no. 37, p. 28.
38. *Ibid.*, no. 93, p. 56.
39. *Ibid.*, no. 93, p. 57.
40. *Ibid.*, no. 92, p. 57.

that honors his/her sacrifice. Such a death presupposes a reciprocity between the 'hero' and the community. The person who gives up his/her life does so as a member of the community; his/her sacrifice feeds on, and strengthens, the 'we' universe of that community. This 'we' universe gives meaning to the 'beautiful death'; it is painfully absent in the tragedy of Auschwitz, and this on two counts.

First, the Jews who were killed were not given a chance to give up their lives for their community, so that this community may survive or uphold its honor. All of them were, in isolation, deprived of their lives, slaughtered one after the other, in the absence of any common will to martyrdom. The only feeling they shared was that the SS wanted everybody's extermination, the extermination of the Jewish race. All of them fell prey to a killing, from which there was no escape. There was no longer a 'we' that could give meaning to what was happening. For this reason it became difficult for the survivors to make sense, in retrospect, of this slaughter, or to bear witness to it: "No phrase inflected in the first-person plural would be possible: we did this, we felt that, they made us suffer this humiliation, we got along in this way, we hoped that, we didn't think about..., and even: each of us was reduced to solitude and silence. There would be no collective witness."[41] And also no convincing theological reflection about what befell them. There was only "shame and anger over the explanations and interpretations – as sophisticated as they may be – by thinkers who claim to have found some sense to this shit (Especially over the argument that it is precisely because God failed that one should be faithful to him)."[42] So, a 'beautiful death' is out of the question.

Second, Auschwitz is not only the impossibility of a 'beautiful death'; it is the forbiddance of it. The German SS elite troops, in their authoritarian way of commanding, robbed their victims of any legitimate ground for perceiving their death as beautiful. The Jews can only react to the command '*That he/she die, I decree it*' by taking cognizance of the order: '*That I die, s/he decrees it*'. The whole accent is on the legislative power of the SS (the addressor). Any form of reciprocity had been obliterated; the SS command death, the deportees undergo it. This predicament deprives them of the privilege of freely giving their life, a life to which they no longer have any acknowledged right. Because their lives are deemed worthless, the Jews cannot even be regarded as addressees. The universe of prescription, in the moral sense of the word, no longer exists; it has been replaced by the brute exercise of an authority that sets itself

41. *Ibid.*, no. 155, p. 98.
42. *Ibid.*, no. 155, p. 98.

apart: "The authority of the SS comes out of a 'we' from which the deportee is excepted once and for all: the race, which grants not only the right to command but also the right to live, that is, to place oneself [as a 'we'] in the various instances of phrase universes. The deportee, according to this authority, cannot be the addressee of the order to die, because one would have to be capable of giving one's life in order to carry out the order. But one cannot give up a life one does not have the right to have. Sacrifice is not available to the deportee, nor for that reason access to an immortal, collective name."[43]

With the help of language pragmatics, Lyotard shows that the two universes, that of the German SS and that of the Jewish deportees, have no possible common application; the deportees are not even addressees in the SS phrase universe. The SS do not say *'die, I decree it'*. They, instead, say *'That he/she die, I decree It'*, or in a variant *'That he/she die; that is my law'*. The SS planning bureau has decreed: the Jews must be exterminated; the addressees of this order are other Nazis who are going to execute the order. The Jewish deportees are never directly confronted with somebody who addresses them as persons sensitive to moral obligations. Because of this lack of direct contact they can only tell among themselves *'That I die, s/he decrees it'*, or *'That I die; that is his/her law'*. In other words, the Jewish deportees are in the impossible position of linking to this order a sentence in which they are located as a respondent (addressee) and a speaker (addressor); this position in the phrase universe of legitimating linkages is denied to them: they are from the outset the 'excluded', they have no right to live: "Dispersion is at its heights. My law kills them who have no relevance to it. My death is due to their law to which I owe nothing. Delegitimation is complete."[44] A broader 'we' called humanity can no longer be invoked: "Auschwitz is indeed the name for the extinction of that name."[45]

The extinction of the 'we' of humanity in Auschwitz cannot be rescued by a speculative concept of reconciliation. There is no third party capable of establishing a higher (Hegelian) synthesis between the torturer and the victim. Such a third party, if it existed, would have to be capable of living, first, in the phrase universe of the SS ('my law kills them who have no relevance to it') and then, second, in that of the deportees ('my death is due to their law to which I owe nothing'). But what would be the result of such an alternation of positions? For Hegel, one and the same Subject would be able to traverse the two opposite worlds and to dialectically

43. *Ibid.*, no. 157, p. 101.
44. *Ibid.*, no. 157, p. 101.
45. *Ibid.*, no. 157, p. 101.

bring them in a rapprochement the one to the other, thus opening the perspective of a new beginning for humankind. Lyotard disallows this speculative reconciliation. The atrocities of Auschwitz have shown that such an enduring Subject capable of reassembling a divided humanity – the Spirit of history – is a sheer illusion. Recourse to the encompassing 'we' of humanity is part and parcel of Hegel's speculative trickery. But in fact, the only 'we' that is left – Lyotard and the readers he inspires – is a much more humble 'we': it is a 'we' that is engaged in thinking the impossibility of a higher totality: "This 'we' is certainly not the totalization of the I's, the you's and the s/he's in play under the name of Auschwitz, for it is true that this name designates the impossibility of such a totalization. Instead, it is the reflective movement of this impossibility."[46]

For Lyotard, the clash between the SS universe and the deportees' universe is worse than a differend; it is the extreme case of a differend. The Nazi-ideology exalts the 'Arians' at the expense of the non-Arians. The Jews are by definition the 'intruders' that must be eliminated. They are not even given the chance to speak up for themselves; from the outset they are condemned to death: "It is a 'terror' without a tribunal, and without a pronounced punishment. Death is sufficient, since it proves that what ought not to live cannot live. The solution is final."[47] The Final Solution is the logical consequence of political or social Darwinism. The 'Arians' act as if they were the elected people, but instead of linking this election, as in Judaism, to a basic attitude of 'listening', they link it, in a primitive manner, to an ethnic narrative that is established on the basis of the exclusion of aliens: "Whoever is not of this people cannot hear, cannot tell [the founding story], and cannot die well. The people alone is made up of 'true men', that's the name one ethnic group calls itself by. It marks the founding exception. That is why savages make war."[48] The 'Arians' exterminate those who do not belong to the 'chosen people' as they have redefined the term; they put pressure on their members to denounce and harass strangers whose blood is not pure. For inflicting these harassments no special blessing from a tribunal is needed.

Exposure to this differend plunges one into wordless silence, into a melancholy that testifies to the unpresentable Idea. This silence and its search for further linkages come back in Lyotard's reflections on how we have to look, in retrospect, at what happened in Auschwitz. One thing is certain: a beautiful concept of reconciliation cannot result from this

---

46. *Ibid.*, no. 158, pp. 102-103.
47. *Ibid.*, no. 159, p. 103.
48. *Ibid.*, no. 160, p. 105.

yawning abyss: "It is not a concept that results from 'Auschwitz', but a feeling, an impossible phrase, one that would link the SS phrase onto the deportees' phrase, and vice versa."[49] This statement betrays a reflective mood that is already anticipating questions about the future of Europe at this moment when the Nazi regime belongs to the past, and the victims are dead. How to find a phrase, today, that expresses the feelings that come up when reflecting on the atrocities of the Shoah?

For Lyotard, that phrase should make us feel the vehemence of a clash of civilizations: the Germans pitted against the Jews, two worlds apart. "There are no stakes held in common by one and the other. In exterminating the Jews, Nazism eliminated a phrase regimen where the mark is on the addressee (*Listen, Israel*) and where identifying the addressor (the Lord) or the sense (what God wants to say) is a dishonorable and dangerous presumption. The genre of discourse, called Cabbala (tradition) is, in terms of questioning and interpretation, at the furthest removed from the savage narrative tradition. The latter is placed under the regimen of the already there, the Jewish idiom placed under that of the *Is it happening?* Nazism assails the occurrence, the *Ereignis*. It thereby attacks the time of all of modernity."[50] 'Modernity' in this context means: critical reason and interrogative philosophy, which already for long has brought to ruin the savage narrativity of the tribe. Nazism attacks that type of modernity; it eliminates the tradition of those who 'listen' and 'decipher', and look for the unexpected and the 'impossible' to happen. True, nowadays, Nazism is gone, it has been defeated. Yet, one can never be sure, Lyotard underlines, that its spirit will not return in the future. Hence again, in the face of this insecurity, the need for "silences, instead of a *Resultat* [a conclusive concept]."[51]

IV. AUSCHWITZ: REMEMBER! *HEIDEGGER AND "THE JEWS"*

In *Heidegger and "the jews"* (1988) Lyotard delves into the question of forgetting and remembering. Heidegger is the philosopher who denounced the forgetfulness of Being; but why, then, did he forget to reflect on the scandal of the Holocaust? It is very well known that Heidegger, in the late 1930s as rector of the university of Freiburg, compromised himself with the Nazi-regime. The only text in which he mentions the death camps is a statement from 1949, three years after the end of World War II. There he says "Agriculture is now a mechanized food

49. *Ibid.*, no. 159, p. 104.
50. *Ibid.*, no. 160, p. 106.
51. *Ibid.*, no. 160, p. 106.

industry; in essence it is no different than the production of corpses in the gas chambers and the death camps, the embargoes and food reductions to starving countries, the making of hydrogen bombs."[52] What interests him is apparently the analysis of the forgetfulness of Being: the more techno-science is making inroads in every day life, the more people become insensitive to what really matters in their lives. But, Lyotard argues, with this concern Heidegger still moves within the framework of a Greek-Christian metaphysics of Being. That is why he did not raise his voice of protest against the extermination of the Jews, a people who are notorious for their lack of interest in metaphysics. Already the young Hegel had ascribed the wretched life circumstances of the Jews to their fate: "By this fate – an infinite power that they set over against themselves and could never conquer – they have been maltreated and will be continually maltreated until they appease it by the spirit of beauty and so annul it by reconciliation."[53]

Lyotard was born a Catholic. In his youth, he even thought of entering the Dominican order. Later, under the influence of Levinas, he became fascinated by the particularity of the Jews, a people who continue to remember that they are taken hostage by a 'voice' and a 'law' they did not ask for. Commenting on Freud's explanation in *Moses and Monotheism*, he says: The Jews live from "a promise made to a people who did not want it and had no need for it, an alliance that has not been negotiated, that goes against the people's interests, of which it knows itself unworthy [...] This simple people is taken hostage by a voice that does not tell it anything, save that it (this voice) is, and that all representation and naming of it are forbidden, and that it, this people, only needs to listen to its tone, to be obedient to a timbre."[54] Like all surrounding peoples this 'elected' people had to engage in organizing itself, in setting up economic relations to make the nation prosper. Yet, it realized that the mechanisms of these worldly activities must never be divinized. The only respect to be paid is that to the unnamable voice that can never be forgotten, even if they would like to relegate it to oblivion. The shock of that voice asks to be remembered: The 'elected' people "is

---

52. J.-F. Lyotard, *Heidegger and "the jews"*, trans. D. Caroll and A. Michel (Minneapolis, MN: University of Minnesota Press, 1990) 85, citing W. Schirmacher, *Technik und Gelassenheit: Zeitkritik nach Heidegger* (Freiburg: Alber, 1984) 25. Originally published as idem, *Heidegger et "les juifs"* (Paris: Galilée, 1988).

53. J.-F. Lyotard, *Heidegger and "the jews"*, 89, citing G.W.F. Hegel, "The Spirit of Christianity and its Fate," in idem, *Early Theological Writings* (Chicago, IL: University of Chicago Press, 1948) 199-200.

54. J.-F. Lyotard, *Heidegger and "the jews"*, 21.

forced to renounce itself, it inscribes this misery into its tradition, it turns into memory this forgotten and makes a virtue of having a deep regard for memory, the *Achtung*, the Kantian 'respect'."[55]

In the title of this work Lyotard writes the term "the Jews" in brackets and without capital letter: *Heidegger and "the jews"*. He does so intentionally because, to his way of thinking, unconventional philosophers and artists can also be called 'jews': unruly individuals that refuse to let themselves be assimilated into the mainstream Greek-Christian culture: "'the jews' are within the 'spirit' of the Occident that is so preoccupied with foundational thinking, the entity that resists this spirit [of the Occident]."[56] This resistance is born from their listening to a 'voice' that cannot be named and that holds them hostage like the native Jews.

Elsewhere Lyotard calls this voice, with Freud, an 'unconscious affect'. This affect acts like a shock that unsettles the vital forces of the psychic system, in such a violent way that it cannot even be consciously felt by it. The shock acts like an excitement that infiltrates the system, but which the system itself is unable to locate or to represent. The 'unconscious affect' defies any structuration in categories of time and space, because it is 'in excess': "Its 'excess' (of quantity, of intensity) exceeds the excess that gives rise (presence, place and time) to the unconscious and the pre-conscious. It is 'in excess' like air and earth are in excess for the life of a fish."[57] It is a mysterious a-temporal anteriority which Lacan calls 'the Thing',[58] and which Derrida evokes as a non-place of disturbance (*khôra*). Later, the excitement will make itself felt in the system, in the form of a dispersed energy or of a formless anxiety. One might call it the aftereffect of the initial shock that remained unperceived: "Something, however, *will make* Itself understood, 'later'. That which will not have been introduced [by a conscious decision] will have been 'acted', 'acted out', 'enacted', 'played out' in the end – and thus re-presented. But without the subject recognizing it."[59] Lyotard calls this aftereffect a second blow. The first blow "is a shock without effect. With the second blow there takes place an affect without a shock: I buy something in a store, anxiety crushes me. I flee, but nothing had really happened. The energy dispersed in the affective cloud condenses, gets organized, brings on an

---

55. *Ibid.*, 21.
56. *Ibid.*, 22.
57. *Ibid.*, 12.
58. See J.-F. Lyotard, *The Inhuman: Reflections on Time* (Cambridge: Polity Press, 1991) 33. Originally published as idem, *L'inhumain: Causeries sur le temps* (Paris: Galilée, 1988).
59. J.-F. Lyotard, *Heidegger and "the jews"*, 13.

action, commands a flight without a 'real' motive. And it is this flight, the feeling that accompanies it, which informs consciousness *that* there is something, without being able to tell *what* it is."[60]

For Lyotard, there is always an uninvited stranger in the house whose presence is signaled, but whose identity one is unable to determine. What psychoanalysis and intrapsychic examination try to do is to identify this stranger, that is to locate, through anamnesis, the first hidden shock. At this juncture a discrepancy comes to the fore. To the extent one draws a continuous line between the first hidden shock and its felt aftereffect experienced in circumstances that have nothing to do with the shock, one disregards the special time in which the first shock took place, a 'time' that cannot be captured in the current chronologization of facts: "Ungraspable by consciousness, this time threatens it. It threatens it permanently. And permanence is the name for what happens in the lexicon of consciousness of time. In truth, it is not even permanence. It has nothing of the *per-*, of crossing, of passing in it [...] it merely has *manere, sistere* in it: menace, manence."[61] Freud tried to find a reason for the clandestine entry and unnoticed stay of that menacing stranger by reconstructing a seduction perpetrated on the child. Whatever the nature of this clandestine entry might be, what Freud sought to highlight is "the unpreparedness of the psychic apparatus for the 'first shock'."[62] We are always torn between a too early and a too late: "the too early of a first blow dealt to the apparatus that it does not feel, and the too late of a second blow where something intolerable is felt."[63] In both cases "the soul is exceeded, dispossessed, passed beyond, excised through and by this something. This is the constitutive infirmity of the soul, its infancy and its misery."[64]

Freud's original repression (*Urverdringung*) – evoked by the 'unconscious affect', 'the Thing' that is 'external' to consciousness while inhabiting it as a 'permanent' menace – serves as a basic pattern, for Lyotard, with which to characterize what is typically Jewish: the Jewish community is taken hostage by a strange voice whose shock it is unable to locate but whose aftereffect continues to haunt and command it. This voice dispossesses them by imposing its covenant whose law brings them into a situation of dispossession and surprise. They always live in "the too early – too late: a people unprepared for the revelation of the alliance, always

60. *Ibid.*, 16.
61. *Ibid.*, 17.
62. *Ibid.*, 17.
63. *Ibid.*, 20.
64. *Ibid.*, 17.

too young for it; and as a result, too old, too paralyzed by preoccupations, idolatries, and even studies to achieve the sanctity required by the promise."[65] In that 'too old', they will perhaps attempt to give the shock of the voice a place in the ordinary chronologization of time, thus making the unpresentable present in historical memory, but at the same time forgetting that the unpresentable shock is part of an 'archaic' pre-history. Yet always will they be asked to remember what not ought to be forgotten. Citing Elie Wiesel in *Souls on Fire*, Lyotard notes that "it must even be sufficient that one remembers that one must remember, that one should; and it must be sufficient that one remembers that one does not remind oneself of it anymore; it must be sufficient to save the interminable and the waiting."[66]

Asking himself the question as to why the "jews" were hated, so much so that the Nazi-regime decided to exterminate them and to eradicate their memory, Lyotard conjectures that it must have been their tenacious remembrance of the covenant and the law that made them unwanted persons in the new Nazi world order 'beyond Good and Evil'. True, Judaism has always been the hidden 'other' of the Greco-Roman inspired Western civilization. But in the totalitarian regime of Nazi Germany this otherness was resented, and became the object of the Final Solution. The Jews are, from their origin, nomads without a stable place; this was perhaps still tolerable, but not their interminable recollection of the covenant. Lyotard writes: "'The jews' do not appear evil, or inapt, to take on the challenge of mobilization, because they are the nomadism of thought, not riveted to their roots, but essentially transportable, like books, money, jewels, the violin. But they are evil if they are riveted to their book, to the stupor of a covenant, of an immemorial 'shock' whose affection they try to reserve against all compromise. This present 'society' that has no need for this affection nor for its preservation forecloses on it more than any other."[67] Just as vehemently as Heidegger, Lyotard denounces a society ruled by pure calculation, but he does so for a different reason: not in order to rescue the awareness of Being, but of the 'soul'. Wall Street and NASA have forgotten the memory of such an immemorial 'shock'; the only thing that matters to them are the shocks and agitations that make the system grow. But in doing so, he adds, they ignore what "is not an

---

65. *Ibid.*, 37.
66. *Ibid.*, 38. The reader's attention is drawn to the Jewish nuance in the above text: To forget, to 'no longer remember', is a betrayal which should haunt the one who has chosen to forget.
67. *Ibid.*, 40 [translation modified].

object or what has no object – and thus the soul, if 'soul' means a spirit disturbed by a host that it ignores, 'nonobjectal', nonobjective."[68]

Right from the outset Lyotard made it clear that his reading of the term "the jews" will be based on both Kant and Freud. No wonder that, in order to describe the feelings of the 'soul', he has recourse to Kant's analysis of the sublime. The feeling of the sublime is not an experience of the senses: it is a feeling of the 'soul' (*die Seele, das Gemüt*) at the moment during which the sensitive imagination experiences an urge to render present the absolute, and fails to produce this presentation. This collapse of the imagination has a deep repercussion on the soul. The soul feels overwhelmed by a sublime pain and delight that "bears witness to the fact that an 'excess' has 'touched' the mind [*das Gemüt*], more than it is able to handle."[69] This is Kant's manner of describing the disturbing 'shock' of the alliance which Judaism feels it must continue to remember without any betrayal. Lyotard remarks that Longinus, the rhetorician of antiquity who launched the notion of the sublime, of the uplifting of the 'soul' (which Kant revisited) comes not from a Greek but from a Jewish-Christian milieu.

In this tradition aesthetics or *aisthesis* cannot possibly lead to the sublime feeling, because the latter bears witness to the unpresentable beyond the realm of the senses: "Nothing can lead from *aisthesis* to the hidden feeling, to the sublime pain and joy that are the inimitable deposit left by the unfelt shock of the alliance, unreachable by any artifact, even when it is of pious speech."[70] Aesthetics and *aisthesis* are part of nature, of our natural energy, whereas the sublime pain-and-joy is not. Aesthetics, in the Greek tradition, is rooted in an imitation that uses its own codes of inscribing experiences; the sublime feeling is bereft of proper codes of writing, it emerges from a dispossession under the shock of the irruption of an 'alterity'. The latter can only by received in utter passibility, through a mere *pathos* of undergoing: "The sublime is the agitated emotion of [the] defection [of encoding writing], a defection that cannot be felt through *aisthesis* but only through *pathos*. This is an insensible passibility, and thus an anesthesia, but one that leaves the soul open to an affection more 'archaic' than the givens of nature and that cannot be equaled by any imitation through form and figure."[71] In drawing the distinction between imitation/figure and shock/disfigurement Lyotard alludes to the

68. *Ibid.*, 41.
69. *Ibid.*, 33.
70. *Ibid.*, 38.
71. *Ibid.*, 44-45.

special art form of the avant-garde, a topic I will examine in more detail below.

In conclusion, since Lyotard is writing on *Heidegger and "the jews"* let us examine precisely where Heidegger misses the point of the sublime. It is, as Derrida already pointed out in his study on Heidegger,[72] on the topic of art. And this in a double manner. Heidegger, first of all, defines art in terms of *mimesis* "which supplements nature by imitating it."[73] Secondly, for Heidegger, politics is also a work of art, of 'fashioning' the mentality of a people, which was in the late 1930's a dangerous statement, if not a legitimization of the Nazi propaganda machine. Now, at a certain moment Heidegger appeared to break with art as *mimesis* by stressing, with the classic German poet Hölderlin, that in the face of imminent disasters the only defensible attitude is to 'wait for God'; and also that the poet will have to assume the task of acting as 'the guardian of the memory of the forgotten'. Both elements – 'waiting for God' and the 'guardianship of the memory of the forgotten' – are typical of Heidegger's turn (*Kehre*). They even seem to intimate a closeness to Jewish thought, although this impression will prove to be incorrect. Lyotard comments on the *Kehre* as follows: "Here, I would say, is the 'moment' in Heidegger's thought where it approaches, indeed, touches the thought of the 'jews'. If there is *mimèsis* in this art of waiting, it can only be acted out there, it would seem, as a prohibition. There should remain only that trace, distant as Egypt, which is the cry for a lost home, the temptation perhaps to represent once again the father's 'house' through some simulacrum, some golden calf, but a longing hereafter principally banned and ridiculed."[74]

Heidegger, however, apparently succumbs to the temptation of the golden calf. His waiting for God includes the waiting for a 'house', for a 'place' where the people (in his case: his people, the German people) may dwell in a secured geographical setting. By contrast, the 'jews' have no fixed place for their home; they are the 'nomadism of thought'. Further, Heidegger's new insight into 'the guardianship of the memory of the forgotten', close as it appears to be to Judaism, is, in the final analysis, a deviation from it. In Judaism "it is the Forgotten that holds the people hostage whatever their 'fashion' of being together,"[75] whereas the Heidegger of the *Kehre* longs for a stupendous come back of the forgotten,

---

72. See J. Derrida, *Of Spirit: Heidegger and the Question* (Chicago, IL and London: University of Chicago Press, 1989). Originally published as idem, *De l'esprit: Heidegger et la question* (Paris: Galilée, 1987).

73. J.-F. Lyotard, *Heidegger and "the jews"*, 76.

74. *Ibid.*, 79-80.

75. *Ibid.*, 80.

in line with the Greek cyclical periodization of history: an epoch of past splendor has been relegated to oblivion; yet, the poetic philosopher already lives from the vision of its expected recurrence. This leads Lyotard to the conclusion that Heidegger "remains bound to sacrality, but completely ignores the Holy." In his writings the "movement of an exodus towards the Law does not take place."[76]

A further analysis of Heidegger's notions of temporality and space corroborates the above reflections. In his early work *Being and Time* Heidegger 'deconstructed' the substantial (transcendental) subject that, since Descartes, has come to dominate the European philosophical scene. Heidegger did so by calling attention to the flux of time: we are 'thrown into an existence-unto-death', which also means: 'into a temporality characterized by dispersal and dissipation', which forecloses any attempt at reaching a stable platform from which to assess reality. This aspect of dispersal has been hailed by Lyotard and his generation of deconstructive philosophers. A critical rereading of *Being and Time*, however, shows that the dissipative approach to time did not affect the notion of place – that is: of place and those having their home in it, the people (*Volk*): "The term *Volk* resists the deconstruction of the subject in *Sein und Zeit* (*Being and Time*)."[77] After Heidegger's *Kehre* and the introduction of 'guardianship' and 'awaiting', this focus on place and people becomes even stronger. It gives rise to a geophilosophy, and to the "sacralization of a territory for this people."[78] Awaited is the moment when the rebirth of the people – the German people – is going to 'take place', in a particular geographical setting with its familiar landscape: "The images of 'the earth' have continued to flower, if I may say so, from the beginning to the end of these writings. The same peasant (pagan) unthought is at work in the obstinate digging out of the roots of language, obviously maternal, as well as the 'discovery' that they share a common bond with the Greek language, the language of the beginning. Anxiety is bound up with time, but space, or rather taking place, dwelling, *technè* as the art of forestry and agriculture, the 'field' of language, cannot mislead."[79]

In laying bare the root metaphors 'place', 'dwelling', and 'beginning' in Heidegger's philosophy even after the *Kehre*, Lyotard is able now to answer the question of Heidegger's mute silence on the Shoah. Heidegger 'forgot' to raise a voice of protest because he overlooked that only a

---

76. *Ibid.*, 80.
77. *Ibid.*, 91.
78. *Ibid.*, 92.
79. *Ibid.*, 92 [translation modified].

thought without beginning and without foundation can escape the pitfall of an ideology of place and dwelling, the ideology of Hitler's National Socialism. His attempts at giving a place again to a 'groundless Ground' of Being that cannot be domesticated by modern technology brought him only half way to a way of thinking without foundation. Heidegger reintroduced the sacred but not the Holy whose presence is felt by one's respect for the Law. Heidegger's thought "hermetically seals his silence on the question of the Holocaust. This silence *is* this nonquestion, this closure and foreclosure: the 'forgetting' that thought is without beginning and unfounded, that it does not have to 'give place' to Being but is owed to a nameless Law."[80]

V. Testifying to the Unpresentable: The Vocation of the Artist

Feelings play an important role in Lyotard's political ethics. They basically relate to an attitude of possibility, listening, the awareness of infancy (always too early/always too late), and the recovery of what he calls 'soul'. These attitudes accompany, and are indicative of, one's felt contact with the supersensible, at the other side of ordinary consciousness. They presuppose that life will be governed by the acceptance of a 'heteronomy' that will come to replace the 'Big organizing Ego'. This 'heteronomy' includes 'obedience', respect for the moral law, and commitment to an unasked-for covenant. To identify this as the aesthetic side of Lyotard without further nuances, however, would fail to do justice to him, because what he is in search of is 'soul', and not pleasure arising from a sensitive appreciation of beautiful forms. His aesthetics is not an aesthetics of the beautiful that appeals to the senses, but an esthetics of the sublime that appeals to the mind and its willingness to be disoriented by the shock of the supersensible. No wonder that, in many passages of his work, he analyzes what artists have to say about this shock and how they set out to communicate it in their works of art. Musing on Vermeer's painting 'View of Delft', a city in the Netherlands, he describes how the intensive yellow used by this 17th century Dutch painter had the effect on him of a 'suspension': "It happens that a yellow, the yellow in Vermeer's view of Delft, can suspend the will and the plot [...] It is this suspension that I should like to call soul: when the mind breaks into shards (letting go) under the 'effect' of a colour (but is it an effect?)."[81]

80. *Ibid.*, 94.
81. J.-F. Lyotard, *The Inhuman*, 151.

The question in brackets 'but it is an effect?' already points to the difficulty that confronts a painter when trying to convey an emotion of the soul by means of sensible images and colors. Is the soul-stirring 'suspension' that occurred to Lyotard when gazing at Vermeer's painting the effect of the color on the canvas? Or is the intensive yellow of the canvas only the medium through which a voice is heard that enjoins listening, 'passibility' and 'infancy'? How can this commanding voice be presented, without this visibility interposing a screen between the message and the addressee? This is the problem Lyotard tackles in his reflections on the sublime and the avant-garde. The movement of the avant-garde began with the advent of the photographic industry around the 1880s, which forced painters to define their vocation in a new way. In this search for identity the vanguard painters discovered that they had to "present that there is something that is not presentable according to the legitimate construction [of the photographic industry.] They began to overturn the supposed 'givens' of the visible so as to make visible the fact that the visual field hides and requires invisibilities, that it does not simply belong to the eye (of the prince) but to the (wandering) mind."[82]

What is called here the 'eye of the prince' is the usual habit of looking at things in an instrumental, consumerist fashion. In contrast to this, the vanguard artists affirm their independence from that objectifying look and claim the 'visual field' as the domain in which to depose the account of the 'wandering' of their mind. They stop pleasing their public; they break with a facile notion of *sensus communis* that takes universal communicability of the judgments of taste for granted: their art is not meant to be understood by each and every person; its grasp is the privilege of the like-minded, of those sensitive to the interrogative character of their works. Lyotard subscribes to this view. He observes that "Kant only refers to [this universal communicability] when writing about beauty, not the sublime."[83] Two major elements of Kant's analysis of the sublime return in avant-garde paintings: First, the formless, chaotic element: "These works appear to the public of taste to be 'monsters', 'formless' objects, pure 'negative' entities."[84] Second, the 'unpresentability' of the Idea for which there can be only an indirect evocation: "One cannot present the absolute. But one can present that there is some absolute. This is a 'negative' (Kant also says 'abstract') presentation. The current of

82. *Ibid.*, 125.
83. *Ibid.*, 104.
84. *Ibid.*, 125.

'abstract' painting has its source, from 1912, in this requirement for indirect and all but ungraspable allusion to the invisible in the visible."[85]

The combination of these two elements, the formless and the evocation of unpresentability, is the means par excellence to allude to the invisible (the supersensible). A great many contemporary artists follow this line of thought. They were preceded, however, by a generation of 'modern' painters who gave expression to their nostalgia for the absent content (the withdrawal of an encompassing sphere of meaning) by using compositions with pleasing, vivid colors. The nostalgia for the 'lost origin' was evoked by scenes and landscapes that pointed to another 'world' that has evaporated: "The modern aesthetic is an aesthetic of the sublime. But it is nostalgic; it allows the unpresentable to be invoked only as absent content, while form, thanks to its recognizable consistency, continues to offer the reader or spectator material for consolation and pleasure."[86] Examples of this trend are romantic (Turner) and impressionistic painting (Monet). A turning point came with the radical avant-garde. They began to shock their public with disturbing, non-figurative paintings. This phenomenon can be witnessed, for example, in cubism, in Picasso (distorted bodies) and in Barnett Newman (canvases with massive colored bars, one placed above the other). Their aim and purpose was to evoke unpresentability itself: "The postmodern would be that which in the modern invokes the unpresentable in presentation itself; that which refuses the consolation of correct forms, refuses the consensus of taste permitting a common experience of nostalgia for the impossible, and inquires into new presentations – not to take pleasure in them, but to better produce the feeling that there is something unpresentable."[87]

Lyotard's favorite painter is Barnett Baruch Newman (1905-1970), an American non-figurative artist who, while engaged in painting, reflected on his Jewish roots. Newman, who is renowned for his visualizing of an interrupting 'now', combines, in an original way, Kant's approach to the sublime with that of Edmund Burke (1729-1797). Kantian in his approach is the mixture of pain and pleasure felt at the moment that the imagination – or the faculty of presentation – has to admit its incapacity for presenting all the power of the supersensible. In confessing this incapacity, the imagination thus 'negatively' testifies to the unpresentable Idea. At various times, Lyotard emphasizes the Kantian influence which can be

85. *Ibid.*, 126.

86. J.-F. Lyotard, *The Postmodern Explained*, trans. D. Barry et al. (Minneapolis, MN and London: University of Minnesota Press, 1992) 14. Originally published as idem, *Le postmoderne expliqué aux enfants* (Paris: Galilée, 1988).

87. *Ibid.*, 15.

observed in Newman's art, which at the same time is enriched by a return to Burke. Lyotard's comment on Theodor Adorno's notion of 'micrologies' will make this clear. For Adorno, "[T]hought 'that accompanies metaphysics in its fall' can only proceed in terms of 'micrologies'."[88] Micrologies are not the same as microstories 'little stories of resistance – which Lyotard himself deems important for reacting against the oppressive force of grand narratives, although something of this resistance also resonates in them. For Adorno, "Micrology inscribes the occurrence of a thought as the unthought that remains to be thought in the decline of 'great' philosophical thought."[89]

This succinct definition contains two strains of thought. First, 'what ought to be thought is the unthought that remains to be thought' is a clear allusion to Kant. For Kant, the supersensible Ideas give a direction to the persons' actions (he sometimes calls them 'regulative Ideas'); they are part and parcel of human thinking; we are forced to think them, although without fully understanding them, in order to judge humankind's progress in matters of ethics. Things are different, however, in a post-metaphysical era, that of the decline of 'great' philosophical thought. Here the supersensible Idea becomes rather the 'unthought' – in a pragmatic setting people stop thinking about them – but that Idea nonetheless ought to be thought, if humankind is not going to lose its sense of human dignity. Second, and this is already consistent with Burke's thought, Adorno insists that the thinking of this 'unthought' must be inscribed as an occurrence – an event – in the decline of metaphysics. The decline must be suspended for a while by the eventful occurrence of 'thinking the unthought that remains to be thought'. In terms of painting, this means that the decline of figurative painting is suspended by the expectation of a sensuous 'now': "The avant-gardist attempt inscribes the occurrence of a sensuous now as what cannot be presented and which remains to be presented in the decline of great representational painting. Like micrology, the avant-garde is not concerned 'with what happens to the subject', but [rather] with 'does it happen?'"[90]

The question is: '*Is it happening?*', a question that keeps one in suspense. The sensuous now unsettles; it deprives one of one's equilibrium, and therefore belongs to the aesthetic of the sublime. The focus on '*Is it happening?*' – on the suspending/unsettling 'now moment' – can hardly be explained from a Kantian perspective. It is here that the influence of

88. J.-F. Lyotard, *The Inhuman*, 103.
89. *Ibid.*, 103.
90. *Ibid.*, 103.

Edmund Burke comes to the fore, the author who in the 18th century reclaimed the notion of the sublime, but whose account of terror and delight was in Kant's eyes overly identified with empiricism. In reaction to Burke, Kant situated the contrast experience of the sublime in one's encounter with the supersensible: for him, the shock of the Idea is what unsettles and calls forth terror and delight. The shock felt in the sublime feeling is a 'spiritual' shock, having a bearing on one's ethical conduct, an element Lyotard highly appreciates. Yet, by situating the shock in the 'spiritual', Kant downplayed what was essential to Burke's approach: the 'now moment' of time, plus the fear that this 'now moment' will fade away. Lyotard writes: "The question of time, of the *Is it happening?*, does not form part – at least not explicitly – of Kant's problematic. [... Kant's reworking of the sublime] strips Burke's esthetic of what I consider to be its major stake – to show that the sublime is kindled by the threat of nothing further happening."[91]

The notions of 'terror' and 'delight', which Kant also uses, function in Burke's aesthetics of the sublime as follows. One's first reaction to some awesome threat is a feeling of terror and privation: "Terrors are linked to privation: privation of light, terror or darkness, privation of others, terror of solitude, privation of language, terror of silence, privation of objects, terror of emptiness, privation of life, terror of death. What is terrifying is that the *It happens that* [the moment of relief of the privation] does not happen, that it stops happening."[92] Indeed, delight, still mixed with the aftershock of terror, only takes place when the terror-causing threat is suspended. This suspension brings relief, felt as immense delight: a temporary removal of the privation of life, darkness, emptiness, etc, but still accompanied by the apprehension that the relief will not last. Hence the anxious question, 'Will the relieve continue to be felt?' 'Will it perhaps stop happening?' What is sublime for Burke "is the feeling that something will happen, despite everything, within this threatening void, that something will take 'place' and will announce that everything is not over [that the terror is removable]. That place is a mere 'here', the most minimal occurrence."[93]

Burke was convinced that the shocking power of poetry would be able to announce 'the now' of deliverance, the advent of the 'angel of the Lord'. For him, this role could be played by experiments in literature, but not, however, in painting. Its reluctance to painting stems from his conception of painting as figurative painting: no canvas presenting an

91. *Ibid.*, 99.
92. *Ibid.*, 99.
93. *Ibid.*, 84.

angel-with-wings will be able to convey the deep sensation, evoked in poetry, of the annunciation of the 'angel *of the Lord'*. For Newman, the Jewish painter, this objection does not create any problem. He firmly believes that the 'now moment' (*'Is it happening?'*) can be evoked with the help of the shock-effects used in non-figurative painting. Lyotard stresses that Kant had already laid down the foundation for such a negative evocation: "One cannot present the power of infinite might or absolute magnitude within space and time because they are pure Ideas. But one can at least allude to them, or 'evoke' them by means of what [Kant] baptizes a 'negative presentation'."[94]

Barnett Newman's subject matter of painting is 'chaos' and the 'light that brings about separation', as narrated in the first creation story in *Genesis*. The instant 'light' is the moment of creation, it bursts forth from a mysterious place, or better non-place, outside and prior to the chaos. For Newman, creation has no beginning in time; it falls from an immemorial pre-history each time when a 'sensuous now moment', fragile as it may be, makes itself felt. Most of his canvases suggest "a flash of lightening in the darkness, or a line on an empty surface [...] The world never stops beginning. For Newman, creation is not an act performed by someone; it is what happens [...] in the midst of the indeterminate. If then, there is any subject mater [in his paintings], it is immediacy. It happens here and now."[95] The *'that it happens'* (*quid*) is more important than *'what'* (*quod*) happens, since it is the astonishing occurrence that directly reveals the creative might of YHWH.

In fact, this Creator is the hidden actor in Newman's paintings. Even when a canvas is given a title with a biblical connotation – Abraham, The Name, Joshua – these canvases never convey a story; they only evoke the essence of it in the style of 'minimal art'; this essence is that which speaks to us. Lyotard remarks that Newman's canvases are no longer "organized around a sender, a receiver, and a referent. The message speaks of 'nothing', it emanates from no one. It is not Newman who is speaking, or who is using painting to show us something. The 'message' (the painting) is the messenger. It says: *'Here I am'*, in other words, *'I am yours'*, or *'Be mine'*."[96] Newman succeeds in presenting – evoking with color, line and rhythm – an obligation that is more ethical than purely aesthetic. The painting – or better, what happens in it – is the visible medium that renders present the invisible Creator's commanding

94. *Ibid.*, 85.
95. *Ibid.*, 82.
96. *Ibid.*, 81.

voice. Lyotard prefers to focus on the notion of 'obligation', because it summarizes the Jewish world view and what distinguishes it from Greek thought. He says: Newman's "model cannot be *Look at this (over there)*; it must be *Look at me*, or, to be more accurate: *Listen to me*. For obligation is a modality of time rather than of space and its organ is the ear rather than the eye."[97]

This shows again to what extent Lyotard appropriated the Jewish way of 'being in the world'. For the Greek, and also for Heidegger, the ideal is 'seeing', 'contemplating', 'beholding' a place that reveals the sacred character of nature. Judaism, on the contrary, does not stick to a place: the wandering Jews feel they have to listen to the commanding voice of the Holy, to hear a sound emerging from the silence. Newman, Lyotard explains, attempts to visually evoke this voice and how it speaks to the listening ear: "No one, and especially not Newman, makes *me* see [the picture] in the sense of recounting or interpreting what I see. I (the viewer) am no more than an ear open to the sound which comes to it from out of the silence: the painting is that sound, an accord. Arising (*se dresser*), which is a constant theme in Newman, must be understood in the sense of pricking up one's ears (*dresser son oreille*), of listening."[98] This act of listening, of pricking up one's ears, allows one to realize who one is, a 'person present to oneself' because of the listening.

The voice that comes from Newman's painting commands one: 'be', or 'know before whom you stand': the Creator. For Newman, the command 'be' and the empowerment or psychic intensification that flows from it is a contrast experience, linked to a place upon which falls the 'now' of creation that shines in the midst of chaos. Newman describes how he was overwhelmed by this 'now moment 'of creation when visiting the mounds built by the Miami Indians in southwest Ohio in the United States. He describes it as follows: "Looking at the site, you feel, Here I am, *here* ... and out beyond there (beyond the limits of the site) there is chaos, nature, rivers, landscapes ... but here you get a sense of your own presence ... I became involved with the idea of making the viewer [of my paintings] present: the idea that 'Man is present'."[99] When introducing the maquette for a synagogue he made for the Recent American Synagogue Architecture Exhibition, Newman explained that the words that guided him when designing the maquette were: 'Know before whom you stand'. He imagined the effect these words would have on

97. *Ibid.*, 81.
98. *Ibid.*, 83-84.
99. *Ibid.*, 86.

those who are called from their seats to proclaim the Torah in the synagogue. They are reminded that they are not asked to ascend to a stage but "to go up to the mound where, under the tension of that 'Tzim-tzum' that created light and the world, he can experience a total sense of his own personality before the Torah and His Name."[100]

At this juncture Lyotard brings up the notion of a 'Jewish space' that is different from the Greek notion of place and space, because it is linked to the experience of 'presence' – of the now moment of creation that places one before the nameless Holy. This presence interrupts and expels the chaos: "Presence is the instant which interrupts the chaos of history and which recalls, or simply calls out 'that there is' even before that which is has any signification."[101] The chaos inspires terror, a terror that "surrounds the event, the relief that *there is*."[102] Terror and relief are, as we have seen, the key notions in Burke's analysis of the sublime.

For Lyotard, the 'now moment' (*'Is it happening?'*) brings one into a dislocated time experience where one feels uprooted and dispossessed, open to the unexpected, commanded to 'listen'. The 'that something happens', the event, is inscribed in this openness to the unexpected: "The expression 'it happens that...' is the formula of non-mastery of self over self. The event makes the self incapable of taking possession and control of what it is. It testifies that the self is essentially passible to a recurrent alterity."[103] This openness to the unexpected is crucial to Lyotard. It makes him alert, in his language pragmatics, to the fact that each sentence is a 'now' that 'right now' presents a meaning, a referent, a sender and an addressee. It makes him protest whenever this eventful 'now' of the sentence is reduced to a past in that a pre-ordained mode of linking sentences determines whether or not this 'now' will become part of the linkage. The 'now' of the event resists and blasts any synthesis.

This is the reason why avant-garde artists, who tenaciously call attention to this disturbing 'now', are suspect to the demagogic planners of society. During Nazism the *'Is it happening?'* had been changed into 'Is the *Führer* coming?' In this way the sublime had been turned into a myth, the myth of the superiority of the 'Arian' race. But today the degeneration of the sublime comes from elsewhere; it "proceeds 'directly' out of market economics [...since] there is a kind of collusion between capital and the avant-garde."[104] Both try to capture the attention of their public

100. *Ibid.*, 86-87.
101. *Ibid.*, 87.
102. *Ibid.*, 88.
103. *Ibid.*, 59.
104. *Ibid.*, 105.

with unexpected innovations. Also in information technology the '*Is it happening?*' gives a thrill to the software engineers who look for a new and unexpected innovation. On the whole, however, Lyotard observes, a basic difference remains between the avant-garde and market economics. The difference lies in the notion of time. Market economics "will affirm its hegemony over time;"[105] the aim and purpose of economics consists in 'gaining time' – in reducing the time it takes to sell a certain product on the market. The avant-garde artists are deprived of this sort of time-manipulation. They are taken hostage by a 'now moment' that reaches them from an immemorial past before and anterior to the coordinates of time and space and their possible manipulations.

VI. THE JEWISH ROOTS OF THE FEELING OF THE SUBLIME

In this concluding section I will bring together, in a more systematic way, the fragmented description Lyotard gave of the Jewish soul, and how Kant's notion of obligation as well as his understanding of the feeling of the sublime exhibit an intimate affinity with this Jewish soul. I start with Lyotard's characterization of Jewishness.

1. In his examination, in the *Differend*, of the scandal of Auschwitz Lyotard made it clear that Nazism wanted to exterminate a people they resented because of their listening to a voice they are forbidden to name and which holds them hostage. Nazism eliminates the tradition of a people who 'listens' and 'deciphers', and looks for the unexpected and the 'impossible' to happen. In this tradition "the mark is on the addressee (*Listen, Israel*)," whereas any attempt at "identifying the addressor (the Lord) or the sense (what God wants to say) is a dishonorable and dangerous presumption."[106] Already in *Just Gaming* Lyotard pointed out that in ancient cultures the element of 'listening' is central, whereas Western thought has virtually forgotten to 'listen'. Ever since Descartes, Western philosophers have come up with theoretical constructs to tell how the world should look like, without lending an ear to what is being told to them. Judaism, on the contrary, is characterized by a basic attitude of 'heteronomy': the Jews are subjected to a law and to a covenant they did not ask for, but which was imposed on hem by a strange, unnamable voice.

105. *Ibid.*, 107.
106. J.-F. Lyotard, *The Differend*, no. 160, p. 106.

In *Heidegger and the "jews"* Lyotard delves deeper into this 'heteronomy'. He explains it, as we have seen, with the help of some basic insights of Freud's psychoanalysis. The covenant is compared to a trauma that leaves an immemorial shock in the psyche. Through this shock and its aftereffects "the soul is exceeded, dispossessed, passed beyond, excised through and by this something."[107] As a matter of fact, the Jews were unprepared for the covenant: it always comes too early (they did not expect its irruption) and too late (they already busied themselves with other pre-occupations). Yet always will they be asked to remember what not ought to be forgotten. This cannot be done by giving that feeling a place in the chronologization of ordinary consciousness. The unpresentable shock is part of an 'archaic' pre-history. From there it confronts them with the demand 'remember', 'be just'. This command holds them captive: it forces them to remember that they must keep remembering the immemorial shock. That is why they intensely study the law and meditate on the effects it has on their lives. But precisely this attitude made them suspect to the Nazis and their obsession with the modern 'Arian' civilization. The Jews are the nomadism of thought. They became to be perceived as evil because they were "riveted to their book, to the stupor of a covenant, of an immemorial 'shock' whose affection they try to reserve against all compromise."[108] In short, the Jews do not fit in the civilization of the Occident. They have no speculative metaphysics; they have always avoided to develop one. Therefore they are blamed for being unruly, for refusing to let themselves be assimilated into the mainstream Greek-Christian culture: "'the jews' are within the 'spirit' of the Occident that is so preoccupied with foundational thinking, the entity that resists this spirit [of the Occident]."[109]

Resistance to foundational thinking is also to be found in Martin Heidegger. But because he drew his inspiration from the ancient Greeks, he rediscovered the sacred in nature, not the holiness of the commanding voice. For that reason he kept silent before the atrocities of the Shoah. "This silence *is* [...] the 'forgetting' that thought is without beginning and unfounded, that it does not have to 'give place' to Being but is owed to a nameless Law."[110] Heidegger attempted to deconstruct the substantial (transcendental) Ego by calling attention to the flux of time. This dissipation of time, however, did not affect his notions of place and dwelling. He finally sacralized a privileged territory, that of the German race.

---

107. J.-F. Lyotard, *Heidegger and "the jews"*, 17.
108. *Ibid.*, 40.
109. *Ibid.*, 22.
110. *Ibid.*, 94.

Not so for the Jewish abstract painter Barnett Newman. For him, the awareness of the sacredness of a place can only proceed from one's listening to the voice of the Holy. This voice is the voice of the Creator who each moment repels the menace of chaos. Barnett's abstract paintings evoke this recurrent moment of creation ('Is it happening?'). They do not tell a story but catch, through their colorful effect, the attention of the viewers in order to sensitize them to the impact of the commanding voice: "I (the viewer) am no more than an ear open to the sound which comes to it from out of the silence: the painting is that sound, an accord. Arising (*se dresser*), which is a constant theme in Newman, must be understood in the sense of pricking up one's ears (*dresser son oreille*), of listening."[111] The effect of this listening is double: the viewer feels that he/she is standing before the Creator: 'Know before whom you stand', and experiences a baffling presence to oneself. If there are sites, like the mounds built by the Miama Indians, that create an atmosphere in which on feels 'who one is', this awareness ultimately flows from one's standing, with awe, before the Creator and his intriguing 'now moment' of creation. The feeling of being present to oneself before the Creator comes from listening, from "non-mastery of self over self."[112]

2. Lyotard does not conceal his indebtedness to Emmanuel Levinas, the author from whom he learned the significance of heteronomy (or the sense of 'transcendence') for a mature ethics. As a Jewish philosopher Levinas does not rely on a metaphysical system from which to derive obligations. The obligation comes from receptivity to a commanding voice. The same is true for Kant's categorical imperative which is also typically Jewish. Kant, too, rejects a derivation or a deduction of the 'you must' from an intellectual construct. In his *Critique of Practical Reason* he clearly stated: "The objective reality of the moral law can be proved through no deduction, through no exertion of the theoretical, speculative, or empirically supported reason."[113] Only the feeling of respect that arises when being addressed by the categorical imperative proves the objective reality of the moral law. The commanding law turns out to be as hidden and concealed as the unnamable voice of JHWH. It cannot be perceived by the senses, but only by the will and its unsettling feeling of respect. This presupposes a listener, not an author who speaks and theorizes: "Only if

111. J.-F. Lyotard, *The Inhuman*, 83-84.
112. *Ibid.*, 59.
113. I. Kant, *Critique of Practical Reason, Original* edition, 82, trans. L. Beck (Indianapolis, IN: Bobbs-Merrill Educational Publishing, 1956) 48, cited in J.-F. Lyotard, *The Differend*, 119.

[this pole of the author] is neutralized, will one become sensitive, not to what it [the obligation] is, but to the fact that it prescribes and obligates ... [In the game of the just] one speaks as a listener, and not as an author. It is a game without an author. In the same way as the speculative game of the West is a game without a listener."[114] The feeling of being obligated is all that matters: the shock that results from the command 'be just'. It is only from this shock that one begins to reflect on what one must do in the concrete, just as the Jews, in their Talmudic study, used to meditate on the effects the commanding voice has and must have on their lives. Kant massively stresses the obligation without specifying what has to be done in the concrete, an issue which Hegel, the system builder, found so objectionable.

For Kant the feeling of being obligated suffices to reflect on what one has to do. This reflection, however, will take on the style of a reflective judgment and its focus on the particular. The command 'be just' has political implications. Lyotard is not tired of repeating that politics is the art of dealing with singular facts. In spite of the semblance of the contrary, Kant's categorical imperative obligates the ethical person to make his own decision. This imperative has, to be sure, a universal character, yet this universal perspective does not tell what one has to do in the concrete. That is an issue every body will have to make out for themselves with the help of a regulative Idea that guides one's reflection. Lyotard places a heavy accent on this point in his explanation of Kant's dictum: "To be just is to act in such a way that (*so dass*; says the German) the maxim of the will may serve as a principle of universal legislation."[115] He comments on it as follows: "The famous *so dass* [so that] of the imperative does not say: 'if you want to be this, then do that'. [...] The *so dass* marks the properly reflective use of judgment. It says: Do whatever, not on condition that, but *in such a way as* that which you do, the maxim of what you do, can always be valid as, etc. We are not dealing here with a determinant synthesis but with an Idea of human society [This supersensible Idea] *does not* determine *what* I have to do. It regulates me, but without telling me *what* there is to be done."[116]

The result is again a feeling; no longer just a feeling of respect for the law that obligates, but a feeling that already borders on a feeling of the sublime: the felt contact with the supersensible Idea of totality (the Idea

114. J.-F. Lyotard and J.-L. Thébaud, *Just Gaming*, 71-72.
115. *Ibid.*, 47.
116. *Ibid.*, 85.

of human society) that smashes all our attempts at presenting it in empirical reality. That is why the feeling of the sublime is a compounded feeling of terror and delight. Such a feeling is born from the awareness of the immense task that befalls us: to act in such a way that one's decisions may help steer the course of human history. It is up to us to take steps that bring humanity closer to its final ethical vocation. Such a view is, again, in line with the Jewish idea of history. History in Judaism, Lyotard underlines, is "what is to be done. That is all that is important. It is a game of the history of the human community in as much as it is held by prescriptions and only by that."[117] In order to know what is to be done one must ponder the consequences of one's actions. This involves that one makes use of one's creative imagination in view of letting one's decisions be steered by a guiding finality: "To be just [in Judaism] is to venture to formulate a hypothesis on what is to be done, and that is where one gets back to this 'Idea'; one regulates oneself upon the imagining of effects, upon a sort of finality. It is the imagining of the effects of what one will decide that will guide the judgment."[118]

3. This brings us to the Jewish roots of Kant's feeling of the sublime. The feeling of the sublime is not an experience of the senses: it is a feeling of the 'soul' (*die Seele, das Gemüt*) at the moment during which the sensitive imagination experiences an urge to render present the absolute, and fails to produce this presentation. This collapse of the imagination has a deep repercussion on the soul. The soul feels overwhelmed by a sublime pain and joy that "bears witness to the fact that an 'excess' has 'touched' the mind [*das Gemüt*], more than it is able to handle."[119] In this description one hears an echo of the 'shock' of the alliance which Judaism feels it must continue to remember without any betrayal. Aesthetics or *aisthesis* cannot possibly lead to the sublime feeling, because the latter bears witness to the might of the unpresentable beyond the realm of the senses: "Nothing can lead from *aisthesis* to the hidden feeling, to the sublime pain and joy that are the inimitable deposit left by the unfelt shock of the alliance, unreachable by any artifact, even when it is of pious speech."[120] In this respect Lyotard likes to quote Kant's reference to the biblical prohibition of presenting JHWH: "Kant cites the passage 'Thou shalt not make unto Thee any graven image' ...

---

117. *Ibid.*, 53.
118. *Ibid.*, 65.
119. J.-F. Lyotard, *Heidegger and the "jews"*, 32.
120. *Ibid.*, 38.

(Exodus 20:4) as the most sublime in the Bible, in that it forbids any presentation of the absolute."[121] And, Kant adds: "This commandment alone can explain the enthusiasm that the Jewish people in their civilized era felt for their religion when they compared it with that of other peoples."[122]

It is this 'enthusiasm' that Lyotard perceives in avant-garde painters like Barnett Newman: "they dedicate themselves to allusions to the unpresentable through visible presentations."[123] Their disturbing non-figurative paintings aim at producing the feeling that there is something unpresentable, a feeling that for Kant has a bearing on one's ethical conduct. For this 'something unpresentable' there can be only an indirect allusion. In Kant this allusion takes on the form of a feeling of dispossession that entails both pain and delight and which testifies to the power of the infinite. Abstract or non-figurative painters try to evoke this dispossession in their often formless and chaotic works: "One cannot present the power of infinite might or absolute magnitude within space and time because they are pure Ideas. But one can at least allude to them, or 'evoke' them by means of what [Kant] baptizes a 'negative presentation'."[124] Negative presentation means: "One cannot present the absolute. But one can present that there is some absolute [...] The current of 'abstract' painting has its source, from 1912, in this requirement for indirect and all but ungraspable allusion to the invisible in the visible."[125]

At times Lyotard brings in a variation on the theme of the sublime. He does so in those passages in which he goes beyond Kant by giving a new content to 'totality' as a total release of heterogeneous perspectives. In this new understanding, the ethical obligation that befalls one is oriented towards the guiding Idea of a 'sacrosanct plurality'. This guiding Idea will call forth a strong feeling of commitment to an 'impossible' task (hence the resonances of terror and delight). The new device is: no perspective is allowed to assume a dominant position; the 'silenced party' must be honored by calling attention to a differend that must not be stifled. In this context Lyotard brings up a sublime feeling of pain that arises in the face of the silence to which the wronged party is reduced, and also a feeling of pleasure when one succeeds in tentatively finding a new idiom by which to make the wronged party heard. Feelings of anguish and

121. J.-F. Lyotard *The Postmodern Explained*, 11.
122. I. Kant, *Critique of Judgment*, Akademie edition, 274, trans. W. Pluhar (Indianapolis, IN: Hackett Publishing Company, 1987) 135.
123. J.-F. Lyotard, *The Postmodern Explained*, 11.
124. J.-F. Lyotard, *The Inhuman*, 85 [translation modified].
125. *Ibid.*, 126.

pain come to the fore in Lyotard's paradigmatic differend: the denial of the existence of gas chambers in Auschwitz.

It is in this perspective of the 'differend that must not be stifled' that one must place the anxious question 'Is it happening?' 'Is it happening that the existence of the gas chambers is no longer denied?' 'Is it happening that the linkage of phrases is no longer dominated by a pre-established logic of domination?' Or, to ask the same question in the parlance of Barnett Newman: 'Is it happening that the light of the creator dispels the menace of chaos?' And if the moment of relieve ('delight') occurs, 'will it last long enough to interrupt the terror of the threat?' Barnett Newman, as we have seen also assimilated elements from Burke's notion of the sublime with its heavier accent on time sequences and their sudden interruption. What is sublime for Burke "is the feeling that something will happen, despite everything, within this threatening void, that something will take 'place' and will announce that everything is not over,"[126] that an 'event' or 'occurrence' is still possible. For Lyotard, also Burke's version of the sublime leads us back to Jewish roots. Indeed, the 'now moment' (*'Is it happening?'*) that Barnett Newman evokes in his paintings brings the viewer into a dislocated time experience where one feels uprooted and dispossessed, open to the unexpected, commanded to 'listen'. "The expression 'it happens that...' is the formula of non-mastery of self over self. The event makes the self incapable of taking possession and control of what it is. It testifies that the self is essentially passible to a recurrent alterity."[127] The secret which allows one to say 'it happened that' is receptivity.

126. *Ibid.*, 84.
127. *Ibid.*, 59.

CHAPTER FIVE

UNIVERSALITY REVISITED

'Universality' is the benchmark of modernity, the benchmark against which to measure progress in civilization. Lyotard appears to seriously question this criterion. For him, the grand narratives of modernity, all of which use universal schemes – such as "the dialectics of Spirit, the hermeneutics of meaning, the emancipation of the rational or working subject, or the creation of wealth"[1] – turn out to be oppressive; they are disrespectful of the 'different': of deviating opinions and habits, of civilizations regarded as 'lagging behind' in their assimilation of Western rationality. This aversion to the grand narratives that confuse concept with reality prompts him to reject totalizing thinking. As he writes in *The Postmodern Explained*: "[Let us abandon] the nostalgia for the all and the one, for a reconciliation of the concept and the sensible, for a transparent and communicable experience. Beneath the general demand for relaxation and appeasement, we hear murmurings of desire to reinstitute terror and fulfill the phantasm of taking possession of reality. The answer is this: war on totality."[2]

Lyotard wagers, thus, a war on modernity's program of universality and totality. Yet, does this imply that he simply abandons the pure Idea of universality? For a philosopher so deeply rooted in Kant this would be rather astonishing. True, Lyotard seriously deviates from Kant with his appeal to radical heterogeneity; yet this deviation apparently does not invalidate his faithfulness to Kant's understanding of the sublime, of the unpresentability of the Ideas of reason, and of the primacy of the reflective judgment in search of its rules in order to judge singular facts. Could it not be the case, then, that Lyotard is, in fact, advocating a new type of universality, one that has left behind the exclusion mechanisms

1. J.-F. Lyotard, *The Postmodern Condition*, trans. G. Bennington and B. Marsuni (Minneapolis, MN: University of Minnesota Press, 1984) xxiii. Originally published as idem, *La condition postmoderne: Rapport sur le savoir* (Paris: Les Éditions de Minuit, 1979).

2. J.-F. Lyotard *The Postmodern Explained*, trans. D. Barry et al. (Minneapolis, MN and London: University of Minnesota Press, 1992) 15-16. Originally published as idem, *Le postmoderne expliqué aux enfants* (Paris: Galilée, 1988).

inherent in the organization of modern societies? We would thus be confronted with a new type of universality, which for lack of a better designation I would call, with Derrida, an 'impossible' universality, a universality to come,[3] one that cannot possibly be presented in empirical reality, for the simple reason that it is a (Kantian!) Idea of Reason. This is the line of thought I will develop in this chapter: the 'impossible' universality upheld by Lyotard, the coryphée of the postmodern condition.

The division of the chapter is as follows. In the first part I will examine the question as to where one has to place Lyotard: is his philosophy a rupture with modernity, or, on the contrary, a radicalization of modernity? This question already presupposes a description of modernity as an era that is constantly in search of its rules. Indeed, modernity can be characterized as an era in which constant change is ushered in. Traditional societies owe their static character to their tendency to reproduce local habits and organizational patterns from generation to generation in the same way. Identical re-enactment of the age-old, unchangeable customs was, in premodern times, the rule. Modernity, on the contrary, has developed the tools that enable people to break away from the selfsame reproduction of social life. For with the help of abstract time- and space-concepts, used in techno-science, it now becomes possible to dissolve the constraints of the traditional network of social relations, and to drastically reshape social reality in the direction of constant innovation. This phenomenon allows us to understand the philosopher's interest in a never-ending search for the rules, a search that will never be fully rewarded.

In the first section of part one I will deal with the topic 'invention of new rules'. More particularly, I will examine the extent to which Lyotard goes beyond Habermas' theory of communicative action. Habermas' aim is to arrive at a consensus about norms among various discussion partners, even when this consensus is only provisionally binding. For Lyotard, as we will see, Habermas' stress on consensus blocks, in fact, the impetus for novelty and innovation that is inherent in the modern way of life. The second section will study the phenomenon that Nietzsche evoked with the term 'nihilism'. Modernity is the epoch of the fall of metaphysics. This implies that modern people are living with the awareness of 'how little reality there is in reality'. Thus, they have, time and again, to decide what reality means for them in the domains of knowledge and commitment, on the basis of a consensus. It is here that one has to locate the process of consensus formation that Habermas pursues in his theory

---

3. See my analysis of Jacques Derrida which follows.

of communicative action. Lyotard reminds us that modern artists know about this 'withdrawal of the real': they react to it with nostalgic paintings. Non-figurative, postmodern artists, on the contrary, react to this situation by alluding – through inventive moves and gestures – to the 'real' that has withdrawn to its domain of unpresentability.

The third section will examine Lyotard's dictum that the postmodern mind is, in a sense, already part of modernity. The postmodern does not chronologically come after the modern. It is rather modernity 'in its infancy'. Infancy knows about dreaming, memory, question, invention; it is openness for astonishment, for the 'Is it happening?', for the event. That is why the 'postmodern' artist and writer live in a 'future anterior': they will only understand the rules 'after the fact'. Their works come too early and too late, just as in Judaism the commanding voice speaks too early – one is unprepared for the shock – and too late, because of a forgetfulness of 'infancy'.

The second part of the chapter will turn to Lyotard's critical analysis of the grand narratives, which as the term itself reveals, are narratives that have forgotten their 'infancy'. For that reason they must be regarded as degenerations of modernity: they arrogate to themselves the status of substitutes for the divine in that they attempt to 'provide reality' to the unpresentable, and so fulfill the phantasm of taking possession of reality. Yet any effort to provide reality to the unpresentable must proceed with deceitful practices. Lyotard points to the deliberate confusion of phrase regimes: the grand narratives jump from cognitive phrases to speculative phrases and carry out illicit passages from the particular to the universal. There are several examples of grand narratives: the Marxist narrative of emancipation from exploitation; the capitalist narrative of emancipation from poverty through development. In all of them the givens arising from events (ignorance, poverty) are forcibly cast into the self-moving logic of history whose speculative final end – the attainment of universal freedom – cannot be verified empirically. On the other hand, the postulated philosophical schema is so persuasive that all those who are reluctant to submit to it are logically put in the wrong: in its name, they must be eliminated. The universal promise of the grand narratives, thus, cannot be truly universal.

Moreover, grand narratives work with extrapolations. The 'we' that promulgated the *Declaration of the Rights of Man and of the Citizen* (1789), e.g., is an extrapolation of the 'we' of a particular nation, the citizens of the French Republic after the revolution. The 'we' of that Republic feels itself entitled to represent the whole of humanity. But this again is an illicit passage. For who is able to represent the whole of humanity, and an Idea of reason that is not to be found in empirical reality? The pretension of the promulgating 'we' is dangerous: those who refuse to accept their message will be reduced to second class citizens, and this on a world scale. Exclusion is the cynical outcome of the passage from the particular to the universal. The philosophically postulated universality is, finally, open to manipulation by strong and potent nations. From the pretense of speculative-philosophical universality, these nations derive the legitimization for what they regard as their noble civilizing mission. The encroachment of the national interests on the 'universal' leads to a world order of rulers and ruled.

The third part of the chapter will present three strands of thought which, taken together, constitute the blue print for a true universality without exclusion. The first section spells out that only an attitude of bearing witness to the unpresentable truly creates an openness to authentic universality. It, first, emphasizes that the more the Kantian Ideas are universal, the more they resist their presentation in empirical reality. This is a source of sublime feelings for those who testify that true universality is not lost. But, it also specifies that, in an era dominated by grand narratives, only a deep respect for a plurality of perspectives – indeed, for a release of heterogeneous purposes – bears witness to the unpresentable. The second section reflects on the Jewish methodology of the concrete, showing that this methodology cannot be dismissed as provincialism. Lyotard's 'jewish' penchant for the particular keeps alive the prospect of a 'cosmopolitanism without exclusions'. The just resolution of the particular case is the yardstick against which to measure true universality. The third section elaborates that true universality consists in justice done to a multiplicity. There must not only be a multiplicity of justices, but also a justice of multiplicity. This notion is not easy to grasp since it only shows up at the other side of a monopolistic universality that for so long has governed Western thought. The last section corroborates the working hypothesis of the whole chapter: Lyotard's deconstruction of the universality claims of the grand narratives paves the way for a true universality without exclusion.

I. RUPTURE WITH MODERNITY OR RADICALIZATION OF MODERNITY?

1. *Invention of the Rules: Beyond Habermas' Consensus Theory*

A first question to be asked is: what is Lyotard's postmodernism, and how does it relate to modernity? The best way to answer these questions is with a comparison to Jürgen Habermas and his view of modernity as an 'unfinished project'. About Habermas I have written elsewhere;[4] in what follows I rely primarily on an article by Emilia Steuerman, 'Habermas vs Lyotard, Modernity vs Postmodernity'.[5] Steuerman examines the commonalities between Habermas and Lyotard, as well as the precise point at which they depart from each other; she also touches the question as to where to position Lyotard: in a rupture with modernity or in a radicalization of modernity? Her basic thesis is that "the postmodern suspicion of the great narrative is *modernity's challenge* rather than a challenge to modernity,"[6] and that this concern is shared both by Habermas and Lyotard. In order to answer modernity's challenge – how to avoid the permanent dominance of a grand narrative? – both make a move toward language, but with different accents. Steuerman writes: "The move to language is for both Habermas and Lyotard a way of answering modernity's challenge. But whereas Habermas [argues] that communication is grounded on the possibility of giving reasons in language for the claims we raise in speech, Lyotard's approach to language as strategic game stresses the dimension of language which, although rule-governed, is not reducible to rational validation."[7] I will explain what this means.

For both Habermas and Lyotard, what is at stake today is the deconstruction of the big (transcendental) subject, of a totalizing thinking that presses the various domains of rationality into a superior, steering unity. This deconstruction we have seen at work in Lyotard's *Lessons on the Analytic of the Sublime*, where he set out to obliterate even the vestiges of a substantial subject – of the Cogito, of the organizing transcendental Ego. For him, the subject is always in the making; it is never complete. It 'comes into being' again and again under the impulse of feelings – of feelings that prompt one to think. A similar reaction to the grand unifying subject is to be found in Habermas. He is dissatisfied with a grand unifying subject, that (especially in Hegel's philosophy) functions as the grounding principle of rational conduct, and dissolves it into an (ever new) process of consensus formation among responsible discussion partners. It is incumbent on these discussion partners to decide what, in the given circumstances, is normative on the basis of a shared, rational argumentation.[8]

4. G. De Schrijver, "Wholeness in Society: A Critical Appraisal of Habermas' Theory of Communicative Action," *Tijdschrift voor de studie van de Verlichting en van het vrije denken* (Brussels) 12, 3-4 (1984) 377-404.

5. E. Steuerman, "Habermas vs Lyotard, Modernity vs Postmodernity," *Judging Lyotard*, ed. A. Benjamin (London and New York: Routledge, 1992) 99-118.

6. *Ibid.*, 111.

7. *Ibid.*, 113.

8. See J. Habermas, *Der philosophische Diskurs der Moderne* (Frankfurt am Main: Suhrkamp, 1985) 347-348.

Once this unifying transcendental Ego has been dissolved, a typical dimension of the modern era – the promotion of novelty – can prosper again: Modernity is "an age that sees itself as continuously breaking with the past. [It] can no longer rely on any 'given' criteria."[9] What is at stake is the continuous, ever repeated invention of criteria. This is what Habermas' program of *Communicative Action* is all about. His basic model is liberal democracy in its pure form. He, therefore, speaks of an ideal community of communication that always anticipates the possibility of a rational consensus, in ever changing circumstances. As far as Lyotard is concerned, he also recognizes that modernity is continuously breaking with the past, but he goes much further than Habermas when it comes to inventing criteria and norms. For him, the consensus model of liberal democracy which aims at reaching a well-founded agreement on norms, in fact, blocks this free invention because of the dominance of procedures with an epistemological undertone. Habermas, to be sure, differentiates between the gamut of speech acts – in science, ethics, and esthetics – but in each case the discussion partners will have to account for their correctness by advancing rational arguments. What matters is the validation or rational foundation of the differentiated claims: claims of truth (science), of rightness (ethics) and of authenticiy (aesthetics), rationality passing for the only tool that binds the discussion partners together. But, on the whole, this validation overemphasizes the cognitive aspect of language, with the exclusion of other dimensions. This is what Emilia Steuerman implies with the term 'rational validation': Habermas' consensus theory is "grounded on the possibility of giving reasons in language for the claims we raise in speech."[10]

Lyotard's approach is different. For him, language is a strategic game which is rule-governed, but not reducible to rational validation. Feelings and emotions play an important role in the strategic moves between addressor and addressee in a particular genre of discourse. These moves are not without rules, but the rules are often found or redefined in the very moment that a daring move takes place, a move which explodes the common expectation: "The moves in language are never predetermined but are continuously being made."[11] Lyotard, thus, radicalizes what runs as a thread through Habermas' program: modernity's search for criteria and norms. For him, the rules and norms of which one is in search necessarily escape the control of rational validation; they are the result of 'moves',

---

9. E. Steuerman, "Habermas vs Lyotard," 110.
10. *Ibid.*, 113.
11. *Ibid.*, 111.

that is: of agonistic fights over shaping and reinventing 'reality'. In his reflections on art, Lyotard made it clear that "modernity rather than post-modernity is the recognition of how little reality there is in reality (the *'peu de réalité'*)." In terms of language pragmatics this means: "What is to count as reality in a certain language game is fought over in language. Reality is constantly being invented and fought over in localized games. The challenge of modernity is the invention of rules. Postmodernity is the taking up of this challenge."[12]

2. *Lyotard's Response to Nihilism – the Awareness of the 'Little of Reality'*

In *The Postmodern Explained* Lyotard delves more deeply into the question as to how postmodernity relates to modernity. At this point I will turn to what Lyotard himself has to say about this subject. Right from the start he clarifies what he means when he speaks of the modern awareness of 'how little reality there is in reality'. He links this to the procedures used by scientists and managers of capital to 'validate' their performance. One of the rules of this validation is "that there is no reality unless it is confirmed by a consensus between partners on questions of knowledge and commitment."[13] But then he points to the 'desacralization' that took place in modernity, which emancipated itself from "the metaphysical, religious, political assurances the mind once believed it possessed."[14] As a result, modernity only acknowledges a 'metaphysics in its fall' (Adorno). This implies reality's retreat from erstwhile firm anchorages. Hence the 'little of reality' that is left in the empirical setting of our lives, a disenchantment that, on the other hand, became the cradle of modern science and capitalistic organization. He writes: "This retreat [from the old assurances] is indispensable to the birth of science and capitalism. There would be no physics had doubt not been cast on the Aristotelian theory of movement; no industry without the refutation of corporatism, mercantilism, and physiocracy. Modernity, whenever it appears, does not occur without a shattering of belief, without a discovery of *the lack of reality* [*'peu de réalité'*] in reality – a discovery linked to the invention of other realties."[15]

It is interesting to observe how Lyotard connects the recognition of performances in science and the capitalist economy to a consensus theory.

12. *Ibid.*, 112.
13. J.-F. Lyotard, *The Postmodern Explained*, 9.
14. *Ibid.*, 9.
15. *Ibid.*, 9.

In order for a scientist to have his/her scientific discovery recognized, s/he needs the common agreement of the scientific community. The same is true for laying claim to a legally protected patent in order to secure the revenues flowing from the discovery. In a world whose reality-sense is weakened because of its disengagement from metaphysical truths, no new reality can be created without this consensus. Habermas' project is also constructed on this premise. His aim and purpose was to start a commonly shared reflection on the values that should be upheld in the human 'life world', with the finality of resisting the colonization of that life world by technocratic rationality. Given the 'little of reality' even in this life world, however, he too felt obliged to resort to a consensus formation that creates 'reality', that of commonly agreed-upon values – realizing that such a consensus is only provisional; it only holds until the next revision is imperative. This ever-provisional character of the consensus begs the question as to whether alternative solutions exist to cope with the 'how little reality there is in reality'.

Lyotard admits that the awareness of what he calls the 'how little reality there is in reality' has been captured by Nietzsche with the term 'nihilism'. Yet prior to Nietzsche, this awareness of 'lack' or 'inadequacy' had been rendered thematic by Kant in his notion of the sublime. The sublime feeling honors the unpresentability of the Ideas of Reason and the role these Ideas play in uplifting the 'soul' (*das Gemüt*), an 'event' that momentarily interrupts the everyday experience of reality, and which in its eventfulness can never be reduced to this everyday experience. That is why the sublime results in a mixed feeling of pleasure and displeasure, occasioned by the felt inadequacy of the imagination to render present the unpresentable Idea. For Kant, the sublime hinges on the hiatus between the 'capacity to present' and the 'capacity to conceive'. The Idea of the infinite ('reality') can only be hinted at through a negative presentation, through the collapse of the creative imagination when confronted with the magnitude of the conceived Idea.

Lyotard's solution, thus, to the 'lack of reality' in our ordinary experiences lies in a resort to the aesthetic of the sublime. He detects traces of it in modern art and, more explicitly, in the avant-garde. He writes: "The aesthetic of the sublime is where modern art (including literature) finds its impetus, and where the logic of the avant-garde finds its axioms."[16] Modern art is characterized by a continuous questioning of the rules that govern images and narratives. In modern painting this leads to

---

16. *Ibid.*, 10.

a rapid succession of schools and styles. Cézanne challenges the space of the impressionists, Picasso and Braque challenge the objects in Cézanne's painting etc. The 'real' or the 'reality' they want to bring into focus always recedes from their attempts at presentation. As modern artists, the feeling they have is that: "[m]odernity unfolds in the retreat of the real and according to the sublime [incommensurable] relationship of the presentable with the conceivable."[17] Modern art finds it inspiration in the sublime, and as such prepares the way for the specific style of postmodern non-figurative art. The distinction between both is a question of accents. Modern art is fascinated by the retreat of the 'real' and develops a nostalgia for its presence, realizing that this presence escapes any pictorial presentation. The accent thus falls "on the inadequacy of the faculty of presentation."[18] The unpresentable is invoked as an absent content, while the form of the painting continues to offer material for pleasure and consolation, so to speak, in order to dulcify the pain occasioned by the absent content.

Confronted with the same absent content (the retreat of the real), postmodern artists also feel the inadequacy of the power of presentation, but place "the accent on the faculty to conceive." They are no longer concerned with "whether or not the human sensibility or imagination accords with what it conceives;" their whole focus is on the invention of "new rules of the game, whether pictorial, artistic or something else."[19] In their paintings there is no nostalgia for the impossible. Invention is what matters, not of forms or colors that might allude to the absent unpresentable, but of forms or colors that signal, in their effect on the addressees, the total unpresentability of the unpresentable. "The postmodern [...] refuses the consensus of taste permitting a common experience of nostalgia for the impossible, and inquires into new presentations – not to take pleasure in them, but to better produce the feeling that there is something unpresentable."[20] Here the aesthetic of the sublime reaches its apogee: the 'real' has really withdrawn into its domain of unpresentability. The artist is taken hostage by the majesty of that hidden power. His vocation is to testify to this unnamable majesty by engaging in a search for rules and codes that are not yet given, in order to give expression, through them, of one's dedication to the unpresentable.

17. *Ibid.*, 13.
18. *Ibid.*, 13.
19. *Ibid.*, 13.
20. *Ibid.*, 15.

3. *The Meaning of 'Always too Early/Always too Late': In Search of the Rules*

It is in this context that Lyotard introduces the intriguing definition of postmodernity in terms of the 'future anterior'. "The postmodern artist or writer [...] is not in principle governed by preestablished rules and cannot be judged according to a determinant judgment, by the application of given categories to this text or work. Such rules and categories are what the work or text is investigating. The artist and the writer therefore work without rules and in order to establish the rules for what *will have been made*. This is why the work and the text can take on the properties of an event; it is also why they would arrive too late for their author, or, what amounts to the same thing, why the work of making them would always begin too soon. *Post-modern* would be understanding according to the paradox of the future *(post)* anterior *(modo)*."[21] This intriguing definition requires some explanation and comment.

First, Lyotard makes it clear that the postmodern is not a historical period coming after modernity. In that sense Emilia Steuerman is correct when she says that "postmodernity is not 'the other' or the overcoming of modernity, but its radicalization."[22] It is the radicalization of modernity's engagement in an incessant search for the rules. The postmodern artist and writer do not work with preestablished rules; they feel themselves guided by intuitions and feelings, and by a reflection on the consequences of their day-to-day choices. If this adventure lasts long enough, these intuitions, feelings and reflections will perhaps crystallize into a rule, which will be understood then as the fruit of a search that had been going on for a long time, on the basis of specific feelings. In that sense the rule is the rule of *what will have been made*. This is the meaning of the famous 'future anterior'. What in the future will perhaps be understood as a rule, has already been 'unconsciously' at work long before its conscious formulation, after the fact. This principle is analogous to one in quantum physics. Here, as process philosophers explain, the possible causal chains that might have had a bearing on the choices or leaps of the quanta can only be traced in retrospect. It is only by looking at the processes of becoming 'backward in time' that one can spot the formation of a 'line of thought' or of a 'consistency of action' that was not predictable in advance, but which slowly crystallized in the very adventure of the search carried out without any clear-cut rule as a pre-given norm.

21. *Ibid.*, 15.
22. E. Steuerman, "Habermas vs Lyotard," 114.

This comparison with quantum physics is, of course, only an illustration of what Lyotard has in view; it does not explain the whole depth of his thinking.

Second, the fact that the postmodern 'future anterior' is the radicalization of modernity's search for rules also explains why, for Lyotard, certain modern painters and writers can already be called 'postmodern': "A work can become modern only if it is first postmodern. Thus understood, postmodernism is not modernism at its end, but in a nascent state, and this state is recurrent."[23] By this he means that the modern work of art, insofar as it meets the minimum conditions for being called an aesthetic of the sublime, must originate with a sudden awareness of the 'too early' and the 'too late'. The rules and norms the artists begin to perceive 'arrive too late for their authors' – these rules and norms were already 'unconsciously' working in them before coming to a clear articulation; whereas the work or the text in which they were engaged 'would always have begun to soon'. So, these artists were postmodern in their nascent state, before turning modern; it is only by giving in to the modern nostalgia for the impossible that they almost forgot this infancy. This makes us understand the meaning of the French title of the work (which is lost in the English translation): The Postmodern Explained to Children (*Le postmoderne expliqué aux enfants*), in which the French word '*enfants*' carries with it the resonance of 'infants', 'infancy', those who are not yet able to properly speak, who are still learning how to speak. In describing infancy, Lyotard writes: "Infancy [...] which knows about broken promises, bitter disappointments, failings, and abandonment, but which also knows about dreaming, memory, question, invention, obstinacy, listening to the heart, love, and real openness to narratives. Infancy is the state of the soul inhabited by something to which no answer is ever given. It is led in its undertakings by an arrogant fidelity to this unknown guest to which it feels itself hostage."[24] Infancy is openness for astonishment, for the 'Is it happening,?' for the event.

Third, the 'too early/too late' also figures in Lyotard's texts with the Jewish undercurrent I examined in the previous chapter. There the 'too early/too late' was used to describe the effect on the Jewish community of its encounter with the voice of the Unnamable. The Jews are taken

23. J.-F. Lyotard, *The Postmodern Explained*, 13.

24. J.-F. Lyotard, R. Harvey and M. Roberts, *Towards the Postmodern* (Atlanic Highlands, NY: Humanities Press, 1993) 148-149. For the importance of the theme 'infancy' in Lyotard's writings, see: Ch. Fynsk, "J.-F'.s Infancy," *Minima Memoria: In the Wake of J.-F. Lyotard*, ed. Cl. Nouvet et al. (Stanford, CA: Stanford University Press, 2007) 123-138.

hostage by a strange voice whose shock they are unable to locate but whose aftereffect continues to haunt and to command them. This voice dispossesses them by imposing an unsought alliance. They always live in "the too early – too late: a people unprepared for the revelation of the alliance, always too young for it; and as a result, too old, too paralyzed by preoccupations, idolatries, etc."[25] The too early/too late comes back in a description of the Jewish soul in terms of Freud's 'original repression' (*Urverdringung*) – evoked by the 'unconscious affect' (the 'Thing') –: We are always torn between a too early and a too late, "the too early of a first blow dealt to the [psychic] apparatus that it does not feel, and the too late of a second blow where something intolerable is felt."[26] In both cases "the soul is exceeded, dispossessed, passed beyond, excised through and by this something. This is the constitutive infirmity of the soul, its infancy and its misery."[27]

Lyotard is well aware that this Jewish background also surfaces in Kant's analysis of the sublime. Attentiveness to it brings us to an area which remained unexplored in our considerations as to how the post-modern relates to the modern. There we examined this relationship in the context of the European Enlightenment with its picture of the scientist who keeps on searching for the rules. Yet, a focus on the Jewish context shows that there is an alternative reading in this search: the Talmudic tradition of pondering the divine command 'be just' and 'remember'. Awareness of the Jewish tradition helps us to better understand the origins of the obligation to 'reflect on what one ought to do' – and to 'search for the rules'. The obligation comes from the shock of feeling oneself hostage to the Unnamed, to the 'unknown guest'. This shock urges one to embark on a nomadic journey of continuous search, far beyond the rules established by a consensus of human dialogue partners. To go beyond these consensual norms (alterable as they are) is part of the shock of the unsought alliance.

From a Jewish perspective, the notion 'unpresentable' also takes on a different meaning. From the perspective of the 'decline of metaphysics' it might look as if the total unpresentability of the 'absolute' would flow from the 'retreat of the real' from the contours of human existence, a phenomenon called 'nihilism' or (in the assessment of religion) 'secularization'. The mourning for 'metaphysics in its fall' takes place in the

---

25. J.-F. Lyotard, *Heidegger and "the jews"*, trans. D. Caroll and A. Michel (Minneapolis, MN: University of Minnesota Press, 1990) 37. Originally published as idem, *Heidegger et "les juifs"* (Paris: Galilée, 1988).

26. *Ibid.*, 20.

27. *Ibid.*, 17.

modern version of the sublime: in the nostalgia for the [lost] contact with the 'real' (the highest Being). Yet, when closely examining the post-modern accent in the aesthetic of the sublime, one discovers in it some typically Jewish traits. In this respect, Lyotard quotes Kant's reference to the biblical prohibition of presenting JHWH: "Kant cites the passage 'Thou shalt not make unto Thee any graven image' ... (Exodus 20:4) as the most sublime in the Bible in that it forbids any presentation of the absolute."[28] This concern is also to be found among the avant-gardes: "they dedicate themselves to allusions to the unpresentable through visible presentations."[29] The shock of this kind of unpresentability has a much deeper impact on the avant-gardes than the version of unpresentability that flows from the secularization of western culture – that is: from the retreat or withdrawal of the sacred from Western consciousness. In all likelihood, this is why artists and philosophers like Lyotard, who breathe the air of the secularized milieu, have no problems at all testifying to the unpresentable; rather, they feel urged to bear witness to it. This urge is not that surprising; it can be explained: Judaism has never developed a metaphysics. It does not, therefore, suffer from the decline of metaphysics; on the contrary it has always challenged metaphysical foundations: "The 'jews' are – within the 'spirit' of the Occident that is so preoccupied with foundational thinking – [the cultural element that] resists this spirit."[30] This resistance is born from their listening to a voice that takes possession of them.

II. THE QUESTIONABLE UNIVERSALIZATION INHERENT IN THE SPECULATIVE PHRASE

Lyotard's characterization of the postmodern in *The Postmodern Explained* ends with a warning. He says: "[...] It should be made clear that it is not up to us to provide reality, but to invent allusions to what is conceivable, but not presentable."[31] This is a warning against the construction of totalizing absolutes, as happened in the grand narratives of modernity. These totalizing absolutes have definitely forgotten their infancy; they arrogate to themselves the status of substitutes for the divine; they are attempts at giving the absolute a this-worldly shape and

---

28. J.-F. Lyotard, *The Postmodern Explained*, 11.
29. *Ibid.*, 11.
30. J.-F. Lyotard, *Heidegger and "the jews"*, 22.
31. J.-F. Lyotard, *The Postmodern Explained*, 15.

figure – in Lyotard's words: attempts at 'providing reality' to the unpresentable, and so "to fulfill the phantasm of taking possession of reality."[32] There are several examples of such totalizing absolutes: "The *Aufklärer* narrative of emancipation from ignorance and servitude through knowledge and egalitarianism [...], the Marxist narrative of emancipation from exploitation and alienation through the socialization of work; and the capitalist narrative of emancipation from poverty through technoindustrial development."[33] These grand narratives may clash with each other, but "in all of them, the givens arising from events are situated in the course of a history whose end, even if it remains beyond reach, is called universal freedom, the true fulfillment of all humanity."[34] In the face of these new absolutes, centered around the promise and attainment of '*universal* freedom' and the true fulfillment of *all humanity*, Lyotard exclaims: "War on totality. Let us attest to the unpresentable, let us activate the differends and save the honor of the name."[35]

Texts like these seem from the outset to foreclose the working hypothesis I introduced in the opening page of this chapter: 'Could it not be the case that Lyotard is, in fact, advocating a new type of universality, one that has left behind the exclusion mechanisms inherent in the organization of modern societies?' So, it is imperative to carefully analyze what the above texts precisely say. They warn against modern grand narratives. These modern narratives differ from premodern narratives (such as the story that narrates the origin of the behavioral codes of the Cashinahua Indians) in that they are 'cosmopolitical', as Kant would say. They use a universal language addressed to the whole of humanity. This universality is conceived by "speculative thought" and is "applied to human history"[36] as it should logically evolve. Lyotard reacts against the use and abuse of this speculative approach, and this for various reasons.

First, to posit that the speculative Idea of totality should also apply to the history of humanity – that is: should be verifiable in empirical reality – is in Kantian parlance a 'transcendental illusion'. A philosopher who thinks along these lines "confuses what can be presented as an object for a cognitive phrase and what can be presented as an object for a speculative and/or ethical phrase."[37] We have seen this confusion at work in

---

32. *Ibid.*, 16.
33. *Ibid.*, 25.
34. *Ibid.*, 25.
35. *Ibid.*, 16.
36. *Ibid.*, 34.
37. J.-F. Lyotard, "The Sign of History," *The Lyotard Reader*, ed. A. Benjamin (Oxford: Blackwell, 1989) 399.

Marx's usage of the term 'proletariat'. Marx coined this term to designate the rebellious workers in many European countries. In doing so he brought in a speculative universalization, he jumped to a universal statement with ostensive power: 'When you look for a new universal class, here it is: the proletariat whose suffering is universal'. This new universal class must of necessity assume the hegemonic position which the bourgeoisie has been holding till now. In order to guarantee this dominant position the communist party, in its Leninist organization, will see to it that the 'real existing proletariat' will live up to the ideal of the new universal class to which it had been promoted. The party apparently knows the rules and norms of this ideal class, and imposes them on the existing proletariat, if necessary by force and coercion. The story ends, as we know only too well, with repression and with concentration camps like Kolyma.

Reflecting on this history makes clear what Lyotard means when he writes: "[In the modern grand narratives] givens arising from events are situated in the course of a history whose end, even if it remains beyond reach, is called universal freedom, the true fulfillment of all humanity."[38] In the case of the proletariat the 'given' of rebellion of European factory workers is placed in the course of a history which is speculatively conceived of as moving toward the worldwide emancipation of the new universal class, the proletariat ('the true fulfillment of all humanity'). Once this given has been forced into the speculative logic of history, the victory of the proletariat can no longer be obstructed. This idea legitimates the organized proletariat, in the person of the party, to liquidate those who still think it can be stopped. The speculative logic of history demands their liquidation.

Second, the confusion of two language games – the speculative phrase and the cognitive phrase – does not happen automatically; it presupposes a 'we' that arrogates to itself the right to link phrases and phrase regimes so that they may serve the end and purpose this 'we' sets for itself. In modernity this aim takes on a universal scope, which in turn requires a speculative phrasing. Since a universal 'we' is not part of empirical reality, it ought to be postulated philosophically. Recourse to speculative thought (to the 'speculative phrase') becomes unavoidable, although this will create new problems. For who is authorized to prescribe in general, and to take the world community as its addressee? A case in point is, for Lyotard, the *Declaration of the Rights of Man and of the Citizen* (1789). Here an Assembly of the French nation arrogates to itself the

---

38. J.-F. Lyotard, *The Postmodern Explained*, 25.

right to issue a universal declaration of human rights. The enjoyment of civil rights in the new republic after the French Revolution was for the French citizens such a decisive step in the advance of civilization that a French Assembly deemed it necessary to solemnly declare that these rights are universal rights, to be shared by all humans on the globe.

But again two entities are lumped together that cannot be equated: the particular, historical French nation and the whole of humanity (which is a speculative Idea). In order to resolve the tension between the two disparate entities, the name of the Supreme Being is invoked: "By soliciting its presence and by imploring its recommendation, the Assembly authorizes itself not only as French but also as human."[39] The fact that a French Assembly invokes the Supreme Being, the source of (modern) 'rationality', clothes these French addressors with the dignity of 'being human', of 'being the universally human': they feel entitled to represent the whole of humanity. They exceed, in a sense, the soil of the French nation, to become 'universal'. Yet the impossible passage will create problems and ambiguities: "The revolution in politics that is the French Revolution comes from this impossible passage from one universe to another. Thereafter, it will be no longer be known whether the law thereby declared will be French or [universally] human, whether the war conducted in the name of rights is one of conquest or one of liberation, whether the violence exerted under the title of freedom is repressive or pedagogical (progressive), whether those nations which are not French ought to become French or to become human by endowing themselves with Constitutions that conform to the Declaration, be they anti-French."[40] A differend without solution was born.

The passage from the French nation to the 'universal' (the 'speculative phrase') provided the French nation with a legitimation for exporting its experience of civil rights to the whole world. The question had hardly been asked as to whether the other nations would be eager to welcome the new political organization that had been declared 'universal'. The post-revolutionary French simply regarded their achievement as the future of the world. Nations reluctant to adopt it were from the outset regarded as wrong and decried as backward. The universalizing logic of the 'speculative phrase' is of necessity a logic of conquest – and exclusion.

Third, for Lyotard, the universalism of the 'speculative phrase' can hardly preserve its purity, given its origin in the particular history of a nation. The universal Idea is open to manipulation by the particular – by

---

39. J.-F. Lyotard, *The Differend: Phrases in Dispute*, trans. G. Van Den Abbeele (Manchester: University of Manchester Press, 1988), Declaration of 1789, 5, p. 146. Originally published as idem, *Le Différend* (Paris: Minuit, 1983).

40. *Ibid.*, Declaration of 1789, 5, p. 147.

particular influential nations that appropriate the legitimating power of the 'universal' to consolidate their empires. A telling example is what happened with the Communist International. "In theory, its internationalism meant that the legitimacy of the class struggle derived not from local (popular or labor) traditions but from an Idea to be realized – the Idea of the worker emancipated from the proletarian condition."[41] From the time of the Franco-Prussian war of 1870-71, however, the International found itself in an impasse over the issue of Alsace-Loraine – should it be German or French territory? –, whereas in the First World War French Socialists voted for a national war budget in the country's struggle with the Germans. Local politics was apparently stronger than internationalism. Eventually Stalin dealt a death blow to the International with the dictum 'socialism in each country'. Communists world-wide had to align with the Soviet Union's definition of internationalism.

A similar encroachment of national interests on the 'universal' is manifested in the modern financial world. The motto that money must freely flow throughout the globe, not to be hampered in the least by national barriers or by protectionism, more often than not turns out to be pure rhetoric. The wealthy nations require other nations to comply with this rule, and to tolerate multinational banks and companies on their territory, but they do not feel themselves bound by the same rule: whenever deemed necessary, they have recourse to protective measures: "There is no trace of a cosmopolitan perspective to be found in the way the world market reconstituted itself after the Second World War, or in the intense economic and financial battle now being conducted for domination of the market by multinational banks and companies – with the support of national states."[42] Even the most liberal economic programs only open the prospect of combating poverty, but fail to achieve this goal: the gap between the rich and the poor keeps on widening. "The capitalist narrative of [universal] emancipation from poverty through technoindustrial development"[43] is less and less verifiable in empirical reality. The goals set by liberal economics can not be given any credit: "Obviously their game, far from reducing the inequalities in the world, exacerbates it, and far from breaking down barriers, exploits them for commercial and monetary speculations. The world market does not constitute universal history in the modern sense."[44]

Lyotard is just as critical of modern development programs. For him, they are only a new edition of the old dream of progress and emancipation

41. J.-F. Lyotard *The Postmodern Explained*, 35.
42. *Ibid.*, 35.
43. *Ibid.*, 25.
44. *Ibid.*, 36.

through techno-science. But instead of helping the developing nations grow, they plunge them deeper into misery. The programs are counter-productive, not because of a lack of implementation, but because they are carried out. Their failure lies, again, in the ideology that legitimates them. Development programs draw their legitimacy from the universal Idea of human emancipation, but this universal Idea is constantly being abused. In the name of this Idea wealthy nations fortify their leading position in the world, convinced that theirs is the universal mission to spear-head the break-through of a higher civilization. But in giving this new direction, they ruin the poor countries with their development programs: "The new illiteracy, the impoverishment of people in the South and the Third World, unemployment, the tyranny of opinion, and the prejudices then echoed in the media, the law that performance is the measure of the good – all this is due not to a lack of development, but to development itself. That is why we would no longer dream of calling it progress."[45]

In conclusion, the speculative phrase falls short of bringing about true universality, and this on three counts: (1) It postulates a philosophical universality that cannot be proven to exist in empirical reality but which it nonetheless seeks to render present in empirical reality; for that reason it ends up with eliminating those who do not fit in the postulated philosophical schema. Repression lurks around the corner. (2) The 'we' of the philosophical phrase is the extrapolation of the 'we' of a particular, historically existing nation. Consequently this historically existing nation feels itself entitled to represent the whole of humanity. This, in turn, leads to a policy of valuation whereby the 'qualified' (the 'enlightened' citizens) are pitted against the 'unqualified' (the backward people). Exclusion is the cynical outcome of the passage from the particular to the universal. (3) The philosophically postulated universality is, thus, open to manipulation by strong and potent nations. From the pretense of philosophical universality, these nations derive the legitimization for what they regard as their noble civilizing mission. The encroachment of the national interests of the world powers on the 'universal' leads to a world order of rulers and ruled. Division reigns where cooperation should be the rule.

In 'deconstructing' the questionable universalization of the grand narratives, Lyotard made use of language pragmatics: he called attention to the illicit transition from cognitive phrases to speculative phrases, as well as from a particular 'we' to a universal 'we'. This neat use of language pragmatics was put at the service of a philosophical program: Lyotard's target is in fact the Hegelian system with its subordination of facts to the

45. *Ibid.*, 95-96.

speculative genre: facts are only genuine facts to the extent they allow themselves to be incorporated into the speculative logic of history. This speculative logic is steered by an Idea of progress that *must* come true, that cannot be resisted. This invincible Idea of development imposes a coercion on the human race: whoever is not willing to follow, is blamed; whoever are not able to follow are pitied. Hegel's disdain, e.g., for the Africans, is notorious: "What we properly understand by Africa, is the Unhistorical, Undeveloped Spirit, still involved in the conditions of mere nature, and which had to be presented here only as on the threshold of the World's History."[46]

In order to 'undo' this stringent logic of history, Lyotard goes back to Kant. This step can be compared to Paul Ricœur's post-Hegelian return to Kant in his publications of the late 1960s. Here, Ricœur distances himself from the closed Hegelian system in order to develop a philosophy of expectancy and hope inspired by Kant. He says: "A philosophy of the limits which is at the same time a practical [but not a logical] exigency of totalization that is for me the element that philosophically corresponds to the Christian kerygma of hope."[47] Indeed, Kant presents a philosophy of the limits of human knowledge which is, at the same time, an orientation towards limitless Ideas of 'totality'. Lyotard appreciates both aspects, and the tension between them. When speaking about 'how little reality there is in reality', given the decline of metaphysics, he explicitly mentions that (prior to Nietzsche) Kant had rendered this 'lack' or 'inadequacy' thematic in his notion of the sublime. The sublime hinges on the hiatus between the 'capacity to present' and the 'capacity to conceive'. The Idea of the infinite ('reality') can only be hinted at through a negative presentation that bears witness to the unpresentable.

III. TOWARDS A UNIVERSALITY WITHOUT EXCLUSION

1. *Only an Attitude of Bearing Witness to the Unpresentable Creates an Openness towards True Universality*

In the previous section I examined what Lyotard understands by grand narratives and why they are doomed to lead to repression, exclusion, and inequality. The insight into these mechanisms makes us appreciate

46. G.W.F. Hegel, *The Philosophy of History*, trans. J. Sibree (New York: Dover Publications, 1956) 99.

47. P. Ricœur, "Freedom in the Light of Hope," in idem, *The Conflict of Interpretations: Essays in Hermeneutics* (Evanston, IL: Northwestern University Press, 1974) 416.

Lyotard's insistence on witnessing to the unpresentable, to the one who, so to speak, looks through these mechanisms: "It is not up to us to provide reality, but to invent allusions to what is conceivable, but not presentable."[48] It is not up to us to provide a reality corresponding to the universal Idea, as the grand narratives mistakenly did, but to invent allusions to the universal Idea (or to the Idea of the universal), in the knowledge that this Idea is conceivable – it must be thought, we cannot afford not to think it, on the penalty of turning barbaric – but that it resists all presentation. Only in this double qualification, conceivable but not presentable, can the Idea of universality – of a true universality – become productive for the betterment of humankind. The capacity to have Ideas is for Lyotard of paramount importance. This becomes evident in the fear he uttered that a civilization governed by techno-science might loose this capacity. He writes: "[Under the spell of techno-science] humans will thereby no longer feel even sorrow before the incommensurability between realities and Ideas, since they will loose their capacity to have Ideas."[49] Yet, it is only this capacity that allows them to ask *"Is it happening?"*[50]

Ideas, in the Kantian sense of the word, are universal. In his *Critique of Pure Reason* Kant defines what transcendental ideas are: they are 'Ideas of totality' which we are able (and urged) to think, but whose presence is not to be found in empirical reality. Yet, they are not superfluous or without importance for human knowledge. They function, in a fundamental and unnoticed way, as a canon for the understanding (*Verstand*) that is geared towards knowing objects, allowing the understanding to broaden and sharpen its view, not by making it know some supplementary object but by giving a direction to its cognition of objects. Through this canon the understanding "cognizes no more objects than it would cognize through its concepts, yet in this cognition it will be guided better and further."[51] For the scientists, this means that their research is guided by what one might call a horizon of 'totality of understanding' to which they gradually, though asymptotically, draw near with the results

48. J.-F. Lyotard *The Postmodern Explained*, 15.
49. J.-F. Lyotard, *The Differend*, no. 260, p. 181.
50. *Ibid.*, no. 263, p. 181.
51. "Although we have to say of the transcendental concepts of reason: *they are only Ideas*, we will by no reason regard them as superfluous or nugatory. For even if no object can be determined through them, they can still, in a fundamental and unnoticed way, serve the understanding as a canon for its extended and self-consistent use, through which it cognizes no more objects than it would cognize through its concepts, yet in this cognition it will be guided better and further." I. Kant, *Critique of Pure Reason*, B 386/A 329, trans. P. Guyer (Cambridge: Cambridge University Press, 1998) 403.

of their research. Transcendental Ideas are, thus, guiding principles, allowing us to place facts and objects of knowledge in a broader, encompassing perspective, realizing that this broader perspective is not part of, but surpasses, empirical reality.

Lyotard knows about the Kantian notion of the 'Idea of totality', but, as we have seen, he also dissociates himself from it: "The problem that faces us, even if it is put in terms of Idea and reflective judgment, is that it is no longer a matter, for us, of reflecting upon what is just or unjust against the horizon of a social totality, but, on the contrary, against the horizon of a multiplicity or of a diversity."[52] He does not give up the notion of the transcendental Idea or the reflective judgment that goes with it. The sole element he desperately wants to eliminate is the connotation of totality, which in Post-Hegelian thinking has been the source of so many social disasters. This means that if we are still guided by a universal Idea of justice, this Idea itself must be seen as unpresentable, first, and, second, it must be characterized by a pluralization. One ought not only to respect the incommensurability between Ideas and realities, but one ought also to take seriously the legitimate heterogeneity of 'phrase universes'. He writes: "[A step forward] would consist in the fact that it is not only the Idea of a single purpose which would be pointed to in our feeling [of the sublime], but already the Idea that this purpose consists in the formation and free exploration of Ideas in the plural, the Idea that this end is the beginning of the infinity of heterogeneous finalities."[53]

For Lyotard, this is not at all an invitation to stroll lightheartedly on the avenues of a fragmented world, nor is it a plea for allowing everybody to enjoy life in a libertarian fashion, freed from any center of control, as pluralism is often understood. No, Lyotard's message is that of a philosopher, an ethicist and a political thinker. In this quality he wants to breathe life again into the notion of universality. For him, universality is no longer patterned on the Newtonian model of science (which Kant to a great extent assimilated) with its universal laws of nature, all acting in a uniform and concerted way. Rather, the new universality that awakens in Lyotard the feeling of the sublime consists in the 'universal' release of incommensurable, heterogeneous perspectives and 'phrase universes' that previously had been forced into the straight jacket of absolute sameness and uniformity. Such a release forms the basis for the exploration

---

52. J.-F. Lyotard and J.-L. Thébaud, *Just Gaming*, trans. W. Godzich and S. Weber (Minneapolis, MN: The University of Minnesota Press, 1985) 87-88. Originally published as iidem, *Au Juste: Conversations* (Paris: Christian Bourgeois, 1979).

53. J.-F. Lyotard, "The Sign of History," 409.

of Ideas in the plural, for a myriad of initiatives where people engage in a 'thinking' that is still in search of the rules 'of what will have been made'. Apparently, however, this exploration of Ideas in the plural is often blocked by agencies that lay a claim on monopolies and so dictate the linking of phrases.

The Newtonian model of mono-causality has, unfortunately, not yet given way to the model of quantum physics that allows for an infinity of finalities: "In the matter of language the revolution of relativity and of quantum theory remains to be made."[54] The revolution of quantum theory consists in the insight that unexpected new moves ('quantum leaps') can take place and that no instruments of measurement used in classical physics will be able to account for them. In terms of language pragmatics this means that openings must be created between the usual linkage of sentences, so that novelty and *Ereignis* may occur. To require such an opening is to engage in a differend. The differend indicates that something would like to pass into language but that its place is already occupied (or is threatened to be occupied) by a quasi-automatic further rolling of linkages of phrases. As Lyotard himself writes: "No matter what its regimen, every phrase is in principle what is at stake in a differend between genres of discourse. The differend proceeds from the question, which accompanies any phrase, on how to link onto it. And this question proceeds from the nothingness that 'separates' one phrase from the 'following'. There are differends because, or like, there is *Ereignis*. But that is forgotten as much as possible: genres of discourses are modes of 'forgetting' the nothingness or of 'forgetting' the occurrence; they fill the void between phrases."[55]

When confronted with this forgetting the philosopher who wants to testify to the unpresentable – and to the fragile birth of an infinity of heterogeneous finalities – will come up with the anxious question: 'is it happening?' 'Is it happening that the break-through of a heterogeneous language (phrase universe) occurs?' 'Is is happening that the 'nothingness' – on which the new birth depends – acquires recognition?: "This nothingness is, nevertheless, what opens up the possibility of finalities proper to the genres. If the manner of linking were necessarily filled [in], there would not be several modes, no void would leave room for that causality exerted from afar, namely 'final causality' [in the plural]."[56] More simply phrased: if the nothingness between the last phrase and the next one is automatically filled in without giving other possible linkages a

54. J.-F. Lyotard, *The Differend*, no. 188, p. 137.
55. *Ibid.*, no. 188, pp. 137-138.
56. *Ibid.*, no. 188, pp. 137-138.

chance, the birth of new, heterogeneous finalities is aborted: no event (*Ereignis*) that appeals to the feeling of the sublime can take place. There is no 'room' for it.

Indeed, the question 'Is it happening?' directly relates to the sublime. For Lyotard, the quasi-automatic linkage of phrases has the disheartening effect of a menace and a distress. The avalanche of linkages that are determined in advance conjures up the specter of a civilization ruled by pure calculation and rational efficiency, with no concern for 'soul' or 'heart'. In the words of Burke, the feeling it generates is one of terror. The question then 'Is it happening that this terror stops?' brings relief, but not a total relief. The successful moment of 'nothingness' as the birth place of the insertion of heterogeneous phrases might in the next instant suddenly be ignored. Yet, even knowing about this fragility, the philosopher feels obliged to keep asking the question 'does it happen?' S/he is held hostage by this question, just as the Jews (or should one put the 'jews?') are held hostage by a voice that plunges them in the misery of a covenant they did not seek. Even if they tried to relegate this voice to the background, it will visit them anew and will demand that they listen from the depths of their very being.

2. *The Jewish Methodology of the Concrete*

Previously I mentioned in passing that Immanuel Kant largely assimilated the Newtonian model of science. This is true for his *Critique of Pure Reason* (science) but not for his *Critique of Practical Reason* (morals); nor for his notion of the sublime. Rather, in these instances one can identify a Jewish inspiration. In the *Critique of Practical Reason*, as we have seen, two Jewish elements come to the fore. First, the moral obligation is not deduced from a system of knowledge, but results from listening to a voice; second, the guiding principle 'act in such a way that the maxim of your will may serve as a principle of universal legislation' does not tell us in the concrete what we have to do, but only steers our ethical reflection in a particular direction, namely to act in such a way that through our action the Idea of a just society may become more tangible.

Lyotard specifically highlighted this Jewish inspiration in Kant, just as he himself borrowed insights from Levinas and the Talmudic tradition. This Jewish inspiration, however, raises some pertinent questions. Among Jewish scholars there is an ongoing discussion as to whether the thought of Judaism is to be regarded as particular or universal. To the extent that 'universal' is understood as a truth or a principle that is in force everywhere, in all places and all times, most Jewish scholars opt, instead, for the particularity of Judaism. This seems to be confirmed by Lyotard when he stressed that Judaism, unlike the Greek-Roman civilization, never developed a metaphysics. Judaism listens to a voice that commands particular actions (without revealing what these particular actions are in the concrete). The American Jewish author Abraham Heschel puts this as follows: "The most significant intellectual act is to decide what the most fundamental question is to live by. Ontology inquires: What is being? Epistemology inquires: What is thinking? The heart of man inquires: What is expected of me? Or in the language of the Bible: what is required of me?"[57]

When one asks what is so particular about Judaism, then the answer is: a focus on listening and on doing what the voice demands, a concrete ethical attitude, thus, one that does not start from a theoretical cognitive construct. Such a concrete ethical attitude can be seen as part of the genius of a people, yet it does not exclude an orientation towards the world community, on the contrary. It is, in the first place, a particular outlook on life, a 'methodology', if you like, rather than an option for a ghetto-like provincialism. Viewed as a methodology, this concrete Jewish ethical attitude is to be valued as part of the world cultural heritage: it can even be shared by persons who have developed a similar ethical sensitivity. This is what Lyotard meant when, in *Heidegger and "the jews"*, he referred to the 'jews' without a capital letter, suggesting that he himself had begun to practice the methodology of the concrete along with the emotional undertone that resonates with it. It is this methodology that finally prompted him to engage in a painstaking examination of the differend. His concern for universal justice urged him to lay his finger on particular injuries that are normally glossed over by modern consensus theories. Grasped by the unpresentable Idea of justice – and its universal demand –, and spurred on by his mixed feelings of terror and delight, he felt he had to call attention to the wrong done to the party that formally is put in the wrong because of its inability to prove its case in the idiom of the powers that be. Let us recall Lyotard's definition of the differend: "A case of differend between two parties takes place when the 'regulation' of the conflict that opposes them is done in the idiom of one of the parties while the wrong suffered by the other is not signified in that idiom."[58] The method is, again, 'listen' and 'remember': 'remember that you have been a stranger in Egypt'. Listen to the complaints of the voiceless, of those who are the helpless victims of a differend, precisely

57. A. Heschel, *Who is Man?* (Stanford, CA: Stanford University Press, 1965) 107.
58. J.-F. Lyotard, *The Differend*, no. 12, p. 9.

because they are not allowed to speak up for themselves in their particular, heterogeneous idiom.

Lyotard's commitment to justice obeys the 'jewish methodology of the concrete', to judge particular cases. Yet it would be too simplistic to belittle this methodology as particularistic, as if it were disconnected from any universal concern. Lyotard's 'jewish' penchant for the particular might seem to be provincial and focused on the local; yet it keeps alive the prospect of a 'cosmopolitanism without exclusions'. The just resolution of the particular case is taken as a yardstick against which to measure true universality. This means that whenever a 'minority' – an entity 'without a voice' – is being wronged and injured by the totalitarian claims of a monopolistic universalism, no true universality has been attainted. Or to put in differently: the Idea of true universality must, as an achievement, be deferred as long as differends exist, whereas, on the other hand, the existence of differends must be constantly uncovered in order to show that the modern tendency of concealing their existence through procedures of consensus formation is and remains the root cause of the silencing of such 'minorities'.

3. The Notion of True Universality: Justice of Multiplicity

I bring forward the notion of true universality in order to highlight the ethical character of Lyotard's dealing with differends. Without true universality no genuine ethics can prosper. It is important to underline this aspect, lest one would regard Lyotard solely as a proponent of deconstruction. Yet, this notion of 'true universality' is not easy to grasp, since it only shows up at the other side of monopolistic universalism. Its reality is only hinted at in the criticism of monopolistic universalism. This becomes evident in the words of David Carroll: "The *differend* has as its critical-political goal the uncovering of *differends* where they have been repressed or supposedly resolved; it argues for the necessity of listening to the idiom not given its day in court, to the silence imposed on the victims of oppression and injustice. It attacks all mechanisms of repression, all courts, institutions, systems of thought that perpetrate the injustice of universal judgment and thus do not recognize the silence imposed on their victims."[59] What Carroll calls 'universal judgment' is what I have termed monopolistic universalism. It is a judgment that relies on the universality of Western cognitive systems, whereas Lyotard has shown (with

---

59. D. Carroll, "Rephrasing the Political with Kant and Lyotard: From Aesthetics to Political Judgment," *Diacritics* 14, no. 3 (1984) 78.

Kant) that ethical obligation cannot be deduced from cognitive constructs. When looking at the procedures of courts, and how they make victims with their cognitive apparatus, Lyotard is saddened, a sadness which is a 'sublime' feeling that testifies to the 'unpresentable', to that which I am calling true universality. The feeling of the sublime signals that the Idea of true universality is not lost, even if its realization is absent from empirical reality.

The problem Lyotard is wrestling with is the Idea that humanity must form a whole that is truly diverse, not to be reduced to a totality, and nonetheless steered by an Idea of justice with a universal scope. In her article 'Lyotard and the problem of justice', Anne Barron puts this as follows: "Kant introduces as a regulator the Idea of a totality: humanity must form a whole. Postmodernism, however, must invoke an Idea of society as a non-totalizable universe of diverse language games, an Idea which has not already been made present: but which 'remains to be attained, it is ahead of us' (Lyotard and Thébaud, *Just Gaming*, 83). There must be 'not only a multiplicity of justices, but a justice of multiplicity' (*ibid.*, 100)."[60] In the wake of Kant, Lyotard remains fascinated by a regulative Idea 'that remains to be attained and is ahead of us' – the Idea of a universal justice; unlike Kant, however, he maintains that this universal justice, to be genuine, must be a justice of multiplicity: justice done to the multiple, the heterogeneous.

Can examples be given of this 'justice of multiplicity?' It is, unfortunately, much easier to quote counterexamples, which give much to ponder in that they call for a conversion from centralizing thinking. The most telling counterexample Lyotard himself offers is that of the *Shoah*, the extermination of the Jews, the unwanted 'others' in Western civilization. Authors, who set out to apply Lyotard's thinking to contemporary cases, currently come up with differends in which foreigners are silenced: immigrants who resist assimilation, indigenous people who are unable to prove the possession of their lands, undocumented residents and 'guest workers' who are harassed because they have no 'green card', races and especially dark-skinned people who are looked upon as being primitive and inferior. The moral of this analysis is that Western people must come to realize to what extent they have perpetrated 'universal' injustice by imposing their 'universal' concepts on heterogeneous cultures. Questionable in each case is the evidence that leads Westerners to take their particular 'we' for a universal 'we', a 'we' that is put forth as representing the whole of humanity. Through

60. A. Barron, "Lyotard and the Problem of Justice," *Judging Lyotard*, ed. A. Benjamin (London and New York: Routledge, 1992) 34.

the tricks of the trade, Westerners have come to present their norms as universally binding norms. It is time that we admit that such a trick is deceptive and unfair, that it blocks the break-through of a 'justice of multiplicity'.

In his article 'Pagans, Perverts, or Primitives' Bill Readings analyses, in the style of Lyotard, the conflict that Herzog evoked in his film 'Where the Green Ants Dream'. An Australian mining company and an Aboriginal tribe are locked in a conflict over land. The Aborigines complain that the blasting tests conducted by the mining company for mineral deposits disturb the dreaming of the green ants, and when this dream is disturbed 'the universe world' will come to an end. An important element of the story is that the Aborigines can only show some wooden objects carved with undecipherable markings to prove their 'property rights', but these objects do not make any sense to the Western mind: they cannot be regarded as legal documents. Still more interesting is the totally different understanding of the concept of 'land' the Aborigines have. For them, the land is the region to which everything, including the ants and themselves, 'belong'. The aboriginal people, and all created things, constitute, with the land, one organic whole. It is not just a territory 'on which' they live and which they treat merely as a 'natural resource'. Land is sacred, and the sacredness of the land is, in fact, the basis for the sacredness of the people themselves. This view sharply contrasts with the Western notion of land as a commodity, something that can be successively utilized for many purposes, mining included: the Western abstract notion of space that goes hand in hand with legal possession, which in turn puts the land in the service of industrialization and development.

The two irreconcilable notions serve to help Readings illustrate a clash of civilizations underneath the 'differend' they are experiencing about land. This clash, when taken seriously, rebuts the Western understanding that all cultures are, in essence, the same, and thus can be Westernized: "The suggestion that all cultures are fundamentally the same is the trade mark of the imperialism of modernity, which seeks to erase rootedness and difference, to reduce everyone to a blank abstract humanity, a bleached-out indifference."[61] It is against this 'indifference' that Lyotard reacted with his battle cry: "Let us activate the differends."[62] Justice cannot be done to the Aborigines by ignoring their particular understanding of the land, which is part of their culture. The only lesson Westerners

---

61. B. Readings, "Pagans, Perverts, or Primitives?," *Judging Lyotard*, ed. A. Benjamin (London and New York: Routledge, 1992) 184.
62. J.-F. Lyotard, *The Postmodern Explained*, 16.

can learn from this differend, is to ask themselves 'Who are we to speak?' For Readings, this is the crucial question because it has the power to 'de-center' us: "To ask, as I have done, 'Who are we to speak?' is not to entrench that 'we' more firmly but to displace it. To say that we speak radically heterogeneous language games (even to 'ourselves') is not a recipe for isolation or solipsism – but a thought of our interaction other-wise than in terms of consensus, unity and self-domination."[63]

4. *Sharpening our Working Hypothesis*

I began this chapter by asking: 'Could it not be the case that Lyotard is, in fact, advocating a new type of universality, one that has left behind the exclusion mechanisms inherent in the organization of modern soci-eties?' We are able now to answer this question and to sharpen what remained vague in the working hypothesis. The new type of universality that emerged from our analysis can be formulated now more positively: it is a universality without exclusion, one that pays respect to cultural differences, without trying to erase them. With Derrida one could call this a belief in the 'impossible' idea of a world-wide cosmopolitanism. What Lyotard advocates is a co-existence of heterogeneous perspectives in a creative tension, perspectives that interact with each other 'in terms other than consensus, unity and domination'.

The new type of universality not only pays attention to cultural dif-ferences; it also honors the rootedness of these cultures in local practices, in a particular geography, with a particular history of habits and beliefs. This particularity, again, calls into question the abstract universalism of modernity, a universalism one could see at work, e.g., in Marxist-gov-erned countries, which all tended to suffocate local practices. The same is analogously true for Western democracies. Lyotard, and, as we will see, Derrida, questions the rationale of the modern nation state. This state is founded on, and strives to enhance the identity of, a homogeneous, unified 'we'. The device by which this identity is to be attained is the con-stitution and the laws flowing from it. The republican 'we' is, again, an abstract universalizing concept: all citizens are supposed to share a com-mon rationality, which enables them to avoid dissent. This abstract 'we' triumphs over the possible differences in ways of life, religious convic-tions, and ethnic varieties. Tensions arising from these particularities are evidently obliterated ad intra. Ad extra a wall is being built to keep out

63. B. Readings, "Pagans, Perverts, or Primitives?," 184.

unwanted strangers, whereas those who are admitted are forced to assimilate. Multiculturalism and the coexistence, in a creative tension, of heterogeneous groups is from the outset discouraged. The possibility of a true universality is confused with the achievement of a sterile uniformity, and thus true universality is never allowed to blossom. For Lyotard, this imposition of uniformity can only result in an impoverishment of the multiplicity of vibrant human life forms to be found in diverse cultures and civilizations.

Lyotard's program of a new universality may sound like a utopia, and in a sense it is. On the other hand, he offers a device for change: the differend. He is convinced that the modern mentality of making arrangements, of engaging in negotiations, which is so typical of economics and world-politics at large, will of necessity create new differends: "The differend is reborn from the very resolutions of supposed litigations."[64] This means that those involved in the conflict who will be silenced because they are not able to defend their cause in the idiom of the hegemonic partner will be urged to look for a new idiom by which to phrase the wrong that has been done to them. This search for new idioms to cope with the pain caused by one's being silenced in the differend will be a step forwards in humankind's march towards true universality. Each time the philosopher observes such a small step, he cannot help but asking: 'Is it happening'? 'Could it be that the unpresentable Idea of the release of heterogeneities – the Idea of true universality – is drawing near in its quasi-impossible break-through'?

---

64. J.-F. Lyotard, *The Differend*, no. 263, p. 181.

PART TWO

JACQUES DERRIDA

Chapter Six

THE NIETZSCHEAN INFLUENCE

In 2005 Jean-Michel Salanskis published an article, 'The Philosophy of Jacques Derrida and the Specificity of Deconstruction Within the Philosophies of the Linguistic Turn', in which he drew an elucidating distinction between Derrida's inspiration and his lasting philosophical achievement. Salanskis terms this inspiration a *Stimmung*, a German word that is hard to translate. In *Stimmung* resonates the word *Stimme*: voice. So, *Stimmung* means to be attuned to a voice, to hear this voice as a sweet sound of music that accompanies one's ordinary doings – that brings one into a particular atmosphere: into a vivid awareness of inspiration: "The authors who appeal to Derrida from the viewpoint of what one might call his *Stimmung* are Nietzsche and Heidegger. But he affirms himself as the Derrida whom we know – with his proper terminology and concepts – in his critical interpretations of Husserl and Levinas (whose philosophies he twisted against themselves)."[1]

In this chapter I will dwell primarily on Derrida's *Stimmung* which indeed can be traced back to his early acquaintance with Nietzsche, from whose perspectivism he engaged in a critical dialogue with Heidegger. In his biography of Derrida (1930-2004), Jason Powell points out that from the period of his higher studies in Paris, Derrida – born in a Jewish family in the then French North African colony Algeria – began to read André Gide, Jean-Jacques Rousseau, and Friedrich Nietzsche in an attempt to free himself from his Judaic background. From as early as 1948, Derrida "would develop the kind of writing he dreamed of, following Rousseau and Nietzsche, transfiguring his identity and his religious intuitions, which had been refined against the disappointment of his familial Judaism."[2]

The first part of this chapter examines Nietzsche's vitalism and perspectivism. It brings to the fore Nietzsche's anti-Platonic stand in that Nietzsche, in opposition to Plato, gives primacy to the world of becom-

---

1. J.-M. Salanskis, "La Philosophie de Jacques Derrida et la spécificité de la déconstruction au sein des philosophies du *linguistic turn*," *Derrida: la déconstruction*, ed. Ch. Ramon (Paris: Presses universitaires de France, 2005) 42 [translation mine].

2. J. Powell, *Jacques Derrida: Biography* (London and New York: Continuum, 2006) 22.

ing and to the sensuous basis of our life-force. In tandem with his negation of the permanent status of the Platonic world of ideas, Nietzsche also
questions the permanence of the knowing subject. The only knowledge
we have at our disposal in a world of continuous change is that of successive, partial perspectives: Apollonian clarity is time and again scattered by the eruptive Dionysian rhythm of ever new creations through
ever new destructions. It is this Dionysian aspect that also surfaces in
Nietzsche's vitalism, in which the strong person affirms his/her 'will to
power' through the embrace of vital tensions in the person: it is only by
facing up to one's condition of degeneracy and sickness that one succeeds in growing ever stronger, so as to discover one's deep craving for
a vital affirmation of life.

The second part of the chapter deals with Derrida's appropriation of
Nietzsche. In a detailed analysis it will show that although Derrida is not
ignorant about Nietzsche's vitalism, he on the whole is more interested
in Nietzsche's perspectivism: the incessant dissemination of fragments of
knowledge after the collapse of the erstwhile unifying center. Indeed,
whenever Derrida brings up Dionysian elements in two of his studies on
Nietzsche – *Otobiographies* and *Spurs: Nietzsche's Styl*es – the polar
tensions that resonate with them are attenuated and channeled into a linguistic system that focuses on dissimulation and undecidability at the
expense of undisputable clarity. The tension between sickness and great
health, so central in Nietzsche's vital affirmation, is reduced to a wavering between extreme states of the mind, which as such give birth to a
variety of styles. A same reduction is carried out with respect to Nietzsche's exaltation of the eternally feminine, which in Derrida's reading
no longer functions as a source of artistic rapture, but as an exhortation
to suspend the decidable opposition between truth and untruth. This weakening of vitalism in Derrida's reception of Nietzsche is confirmed by
Michel Haar, who in his article 'The Play of Nietzsche in Derrida'
showed that the latter substituted Nietzsche 'play of physical cosmic
forces' with an endless play of shifting signifiers. In Haar's interpretation,
Nietzsche's 'play of the world' is not mere symbolism – the 'play of signifiers' as Derrida sees it – but a manifestation of the force of the physical reality of the world.

The third part of the chapter examines Derrida's radicalization of Heidegger's deconstruction of Western metaphysics. In order to understand
this radicalization one must know something about Derrida's assessment
of semiotics. In this field de Saussure drew the distinction between the
signified and the signifier: the written word (the signifier) stands for the
signified (the concept of the mind). Derrida rejects this subordination of

the signifier to the signified, because it smacks of what he refers to as 'logocentrism' and 'phonocentrism'. Instead, he opts for a linguistic system in which written words (signifiers) refer to other written words (signifiers), in such a way that an unrestrained substitutability of signifiers can take place – a boundless play of signifiers that are no longer anchored in (or restrained by!) some notion of an ideal 'origin' that could be appealed to as the final arbiter of their meaning. It is from this background that Derrida enters in conversation with Heidegger. He, first of all, appreciates Heidegger's attempt at rescuing the realm of Being from the tentacles of the purely calculating logic of Western techno-science, which Heidegger accomplishes by introducing the ontological difference between 'Being' and 'beings'. In this way the poetic aspect of our 'being in the world' has been saved. On the other hand, Derrida opines that Heidegger does not succeed in transcending the logocentrism he sought to overcome, in so far as his distinction between 'Being' and 'beings' is framed in the binary schema of a signified ('Being') to which all the signifiers (the 'beings') refer. So, Derrida pleas for the acceptance of a 'difference' that is older than Heidegger's ontological difference, namely a pulsating process of differing and differentiating – in his own technical language: a *différance* – that sets in motion the play of the incessant substitution of signifiers by other signifiers. To engage in such a play of signifiers is, for Derrida, his own way of enacting the Nietzschean ideal of eternal becoming, without any regret about the fact that the alleged origin is lost.

I. NIETZSCHE'S VITALISM AND PERSPECTIVISM

Friedrich Nietzsche (1844-1900) can be termed a 'vitalistic' thinker. In order to safeguard the realm of feelings, he rejects the imposition of patterns of rational conduct on a person's life. He is the first author to seriously question the *Weltanschauung* of modernity. Weary of modern clarity and planning, he wagers on a deep affirmation of life that hinges on one's ability to face up to the tensions between polar opposites, such as sickness and health, the genius and the insane. He is convinced that the endurance of these tensions results in a genuine growth in the discovery of one's life-force. One's life history is not only made up of ever changing perspectives; it is also basically governed by the clash of polar tensions. That is why, for him, the whole of existence can only be 'justified' in terms of art and aesthetics: the experience of the rare beauty that springs from the collision of opposites is the real motive for accepting life

as it is. Modern rationality tends to appease the polar opposites by channeling them into a dialectical process that prepares the triumph of a higher
synthesis. A case in point is the Hegelian system with its three logical
steps: thesis, antithesis, and synthesis. In this logical concatenation the
polar opposites are domesticated (*aufgehoben*) and brought under control.
Nietzsche, on the contrary, opts for allowing the polar tensions to be tensions, so that they may fuel one's life energy. Whereas the 'mediocre
individual' tends to remain aloof from tensions and pain, the 'strong individual' (*Übermensch*) embraces them and uses them to energize his/her
'will to power'. One's fascination for the world's 'beautiful appearance'
grows if one dares to interpret that world according to a rhythm of polar
tensions. This world view can be analyzed along two lines of thought
which, taken together, constitute Nietzsche's legacy: perspectivism and
vitalism.

1. *Perspectivism*

Decades before Whitehead elaborated his process-cosmology with its
focus on the principle of creativity and novelty, Nietzsche had recovered
the memory of the pre-Socratic philosopher Heraclitus and launched the
idea of a 'cosmos of ongoing becoming'. His aesthetic perception capitalizes on this new awareness: If the world is, indeed, caught up in eternal becoming, this has tremendous implications for a theory of knowledge. The knowing person ought to abandon his/her classical presumption
that knowledge consists in taking hold of the phenomena of the 'tran-
sient' world as if they had a 'solid', 'substantial' substratum. Such an
underlying solid substratum does simply not exist; it is a projection of the
human mind which, also for itself, upholds the illusion of substantiality.
In order, thus, to do justice to reality, knowledge should espouse the natural rhythm of 'emergent becoming'. This can only be achieved by a
knowledge that realizes its basically perspectival and provisional character. Any so-called solid gathering of knowledge must be released again
and again. The clear, Apollonian idea must allow itself to be shattered into
a diversity of ever changing perspectives. Nothing can be known twice
in the same manner, just as one cannot step twice into the same river, as
Heraclitus maintained in antiquity. What we have at our disposal are ever-
changing perspectives, for the simple reason that the Apollonian element
of clarity is created by a momentary eruption of the Dionysian dark
ground whose creative force acts through destruction. The Dionysian is
the overflowing principle that washes away any clear form that would

lay a claim on permanence. The result is the ever-renewed birth of partial perspectives.

Peter Pütz puts this as follows: "The Apollonian fixes unambiguous detail and captures a part of reality. The Dionysian strives after the unity of the *whole* and the Apollonian aspires to the clarity attainable from a particular *perspective*. Despite their antagonism, the two elements are necessarily related, for left to itself, the Dionysian principle represents a chaotic and permanent pursuit of excess. It thus requires the simplifying, ordering, and crystallizing function of the Apollonian principle. If, however, the latter were to isolate itself, it would become fossilized and barren. Hence its dependence on the rich, the whole, the overflowing principle. The totality of the world is constantly breaking down the one-sided, partial perspective, and restoring the claims of the Dionysian principle. This in its turn can only manifest itself in ever-renewed Apollonian forms of partial expression."[3]

Perspectivism captures Nietzsche's new experience of the world. Since ever-renewed becoming is the most fundamental reality, it is untruthful to argue that the cognitive faculty is able to give an objective, long-lasting picture of the 'sea of becoming'. Becoming cannot be grasped in stable categories. The Platonic world of ideas which erects unchangeable paradigms above the world is thus nothing but sheer illusion, or as Nietzsche himself terms it: a fable. For him, Western philosophy, from Antiquity onward, has privileged reason and conceptual thought at the expense of the senses. In this way that which the senses perceive – namely becoming, passing away and change – has been devalued and judged to be only unreliable impressions. Only the conceptual worlds, conceived in reason, are given the status of the 'true world'. Hence the actual world is judged to be lacking in Being, and is dismissed as impermanent, transitory, aleatory, as false – it consists in mere appearance. But, Nietzsche exclaims, "the 'apparent' world [*Die "scheinbare" Welt*] is the only one; the 'true' world is merely added by a lie."[4] It is "the prejudice of reason," which "forces us to posit unity, identity, permanence, substance, cause, thinghood, being," so that we are "ourselves somehow caught in error, compelled into error."[5] This 'true world', which has been constitutive of the philosophical discourse of the West, for more than two millennia

---

3. P. Pütz, "Nietzsche: Art and Intellectual Inquiry," *Nietzsche: Imagery and Thought*, ed. M. Pasley (London: Methuen, 1978) 19.

4. F. Nietzsche, "Twilight of the Idols," 2, *The Portable Nietzsche*, trans. W. Kaufmann (New York: The Viking Press, [1954] 1968) 480.

5. F. Nietzsche, "Twilight of the Idols," 5, *The Portable Nietzsche*, 482.

– "this entire apparatus of our intelligibility itself, Nietzsche attacks with his celebrated 'critique of pure fiction'."[6]

In his unrelenting critique of what he regards as pure fiction, Nietzsche goes so far as to dismantle the rational subject that invented this fiction. The positing of a stable cognitive faculty capable of extracting substantial forms from the data of the sense impressions proves highly artificial. Whatever the classical theories of knowledge from the time of Socrates may maintain, there is no such a thing as a fixed knowing subject. Just as the world continually changes, so too the knowing subject lacks permanence. Being merely a part of the ever-changing universe, the knowing subject is relentlessly forced to adopt new perspectives of perception, along with the ever new emergence of the world.

2. *Vitalism*

Nietzsche's perspectivism cannot be disconnected from his 'will to power' (*Wille zur Macht*) which thrives on the valuation of the clash of polar tensions. Nietzsche's world-view is basically vitalistic. He firmly believes that our perspectival interpretations will engage us in a play that both remains on the surface and espouses the rhythm of the abysmal 'ground' of untamed, composite beauty. Nietzsche understands that the phenomena of the world are to be appreciated both as 'surfaces' (ever changing appearances) and as 'manifestations' of the chaotic ground of Dionysian rapture. The appearance is like the sweet sound of music that reveals an underlying ocean of rhythmic, dissonant musicality. Nietzsche invites us to have the courage to embrace life, with its multifarious clashing antagonisms, as something that we can affirm so deeply that we eagerly desire for it to happen and to happen again as it happens (and is bound to happen again, and again). This theme of the 'eternal recurrence of the same' joins forces with that of the *Übermensch*. Indeed, if one succeeds in affirming the eternal recurrence of the same, one will succeed in bringing the horror of life into fusion with some overwhelming beauty. He sees it possible for human courage to welcome – again and again – the dark sides of existence, sides which precisely add to the greater richness of life and its joyful exultation. It is our vocation to live our lives as the 'great yea-sayers', even to pain and suffering.

Nietzsche's idea of the *Übermensch* crowns, in a sense, also his theory of perspectivism. The great 'artist' is expected to unite in his/her affirmation a clashing variety of opposite perspectives. One's intensity of

6. D. Allison, "Iconologies: Reading Simulations with Plato and Nietzsche," http://www.sunysb.edu/philosophy/research/allison_2.html.

'being in the world' grows to the extent that one is able to integrate as many perspectives as possible into one's life history. The endurance of tensions in the midst of an irreconcilable plurality of perspectives proves to be heroic and realistic.

II. DERRIDA'S APPROPRIATION OF NIETZSCHE

1. *Weakening of Nietzsche's Vitalism*

Derrida is not oblivious to Nietzsche's vitalism, although he is much more interested in his perspectivism. But, as already said, both aspects are intertwined. In *Otobiographies*, when commenting on Nietzsche's autobiographical statements which he sees marked by ambiguity, if not by a 'contradictory duplicity', he brings up what I have termed Nietzsche's vitalism (endurance of tensions). For Derrida, Nietzsche's 'confessions' are, in their straightforwardness, accompanied by a dark and mischievous shadow history, which renders all statements about his life "at once possible (Nietzsche said it all, more or less) and necessarily contradictory (he said the most mutually irreconcilable things, and he said that he said them)."[7] In other words, in Nietzsche's self-presentation we find a lot of dissimulations which can be attributed to the duplicity he ascribes to himself.

As Derrida sees it, these dissimulations are inevitable in a genuine autobiography. In order to substantiate his point, he borrows two antagonistic elements from the Freudian discourse: the principle of life, or the urge to speak about oneself, and the principle of death, or the neutral scientific approach to presenting a biography (ironically called a thanatography): "It is *painfully difficult* for life to become an object of science [...] with [its] legal status of scientificity."[8] This scientificity tends to dominate its object of research without due attention to the detail or respect for the unsaid, whereas the science of life must necessarily deal with 'delays' and 'residues', that is, with aspects that cannot be captured in a methodological approach. So, it is quite normal that Nietzsche defies the neutral scientific approach; he does so by calling attention to the various layers in his personality, a plurality that bears the mark of a play with masks. For Derrida, Nietzsche should be read "beginning with the scene from *Ecce Homo* where he puts his body and his name out front, even

---

7. J. Derrida, "Otobiographies," trans. A. Ronell in idem, *The Ear of the Other: Otobiography, Transference, Translation* (New York: Schocken Books, 1985) 15. Originally published as idem, *L'oreille de l'autre: Textes et débats* (Montréal: Sopra-vivere, 1982).
    8. *Ibid.*, 6.

though he advances behind masks or pseudonyms without proper names."[9] Masks or plural names belong to that "protection" and "surplus value in which one may still recognize the ruse of life,"[10] for life is dissimulation. The ruse of life must not be suffocated by objectively written biographies. The ruse of life and the masks protecting it are gestures that crave to carve a margin or an empty space within those scientific bodies. The margin has the potency to break up the centered reading of the scientific text, in order to allow the very eruptions of the life force to occupy the stage.

In his analysis of Nietzsche's autobiographical statements, Derrida also comments on the 'principle of contradiction' or 'the double truth' that is operative in Nietzsche's life. In the first chapter of *Ecce Homo*, 'Why I am so Wise', Nietzsche says that the good fortune of his existence lies in his fatality: "I am, to express it in the form of a riddle, already dead as my father, while as my mother I am still living and becoming old."[11] For Derrida this statement reveals the existence of a contraction in Nietzsche's life: the contradiction "between the principles of death and life, the end and the beginning, the high and the low, degeneracy and ascendancy, etcetera."[12] The father is the principle of death, whereas the mother (who survived the father) is the principle of life that tenaciously goes on. Nietzsche knew to combine both principles: "I know both, I am both,"[13] he wrote. Indeed, in his many days of sickness (migraine, vomiting) he knew from experience what the shadow of death meant, but he also used this experience as a springboard to appreciate the brightness of life. This did not just lead him to an ever repeated alternation of the experiences of 'degeneracy and ascendancy'; it enabled him to look at his life – and life as such – from a double perspective. His program thus became one of "looking from the perspective of the sick toward *healthier* concepts and values, and, conversely, looking again from the fullness and self-assurance of a *rich* life down into the secret work of the instinct of decadence." And he adds: "In this I have had the longest training, my truest experience; if in anything, I became master in *this*. Now I know how, have the know-how to *reverse perspectives:* the first reason why a revaluation of values is perhaps possible for me alone."[14]

9. *Ibid.*, 7.
10. *Ibid.*, 7.
11. F. Nietzsche, *On the Genealogy of Morals and Ecce Homo*, trans. R. Hollingdale and W. Kaufmann (New York: Random House, 1967) 222, cited in J. Derrida, "Otobiographies," 15.
12. J. Derrida, "Otobiographies," 15.
13. *Ibid.*, 17.
14. F. Nietzsche, *On the Genealogy of Morals and Ecce Homo*, 223. I took this text from Behler's comment on "Otobiographies," see: E. Behler, *Confrontations: Derrida/Heidegger/Nietzsche* (Stanford, CA: Stanford University Press, 1991) 128.

Derrida fails to properly delve into the question as to whether sickness (or *thanatos*) actually fuels the 'will to power' or the 'ruse of life'. In my presentation of Nietzsche I have emphasized this aspect. Derrida only underlines that "the contradiction of the 'double' [the *Doppelgänger*] goes beyond whatever declining negativity might accompany a dialectical opposition."[15] Derrida is apparently more interested in the fading of the oppositions under the pressure of the richness of the undecidability that flows from one's disillusionment with clear concepts. Undecidability creates a margin that allows previously censured voices to be heard. These voices can be extremely skeptical: 'Is what has been called sickness or degeneracy also in actual reality sickness and degeneracy?' 'Is what has been called health or ascendancy also in actual reality health and ascendancy?' This skeptical questioning, which enabled Nietzsche to reverse perspectives, is unmistakably present in his corpus. But, in addition to this skepticism, we also find the vital affirmation of the life force: the life force grows in intensity the more it feels exposed to powers of decline. The ruse and the cunning of life remain weak without the spur of pain. Derrida's interest in textual analysis and 'writing' results in his overlooking the point of Nietzsche's vital affirmation, his unreserved 'yes to life'. Moreover, it is this 'yes to life' that turns the latter into an intrepid explorer of skeptical questions.

Writing as early as *Spurs: Nietzsche's Styles* (1978), Derrida highlighted the theme of the mother – or better: of the woman – as the principle of life in Nietzschean thought. *Spurs*, a text which was Derrida's contribution to the July 1972 Colloquium at Cerisy-la-Salle 'Nietzsche Today?' (*'Nietzsche aujourd'hui?'*), is totally dedicated to the study of femininity, a symbol for the soul of the artist philosopher. One of the intriguing questions Derrida tackled in it is why Nietzsche, who ridiculed the nascent feminist emancipation, chose the metaphor 'woman' to suggest his own attitude to life, art, and truth. The answer to this question lies in Nietzsche's assessment of western philosophy. This philosophy defines truth in terms of the male's preference for clear concepts: "'I, Plato, I am the truth',"[16] whereas for Nietzsche this authoritarian notion of truth has lost its credibility: for him, truth is feminine: "that element in truth which refuses to allow itself to be captured is: the feminine."[17] Nietzsche's new idea of truth is one that seduces, teasingly veils its pudenda, dissimulates and is fond of 'playing on the surface' (instead

---

15. J. Derrida, "Otobiographies," 6.
16. J. Derrida, *Spurs: Nietzsche's Styles*, trans. B. Harlow (Chicago, IL and London: University of Chicago Press, 1979) 87. Originally published as idem, *Eperons: Les styles de Nietzsche* (Paris: Flammarion, 1978).
17. *Ibid.*, 51 [translation modified].

of being profound). This feminine approach to truth is identical with what
Nietzsche in the *Gay Science* said about the charm of life: "I mean to say
that the world is overfull of beautiful things but it is nevertheless poor,
very poor in beautiful things. But perhaps this is the most powerful charm
of life: it puts a golden-embroidered veil of lovely potentialities over
itself, promising, resisting, modest, mocking, sympathetic, seductive. Yes,
life is a woman!"[18]

Derrida quotes from and comments on a gamut of suggestive Niet-
zsche-texts. One of them is the 'parable' of a young man sitting at the
shore of a stormy ocean. Overwhelmed by the bustling noise of the
waves, he is suddenly transported to a dream world in which he feels at
home. In a vision he sees a large sailboat gliding along as silently as a
ghost. This elegant sailboat acts upon him as the symbol of happiness and
quietude of mind: a magic that must keep itself at a distance in order to
retain its seductive power. So too, is it with woman/truth; she exerts a
fascination from a distance. And Nietzsche adds: "The enchantment and
the most powerful effect of woman is, to use the language of philosophers, an effect at a distance; an *actio in distance*; there belongs thereto,
however, primarily and above all – *distance*."[19] Derrida emphasizes both
aspects: (a) truth appears enchanting only when perceived from a distance; and (b) 'the lovers of truth' must respect that distance; as soon as
they think they have 'captured' it, that they are in possession of it, it will
disappear: truth is not obtained through rape.

What strikes us in this description is the aesthetic component which is
at the root of Nietzsche's styles. In addition, parody and irony enter into
play: "Woman is but one name for that untruth of truth."[20] "There is no
such thing as the essence of woman because woman averts, she is averted
of herself."[21] "She does not *want* truth: what is truth for a woman! From
the very first nothing has been more alien, repugnant, inimical to woman
than truth – her great art is the lie: her supreme concern is appearance
(*Schein*) and beauty."[22] "Maxims and Arrows 16: Among women:
'Truth? Oh, you don't now truth. Is it not an attempt to assassinate all
our *pudeurs*?'"[23]

18. *Ibid.*, 52-53, citing F. Nietzsche, *The Gay Science*, trans. W. Kaufmann (New York:
Random House, 1974) 271-272.
19. J. Derrida, *Spurs: Nietzsche's Styles*, 47, citing from F. Nietzsche, *The Gay Science*.
20. J. Derrida, *Spurs: Nietzsche's Styles*, 51.
21. *Ibid.*, 51.
22. *Ibid.*, 67.
23. *Ibid.*, 83.

Derrida is particularly interested in Nietzsche's story of 'How the true world finally became a fable' recounted in 'The History of an Error' in *Twilight of the Idols*. This text had already caught the attention of Heidegger, who not only took seriously the reversal of the true world into the world of appearance, but also noted the way in which this reversal implied a "transformation of the very value of the hierarchy itself."[24] Yet, Heidegger was apparently not able to decipher Nietzsche's enigmatic saying: "With the true world we have also abolished the apparent one,"[25] because of his undue preoccupation with philosophical hermeneutics. He seemed not to have grasped Nietzsche's break with the philosophical system, the very order that Nietzsche wanted to "put out of order."[26] Moreover, at a crucial moment, Heidegger overlooked the importance of *femina vita* in Nietzsche. In his comments on 'The History of an Error', Heidegger skirted the saying: "truth: it becomes female,"[27] all the more reason for Derrida to read 'The History of an Error' through the lens of the women's role in the weakening of philosophical truth. Truth has a history; this history evolves in the direction of the feminization of truth.

For Plato, only the male conceptualization of the world of ideas is able to establish the truth. In the classical Greek world, women were thought to be debased: their lives were seen as enmeshed in the world of appearance; theirs is the domain of the probable, of the impressions. But then starts the metamorphosis of truth: truth becomes feminine. How is this 'turn' to be explained? The starting point is the distance of the world of ideas from every day life, as Plato suggested. This 'placing at a distance' instigates a cleavage between the philosopher and the truth. Truth begins to be seen as inaccessible. "Distance – woman – averts truth – the philosopher. She [the feminine distance] bestows the idea. And the idea withdraws, becomes transcendent, inaccessible, seductive. It beckons from afar. Its veils float in the distance. The dream of death [of the true world] begins. It is woman."[28] The 'lure from afar' turns into feminine seduction, an enchantment that speaks to the artist/philosopher. Yet, this new epoch in history is again blocked by yet another metamorphosis: having said "truth becomes female," Nietzsche adds a parenthesis: "truth becomes Christian."[29]

24. *Ibid.*, 81.
25. *Ibid.*, 81.
26. *Ibid.*, 83.
27. *Ibid.*, 85.
28. *Ibid.*, 89.
29. *Ibid.*, 89.

This parenthesis introduces a new plot: "The true world – unattainable for now, but promised for the sage, the pious, the virtuous man ('for the sinner who repents'),"[30] becomes part of the Christian message, with its focus on conversion. The female truth will, thus, have to feign its adaptation to Christianity. She does so by simulating castration. She plays at giving up wants and desires in order to be accepted by the phallocentric world of the dominant culture, which she seeks to conquer by deceit. She feigns to feel at home in the Christian world of extirpation ('if thy eye offends thee, pluck it out'), with the ultimate purpose, however, of seducing the master. She subtlety insinuates that every attempt at eradicating the passions will be in vain, and that it would be much better to put the senses in the service of the great affirmation of life. Derrida quotes Nietzsche: "The church fights passion with excision (*Ausschneiding*, severance, castration) in every sense: its practice, its 'cure' is *castratism*. It never asks 'How can one spiritualize, beautify, deify a craving? It has at all times laid the stress of discipline on extirpation (of sensuality, of pride, of the lust to rule, of avarice, of vengefulness). But attack on the roots of passion means an attack on the roots of life: the practice of the church is *hostile to life*."[31]

The final phase of 'The History of an Error' consists in a plea for honoring the vital forces of life. This last episode is Nietzsche's answer to the devaluation of the senses that paradoxically took place at the moment when the 'true world' disappeared. In describing this last segment, Derrida makes use of Nietzsche's Dionysian vocabulary. In this phase, he says, "woman is recognized and affirmed as an affirmative power, a dissimulatress, an artist, a dionysiac. And no longer is it man who affirms her, she affirms herself, in and of herself, in man."[32] This Dionysian vocabulary surfaces again in a passage in which Nietzsche attributes the plurality of his styles to his knowledge of the feminine: "I am capable of many kinds of style," because "I know women [or rather: the female]. This knowledge is part of my Dionysian patrimony. Who knows? Maybe I am the first psychologist of the eternally feminine?"[33]

Instead, however, of dwelling at length on the secret of this affirmative power, which we have termed Nietzsche's vitalism, Derrida resumes his usual agenda of textual criticism: the eternally feminine dissolves

---

30. *Ibid.*, 89.
31. *Ibid.*, 93, citing from F. Nietzsche, *Twilight of the Idols*, trans. W. Kaufmann.
32. J. Derrida, *Spurs: Nietzsche's Styles*, 97.
33. *Ibid.*, 107, citing from F. Nietzsche, *Ecce Homo* (*Why I Write Such Good Books?*), trans. A. Ludovici.

regimens of knowledge that erect firm oppositions between truth and untruth ("the question of the woman suspends the decidable opposition of true and non-true."[34]); from now onward these oppositional terms must be made fluid, kept in suspense. The eternally feminine disqualifies also these hermeneutics that look for the sense – the sole and true sense – of the text: "The hermeneutic project which postulates a true sense of the text is disqualified under this regime."[35] The eternally feminine even questions Heidegger's program of the search for the truth of Being: "Reading is freed from the horizon of the meaning or truth of being [a horizon which still presupposes a sole producer or giver of meaning], liberated from the values of the product's production or the present's presence. Whereupon the question of style is immediately unloosed as a question of writing."[36] For Derrida, the Dionysian affirmation of life is from the onset seen in its results: the setting free of the dissemination of writing. Its vital kernel is presupposed, not deemed worthy of further analysis.

2. *The Legacy of Nietzsche's Perspectivism*

Both in *Nietzsche's Otobiographies* and in *Spurs: Nietzsche's Styles*, Derrida touches upon Nietzsche's vitalism – his Dionysian patrimony – without exploring its depth. He seems rather to *refer* to Nietzsche's Dionysian rapture than to take part in it himself. The critical assessment I have made here is confirmed and corroborated by Michel Haar in his article 'The Play of Nietzsche in Derrida'.

In his article Haar, first of all, points out that Derrida hardly gives a critical reading of Nietzsche, as he does with other authors – e.g. Heidegger and Freud – whom he accuses of adhering to a centralizing system, called logocentrism. For Derrida, Nietzsche is the inaugurator of a new era in philosophy, an era in which he places himself: namely the post-logocentric era. He is given credit of inviolability: "Whereas Freud, Levinas, and especially Heidegger, are, to a greater or lesser degree, convicted in turn of belonging to metaphysics, Nietzsche alone is, if not absolutely spared, at least subtly accommodated."[37] And accommodation there is; in Derrida's appropriation of Nietzsche one will have to look in

34. J. Derrida, *Spurs: Nietzsche's Styles*, 107.
35. *Ibid.*, 107.
36. *Ibid.*, 107.
37. M. Haar, "The Play of Nietzsche in Derrida," *Derrida: A Critical Reader*, ed. D. Wood (Oxford: Blackwell, 1992) 53.

vain for traces, and here Haar is explicit, of "Nietzschean *physics* of forces" or "a philosophy of life and the cosmos."[38] For Derrida, Nietzsche is the prototype of a philosopher who, with his radicalization of "the concepts of *interpretation, perspective, evaluation, difference* [...] contributed a great deal to the liberation of the signifier from its dependence or derivation with respect to the logos and the related concept of truth or primary signified."[39]

Being aware of this accommodation, Haar seeks, in a second step, to demonstrate that – in addition to the destruction of logocentrism which Derrida so thoroughly appreciates – Nietzsche, has developed a notion of language, and also of writing, that is alien to Derrida's linguistic and grammatological considerations. Haar makes it clear that, for Nietzsche, every word, every concept is derived – not from an intralinguistic play of signifiers, as Derrida would have it – but from sensible impressions: "Nietzsche's constant position is that language ensues from a prelinguistic experience commanding it and to which it is unknowingly subordinated: this experience is in essence 'aesthetic' or rather 'artistic', it is a fictional process."[40] Language is the code one needs for social communication; but this code is only a weakened echo of the emotions and feelings that thrive on the artistic will to power and its clashing pulsations of pleasure and pain. Every concept results from a metaphor that has forgotten the original experience from which it emerged. Spoken and written language are an "impoverished, that is, formal and luminous Apollonian analogy of the nocturnal Dionysian depth where the original melody of pleasure and displeasure is played out."[41] For Nietzsche, language cannot properly 'translate' the fluctuations of one's affective intensity; it is only able to convey "an echo of what Nietzsche calls *the music of the heart*, or less lyrically, *the life of drives*."[42] As far as writing is concerned, it can, up to a certain point, reverse the entropy of language. Especially by using aphorism the writer can evoke the music of the heart that is lost in the common language of social communication.

With Nietzsche we are worlds apart from Derrida's notion of writing, which amounts to a an entirely intra-linguistic 'play'. For Derrida, "the

38. *Ibid.*, 53.
39. *Ibid.*, 53, citing J. Derrida, *Of Grammatology*, trans. G. Spivak (Baltimore, MD: Johns Hopkins University Press, 1974 [1976]) 19. Originally published as idem, *De la grammatologie* (Paris: Minuit, 1967).
40. M. Haar, "The Play of Nietzsche in Derrida," 55.
41. *Ibid.*, 56.
42. *Ibid.*, 57.

advent of writing is the advent of this play,"[43] a "systematic play of differences,"[44] a game that can be played out thanks to "an absence of origin and [an] absence of foundation."[45] Haar, however, makes it clear that Nietzsche's writing – his aphoristic style, combined with parody – is most definitely *not without* a foundation and an 'origin': "The world of Nietzsche is not a *groundless chess board*. The *chaos of forces*, another name for the cryptic phusis, sustains and maintains the human being [...]. Language, the play of language, namely the style, are for him *equivalents of a living body*."[46] The style of writing must be such that it gives the reader a kick ('makes the reader feel like dancing'). Therefore, the best style is obtained by 'imitating' the most vivid utterances of the spoken language. The intonation of the voice – which comes from the body and its musical *Stimmung* – must be heard in the cunning stylistic means the artist employs to express his/her affective intensity: "One must *desire to be cunning* with language, so as to thwart and disarticulate the codes. This voluntarist therapeutics can be a shock therapy."[47]

While Haar concedes that Derrida successfully appropriates Nietzsche's cunningness with language, he at the same time makes the case for the fact that Derrida appropriates Nietzsche only partially; that Derrida ignores, if not rejects, Nietzsche's basic world view: "The Nietzschean poetics of writing, poetics of diversion and of parody, of aphorism and fragment [...] this hyperconscious and hypercalculated politics of severity towards language Derrida makes his own, without at all assuming the Nietzschean motifs, without in the least adhering to Nietzsche's fundamental thesis."[48] Derrida refuses to accompany language towards the tone of the song that surfaces in the midst of the fragmentary: the hymn or dithyramb "that *sings* the yes, without worrying about the no."[49] Derrida is apparently not willing to join in this drunken song of excessive affirmation, for fear that it may frustrate any further neutral reflection on the meaning of language. Nietzsche's eruptive song of the 'yes to the earth' is no longer in control of its effects: "Its finality is no longer that of meaning, but the unconceptualizable melody of affects, a

---

43. *Ibid.*, 57, citing J. Derrida, *Of Grammatology*, 7.
44. M. Haar, "The Play of Nietzsche in Derrida," 57, citing J. Derrida, *Margins of Philosophy*, trans. A. Bass (Chicago, IL: University of Chicago Press, 1982) 11. Originally published as idem, *Marges de la philosophie* (Paris: Minuit, 1972).
45. M. Haar, "The Play of Nietzsche in Derrida," 57.
46. *Ibid.*, 57.
47. *Ibid.*, 59.
48. *Ibid.*, 59.
49. *Ibid.*, 59.

thought of the body, whose symbolization flows back infinitely to its unsayable 'physical' source."[50]

In a third step, Haar points to two hyper-Nietzschean strategies in Derrida: the reversal and displacement of the system, and a certain cruelty with regard to language. As far as the first is concerned, Derrida, in a Nietzschean fashion, reverses the given hierarchical order: the element that commanded, the *arche*, is no longer the true master of the game, whereas the elements that used to obey (the results) are set free from the constraint of the *arche*. Yet, Derrida also goes beyond Nietzsche in dissolving classical oppositions like inside and outside, active and passive, originary and derivative. He transposes these oppositions "toward their undecidable limits so as ultimately, if not to neutralize them, at least to thwart their functioning as a restoration of the proper and of essence."[51]

An example in case is the way in which Derrida dissolves Plato's opposition of speech and writing (of memory and the written text, as aid of memory, respectively). Plato privileges memory, and its unmediated contact with the presence of the 'idea', over writing that, in his eyes, is a pseudo-remedy against forgetting: *pharmakon* means both remedy and poison. For Plato, writing and written testimonies distance us from the direct, vivid contact with the idea; it may distort the clear vision of that direct contact; the *inside* must not be contaminated with a product from the *outside*: *inside* and *outside* are strict opposites. Derrida, however, shows that the *outside* – the realm of the contingent, of changing circumstances – is needed to make the *inside* – memory and recollection – work properly. Recollection in its pure form is illusory. Whoever wants to live by that illusion tends, like Plato, to keep contaminations that stem from the outside at bay. The celebration of purity is an option made by the philosophy of presence. Yet this philosophy forgets the contingent character of the world of writing – a contingency which obliges us to rely on temporalized, fragmented bits of memory, which as a whole cast doubt on the purity and the sameness of the allegedly once-and-for-all contemplated idea: "The outside [the fragmented] is already *within* the work of memory [the inside]. The evil slips in within the relation of memory to itself, in the general organization of the mnesic activity. Memory is finite by nature."[52] Derrida's interest in the dissolution of traditional philosophical opposites dates back to his study of Husserl's phenomenological approach to geometry: Is our knowledge of geometry the result of a direct

50. *Ibid.*, 59.
51. *Ibid.*, 61.
52. J. Derrida, *Dissemination*, trans. B. Johnson (Chicago, IL: The University of Chicago Press, 1981) 109. Originally published as idem, *La dissémination* (Paris, Seuil, 1972).

contact with the platonic idea, or does it also contain elements that are contingent in origin?

For Derrida, writing is an enterprise that takes place in the fragmentation of time. From this it follows that writing becomes an ever-repeated 'play in language'. The style Derrida adopts in this play is often cruel, more cruel than is the case with Nietzsche's stylistic strategies. Indeed, Derrida holds that the oppositions erected by autistic philosophies of presence "cannot be erased without some carnage of language."[53] Hence his summons: "Consume signs right down to their ashes, but first and more violently, with an irritated verve, dislocate verbal unity ... a ceremony both joyful, irreligious and cruel (let them dance with the pieces)."[54] For Haar, this 'carnage of language' is hyper-Nietzschean: it intimates a destruction without an organic link to the 'wild' eruption of new, exuberant creations. Rage prevails over Dionysian rapture. The ceremony alluded to is, at bottom, the "parade of a parody, so little Nietzschean."[55]

Haar's fourth step is a critical examination of Derrida's notion of 'play', more particularly of 'play of the world'. He points out that "the motif of play, everywhere at work in Derrida's text, has a very wide range, too much so." Haar cites the following examples: (a) Play is the equivalent of writing: "writing is a game within language."[56] (b) Play comes before the metaphysical oppositions, and is older than them: "the concept of *play* ... announces, on the eve of philosophy and beyond it, the unity of chance and necessity in calculations without end;"[57] it thwarts, in other words, all the obligatory oppositions. (c) Play is the mysterious source of metaphysical oppositions, before these oppositions even come into existence: Play is then "no longer simply a concept, but the possibility of conceptuality, of a conceptual system and process in general."[58] (d) Play is the erased origin of conceptual differences; it plays out the play of the absence of origin: "One could call *play* the absence of the transcendental signified as limitlessness of play."[59] (e) Play crosses and

53. M. Haar, "The Play of Nietzsche in Derrida," 62, citing J. Derrida, *Margins of Philosophy*, xv.

54. M. Haar, "The Play of Nietzsche in Derrida," 62, citing J. Derrida, *Ecarts* (Paris: Fayard,1973) 311.

55. M. Haar, "The Play of Nietzsche in Derrida," 63.

56. M. Haar, "The Play of Nietzsche in Derrida," 63, citing J. Derrida, *Of Grammatology*, 50.

57. M. Haar, "The Play of Nietzsche in Derrida," 63, citing J. Derrida, *Margins of Philosophy*, 7.

58. M. Haar, "The Play of Nietzsche in Derrida," 63, citing J. Derrida, *Margins of Philosophy*, 11.

59. M. Haar, "The Play of Nietzsche in Derrida," 63, citing J. Derrida, *Of Grammatology*, 50.

exceeds the 'question of being', since it is "not a play *within the world*;"[60] rather, especially in an epoch in which onto-theology vacillates and 'being' becomes dispersed one should conceive this play as 'play of the world': "it is ... *the play of the world* that must first be thought, before attempting to understand all the forms of play in the world."[61] From this wide range of meanings Haar selects the intriguing Derridean notion of 'play of the world' in order to find out the extent to which it might differ from Nietzsche's notion of the same concept. That the term 'play of the world' is Nietzschean needs hardly to be proven. One ought only to think of Nietzsche's saying: "The imperious play of the world mixes being and semblance."[62] Yet, the fact that Derrida uses the identical term should not be taken to imply that he understands it in the same way.

Haar makes it clear that Nietzsche's notion of play, 'play of the world' for that matter, thrives on an "over-abundance of plastic forces, a *surplus of force*, All play is the exercise, the deployment of a 'drive of play' (*Spieltrieb*) ... It is the 'incessant reawakened drive of play that 'calls new worlds to life' ... The world 'plays', it has play ... it pulsates, contracts and expands, propels and expels ... 'Fire always plays with fire' – the living fire, the burning, invisible harmony which incessantly unites creation and destruction in the world as a work of art that produces itself."[63] Haar crowns this characterization, woven together with Nietzschean sayings, with the following quote from Nietzsche: "Thus the eternally living fire plays, like the child and the artist; thus it builds and destroys, in all innocence ... and this play is the Aion playing with itself."[64] Nietzsche's play of the world is, basically "cosmological: It belongs to *Phusis*. Its attributes of 'eternity' and 'innocence' signify that it is not subject to a 'moral', that is, anthropological teleology."[65]

For Haar is it obvious: this cosmological, non-anthropological view of the 'play of the world' is foreign to Derrida. Also alien to Derrida is the

---

60. M. Haar, "The Play of Nietzsche in Derrida," 63, citing J. Derrida, *Of Grammatology*, 50.
61. M. Haar, "The Play of Nietzsche in Derrida," 63, citing J. Derrida, *Of Grammatology*, 50.
62. F. Nietzsche, *The Gay Science*, trans. W. Kaufmann (New York: Vintage, 1974), 'Songs of Prince Vogelfrei'.
63. M. Haar, "The Play of Nietzsche in Derrida," 64, citing from F. Nietzsche, *The Will to Power*, trans. W. Kaufmann (New York: Vintage, 1968) section 797, and *Kritische Studienausgabe*, T 1, 833.
64. M. Haar, "The Play of Nietzsche in Derrida," 59, citing F. Nietzsche, *Kritische Studienausgabe*, T 1, 833.
65. M. Haar, "The Play of Nietzsche in Derrida," 59.

Dionysian undertone of this cosmological vision. Derrida's understanding of 'play of the world' is, basically Apollonian. It is a play of signifiers and their successive substitutions, a symbolic play that has lost track of the 'eternally living fire', which *in the physical reality of the world*, in all innocence, plays the artistic play of building and destroying – as this occurs outside the house of language, which solely comprises the language games human beings make use of to live out and organize their lives. In short, Derrida's thinking is "Apollonian thinking, if there is such a thing, inscribed upon the forgetting of its anchor [in the materiality of the world], upon the forgetting of the black ink [drawn from the earth] of its graphic."[66] Nietzsche's 'play of the world', on the contrary, "is not [as in Derrida], symbolically, a play of signifiers, but a manifestation of force."[67]

At this juncture Haar asks himself the question as to whether Derrida would accept a force that is extra-linguistic. The answer is 'no'. True, Derrida broached the question of force in his discussion with structuralism, which for him is patterned on Husserl's phenomenology. He blamed structuralism for its obsession with form and structure at the expense of force, that is: of creativity and fantasy. In this context he said: "One would seek in vain a concept in phenomenology which would allow one to think intensity or force." He also gave the following definition of force: "Force is the other of language without which language would not be what it is."[68] For Haar, however, this definition does not at all involve a leap outside of language. In it, force is seen as the intralinguistic element – the 'other-of-itself' of language, in Hegelian parlance, that sets language in motion. Force inhabits the circulation of signifiers, a circulation that only starts moving once the transcendental signified, the all controlling center, has been obliterated.

Force, in other words, inhabits writing; it accounts for the *perpetuum mobile* of writing: "I define writing," Derrida says, "as the impossibility of a chain arresting itself on a signified that would not relaunch it, so as to have already put itself in the position of the signifying substitution."[69] It is thus the absent transcendental signified – the alleged origin in the philosophy of presence – which, in its slipping away, acts as the fictive *primum*

---

66. *Ibid.*, 65.
67. *Ibid.*, 64.
68. *Ibid.*, 65, citing J. Derrida, *Writing and Difference*, trans. A. Bass (Chicago, IL: University of Chicago Press, 1978) 27. Originally published as idem, *L'écriture et la différence* (Paris: Seuil, 1967).
69. M. Haar, "The Play of Nietzsche in Derrida," 66, citing J. Derrida, *Positions*, trans. A. Bass (London: Athlone, 1972) 82. Originally published as idem, *Positions* (Paris: Galilée, 1992).

movens of the chain. The force Derrida alludes to, in his discussion with structuralism, is nothing else than the free circulation of signifiers, made possible by the evaporation of the transcendental signified. The vanished transcendental signified has lost its authority for dictating the formation of fixed structures; that is why an incessant process of substitutions can begin proliferating. Haar puts is as follows: "No alien force, no force of phusis, of earth, of body, or *of Stimmung* drives or animates the play of writing. Yet, this play is not 'without why'. What sets the chain of signifiers in motion does not possess any 'cosmic' or 'phusical' character. On no account is it a play of the world. It is solely the logic of the 'supplement', namely an indefinite process of substitutions or permutations."[70] In order to corroborate this insight Haar examines Derrida's notion of place. He finds out that Derrida defines place in purely relational terms, and exclaims: "Is not the 'play of the world' reduced to a purely formal world-hood, to an abstract network of relations? ... [Yet], a world which would be constituted only by references would no longer have a *place* to be."[71]

Haar is a specialist in Heidegger. This explains his insistence on the earth as the dwelling place of human beings. As we have seen in our analysis of Lyotard, Heidegger dissolved the compact notion of time and replaced it with the fluidity of temporal sequences, as the index of finitude; he did, however not obliterate the human beings' insertion in the physical springing forth, which is the earth. At the same time Haar looks for attempts, in the late Derrida, to break away from the incessant but closed chain of substituting signifiers. A first break consists in attending to the unfathomable character of the gift, which already impressed Heidegger. A second break follows when Derrida becomes alert, in line with Levinas and Blanchot, to the imperative/affirmative 'come' addressed to me by the 'other'. A third break occurs in the Nietzschean emphasis, which the late Derrida will make his own, on 'affect' beyond calculation. I will come back to these breaks in due time.

III. RADICALIZATION OF HEIDEGGER'S DECONSTRUCTION OF WESTERN METAPHYSICS

1. *Heidegger and the Question of Being*

Heidegger is renowned for his attempts at deconstructing the onto-theological heritage in metaphysics. He showed that, in the course of

---

70. M. Haar, "The Play of Nietzsche in Derrida," 66.
71. *Ibid.*, 67.

Western philosophy, the divine or the absolute had come to be understood as the corner stone in the immense cathedral of all that is: the supreme reality in the chain of beings. Ever since Aristotle (or was it even Plato?), this supreme reality has been defined as self-knowledge. The supreme God is immediately present to the thoughts of His mind, just as these are present to Him in His act of contemplation.[72] Moreover, the deity's self-presence constitutes the foundation and the model of growth and development in the world. To reach self-transparency and to be fully present to one self becomes the ideal of philosophers and contemplative monks alike. Translucency towards their inner core and towards the ultimate ground of Being makes them participate in the deity's bliss of self-possession. This is the basic pattern handed down from antiquity: the 'mirror relationship' between the deity's self-possession and the human person's awakening to self-identity.

Modernity inherits this pattern, and gives it a twist. This becomes evident in Descartes. Having gone through a period of methodological doubt, he postulates the necessary existence of God. The deity's self-sameness and transparency must guarantee the permanence of the Ego, of the Ego which tells itself: *'cogito ergo sum'*. 'I think, therefore I am'. The act of thinking presupposes and discloses one's desire for self-possession. New in this approach is that God's veracity is, first of all, needed to reinforce the human mind's awareness of presence to itself. But that, second, God is also needed to warrant the successful conquests of the human mind, the organization of the world. That which is founded can never be without the assistance of the foundation. The mind's wager is never without the deity's backing.[73] The human intellect must project above itself a superstructure which provides greater evidence for the certainties one already has. In modernity, God, understood as the absolute, becomes the secret code for the unshakable trust in the triumphant unfolding of a logic that cannot be halted by the slightest remainders of doubt.

Heidegger felt compelled to deconstruct this age-long metaphysical tradition, because he foresaw that it would ultimately lead to the technologization of the world and of the human under the guidance of instrumental reason. He set out to retrieve what had been relegated to the background in the metaphysics of conquest: our rootedness in the earth with all the poetic wealth this involves. In order to accomplish this retrieval, he had to remove two major obstacles: the priority of permanence over

---

72. See Aristotle, *Metaphysics* XII, vii, 1072b 22-31.
73. For Heidegger's analysis of Descartes, see M. Heidegger, "Die Zeit des Weltbildes," in idem, *Holzwege* (Frankfurt: Klostermann, 1950 [1963]) 87-104.

becoming, and the tyranny of 'sameness'. In order to dissolve Descartes' fixed starting point in the Ego (or Kant's transcendental subject for that matter) one must take temporality seriously. This is what Heidegger's does with his definition of 'being' as 'being unto death' (*Sein zum Tode*). His analysis of 'being and time' (*Sein und Zeit*) places a heavy accent on our 'thrownness into the world', into a fluidity of time whose erring flow is more potent than our will to mastery. Temporality bereft of a clear teleology calls into question modernity's schemes of progress and development; it plunges one into an anxiety from which only a poetics of awe and wonder may offer salvation. From this background Heidegger reflects on the abyss that separates Being and beings (das *Sein und die Seienden*). Being (*Sein*) is an unfathomable reserve of gracious possibilities, erupting from an original chaos of indeterminacy. This is why these possibilities will always exceed the capacity of the entities (*die Seienden*) in the world, that is to say, of the human beings and the things at their disposal. The ontological difference between 'Being and beings' shatters modernity's illusion that our world is makeable; the abyss of Being (*Abgrund des Seins*) is beyond calculation.

This realization leads Heidegger to meditate on Being's mysterious presence, a presence that borders on the uncanny. Commenting on Parmenides' *estin gar einai*: 'Being is there, it is given' (in German: '*Es gibt das Sein*'), he makes it clear that the unfathomable 'Ground' of all that is, is not yet fully understood when one defines it as a factual 'being there'. Besides 'being there', the unfathomable Ground ('Being') also communicates itself. '*Es gibt das Sein*' also means: 'Being gives, donates itself' ('*Es gibt sich*'). This act of self-giving, however, is something quite unique. In 'giving itself', Being withdraws into a sacred anonymity (*Es*) at the very moment in which it opens up the space for the beings to receive their destiny: "Being enters the domain of destiny in that it [Being] gives itself. This means, in terms of destiny: Being gives and withholds itself in the same gesture."[74]

This leads, in a second step, to a reflection on the reciprocity of Being and receptive thought. Heidegger reads this reciprocity in another dictum of Parmenides: '*to gar auto noein esti kai einai*': '*The same is receptive thought and Being*' ('*Das Selbe nämlich ist Vernehmen so sowohl als auch Sein*'). He explains it as follows: "Receptive thought and Being pertain to the same, therefore they belong together."[75] This mutuality

---

74. M. Heidegger, *Über den Humanismus* (Frankfurt: Klostermann, 1949 [1968]) 23 [translation mine].

75. M. Heidegger, *Identität und Differenz* (Pfullingen: Neske, 1957) 14 [translation mine].

entails a whole program. Human beings can only live up to their destiny if they shield the truth of Being from profanation. Humans are the 'shepherds of Being' (*Hirt des Seins*).[76] In order to carry out this task they must acknowledge their place within the 'fourfold' (*das Geviert*). The scene upon which their shepherdship takes place is the plane formed by two intersecting polarities, the polarity of 'earth and sky' and the polarity of 'mortals and deities'. The Being to be shielded is neither God in the heavens nor the foundation of the earth. Rather Being shines forth through the entities in the *Geviert*, a shining forth that alternates between utmost simplicity and chaotic agitation (Heidegger's rendering of the Apollonian and the Dionysian).

When, in his *Letter on Humanism*, Heidegger raises the question 'What is Being?', he gives the following enigmatic answer: 'Beings is what it is: itself' (*Es ist Es selbst*).[77] It is 'itself' in its anonymous epiphany (*Lichtung*) and withdrawal; in this quality it is perhaps the farthest away, but the closest to our poetic, ecstatic capacity. While the anonymous abyss of Being manifests itself in a variety of beings (in forests, rocks, animals, works of art, tools and instruments, angels and gods), it is, at bottom, nearer to us than all these mediating entities. Indeed, through all these mediations Being remains what it is: 'itself', just as the sacredness of its *Ereignis* remains 'itself'. This makes us eventually understand the unity of Being and reflective thought. It is precisely because Being *manifests and withdraws* itself simultaneously that reflective thought feels encouraged to conceive of Being in terms of a variety of manifestations. Being's concealment in the sanctuary of 'itself' (*Es Selbst*) paradoxically renders possible the marvel of its diverse, changing appearance – registered by receptive thought.

Having given this succinct account of Heidegger's achievement, I now turn to Derrida's assessment of it. This assessment is both mild and severe. It is mild because Derrida acknowledges the enormous service Heidegger rendered to philosophy by introducing the ontological difference between 'Being and beings': in its free manifestation Being remains beyond our grasp. On the other hand, Derrida would like to show that Heidegger's ontological difference is still caught in the schemes of the very onto-theology he sought to demolish. Derrida employs linguistics as a tool in proving his claim. Therefore, I will first have to explain Derrida's engagement with semiotics, the study of linguistic signs.

76. M. Heidegger, *Über den Humanismus*, 19.
77. *Ibid.*, 19.

2. Derrida's Critical Assessment of Semiotics

Derrida opts for a linguistics that refuses to understand the signification of words by relating them to referents outside of the text: "There is nothing outside of the text."[78] In his reflections on language Derrida retrieves the nominalistic tradition (there are no concepts prior to the names), and Nietzsche's 'empiricism' with its emphasis on the fragmentary, evaluative reading of signs instead of deducing meaning form pre-given, Platonic ideas. This critical dialogue with Western philosophy distinguishes Derrida from the analytic philosophy en vogue in the UK and the USA. The dialogue comes to the fore in his dismissal of the Book, the symbol of religious doctrines and philosophies that attempt to present absolute truth. Derrida is convinced that our epoch is the epoch of the closure of the book. He therefore opts for writing, an activity freed from the dictates of a centralizing logic. Free writing must come to replace logocentrism.

For Derrida, writing must be released from the subordinate place it was given by Plato (and later also by Rousseau). Plato gave primacy to the voice in order to express one's vivid contact, in the depth of one's psyche, with the world of ideas, whereas he considered the written word at most as an aid of memory, a codified text in which this vivid contact no longer resonates: "While the phonetic signifier [speech] would remain in animate proximity, in the living contact of mneme or psyche, the graphic signifier [writing], which reproduces it or imitates it, goes one degree further away, falls outside of life; all life is distilled out of it and is put to sleep in the type of its double."[79] Logocentrism goes hand in hand with phonocentrism: the perception of absolute truth in the world of ideas entails an enhanced self-presence of the knowing person. Whoever engages in a logocentric philosophy engages also in a philosophy of presence which, in turn, has recourse to the voice in order to convey this vivid awareness (to oneself and to others).

Derrida takes his lead from Ferdinand de Saussure, the Swiss originator of the study of the sign, at least insofar as de Saussure stressed the non-referential aspect of the sign, that is: "the sign as having a meaning determined by its relations with other elements in a system rather than as a tie with an object in the world."[80] Within this system of relations de Saussure drew the distinction between 'signified' and 'signifier'. The written word (the signifier) stands for the signified (the concept in the mind); it provides

78. J. Derrida, *Of Grammatology*, 158.
79. J. Derrida, *Dissemination*, 110 [translation modified].
80. B. Stocker, "Editor's Introduction," *Jacques Derrida: Basic Writings*, ed. B. Stocker (London and New York: Routledge, 2007) 7.

the notions conceived in the mind with a sensible exteriorization: "The constitutive mark of any sign in general and of any linguistic sign in particular is its twofold character: every linguistic unit is bipartite and involves both aspects – one sensible and the other intelligible, or in other words, both the *signans*, 'signifier' (Saussure's *significant*) and the *signatum*, 'signified' (*signifié*). These two constituents of a linguistic sign (and of sign in general) necessarily suppose and require each other."[81] For Derrida, this view of language betrays its logo-phonocentric heritage. This heritage comes to the fore in the classical division between the intelligible (the signified) and the sensible (the signifier) which de Saussure incorporates in his semiotics. The division goes back to Plato's prioritizing of the true world of ideas over the realm of sense impressions. In the same way the signifier (the written word) is made subordinate to the signified (the idea).

Derrida contests this subordination of the signifier to the signified. He writes: "The written signifier is always technical and representative. It has no constitutive meaning. This derivation is the very origin of the notion of the 'signifier'. The notion of the sign always implies within itself the distinction between signifier and signified, even if, as Saussure argues, they are distinguished simply as the two faces of one and the same leaf. This notion remains therefore within the heritage of that logocentrism which is also a phonocentrism, absolute proximity of voice and being, of voice and the meaning of being, of voice and the ideality of meaning."[82] In order to put an end to this subordination of the signifier (the written word) to the signified (the ideal meaning) Derrida pleads for a semiotics in which signifiers refer to signifiers, in a – purely horizontal – unrestrained rhythm of substitutability, without any further interference of the ideality of meaning associated with the notion of 'the signified'.

In order to appreciate Derrida's new 'horizontal' program one must place it within the context of a malaise with the age-long tradition of onto-theological metaphysics, an age which is now coming to a close. Phonocentric semiotics are, at bottom, theological: "The sign and divinity have the same place and time of birth. The age of the sign is essentially theological."[83] The *phone* proclaims a message of eternal, unshakeable truth, to be transmitted and dispatched by the signifier in the same way as a postman delivers a letter. Hardly is there room left, in this transmission, for valuations and interpretations with a temporal, empirical origin (every new 'becoming' develops its own perspective on the whole).

81. J. Derrida, *Of Grammatology*, 13.
82. *Ibid.*, 11.
83. *Ibid.*, 14.

Nor is there an opportunity for replacing existing valuations and interpretations with novel ones, in response to the next wave of 'becoming' – the Nietzschean point of view, which Derrida makes his own, and summarizes with the catch phrase 'substitutability of signs'.

Yet, if one would take seriously these successive waves of temporal becoming, one would have to devalue the notion of an unchangeable truth associated with 'the signified'. It would dawn upon the practitioners of semiotics that their prioritization of the signified as the possessor of an unalterable truth (or fixed signification) that only waits to be put into words, without these words having the slightest ability to modify the signification, is part and parcel of the metaphysics of a bygone age. That which pretends to be an eternally valid 'signified' must be dethroned, deconstructed, and debunked as a hollow phrase, especially in an epoch in which people have begun to feel at home in the ever changing 'house of language'. So, would it not be better to venture to re-baptize the eternally valid 'signified' as something more modest, as a 'provisionally privileged *signifier*' (that is: a provisionally privileged carrier of signification, to be replaced with a next provisional carrier of signification etc.)? This, however, would be a hazardous enterprise. For after awhile one would have to admit that such a renaming does not drastically dislocate the prioritization of the transcendental 'signified'. Having been conceived within the parameters of the metaphysics of presence, the binary unit 'signified/signifier' proves to be hard to dissolve. Even if one's efforts meet with a certain success, the inherited metaphysical background will finally reappear. That is apparently why the prioritization of the alleged 'signified' can not be effaced without remainder. Even if effaced, it will still be legible as a trace.

The question is, indeed, why has there been for so long a privileged, eternally valid 'signified' in Western metaphysics? Derrida's answer reads as follows: "The privilege of the *phone* does not depend upon a choice that could have been avoided. It responds to a moment of *economy* (let us say of the 'life' of 'history' or of 'being as self-relationship)'. The system of 'hearing (understanding) oneself speak' through the phonetic substance – which *presents itself* as the non-exterior, nonmundane, therefore nonempirical or noncontingent signifier – has necessarily dominated the history of the world during an entire epoch, and has even produced the idea of the world, the idea of world-origin, that arises from the difference between the worldly and the non-worldly, the outside and the inside, ideality and nonideality, universal and nonuniversal, transcendental and empirical, etc."[84] In other words, the work of deconstruction is not

---

84. *Ibid.*, 7-8.

yet finished. One should not underestimate the persistence of the meta-physico-theological roots in the Western philosophical tradition. The start-ing point is always "a signified, able to 'take place' in its intelligibility, before its 'fall', before any expulsion into the exteriority of the sensible here below. As the face of pure intelligibility it [the signified] refers to an absolute logos to which it is immediately united."[85] Realizing this tenacious persistence, Derrida wonders whether this supremacy of 'pure intelligibility' and 'absolute logos' will ever be broken: "Perhaps it will never *end*. Its historical *closure* is, however, outlined."[86]

3. *Derrida's Criticism of Heidegger*

It is at this juncture that Derrida instigates his criticism of Heidegger. As previously noted, Derrida deeply admires Heidegger's goal of rescu-ing the realm of Being from the tentacles of the purely calculating logic of techno-science. Derrida is, however, dissatisfied with the manner in which Heidegger performed this rescue operation, by positing an onto-logical difference between Being and the factual beings in the world. For him, this ontological difference is still caught in the logocentrism Hei-degger sought to undermine. He writes: "Heideggerian thought would reinstate rather than destroy the instance of the logos and of the truth of being as '*primum signatum*': [as] 'the transcendental signified'."[87] Derrida corroborates this statement by critically examining the necessary condition whereby this ontological difference could be effective. This necessary con-dition involves a difference and a subordination. There must, first of all, be a real difference between the two entities ('Being' and the 'beings'). But there must also be a subordination. As the designations 'Being' and 'beings' suggest, beings owe their existence to Being. This implies the subordination of the beings to the realm of Being. Being functions as the 'first signified' (*primum signatum*); beings refer to Being as mere signi-fiers. In other words, the ontological difference, developed by Heidegger, presupposes the binary unit 'signified/signifier', and consequently rein-states the metaphysics of presence with its focus on logos and *phone*: "[Heidegger's] 'Thought obeying the Voice of Being' is the first and last resource of the sign, of the difference between *signans* and *signatum*. There has to be a transcendental signified for the difference between signifier and signified to be somewhere absolute and irreducible."[88]

85. *Ibid.*, 13.
86. *Ibid.*, 14.
87. *Ibid.*, 20.
88. *Ibid.*, 20.

For Derrida, phonocentrism – *'hearing (understanding) oneself speak* through the phonetic substance that *presents itself* as the signified' – is the clearest indication of logocentrism, of the metaphysics of presence. Therefore he calls attention to the role of the voice in Heidegger's philosophy: "It is not by chance that the thought of being, as the thought of this transcendental signified, is manifested above all in the voice: in a language of words *(mots)*.The voice is *heard* (understood) – that undoubtedly is what is called conscience – closest to the self as the absolute effacement of the signifier: pure auto-affection that necessarily has the form of time and which does not borrow from outside of itself, in the world or in 'reality', any accessory signifier, any substance of expression foreign to its own spontaneity."[89] In this concise text Derrida identifies the essence of phonocentrism. Whereas in logocentrism he detected an undue *subordination of the signifier* to the signified (the signifier has no other function than to transmit the eternal verity of the signified), he focuses, in his critique of phonocentrism, on the self, on the self-consciousness that hears and understands, in pure auto-affection, the logos of the transcendental signified. Just as the transcendental signified is autarkic – not even standing in need of a signifier – so too absolute self-consciousness can dispense of any accessory signifier: that is 'of any substance of expression foreign to its own spontaneity'. That is why this solipsistic spontaneity is called: 'the *absolute effacement of the signifier*'.

The phrase cited above – 'Thought obeying the Voice of Being' – is a citation from Heidegger. Derrida reads it in such a way as to show that Heidegger still moves within the philosophy of presence. Heidegger must be regarded as belonging to the history of the philosophy of presence, which is slowly coming to a close. When commenting in *Speech and Phenomena* on Husserl, whom he also suspects of adhering to a solipsistic philosophy of presence, of auto-affection, Derrida writes: "*The history of metaphysics therefore can be expressed as the unfolding of the structure or schema of an absolute will-to-hear-oneself-speak.*" And, in a prophetic gesture he continues: "This history is closed when this infinite absolute appears to itself as its own death. *A voice without différance, a voice without writing, is at once absolutely alive and absolutely dead.*"[90] For Derrida, the schema of an absolute will-to-hear-oneself-speak repels any mediation from outside, anything foreign to its

---

89. *Ibid.*, 20.
90. J. Derrida, *Speech and Phenomena*, trans. D. Allison (Evanston, IL: Northwestern University Press, 1973) 102. Originally published as idem, *La voix et le phénomène* (Paris: Presses universitaires de France, 1967).

own spontaneity. That is why it is absolutely alive – absolutely self-sufficient – but also absolutely dead – absolutely sterile. It is only if the input of what is foreign to one's own spontaneity is allowed to penetrate the 'inside' of the self so as to blow up its inherent self-sufficiency that a new epoch will see the light of day. The remedy is, indeed, the admission of *différance*, which in Derrida's parlance means: a 'differing' and a 'deferring': a differential that generates an incessant deferral of self-presence – the opposite thus of "the history of being as presence, as self-presence in absolute knowledge, as consciousness of self in the infinity of *parousia*."[91]

In his analysis of Heidegger in *Of Grammatology*, Derrida sets out to find some prefigurations, in Heidegger, of a break with the metaphysics of presence. He sees the inauguration of a break when, in the words of Emilio Brito,[92] Heidegger shifts from phenomenology to aphanology: from appearance to non-appearance, from speech to cessation of speech, from voice to a 'resonance of silence'. In his later writings, Heidegger continues to invoke a "voice of being" arising from the depths of hidden sources; but "the voice of the sources is not heard." From this Derrida concludes that what has taken place is "[a] rupture between the originary meaning of being and the word, between meaning and the voice, between 'the voice of being' and the *phone*, between 'the call of being', and articulated sound." And, he continues, "[this rupture] translates the ambiguity of the Heideggerian situation with respect to the metaphysics of presence and logocentrism. It [the rupture] is at once contained within [the metaphysics of presence] and transgresses it."[93]

The rupture announces itself from the moment Heidegger begins to speak of the concealment of Being: Being manifests *and* withdraws itself at once, in one and the same gesture. Derrida points out that "from the *Introduction to Metaphysics* onward, Heidegger renounces the project of, and the word, ontology," and stresses "[t]he necessary, originary, and irreducible dissimulation of the meaning of being, its occultation within the very blossoming forth of presence, that retreat without which there would be no history of being which was completely *history* and history of *being* [...] All this clearly indicates that fundamentally nothing escapes the movement of the signifier and that, in the last instance, the difference

---

91. *Ibid.*, 102.
92. Emilio Brito points out that Heidegger's thought oscillates between a phenomenological approach and an aphanology, ending up with a 'resonance of silence'. See E. Brito, *Heidegger et l'hymne du Sacré*, BETL, 141 (Leuven: Leuven University Press, 1999) 732.
93. J. Derrida, *Of Grammatology*, 22.

between signified and signifier is *nothing*."[94] If in the metaphysics of presence the auto-affection of the self entailed the effacement of the signifier (expressions foreign to the self's spontaneity being simply ignored), this effacement is now reversed: the irruption of occultation in the blossoming forth of presence leads to the effacement of the solipsism of the signified. In this sense the difference between signified and signifier evaporates. A beginning of writing is inaugurated: the timid birth of 'différance' – of an incessant deferral of self-presence.

It is, indeed, a timid birth. Derrida remarks that Heidegger's "proposition of transgression [is] not yet integrated into a careful discourse [and therefore] runs the risk of formulating regression itself."[95] He makes this clear by pointing to the ambivalence that persisted even when Heidegger, in *Zur Seinsfrage*, graphically crossed out the word Being, suggesting that his use of the term was to be understood in contradistinction from the usage employed in lexica and grammars, and specifically in the linguistic articulation of Western philosophy. In asking the 'question of being', Derrida goes on, Heidegger seemed to realize that the language that gave a fixed meaning to Being has an inescapable historical origin: "Western metaphysics, as the limitation of the sense of being within the field of presence, is produced as the domination of a linguistic form."[96] It is precisely because Heidegger wished to call this domination into question that he graphically crossed out the word 'Being' whenever he used it in his text. While he appreciates this gesture, Derrida ventures that Heidegger did not go far enough. The reason is obvious: under the mark of deletion the old dominating language continues to be visible and to exert its fascination. Derrida writes: "That deletion is the final writing of an epoch. Under its strokes the presence of a transcendental signified is effaced, while still remaining legible. Is effaced while still remaining, is destroyed while making visible the very idea of the sign."[97]

Derrida himself seeks to go further and to articulate the horizon that has been opened by the Heideggerian path. In this articulation he clearly states that the transcendental, trans-epochal signified must be reduced to what, in fact, it is: a signifying trace. Derrida justifies this reductive transformation. He points out that the 'signified body' is itself derivative with regard to a difference that is more radical than Heidegger's ontological difference, namely the interruptive pulsation of 'differing/deferring' that

---

94. *Ibid.*, 22-23.
95. *Ibid.*, 23.
96. *Ibid.*, 23.
97. *Ibid.*, 23.

resonates in the notion 'différance'. He writes: "[T]he sense of being is not a transcendental or trans-epochal signified (even if it was always dissimulated within the epoch) but already, in a truly *unheard of* sense, a determined signifying trace [...] The ontico-ontological difference and its ground (*Grund*) are not absolutely originary. *Différance* by itself would be more 'originary'."[98] The statement that différance's production of interrupting waves of differing/deferring' – the puncturing and suspension of presence – is more 'originary' does, however, by no means imply that one should call it 'origin' or 'ground', since these fixed terms belong to the metaphysics of presence. The notions 'origin' and 'ground "belong essentially to the history of onto-theology, to the system functioning as the effacing of difference."[99]

4. *Back to the Nietzschean Influence*

At times Derrida evokes what he understands by 'différance', the production of differing/deferring', with Nietzschean metaphors of play. He contrasts these metaphors with another type of play that is to be found in Heidegger (and also, via Husserl, in structuralist analysis). He defines play as the disruption of presence. Yet this disruption can lead to two opposed interpretations of play. "The one seeks to decipher, dreams of deciphering a truth or an origin which escapes play and the order of the sign, and which lives the necessity of interpretation as an exile. The other, which is no longer turned toward the origin, affirms play and tries to pass beyond man and humanism, the name of man being the name of that being who, throughout the history of metaphysics or of ontotheology – in other words, throughout his entire history – has dreamt of full presence, the reassuring foundation, the origin and the end of play."[100] Heidegger and Lévi-Strauss seem to experience the necessity of having to interpret the meaning of life (the sense of being) as an exile; they are haunted by the lost origin, in the awareness that it never can be recovered. To their notion of play is a "saddened, *negative*, nostalgic, guilty side"[101] – a nostalgia for a unity thought to have been experienced in some originary past, but since broken.

Derrida himself opts for the Nietzschean affirmation, for a play that feels no longer guilty when gleefully dismantling august cathedrals of humanity's age-long dream of full presence – dismantling them as if they

---

98. *Ibid.*, 23.
99. *Ibid.*, 23.
100. J. Derrida, *Writing and Difference*, 292.
101. *Ibid.*, 292.

were sandcastles to be washed away by ever new waves of becoming. In this context Derrida refers to Nietzsche's affirmation of 'the play of the world', without, as I have argued earlier, espousing the latter's vitalistic, Dionysian undertone (the clash of opposites fueling one's life force so as to give birth to ever new creations, through destruction). Derrida's critical dealing with semiotics takes the edge off of this vitalistic undertone. The play of new creations through destructions is transposed to the Apollonian key of a substitutability of signifiers with other signifiers. Freed from any uniting center (the 'signified'), bits of writing add themselves to other bits of writing, indirectly replacing them and substituting their hints with new, unexpected hints. The house of language is open ended. The avalanche of interpretations never stops. Its play of changing perspectives lacks any clear finality steered by a metaphysics of presence. Every new interpretation, necessitated by a new wave of becoming, turns out to be a seminal adventure of a trace – a dissemination – that joyfully affirms its liberated drifting away from the center.

Derrida encapsulates his appropriation of the Nietzschean affirmation as follows: "The joyous affirmation of the play of the world and of the innocence of becoming. The affirmation of a world of signs without fault, without truth, and without origin which is offered to an active interpretation. *This affirmation then determines the noncenter otherwise than as loss of the center*. And it plays without security. For there is a sure play: that which is limited to the *substitution of given, existing, present* pieces. In absolute chance, affirmation also surrenders itself to *genetic* indetermination, to the *seminal* adventure of a trace."[102] The play is without security but also sure. It is 'without security' if one looks at it from the vestiges of a metaphysics of presence; but it can be 'sure' of its prognosis that provisional interpretations ('signifiers') will be substituted with other provisional interpretations 'signifiers'); the play can be sure that this adventure will not be brought to a close. Dissemination ('the seminal adventure of a trace') crosses all sorts of borders and limits. There is a dispersal of meaning, because every word can be connected to all sorts of other words in ever new contexts. This incessant interweaving cannot be arrested by any authoritative source. This is Derrida's new assurance, in the wake of Nietzsche, after the evaporation of the erstwhile reassuring foundation of metaphysics.

102. *Ibid.*, 292.

CHAPTER SEVEN

DERRIDA AND PHENOMENOLOGY

As so many others of his generation, Jacques Derrida (1930-2004) began his career by studying and critiquing phenomenology. He learned phenomenology from Paul Ricœur and Emmanuel Levinas, both of whom had earlier studied with Edmund Husserl, the 'father' of phenomenology, in Freiburg, Germany. Derrida employed the writings of Jean-Paul Sartre, among others, in his critique. Sartre had already questioned Husserl's focus on self-presence and his bracketing (*epoche*) of contingency and our natural attitude of experience and thought.[1] A similar criticism is to be found in Derrida's early publications which all explore, with a 'rigor' he learned from Husserl, the hidden tensions and unexamined presuppositions in Husserl's methodological approach. As Derrida declared in an interview published in 1982, "I never shared Husserl's pathos for, and commitment to, a phenomenology of presence. In fact, it was Husserl's method that helped me to suspect the very notion of presence and the fundamental role it played in all philosophies."[2]

I. HUSSERL'S PHENOMENOLOGY

Phenomenology as practiced by Edmund Husserl (1859-1938) aims at describing the world of phenomena as it presents itself to consciousness. It aims at overcoming the clash between an empiricist and an idealist approach to reality as well as the ideological anti-metaphysical or metaphysical stands characteristic of those two systems. Having been trained as a mathematician, Husserl wanted to return 'to things themselves' ('*zu den Sachen selbst*'), and to view them in a way unencumbered by theories of psychology or general world views. His main instrument was the notion of '*epoche*' or phenomenological reduction. This reduction consists, as the name itself implies, in letting phenomena present themselves

---

1. For this Sartrean influence see: Chr. Howells, *Derrida: Deconstruction from Phenomenology to Ethics* (Cambridge: Polity Press, 1999) 27-28.
2. R. Kearney, *Modern Movements in European Philosophy* (Manchester: Manchester University Press, 1986) 114.

to consciousness, not hindered by elements that might interpose themselves *between* the phenomena and consciousness, such as one's personal history, one's nationality, one's position in society, one's esthetic preferences, one's idea of social commitment, one's gender etc. "Phenomenological reduction puts aside, or 'brackets off' the contingent and personal to reveal the underlying universal structures of, for example, imagination, or perception. It abandons the 'natural attitude' in an effort to describe, without preconception, what appears to consciousness, that is: phenomena as they are 'intended' by consciousness."[3]

1. *From Static to Genetic Phenomenology*

To the axioms of phenomenology belong: the phenomenon, phenomenality, appearance, meaning, and intuition.[4] The empirical sciences, too, deal with facts, appearance and intuition; they develop an empirical intuition of concrete facts in empirical reality. Phenomenology, however, does not take its point of departure in *empirical facts*. Its subject matter is not obtained from, nor grounded in, empirical experience; its business is to supply a logical ground for *ideal possibilities*. This becomes evident in geometry. The subject matter of geometry is not a collection of empirical data, but the ideal form, e.g., of a triangle. In this case essential insight (*Wesensschau*), or insight into the essence of a triangle comes to the fore. This essential insight tells us that in Euclidean geometry the relations among the angles of a triangle add up to 180 degrees: this is a necessity, a given that can be apodictically stated, without recourse to empirical tests. In his work *Ideas: General Introduction to Pure Phenomenology* (1913), Husserl puts it as follows: "For the geometer, who studies not actualities, but 'ideal possibilities', not actual, but essential relationships, *essential* insight, and not experience is the act that supplies the ultimate grounds."[5] Elsewhere Husserl calls the 'essential insight': 'eidetic intuition', a direct intuition of the essence of a thing or of an ideal state of affairs.

The 'object' viewed in the eidetic intuition can be compared to the platonic idea, with this crucial difference that, for Husserl, the essence or *eidos* cannot be dissociated from the consciousness to which it appears.

3. Chr. Howells, *Derrida: Deconstruction from Phenomenology to Ethics*, 7.

4. See J. Caputo and M. Scanlon, *God, The Gift and Postmodernism* (Indianapolis, IN: University Press, 1999) 60-61.

5. E. Husserl, *Ideas: General Introduction to Pure Phenomenology*, trans. W.R.B. Gibson (London: George Allen and Unwin, 1933) 62.

The *eidos* comes into presence through an act of consciousness: "the *eidos* is given primordially in ideation as the originating act of consciousness through which alone the object comes into presence."[6] Ideation or *Wesensschau* is not a process of abstraction or of conceptualization; it rather parallels the manner in which an individual entity is grasped in empirical intuition. Analogous to empirical intuition, consciousness intuitively grasps the *eidos*. Yet, the content of this grasp is different. In the *Wesensschau* (essential insight) the 'object' grasped is not a physical object that factually exists – or may exist – in empirical reality, but a lasting essence that is of an imaginary, eidetic order:[7] "Essences and their intuitions are independent of facts and their intuitions since they need not to be based on fact. Ideation is the bringing to presence of essences, but makes no assertions of existence within the realm of the empirical."[8]

The essential insight may start from the awareness of an empirical intuition, but as soon as the *eidos* is grasped, the empirical realm is put aside. This 'bracketing off' is a first step in the phenomenological reduction. This reduction will enable Husserl to get access to a domain from which to critique the possible aberrations of the physical sciences – their tendency to give a utilitarian orientation to their research, a criticism which Heidegger, a disciple of Husserl's, will pursue in *Sein und Zeit* (*Being and Time*), when denouncing the devastating effects of modern techno-science on the human life-world.

The *Wesensschau* provides sense (*Sinn*) to consciousness. This sense cannot be derived from the world in its 'matter-of-factness'. That is why the brute materiality of the world must be 'bracketed off' – waiting, so to speak, to receive a clarification from the philosopher's dealing with the eidetic realm that holds out the promise of a recovery of the 'lived sense'. In his *Crisis of the European Sciences* (1936), Husserl deals at length with the loss of meaning in the human life-world due to the rise of modern science. For him, Galileo's ground-breaking study of the laws of physics inaugurated an era of technological dominance with catastrophic side-effects. Galileo stands as symbol for the historical development of

6. W. Fuchs, *Phenomenology and the Metaphysics of Presence: An Essay in the Philosophy of Edmund Husserl*, Phaenomenologica, 69 (The Hague: Martinus Nijhoff, 1976) 23.

7. This does, of course, not mean that the *eidos* is the product of 'imagination' as a 'modification' of empirical experience: "In particular essential insight is a primordial dator act, and as such analogous to sensory perception, and not to imagination." E. Husserl, *Ideas*, 92.

8. W. Fuchs, *Phenomenology and the Metaphysics of Presence*, 25.

physics between 1600 and 1700 as well as for the ensuing scientific dis-coveries (Einstein, quantum physics). Modern science is characterized by the 'mathematization' of nature, which led to the prevalence of merely fact-minded sciences and the shaping of merely fact-minded people. He writes: "The exclusiveness with which the total world-view of modern man, in the second half of the nineteenth century, let itself be determined by the positive sciences and be blinded by the 'prosperity' they produced, meant an indifferent turning-away from the questions which are decisive for a genuine humanity. Merely fact-minded sciences make merely fact-minded people."[9]

In order to ward off this positivistic tendency, Husserl sees only one solution: to show that the mathematical abstractions with which positivist scientists work are a far cry from what was originally meant in the grounding act of Greek geometry. This geometry was built on the dis-covery of the unchanging patterns of mathematic idealities, a discovery which was a real source of wonder. In order to recover this Greek ideal, Husserl, consistent with his phenomenological method, underlines the importance of the two following aspects: 1. The world of idealities (the eidetic realm) is of such magnitude that it can never be exhausted by the human mind. The idealities can only be 'intended' in ever repeated attempts, whereas a rational all-encompassing science works with frozen idealities that no longer refer to the idealities' inexhaustible wealth. 2. The contact with the world of idealities presupposes active and creative human persons who, through their intuitive grasp of idealities, are able to make sense of their human life-world, and to live in the certainty that life is directed towards a goal or *telos*, an aspect which escapes the men-tality of merely fact-minded people.[10] So, it is imperative to reactivate the 'eidetic power' that was *en vogue* before the rise of a positivistic mas-tery of the world. Only then will it dawn upon us that the things we have at our disposal are not just cold, positivistic data, but can be enriched with meaning on the basis of lived experiences.

In his later works, Husserl transforms his static phenomenology into a genetic, transcendental phenomenology. The aim and purpose of this genetic approach is to describe the various possible reenactments, throughout history, of the original grounding event (*Erlebnis*): the phe-nomenological perception that emerged in Greek geometry. Such a

---

9. E. Husserl, *The Crisis of the European Sciences and Transcendental Philosophy*, trans. D. Carr (Evanston, IL: Northwestern University Press, 1970) 6.

10. See K. Mai, *Die Phänomenologie und ihre Überschreitungen: Husserls reduktives Philosophieren und Derridas Spur der Andersheit* (Stuttgart: M und P Verlag für Wis-senschaft und Forschung, 1996) 35-37.

description works with a concept of history that links the emerging origin with its orientation towards a *telos*. What Husserl seeks to reconstruct is the genuine unfolding, in history, of the initial intuitive grasp of the idealities, against the deviations caused by positivistic science. In this reconstruction Husserl opts for a transcendental method that has the life-world as its correlate. This method takes its point of departure from the reflection of a transcendental ego on its own ability to transform the pre-given life-word into a place where humans are able to make sense of their lives. The transcendental ego stands for the ideal form of what it means to be a critical, responsible person. For this reason, Husserl's reconstruction of this history will not consist in offering a history of facts (observable in the life-world) but in uncovering an 'intrinsic intentional history', in which the transcendental ego looks back at the various revitalizations of 'lived sense' that occurred in the past in order to anticipate new significant accretions of it in the future.[11]

2. *Comparison with Kant's Tanscendental Approach*

The introduction of the notion of a transcendental ego calls to mind the transcendental method of Immanuel Kant. So, a short comparison with Kant is in order. In his *Critique of Pure Reason* Kant examines, with his transcendental method, the 'a priori conditions' of human knowledge. He says: "I entitle *transcendental* all knowledge which is occupied not so much with objects [of experience] as with the mode of our knowledge of objects, in so far as this mode of knowledge is to be possible *a priori*."[12] What matters is to apply the 'a priori categories' (of causality, relation, substance, etc) to the empirical phenomena that enter our perception. In this approach, the phenomena offer only the ephemeral material out of which reliable knowledge is to be processed. They are the 'appearance' of a thing-in-itself that in itself remains totally unknown. Kant, thus, operates with a distinction between *phenomenon* and *noumenon* (the thing-in-itself that can be thought but not observed or experienced). Husserl's concept of phenomenon, is, as we have seen, different. For him, the phenomenon is the disclosure of an *eidos* or ideality that manifests itself to consciousness. Because it is unrelated to the empirical materiality of the world, this *eidos* can only be perceived on the basis of a phenomenological reduction that brackets off the sense impressions. That is why

11. *Ibid.*, 187.
12. I. Kant, *Critique of Pure Reason*, A 12/B 25, trans. N. Smith (London and Basingstoke: The Macmillan Press, 1929 [1982]) 59.

Husserl's phenomenon is closer to the Kantian *noumenon*, that is: to the supersensible 'thing-in-itself' that Kant introduced in the *Critique of Pure Reason*, and which makes it reappearance in the *Critique of Practical Reason* and in the *Critique of Judgment*. In Kant's later works, the *noumenon* has a double function. It, first of all, founds the moral obligation of the categorical imperative, and holds out the perspective of wholeness and totality in the mode of supersensible Ideas of Reason that cannot be presented in empirical reality (an aspect on which I dwelt at length in my analysis of Lyotard).[13]

A second element that allows for a comparison with Kant is Husserl's notion of intentionality. While Kant discriminates between the spontaneous activity of the mind (linked to the use of 'a priori categories') and the passivity with which the mind takes in the sense impressions, Husserl eliminates this distinction. For Husserl, consciousness definitely plays an active role in welcoming the intended disclosure of idealities. This active role can take on various shades: whereas receptivity is the lowest degree of activity, spontaneity forms its culmination.[14] A similar oscillation returns in Husserl's two poles of the intentionality of consciousness: *noesis* and *noema*. *Noesis* is the active side of consciousness that spontaneously welcomes and 'intends' the *noema*, whereas the *noema* (the disclosure side of the idealities) appeals to consciousness' passivity of reception. This fluidity between spontaneity and receptivity is, in fact, basic to Husserl's principle that the "essence of consciousness is intentionality."[15] Intentionality, too, has two sides: the object intended and consciousness' straining to be filled by the object intended. On close inspection, this principle is linked to the metaphysical notion of 'presence' which Derrida is going to criticize. In his essay *Phenomenology and the Metaphysics of Presence*, Wolfgang Fuchs describes the link between the intentionality of consciousness and the (Greek) metaphysics of presence as follows: "The intended object is totally present to the intending consciousness [...] The intention has 'fullness' because the object [*noema*], given to it completely, also completely fulfills the intention [*noesis*]. The intending refers to nothing 'other', nothing alien, nothing absent to what is given: the object in total presence. This is *total presence;* the object is totally present to the intention, but also the intention is totally present 'in' the object, is exhausted by it."[16]

---

13. See K. Mai, *Die Phänomenologie und ihre Überschreitungen*, 172-173.
14. *Ibid.*, 177.
15. W. Fuchs, *Phenomenology and the Metaphysics of Presence*, 33.
16. *Ibid.*, 50.

The third element in Husserl's thought that is reminiscent of Kant is his notion of time as *Erlebnis*: lived time. Here too, the metaphysical notion of 'total presence' comes to the fore. Aristotle posed the question as to whether time would exist if there were no humans to register it. His answer was: yes, time exists at a cosmological level and is characterized by a now, preceded by a past and followed by a future. Kant, for his part, downplayed the objective presence of physical time; for him, time and space are 'a priori intuitions' (in the Kantian sense) that prepare the ground for the application of 'a priori categories' to the data of sense-perception. This relocation of time in transcendental subjectivity, however, continues to operate within the scheme of 'past, present, and future' set forth by Aristotle. Compared to Kant, Husserl breaks new ground. With his phenomenological description he 'brackets off' the objective time sequences that can be measured by clocks in empirical time. Such a reduction (*epoche*) allows him to access time as *Erlebnis* – to a 'lived time' that displays the vibrant features of a consciousness in search for its fulfillment by the 'intended' objects.

The phenomenological approach directs one's attention to the particular phenomenon of duration. Consciousness, which is always 'consciousness-of' an object (*noema*) turns out to be constituted by temporalization. Indeed, the intentionality of consciousness is, in fact, laid out in various acts of 'intending' a fulfillment through the disclosure of an object. This creates in the 'intending' consciousness the sense of a flow of time, an awareness that is fortified by the realization that also the 'intended' objects appear as endowed with temporal extension: "[...] a phenomenological analysis of time cannot explain the constitution of time without the constitution of the temporal Object. By temporal Objects, in this *particular sense*, we mean Objects that are not only unities in time but also include temporal extension in themselves."[17] Temporal extension also means temporal succession. When delivering his lectures *The Phenomenology of Internal Time Consciousness*, published in 1928, Husserl was well aware of phenomenology's original contribution to the experience of the duration of time. A critical reading of these lectures, however, shows that Husserl, in his analysis of internal time consciousness, was not always consistent with his phenomenological method. This analysis was, as Wolfgang Fuchs points out, tainted by his unquestioned acceptance of a metaphysics of presence.

In his phenomenological reflection on duration, Husserl introduces the notions of retention and protention. Indeed, if there is duration, one ought

---

17. E. Husserl, *The Phenomenology of Internal Time Consciousness*, ed. M. Heidegger, trans. J. Churchill (Bloomington, IN: Indiana University Press, 1964) 43, cited in W. Fuchs, *Phenomenology and the Metaphysics of Presence*, 62.

also to pay attention to its successive phases. This becomes evident when listening to a musical tone or a melody. In Wolfgang Fuchs' words: "The tone appears in a continuous flux, but as different modes within the flux since I am conscious of the beginning point of the tone and the interval from then to 'now'. And when the tone has ended, in being conscious of its 'end-point' as now, I am still conscious of the tone in its retention, as 'having been', and of having been a unitary duration."[18] The melody forms, so to speak, a flux that is laid out in temporal sequences which form an organic unity among themselves. Central in the act of listening is the 'now' moment – the sound structure one perceives in the moment, as the sound is created. The sound structure perceived in the 'now', has been preceded by a sound structure (a 'previous now') that is already vanishing into the past. Consistent with the logic of intentional consciousness, however, the hearer seeks to retain this vanishing 'primordial impression' and to blend it with the 'primordial impression' of the now moment. This is what Husserl calls retention. Something similar happens in the transition to the next part of the melody that begins to announce itself. The listener already anticipates this new sound structure through what Husserl calls a protention. In conclusion, phenomenologically speaking, the 'now' moment is accompanied by the ebb of what 'has been' and the flow of what is about to appear. This double accompaniment gives the hearer, emotionally, a sense of internal time duration and of depth: "Retention and protention are the elements that provide the now moment with the quality of duration and depth."[19]

Because of the important role of retention and protention in enhancing the quality of the 'now' moment, Husserl tends to regard them, at this juncture, as 'primordial impressions', on the same footing as the 'primordial impression' of the now moment. He writes: "An Objectivity such as a melody cannot itself be originally given except as 'perceived' in this form. The constituted act constructed from now-consciousness and retentional consciousness, is *adequate perception of the temporal Object*."[20] Elsewhere, however, when reflecting on the element that gives validity to the perceived object, notably 'presence to consciousness', which precisely provides 'evidence', the 'now moment' takes precedence over all the rest. In it alone the living presence of the intuition is safeguarded in all its purity. Retention and protention are downgraded to

18. W. Fuchs, *Phenomenology and the Metaphysics of Presence*, 62.
19. K. Mai, *Die Phänomenologie und ihre Überschreitungen*, 282 [translation mine].
20. E. Husserl, *The Phenomenology of Internal Time Consciousness*, 60, cited in W. Fuchs, *Phenomenology and the Metaphysics of Presence*, 69.

derivatives. The reason is quite simple: "The living presence cannot be made dependent on something that is alien to it; it must constitute the ultimate, ideal and absolute ground of the ensuing philosophical reflection on how to substantiate the validity claim of scientific evidence."[21] Metaphysics of total presence remains in full force, against the new possibilities opened up by the phenomenological approach. From this wavering between phenomenological openness and dogmatic foundationalism, Derrida will deduce that Husserl is afraid of admitting that presence can only appear against the background of non-presence (receding presence; advancing presence respectively).

A fourth domain in which Husserl refers to Kant is his reconstruction of the suspended life-world. Husserl's genetic, transcendental phenomenology aims at the ongoing transformation of a world of volatile opinions into a realm of validated certainties. This aim is encapsulated in the device 'back to the things themselves' (*zu den Sachen selbst*), that is: back to things with undeniable truth. In order to get at these 'true things' the whole domain of the life-world must be suspended. The entire empirical world must be 'bracketed off', in order for the true world to appear to intentional consciousness. This reduction provides Husserl with a platform from which to shed a new light on the 'natural' empirical world. Indeed, as Hans-Georg Gadamer (1900-2002) remarked: once the phenomenological reduction has been completed, Husserl can engage in a process of "reconstruction" – a reconstruction which "becomes the main theme of his phenomenology as transcendental philosophy."[22]

It is precisely in this 'reconstruction' or 'rebuilding' of the suspended ('reduced') life-world that Husserl has recourse to Kant's regulative Idea of Reason (a recourse that, as we will see in further detail, is objectionable, since it cannot be accounted for with the phenomenological method). To the extent that Husserl transforms his static phenomenology into a genetic, transcendental phenomenology he is forced to rethink the relationship between transcendental subjectivity (the transcendental ego) and the natural, empirical world. This rethought relationship is dialectical – it runs in two directions. On the one hand, transcendental phenomenology is a philosophy centered on the unrestrained operations of transcendental subjectivity. Yet, on the other, this transcendental subjectivity

21. K. Mai, *Die Phänomenologie und ihre Überschreitungen*, 282-283 [translation mine].

22. H.-G. Gadamer, *Kleine Schriften*. III: *Idee und Sprache, Plato, Husserl, Heidegger* (Tübingen: Mohr, 1972) 178, cited in K. Mai, *Die Phänomenologie und ihre Überschreitungen*, 140 [translation mine].

can only become fully conscious of itself by acting upon a world that is its correlate or external domain of action (the domain it seeks to transform). This correlation has far reaching implications. First of all, the world must be conceived as a universal horizon against the backdrop of which the transcendental subjectivity must unfold itself – must activate its potential for establishing validated certainties –, if this subjectivity is to become aware of its own quasi-infinite depth. Without the universal horizon of the world, no genuine depth of transcendental subjectivity can be attained. Second, the quasi-infinite depth of transcendental subjectivity cannot be reached at once. It is a final stage to which each and every philosophical reflection is directed. Third, if this is the case, then the world as universal horizon must also take on the form of an infinite Idea, whose total content cannot be made visible. Katharina Mai puts it as follows: "The universal horizon of the world is constitutive of each and every philosophical reflection. The world as horizon is an infinite Idea in the Kantian sense – the content of which can never be exhausted, but which is always presupposed and 'intended' [as Husserl sees it] in our acts of knowledge, in our orientation towards the world."[23]

With this assessment Katharina Mai is alluding to Derrida's later criticism, namely that Husserl builds his phenomenological method on a Kantian foundation. For Derrida, the idealizations which Husserl pursues "are thought as an infinite process that has its correlate in an Idea [of Reason]." Consequently, "Husserl has overstepped the boundaries of phenomenology; he is no longer able to uphold his principle of absolute evidence, since the [Kantian] Idea [to which he has recourse] is not presentable,"[24] i.e., cannot be described with the tools of phenomenology. Mai gives further examples of Husserl's 'Kantianism': The more Husserl engages in a reconstruction of the domain that he previously 'bracketed off' (the natural world), the more he will have to admit that his proposed reconstruction is far from being complete. The reconstruction always remains to be perfected: "The real object can never coincide with its ideal form. This non-coincidence turns the object into a [never fully attainable] Idea in the Kantian sense."[25]

In his work the *Crisis of the European Sciences*, Husserl raises the topic of derailments and deficiencies in history. Here again, as Paola Marrati-Guénoun points out, the deficiencies are seen as merely provisional: they can be overcome, provided one firmly believes in the finality (*telos*)

---

23. K. Mai, *Die Phänomenologie und ihre Überschreitungen*, 84 [translation mine].
24. *Ibid.*, 186-187 [translation mine].
25. *Ibid.*, 183 [translation mine].

of history, a finality that runs parallel to the finality transcendental subjectivity sets for itself. The *telos*, much more than the actual vivid awareness of presence, gives the phenomenological enterprise its final orientation. This again shows the Kantian influence: "The phenomenological project turns out to be a project conducted against the horizon of an infinity that, without ever acquiring the form of a full presence, has the status of a *telos*, of an Idea in the Kantian sense of the word. Yet, Husserl never gives up the metaphysical idea of total presence, which, also when its presence fades away and is incessantly postponed – no less remains the purpose to be attained."[26]

II. DERRIDA'S NOTION OF DECONSTRUCTION

Husserl's alternation between a metaphysics of full presence and presence as a purpose to be attained reveals the failure of his phenomenological project. His successors will be more prudent in carrying out 'reductions', which, in Husserl's approach, are mainly meant to safeguard the purity of the intuiting subject. Merleau-Ponty (1908-1961) had earlier warned against an excessive use of reductions. In his work *Phenomenology of Perception* (1945) he notes: "The most important lesson of [phenomenological] reduction is the impossibility of a *complete* reduction."[27] His phenomenology gives a central place to the body and to bodily existence, aspects which Husserl had 'bracketed off' in his reduction of the human life-world. With this change in emphasis, important new themes can be examined that escaped Husserl's attention, such as interpersonal relations and the fragility of human existence – or in the variant of Martin Heidegger (1889-1976) in *Being and Time* (1927) – our situation of 'being thrown into the world', of having to live 'an existence-unto-death'. Jacques Derrida, too, will include in his philosophical inquiry the threat of death, disappearance, and absence. From the backdrop, however, of his Paris intellectual milieu he will treat these themes by giving a linguistic turn to Husserl's phenomenological investigations. The inspiring figure behind this linguistic turn is, as already mentioned, Ferdinand de Saussure who built his semiotics on the principle that presence presupposes a background of absence: What a word or sign positively means

26. P. Marrati-Guénoun, *La genèse et la trace: Derrida lecteur de Husserl et Heidegger*, Phaenomenologica, 146 (Dordrecht, Boston and London: Kluwer Academic Publishers, 1998) 97 [translation mine].
27. M. Merleau-Ponty, *Phänomenologie der Wahrnehmung* (Berlin, 1966) 11 quoted in K. Mai, *Die Phänomenologie und ihre Überschreitungen*, 159 [translation mine].

cannot be dissociated from the anonymous structure of language in which it is embedded. This dark, hidden environment arises along with the clarity of the intended meaning-utterances, with the effect of lessening the impact of their occurrence.

A rereading of Husserl from the linguistic perspective must necessarily place new accents within the fabric of Husserl's texts. In his further elaboration of phenomenology, Husserl increasingly focused on the active role of transcendental subjectivity. In this approach, the transcendental 'I' – not in the least hindered by its surrounding empirical realm (the 'non-I') – lets its clarifying light shine upon all the rest. Derrida's linguistic reading, on the contrary, drastically reduces the original input of transcendental subjectivity, to the point of demolishing the reputable edifice of Husserl's phenomenology of full presence. This demolition is what one would spontaneously associate with the term 'deconstruction'. Yet, what does Derrida precisely understand by the term?

In an interview in 1990, Derrida states that his use of the term 'deconstruction' was meant to translate Heidegger's notions of *Abbau* and *Destruktion*, concepts that have no negative connotation in themselves, since they aim at clearing away the distorting encrustations of the philosophical tradition that occlude the originary character of an experience.[28] Deconstruction is "not destructive, not having the purpose of dissolving, distracting or subtracting elements in order to reveal an internal essence. It asks questions about the essence, about the presence, indeed about this interior/exterior, phenomenon/appearance schema" – it intervenes in texts and contexts that are ruled by essence and presence.[29] With this statement Derrida keeps his listeners and readers in suspense. When explaining that deconstruction is not destructive, he intimates that it is phenomenology, with its methodological *epoche* ('reduction'), which is truly destructive, since it 'dissolves, distracts or subtracts elements in order to reveal an internal essence'. Viewed in this light, Derrida's 'deconstructive' reading of texts seeks to repair the damage done by phenomenology's methodological *epoche;* it endeavors to eliminate the undue oppositions and exclusions called forth by phenomenology's extreme desire for purity, such as the binary oppositions interior/exterior and phenomenon/appearance. With his 'deconstruction', Derrida, like a medical doctor, offers a *pharmakon* to these

---

28. For this definition of *Abbau* and *Destruktion*, see: M. Yar, *The Internet Encyclopedia of Philosophy*: http:/www.iep.utm.edu/a/arendt.htm (accessed on March 3, 2007).
29. R. Mortley, *French Philosophers in Conversation: Levinas, Schneider, Serres, Irigaray, Le Doeuff, Derrida* (London: Routledge, 1991) 96-97.

purists: a 'medicine' to cure them – or should one read: 'a poison' to make them stop excluding what they deem to be contaminations and impurity?

In an earlier interview, broadcast in 1986 by the German radio station '*Bayerische Rundfunk*', Derrida refused to call his deconstructive reading of texts a method, a systematic approach with solid foundations. Is his deconstruction a method? The answer again is: 'no'. "What I call deconstruction is, of course, able to produce rules, procedures, and techniques, but basically it is not a method and also not a scientific critique. A method is a technique of questioning or reading which without taking into account the idiomatic features should be repeatable in other contexts. Deconstruction is not such a technique. It deals with texts, particular situations, autographs, in fact, with the whole of the history of philosophy in the course of which the notion of method has been formed. When deconstruction examines the history of metaphysics and of the concept of method, it cannot simply present itself as a method."[30] Here, again, method is defined in terms of Husserl's phenomenological enterprise. For Husserl, the essential intuition (*Wesensschau*), because of its unchangeable character, is to be repeated in exactly the same way in other circumstances and contexts. This is a conviction he inherited from the history of science, and behind that, from the history of philosophy, in which the concept of method as a generalizable procedure to resolve particular problems took shape. Also this partial answer, because it is only negative – telling us what deconstruction is not – does not lead us significantly further. Still, the interview gives us the beginning of a clue: Derrida seems to admit that, in the absence of a method in the precise sense, he has developed strategies and techniques to read a text, as we will see, often against the grain of the author's intention.

In an interview with Henry Ronse, conducted as early as 1967, Derrida gives us a good idea of such a deconstructive strategy. At a certain moment Ronse complained that is was so difficult to locate the style of Derrida's comments on Rousseau, Artaud, Jabès etc: is this style still philosophical or is it something else? "It seems almost impossible to situate the style of your discourse," Ronse said. In reaction to this remark Derrida answered that he tried to keep himself "at the *limit* of philosophical discourse," for the simple reason that the latter "defined itself as the *episteme* [true knowledge], functioning within a system of fundamental constraints, conceptual oppositions without which the philosophy

30. F. Rötzer, *Französische Philosophen im Gespräch* (München: Klaus Boer Verlag, 1986) 70 [translation mine].

becomes impracticable." 'At the limit' apparently means 'at the border', 'at the fringes', 'at the periphery' of philosophy. In the course of the conversation, Derrida makes it clear that this positioning in the periphery allows him to shed a critical light on the center – on what it is promoting and on what it is repressing. He says: "I try to respect as rigorously as possible the internal, regulated play of philosophical or epistemological propositions by making them slide – without mistreating them – to the point of their nonpertinence, their exhaustion, their closure. [I make them slide into this exhaustion] by means of a double gesture, marked in certain decisive places by an erasure which allows what it obliterates to be read, violently inscribing within the text that which attempted to govern it from without."[31] In plain English: Derrida tries to read the text in such a way that the cracks and fissures he discovers in it show that the straightforward thesis of the work cannot be upheld. In this deconstructive reading he makes use of a twofold strategy: (a) he sheds doubt on central terms of Western philosophy: he crosses them out in order to make them say much more (or much less) than they enunciate – with the old meaning still being legible under the erasure, a strategy he borrowed from Heidegger, who at a certain moment graphically crossed out the notion of Being; and (b) he calls attention to ideological elements that infiltrated into the text so as to drive the linkage of its sentences.

With the description of this strategy, Derrida gives a clear picture of what he intends with deconstruction. He says: "To 'deconstruct' philosophy, thus, would be to think – in the most faithful, interior way – the structured genealogy of philosophy's concepts, but at the same time to determine – from a certain exterior that is unqualifiable or unnamable by [logocentric] philosophy – what this history has been able to dissimulate or to forbid, making itself into a history by means of this somewhere motivated repression."[32] Let us notice in passing the usage, in this definition, of the Nietzschean term 'genealogy', which Derrida immediately complements with the Freudian notion of 'symptom' – a symptom that is "necessarily and structurally dissimulated for reasons and along pathways that I attempt to analyze."[33]

Having noticed the influence of Nietzsche and Freud, two famous masters of suspicion, on Derrida's subversive program, we are now able to

31. J. Derrida, "Implications. Interview with Henri Ronse," in idem, *Positions*, trans. A. Bass (London and New York: Continuum, First South Asian Edition, 2005) 5 [translation modified]. This interview has been first published in *Lettres françaises* no. 1211, 6-12, December 1967.
32. *Ibid.*, 5.
33. *Ibid.*, 6.

highlight the twofold task of deconstruction that Derrida sets for himself: (a) to delve into the genealogy of Western philosophy – its Greek origin that has internally shaped and structured all its subsequent developments; and (b) to scrutinize under which external conditions this genealogical history has come to establish a reign of domination and repression. This twofold task corresponds to the above described twofold strategy: (a) to shed doubt on central themes of logocentric philosophy and (b) to lay bare the ideology that has infiltrated into these themes, an ideology which this philosophy attempts to dissimulate, but which a deconstructive reading seeks to expose as symptom of a malady. What is at stake in this twofold task is liberation from a totalitarian way of philosophizing. In this respect Derrida likes to refer to Emmanuel Levinas who in his work *Totality and Infinity* (1961) explores a thought that (in Derrida's words) "seeks to liberate itself from the Greek domination of the Same and the One (other names for the light of Being and of the phenomenon) as if from oppression itself – an oppression certainly comparable to none other in the world, an ontological or transcendental oppression, but also the origin and alibi of all oppression in the world."[34] Levinas' thought is, without doubt, inspired by a deep ethical concern. So, too, is Derrida's.

In her comparative study of Husserl and Derrida, Katharina Mai points out that Derrida, in counterpoint to Husserl's device 'back to the things themselves', engaged in a search for the 'things concealed' in the philosophical text. This results in a "praxis of text-transformation," i.e. in a textual analysis that, if necessary, deviates from the explicit intention of the author. The aim and purpose of this transformation is to uncover suppressed strata in the text: elements that have been partially or entirely discarded from the flow of the writing process, not so much because, linguistically speaking, each enunciation necessarily bars the way for other similar enunciations, but because these elements are repressed in the name of a dominant philosophical tradition. In other words, their partial or total repression is not random; the repression is planned, carried out by instinct. To call attention to this state of affairs is, therefore, "a political praxis."[35]

Derrida's political praxis is primarily an act of resistance: this will become evident in our next chapters. Yet, resistance is each time a confrontation, a clash with a system that is not going to disappear overnight.

---

34. J. Derrida, "Violence and Metaphysics," in J. Derrida, *Writing and Difference*, trans. A. Bass (London: Routledge, 1978) 83. Originally published as idem, *L'Écriture et la différence* (Paris: Seuil, 1967).

35. K. Mai, *Die Phänomenologie und ihre Überschreitungen*, 240.

In that sense, Derrida's deconstructive reading of philosophical texts continues to presuppose the persistence of the 'logocentrism' of these texts. He paradoxically stands in need of them, in order to vehemently confront them. In the words of Rudolf Bernet: "Derrida's deconstruction is not a destruction [of logocentrism], for the simple reason that his deconstruction owes everything to the [logocentric] text it deconstructs: it owes to that text both its limitation and its delimitation."[36] Part of this 'delimitation' is Derrida's commitment to the other: to the person who is not given a place in the dominant system of 'the Same and the One'. It is this commitment that gives a positive connotation to his deconstructive praxis. In an interview given in 1984 Derrida states: "Deconstruction is, in itself, a positive response to an alterity which necessarily calls, summons or motivates it. Deconstruction is, therefore, a vocation – a response to a 'call'." [37] In the 1986 interview referenced above, he declares: "I would like to underline that deconstruction is far from being [the] amoral or unethical nihilism for which it is often taken. Deconstruction is an affirmative thought, the source of an ethics to come, of commitment at the other side of pure calculation. The concern for responsibility is at the heart of the deconstructive experience."[38]

III. The Rise of Deconstruction: Derrida's Early Studies of Husserl

In 1959 the young Derrida read a paper at a conference in Cerisy-la-Salle in which he critically examined the relationship between 'Genesis and Structure in Husserl's phenomenology'. This paper was, with some slight modifications, published for the first time in 1965 in the Proceedings of the conference.[39] In 1967 Derrida published it, with further revisions, as a chapter in his work *Writing and Difference*. In that same year, Derrida also published *Of Grammatology*, and *Speech and Phenomena*, the

---

36. R. Bernet, "Differenz und Anwesenheit: Derridas und Husserls Phänomenologie der Sprache, der Zeit, der Geschichte, der wissenschaftlichen Rationalität," *Studien zur neueren französischen Phänomenologie*, Phänomenologische Forschungen, 18 (Freiburg and München: Alber, 1986) 62-63 [translation mine].

37. R. Kearney, *Dialogues with Contemporary Continental Thinkers: Paul Ricœur, Emmanuel Levinas, Herbert Marcuse, Stanislas Breton, Jacques Derrida* (Manchester: Manchester University Press, 1984) 118.

38. F. Rötzer, *Französische Philosophen im Gespräch*, 77-78 [translation mine].

39. M. de Gandillac, *Entretiens sur la notion de genèse et de structure* (Paris: Mouton, 1965) 253-270.

work that is renowned for its characterization of Husserl's phenomenology as a metaphysics of presence. The fact that Derrida refined the 1959 paper twice reveals the importance Derrida attached to it. Indeed, the paper 'Genesis and Structure' forms the hinge between Derrida's dissertation *The Problem of Genesis in Husserl's Phenomenology*, written in 1953/1954 and published in 1990, and Derrida's long *Introduction* to his French translation of Husserl's *The Origin of Geometry*, published in 1961.

I will start this section with an analysis of 'Genesis and Structure' (leaving out the further accretions[40]). In a second step I will go back in time to *The Problem of Genesis in Husserl's Phenomenology*; only then will I dwell on Derrida's *Introduction* to his translation of Husserl's *The Origin of Geometry*. *Speech and Phenomena* will be discussed in the next chapter. It is in that work that the linguistic turn I alluded to earlier will be fully realized. The previous studies merely lay the foundations for this turn, which does not mean that their importance can be minimized: they show, through a meticulous philosophical analysis, Husserl's transgression of the limits of phenomenological description under the spell of the horizon of the infinite opened up by Kant's Ideas of Reason.

1. *Genesis and Structure in Husserl's Phenomenology*

In his study *Derrida and Husserl: The Basic Problem of Phenomenology*, Leonard Lawlor observes that although some scholars "place Derrida firmly in the tradition of Husserl's interpretation, Derrida's interpretation of Husserl [in 'Genesis and Structure'] must be seen as a critique of Husserlian phenomenology."[41] Indeed, in 'Genesis and Structure', Derrida admits that the hypothesis on which he bases his analysis "seems to go against the grain of what is most clear in Husserl,"[42] the latter's rejection of metaphysics. Derrida's reading of Husserl is thus 'subversive', 'deconstructive' in the sense I have explained. How does Derrida proceed? First of all, he calls attention to Husserl's aversion for debate, for dilemma, "for a reflection in the alternative mode," because he fears it will force the philosopher to take a decision "that would be the result of a speculative or 'dialectical' attitude."[43] Such a speculative attitude would

40. For a listing of these additions, see L. Lawlor, *Derrida and Husserl: The Basic Problem of Phenomenology* (Bloomington, IN and Indianapolis, IN: Indiana University Press, 2002) 31-33.
41. *Ibid.*, 24.
42. *Ibid.*, 25.
43. J. Derrida, "Genesis and Structure in Husserl's Phenomenology," in idem, *Writing and Difference*, 154.

smack of metaphysics, that is, of speculation without evidence or intuition. Husserl, thus, refuses to pit genesis and structure against each other.
Depending on the case to be examined he will give a separate phenomenological description of structure, and of genesis: "the thing itself determines whether a genetic or a structural description is appropriate: the
thing itself [the perceived phenomenon] keeps itself open to continuous
interpretation."[44]

In a second step, Derrida shows that Husserl's technique of 'skirting
around' the problem results in positing a teleological orientation within the
structured element – thus wagering on a *telos* that is steered by an origin.
He writes: "[Husserl appears] to move towards a metaphysics of history,
in which the solid structure of a Telos would permit him to reappropriate [...] an untamed genesis which grew to greater and greater expanse."[45]
In other words, it is by perceiving a finality – a teleological development –
in the structure that Husserl infers the existence of a steering origin, which
remains at work within the eidetically perceived structure. This, however,
leads, for Derrida, to the elaboration of a 'metaphysics of history'. Derrida
coins this term himself. Husserl only speaks of a 'logos that animates history' and which, from his perspective, can be perceived in phenomenological intuition. In characterizing this enterprise as a 'metaphysics of history'
Derrida already anticipates his further criticism that an eidetic perception
of the logos of history threatens to exceed the capacity of phenomenology.

In order to corroborate the hypothesis that Husserl tends to move
towards a metaphysics of history with a solid finality (*telos*), Derrida analyzes some passages in which Husserl has recourse to the Kantian Idea
of Reason in order to ward off empiricism and positivism. A case in point
is Husserl's refutation of Dilthey's philosophy of history which he finds
too empiricist. For Husserl, Dilthey is engaged in a "genetic description
[of history] which borrows its schemas from naturalism and causalism,
and depends upon a science of 'facts' and therefore on an empiricism."
Dilthey's account of history, therefore will smack of relativism and "be
incapable of insuring its own truth."[46] Derrida observes that this attack
on Dilthey comes as rather a surprise, since Husserl appreciates a great
many of Dilthey's achievements: (a) his overcoming of historicism
through a 'philosophy of life' in which experience plays an important
role; and (b) his understanding of philosophy as an activity which brings
life to consciousness, which in turn presupposes the existence of persons

44. L. Lawlor, *Derrida and Husserl*, 25.
45. J. Derrida, "Genesis and Structure," 157.
46. *Ibid.*, 159.

capable of re-living their intense experiences. Yet, it is not this 'philosophy of life' that creates a problem for Husserl. What makes him depart from Dilthey is the latter's concept of 'world view' (*Weltanschauung*), which, in Husserl's eyes, is grounded in pure subjectivity. The controversy pivots around the opposition between philosophy as a rigorous science – Husserl's phenomenology – and Dilthey's philosophy in terms of 'world view'. For Husserl, this philosophy has no other norm than 'historical facticity', and thus confuses *truths of reason* with *truths of fact*: "Pure truth or the pretension to pure truth is missed in its *meaning* as soon as one attempts, as Dilthey does, to account for it from within a determined historical totality, that is, from within a factual totality, from within a finite totally" the cultural manifestations of which are "all regulated by the same function, by the same finite unity of a total subjectivity."[47] In other words, Dilthey only offers a semblance of objectivity when calling attention to the basic coherence of, and similarities between, diverse cultural manifestations. Yet, Husserl objects, it is not by seeing the same basic patterns at work in a variety of domains that one accounts for their objective truth, since all these structures are solely finite totalities, with no other yardstick than their proper finitude. The real meaning of truth, on the contrary, is only to be found in "the requirement of an absolute, infinite omni-temporality and universality, without limits of any kind. The Idea of truth, that is the Idea of philosophy or of science, is an infinite Idea, an Idea in the Kantian sense. Every [empirical] totality, every final structure is inadequate to it [...].On the basis of the structural description of a *vision of the world* (*Weltanschauung*) one can account for everything except the infinite opening to truth, that is, philosophy."[48] The Kantian Idea opens an absolute, universal horizon from which alone a real 'infinite opening' to truth is to be expected.

A second example of Husserl's recourse to the Kantian Idea is the manner in which he distances himself from a purely positivistic use of mathematics and geometry in the style of Galileo. Here Derrida dwells on Husserl's distinction between the exactness of mathematics and the inexact character of phenomenology, an 'inexactness', which, as we will see, is paradoxically required in order to break away from closed systems: "An eidetic descriptive science, such as phenomenology, may be rigorous but, it is necessarily inexact – I would rather say 'anexact' – due to no failure on its part."[49] Derrida prefers the term 'anexact' over

47. *Ibid.*, 160.
48. *Ibid.*, 160.
49. *Ibid.*, 162.

'inexact' because phenomenology has a different type of rigor than geometry. Geometry is a 'material' and 'abstract' science – dealing with abstract eidetic elements such as spatiality and the mathematical manifold. Because of the axioms that regulate geometry this science is comprehensive but also closed: the mathematical manifold is ruled by a closure. In order to explain this closure Derrida quotes in a footnote a passage from Husserl's work *Ideas* in which this issue is treated: "The essential generic nature of the domain of geometry, and in relation thereto the pure essential nature of space, is so ordered that geometry can be fully certain of being able to control with exact precision, through its method, really all the possible cases [...] A finite number of concepts and propositions ... determines completely and unambiguously on lines of pure logical necessity the totality of all possible formations in the domain, so that in principle, therefore, nothing further remains open within it."[50] The eidetic perception is of a different nature. What Husserl wants us to retain from this comparison with geometry, Derrida says, is "the structural impossibility of closing a structural phenomenology. It is the infinite opening of what is experienced, which is designated at various moments of Husserlian analysis by reference to an *Idea in the Kantian sense*, that is, the irruption of the infinite into consciousness."[51] This irruption has the effect of unifying "the temporal flux of consciousness just as it unites the object and the world by anticipation, and despite an irreducible incompleteness."[52] Anticipation of an ever-fuller, inexhaustible reality, despite irreducible incompleteness of the momentary eidetic perception, is what Husserl associates with the Idea in the Kantian sense. To believe in the power of this Idea is for him the antidote to the closeness of positivistic, axiomatic systems.

Derrida's third step consists in showing, or at least in strongly insinuating, that wherever Hussserl has recourse to the Idea in the Kantian sense, he threatens to overstep the limits of phenomenology. Unlike the notion of a 'metaphysics of history', which is not to be found in Husserl's texts, but which Derrida coined in order to pass a judgment on Husserl, the reference to Kantian ideas is genuinely Husserlian. So, Derrida has a firm basis on which to stand when he writes: "The presence of *Telos* or *Vorhaben* – the infinite theoretical anticipation which simultaneously is given as an infinite practical task – for phenomenological

50. E. Husserl, *Ideas I*, trans. W.R. Gibson (London: Allen and Unwin, 1931) sec.72, 204, cited in J. Derrida, "Genesis and Structure," 322n14.
51. J. Derrida,, "Genesis and Structure," 162.
52. *Ibid.*, 162.

consciousness is indicated every time that Husserl speaks of the *Idea in the Kantian sense*. The latter is offered within phenomenological self-evidence as evidence of an essential overflowing of actual and adequate self-evidence."[53] Indeed, every time this Kantian Idea is mentioned, Husserl effects a broadening of the phenomenological perception (the things immediately present to consciousness), under the guidance of a *telos* which is infinitely anticipated. The phenomenological perception intuits the structure, or the *eidos*, as already moving on to its next stage of disclosure to consciousness. Moreover, the phenomenological perception also seems to intuit the widening effect of the Kantian Idea: this Idea being an Idea of 'totality', always 'overflows' every successive, actual stage of phenomenological perception; it gives an *a priori* guidance and orientation to this succession of possible next moments, in a manner that seems to contradict Husserl's initial phenomenological approach.

This allows us to understand Derrida's pertinent remark: "One would have to examine quite closely the intervention of the Idea in the Kantian sense at various points along Husserl's itinerary. Perhaps it would appear then that this Idea is the Idea or very project of phenomenology, that which makes it possible by overflowing its system of self-evidences or factual determinations, or by overflowing this system as phenomenology's source and end."[54] As we will see in our further analyses of Derrida's studies on Husserl, this recourse to the Idea in the Kantian sense will become more and more the target of Derrida's 'deconstruction'. Such a 'deconstruction' is already foreshadowed in *The Problem of Genesis in Husserl's Phenomenology*, the young Derrida's dissertation.

2. *The Problem of Genesis in Husserl's Phenomenology*

Derrida's dissertation *The Problem of Genesis in Husserl's Phenomenology* is, of course, a serious scholarly work. Yet, in the manner in which it interrogates, and points to certain aporias, in Husserl's work, it lays the foundation for Derrida's further conversation with Husserl. I select from this dissertation two topics: Derrida's presentation of Husserl's recourse to the Idea in the Kantian sense, and Husserl's idealistic concept of science. The first topic made its appearance in Derrida's essay 'Genesis and Structure in Husserl's Phenomenology', while the second topic,

---

53. *Ibid.*, 167.
54. *Ibid.*, 167.

Husserl's concept of history, will be studied again in Derrida's *Intro-duction* to Husserl's *Origin of Geometry*, under the aspect of the trans-mission of scientific insights in language and writing.

a) The Temporality of the Perceiving 'I'

In *The Problem of Genesis* Derrida, first of all, reveals that there is, indeed, a problem with genesis in Husserl's phenomenology. The notion of a genesis or origin becomes problematic for a philosophy that methodologically brackets off the natural, empirical realm from which one would expect something new to emerge. Husserl, as we already know, rejects psychologism and empiricism. So, genesis must be demon-strated to play a role in the intentional consciousness as it intuits the *eidos*. Yet, that which consciousness perceives is an existent, already constituted *eidos* that shows itself in evidence to consciousness. Where this *constitute*d *eidos* comes from, in terms of genesis and origin, is at this moment of Husserl's research not yet seen as a problem. The ques-tion of the origin (that which *constitutes* things) only comes up when Husserl reflects on the temporality of the perceiving 'I' (of the transcen-dental ego respectively). It is here that the Idea in the Kantian sense is going to play a role.

Husserl already broached the topic of the temporality of the perceiv-ing 'I' in his lectures on *The Phenomenology of Internal Time Con-sciousness* (1905). He repeated and deepened this analysis in his work *Ideas* (1913). Derrida focuses on the elucidations in *Ideas*, because this work inaugurates Husserl's transcendental turn, that is, his preoccupation with a reflection on the pure activities of the transcendental ego, the reduced, 'abstracted' seat of the unity of the stream of consciousness. In his first step Derrida examines a line of thought that could also have been taken from *The Phenomenology of Internal Time Consciousness*. This line of thought runs as follows: In internal time consciousness one becomes aware of duration, of a succession of various *now* moments: the actual *now* moment arising from a previous *now* moment that is still vaguely felt to persist as if kept in *retention* – and preparing the emergence of the next *now* moment towards which it already reaches out in *protention*. The notions *retention*, the echo of what some seconds ago has been, and *protention*, the expectation of the next sequence to come, are apparently introduced to highlight the centrality of the actual *now* moment in the perception of duration. The following quotation from Husserl makes this clear: "The actual *now* is necessarily something punctual and remains so, *a form [of consciousness] that persists through continuous change of*

content."⁵⁵ Derrida has problems with Husserl's insistence on the persistence of this punctually perceived actual *now*, since this insistence
tends to divert one's attention away from the fact that the punctual *now*
has been preceded and influenced by a prior punctual *now*, which in turn
was preceded and influenced by another punctual *now*, etc. When this is
the case, Derrida reasons, the purity of the punctually perceived actual
now – which Husserl wants to uphold – is not that pure at all: it owes its
vividness to something else, to something absent: "its absolute consists
in being taken in a lived 'relation' [with past and future]; its purity reveals
itself and is enriched in what is not itself."⁵⁶ Derrida thus concludes that
a convincing explanation of the genesis and duration of internal time consciousness has not been given.

In his next step, Derrida examines Husserl's attempt at giving a future
orientation to the duration of the internal time consciousness. In this
attempt Husserl is in search of the 'pure unity of the ego and of the temporal form'. Yet, because this pure unity or synthesis cannot be given in
a punctual now, Husserl holds out the prospect of a future stage in which
the transcendental ego will be aware of its uninterrupted flow of duration
(its fulfilling temporal form). But this attempt, too, is not without creating problems: (a) It, posits and requires "the form of a 'totality',"⁵⁷ that
is: of an 'infinite succession' of possible 'nows'. But (b) It is questionable whether such an 'infinite succession' can still be grasped in phenomenological intuition. Husserl maintains that this 'infinite succession
is graspable in a very special way. He writes: "In principle this *whole*
connection [of possible successive 'nows'] is never one that is or can be
given through a single pure glance. Notwithstanding, even then it is in a
certain, though in an intrinsically different, way intuitively graspable,
namely, along the line of a *'limitlessness in the progressive development'*
of immanent intuitions."⁵⁸ So, Husserl makes it clear that the intuitive
grasp of this limitless development is of a different nature than the (static) intuition with which the *eidos* is grasped: it is a grasp that intuits, as
it were in anticipation, the concatenation of the infinite succession of the
totality of possible 'nows'. It is here that the Idea in the Kantian sense
makes its appearance. Husserl says: "Advancing continuously from one

55. E. Husserl, *Ideas: General Introduction to Pure Phenomenology*, 237, cited in
J. Derrida, *The Problem of Genesis in Husserl's Phenomenology* (Chicago, IL and London: University of Chicago Press, 1990) 97. Originally published as idem, *Le Problème
de la genèse dans la philosophie de Husserl* (Paris: Presses universitaires de France, 1990).
    56. J. Derrida, *The Problem of Genesis*, 97.
    57. *Ibid.*, 97.
    58. E. Husserl, *Ideas*, 239, cited in J. Derrida, *The Problem of Genesis*, 97.

apprehension to another, we apprehend in a certain way, I remarked, *the stream of experience as a unity also*. We do not apprehend it like a single experience, but after the fashion of an *Idea in the Kantian sense*."[59] And a little farther on, Derrida adds, "Husserl speaks of 'an intuition of this Idea in the Kantian sense'."[60]

Here, again, Derrida's question is: how can this solely anticipated, not yet given, indefinite/infinite succession of possible 'nows' lead to the apprehension, in immediate self-awareness, of the 'stream of consciousness' as an enduring unity? True, Husserl's approach is different from that of Kant. So, one cannot blame Husserl for not complying with the Kantian warning that the Idea of totality is not presentable in empirical reality. Yet, in having recourse to the Kantian Idea, Husserl turns out to disregard the basic principle of phenomenology itself that "intuition must be that of a lived experience."[61] Indeed, Derrida wonders, "how is an intuition of what is not yet there possible? How can nonbeing and absence be immediately and concretely apprehended? [...] This totality [which Husserl associates with the Kantian Idea] remains formal and the intuition that claims to aim at it cannot be 'fulfilled' by an originary presence,"[62] i.e. by the lived experience of phenomenological perception. Derrida's remark seems to echo the opposition of Husserl's former students who had attended his courses at the University of Göttingen, before Husserl moved to the University of Freiburg where he began to teach his transcendental phenomenology. Some of these former students, like Edith Stein and Roman Ingarden, had become themselves famous philosophers precisely by applying and deepening Husserl's early phenomenological insights. They were surprised at the idealistic passages in Husserl's work *Ideas*, and set out to prove that this idealistic orientation went against the grain of the experiential side of phenomenology – the lived experience of the phenomenological perception of the *eidos*.[63]

b) Questioning Husserl's Idealistic Concept of Science

This brings us to the second topic, Derrida's questioning of Husserl's 'idealistic concept of science'. To realize what is at stake one ought to delve into Husserl's turn to transcendental idealism. This is what Derrida does in his comments on Husserl's Fourth Cartesian Meditation. In the

---

59. E. Husserl, *Ideas*, 240, cited in J. Derrida, *The Problem of Genesis*, 98.
60. J. Derrida, *The Problem of Genesis*, 98.
61. L. Lawlor, *Derrida and Husserl*, 73.
62. J. Derrida, *The Problem of Genesis*, 98.
63. See *ibid.*, 135 where Derrida alludes to this protest.

Cartesian Meditations (1930) Husserl set for himself the goal of elaborating a notion of absolute science premised on a resolute finality. The elaboration of such an absolute science is only possible at the level of a strictly transcendental phenomenology that abstracts from the perceptions of the empirical ego in order to focus on the pure essence of an active ego. Such a monadic, pure ego is not only freed of all vicissitudes and alterations, but also defines the limits within which alterations will be allowed to come into play.

Derrida right away goes to the heart of the matter: how will Husserl be able to resolve the question of the infinite succession that is comprised in the teleological Idea of science? He writes: "The teleological Idea of an absolute science, of the experience of a limitless theoretical intention [...] cannot be clarified as such except by a meditation and a mediation which are infinite [...] Thus Husserl situates it [the teleological Idea] on the methodological path that leads to the synthesis of the constitution of the transcendental ego"[64] In other words, the teleological Idea of an absolute science will lead to the infinite task of intellectual clarification, which will have to be carried out again and again (the 'infinite mediation'). But in order to warrant the success of this task, each of its stages of performance must be connected to a subject that continuously creates and reaffirms itself. The infinite task of the scientific enterprise requires the continuous self-constitution of the transcendental ego. The question of genesis seems, at least at this level, to be resolved. Let us notice, however, in passing, that in *The Problem of Genesis* (1953/1954) Derrida presents a rather polemic description of Husserl's turn to transcendental phenomenology. This however will change. As we will see in the next chapter, in his article 'Violence and Metaphysics: An Essay on the Thought of Emmanuel Levinas' (1964) Derrida will acknowledge that, thanks to the transcendental phenomenology he developed in the *Cartesian Meditations*, Husserl was able to reflect on human intersubjectivity and on the respect one owes to the unfathomable depth of the 'other'.

In the *Problem of Genesis* Derrida only focuses on the self-constitution of the transcendental ego. This self-constitution is what Husserl sets out to demonstrate in the Fourth Cartesian Meditation: "The ego is himself existent for himself in continuous evidence, thus, in himself, he is *continuously constituting himself as existing*."[65] This is further specified as follows: "The ego grasps himself not only as a flowing life but also

64. *Ibid.*, 135.
65. E. Husserl, *Cartesian Meditations*, trans. D. Cairns (The Hague: Martinus Nijhoff, 1966) 66, cited in J. Derrida, *The Problem of Genesis*, 136.

as I, who live this and that subjective process, who live through this and that cogito, *as the same I.*"[66] The personified language – 'he' and 'him' – should not deceive us. Husserl speaks at the highest level of phenomenological reduction, with a pure focus on the conditions of possibility that must be fulfilled in order for a teleological science to be absolute, that is: to perform its infinite, never accomplished task of shedding its light of understanding and meaning on the world and on human history. A basic condition in this respect is the uninterrupted flow of an 'I' that continuously constitutes itself as existing – as existing as the ever new and ever selfsame living 'I'.

One can already foresee Derrida's critical remark: how will such a philosophy of the monadic ego be able to substantiate its claim of continuously shedding an intellectual light on the natural world? This claim can only be corroborated when it is also shown that the ego is willing to answer questions that properly arise from states of affairs in the existing world. This presupposes a *receptivity* to empirical facts, a receptivity that is not evidently given with a self-constituting transcendental ego. It is in this context that Derrida examines the passive side of the sense-conferring transcendental ego. It is through this 'passive side', technically called 'passive genesis', that Husserl attempts to ward off the monadic ego's splendid isolation from the pre-given things in the world.

In this examination Derrida finds out that Husserl makes the monadic ego look at pre-given things as if it had already the power to master them. The 'things' outside the realm of the transcendental ego are only there to be apprehended by the transcendental ego, in accordance with its own mode of comprehension: "Whatever may be the product of a genesis whatsoever, it will be comprehended and organized by the structural form of the known,"[67] that is: it will always be processed by the ego's *a priori* intuitions. It is on the basis of these *a priori* intuitions that the empirically pre-given things are raised to the status of 'the known'. At this juncture Derrida mentions the importance Husserl attaches to the 'goal form' which the ego always already intuits in advance: "It [this goal form] itself points back to a 'primal instituting' (*Urstiftung*) of this form. Everything known to us points to *an original becoming acquainted. What we call unknown has, nevertheless, a known structural form*, the form 'object', and, more particularly, the form 'spatial thing', 'cultural object',

---

66. E. Husserl, *Cartesian Meditations*, 66, cited in J. Derrida, *The Problem of Genesis*, 136.

67. J. Derrida, *The Problem of Genesis*, 146.

'tool', and so forth."[68] In order to grasp and to make sense of the pre-given things in the world it suffices for the scientist to classify them under their suitable rubric or structural form which the scientist, in line with the transcendental ego's *a priori* functioning, at all times knows in advance. In Husserl's idealism passive genesis (receptivity to the pre-given things in the world) is naturally transformed in active genesis (the imposition, on them, of *a priori* known structural forms).

For Derrida, the idealistic transformation of passive genesis into active genesis does not totally resolve the problem of genesis. If one looks at the history of science, then it is obvious that this history did not just have a formal beginning in the continuous self-constitution of the transcendental ego: it also had a beginning in the empirical time of human history. This is the question which Husserl broaches in his works *The Crisis of the Human Sciences*, and *The Origin of Geometry*. Because Derrida will treat this question at length in his *Introduction* to Husserl's *The Origin of Geometry*, I limit myself to Derrida's basic criticism voiced in his dissertation. This criticism relates to Husserl's resolution of problems at a formal *a priori* level. If it is true, Husserl tells us, that the self-constituting ego has, in concert with the infinite task of the scientific enterprise, a teleological orientation, then it is easy to understand that everything having a teleological orientation must also by necessity have had a beginning, an origin. In a further derivation, this origin can be extrapolated, then, and catapulted in the empirical time of humankind's history. Strictly speaking, the formal, *a priori* understanding of a beginning is enough; compared to it, the precise location, in time, of this origin – its emergence with Greek geometry – is of secondary importance.

3. *Introduction to Husserl's* Origin of Geometry

Derrida's *Introduction* has no precise title. If one were to give it a title, it should read: 'The origin of truth' (in the style of Merleau-Ponty) or 'On the essence of truth' (in the style of Heidegger), titles that underline how important it is to "make oneself responsible for the truth, by regressively inquiring into its origin."[69] Also the chapters of the work have no title; they are classified with the help of Roman numbers, from I till XI. This, too, makes the *Introduction* no easy reading. Some commentators call it a labyrinthic work: Derrida spends 153 pages to 'introduce' Husserl's *The Origin of Geometry* (1939), a readable essay that comprises only

---

68. *Ibid.*, 145.
69. L. Lawlor, *Derrida and Husserl*, 104.

23 pages.[70] Moreover, Derrida has constant recourse to Husserl's other writings, as well as to studies by Ricoeur, Fink, Merleau-Ponty, and others. A special source of inspiration was Jean Hyppolite's *Logic and Existence* (1952), a work that "stresses the irreducible role that language plays in Hegel's dialectical genesis (in Hegel's movement of idealization)."[71] Hyppolite was a specialist in Hegel. As a student in Paris, Derrida had admired Hyppolite, – he took him as the director of one of his papers. Now he took Hyppolite's study as a model to investigate the role of language in Husserl's *Origin of Geometry* (1961). It is also in Hyppolite's interpretation of Hegel that "the very root of Derrida's law of contamination can be found; it is the source of the concept of *différance*."[72]

When asked, in an interview in 1983, what in retrospect was the central concern of his *Introduction*, Derrida answered: the 'historicity of ideal objects' as well as the question of the linguistic and more in particular the graphic expression of this historicity of ideal objects. And he added: "this concern has also become pivotal in the whole of my work."[73] It is interesting to observe that these very topics are also central in Husserl's essay. When Derrida asserts their centrality for him, he has, of course in view his deconstructive reading of these topics. On the other hand, this deconstructive reading is not devastating; it is rather a meticulous reading of Husserl's texts that at the same time draws attention to certain hesitancies and lacunas in Husserl's explanations. Yet, on the whole, Derrida faithfully followed Husserl's reasoning because he felt that Husserl in the *Origin* was breaking new ground. Till now Husserl had mainly examined how an *already constituted* ideal object affected consciousness's intuitive grasp of it. In his later works he tackled the more thorny problem as to how the ideal object – in this case the mathematical and geometrical ideal object – had *started off* in the history of humankind, and under which conditions it could have been transmitted from generation to generation in its quality of quasi-unchangeable, universally accepted ideal object. Husserl also understood that language and writing played an important role in this transmission, and this because of his acquaintance with Hegelian philosophy.

70. I refer to the pages of the English edition: J. Derrida, *Edmund Husserl's Origin of Geometry: An Introduction* (Lincoln, NE and London: University of Nebraska Press, 1989). Originally published as idem *Edmund Husserl, l'Origine de la géometrie*, trans., introd. (Paris: Presses universitaires de France, 1962).

71. J. Derrida, *Edmund Husserl's Origin of Geometry*, 89.

72. L. Lawlor, *Derrida and Husserl*, 103. Leonard Lawlor spent many pages demonstrating the influence of Hyppolite's study of Hegel on Derrida's deconstructive reading of Husserl.

73. J. Derrida, "The Time of a Thesis: Punctuations," *Philosophy in France Today*, ed. A. Montefiori (Cambridge: Cambridge University Press, 1983) 39-40.

Husserl's *The Origin of Geometry* must be placed in the context of his other work, *The Crisis of the European Sciences* (1936), in which he accused the hard sciences of having, with their positivism, lost track of the humanistic, sense-creating, origins of European sciences. So, the recovery of these origins will be the main objective of *The Origin of Geometry*. Methodologically, such a recovery must follow a specific path. Phenomenological reflection can only start from what immediately appears to consciousness. So this past origin can only be reached through a return inquiry (*Rückfrage*) into a message that has, so to speak, been posted more than two millennia ago, and whose cumulative effects, after so many sequences of transmission, now finally reach us. In this return inquiry one asks oneself the question as to how, why, and in view of which this past message is still speaking to us with a vital concern: "Husserl uses, just like Freud, an archeology, which is not [primarily] interested in the original fact, but asks the question as to how this original fact had in retrospect been able to acquire such an eventful and never definitely exhausted meaning."[74]

The method of return inquiry (*Rückfrage*) is an antidote to the procedures of historicism. Historicism is merely interested in historical facts that can be documented. For it, historiography must end up in fantasy, if the validity of these facts is not carefully established. For Husserl, and Derrida follows suit,[75] facts alone are not able to disclose their 'lived sense' except when placed within a horizon in which one becomes conscious of historicity, i.e. in which one realizes the necessity of an incessant quest for the meaning of life in evolving cultural circumstances. In his preface to the English edition of Derrida's *Introduction*, John Leavey puts this as follows: "Historicity is always a *sense-history*. It operates on the level of sense and is related to the problems of language, ideality, truth, and humankind in its Living Present – the source of all sense and history."[76] The historical awareness goes beyond the mere knowledge of historical facts. It sensitizes us to the presence and shifting of broad cultural horizons: every cultural present is linked to the totality of the past. In paraphrasing Husserl's understanding of historicity, Derrida

74. R. Bernet, "Vorwort zur deutschen Ausgabe," in J. Derrida, *Husserls Weg in die Geschichte am Leitfaden der Geometrie* (München: Wilhelm Fink Verlag, 1987) 16 [translation mine].

75. For the fact that Derrida, in his *Introduction*, makes his own, without any further criticism, Husserl's notion of historicity, see: R. Bernet, "Vorwort zur deutschen Ausgabe," 15.

76. J. Leavey, "Preface," in J. Derrida, *Edmund Husserl's Origin of Geometry: An Introduction* (Lincoln, NE and London: University of Nebraska Press, 1989) 11.

writes: "Whatever our ignorance on the subject of actual history, we know *a priori* that every cultural present, therefore every scientific present, implicates in its totality the totality of the past."[77] With respect to the question of the origin of geometry, this implies that, for Husserl, the documented knowledge of who exactly discovered the ideal objects of geometry – Thales of Milletus or some other contemporary – is less important than the study of the magnitude of this inaugurating act, a study that can only be successful if one takes into account the felt impact of this inaugurating act on our present condition of being-in-the-world.

Derrida lists three elements that make, for Husserl, such a felt impact possible. (a) The discovery of the ideal *eidos* of geometry is a unique event in humankind's history. One must, therefore, term it an irreplaceable inaugural act. (b) In spite of this irreplaceable character, the inaugural act can be reactivated in the course of history: the inaugurating act is not for ever buried under contingent, historical sedimentations that accompany its transmission; it lends itself to be reawakened. (c) This reactivation differs from the repeated access to an already constituted *eidos* in static phenomenology, where the same *eidos* is intuited repeatedly by carrying out the bracketing of empirically existing things. Historic phenomenology is of a different nature in that its reflection focuses on the historical reactivations of the first inaugurating act: "Instead of repeating the constituted sense of an ideal object [as in static phenomenology], we have to reawaken the dependence of sense with respect to an inaugural and institutive act concealed under secondary passivities and infinite sedimentations – a primordial act which created the [ideal] object whose [...] inaugural signification is always reproducible."[78] And, Derrida concludes: "Only under these conditions can Husserl write: 'our interest shall be the inquiry back into the most original sense in which geometry once arose, was present as the tradition of millennia ... we inquire into that sense in which it appeared in history for the first time – in which it *must have appeared* [Derrida's emphasis], even though we know nothing of the first creators and are not even asking after them."[79]

This emphasis on '*must have appeared*' already prepares the critical questions which Derrida is going to raise: "This *must* [have appeared] marks the necessity now recognized and timelessly assigned to a past fact of an eidetic pre-scription and of an *a priori* norm."[80] That which, for the

77. J. Derrida, *Edmund Husserl's Origin of Geometry*, 108-109.
78. *Ibid.*, 47-48.
79. J. Derrida, *Edmund Husserl's Origin of Geometry*, 49, citing E. Husserl, *The Origin of Geometry*, in idem, *Edmund Husserl's Origin of Geometry*, 158.
80. J. Derrida, *Edmund Husserl's Origin of Geometry*, 49.

first time, had been discovered, is precisely the *a priori* norm that is handed down through the various subsequent reactivations. At this juncture Husserl installs a *'zigzag'* way of proceeding. On the one hand, the inaugural act of origin sheds a light on all the subsequent reactivations. Yet, in order to get a deeper insight into the innovative character of the inaugural act, one paradoxically ought to start from what we, in our actual reactivation, are able to see as the essence of geometry. This is the only way to go back to the origin, which, as Derrida underlines, is intimately linked to a *telos* – to geometry's fuller deployment that also nowadays continues to inspire the actual generation of geometers: "Whoever *in fact* the first geometers were, and whatever *in fact* the content of their acts was, it is *a priori* necessary that the establishing gestures had a sense, such that geometry issued from them *with the sense as we now know it*."[81] The *'zigzag'* way of proceeding is carried out on the basis of phenomenological method ('as things appear to consciousness'). That is why this circularity paves the way for the elaboration of an 'intentional and intrinsic history', from which to critique positivistic scientific developments. The circularity between the origin and our actual historical experience of it "permits the neutralization of worldly history. Neutralization then opens the space for an intentional and intrinsic history of this very circulation and permits the comprehension of how a tradition of truth is possible in general."[82]

a) Criticism of Husserl's Univocal Use of Language

This brings us to the first area in which Derrida will ask some critical questions concerning tradition and language. In order to launch a tradition the first geometer must have realized that he took a step forward by introducing the ideal object 'circle', whereas pre-geometrical people only worked with the notion 'roundness'. He must also have realized that this ideal object is such that it can be universally grasped and communicated. So, in a first step, the discoverer will, in an interior monologue, express his astonishment about the insights flowing from the first discovery, insights which lend themselves to communication in language. It is here that the question of the 'ideality of sense' communicated in speech comes to the fore. Derrida points out that Husserl drew a distinction between 'bound' ideality and 'free' ideality. A 'bound' ideality is e.g. the notion of lion (or *Löwe* in German). This notion is translatable in all languages

81. *Ibid.*, 50.
82. *Ibid.*, 51.

used by people who know or have heard of lions. Because of this virtual universalization, the notion of lion is supra-regional, and supra-temporal, but remains, in the last resort, bound to a reference to empirically existing lions. Geometry, on the contrary, works with free idealities whose supra-spatiotemporal existence is not in the least 'bound' to empirically existing things. That is the reason why Husserl can say that geometry's 'ideality of sense' is always the same, exists only once: "The Pythagorean theorem, indeed, all of geometry, exists only once, no matter how often or even in what language it may be expressed. It is identically the same in the 'original language' of Euclid, and in all 'translations'; and within each language it is again the same, no matter how many times it has been sensibly uttered, from the original expression and writing – down to the innumerable oral utterances and written or other documentations."[83]

In his further elucidation of the identical sameness of the geometrical free ideality Husserl found it necessary to reflect on the role of written texts. To Derrida's contentment, Husserl attributes to the written documents the role of freeing geometry's free ideality from the subjective awareness of the initiator and his contemporary followers: the written documents bring the geometrical theorems in free circulation: "Without the ultimate objectification that writing permits, all language would as yet remain captive of the de facto and actual intentionality of a speaking subject or community of speaking subjects. By absolutely virtualizing dialogue, writing creates a kind of autonomous transcendental field from which every present subject can be absent."[84] Derrida also welcomes the fact that Husserl admits that in this free circulation, which is absolutely necessary for a genuine transmission of tradition in the subjectless field of communication, misunderstandings and deviations can also occur. But he is less enthusiastic when he sees that these deviations are, for Husserl, rather accidental and thus correctible, whereas for Derrida himself deviations belong to the very practice of tradition: "Are not non-communication and misunderstanding the very horizon of culture and language?"[85] he asks. And if this is so, must not misunderstanding and disagreement be seen as part of the transmission of tradition, of a transmission that takes place in the house of language and writing?

Indeed, for Husserl misunderstanding and deviations are accidental and never total. When he admits of the necessity for thought to incarnate itself

83. *Ibid.*, 72, citing E. Husserl, *The Origin of Geometry*, in idem, *Edmund Husserl's Origin of Geometry*, 160.
84. J. Derrida, *Edmund Husserl's Origin of Geometry*, 87-88.
85. *Ibid.*, 82.

in language and writing, he at the same time tends to 'spiritualize' the corporeality of the written text. For Husserl, writing is much more than a merely constituted sensible body (*Körper*, or material, inanimate body) – the codified text –; writing is also, and primordially, a constituting body (*geistige Leiblichkeit* or living body) – the act of conveying/creating 'living truth-sense'. It is this latter aspect that safeguards the purity of the selfsame free ideality, even as it is embodied, and makes use of this embodiment, to bring itself objectively in free circulation in the materiality of graphic signs. Yet, even so, degradation may occur. In Husserl's reflections on language and writing "[t]ruth depends on the *pure* possibility of speaking and writing, but is independent of what is spoken or written, in so far as they [speaking and writing] are in the world. If therefore, truth suffers in and through its language from a certain changeableness, its downfall will be less a fall toward language [toward the merely material body of written language] than a degradation within language [within the composite whole of living body and material body]."[86] Such a degradation can be overcome through a renewed attempt at reactivating the insight of the first origin: "forgetfulness will never be radical, however profound it may be, and sense can always, in principle and de jure, be reactivated."[87]

Husserl's ideal is that of univocal language: the same word or sign always has the same identical sense and meaning. His concept of language is patterned after the model of logic with its neatly defined, clear concepts. For him, it is this univocity that must be saved from degradation in the process of transmitting and reactivating the original sense of geometrical theorems. For Derrida, however, it is very questionable as to whether in the transmission of tradition, from cultural epoch to cultural epoch, univocal language could still be maintained. Insofar as writing is both a constituting body (the living truth-sense) and a constituted body (the codified text), the univocity of language is always intermingled with equivocity, that is: with the emergence of a deviant 'other' that inflates the obsession with the permanence of an always identical sense. Geometry is no exception to this rule, as becomes evident in the new developments of Riemannian geometry. Further, within the realm of the sciences, new perspectives, and new combinations inevitably emerge and intersect, so that a unitary perspective is ceaselessly postponed. For Derrida, this internal collapse of univocal language can be accounted for with Husserl's phenomenological method: "If, in fact, equivocity is always irreducible,

86. *Ibid.*, 92 [italics mine].
87. *Ibid.*, 98.

that is because words and language in general are not and can never be absolute *objects*. They do not possess any resistant and permanent identity that is absolutely their own. They have their linguistic being from an intention which traverses them as mediations. The 'same' word is always 'other' according to the always different intentional acts which thereby make a word significative (*significant*). There is a sort of *pure* equivocity here, which grows in the very rhythm of science."[88]

Husserl, too, seemed to have realized the inevitable occurrence of '*pure* equivocity', as Derrida puts it. Let us not forget that phenomenology's aim is to get at the purity of things. Further, for Husserl, the univocity of language becomes, increasingly, an ideal that must be pursued but which can never be properly attained. Science always remains a task to be accomplished. Its enterprise is never finished. In a footnote Husserl writes: "Objective, absolute firm knowledge of truth is an infinite idea,"[89] to which Derrida adds: "Absolute univocity is inaccessible, but only as an Idea in the Kantian sense can be."[90]

b) *The Kantian Idea Cannot be Phenomenologically Perceived*

This brings us to the second area in which Derrida will ask some critical questions, or better *the* basic question already raised in his dissertation: the link between origin and *telos* (ultimate end), or what boils down to the same: Husserl's recourse to the Idea in the Kantian sense. Husserl inquired into the origin of geometry because of his dissatisfaction with the 'mathematization' of nature that started with Galileo, and which finally led, under the ensuing impact of scientific positivism, to the technological exploitation of nature. Husserl's main objection is that Galileo lost track of the question of origin: "For Galileo, then, [pure] geometry [as tradition] was given – and of course he quite understandably, did not feel the need to go into the manner in which the accomplishment of idealization originally arose (i.e. how it grew on the underlying basis of the pre-geometrical, sensible world and its practical arts) or to occupy himself with questions about the origin of apodictic, mathematical self-evidence."[91] To make up for this neglect, Husserl set for himself the goal of delving into a domain that lies before the ready-made geometry from

---

88. *Ibid.*, 104.
89. *Ibid.*, 104, citing E. Husserl, *The Origin of Geometry*, in idem, *Edmund Husserl's Origin of Geometry*, 166.
90. J. Derrida, *Edmund Husserl's Origin of Geometry*, 104.
91. *Ibid.*, 36-37, citing E. Husserl, *The Crisis of European Sciences and Transcendental Philosophy*, trans. D. Carr (Evanston, IL: Northwestern University Press, 1970) 29.

which Galileo developed his study of the laws of nature. His aspiration is to get at the founding act of the geometrical 'idealities', and thus at the conditions that make ready-made geometry possible. In this inquiry into the origin, he gives "juridical priority [to] the question of phenomenological origin."[92] For him, this inquiry can only be successful on the basis of a phenomenological approach that focuses on how things and states of affairs appear in evidence to consciousness.

The starting point of this inquiry is "the upsurge of geometry [...] in so far as it has taken place 'once', 'for the first time', starting from a 'first acquisition'."[93] This starting point, as we have seen, paves the way for the emergence of an 'intrinsic', phenomenological sense of historicity, which is crowned by a clear orientation toward a *telos*, a teleological orientation which can never be deduced from the empirical facts of history. In this context Husserl brings up the notion of 'horizon' as a lived experience: "The notion of horizon is decisive here: 'horizon-consciousness', 'horizon-certainty', 'horizon-knowledge', such are the key-concepts of the *Origin*. Horizon is given to a *lived* evidence, to *concrete* knowledge, which Husserl says, is never 'learned', which no empirical moment can then hand over, since it always presupposes the horizon."[94] 'Horizon' contains the promise of a future, or in terms of spatiality: a promise of infinity; in it, we are dealing with "a primordial knowledge concerning the totality of possible historical experiences. Horizon is the always-already-there of a future which keeps the indetermination of its infinite openness intact (even though this future was *announced* to consciousness)."[95] The manner in which Derrida describes this open future already raises the problem as to how this always-already-there of a future that holds out a promise of infinite openness can appear to consciousness, can be announced to a consciousness that structurally remains within the confines of finitude.

In order to get a better grasp of the problem, Derrida critically examines Husserl's notion of '*anticipatory* structure of intentionality'. Crucial in this notion is the striving towards "an infinite approximation," towards "a leap to the infinite." Derrida places these elements in the context of geometry and remarks that if geometry deals with mathematical idealizations, then in order "for the intentional anticipation to leap to the infinite, it [this anticipation] must *already* be ideal [itself]." And, he continues, "It is the presence for consciousness of an *Idea in the Kantian sense*

92. J. Derrida, *Edmund Husserl's Origin of Geometry*, 38.
93. *Ibid.*, 47.
94. *Ibid.*, 117.
95. *Ibid.*, 117.

that at once authorizes and prescribes this idealization of anticipation."[96] In other words, for Husserl, the intentional anticipation is commanded by the Kantian Idea and by the perspective this Idea opens on an infinite progress and approximation. This infinite approximation is to be repeated again an again. Indeed, geometry's 'passage to the limit' is not arbitrary or aimless: it is guided by an 'essence' which can always be anticipated and then 'recognized', a process whose expansion goes on and on: "Essence-limits suppose then an open horizon and the breakthrough toward the infinite of an *'immer wieder'* [again and again], or an *'und so weiter'* [and so on], which is the very movement of mathematical idealization in general."[97]

On close inspection the progression of the mathematical idealization towards the infinite has a double function: (a) to make one aware of the infinite progression and approximation, as a *real possibility*; (b) to sensitize one to the fact that the infinite progression, since it is accomplished by a finite human intellect, is at the same time *never reachable*, and thus an unending task.[98] Unlike Kant, Husserl does not sharply distinguish between theory and practice, between theoretical and practical reason.[99] So, for him, and this is something Derrida appreciates: to take up the unending task of the advance of science is at once also an ethical obligation. "The 'again and again' which hands over exactitude inscribes the advent of mathematics within the ethico-teleological prescription of the infinite task."[100] A bit further he describes this infinite task as radical responsibility: "Husserl's phenomenology starts from this *lived anticipation* as a radical responsibility (something which, when considered literally, seems not to be the case with the Kantian *Critique*)."[101] In a further reflection on this radical responsibility, Derrida already sees as a future task for phenomenology to specify this responsibility as a response to urgent needs, thereby alluding to Emmanuel Levinas (also a critical commentator on Husserl), who in his work *Totality and Infinity* (1961) made the response to the needs and appeals of the 'other' (the naked face) his central ethical theme. In this light Derrida's assessment of phenomenology is rather positive. He writes: "Phenomenology as method of discourse is first of all *Selbstbesinnung* [critical self-reflection], and *Verantwortung* [responsibility], the free resolution to give the matter due consideration, in order to

96. *Ibid.*, 135 [translation modified].
97. *Ibid.*, 135.
98. See: R. Bernet, "Vorwort zur deutschen Ausgabe," 25.
99. J. Derrida, *Edmund Husserl's Origin of Geometry*, 137n162.
100. *Ibid.*, 136.
101. *Ibid.*, 141.

make oneself accountable, through speech, for an imperiled pathway. This speech is historical, because it is always already a *response*."[102]

In spite of this positive appreciation for Husserl's ethical concern, Derrida enters into a polemic with Husserl about phenomenology's ability or inability to bring the Idea in the Kantian sense to visibility (to phenomenological evidence). He first shows (a) that Husserl's 'lived anticipation' of the *telos* capitalizes on the latter's phenomenological description of the actual 'lived now' that 'retains' the projects of the previous 'lived nows' (*retention*) and already anticipates the project of the next 'lived now' (*protension*): "The Now, always in suspense, always tending to a next Now."[103] But then he points out (b) that the unity of these successive now moments presupposes an Idea of indefiniteness or of 'the unity of infinity' whose content cannot be intuitively grasped by consciousness. This Idea is only *"announced* in the Present," i.e. in each stage of the 'lived now'. As already mentioned in our presentation of Lyotard's analysis of Kant, the Kantian Idea can and must be thought, but cannot be rendered present in intuition; yet the unpresentable Idea makes itself known in a specific feeling of being obliged. Derrida renders this Kantian insight by revealing that the unpresentable Idea is *announced* in the tensional 'lived now' of the flux of consciousness. But even then the Idea itself never appears. In Derrida's words: "The unity of infinity, the condition for that temporalization, must then be *thought*, since it is *announced without appearing* and without being contained in a present [...] The Idea in the Kantian sense never phenomenalizes itself."[104]

At this juncture, Derrida remarks that "Husserl never made the [Kantian] Idea *itself* the *theme* of a phenomenological description."[105] If he had done so, he would have realized that any attempt at giving a phenomenological description of this Idea would be doomed to failure. The principle of all principles in phenomenology requires that "the thing itself 'in person'" must be immediately present to consciousness, which implies that "the phenomenally defined or definable thing, therefore [is] the *finite* thing." Yet, the Kantian Idea is not a thing itself 'in person', or a finite thing: it is a regulative Idea, "it is the horizon for every intuition in general [...] The Idea is the pole of a pure intention, empty of every determined object [thing itself 'in person']. It alone reveals, then the being of the intention: intentionality itself."[106] The Kantian Idea is empty of every

102. *Ibid.*, 149.
103. *Ibid.*, 137.
104. *Ibid.*, 137 [last italics mine].
105. *Ibid.*, 137.
106. *Ibid.*, 137-138.

determined object; so there is nothing to say about it. However, "[i]f there is noting to say about the [Kantian] Idea *itself*, it is because the Idea is that starting from which something in general can be said. Its own particular presence then, cannot depend on a phenomenological type of evidence."[107] All this leads Derrida to conclude that it is not possible for Husserl to account for the basic presuppositions of his method with the very tools of that method: "[P]henomenology can never be reflected in a phenomenology of phenomenology [...] Its *Logos* can never appear as such, can never be given in a philosophy of seeing, but (like all Speech) can only be heard or understood through the [material contact with the] visible."[108]

With this criticism of Husserl's phenomenology as an extreme philosophy of idealizing seeing which threatens to forget the requirement of immersing itself in the materiality of the world – of letting itself be 'contaminated' by this materiality –, Derrida brings his 'deconstructive' reading of *The Origin* to a close. In a final chapter he explores some avenues as to how to break out of the closed shell of idealizations, such as difference, delay, and pre-givenness (world, exteriority), topics which he will treat at length in later publications.

107. *Ibid.*, 138-139.
108. *Ibid.*, 141.

CHAPTER EIGHT

DERRIDA'S EXPLORATION OF EXTERIORITY
AND ANTERIORITY

Three years before his famous monograph on Husserl, *Speech and Phenomena* (1967), came out, Derrida published 'Violence and Metaphysics. An Essay on the Thought of Emmanuel Levinas' in *Revue de métaphysique et de morale*. In this article Derrida engages in a dialogue with Levinas' critical reading of Heidegger and Husserl. Given the importance of the new insights Derrida learned from Levinas, as well as of the questions he raises about Levinas' interpretation of Husserl, I will begin this chapter with a presentation of this article. The second part of this chapter will be devoted to Derrida's *Speech and Phenomena*, in which he deconstructs Husserl's phenomenology of presence by showing that the emergence of presence can only be explained as emergence from non-presence. It is in this text that Derrida makes plausible his notion of *différance* (difference plus deferral). The third part of the chapter will deal with the essential characteristics of Derrida thought: trace, *différance*, and *khôra*. Whereas his discussion with Levinas leads Derrida to underline the importance of exteriority (the naked face of the other), trace, *différance* and *khôra* bring us into contact with an immemorial anteriority that renders a metaphysics of presence for ever impossible. In this third part I will also examine Derrida's relation to negative theology.

I. VIOLENCE AND METAPHYSICS: THE QUESTION OF EXTERIORITY

A slightly revised version of 'Violence and Metaphysics' appeared in Derrida's *Writing and Difference* (1967). I will use this edition, taking into account the few modifications it contains and which have been listed by Leonard Lawlor in his study on Derrida and Husserl.[1]

In *Totality and Infinity* Levinas challenged Husserl's phenomenology from the background of Jewish thought, which, as we have seen in our

---

1. L. Lawlor, *Derrida and Husserl: The Basic Problem of Phenomenology* (Bloomington, IN and Indianapolis, IN: Indiana University Press, 2002) 147-156.

analysis of Lyotard, takes its point of departure not in seeing on one's own initiative, but in listening to the commanding voice of YHWH, and that of the needy. So, Levinas' approach basically clashes with Husserl's method of bringing intuited idealities to the immediacy of consciousness. That is why in the opening pages of his article Derrida expresses his admiration for Levinas' innovative insights. On the other hand, Derrida will also raise some critical questions which all relate to Levinas' endeavor to retain what Levinas regards as Husserl's 'essential teaching': fidelity to experience and intentionality. *Totality and Infinity* (1961) works with "an intentionality enlarged beyond its representative and theoretical dimension, beyond the noetico-noematic structure which Husserl incorrectly would have seen as the primordial structure." For Levinas, Husserl lost track of "the true depths of intentionality as desire and as metaphysical transcendence toward the other beyond phenomenality or Being."[2] To make up for these deficiencies Levinas developed his metaphysics of the 'other'. Derrida welcomes this new approach but also problematizes it, from the point of view of language, but also from his own interpretation of Husserl. In my analysis I will focus on three points: (a) the shock Derrida underwent in his contact with Levinas' Jewish thought; (b) Derrida's critical examination of Levinas' new approach, and (c) the strange historical coupling of Judaism and Hellenism.

1. *Derrida's Positive Appreciation of Levinas'* Totality and Infinity

Derrida's positive appreciation of Levinas resonates in the following text which reads as a dithyramb: "[T]he thought of Levinas can make us tremble. At the heart of the desert, in the growing wasteland, this thought, which fundamentally no longer seeks to be a thought of Being and phenomenality, makes us dream of an inconceivable process of dismantling and dispossession [...] This thought summons us to a dislocation of the Greek logos, to a dislocation of our identity, and perhaps of identity in general: it summons us to depart from the Greek site and perhaps from every site in general, and to move toward what is no longer a source or a site (too welcoming to the gods), but toward an *exhalation*, toward a prophetic speech [...]."[3] This thought is developed in its discourse "neither as a theology, nor as a Jewish mysticism [...]; neither as a dogmatics, nor as a religion, nor as a morality. In the last analysis

---

2. J. Derrida, "Violence and Metaphysics: An Essay on the Thought of Emmanuel Levinas," in idem, *Writing and Difference*, trans. A. Bass (London: Routledge,1978) 118. Originally published as idem, *L'Écriture et la différence* (Paris: Seuil, 1967).

3. *Ibid.*, 82.

it never bases its authority on Hebraic theses or texts. It seeks to be understood from within a *recourse to experience itself.* Experience itself and that which is most irreducible within experience: the passage and departure toward to other; the other itself as what is most irreducible within it: Others."[4]

The experience in question is a reversal of perspective. It is no longer the ego that looks for an alter ego. No, the 'other', in its strangeness and separation, takes the ego hostage, renders it captive, and awakens in it the desire for the infinite beyond the closed – and in fact: finite – circularity of a thought that is rounded up in itself as self-defined totality. All systems that reduce the other to the same are under the spell of an idea of totality that tends to violently suppress the deviant other. In Levinas' reversal of perspective only a surrender to the other in its infinite otherness can transpose one into a sphere of peace without violence. Derrida underlines that Levinas uses a language that might seem to be antiquated, but which has its antecedents: for Descartes, the infinite can never become an object of human thought, whereas for Plato 'the Good is beyond [the concept of] Being' (*epekeina tès ousias*). Levinas resumes this line of thought; he underlines that only the experience of an absolute ethical obligation that befalls the person gives access to true infinity, an aspect for which one would look in vain in Heidegger and Husserl. When Husserl brings up infinity, this infinity is basically a project of the cogito itself, which – from the angle of createdness, and receptivity – is absurd: "Husserl 'sees in the cogito a subjectivity with no support from without, constituting the idea of infinity itself, and providing himself with it as object'. Now, the infinite(-ly other) cannot be an object because it is speech [addressing me], the origin of meaning and the world. Therefore, no phenomenology can account for ethics, speech, and justice."[5]

The real point Levinas wants to bring home is that the awareness of the infinite is connected with the naked face of the other, of the 'infinitely other'. The phrase 'the infinitely other' has both a very concrete connotation (the other is the neighbor or stranger in need) and a religious resonance (the character of the 'most high'); both aspects merge in the face: "What neither Plato nor Descartes [...] recognized is that the expression of this infinity is the face. The face is not only a visage which may be the surface of things or animal facies, aspect, or species. It is not only, following the origin of the word, what is *seen*, seen because it is naked. It is also that which *sees*. Not so much that which sees things – a

4. *Ibid.,* 83.
5. *Ibid.,* 106, citing from E. Levinas, *Totality and Infinity.*

theoretical relation – but that which exchanges its glance. The visage is a face only in the face-to-face. As Scheler said: [...] I see not only the eyes of the other; I see also that he looks at me."[6] How does one relate to this infinitely otherness of the naked face? The answer is: not through a relation of reciprocity; one is rather to do with a rupture, with a separation. That is why in speech only the vocative can be used to address the other; to subsume the other under the grammatical accusative would neutralize the face, reduce it to a theoretical construct (in the style of 'these are the elements that condition the nakedness of the face'). The vocative addresses the other in its absolute strangeness; the vocative "is not a category, a *case* of speech, but rather the bursting forth, the very raising up of speech."[7] This makes us understand why in Levinas' metaphysics of the infinite no importance is attached to a "discourse *on* God;" in this metaphysics Levinas only enacts a "discourse *with* God,"[8] with the unseen JHWH: "the Eternal 'speaking face to face with Moses', but saying to him also: 'Thou canst not see my face: for there shall no man see me and live' (Exodus 33:20)."[9]

In this context Derrida explores, with Levinas, the possibility of a phenomenology of non-phenomenality: "What 'other' means is phenomenality as disappearance."[10] The other "must present himself as absent, and must appear as non-phenomenal."[11] This non-phenomenality is also at the heart of Levinas' messianic eschatology. Since the other is beyond any concept, s/he resists all categories, including the structure of anticipation. What is left is the "adventuring outside oneself toward the unforeseeably-other, *without hope of return*. [...] Levinas speaks of an 'eschatology without hope for the self or without liberation in my time'. Therefore, there is no way to conceptualize the encounter: it is made possible by the other, the unforeseeable 'resistant to all categories'. Concepts suppose an anticipation, a horizon within which alterity is amortized as soon as it is announced precisely because it has let itself be foreseen. The infinitely-other cannot be bound by a concept, cannot be thought on the basis of a horizon; for a horizon is always a horizon of the same, the elementary unity within which eruptions and surprises are always welcomed by understanding and recognition."[12] I quoted this text at length

---

6. J. Derrida, "Violence and Metaphysics," 98.
7. *Ibid.*, 103.
8. *Ibid.*, 108.
9. *Ibid.*, 108.
10. *Ibid.*, 129.
11. *Ibid.*, 103.
12. *Ibid.*, 95.

because the same idea, as we will see, will return in Derrida's exploration, in the late 1980s, of the messianic notion of hospitality: 'waiting without any horizon of the wait'; 'a welcoming of the guest without any a priori scheme of welcoming'.

2. *Problematization of Levinas' Metaphysics of the Infinite*

In a second move Derrida problematizes Levinas' metaphysics of the infinite. I select two items from the many questions Derrida raised: (a) did Levinas realize the problems involved in the 'archaic' use of his language? (b) Did Levinas realize the extent to which his prioritizing of the authority of the infinitely-other still presupposes the phenomenological approach which Husserl already used in his reflections on alterity?

By the 'archaic' use of language Derrida means: a strange language that cannot be immediately understood by people with a 'Western education'. So, he will attempt to 'translate' Levinas' basic insights into the language and mindset of Western people, in order to show how difficult it is for them to grasp the meaning of Levinas' classical notion of 'infinity', in an epoch in which belief in an afterlife has begun to fade away. A case in point is Levinas' eschatology of pure peace, as opposed to the violence inscribed in our 'being in the world', which also for Derrida is marked by finitude and mortality. Has not Heidegger already noted: "*Das Sein selbst ist das Strittige* (Being itself is combat)?" and also that "Being itself ... is in itself eschatological?" So, "the relationship between this (Heideggerian] eschatology and [Levinas'] messianic eschatology requires close examination. The first supposes that war is not an accident which overcomes being, but rather Being itself,"[13] whereas for Levinas the messianic era inaugurates the plenitude of peace.

It is at this juncture that Derrida points to a quasi-irresolvable aporia. In order for Levinas to elucidate how eschatological peace is brought about by one's encounter with the 'infinitely other' he must frame his conviction in language. If Levinas were to do so, however, he would quickly find out that language itself is by no means a peaceful instrument of communication, especially not in a context of finitude and struggle for life. Derrida, thus, problematizes Levinas' achievement from the background of a reflection on language: linguistic arrangements call forth, and feed on, violence. He writes: "Peace, like silence, is the strange vocation of a language called outside itself by itself. But since *finite* silence

13. *Ibid.*, 144.

is also the medium of violence, language can only indefinitely tend toward justice by acknowledging and practicing the violence within it. Violence against violence [...] Speech is doubtless the first defeat of violence, but paradoxically, violence did not exist before the possibility of speech."[14] If one were to frame in 'usual' language the absolute ethical obligation that flows from one's encounter with the naked face of the infinitely-other, then one would have to concede as well that this very face exerts a violence on the receptive person who is taken hostage by it. So, in order to suggest a peace 'that is not of this world' Levinas would have to envelop himself in mute silence, only suggesting that he wished that something like eternal peace may happen in this world, and that this wish is his non-violent speech-utterance. Yet, such a non-violent speech-utterance, Derrida remarks, would communicate nothing at all: "A Being without violence would be a Being which would occur outside the existent: nothing; nonhistory; nonoccurrence; nonphenomenality. A speech produced without the least violence, would determine nothing, would say nothing, would offer nothing to the other; it would not be *history*, and it would *show* nothing, in every sense of the word, and first of all the Greek sense, it would be speech without *phrase* [without clear articulation]."[15]

Levinas seems to have grasped Derrida's problematization. In his later work, *Otherwise than Being* (1974) he discriminates between two layers of speech, the *Saying* and the *Said*. In his comparative study of Derrida and Levinas, Simon Critchley puts this as follows: "The Saying is my exposure – corporeal and sensible – to the Other, my inability to refuse the Other's approach. It is the performative stating, proposing, or expressive position of myself facing the Other. It is a verbal or non-verbal ethical performance, whose essence cannot be caught in constative propositions. It is a performative *doing* that cannot be reduced to a constative description."[16] At the same time Levinas feels that what he intended to say with performative language makes its appearance, and is conveyed, in the *Said*, the language of propositions whose conceptuality can be analytically unraveled. The *Said*, thus, both conveys *and* betrays the performative intention of the *Saying*. In *Otherwise than Being* Levinas makes use of a hybrid style, which attempts to do 'violence' to the usual language of the Said: perforating and interrupting this language in the knowledge that always a residue of the interrupted text will remain in place. "Thus,

14. *Ibid.*, 119.
15. *Ibid.*, 147.
16. S. Critchley, *The Ethics of Deconstruction: Derrida and Levinas* (Edinburgh: Edinburgh University Press, 1992 [1997]) 7.

whereas *Totality and Infinity* powerfully articulates the non-ontological 'experience' of the face of the Other in the language of ontology [...], *Otherwise than Being* is a performative disruption of the language of ontology, which maintains the interruption of the ethical Saying within the ontological Said. Whereas *Totality and Infinity* writes about ethics, *Otherwise than Being* is the performative enactment of ethical writing."[17]

The second critical question Derrida addresses to Levinas is whether Levinas sufficiently realized that his metaphysics of the 'infinitely-other' presupposes a phenomenological approach. Put differently: did Levinas realize that the ethical priority he ascribes to the 'infinitely-other' only makes sense on the basis of what Husserl already developed in his phenomenological description of the 'alter ego', that is: of the other whose intimate self-awareness is as particular and irreducible as the particular self-awareness I have of my self? The reader may perhaps be surprised to see Derrida suddenly side with Husserl. Indeed, for Derrida, there are, in fact, two Husserls, the 'superficial' Husserl who was not able to avoid the pitfall of a self-centered philosophy of presence; and the 'deep' Husserl who tried to escape this closed shell in his considerations on temporality, and intersubjectivity. In *Speech and Phenomena* Derrida writes: "Let us note [...] that phenomenology seems to us to be tormented, if not contested from within, by its own descriptions of the movement of temporalization and the constitution of intersubjectivity."[18] It is this 'deep' Husserl that Derrida is going to play out against Levinas, thereby making use of Husserl's *Cartesian Meditations* in which Husserl brings up the question of intersubjectivity.

Derrida begins the discussion by pointing out that Levinas misunderstood the Husserl of the *Cartesian Meditations*. For Levinas, "Husserl [...] missed the infinite alterity of the other, reducing it to the same," from the moment he "made the other the ego's phenomenon, constituted by analogical appresentation on the basis of belonging to the ego's own sphere."[19] In simpler terms: Levinas accuses Husserl of not respecting the infinite alterity of the other, precisely by making the other an 'object' of phenomenological description. Derrida repudiates this accusation as unfounded. He underlines that no understanding of a thing whatsoever is

17. J. Derrida, "Violence and Metaphysics," 8.
18. J. Derrida, *Speech and Phenomena: Introduction to the Problem of Signs in Husserl's Phenomenology*, trans. D. Allison (Evanston, IL: Northwestern University Press, 1973) 6. Originally published as idem, *La voix et le phénomène: Introduction au problème du signe dans la phénoménologie de Husserl* (Paris: Presses universitaires de France, 1967).
19. J. Derrida, "Violence and Metaphysics," 123.

possible without this thing *appearing* for an ego. "It is impossible," he writes, "to respect the alter ego in experience and in language, if this other in its alterity does not *appear* for an ego (in general)."[20] Derrida formulates this statement in the technical language of Husserl's *transcendental* phenomenology, according to which the ego is not just an individual particular ego, but an 'ego in general' (the *eidos* ego). Transcendental phenomenology brackets the particular ego. The only center to which, in this 'reduction', phenomena appear is the 'ego in general'. So, what is determined of this ego in its interaction with the world applies to each and every (empirical) ego: to each and every 'me' in their interaction with the world.

This basic insight that the same 'structure' applies to each and every ego opens the perspective on intersubjectivity, on the recognition of the other in its irreducible alterity. Quoting from Husserl's *Cartesian Meditations*, Derrida writes: "They (the other *egos*), however, are not simply representations or objects represented within me, synthetic unities of a process of verification taking place 'within me', but precisely 'others' ... subjects for this same world ... subjects who perceive the world ... and who thereby experience me, just as I experience the world and in it: others."[21] And, Derrida adds: "it is this appearance of the other as that which I can never be, this originary non-phenomenality, which is examined as the ego's *intentional phenomenon*."[22] So, a 'philosophy of the presence' that would reduce the other to the sphere of the same (the ego without otherness) is definitely ruled out. What phenomenologically appears for the subject (the 'me') is the existence of an 'other me' that is *not* 'me'.

This 'not me' is the reason why Husserl spoke of an 'analogical appresentation', that is: of a 'rendering present to me' (to my consciousness) that is only analogous to the way in which consciousness 'scientifically' validates neutral objects in a process that is termed: 'presentation' of objects in and for consciousness. The irreducibly 'other' can never be grasped ('presented' in and for consciousness) as an neutral object, for the simple reason that I can never have the intimate experience the other has of herself, of the world, and of me, just as the other can never have my intimate experience of the world, of me and of her: "The necessary reference to analogical appresentation, far from signifying an analogical, and assimilatory reduction of the other to the same, confirms and respects separation, the unsurpassable necessity of (non-objective) mediation [...]

20. *Ibid.*, 123.
21. *Ibid.*, 123, citing from E. Husserl, *Cartesian Meditations*.
22. J. Derrida, "Violence and Metaphysics," 123.

The stranger is infinitely other because by his essence no enrichment of his profile can give me the subjective face of his experience *from his perspective*, such as he has lived it. Never will this experience be given to me originally, like everything which is *mir eigenes*, which is proper to me."[23]

Derrida concedes that Husserl's view on the irreducible otherness of the other is not exactly the same as Levinas' ethical approach according to which the other, the naked face of the other, addresses and commands me, in such a way that no longer a symmetrical but an asymmetrical relation is in place. Yet, Derrida maintains, without the realization of the symmetry, as elaborated by Husserl, the specific ethical asymmetry which Levinas highlights would provoke no shock, would have no proper resonance of its own. Derrida writes: "Even if one neither seeks nor is able to thematize the other *of which* one does not speak, but *to whom* one speaks, this impossibility and this imperative can be thematized (as Levinas does) only on the basis of a certain appearance of the other as other for an ego."[24] In other words, one must already be sensitive to interpersonal relations that respect the irreducible alterity of the other, in order to feel oneself summoned by the other-in-need. One would never be able to respond to the categorical demand of the naked face, if one did not yet know that this command is given by a real human person with their own irreducible sensitivities: "The egoity of the other permits him to say 'ego' as I do; and this is why he is Other, and not a stone, or a being without speech *in my real economy*. This is why, if you will, he is face, can speak to me, understand me, and eventually command me. Dissymmetry itself would be impossible without this symmetry."[25]

3. *The Strange Coupling of Judaism and Hellenism*

These considerations land us in what Derrida, at the end of this article, terms as 'the strange historical coupling of Judaism and Hellenism'. Judaism and Hellenism (which means the whole of Western philosophy) have distinct characteristics, which nonetheless are such that they stand in need of mutual complementarity. If Hellenism stands for clarity of thought and for a theoretical approach, and if Judaism stands for ethical concern and attention to the particular, then each of these approaches should allow itself to be cross-fertilized by the other. This is what Derrida has tried to demonstrate in his double problematization of Levinas'

23. *Ibid.*, 124.
24. *Ibid.*, 124.
25. *Ibid.*, 125-126.

Totality and Infinity, knowing that Levinas himself aspired for such an 'impossible' complementarity. In *Difficult Liberty* Levinas spoke up for espousing, as far as possible, "Greek civilization and what it produced: the logos, the coherent discourse of reason, life in a reasonable state."[26]

This 'impossible' complementarity is, in fact, also Derrida's ideal; it is, on closer inspection, at the heart of his practice of deconstruction. Indeed, in the course of his analysis of Levinas Derrida brings up the "necessity of lodging oneself within traditional [read: Greek] conceptuality in order to destroy it," all by being aware of a possible return of the "indestructible and unforeseeable resource of the Greek logos." The Greek logos has such a "power of envelopment" that one might fear that "he who attempts to repel it would always already be *overtaken*."[27] The only means, perhaps, to neutralize the grip of these tentacles would be to "accommodate duplicity and difference within speculation, within the very purity of philosophical meaning."[28] This is the path Derrida explores in *Speech and Phenomena*.

II. SPEECH AND PHENOMENA: INTRODUCTION TO THE PROBLEM OF SIGNS IN HUSSERL'S PHENOMENOLOGY

The full title of this book is *Speech and Phenomena: Introduction to the Problem of Signs in Husserl's Phenomenology* (1967). It is in this work that Derrida's 'linguistic turn' makes its appearance, as well as his questioning of Husserl's 'metaphysics' of presence. Indeed, the 'principle of principles' in Husserl's phenomenology is "the original, self-giving evidence, the *present* or *presence* of sense to a full and primordial intuition."[29] As already mentioned, this focus on (self-)presence has, against the grain of Husserl's basic framework, been weakened in two instances: in Husserl's late discovery of intersubjectivity, and in his reflections on the temporal flow: "In these two decisive moments of description," Derrida comments, "we recognize an irreducible nonpresence as having a constituting value, and with it a nonlife, a nonpresence or nonself-belonging of the living present, an ineradicable nonprimordiality."[30] In *Speech and Phenomena*, Derrida will touch again on these two 'breaches' in Husserl's thinking, with the explicit purpose, however,

26. *Ibid.*, 152, citing from E. Levinas, *Difficult Liberty*.
27. J. Derrida, "Violence and Metaphysics," 111-112.
28. *Ibid.*, 113.
29. J. Derrida, *Speech and Phenomena*, 5.
30. *Ibid.*, 6-7.

of showing that, from the onset, in his *Logical Investigations* (1900-1901), up to the fourth edition of that work (1928) Husserl was not willing to abandon his basic framework in spite of the difficulties that arose with it. From the first to the fourth edition, "there was no fundamental change, no determined re-examination"[31] of the founding value of presence. On the contrary, whenever Husserl ran into problems, he set out to bring in new distinctions and modifications, rather than abandoning his 'principle of principles'.

It is against this background that Derrida examines the notion of sign (*Zeichen*), or better, signs, in Husserl's *Logical Investigations*, in order to show that this notion obeys the logic of a metaphysics of presence, and is not at all in keeping with what later semiotics reveals about the function of linguistic signs. I will select three domains for comment: 1) the idealistic bias in Husserl's theory of signs; 2) Derrida's plea for accepting a non-repressed non-presence in the constitution of presence: his notion of *différance*; 3) Derrida's demonstration that the 'mature' Husserl had already laid down the foundations of his own notion of *différance*.

1. The Idealistic Bias in Husserl's Theory of Signs

Derrida points out that Husserl works with a twofold notion of sign: first, a sign that is an expression (*Ausdruck*) of meaning (*Bedeutung*) – an inner word through which consciousness speaks to itself the meaning (the meaningful evidence) which the intuited object has for its lived experience – and, second, sign as indication (*Anzeige*): e.g., empirical objects or states of affairs that 'point to' a truth without obtaining the certainty inherent in the meaning-conveying expressive utterance (*bedeutungsvoller Ausdruck*). In other words, unlike 'expression' (*Ausdruck*), an 'indication' or 'indicative sign' (*Anzeige*) does not yield clear evidence; it remains conjectural. Derrida gives some examples of such conjectural indications: He writes: "What is an indicative sign? It may be *natural* (the canals of Mars *indicate* the possible presence of intelligent beings [on that planet]), as well as *artificial* (the chalk mark, the stigmata, all the instruments of conventional designation)."[32] To the natural indicative signs also belong "the facial expression and the various gestures which involuntarily (*unwillkürlich*) accompany speech without communicative intent, or those in which a man's mental states achieve understandable 'expression' for his environment, without the added help of speech."[33]

---

31. *Ibid.*, 3.
32. *Ibid.*, 27.
33. *Ibid.*, 35, citing E. Husserl, *First Logical Investigations*, §5.

The facial expression and accompanying gestures tell something about the inner vivid experience of the person in question, but only by way of conjectural indications

The whole focus is, thus, on the meaning-conveying expression, which, in its purest form, takes place in a soliloquy in the 'solitary mental life'. It is from this 'solitary mental life' that the will or the pure intention to express meaning originates: "Pure expression will be the pure active intention (spirit, *psyche*, life, will) of an act of meaning (*bedeuten*) that animates a speech whose content (*Bedeutung*) is present."[34] Yet, Derrida observes, such a purity of expression can, for Husserl, only be obtained through a 'bracketing off' (*epoche*, reduction) of the whole empirical realm, including the indicative sign which is part of it: "The meaning is therefore *present to the self* in the life of a present that has not yet gone forth from itself into the world, space, or nature. All these 'going-forths' effectively exile this life of self-presence to indications."[35] At this juncture Derrida asks the question as to how, from this perspective, communication with the outer-world, with 'the other' will still be possible. Indeed, at a certain moment Husserl opened the perspective of such a communication on the basis of a movement in which the interior pure expression would be intertwined with an indicative sign that could be grasped by a dialogue partner. Such an intertwining, if it were really to happen, is crucial for Derrida: it would reveal that the purity of Husserl's phenomenology of presence is not pure, but contaminated by elements from the empirical world. Husserl is aware of this difficulty. He therefore states that such an intertwining only leads to a lesser form of 'expression', since the other can never grasp the lived experience of what the 'I' feels in its purely inner expression.

The reasoning that follows shows a resemblance with what Husserl later develops in the *Cartesian Meditations*, namely that the subjective side of an experience, including its communication through gestures and indicative signs, can never be experienced as such by the dialogue partner. In the *Cartesian Mediations* this basic insight leads, as we have seen in Derrida's discussion with Levinas, to the recognition of the irreducible otherness of 'the other'. At this stage of Husserl's thought the phenenological description has evolved into a *transcendental* phenomenology, in which the transcendental ego occupies a rather objective, encompassing position that departs from the monological phenomenology of the

34. J. Derrida, *Speech and Phenomena*, 40.
35. *Ibid.*, 40.

earlier works, and thus is able to acknowledge various centers of 'personalized thinking', all existing in mutual respect for one another. In the *Logical Investigations* this transition to intersubjectivity has not yet taken place. Here, the sole question to be treated is whether the purity of the inner meaning-content of expression in the solitary mental life can be communicated *as such* to the external other. The answer is: no; the subjective side of the experience cannot be communicated through indicative signs. If I were to place myself at the receiving end, then I would be able to grasp the indicative sign but not the inner core from which it proceeds: "the subjective side of [the other's] experience, his consciousness, in particular the acts by which he gives sense to his signs, are not immediately and primordially present to me."[36]

For Derrida, Husserl is compelled to underscore the weakening character of the indicative sign, in order to safeguard his phenomenology of pure presence. This leads him to examine the extent to which Husserl, in his theory of signs, admits of any mediating sign by which the meaning-content of expression is to be mediated to consciousness, within the confines of one's interiority. He observes that Husserl introduces a further distinction to ward off contact with the empirical world. For Husserl, the interior expression of meaning cannot stand in need of an indicative sign, since this indicative sign is part of the empirical world: a facial expression, an intonation of the voice, etc. So, its mediating sign must be of a different nature: this mediating sign is now called a 'pointer' (*Hinzeige*) instead of an 'indicator' (*Anzeige*). The signs that 'point to', that help to communicate to, consciousness the meaning-content of expression are imaginative representations (*Phantasievorstellungen*). Derrida extensively quotes Husserl: "[In solitary discourse] we are in general content with imagined rather than with actual words. In imagination a spoken or printed word floats before us, though in [empirical] reality it has no existence. We should not, however, confuse imaginative representations (*Phantasievorstellungen*), and still less the image-contents they rest on, with their imagined objects. The imagined verbal sound, or the imagined printed word does not exist, only its imaginative representation does so. The difference is the difference between imagined centaurs and the imagination of such beings [It is this last element that matters]."[37]

The next question is: what is the function of these imaginative representations? They mainly serve to make the repetition of the same 'meaning-content of expression' possible, without substantially altering it in

---

36. *Ibid.*, 38.
37. *Ibid.*, 44.

the successive acts of repetition. If the number 'nine' is a 'meaning-content of expression' *presented* to consciousness, then the subsequent repetition of this same number 'nine' is its renewed presentation, or *its re-presentation* to consciousness. This leads Derrida to ask the question as to how precisely, for Husserl, in this system of repeatability, the re-presentation (the 'signifier') relates to the first presentation (the 'signified'). His fears are that the imaginative re-presentation (the 'signifier') will be regarded as derivative and subordinate to the first presentation (the 'signified'). Indeed, in Husserl's phenomenology of presence, the first presentation is immediately present to consciousness, and it is this immediacy that will also govern the subsequent re-presentations in the future. At this juncture Derrida remarks that, for Husserl, ideality and repeatability presuppose each other. The selfsame transmission of the meaning-content takes place in the sphere of ideality: "What constitutes the ideality of meaning for Husserl is the possibility of its being repeated an infinite number of times."[38]

If one would abandon this ideality, and return to semiotics, which is what Derrida does, repetition in language would open up a different perspective, one that is catapulted into the past. In semiotics, repetition, as a real and primordial possibility, *precedes*, and is operative in, the constitution of meaning. Derrida writes: "When I *effectively* use words [...] I must from the outset operate (within) a structure of repetition whose basic element can only be representative. [...] A sign which would take place but 'once' would not be a sign; a purely idiomatic sign would not be a sign."[39] So, repeatability is the foundation of language as it actually functions. In this repeatability signs refer to other signs, which they also occasionally modify. According to this logic, Husserl's exalted idealities must also be regarded as signs by which a chain of transmitting signs are derived from signs (impressions) of empirical objects. This leads Derrida to write: "The [idealized] presence-of-the-present is derived from repetition and not the reverse."[40] Let us notice that in this semiotic notion of repetition (repetition that comes first), no mention is made of a 'signified': there is only a play of signifiers through acts of substitution or representation. This is not at all the case with Husserl. For him, repetition is intrinsically connected with ideality; it takes its point of departure in the ideality of the thing that is directly present to consciousness, and which is the 'signified' to be transmitted through repetition: "Absolute

---

38. D. Allison, "Translator's Introduction," in idem, *Speech and Phenomena*, xxxv.
39. J. Derrida, *Speech and Phenomena*, 50.
40. *Ibid.*, 52.

ideality is the correlate of a possibility of indefinite repetition [of the *same* meaning-content]."[41]

Since *Speech and Phenomena* does not contain a study of Husserl's later works, hardly a mention is made of the transmission of the original meaning-content through codified texts, through writing. Instead, Derrida remarks that the indefinite repetition of the ideality brackets off the whole empirical realm, included the elements of finitude and mortality. He points out that Husserl must have realized the oddity of this elimination, since for the indefinite repetition of the ideality to take place, an infinite series of human transmitters is needed, who are all replaceable and mortal. From this Derrida concludes that the phenomenology of presence both suppresses and dissimulates the relationship with death and disappearance: "The relation with the presence of the present as the ultimate form of being and of ideality is the move by which I transgress empirical existence, factuality, contingency, worldliness etc. – first of all, *my own* empirical existence. [...] The relationship with *my death* (my disappearance in general) thus lurks in this determination of being as presence, ideality, the absolute possibility of repetition."[42] This relationship with disappearance is what Derrida terms 'the presence of absence' which is negated and dissimulated in the phenomenology of presence. If one would dare to take leave of this 'determination of being as presence', which has dominated the whole history of Western metaphysics, then one would have to acknowledge that non-presence is intertwined with the affirmation of presence. One would understand that "the possibility of my disappearance in general must somehow be experienced in order for a relationship with presence in general to be instituted."[43]

2. *The Role of Non-Presence in the Constitution of Presence*

This brings us to the second point: Derrida's plea for accepting a non-repressed non-presence in the constitution of presence: his enigmatic notion of *différance*. In tackling this question, Derrida again examines the relationship between 'retention, now moment, and 'protention' which Husserl developed in his *Phenomenology of Internal Time Consciousness*. What is at stake in this examination is the consistency of Husserl's whole project: "If the punctuality of the instant is a myth, a spatial or mechanical metaphor, an inherited metaphysical concept, or all that at once, and

41. *Ibid.*, 52.
42. *Ibid.*, 53-54.
43. *Ibid.*, 54.

if the presence of self-presence is not *simple*, if it is constituted in a primordial and irreducible synthesis [with non-presence], then the whole of Husserl's argumentation is threatened in its very principle."[44] As mentioned earlier, in his analysis of internal time consciousness, Husserl discovered the notion of duration or the lived experience of the flux of time. In describing this lived experience he suggested a 'spreading out' of the perception of duration in a past moment (that still is retained), an instantaneous now moment, and the anticipation of the next now moment (protention).

Yet, Derrida remarks, since Husserl's whole focus is on evidence and the 'presence of the present', he still prioritizes, even in his description of duration, the punctuality of the instant: "This spread is nonetheless thought and described on the basis of the self-identity of the now as point, as a 'source-point'. In phenomenology, the idea of primordial presence and in general of 'beginning' [...] always refers back to this source point."[45] In order to corroborate this view, Derrida quotes a text from Husserl's *Ideas*: The 'I', the self, can only be constituted as the result of "[t]he actual *now* [which is] necessarily something punctual *(ein Punktuelles)*, and remains so, a form that persists through continuous change of matter."[46] Nonetheless, there are passages in which Husserl also characterizes retention and protention in terms of non-perception: In a description of retention as 'primary remembrance' and protention as 'primary expectation', Husserl admits that in these instances one is concerned with a situation "whereby *perception and non-perception continually* pass over into one another."[47] For Derrida, this implies that "the presence of the perceived presence can appear as such only inasmuch as it is *continuously compounded* with nonpresence and nonperception [...] These nonperceptions are neither added to, nor do they *occasionally* accompany, the actually perceived now; they are essentially involved in its possibility."[48]

Husserl apparently tries to harmonize two irreconcilable approaches. On the one hand, in fidelity to the experience of the 'things themselves', he cannot but categorize retention as 'non-perceived' in the actual now moment; on the other, the only source of certitude is the presence of the present: on this basis he tries to keep the retention in the sphere of the actual now moment. From this wavering between two extremes, Derrida

44. *Ibid.*, 61.
45. *Ibid.*, 61-62.
46. *Ibid.*, 62, citing E. Husserl, *Ideas* I, §81.
47. J. Derrida, *Speech and Phenomena*, 65, citing E. Husserl, *Phenomenology of Internal Time-Consciousness*, §16.
48. J. Derrida, *Speech and Phenomena*, 64.

concludes that it would be more logical to see an affinity between 'retention' and 'representative repetition', and to admit that it is repetition (in the sense of semiotics) that "makes possible the ever renewed upsurge and virginity [of the actual now moment]."[49] It is here that Derrida brings up the notion of *différance*: "[On closer inspection] the presence of the present is thought of as arising from the bending-back of a return, from the movement of repetition, and not the reverse [...] This trace or *différance* is always older than presence and procures for it its openness [its loss of the characteristic of self-identity]."[50] Once one admits that presence arises from the region of the *non-identical* which Derrida associates with trace and *différance*, presence becomes an open presence, and no longer stands in need of affirming its irreducible character of 'being absolutely identical to itself'. Derrida realizes that, by entering a domain 'that is older than presence', he is venturing into a new understanding of space and time, one that no longer bears the imprint of a metaphysics of presence.

In a first move to explore this domain, Derrida further meditates on the correlation between the 'presence of the present' and the awareness of 'absolute self-identity'. He does so by pointing out that a phenomenology of presence not only smacks of logocentrism, but also of phonocentrism: 'hearing oneself speak'. In his analyses of phonocentrism Derrida has at various times recourse to the thought of Hegel. In the pages devoted to phonocentrism and auto-affection, references to Husserl are minimal. This Hegelian inspiration leads Derrida to adopt a dialectical reasoning in which what is first affirmed (absolute unity) is, in a second step, erased (the emergence of difference within unity). In a first moment Derrida shows that the voice is the most appropriate metaphor to suggest unbroken unity; the speaker hears his/her own voice speak without any intermediary: "The subject does not have to pass forth beyond himself to be immediately affected by his expressive activity. My words are 'alive' because they seem not to leave me: not to fall outside me, outside my breath, at a visible distance; not to cease to belong to me, to be at my disposition 'without further props'."[51] The signified is, in other words, immediately present to itself; any mediating signifier evaporates: "the soul of language seems not to separate itself from itself, from its own self-presence."[52] To hear oneself speak is pure auto-affection. But then

49. *Ibid.*, 66.
50. *Ibid.*, 68.
51. *Ibid.*, 76.
52. *Ibid.*, 77.

comes the dialectical reversal: Whenever the 'I' affects itself in speech, a 'space of difference' is opened in the interior of this auto-affection. From this cleavage emerges the possibility of 'otherness' which auto-affection thought it could eliminate. Derrida writes: 'Taking auto-affection as the exercise of the voice, auto-affection supposed that a pure difference comes to divide self-presence. In this pure difference is rooted the possibility of everything we think we can exclude from auto-affection: space, the outside, the world, the body etc."[53]

This recourse to Hegel serves Derrida as a springboard from which to shed light on what I earlier termed the 'deep' Husserl. Indeed, as Derrida sees it, Husserl, with his reflections on time-consciousness, laid down the foundation of what Heidegger rendered thematic as the temporalization of existence. The experienced 'time flow' cannot be arrested by consciousness, however much the 'superficial' Husserl tried to achieve this with his incorporation of retention into the punctual now moment. Once, however, one abandons this attempt at mastery, things become different; it becomes evident, then, that temporalization is already at work within the auto-affection of the 'I', the seat of allegedly uncontaminated self-identity. Even at that level, the trace of non-identity infiltrates self-identity. For Derrida, this insight reveals the power and the limit of the phenomenological method. He writes: "Temporalization is at once the very power and limit of phenomenological reduction [...] phenomenological reduction is a scene, a theater, a stage."[54] On the one hand, phenomenological reduction allows one to give a pure description of what appears to consciousness by bracketing domains that are not deemed essential to that description. On the other hand, exactly this rigorous phenomenological description showed that the phenomenological voice which thinks to hear itself speak without external contamination, can only engage in this activity on the basis of a process of self-relation within self-difference: "Auto-affection is not a modality of experience that characterizes a being that would already be itself (*autos*). It produces sameness as self-relation within self-difference; it produces sameness as the non-identical [...] The movement of *différance* is not something that happens to a transcendental subject; it produces a subject."[55]

This is also true for the actual now moment. Retention is not something that happens to the subject in its punctual now experience. Rather, this

---

53. *Ibid.*, 82.
54. *Ibid.*, 86.
55. *Ibid.*, 82.

punctual now experience is produced by an otherness that precedes its emergence: "The process by which the living now [...] must, in order to be a now and to be retained in another now, affect itself without recourse to anything empirical [...], this process is indeed a pure auto-affection in which the same is the same only in being affected by the other, only by becoming the other of the same."[56] Temporalization dethrones any ego that would deem itself to be purely self-identical: there is no 'inside' (seat of egoity) without being punctured by an 'outside'. For Derrida, it is imperative to link temporalization with spatiality and spacing. It is only this combination with an interrupting spacing that makes us aware of a temporality that is not marked by sameness. As we will see in a moment: the intriguing term difference, or *différance* for that matter, has both a temporal and spatial connotation. He writes: "As soon as we admit spacing both as 'interval' or difference and as openness upon the outside, there can no longer be an absolute inside, for the 'outside' has insinuated itself into the movement by which the inside of the nonspatial, which is called 'time', appears, is constituted, is 'presented'. Space is 'in' time; it is time's pure leaving-itself; it is the 'outside-itself' as the self-relation of time."[57] Related to this notion of space, is the notion of trace, which Derrida defines as "the openness upon exteriority in general, upon the sphere that is not 'one's own' etc." [58]

3. *Elements in Husserl that Prepared the Way for* Différance

In a last section Derrida examines the extent to which there are elements in the 'deep' Husserl that prepare the way for Derrida's own notion of *différance*. This examination focuses on Husserl's theory of speech which says that the correctness of speech does not depend on its ability to make knowledge possible. The rules for speech are not the same as the rules for knowledge; they function without being bothered about the intuited 'givenness' of truth; they function, in other words, without presupposing the notion of 'presence'. Against this background Derrida gives a succinct definition of *différance*: "[*Différance* is] the operation of differing which at one and the same time both fissures and retards presence, submitting it simultaneously to primordial division and delay. *Différance* is to be conceived prior to the separation between deferring as delay and

56. *Ibid.*, 85.
57. *Ibid.*, 86.
58. *Ibid.*, 86.

differing as the active work of difference."[59] In *différance* there is, thus,
a spatial element: that of the delay of plenitude of presence *and* a temporal element: presence being repeatedly fissured by non-presence, self-
identity being repeatedly invaded by non-identity.

Derrida's examination focuses on speech, and more precisely, on expression (as distinct from indication). The basic question is "in what respect
expression itself implies, in its very structure, nonplenitude?"[60] Derrida
welcomes the fact that, in order to attain the purity of expression, Husserl
brackets off, as non essential, the act of intuitive knowledge which 'fulfills' the intention. An expression is valid when it aims at an object, and
also when this object is not given in the immediacy of fulfillment. For an
expression to be correct, it is enough that, in speech, an object is intended;
the fulfillment by an intuition that 'sees' the object is not required. The sole
intentionality, isolated from the object-presenting intuition: that is all that
matters. With this formal approach Husserl is able to draw a distinction
between expressions that are contradictory without becoming nonsense
('a golden mountain') and pure nonsensical expressions ('green is where').
For Derrida, this formal approach comes close to contemporary linguistics
for which the absence of the author, and the disappearance of the objects
this author was able to describe, are required for the formal validity of the
statement. He writes: "The absence of intuition – and therefore of the subject of the intuition [that is, of the person to whom the intuition occurs] –
is not only *tolerated* by speech [as in Husserl's theory]; it is *required* by
the general structure of signification, when considered *in itself.*"[61]

The problem, however, is that Husserl occasionally relapses into the
framework of a metaphysics of presence. This is specifically the case
when he examines particular subjective expressions in which the 'I' of the
speaker – 'see, here I am' – reveals something about him/herself: e.g.
'I am alive'. In this case Husserl tends to require a fulfilling intuition (of
'presence to oneself') to validate the statement, whereas for Derrida, this
is absolutely not necessary: "Whether or not I have a present intuition of
myself, '*I*' expresses something, whether or not I am alive; *I am* 'means
something'. Here also the fulfilling intuition is not an 'essential component' of expression."[62] In other passages Husserl seems to realize that
essentially subjective expressions, as the above example, pose a problem.
Unlike objective expressions, they lack absolute ideality and objectivity.

59. *Ibid.*, 88.
60. *Ibid.*, 89.
61. *Ibid.*, 93.
62. *Ibid.*, 95.

Given their strictly personal character, the essentially subjective expressions can not even be subsumed under the general statements of objective expressions. The only solution is to regard them as if they were underway to approximating the ideal of objective expressions, without ever reaching it. Derrida quotes the following text from Husserl: "We are infinitely removed from this ideal [of fully attaining at truth] … Strike out the essentially occasional [that is: the essentially subjective] expressions from one's language, try to describe any subjective experience in unambiguous, objectively fixed fashion: such an attempt is always plainly vain."[63] Later on, in *The Origin of Geometry*, Husserl will put it still more clearly: "Objective, absolute firm knowledge of truth is an infinite Idea,"[64] the Idea in the Kantian sense.

From these hesitancies in Husserl, Derrida concludes, that for Husserl as well the Idea in the Kantian sense is, ultimately, never fully realized – that the intention which was the point of departure of Husserl's theory of expression is never fully fulfilled by an intuition to which the ideal *eidos* is immediately present. This conclusion runs, of course, counter to Husserl's basic framework of a phenomenology of presence, a framework which Derrida, however, observes to be gradually fading away in the 'deep' Husserl. On the basis of this presupposition – the fading away of a phenomenology of presence – Derrida ventures to state that the Kantian Idea must no longer be seen as an ideal towards which we are under way in an unending approximation. The Kantian Idea is nothing else than a *telos* whose attainment must be endlessly deferred. If this is true, Derrida continues, one can not suspect Husserl of professing an absolute idealism in the fashion of Hegel. Derrida writes: "That Husserl always thought of infinity as an Idea in the Kantian sense, as the indefiniteness of an '*ad infinitum*', leads one to believe that he never […] believed in the accomplishment of an 'absolute knowledge'. […] What he shows us of the movement of temporalization leaves no room for doubt on this subject."[65] Whoever says temporalization, also says 'death': disappearance, absence. In the new context of temporalization and finitude, the incessant postponement of fulfillment must of necessity include the infiltration of absence, and 'lack of being'. It is the ever-repeated irruption of absence (which Derrida calls 'a relation to my-death') which

63. *Ibid.*, 100, citing E. Husserl, *Logical Investigations*, §28.
64. J. Derrida, *Edmund Husserl's Origin of Geometry*, 104, citing E. Husserl, *The Origin of Geometry*, in idem, *Edmund Husserl's Origin of Geometry*, 166. Originally published as idem, *Edmund Husserl, l'Origine de la géometrie*, trans., introd. (Paris: Presses universitaires de France, 1962).
65. J. Derrida, *Speech and Phenomena*, 101.

necessitates that we speak about the infinite deferral of presence: "Only a relation to my-death could make the infinite deferring of presence appear [...] The *infinite* différance is itself *finite*."[66]

Having brought back the Idea in the Kantian sense to the contemporary awareness of our basic condition of finitude, Derrida still wonders whether one must not definitely go further. Even by bending the Kantian Idea back to the flux of temporalization and finitude, one still works with modifications of the old schemes of thinking: "As long as we ask if the concept of differing is conceived on the basis of presence or antecedent to it, it remains one of the old signs. [In order to move definitely further] *unheard-of* thoughts are required, sought for across the memory of old signs."[67] For Derrida, the formulation of these new thoughts is a challenge without precedence. In order to free oneself of the fetters of the usual way of thinking, one should have to delve into a domain that is "'older' than the primordial dator intuition, older than the present and full perception of the 'thing itself', older than seeing, hearing, and touching"[68] – one should delve into the archeology of an 'immemorial past' from which waves of subversion reach us with the effect of turning upside down the existing hierarchy, so that 'secondary sign', 'trace', and 'writing', as shocks of disturbance, may get precedence over the 'primary sign' and the 'self-sufficiency of speech', to which these 'secondary elements', for more than two millennia, have been subordinated.

III. The Mythical 'Anteriority' of Trace, *Différance*, and *Khôra*

In his article 'Derrida and Marion: Two Husserlian Revolutions', John Caputo comments on Derrida's analysis of *Speech and Phenomena*. Caputo argues that the liberation of the sign from the dogma of intuitionism (a liberation which, as we have seen, started with the 'deep' Husserl) inaugurates, for Derrida, the beginning of a new era, that of the 'longing for the impossible'. Caputo writes: "[Derrida's] analysis of Husserl is not meant to confine us, negatively, to a hollow and empty play of signifiers [...] but to release the signifying power of the sign,

---

66. *Ibid.*, 102.
67. *Ibid.*, 102.
68. *Ibid.*, 103.

to allow the signifier to head for the future, for the unfilled and unful-fillable coming of something that eye has not seen, nor ear heard."[69] This is an assessment made in retrospect; in the knowledge thus of Der-rida's 'messianic turn' in the late 1980s, the period in which Derrida began to write on ethics and politics. This messianic turn goes hand in hand with Derrida's revolutionizing of Husserl's phenomenology which consists in paying attention to non-phenomenality, non-intuitionism, and non-appearance. In *Politics of Friendship* Derrida has this to say about the special mode of appearance of the 'other': "[T]he other appears as such: this is to say, the other appears as a being whose appearance appears without appearing, without being submitted to the phenomenological law of the originary and intuitive given that governs all other appearances, all other phenomenality as such. The altogether other, and every other [...] comes here to upset the order of phenome-nology."[70]

Derrida thus follows the path of the 'deep' Husserl, who against the principles of his own phenomenology of presence had to acknowledge that the self-experience of the other is not accessible to the intuitionism inherent in phenomenological description: the appearance of the other is without appearance. The same is true for Derrida's messianic notions, such as true democracy, true justice, true hospitality, true gift, and true forgiveness which will occupy a central place in his later works (see the next chapters). Once liberated from intuitionism these notions or signs transport us into a messianic realm whose purity intimates that what is meant by these signs – their true meaning – is not yet given. The full appearance of the meaning of these signs is still to come. In the words of Caputo: "[Derrida's] entire analysis of the Messiah is foreshadowed by the early analysis of the unfulfillable signifier, the sign whose time never comes but is always coming, for whose coming we pray and weep, which keeps us open to the future without binding us to the present, which allows us to see the present as a kind of idol vis-à-vis the messianic age. The deconstruction of the rule of intuition over the signifier is thus like the hammer that Moses took to [demolish] the golden calf in which Aaron tried to trap the divine."[71]

69. J. Caputo, "Derrida and Marion: Two Husserlian Revolutions," *Religious Experi-ence and the End of Metaphysics*, ed. J. Bloechl (Bloomington, IN and Indianapolis, IN: Indiana University Press, 2001) 120.

70. J. Derrida, *Politics of Friendship*, trans. C. Collins (London and New York: Verso, 1997) 232, cited in J. Caputo, "Derrida and Marion," 124. Originally published as idem, *Politiques de l'amitié* (Paris: Galilée, 1994).

71. J. Caputo, "Derrida and Marion," 124.

The word 'future' that Caputo uses is somewhat misleading. One must not read it with the same sense in which it is used in a philosophy of presence. There the future functions as a *telos* that is grasped and anticipated in the present, because of the dynamism set in motion by an origin that steers the whole process of development toward a fixed *telos*. Derrida's future is an 'impossible' future that cannot be captured in our present schemes of expectancy (which obey the rule of intuition). In order to specify the 'unforeseeable' character of this messianic future, Derrida is compelled to delve into an archeology that is older than the dynamic origin-*telos*-construction that characterizes the metaphysics of presence – a 'pre-historic' archeology from which the messianic dream of the 'impossible things to come' may emerge. It is from this archeology that Derrida will continue to address critical questions to the builders of 'closed systems'. In order to secure the strange character of this archeology which is 'older' than the origin-idea in the philosophy of presence, Derrida coined a whole gamut of 'subversive' terms meant to reveal 'cracks' in allegedly indisputable 'solid edifices' – such as 'trace', 'architrace', 'archi-writing', *'différance'*, *'khôra'* etc.

Where does this interest in 'archeology' come from? Some commentators opine that it is mainly due to Derrida's acquaintance with Freud's psychoanalytic studies. This acquaintance can certainly be documented. One ought only to think of *The Post Card: From Socrates to Freud and Beyond*,[72] or *Archive Fever: A Freudian Impression*.[73] Yet, one would fail to do justice to Derrida by just labeling him as a Freudian philosopher, who from a purely psychoanalytical standpoint takes delight in 'puncturing' respected literary texts in the fields of literature, ethnology and philosophy so as to make fun of their secret, repressed libidinal undercurrents. True, some of Derrida's analyses joyously take this direction. To give them overdue weight, however, would divert one's attention from Derrida's philosophical merits. He repeatedly proclaimed that he was not amused with the label of an 'eminent literary critic'; his ambition was to be recognized as a full-blood philosopher facing up to new challenges. So, it is fairer to value his interest in 'archaeology' in connection with his never-ending dialogue with Husserl's phenomenology, and underneath it also with his Nietzschean *Stimmung*. As a matter of fact, in his article 'Différance', Derrida acknowledges his indebtedness to both Freud and

---

72. J. Derrida, *The Post-Card: From Socrates to Freud and Beyond* (Chicago, IL: Chicago University Press, 1987). Originally published as idem, *La carte postale: De Socrate à Freud et au-delà* (Paris: Flammarion, 1980).

73. J. Derrida, *Archive Fever: A Freudian Impression* (Chicago, IL: Chicago University Press, 1996). Originally published as idem, *Mal d'archive* (Paris: Galilée, 1995).

Nietzsche. From these two thinkers he learned to doubt any definition of consciousness in terms of 'full presence'.[74]

1. *Trace*

The first archeological notion I mentioned is 'trace', a notion to be found also in the works of Nietzsche and Freud. The trace is a repressed utterance; it is an important indicator, leading to that for which Derrida is searching: a domain or region that escapes the hegemony of self-identity and presence. Trace, thus, is a signpost pointing to the unsettling domain of alterity – unsettling, at least, for those who are accustomed to following their spontaneous tendency to subordinate the 'other' to the 'self'. Derrida takes the notion 'alterity' or 'otherness' seriously, and therefore speaks of 'radical heterogeneity'. But how to describe this domain of radical otherness or heterogeneity? This seems to be an impossible task, because even the terms employed by linguistic analysis betray an undercurrent of a 'philosophy of presence'. No wonder then that Derrida, when trying to define his archeological key-terms, finds it necessary to issue warnings to his readers, telling them: 'no, it is not this', and 'no, it is not that', thus using a language that brings him close to negative theology, although he himself wants to go even further than negative theology can take him.

For Derrida, the trace is neither a sign, nor an origin, at least not in the sense in which these words are currently used within classificatory systems. These systems, in fact, regard themselves as being immune to temporality; they place themselves outside of the flux of time (even if they mention the notion 'origin', for example, to designate the starting point of a curb in a graph), and this creates a serious problem. With reference to these classificatory systems, the trace cannot be a sign because – in such a classificatory system – the sign always refers to something that precedes it. Yet, the term 'trace', Derrida maintains, can never be the secondary mark of a prior origin. For him, there is simply no prior origin to the trace. One ought rather to say that the trace coincides with 'origin' – on this account he often speaks of the trace as an 'originary origin'.

It will have become clear to the reader that the term 'origin' has in the meantime taken on a different meaning. Origin is no longer, as in current classificatory systems, a single point of origination (projected upon a single plane); it is associated now with 'virtual multiplicity' (spreading into

74. See: J. Derrida, "Différance," in idem, *Margins of Philosophy*, trans. A. Bass (Chicago, IL: University of Chicago Press, 1982) 21. Originally published as idem, *Marges de la philosophie* (Paris: Minuit, 1972).

multidimensional space, so to speak, with dissipating routes that change their position in the course of time), a matrix that radically differentiates itself and makes heterogeneity possible. From this perspective, trace not only comes before meaning and meaning systems, but actually grounds them. Meaning precisely arises where, without any reservation, free access is given to 'difference': only difference that matters gives rise to specific meaning.[75] Or as Derrida puts it: "The trace is in effect the absolute origin of meaning in general. This is a way of saying, once again, that there is no absolute origin of meaning in general. The trace is the *différance* which opens up appearance and meaning."[76]

2. Différance

Derrida's second key-term, *Différance*, is closely connected to the emergence of heterogeneity. It acts like a signal of prohibition, reminding us that any attempt at subsuming the many under the 'one' is illegitimate. In its graphic form it is a French neologism, a deformation of the more common French word '*différence*' (difference in English). Derrida accounts for this neologism by pointing to the two meanings conveyed by the Latin verb '*dif-ferre*' (in French: *différer*). In the first instance, it means an act of 'deferral' or 'postponement'; but at the same time it also means 'to be different', 'to be other', 'to be discernible'. Because 'difference' in common usage designates the aspect of being different, but leaves out that of deferral, Derrida found it necessary to coin the unusual noun '*différance*'. In French this noun is pronounced in the same way as '*différence*'; so one will not hear that something has been changed. Yet even so, the '**a**' of '*différance*' is perceptible in writing; there it acts as a trouble-maker, signaling the deferral of presence in and through the play of differences.

Derrida further points out that in French "the ending -ance [in *dif-férance*] remains undecided *between* the active and the passive."[77] It is rather a 'middle voice'; not to be conceived as agent or patient. This suggests that the notion '*différance*' is to be located at the other side of classical binary oppositions. '*Différance*' seems to operate from 'outside of the system', 'puncturing' systematic thinking and its fixed concepts of mutual exclusion. This brings us back to the sphere of archaeology and

---

75. This insight was already reached in certain linguistic schools.

76. J. Derrida, *Of Grammatology*, trans. G. Spivak (Baltimore, MD: John Hopkins University Press, 1984 [1976]) 95. Originally published as idem, *De la grammatologie* (Paris: Minuit, 1967).

77. J. Derrida, "Différance," 9.

to the way in which, in this region, the 'origin' is replaced with an 'archi-origin': with an origination characterized by a never-ending play of 'dissemination', by a dispersal that never returns to its 'origin'.

Derrida specifies his understanding of this never-ending play by comparing it with what de Saussure reveals about the role of the sign in language. Derrida observes that, for de Saussure, "the play of difference [...] is the condition for the possibility and functioning of every sign:"[78] the sign has both a differential and arbitrary character (one cannot define it in advance). This means that language has neither ideas nor sounds that exist before the linguistic system; language feeds on the conceptual and phonic differences within the linguistic system. Derrida positively appreciates this intra-linguistic view, but at the same time wants to emphasize, beyond de Saussure, that this 'system of differences' is also marked by deferral and delay. He does so by asking the question as to how the sign relates to the thing it represents (to use this classical formulation). His answer reads as follows: "The sign represents the present in its absence. It takes the place of the present. When we cannot grasp or show the thing, state the present, the being-present, when the present cannot be represented, we signify, we go through the detour of the sign. We take or give signs. We signal. The sign, in this sense, is deferred presence."[79] This deferred presence makes us aware of the 'temporization' and the 'spacing' that are inherent in the house of language, within which time and again we wander from sign to sign. Derrida writes: "Whether we are concerned with the verbal or the written sign, with the monetary sign, or with electoral delegation and political representation, the circulation of signs defers the moment in which we can encounter the thing itself, make it ours, consume or expend it, touch it, see it, intuit its presence. What I am describing here in order to define it is the classically determined structure of the sign in all the banality of its characteristics – signification as the *différance* of temporization. And this structure presupposes that the sign, which defers presence, is conceivable only on the *basis* of the presence that it defers and *moving toward* the deferred presence that it aims to reappropriate."[80]

Derrida admits that the idea of the deferred presence is already to be found in de Saussure. Yet, he remarks, de Saussure regarded the substitution of the sign for the 'thing itself' as something provisional and secondary. Classical semiotics expects that, in spite of a provisional substitution, the link with the 'thing itself' will never be lost – which is, in

78. *Ibid.*, 5.
79. *Ibid.*, 9.
80. *Ibid.*, 9.

fact, a remnant of metaphysics of presence. For Derrida, however, the circulation of signs that defers the present is not at all provisional or secondary; it is just a fact we can never escape. The delay of presence is something permanent, just as there is no escape from 'taking the detour of the sign'. *Différance* reminds us that each attempt at resuscitating 'presence' is illusory and dangerous. It therefore questions and shakes every 'kingdom of presence' from its dark 'pre-historic' location that cannot even be called 'being': "It is the domination of beings that *différance* everywhere comes to solicit, in the sense that *sollicitare*, in old Latin, means: to shake as a whole, to make tremble in entirety. Therefore, it is the determination of Being as presence or as beingness that is interrogated by the thought of *différance* [...] *Différance* is not. It is not a present being, however excellent, unique, principal, or transcendent. It governs nothing, reigns over nothing, and nowhere exercises any authority. It is not announced by any capital letter. Not only is there no kingdom of *différance*, but *différance* instigates the subversion of every kingdom. Which makes it obviously threatening and infallibly dreaded by everything within us that desires a kingdom, the past or future presence of a kingdom."[81]

3. Khôra

Equally as mysterious as *différance* is the notion of *khôra* which Derrida discovered in the *Timaeus*, in which Plato gives a mythico-scientific account of the creation of the cosmos. This notion is clearly 'mythical' in that Plato locates it in a 'before' that is difficult to imagine and which can only be grasped in an oneiric dream-state. In the *Timaeus*, *khôra* is a formless spatial receptacle in which the sensible copies of the forms or paradigms (ideas) are going to be received so as to take on concrete existence in the world. *Khôra*, therefore, is likened to a womb that receives and 'gives place' to the sensible things patterned after the self-identical ideas; but taken in herself she is neither sensible nor intelligible. She shares with the pre-existent ideas some form of eternity – *khôra* has always been there and will exist for ever – but this eternity must be conceived as a mythical anteriority, rather than as the selfsame eternity proper to the intelligible paradigms. That is the reason why Derrida calls her a 'non-place', although *khôra* literally means 'place'. On the other hand, *khôra* is also not a sensible thing; she is, on the contrary, the indeterminate receptacle into which the sensible things are going to be inscribed.

---

81. *Ibid.*, 21-22.

We already know of Derrida's predilection for entities that are neither 'this' nor 'that' – a sort of 'third genre' (*triton genos*) whose exact nature is difficult to determine. Plato, too, seems to have been wrestling with this difficulty. He had to admit that a definition of *khôra* exceeds the capacity of systematic thinking; the only access to it is through a 'bastard reasoning' that has an affinity with mythical language. This sits well with Derrida's exploration of the domain that comes 'before clear conceptuality'. For him, *khôra* lies both at the origin of the emergence of binary oppositions with which Western logic works, and completely outside of these oppositions. This gives *khôra* the traits of an a-temporal anteriority: "The *khôra* is a-temporal; it 'is' the a-temporality within being, or better: the a-temporality of being. It anachronizes being."[82] With the 'appearance' of *khôra* the emergence of thought is catapulted into the clouds of an 'immemorial past'.

Khôra is basically an outsider. If the intelligible paradigm forms with the sensible becoming a father/son couple, then *khôra* falls outside of this oppositional couple: "*Khôra* marks a place apart, the spacing which keeps a dissymmetrical relation to all that which, 'in herself', beside or in addition to herself, seems to make a couple with her. In the couple outside of the couple, this strange mother who gives place without engendering, can no longer be considered as an origin. She/it eludes all anthropo-theological schemes, all history, all revelation, and all truth. Preoriginary, *before* and outside of all generation, she no longer even has the meaning of a past, of a present that is past. *Before* signifies no temporal anteriority [in the common understanding of that word]. Her/its [...] nonrelation looks more like the relation of the interval of the spacing to what is lodged in it to be received in it."[83] *Khôra*, described in this way, seems to be the antipode of the demiurge and of the eternal paradigms upon which he fixes his gaze. That is the reason why Derrida, in his reading of Plato, places *khôra* before and outside of history, revelation, and truth, which apparently find themselves on the side of *logos*, eternal verities, and the Godhead (demiurge), the guarantor of truth. Located before and outside of all generation, *khôra* eludes all anthropological and theological schemes. *Khôra* belongs to the dark side of the cosmos; her voice reaches us from an 'immemorial' past, before the adventure of human history.

---

82. J. Derrida, "*Khôra*" in idem, *On the Name*, trans. D. Wood (Stanford, CA: Stanford University Press:1995) 94 [translation modified]. Originally published as idem, *Sauf le nom* (Paris: Galilée, 1993).
83. *Ibid.*, 124-125.

In a further elucidation Derrida reflects on the precise manner in which *khôra* 'gives birth (place)' to the sensitive things patterned after the ideas. As a spatial receptacle, he says, *khôra* receives all the determinations in order to 'give place' to them. But in receiving these determinations – the imprints of the copies of the paradigms – she does not appropriate any of them as her own property. *Khôra* does not possess any thing of her own: "*Khôra* receives, so as to give place to them, all the determinations, but she/it does not possess any of them as her/its own. She possesses them, she has them, since she receives them, but she does not possess them as properties; she does not possess anything as her own. She 'is' nothing other than the sum or the process of what has just been inscribed 'on' her."[84] She also does not give anything, and in this sense *khôra* has no 'being'. Consequently *khôra* does not lend any substantial 'support' to the elements to which she 'gives a place'. She just sets them free on their own without any gesture of a donor-subject. But precisely because of this 'absence of support' – because she is not 'origin' in the conventional meaning of the term – *khôra* is able to act, from her mythical anteriority, as an entity that issues admonitions and warnings against possible derailments in the direction of logocentrism. Derrida writes: "This absence of support, which cannot be translated into absent support or into absence as support, provokes *and* resists any binary or dialectical determination, any inspection of a philosophical *type*, or let us say more rigorously, of an *ontological* type. This type finds itself both defied and relaunched by the very thing that appears to give it place." And, he adds, "the expression *to give place* does not refer to the gesture of a donor-subject, the support or origin of something which would come to be given to someone."[85] In Derrida's reading of the *Timaeus*, *khôra* is not just the receptacle that welcomes the structuring forms or ideas; rather, it receives these in order to confuse their intelligible imprint. *Khôra* is a place of 'negativity' – issuing negative warnings – meant to keep us within the confines of finitude.

In *How to Avoid Speaking? Denials*, an essay on negative theology and on Heidegger's and his relation to it, Derrida makes it clear that for him the negativity of *khôra* is not that of a threshold allowing the transition, as in negative theology, towards a higher form of communication with the Sacred. In a footnote to this essay he quotes a text that already figured in his article 'Différance'. In this text he reacts to critics insinuating that Derrida, with his emphasis on delay and difference, was tacitly

84. *Ibid.*, 99.
85. *Ibid.*, 99-100.

espousing a type of negative theology. His succinct self-defense reads as follows: "So much so that the detours, locutions, and syntax in which I will often have to take recourse will resemble those of negative theology, occasionally even to the point of being indistinguishable from negative theology. Already we have had to delineate *that différance is not*, does not exist, is not a present-being (*on*) in any form [...] It derives from no category of being, whether present or absent. And yet those aspects of *différance* which are thereby delineated are not theological, not even in the order of the most negative of negative theologies." He explains why this is not the case: "[Negative theologies] are always concerned with disengaging a superessentiality beyond the finite categories of essence and existence, that is, of presence, and always hastening to recall that God is refused the predicate of existence, only in order to acknowledge his superior, inconceivable, and ineffable mode of being."[86]

How to Avoid Speaking? Denials is an elaborated version of a paper Derrida read in 1986 at a conference in Jerusalem on *Absence and Negativity*. In it, he responds to the allegations that he may cryptically be engaged in negative theology. The first part deals with certain commonalities between his thought and that of negative theology. Derrida admits that his notions of trace and *différance* can, analogously, also be found in negative theology. As with Derrida's thought, so also in negative theology "the apophatic movement [...] can only indefinitely defer the encounter with its own limit."[87] This is, for him, however, no reason to follow Wittgenstein's advice that one must keep silent (did not Wittgenstein write: "concerning that about which one cannot speak, one must remain silent"?). Derrida himself wants to go further than mute silence – and he suspects that negative theology will follow suit. Three elements allow for overcoming this silence: 1) the keeping alive of the promise, 2) of the secret, and 3) of the place. 1. The promise. Commenting on Wittgenstein's 'one must remain silent', Derrida remarks that he takes seriously solely this 'one must', but not that which Wittgenstein deduces from it: total silence. For him, the 'one must' (*il faut*) "inscribes the injunction to silence in the order of the promise of a 'one must [finally] speak', 'one must – not avoid speaking'; or rather, 'it is necessary (*il faut*) [...] that there have been a trace', a sentence that one must simultaneously turn towards a past *and* toward a future that are as yet

86. J. Derrida, "Différance," 6, cited in J. Derrida, "How to Avoid Speaking? Denials," *Languages of the Unsayable*, ed. S. Budick and W. Iser (New York: Columbia University, 1989) 63n2. Originally published as idem, "Comment ne pas parler? – Dénégations," in idem, *Psyche – Invention de l'autre* (Paris: Galilée, 1987).
87. J. Derrida, "How To Avoid Speaking? Denials," 11.

unpresentable."[88] In other words, even in the midst of speechlessness, there is a trace that obligates one not to avoid speaking. Derrida links the notions of trace and of promise (in which the injunction to silence is inscribed) to an archi-promise that already inhabits language: "even before speech, in any case, before a discursive event as such, there is necessarily a commitment or a promise. The event presupposes the open space of the promise."[89] 2. The secret. The fact that one is compelled to delay speech, even against the background of the promise contained in language, reveals that one is concerned with a secret, a secret that must not be betrayed, but which also resists its non-disclosure. 3. Place. Finally there is the notion of place, or the typology of the secret. On closer inspection, this place must be termed a 'non-place' of manifestation from which an event can 'take place'.

The second part of the essay compares three schools of 'negative theology', the Platonic (or neo-Platonic), the Christian, and the Heideggerian. Derrida begins his review by pointing to two irreconcilable sources in Plato: Plato's considerations about the Good, situated beyond Being (*epekeina tès ousias*), and about *khôra*. The former will be received in Christian negative theology, the latter will surface in Heidegger and in Derrida himself. In his dialogue *The Republic*, Plato places the idea of the Good beyond the beingness of Being: "From what is beyond the presence of all that is, the Good gives birth to Being and to the essence of what is, *to einai* and *tèn ousian*, but without itself being [part of them]."[90] In order to come into contact with this hyperessential Cause of all that exists, the philosopher and the mystic ought to pass through a process of negations. But this "negativity serves the *hyper* movement that produces, attracts, or guides it [...]. This negative form is not neutral. It does not oscillate between *ni ceci – ni cela* (the neither/nor). It first of all obeys the logic of the *sur*, of the *hyper*, over and beyond, which heralds all the hyperessentialisms of Christian apophases."[91]

In the Christian milieu the negations ('what God is not'), radical as they may be, are seen as preparing the way for beholding the supereminent disclosure of God's self-communication from beyond the limits of common understanding. When Pseudo-Dionysius, the prototype of Christianized Neo-Platonic mysticism, for example, says that God is not Being, this does not at all mean that the mystic comes in touch with God as

88. *Ibid.*, 11-12. Here Derrida uses, for the first time, the expression 'unpresentable' we have examined at length in our analysis of Lyotard.
89. *Ibid.*, 13.
90. *Ibid.*, 32.
91. *Ibid.*, 32.

nothingness. The refusal to predicate Being to God rather aims at puri-
fying the notion of its mundane or contaminated connotations, so as to
prepare oneself to be transported into a state of rapture at the encounter
with God's 'luminous darkness'. The mystics are, in other words, drawn
from a non-purified to a purified state, thus crossing a threshold that
brings them to a higher awareness. Crossing this threshold is often
painful, for one has to abandon one's usual ways of thinking and living.
Nonetheless the adventure is worthwhile. Dionysius knows, as is were in
advance, that with God's help, this final leap will be possible. The 'certitude' is expressed in the prayers he addresses to the One-on-the-other-
side, whom he believes will draw him over the threshold.

In his analyses of Dionysius and Eckhardt, Derrida highlights the role
of prayer and praise (*encomium*) in the mystical ascent. Dionysius begins
his *Mystical Theology* with a prayer addressed to the "Trinity beyond
Being," humbly asking that this Trinity "beyond divinity" and "beyond
goodness" may "direct him to the mystical summits more than unknown
and beyond light."[92] In his comment Derrida underlines that Dionysius
seems to realize, first, that the one whom he addresses "is in truth the first
Cause of his prayer and already guides it,"[93] and second that he feels
himself steered by the promise of a revelation. It is here that we encounter
the notion of a 'promise', taken in a stronger sense than Derrida intended.
In accordance with the Christian milieu in which Dionysius lived, the
promise is linked to the specificity of biblical revelation. This biblical
milieu is the 'place' of the mystical union with the hidden divinity; it
also delineates the type of secret that accompanies the mystical ascent, a
secrecy that necessitates an initiation into the mystery (*mystagogia*): "The
identity of this place, and hence of this text, and of its reader, comes from
the future of what is promised by the promise. The advent of this future
has a provenance: the event of the promise. Contrary to what seemed to
happen in the 'experience' of the place called *khôra*, the apophasis is
brought into motion – it is *initiated* in the sense of initiative and initiation – by the event of revelation which is also a promise."[94]

All this is worlds apart from the promise, the secret and the place that
Derrida associates with the negativity of *khôra*. Here the place is not
associated with a mountain – Mount Sinai – upon which the revelation
takes place. Instead of being linked with height – *hyper*, over and beyond
–, *khôra* is associated with a receptacle 'underneath' – a matrix that

92. Ps.- Dionysius Areopagita, *Mystical Theology*, Chapter 1: 9098a.
93. J. Derrida, "How To Avoid Speaking? Denials," 47-48.
94. *Ibid.*, 48-49.

spaces from an immemorial past: "The *khôra* is the atemporality
(*l'anachronie*) itself of the spacing; it (a-)temporalizes (*anachronises*);
it calls fort atemporality, provokes it immutably from the pretemporal
already that gives place to every inscription."[95] Whereas in Christian
negative theology the negation ('this or that is not God') "opens up a
history and a anthropo-theological dimension,"[96] the negativity inherent
in *khôra* is "radically nonhuman and atheological."[97] It is in this form that
khôra makes it reappearance in Heidegger, for whom *khôra*, as spacing,
separates Being from the beings (the ontological difference). In this atheological context Heidegger drops the *apostrophe*, the act of addressing
and naming the 'other', that was so significant in Dionysius: "But there
is never a prayer, not even an 'address' in Heidegger's rhetoric. Unlike
Dionysius he never says 'you'; neither to God, nor to a disciple or
reader,"[98] although one must admit that Heidegger shows respect for
prayer.

As far as Derrida is concerned, he refuses to drop the act of addressing. The appellation 'O *khôra*' makes sense for him, just as a promise *in
sordino* – a promise that is not linked to a history with an anthropologi-
cal-theological dimension – makes sense. In a first moment he states that
khôra gives nothing and promises nothing. Contrasting *khôra* with Heidegger's '*Es gibt das Sein*' (Being is there, and it is there as giving), Derrida points out that *khôra* cannot be conceived of as 'giving something'.
The '*es gibt*' applied to *khôra* only means that *khôra* 'is there', although
in a mode of 'being there' that can never be located in space and time,
since, strictly speaking, *khôra* is before time and history. Moreover, what
certainly cannot be said is that *khôra* 'gives' something (the second meaning of *es gibt*). *Khôra* is not instrumental in bringing about order; it does
not contribute to making human history meaningful; it makes no promise
of an anthropological or theological type; it does not aim at elevating
human beings into semi-gods; it does not lure them into activating poetic
powers which turn them into 'shepherds of Being'. Or, as Derrida himself puts it: "Radically nonhuman and atheological, one cannot even say
that *khôra* gives place or that *there is* the *khôra*. The *es gibt*, thus translated, too vividly announces or recalls the dispensation of God, of man,
or even that of the Being of which certain texts by Heidegger speak (*es
gibt das Sein*). *Khôra* is not even that (*ça*), the *es* or *id* of giving, [since

95. *Ibid.*, 36.
96. *Ibid.*, 49.
97. *Ibid.*, 37.
98. *Ibid.*, 61 [translation modified].

it is itself] before all subjectivity. It does not give place as one would give something. It neither creates nor produces anything, not even an event insofar as it takes place. It gives no order and makes no promise. It is radically ahistorical, because nothing happens through it and nothing happens to it."[99]

Yet, in a second moment, Derrida suggests that precisely the absence of 'the dispensation of God' reintroduces the trace that contains a promise. This reintroduction flows from an experienced injunction that one should address oneself to *khôra*: in the first place by addressing it always in the same way, thus suggesting that *khôra* has a proper name: "One respects the absolute uniqueness of *khôra* by always calling it in the same way – and this is not limited to the name: a phrase is necessary. To obey this injunction with neither order nor promise, an injunction that has always already taken place, one must think of that which – beyond all given philosophemes – has nevertheless left a trace in language [*khôra*, for example in the Greek language]."[100] It is this trace that contains, in its own way, a promise: a linguistic, nontheological promise, if you like. Indeed, the trace is a trace in language; as such it opens new grammatical and philosophical possibilities, some of them having begun to see the light of day. Derrida writers: "However insufficient [these possibilities] may be, they are given, already marked by that unheard trace, promised to the trace that has promised nothing. This trace and this promise always inscribe themselves in the body of language."[101]

The particular promise, then, that arises from one's 'experience' with *khôra*, will become an important theme in Derrida's politic ethics. When speaking of an 'impossible' democracy or hospitality to come, Derrida will always bring up an injunction and a promise that reaches us from the immemorial past of the *khôra*. For Derrida, this promise is universal, that is: going farther than the respective promises that are articulated in the various particular mystical traditions. The study of this politic ethics is the subject of our next chapter.

99. *Ibid.*, 37.
100. *Ibid.*, 38.
101. *Ibid.*, 38.

CHAPTER NINE

DERRIDA'S POLITICAL ETHICS: FOUNDATIONS

In this chapter I will study the foundations of Derrida's political ethics. These foundations, as we will see, flow from his reflections on the gift in a phenomenological perspective, or rather in a perspective that goes beyond phenomenology. The first part of the chapter – The Desire for 'the Impossible' – will deal with this move beyond phenomenology: the excessive, 'impossible' gift cannot be the object of phenomenological description; it explodes the basic framework of phenomenology. The second part of the chapter will examine Derrida's distinctive notion of justice. It will sketch his deconstruction of the self-referential, 'mystical' foundation of authority upon which the enforcement of the law is grafted, and show how this deconstruction paves the way for a desire for an 'impossible justice' at the other side of 'legality', the narrow limits of legal justice. Derrida's move beyond legality does not come out of the blue; it prolongs, as we will see, his move beyond phenomenology. The last part of the chapter will examine the extent to which Walter Benjamin's essay 'Critique of the Force of Law' (1921) has been a source of inspiration for Derrida. In this examination it will become evident that, in spite of his admiration for Benjamin, Derrida is unwilling to subscribe to Benjamin's notion of apocalyptic messianism. Derrida's messianic dream of the 'impossible' will be of a different nature: instead of wagering on a divinely ordained destruction (Benjamin), it radically commits itself to 'things not yet given' at the other side of what is expected to be possible.

I. THE 'DESIRE FOR THE IMPOSSIBLE':
DERRIDA'S MOVE BEYOND PHENOMENOLOGY

Derrida's move beyond phenomenology is most perspicuous in his reflections on the 'impossible gift'. These reflections were published after his elucidation of the notion of justice at the colloquium on 'Deconstruction and the Possibility of Justice' organized in the Cardoso Law School in New York in 1989. In a first step I will analyze Derrida's notion of the 'impossible gift' which he explained in his short essay *Given Time* (1991). This will be followed by an account of the famous discussion between Jacques Derrida and Jean-Luc Marion that took place in 1997 during a Conference on 'Religion and Postmodernism' at Villanova University in Philadelphia, USA. Whereas Marion sought to stretch the method of phenomenology so as to be able to account for excessive, 'saturated' phenomena, such as the gift of revelation and the gift of existence, Derrida radically opts for a non-phenomenality of the impossible gift. Whereas Marion moves within the ambit of mystical theology, Derrida lays down the foundation for a universal political ethics, based on his concept of *khôra*, the universal 'place' or 'non-place' of resistance.

1. *The Impossible Gift*

Derrida is famous for his challenging and disturbing formulations. One of them is the statement that "the conditions of the possibility of the gift (that some 'one' gives some 'thing' to some 'one other') designate simultaneously the conditions of the impossibility of the gift," for the simple reason that "these conditions of possibility define or produce the annulment, the destruction, the annihilation of the gift."[1] This disturbing formulation is to be found in *Given Time* (1991), but already dates back to a seminar Derrida gave in 1977-1978 at the *École Normale Supérieure* in Paris.[2] The shock of the disturbing formulation aims, in fact, at drawing attention to the purity of the gift, or in less technical terms, to the gift understood as excess: excessive giving, in pure gratuity, not blocked or contaminated by any calculation of profit or self-interest. Such an 'excess in giving' is not part of the common understanding; rather Derrida attempts to get access to it through a reflection on the non-phenomenality of the pure gift.

Yet, such a reflection cannot start from scratch. It has no other choice but to take its point of departure in the common understanding of the 'gift', in order to then, in a second step, show that this common understanding is, at bottom, self-defeating, because it tends to reduce the gift to an exchange in the economic order. Let us first consider the common understanding. Here it is evident that in order for a gift to be possible, three elements are required: A gives something (C) to B: "In order for

---

1. J. Derrida: *Given Time. 1: Counterfeit Money*, trans. P. Kamuf (Chicago, IL and London: The University of Chicago Press, 1992) 12. Originally published as idem, *Donner le temps. 1: La fausse monnaie* (Paris: Galilée, 1991).
    2. *Ibid.*, ix.

there to be gift, gift event, some 'one' has to give some 'thing' to someone other, without which 'giving' would be meaningless."[3] The problem
is, however, that in common understanding this type of giving obeys the
logic of the circular exchange (circulation of goods, and monetary signs),
which is reflected in the age-long philosophical understanding of time as
an ongoing circular movement. So, what ought to be shown is that the
gift, although taking place within this circularity, at the same time tears
apart the circularity of both the economic exchange and the concept of
time that is related to it. The reason why Derrida seeks to interrupt this
circularity is obvious: the benefits of the gift as exchange return back to
the originator of the gift, to the donor. As long as there is this return, in
terms of goods or cultural capital (gratitude), to the donor, one cannot
speak of a pure gift: "If the figure of the circle is essential to economics, the gift must remain *aneconomic*. Not that it remains foreign to the
circle, but it must keep a relation of foreignness to the circle. It is perhaps in this sense that the gift is the impossible."[4]

In taking this stand Derrida reacts to the results of Marcel Mauss's
anthropological study, *The Gift: The Form and Reason for Exchange in
Archaic Societies* (1950) in which the schema 'gift, debt, and counter
gift' had been documented in the economic and cultural dealings of
ancient tribes. For him, "Marcel Mauss's *The Gift* speaks of everything
but the gift: It deals with economy, exchange, contract (*do ut des*), it
speaks of raising the stakes, sacrifice, gift *and* counter gift – in short,
everything that in the thing itself impels the gift *and* the annulment of the
gift."[5] A gift – a gratuitous gift – that would escape this annulment, would
strike us as an event, as a shock. But how to get access to the inner structure of such a gratuitous gift? And, can it be done using the tools of the
phenomenological method? This is the real question Derrida raises.

In a first step, Derrida posits as a 'condition' for the occurrence of the
true gift that the giver 'forget' that s/he is the giver. This implies that not
even the generosity of the giver can become a part of the definition of the
pure gift. The giver must forget that s/he is generous, for this generosity
will still be conceived of from the standpoint of an actor who cultivates
his/her own expectation – intentionality – of what generosity means. So,
the requirement to forget includes the requirement to go beyond phenomenology. Indeed, for Derrida, it suffices to perceive that "the *intentional* meaning of the gift […] annuls the gift as gift even before *recog-*

3. *Ibid.*, 11.
4. *Ibid.*, 7.
5. *Ibid.*, 24.

nition becomes *gratitude* [...] *At the limit, the gift as gift, ought not to appear as gift: either to the donee or to the donor.* It cannot be gift as gift except by not being present as gift. Neither to the 'one' nor to the 'other'. If the other perceives or receives it, if he or she keeps it as gift, the gift is annulled. But the one who gives it must not see it or know it either; otherwise he begins, at the threshold, as soon as he intends to give, to pay himself with a symbolic recognition, to praise himself, to approve of himself, to gratify himself, to congratulate himself, to give back to himself symbolically the value of what he thinks he has given or what he is preparing to give."[6]

In this description one recognizes Derrida's apprehension of the metaphysics of presence which he detected as a basic scheme in Husserl's phenomenology. For him, it is clear: if the gift is perceived as given-in-actual-presence, then "the gift can certainly keep its phenomenality or, if one prefers, its appearance as gift. But its very appearance, the simple phenomenon of the gift, annuls it as a gift, transforming the apparition into a phantom and the operation into a simulacrum."[7] It is at this juncture that Derrida has recourse to Heidegger's shift from phenomenology to aphanology: from appearance to non-appearance, from speech to cessation of speech, from voice to a 'resonance of silence', which I mentioned in Chapter Six. Indeed, *Given time* spends a couple of pages on the way in which Heidegger evoked the unfathomable character of the gift of Being and of time, suggesting that Heidegger, in his meditation on the gift, disconnected time from the circularity in which the age-long philosophical tradition had imprisoned it, just as Heidegger also disconnected Being from a dense notion of presence by accentuating the withdrawal of Being in its very manifestation. The Heidegger Derrida has in mind is the Heidegger of the 'turning' (*Kehre*) who related Being to *Ereignis*, to an eventfulness as gift: "Heidegger sometimes says that Being [...] is *Ereignis*. And it is in the course of this movement that Being (*Seyn*) – which is not, which does not exist as being present/present being – is signaled on the basis of the gift."[8]

To summarize: "If there is no gift, there is no gift, but if there is gift held or beheld *as* gift by the other, once again there is no gift; in any case the gift does not *exist* and does not *present* itself. If it presents itself, it no longer presents itself [as excessive gift]."[9] How can such an 'absent'

6. *Ibid.*, 14.
7. *Ibid.*, 14.
8. *Ibid.*, 19.
9. *Ibid.*, 15.

gift – in Lyotard's vocabulary: the 'unpresentable' – stir the deepest roots of human desire? This is the 'secret' Derrida seeks to render thematic. His move is comparable to that of Lyotard, who, in the wake of Kant, underlines the importance of the noumenal Idea that can and must be thought but whose whole content cannot be presented in empirical reality, and which nonetheless signals its felt presence in one's dedication to the sublime: in one's mixed feelings of displeasure and rapture. Derrida's background is not Kant's philosophy, but phenomenology. From this background he initiates a particular way of 'naming' and 'thinking' the excessiveness of the gift, in the knowledge that this excessiveness can never become the object of phenomenological perception. The thinkable excessiveness of the pure gift can never be experienced; if somebody would deem to experience it, the excessive quality of the gift would break down. Now, it is precisely this thinkable excessiveness of the pure gift which eludes all phenomenological perception that elicits an ineradicable desire – a desire whose striving is oriented towards "the [excessive] gift as remaining (*restance*) without memory, without permanence and consistency, without substance and subsistence; at stake is this rest that is without being (it), beyond Being, *epekeina tès ousias*. The secret of that about which one cannot speak, but which one can no longer silence."[10] The gift is not only beyond Being, it is also 'without/beyond memory', for if the gift would continue to resonate in our memory; we would be haunted by the idea that we would have to repay it with a counter gift.

That about which one cannot speak, but which one can no longer silence, is, in one word, the impossible: not just 'something impossible' but '*the* impossible' – *the* impossible that awakens one's desire for *the* impossible: "Finally, if the [excessive] gift is another name of the impossible, we still think it, we name it, we desire it. We intend it. And this *even if* or *because* or *to the extent that we never* encounter it, we never know it, we never verify it, we never experience it in its present existence or in its phenomenon. The gift *itself* – we dare not say the gift *in itself* – will never be confused with the presence of its phenomenon;"[11] it is beyond phenomenality, and therefore intensely desired. In imitation of Jean-Luc Marion (see below) who dared to speak about God as *Dieu sans l'être*, which both means 'God without/beyond Being' and 'God without being God in the usual sense of the word' one could sum up Derrida's notion of the gift as *Le don sans l'être*: 'The gift without/beyond Being' – beyond Being as an accessible horizon of understanding – and thus

---

10. *Ibid.*, 147.
11. *Ibid.*, 29.

also: 'The gift without being a gift in the usual sense of the word'. It is this unusualness or surprise that elicits and awakens one's desire for it: for that which is *the* impossible, beyond the limits of the possible.

Has Derrida, in these considerations, taken leave of phenomenology? In a sense, yes; in another sense, no. He clearly states that the gift's excessiveness *as such* can never become part of human experience, can never appear in its phenomenality. On the other hand, he maintains that the *desire for the impossible* is, in its own way, an experience that is accessible to phenomenological perception. It must be possible to phenomenologically describe the act of *welcoming the unknown* – of that excessive gift which ruins every circularity of calculation. Such a description, however, will itself be caught up in the 'measurelessness' of the in-break of the impossible. For Derrida, there is only genuine thought and desire "where there is this movement still for thinking, desiring, naming that which gives itself neither to be known, experienced, nor lived – in the sense in which presence, existence, determination regulate the economy of knowing, experiencing, and living." From this it follows that the openness for the 'unknown' (the 'unpresentable') will share in the 'measurelessness' of the impossible. "One can sense, one can think, desire, and say only the impossible, according to the measureless measure (*mesure sans mesure*) of the impossible."[12]

It is this mesurelessness that distinguishes Derrida's enterprise from knowledge, science and philosophies that remain within the order of economic calculation. The thinking and desiring of the impossible "lets announce itself what nevertheless cannot *present itself* as such to experience, to knowing, in short; [it deals with] *"a gift that cannot make itself present."*[13] So, from the standpoint of common knowledge and science, such a thinking and desiring might appear to be a 'transcendental illusion' (Kant). Nonetheless, Derrida believes that one can and must account for this 'transcendental illusion'. He writes: "Even if the gift were never anything but a simulacrum, one must still *render an account* of the possibility of this simulacrum and of the desire that impels toward this simulacrum. And one must also render an account of the desire to render an account [...] Whence comes the law that obligates one to give even as one renders an account of the gift? [...] And that forbids one to forgive whoever *does not know how to give?"*[14] Here, Derrida is already hinting at what later on he will call 'the messianic dream', a belief in and a vision

12. *Ibid.*, 29.
13. *Ibid.*, 29.
14. *Ibid.*, 31.

of the 'impossible' things to come. He is not afraid of using terms such as 'simulacrum' and 'transcendental illusion', realizing that in the meantime, in his way of thinking, they have taken on a positive meaning.

In order to show that his vision of the 'impossible gift' does not imply a 'flight from the world' he adds two further remarks: (a) The vision of the 'impossible gif' has practical implications in terms of commitment. (b) This vision must never make us forget that, in reality, we continue to stay within the circularity of economic calculation – a situation one permanently needs to challenge and to address. Our commitment to this challenge consists in keeping alive the thinking of – and the desire for – the impossible, whose injunction is felt by those who allow themselves to be grasped by it: "The effort to think the groundless ground" should not lead to "a simple movement of faith in the face of that which exceeds the limits of experience, knowledge, economy – and even philosophy. On the contrary, it is a matter – desire beyond desire – of responding faithfully but also as rigorously as possible to the injunction or the order of the *gift* ('give')."[15] But since this order is addressed to people who are, in one way or another, infected by the disease of reducing the gift to a calculated exchange of gift and counter gift, it is also imperative to explain for oneself and for others, what one understands by a gift, to the effect perhaps that one has to admit that one's understanding of the gift is self-defeating: "know what you want and want to say when you give, know what you intend to give, know how the [superficial] gift annuls itself, commit yourself even if commitment is the destruction of the gift by the gift, give economy a chance [to revise its presuppositions]."[16]

2. *On the Gift: A Discussion between Jacques Derrida and Jean-Luc Marion*

On September 25-27, 1997, Villanova University (Philadelphia, USA) held a Conference entitled 'Religion and Postmodernism'. In the course of this Conference a public discussion took place between Derrida and Marion on the notion of the gift. I will render in broad strokes the content of this discussion because it will help us to better grasp Derrida's specific understanding of the 'gift beyond Being' (*epekeina tès ousias*), in contrast to Marion's understanding of the same notion. In the discussion allusions are made to the paper Marion read in the same Conference

15. *Ibid.*, 30.
16. *Ibid.*, 30.

"In the Name. How to Avoid Speaking of 'Negative Theology?'" A brief presentation of this paper and of Marion's method is, thus, in order.

1. In his paper Marion, first of all, endeavored to rebuke Derrida's objections that 'negative theology', in its Christian form, surreptitiously reintroduced a positive naming of God after a cascade of negations (the question of the *way of eminence*'). In a second move – and that is the move that interests us here – he set out to translate into the idiom of phenomenology what mystical theology has to say about *kataphasis* (God talk in positive terms), *apophasis* (God talk on the basis of negations) and *via eminentiae* (undoing of knowledge because of excess). He tries to capture these various stages in terms of how, in phenomenology, intention is crowned, or fails to be crowned, by an intuition that fulfills the intention. Defined in Husserlian terms *kataphasis* would mean: "The intention finds itself confirmed, at least partially, by the intuition" and on this basis the truth-claim of the intention is corroborated. *Apophasis* then, in contrast, would mean: "The intention can exceed all intuitive fulfillment, and in this case the phenomenon does not deliver objective knowledge on account of a lack:" Here the concepts that aim at naming God are negated "because of an insufficiency in intuition."[17] These are the two possibilities that are consistent with Husserl's theory: in the first case the intention is fulfilled by the intuition; in the second case the intention remains unfulfilled: there is nothing to be seen. Marion, however, introduces what he regards as a justifiable modification of Husserl's theory in an effort to give an account of the *via eminentiae*; he admits of a third possibility, viz., that "the intention (the concept or the signification) can never reach adequation with the intuition (fulfillment) not because the latter is lacking, but because it exceeds what the concept can receive, expose and comprehend."[18] This is what Marion terms the 'saturated phenomenon', an excess of givenness and corresponding vision: "the excess of intuition overcomes, submerges, exceeds, in short, saturates, the measure of each and every concept."[19]

Marion motivates this turn to the 'saturated' phenomenon by pointing out that Husserl focused his studies primarily on ordinary, 'secular' phenomena ('poor' phenomena in Marion's vocabulary), whereas what Marion has in view are rich, religious phenomena, such as the experience of

17. J.-L. Marion, "In the Name: How to Avoid Speaking of 'Negative Theology?'," *God, The Gift and Postmodernism*, ed. J. Caputo and M. Scanlon (Bloomington, IN and Indianapolis, IN: Indiana University Press, 1999) 39.
   18. *Ibid.*, 39.
   19. *Ibid.*, 40.

love, the gift of the Eucharist, the mystical encounter with God. In his comments on the discussion between Derrida and Marion, John Caputo calls attention to Derrida's and Marion's differing interpretations of Husserl's *Logical investigations*. As we have seen in chapter eight, Derrida welcomed the fact that, in order to attain the purity of linguistic expression, Husserl bracketed off, as non essential, the act of intuitive knowledge which 'fulfills' the intention. A linguistic expression is valid when it aims at an object, even when this object is not given in the immediacy of fulfillment. For an expression to be correct, it is enough that, in speech, an object is intended; the fulfillment by an intuition that 'sees' the object is not required. So, Caputo writes, whereas Derrida "noticed in his reading of the *Logical Investigations* that Husserl had 'discovered' (without taking any joy in it) the formal possibility of a completely empty or blind signifier [a mere intention], operating entirely in the absence of intuitive fulfillment [...], Marion's more radical phenomenology turns Husserl's analysis on its head [by admitting of] the formal possibility of an absolutely plenitudinous givenness exceeding any possible intention."[20] The contrast with Derrida's reading of Husserl could not be any sharper.

A moment ago I noted that Marion deemed it justified to modify Husserl. His motivation is quite simple: to the extent that Husserl still smacks of modern thought – in its attempt to ascertain the validity of knowledge from the position of the judging subject (Descartes, Kant) – this centrality of the judging subject ought to be bracketed off, so as to give room, again, to the marvel of perceiving the givenness of things as pure donation. For him, this 'bracketing off' of the organizing transcendental subject is the logical consequence of the emergence of postmodernism. Postmodernism is precisely a movement that is wary of, and thus without remorse takes leave of, the one organizing center that has been for so long the backbone of modern thought: "The saturated phenomenon comes after the subject, after the reduction [bracketing off] of the subject, after the reduction of modernity's subjective transcendental."[21] Gift or donation, as the basic awareness of being in the world, figures again on the philosophical agenda.

This implies that the gift can no longer be seen as imprisoned in the economic calculus of gift and countergift (Mauss), which precisely, as Derrida has shown, annuls the pure givenness of the gift: "For Marion,

20. J. Caputo, "Apostles of the Impossible: On God and the Gift in Derrida and Marion," *God, The Gift and Postmodernism*, ed. J. Caputo and M. Scanlon, 193-194.
    21. J. Caputo, "Apostles of the Impossible," 194.

the gift must be removed from the horizon of 'economy' – this we learn from Derrida – and re-conducted [...] to the horizon of 'givenness' (French: *donation*; German: *Gegebenheit*), bracketing everything alien to the gift in order to think it in terms that are proper to it. Specifically that means laying aside the metaphysical schema by which a donor (*causa efficiens*) produces an effect in the recipient (*causa finalis*) through the material and formal cause of the gift-object."[22] Marion, thus, sets out to reconstruct various cases that point beyond themselves to the pure horizon of donation. He realizes that the classical three elements required for an (imperfect) gift – viz., the donor, the recipient, and the thing given – when taken together as a solid construct easily lapse into the economic schema of 'gift, debt, and countergift': 'I give you something with the purpose of earning a remuneration'. So, he tries to imagine how this vicious circle can be interrupted. His answer is: whenever one of the three elements constitutive of the (imperfect) gift is left out, we have, at least, the beginning of a pure donation. Examples of such cases can be given: "There can be a gift without a recipient if I give a gift to someone who rejects my gift, as when I love my enemy who rejects my love [...] There can also be a gift without a gift itself [...] Giving without a gift is found when the lover gives his invisible love without a visible token, without a ring. The lover gives his love but he does not give a *thing*, something *present*. Finally there can be a gift without a donor, e.g. when the donor makes an anonymous gift so that the recipient cannot identify the source."[23] In all these cases, one perceives a glimpse of the horizon of donation in which we are generously allowed to participate.

Let us, finally note that Marion has been engaged in a polemic with Derrida for a long time. For him, Derrida's analysis of the gift is extremely negative; in Marion's eyes, Derrida never attains the level of the *way of eminence*, the silent adoration of the source of all that is. Because Derrida takes his point of departure in the economic horizon, his criticism of that horizon, as Marion sees it, never escapes its tentacles: instead, he ends up in a series of vexing aporias, with no real perspective at all on donation. One could even doubt whether he still reckons with the possibility of the gift. True, especially in *Giving Time*, Derrida employs the phenomenological method to demonstrate that, strictly speaking, a phenomenal appearing of the pure gift is impossible. Yet, Marion fears that such a methodological rigor only conceals Derrida's basic conviction that no gift at all is possible. From his analysis of

22. J. Caputo, "Apostles of the Impossible," 201.
23. *Ibid.*, 202.

Derrida's texts Marion concludes "that the impossibility of the phenomenal appearing of the gift as such, and thus of any *phenomenology* of the
gift rigorously conceived involves [for Derrida] the impossibility of the
gift pure and simple."[24]

2. We have sufficient elements at hand now to assess what the 1997
discussion between Derrida and Marion is about. I will sketch out the
various steps of this discussion by which the divergence between the two
authors will increasingly become clear.

(a) The question of givenness in phenomenology. Marion opens the
discussion with an account of what he understands by 'the saturated phenomenon'. He, first of all, points out that, as early as the Husserl of the
Logical Investigations, the "definition of the phenomenon was expressed
in the language of 'being given', in German *Gegebensein*." Unlike Kant's
active construction of knowledge, Husserl developed a more receptive
approach. For Husserl, both intention (signification) and intuition are
'given': "Everything, not only the intuition, is *gegeben* [given], or can
be *gegeben*, or at least, you can ask about any signification whether it is
gegeben or not."[25] In the next move, Marion points to Heidegger's
endeavor to relate Being to the anonymous act of giving: the *es gibt*, or
in French, *cela donne* and stresses that this insight had a bearing on
Ricœur, Levinas and Michel Henry, who all focused on phenomena that
cannot be simply described as 'being there' because of their eventful
character. "So, in fact, they are describing new phenomena, like the self-
affection of the flesh, the ethics of the other, the historical event, narrative, *différance*, and so forth, which, of course, cannot be said to be in any
way objects and should not be said to 'be' at all […] My guess amounts
to saying that the ultimate determination of the phenomenon implies not
to be, but to appear – *as given*."[26] So, the event, that which happens as
given, as donation, to consciousness, is what phenomenology today
should properly study. This also includes religious experience: the
Eucharist, the Word, forgiveness, life in the Spirit etc.

To Marion's preliminary clarification Derrida replies that it is not at all
sure, for him, that Husserl associated the phenomenon that is given, *'that
is there'* (*Gegebenheit* in German) with gift/donation: "I am not sure that
when, of course, Husserl refers, extensively and constantly, to what is
given to intuition, this given-ness, this *Gegebenheit* has an obvious and

24. *Ibid.*, 203.
25. R. Kearny, "On the Gift: A Discussion between Jacques Derrida and Jean-Luc
Marion," *God, The Gift and Postmodernism*, ed. J. Caputo and M. Scanlon, 56.
26. *Ibid.*, 57.

intelligible relationship to the gift, to being given as a gift."[27] Here, Derrida certainly makes a point. To corroborate it, he could have remarked that Marion, in his account, already distorted the Husserlian notion *Gegebenheit* ('being there') by rendering it as *Gegebensein* ('being given'), a term which is not to be found in Husserl. Equally problematic, for Derrida, is Marion's recourse to Heidegger. When Heidegger brings up the *Gabe* (gift in the strong sense) he speaks at a level that is different from the basic phenomenological approach which tells us 'that something is there' (*Gegebenheit*) as a particular phenomenon. So, Derrida makes it clear that what he means by 'gift' is the particular act of giving something to somebody else, a notion of which he had examined the aporias in *Given Time*. He admits that Marion, in his comments on *Given Time*, had a good grasp of the basic aporia, and formulates it again: "As soon as a gift – not a *Gegebenheit*, but a gift – as soon as a gift is identified as a gift; with the meaning of a gift, then it is canceled as a gift. It is reintroduced into the circle of an exchange and destroyed as a gift."[28] However, Derrida contests that Marion drew the right conclusion from this aporia, when stating that he (Derrida) holds that there is no gift at all. For Derrida, this accusation is ill-founded. He therefore explains again what he understands by the impossibility of the gift.

What matters to Derrida is the experience of the phenomenological impossibility of the gift – the gift, *as such*, cannot appear – but this does not at all imply that one would cease having a relationship to the excessiveness of the gift, on the contrary. To clarify this point he refers to Kant's definition of the Ideas of Reason: "I would suggest that what this question of the gift compels us to do, perhaps, is to re-activate, while displacing, the famous distinction that Kant made between knowing and thinking, for instance. The gift I would claim, I would argue, as such cannot be known; as soon as you know it you destroy it. So the gift as such is impossible. [...] The gift as such cannot be known, but it can be thought of. We can think what we cannot know. Perhaps thinking is not the right word. But there is something in excess to knowledge. We have a relation to the gift beyond the circle, the economic circle, and beyond the theoretical and phenomenological determination. It is this thinking, this excess, which interests me."[29] It is this excess that emotionally stirs in him the desire for the impossible. As we will see in a moment this reference to the Kantian Idea, which we can and must think but which

27. *Ibid.*, 58.
28. *Ibid.*, 59.
29. *Ibid.*, 60.

remains totally 'unpresentable' – and thus escapes every phenomenological description – paves the way for Derrida's political ethics.

(b) Stretching the limits of phenomenology, or going beyond phenomenology? The heart of the discussion between Derrida and Marion
is about the limits of phenomenology. Derrida acknowledges that, "strictly
speaking, he is not a phenomenologist anymore;"[30] he rather sides with
Levinas, who wanted "to find within phenomenology the injunction to go
beyond phenomenology [...] to go phenomenologically beyond phenomenology,"[31] in order to do justice to the 'naked face' of the other. This
is exactly what Derrida seeks to do in view of safeguarding the purity of
the gift, a gift that is simply 'impossible' according to phenomenological standards. This is also the reason why he is so critical of Marion's
attempt to stretch the phenomenological method, in such a way that even
Christian revelation can acquire phenomenological status.

At a certain moment in the discussion Marion admits that he, too,
endeavors to describe the excess of the impossible, but, unlike Derrida, he
links this excess to the event of the saturated phenomenon, that is: to the
eruption of the excessive intuition that overflows the intention (the signification). As already mentioned, he sees the beginning of such an eruption
happen whenever one of the three components of the gift – namely donor,
receiver, and the thing given – is suspended. At that moment the rules of
phenomenology seem to be changed, since the notion of instrumental
cause that ruled the 'triadic' structure has been eliminated. He explains:
"[E]ven though the most abstract and common pattern of the gift implies
a giver, an object to be given, and a receiver, you can nevertheless describe
the gift, I would say the enacted phenomenon, the performative of the gift,
by bracketing and putting aside, at least one and from time to time two of
those three features of the gift. And this is new: it makes clear that the gift
is governed by rules that are completely different from those that are
applied to the object or to the being [...] We can describe the gift outside
of the horizon of economy in such a way that new phenomenological rules
appear. For instance, the gift or the given phenomenon has no cause and
does not need any. It would sound absurd to ask what is the cause of the
gift, precisely because givenness implies the unexpected, the unforeseeable, and the pure surge of novelty."[32] For Marion, it is clear: to the extent
that the gift is an unforeseeable event, it explodes the horizon of economy
as well as the phenomenological description that follows suit.

30. *Ibid.*, 66.
31. *Ibid.*, 75.
32. *Ibid.*, 62-63.

Derrida has serious objections to this view. He doubts whether it is possible to give a phenomenological description of the irruption of a pure gift after the 'deconstruction' of the 'triadic' economic structure (into which now a 'lack' has been introduced). In order to substantiate this doubt he quotes a text from Marion that summarizes the latter's enterprise: "You say that what is left is to give up the economic horizon of exchange in order to interpret the gift, *à partir*, starting from, the horizon of donation itself. What remains to be described, you say, is donation, not any more after what it rejects, but as such, *en tant que telle*. Then you add, with a scruple that I would like you to comment upon, *si une telle en tant que telle convient encore*, if such an as such still fits."[33] The specification 'as such' is typical of phenomenology which is interested in the description of the *essence* of a particular phenomenon. So, Marion is invited to explain why he deems that a description of the gift *as such* is possible, and why there are also reasons to weaken the rigor of such a description. Marion's answer reads as follows: "What raises my interest is that we can always give up at least one and perhaps two [of the three elements] and nevertheless keep a genuine and thorough phenomenon [...] which can still be described although it does not amount to an object and not a being either,"[34] since it is pure event 'outside' of the economic circle. Upon Derrida's insistence, Marion then adds that precisely because the pure gift, as phenomenon, reaches us as an event, one would, strictly speaking, have to drop the 'as such', since in the technicality of phenomenology this 'as such' of the description relates to objects or beings, but not to events. To this statement Derrida replies: "if you give up the as such, what is the use that you can make of the word phenomenology?"[35]

Derrida further points out that Marion seems to speak from a theological background in which it is presupposed that the whole of the finite realm is 'given' by God. This implies that what phenomenologists call *Gegebenheit* is immediately qualified as being a gift of the creator: "For you, everything that is given [...] to us in perception, in memory, in a phenomenological perception, is finally a gift to a finite creature, and it is finally a gift of God."[36] It is this mentality that, according to Derrida, motivates Marion to argue that the finite knowing subject does not create the objects, but receives them. So, the horizon of receiving a gift is

33. *Ibid.*, 65.
34. *Ibid.*, 65.
35. *Ibid.*, 66.
36. *Ibid.*, 66.

everywhere presupposed: "Receptivity is interpreted as precisely the situation of the created being, the creature, which receives everything in the world as something created. So it is a gift. Everything is a gift. Is that not the condition for the extraordinary extension that you propose of *Gegebenheit* and of the category of the gift?"[37] This remark, of course, upsets Marion who vividly protests against a trend in France towards identifying his reflections on the gift as being inspired by theology. He therefore underlines that his enterprise is and remains purely phenomenological: "[I]n *Étant donné* I made it my goal to establish that givenness remains an immanent structure of any kind of phenomenology, whether immanent or transcendent."[38] For him, this immanent structure is evident, especially after the dissolution of modernity's transcendental, ordering subject. In the period of postmodernism, Marion maintains, it does not create any problem for philosophers and phenomenologists to adopt an attitude of receptivity: "So my hypothesis, as a phenomenologist is that we should not try to constitute them [the objects], but to accept them – in any sense of accept – as given and that is all."[39]

Derrida is again not satisfied with this answer. For him there remains a double difficulty: (i) He has no doubt about Marion's position, notably that, in the latter's view, it is precisely the excess of the gift that deconstructs the vicious economic circle of 'gift and counter gift'. Yet, he exclaims: "It is difficult for me to understand how an excess of intuition [which gives access to the excess of the gift] can be described phenomenologically." And he adds: "The excess, the structure, in which I am interested, is not an excess of intuition;"[40] it is an excess that jumps out of the schemas of phenomenology, and plunges into the realm of the impossible. (ii) Derrida makes a clear distinction between *Gegebenheit* (something is there) and the gift (something is given); for him, it is only of the former that a phenomenological description can be given, whereas the pure gift, as he sees it, escapes phenomenality. Therefore he goes on criticizing which he feels is Marion's position, namely that every *Gegebenheit* is a gift: "[I]f you say the immanent structure of phenomenology is *Gegebenheit*, and if by *Gegebenheit* you refer to something given, to some common root, then every phenomenon is a gift. Even if you do not determine the giver as God, it is a gift. I am not sure that this is reconcilable or congruent with what I know under the name of phenomenology."[41]

37. *Ibid.*, 67.
38. *Ibid.*, 70.
39. *Ibid.*, 71.
40. *Ibid.*, 71.
41. *Ibid.*, 71.

(c) Derrida's reservations about revelation and revealability. Richard Kearny, the moderator of the discussion, had at various times insisted that the two discussion partners should not lose themselves in the technicalities of phenomenology, but instead should tackle the question of religion, since the general theme of the conference was 'Religion and Postmodernism'. That is why Derrida at a certain moment brought up the notion of revelation which he problematizes from the background of his understanding of *khôra*.

We already know that, for him, *khôra* is the mysterious place of disturbance, the strange voice that declares certain situations to be wrong and intolerable. This disquieting 'place or non-place' which can never be raised to the status of revealability is so crucial to him that he contrasts it to Marion's loyalty to mystical theology. He observes that there is "a strange affinity between negative theology and phenomenology."[42] And, indeed, in his final conclusion, Marion summarizes his phenomenological enterprise with a reference to mystical theology (his term for negative theology). For Marion it is evident that areas, which for a long time were depreciated because they were deemed not to fulfill the conditions of possibility set by the modern transcendental ego, can nowadays be brought to the limelight again without any scruple. In describing these areas – gratitude, revelation, the gift – Marion uses the same vocabulary as Derrida: excess, and desire for the impossible. But when specifying them in terms of 'counter-experiences' to the rationally verified experiences of modern times, he not only refers to feelings of astonishment and awe, but also to Saint Augustine's definition of mystical experience as the awareness of God's incomprehensibility. For him, this awareness results in a particular type of knowledge: "to know [but] without knowing in the mode of objectivation, it is *incomprehensibiliter comprehendere incomprehensibile*, as Augustine said. But this comprehension of and by the incomprehensible is not nothing [...] The incomprehensible, the excess, the impossible are [really] part and parcel of our experience."[43]

It goes without saying that Derrida's 'desire for the impossible' is of a totally different nature. For him, the excess, and 'the impossible' are not linked to a historical revelation, but to a universal structure that comes before the particular *topos* or locality of Christian revelation – and which steers one's great expectation concerning the birth of a new world ethos. As will become evident in a moment, Derrida's interest in this universal

42. *Ibid.*, 76.
43. *Ibid.*, 75.

structure goes hand in hand with his project of a new political ethics whose perspective is broader than Europe and Christianity. As early as his short essay *On the Name* (1993) he was in search of this universal structure in a close reading of, and commentary on, the poetry of the German mystic Angelus Silesius (1624-77). This German mystic is renowned for his imagery of the desert, of 'taking leave of God', and 'wandering there where nobody can go' – a wandering in a boundless region. In these images of de-centering, Derrida deciphers an attempt at universal openness, no longer hindered by, or reduced to, the particular language and topography of Christian revelation, or of any revelation whatsoever: "An immediate but intuitionless mysticism, a sort of abstract kenosis, frees this language from all authority, all narrative, all dogma, all belief – and at the limit from all faith."[44] For him, this is a prefiguration of the notion of *khôra* which he mentions at various points in this essay.

In his discussion with Marion, Derrida asks himself the question as to how he first encountered this notion of *khôra*: was it from the mystics of a particular religion? Or, could it be that *khôra* is a broader, more foundational notion on the basis of which it becomes possible to assess a particular tradition: "I do not know if this structure [of *khôra*] is really prior to what comes under the name of revealed religion or even of philosophy, or whether it is through philosophy or the revealed religions, the religions of the book, or any other experience of revelation that retrospectively we think what I try to think. I must confess, I cannot make the choice between these two hypotheses."[45] At any rate, the universal structure of *khôra is* what fascinates him. In order to describe this merely universal structure Derrida uses a lot of negations: *khôra* is something non-historical; it "remains irreducible to historicization, humanization, anthropo-theologization of revelation [... it remains] the absolute heterogeneity to philosophy, and the Judaeo-Christian history of revelation, even to the concept of history, which is a Christian concept."[46] *Khôra* is a desert within a desert; its neutral 'being there' does not give anything; it is a place of non-gift. It resists history, and as such contains the unforeseeable promise of a true history. In its heterogeneity to history; it makes history possible through its potential for resistance. Compared to a particular historical revelation, or to a particular cultural tradition, *khôra's*

44. J. Derrida, *On the Name*, trans. Th. Dutoit (Stanford, CA: Stanford University Press, 1995) 71. Originally published as idem, *Sauf le nom* (Paris: Galilée, 1993).

45. R. Kearny, "On the Gift," 73.

46. *Ibid.*, 76.

disturbance is truly universal, and provides the occasion for crossing the borders one would be tempted to prefer to this disturbance.

Derrida's final words in the discussion open the perspective on a universal politics, beyond the divisions of religions and continents – of the Jewish religion, the Christian religion, and of Islam: "I think that this reference to what I call *khôra*, the absolutely universal place, so to speak, is what is irreducible to what we call revelation, revealability, history, religion, philosophy, Bible, Europe, and so forth. I think the reference to this place of resistance is also the condition for a universal politics, for the possibility of crossing the borders of our common context – European, Jewish, Christian, Muslim, and philosophical. [...] I use the problematic of deconstruction and negative theology as a threshold to the definition of a new politics. I am not saying this against Europe, against Judaism, Christianity, or Islam. I am trying to find a place where a new discourse and a new politics could be possible."[47] And he adds that he is eager to see how the respective religions – Judaism, Christianity, and Islam – are going to profit from this new insight: "Perhaps, and this is my hypothesis, if not a hope, what I am saying here can be retranslated after the fact into Jewish discourse, or Christian discourse, or Muslim discourse, if they can integrate the terrible things I am suggesting now."[48] Such a – horizontal – universalism beyond the divisions of ethnicity and religion is totally absent in Marion, in spite of his broad view that every thing given is a gift from heaven. One would also look in vain for the beginnings of a political ethics in Marion, a concern that became the heart of the matter in Derrida's late writings.

II. DERRIDA AND THE QUESTION OF JUSTICE

In October 1989 Jacques Derrida was invited by the *Critical Legal Studies* movement to deliver the keynote address at the colloquium on 'Deconstruction and the Possibility of Justice' that took place in the Cardoso Law School, in New York (USA). For lack of time he was only able to read the first part of his paper – the part dealing with the question of justice; the second part he read at a Conference on 'Nazism and the Final Solution: Probing the Limits of Representation' organized by the University of California (USA) on April 26th 1990. The whole, 'Force

47. *Ibid.*, 76.
48. *Ibid.*, 77.

of Law: the Mystical Foundation of Authority', has been published in the *Cardozo Law Review* 11 (1990) 920-1045.

1. *Has Deconstruction Anything to Say about Justice?*

To warm up his audience, Derrida jokingly remarked that, even though he was a Frenchman, he had been asked to speak in English, a language he had satisfactorily mastered but which after all was not the native idiom in which he developed his philosophy. This introductory remark served him as a springboard from which to jump into the question of justice. Had justice, he wondered, been done to him, who under the circumstances had been forced to comply with the language constraint (but how could he have objected since he was granted hospitality in the States)? Or, was justice on the side of the staff of the Law School who had to assure that no infringement be made on the language regime as stipulated by the laws of the United States? With these playful/ironic remarks, which still left somewhat undecided the question as to whether 'justice done to the stranger' was to be preferred to 'justice done to the American nation', Derrida had succeeded in raising the central issue he wanted to tackle: Does justice necessarily flow from abiding by the law? Is justice practiced *per se* whenever the law is being enforced? The more he persisted in asking rhetorical questions like these, the more it became evident to the audience that he was shedding doubt on the 'just' character of the law – that he was submitting law and legality to deconstructive analysis.

The audience was, of course not entirely surprised to see Derrida engage in deconstruction. Yet, for specialists in law and jurisprudence such an approach was rather unsettling. Derrida knew about this. So, he started to ask himself whether with what he was doing – separating and displacing notions that often, for simplicity's sake, are lumped together: justice and legality – he was not demolishing the foundations of the legal system. Being, thus, aware of the fact that he might be perceived as an anarchist, he tried to defend himself by sketching the following scenario and the parting of the ways it includes. He said: "The title [of the symposium] suggests a question that itself takes the form of a suspicion: does deconstruction insure, permit, authorize the possibility of justice? Does it make justice possible, or a discourse of consequences on justice, and the conditions of its possibility? Yes, certain people would reply; no, replies the other party. Do the so-called deconstructionists have anything to say about justice; do they have anything to do with it? Why do they basically speak of it so little? Does it interest them, in the end? Isn't it because, as certain people suspect, deconstruction doesn't permit in itself any just action, any just discourse on justice, but instead constitutes a threat to *droit*, to law or right, and ruins the conditions of the very possibility of justice? Yes, certain people would reply, no, replies the other party."[49]

So, one thing is clear: the simple suggestion that deconstruction may threaten to undermine the foundations of the legal system provokes different reactions which, in fact, divide people. Some will actually welcome 'cracks' in the legal system, while others get furious by only thinking of the possibility of it. For Derrida, this is already an indication that deconstruction compels one to confront serious 'aporias', and, as he will explain later, it is only through the awareness of such 'aporias' that decisive steps in the direction of a refinement of the law can be taken – steps which in the meantime may lead to a 'suspension' of the law. In the course of his talk he will list various areas that, on closer inspection, are beset by aporias. I note two of them:

A first aporia arises when one realizes that justice ought to be done to every single individual (to the 'infinitely other' at the 'other side' of every general treatment), whereas the rule of law is enshrined in universal categories, applicable to each and every person in the same way in spite of different, and often extremely divergent, circumstances. For Derrida, just as for Levinas, the identity and the needs of the 'infinitely other' explode the framework of phenomenological description. This resistance to phenomenological description translates into a resistance to a juridical system that by its own nature brackets off the uniqueness of individual persons so as to transform them into citizens obligated to accept the authority of the law. In this option one recognizes the Jewish emphasis on respect for the particular. Jewish thought, as our analysis of Lyotard has indicated, is weary of the dictates of systematic philosophical thinking. This aporia – the law's inability to do justice to every body – is so basic for Derrida that it forms the undercurrent of his further treatment of the question of justice.

A second aporia, which he addresses right from the start, is the inseparability of 'legitimate authority' and of 'force/violence', two elements that naturally coalesce in the German term *Gewalt*. This notion had already critically been examined by Walter Benjamin in his essay '*Zur Kritik der Gewalt*' (1921), usually translated as 'Critique of Violence',

49. J. Derrida, "Force of Law: The 'Mystical Foundation of Authority'," trans. M. Quaintance; idem, "Force de loi: Le 'fondement mystique de l'autorité'," *Cardozo Law Review* 11 (1990) 921-923.

although Benjamin also had in view a critique of 'legitimate authority', or better: of 'an authority that presents itself as legitimate'. How does it happen that 'authority' has spontaneous recourse to violence? How are we to interpret the fact that the law is commonly associated with the use of force? This connection can, for example, clearly be seen in the English expression: 'to enforce the law'. But where force comes into play, one must also suspect that force is used to defend some hidden interests. In whose interest is it that the law should be strictly enforced? Is it true that law is impartial in all circumstances? How does it happen that those who doubt its impartiality are exposed to violent harassments?

In order to lay his finger on the aporias in the system, Derrida has recourse, primarily, to two methods. The first method consists in analyzing the precise meaning of the terms that are being used or presupposed. That was the case in the above example. Here it became evident that 'justice done to every body [read: as each unique individual] in particular' is not the same as 'enforcing the rule of law on everybody [read: as a collective of persons] in the same standardized way'. Justice and law are apparently not the same thing. Justice relates to the singular, whereas 'the law' resorts to general categories. So, how are we to resolve this 'unevenness'? How are we to reconcile these two conflicting approaches?

The second method engages in historical analysis; it examines the formation of juridical systems in the course of time. In this analysis the aspect of violence is given due attention. Indeed, contrary to appearances, the promulgation of a law is not a neutral fact; it is often preceded by serious battles and even wars, the violence of which still resonates in the institution and promulgation of the law. What Derrida has mainly in view is the formation of the modern nation state which consolidated itself through the enforcement of laws, with the help of the police force, and if necessary of the standing army. These two methods allow him to address the problem of justice – at least in an indirect or oblique way. He says: "Deconstruction, while seeming not to 'address' the problem of justice has done nothing but address it, if only obliquely, unable to do so directly [...] one cannot speak *directly* about justice, say 'this is just' and even less 'I am just', without immediately betraying justice, if not law (*le droit*)."[50]

'Obliquely' means, of course, through the detour of the deconstructive 'dismantling' of allegedly solid foundations. We already know that Derrida in his deconstruction of the metaphysics of presence criticized logocentrism and its tendency to subsume the many under the one. In his

---

50. *Ibid.*, 935.

problematization of the pertinence of legal procedures he will do the same, but in addition he will tackle the component of 'force' used to enforce the law. He says: "to enforce the law [...] cannot become justice legitimately, or *de jure* except by withholding force or rather by appealing to force from its first moment, from its first word. At the beginning of justice," he sarcastically adds, "there was logos, speech or language, which is not necessarily in contradiction to another *incipit*, ' in the beginning there will have been force'."[51]

2. *The Mystical Foundation of Authority*

It is not at random that Derrida joins 'logos, speech' and 'force' together. His objective is to show that the enactment of a law rests on a 'performative force'. He opens his demonstration with a quote from the *Pensées* of Blaise Pascal (1623-62): "It is just that what is just be followed, it is necessary that what is strongest must be followed."[52] In trying to unravel this enigmatic saying, Derrida points out that what Pascal intends to say is that a law ('what is just') that is not strong does not merit the name of just law, since it is totally ineffective. The stronger the law (and its ensuing enforcement) the more effective and the more 'necessary' such a law becomes.

He also explains that this quote must be placed in the context of Pascal's religious pessimism, which holds that humankind is corrupted by original sin and that therefore what one calls 'natural law' cannot be trusted. So, one really needs a positive law that is just *and* strong for the betterment of the human race. From this background one cannot conclude that Pascal is immediately thinking of repression (punishing those who fail to abide by the law); nor that he understands force as a means to obtain economic, political, or ideological power. What he has in view with his insistence on a strong positive law is the idea that the law must have a firm foundation of its own.

When asking himself where the authority of the law (of positive justice) comes from, Derrida lists various conjectures, propounded by Pascal, of which only the last seems to be convincing, namely that custom and tradition are the ultimate ground of the law's authority: "One man says that the essence of justice is the authority of the legislator, another that it is the convenience of the king, another that it is current custom;

51. *Ibid.*, 935.
52. *Ibid.*, 935.

and the latter is closest to the truth: simple reason tells us that nothing is just in itself; everything crumbles with time. Custom is the sole basis for equity, for the simple reason that it is received; it is the mystical foundation of authority. Whoever traces it to its source annihilates it."[53] Derrida is struck by the expression 'mystical foundation of authority', and discovers that the term had, in fact, been coined much earlier by Montaigne (1577-1641), who unambiguously wrote: "Laws keep up their good standing, not because they are just, but because they are laws: that is the mystical foundation of their authority, they have no other [...] Anyone who obeys them because they are just is not obeying them the way he ought to." Elsewhere Montaigne says: "our very law, it is said, has legitimate fictions on which it founds the truth of its justice."[54]

For Derrida, these elucidations are crucial. They show that both Montaigne and Pascal link the 'strength' of the law to the authority it – mystically and fictionally – derives from its solemn promulgation. That is the reason why Derrida speaks of a 'performative force' at the moment of the institution of the law: "The founding and justifying moment that institutes law implies a performative force, which is always an interpretative force."[55] Unlike constative language, which only states or confirms that a certain state of affairs is given, performative language 'brings about' and 'creates' something new: a novel state of affairs. When the president of a university solemnly says 'I declare this academic year to be opened', then that academic year is opened in virtue of the force of his words. The same is true for a wedding. Here the performative language 'From now on the Church shall regard you as husband and wife' institutes a new reality that formerly was not there. Yet, Derrida speaks not only about performative language; he uses the term 'performative force', thus linking this special type of performative language to the institutional power of the state and its laws. The performative language in question derives its force and authority from the institutional power of the state.

But, again, on what precisely is this institutional power grounded? To this question there is only a tautological answer: the institutional power is simply based on itself, supported by institutional legitimacy, and on nothing else. This tautological answer might seem strong to some, but deconstructionists debunk it as weakness, just as they show the frailty of a logos (or self-referential logical system) that is only founded on itself.

53. *Ibid.*, 937, citing Pascal, *Pensées*, 293.
54. *Ibid.*, 939, citing Montaigne, *Essais III, XIII, De l'expérience*, Pleiade, 1203.
55. J. Derrida, "Force of Law," 941.

Derrida's assessment of this tautology reads as follows: "Since the origin of authority, the foundation or ground, the position of the law can't by definition rest on anything else but themselves, they are themselves a violence without ground. Which is not to say that they are in themselves 'unjust', in the sense of 'illegal'. They are neither legal nor illegal in their founding moment. They exceed the opposition between founded and unfounded."[56]

For Derrida, this wavering between a legality that feels it has to present itself as founded, while not being able to strictly prove its claim, was the reason why Montaigne and Pascal brought up the notion of a 'mystical foundation of authority'. To speak of a 'mystical foundation' implies that this foundation stands in for a real one, that no real foundation exists. For every attempt to assert a real foundation would end up in failure. Indeed, even if one would seek to ground certain claims of the modern legislative state on earlier strata of law and jurisprudence that were in vogue in more ancient, premodern times, one would not succeed in establishing the existence of a real foundation. Rather, one would discover that these ancient layers have themselves been instituted by the same process of self-founding legitimization – one that has successfully enacted its 'performative force' to the point of turning its own (self-)interpretation into the dominant interpretation, i.e., 'the truth', which is not to be questioned.

This analysis shows that the authority of the state and of its laws are both founded and unfounded: Founded to a certain extent by reference to earlier developments in state formation and jurisprudence (as historical law studies are able to uncover); unfounded, because, in the last resort, this authority – and also that of the earlier strata on which they may rely – is self-referential and therefore based on force and violence (a violence that still hits all those who question the legitimacy of this self-referential system). The least one can say is that state authority is and remains ambivalent: it is both "legitimate power and the supposedly originary violence that must have established this authority and that could not itself have been authorized by any anterior legitimacy."[57] On account of this ambivalence it is 'deconstructable', and this on two counts. First, in so far as state authority is partially founded on interpretations and reinterpretations of textual strata taken from the past history of law and nation building, this authority proves to be reformable; and what is reformable cannot remain within its closed shell. And second, in so far as the state

56. *Ibid.*, 943.
57. *Ibid.*, 927.

authority is self-referential it lays itself open to deconstructive criticism that is eager to find 'cracks' in the system: the allegedly ultimate foundation of state authority is unfounded; so too are the force and the violence that are used to uphold it.

3. In Search for an 'Impossible Justice' beyond Legality

It will have become clear that the genealogical reconstruction of legal authority tolls at the same time its death knell: it is exposed now to deconstruction. The aim and purpose of Derrida's deconstruction is to take leave of the unstable construct of legal authority and to aspire for a reign of justice beyond legality – to sow already the seeds of this reign of justice in the 'cracks' that became visible in the edifice of 'law and order'. As we will see, Derrida will engage in a campaign for giving hospitality to strangers within the walls of the modern nation states (fortress Europe, fortress USA) that desperately try to keep immigrants at bay.

When asking himself where – against the grain of a legality that reveals itself to be 'unjust' – the desire for a reign of 'impossible' justice comes from, he can only tell that experience shows that the desire is there, that it takes him hostage, that this desire is indestructible, and 'undeconstructable'. This desire lies at the heart of the activity of deconstructive questioning, but escapes any deconstruction itself because of the purity which makes it strive for the 'impossible'. In his literary style he often speaks of an 'impossible' justice, just as he speaks of an 'impossible' gift, an 'impossible' hospitality, etc. whereby the qualification 'impossible' points to something 'excessive' beyond rational calculation. In his address at the Cardozo Law School he is less lyrical and prosaically states: "1. The deconstructibility of law (*droit*), of legality, legitimacy or legitimation (for example) makes deconstrucion possible. 2. The undeconstructibility of justice also makes deconstruction possible, indeed is inseparable from it. 3. The result: deconstruction takes place in the interval that separates the undeconstructibility of justice from the deconsctructability of *droit* (authority, legitimacy, and so on)."[58]

Deconstruction enacted in the name of an 'impossible' justice seeks to redesign the "whole apparatus of boundaries within which a history and a culture have been able to confine their criteriology."[59] In Western civilization this criteriology has privileged the male adult, at the expense of women, children, and animals, to quote these examples; it also used to

58. *Ibid.*, 945.
59. *Ibid.*, 953.

privilege the national language as a decisive factor for being qualified as genuine citizen, thus forcing minority groups to give up their own language. Think, for example, of the linguistic policies of the French nation whose political unity is based on the imposition of the same language on all the regions of the country – aided by a legal system that simply declares what is right and what is not. In order to overcome this narrow criteriology, which privileges and excludes, Derrida speaks up for a serious revision of the legal system on the basis of the desire for an 'impossible' justice, a justice that goes beyond the calculating logic of the law. He hereby invites specialists in jurisprudence as well as judges to sensitize themselves to the aporias that arise when this calculating logic is simply enforced unthinkingly on each and every situation. He treats three such aporias:

A first aporia is that of the rule and its suspension. His starting point here is a reflection on freedom and responsibility. In order to be just, a judge must be able to act as a free human being that assumes responsibility. On the other hand, he cannot afford not to pay attention to the rules. Yet, Derrida observes, this does not mean at all that a judge, like an automaton, would pronounce his judgment by merely applying conventional norms to a particular case; for this oversimplification would not do justice to the heterogeneity and singularity of the persons involved. So, what really ought to be done is to enact a 'fresh judgment', one that *reinterprets* the rule so as to do deal correctly with the particular case and the singular persons.

This means: the decision must be both regulated and without regulation; "it must conserve the law and also destroy it or suspend it enough to have to reinvent it in the reaffirmation and the new and free confirmation of its principle."[60] Genuine responsibility towards justice forces the judge to be lawful and lawless at the same time – to suspend the rule and to reinvent it. This is not an easy task, just as a honest exercise of one's freedom is not easy; it presupposes insightful knowledge of the historical origin of norms, and also a belief in their reinvention. Moreover, a judge acting in this way will feel himself in 'suspension', not knowing for certain whether he has been really fair both to the law and to the circumstances of the particular situation. Yet, this 'suspension' is better than having to regard oneself as merely abiding by 'law and order' in a rote way. Let us remark in passing that this is the reversal of the phenomenological *epoche* in which the particular is suspended in order to attain at the selfsame *eidos* or essence.

60. *Ibid.*, 961.

This leads us to the second aporia: 'the ghost of the undecidable'. A judge, and every responsible person for that matter, will willy-nilly have to make a choice between various options. This obligation to choose leads one to confront the 'undecidable', a notion which in the meantime has become part and parcel of the vocabulary of deconstruction. Yet, the undecidable is not merely the oscillation or the tension between two choices. It really consists in having to make a decision that, so to speak in a lawless manner, does justice to the 'other', to the one who – because of his/her heterogeneity and strangeness – exceeds the order of the calculable, while at the same time trying to reinvent the rule. This explains why 'the ghost' of uncertainty, of a lack of total certainty lingers: is the decision one takes totally right? Think of the painful decisions that have to be taken today in matters of biogenetics. The responsible person will continue to be haunted by this ghost, even when realizing that to endure this 'ghostliness' bestows some dignity upon her. "The ghostliness deconstructs from within any assurance of presence, any certitude or any supposed criteriology that would assure us of the justice of a decision, in each event of a decision."[61] On the other hand, and this is decisive in Derrida's reasoning, the very fact that one feels bereft of any 'assurance of presence' makes one yearn for testifying to the truth of an exceeding 'Idea of justice', even if this Idea seems to withdraw itself from empirical reality.

For Derrida, the 'Idea of justice' is something irreducible, at 'the other side' of performances based on a calculable exchange, "indestructible in its positive affirmation, in its demand of a gift without exchange, without circulation, without recognition or gratitude, without economic circularity, without calculation, and without rules, without reason and without rationality." And, he continues, "we can recognize in it, indeed, accuse, identify a madness. And perhaps another sort of mystique. And deconstruction is mad about this kind of justice. Mad about this desire for justice."[62]

A third aporia arises when one thinks of the urgency with which one has to make a decision. Mostly it is 'right away'. True, the Idea of justice is 'unpresentable', yet ethical decisions cannot be deferred while one waits for its manifestation. The same is true for those who are 'grasped' by this Idea; they cannot delay their decisions until they have exhausted all the theoretical approaches or hypothetical imperatives of jurisprudence that are currently en vogue and on which apparently depends the justification of an act. The urgency to act forces them not

61. *Ibid.*, 965.
62. *Ibid.*, 965.

to look for justifications, how much insane such a gesture might seem. For Derrida, just as for Kierkegaard to whom he refers, the instant of decision – of a just decision – is pure madness; it is always a precipitation in advance of what is reasonable, driven by urgency, and "acting in the night of non-knowledge and no rule. Not [in the night] of the absence of rules and knowledge but [in the night] of a reinstitution of rules which by definition is not preceded by any knowledge or by any guarantee as such."[63] The real agony is thus about the 'night' of not-knowing yet the rules that might provide some guidelines for action in the complex situation in which one has to live up to the demands of an 'impossible justice'.

The urge to conceive rules that are not yet there[64] is for Derrida the ultimate reason why he does not give credit to the Kantian regulative Ideas. Derrida fails to explain what he understands by regulative Ideas. He simply takes it for granted that the reader knows what they are. So, a brief explanation is in order. In his *Critique of Pure Reason* Kant first of all defines what transcendental Ideas are: they are 'Ideas of totality' which we are able (and urged) to think, but whose presence is not to be found in empirical reality. Yet, they are not superfluous or without importance for human knowledge. They function, in a fundamental and unnoticed way, as a canon for the understanding (*Verstand*) that is geared towards knowing objects, allowing it to broaden and sharpen its view, not by making understanding know some supplementary object but by giving a direction to understanding's cognition of objects. Through this canon the understanding "cognizes no more objects than it would cognize through its concepts, yet in this cognition it will be guided better and further."[65] For scientists, this means that their

---

63. *Ibid.*, 968-969.

64. This resonates with Lyotard's preference for the reflexive judgment that is in search of its rules: "The postmodern artist or writer is in the position of a philosopher: the texts he produces are not in principle governed by pre-established rules, and they cannot be judged according to a determinant judgment, by applying familiar categories to the text or the work. Those rules or categories are what the work of art itself is looking for. The artist and the writer, then, are working without rules in order to formulate the rules of *what will have been made.*" J.-F. Lyotard, *The Postmodern Explained* (Minneapolis, MN and London: University of Minnesota Press, 1992) 15.

65. "Although we have to say of the transcendental concepts of reason: *they are only Ideas*, we will by no reason regard them as superfluous or nugatory. For even if no object can be determined through them, they can still, in a fundamental and unnoticed way, serve the understanding as a canon for its extended and self-consistent use, through which it cognizes no more objects than it would cognize through its concepts, yet in this cognition it will be guided better and further." I. Kant, *Critique of Pure Reason, Original* edition, B 386/A 329, trans. P. Guyer (Cambridge: Cambridge University Press, 1998) 403.

research is guided by what one might call a horizon of 'totality of understanding' to which they gradually, though asymptotically, draw near with the results of their research. In this way a quasi-rational horizon of expectancy is being formed, enabling one to make predictions about the future, conceived as a straightforward prolongation of the present.

Kant used these regulative Ideas initially to describe the attitude of scientists who anticipate the successful outcome of their enterprise. But he also used them in his ethics and political theory where they motivate people to persist in committing themselves to a noble cause, in spite of foreseeable frustrations.[66] Let us notice, however, that, in his considerations on the sublime, Kant no longer speaks of regulative Ideas, but of 'Ideas of Reason' that we are able to think, but which definitely defy any visual presentation. It is his latter emphasis that appealed to Lyotard in his summons to testify to the Idea of Reason – for him, the unpresentable Idea of a humanity that fully respects heterogeneity – even if this Idea seems to be relegated to oblivion. It is the same emphasis that comes to the fore in Derrida's desire for 'the impossible', "for that which, as such cannot be known; as soon as you know it you destroy it. So the gift as such is impossible [...] The gift as such cannot be known, but it can be thought of. We can think what we cannot know. [...] It is this thinking, this excess, which interests me."[67]

Derrida finds that these regulative Ideas obstruct rather than help to express what he has in mind when speaking about the urgency to act. He writes: "It is because of this structural urgency and precipitation of justice that the latter has no horizon of expectancy (regulative or messianic[68]). But for this very reason, it may have an *avenir*, a 'to come', which I rigorously distinguish from a future that can always reproduce the present. Justice remains, is yet, to come, *à venir*, it has an, it is *à-venir*, the very dimension of events irreducibly to come." And, he adds: "it is precisely because justice has the pure quality of 'to come' that it will be able to transform and to recast the juridical and political concepts we inherited from the past."[69]

66. For an in-depth analysis of Kant's ethical horizon of expectancy, see P. Ricœur, "Freedom in the Light of Hope," in idem, *The Conflict of Interpretations: Essays in Hermeneutics* (Evanston, IL: Northwestern University Press, 1974) 418-420. Originally published as idem, *Le conflit des interprétations: Essais d'herméneutique* (Paris: Seuil, 1969).
67. R. Kearny, "On the Gift," 60.
68. 'Messianic' is understood here as 'flowing from messianism'. For the distinction between religious messianism and Derrida's universal notion of messianicity, see the next chapter.
69. J. Derrida, "Force of Law," 969.

But how to transform and recast these 'current' juridical and political concepts? Derrida proposes a double strategy. First, one must remind the experts in jurisprudence that the juridical concepts they utilize as if they had always existed, have a contingent origin – in some cases, even a disruptive and violent origin in that their institution often results from a battle against, and a victory over, the then established order. If the jurists would begin to realize the wild irruption that lies at the origin of their neat juridical stipulations, they would no longer be surprised at seeing how a new generation advocates a cross-fertilization of these stipulations by the demands of an excessive notion of justice – one that is not longer based on violence and the force of law.

The other strategy consists in 'negotiation', which is not the same as looking for compromises. It rather means: not to shun the discussion with experts in law and politics, so that one's counter-voice can be heard. This engagement in discussion is crucial, if the Idea of an 'impossible' justice is to have an impact on the domains of law, ethics, politics, and economics. The aim and purpose of such a discussion is to make the incalculable (the 'impossible' justice) enter the domain of the calculable, so that the latter may be recast. However, the relation between the incalculable and the calculable must be negotiated in such a way that the Idea of the 'impossible' justice is not betrayed.

Such negotiation, however, is not an easy task. What ought to be revised is not the exceeding 'impossible' justice, but the judicial system. Yet, the advocates of the 'impossible' justice have only at hand 'a rule that still has to be invented'. Nonetheless they have to regard this 'rule' as a device, forced as they are by the urgency of the decisions to take. Derrida writes: "We must calculate, negotiate the relation between the calculable and the incalculable, and negotiate without [being in possession of] the sort of rule that still will have to be invented there where we are cast, there were we find ourselves."[70] In this situation they will have to raise concerns about pressing world-problems, such as the question of human rights, the abolition of slavery, and other areas of social justice and emancipation. This presupposes a knowledge about the fields in which a 'reinvention of the rule' is at stake. More particularly, Derrida thinks of recent burning problems, such as the issues of organ trafficking, abortion, euthanasia, bio-engineering, medical experimentation, the social treatment of AIDS, the drugs problem, the homeless, and even animal rights.

70. *Ibid.*, 971.

Especially in these new domains one cannot expect the legislation to improve overnight. It took centuries of struggle before slavery in its crudest forms was abolished, and before basic human rights, such as the right not to be tortured or the right of freedom of expression were recognized. So too, the advocates of the invention of 'new rules' in matters of bioengineering, euthanasia etc. will have to reckon with a long period of campaigning and 'negotiating' in order to inaugurate a new 'era of social justice'. This is, of course, not to say that Derrida himself is going to deal with this whole gamut of 'burning questions'. In line with his competence, he will rather tackle the issues of immigrants, cosmopolitanism, and globalization. In the meantime his hopes are that his method of 'deconstructing the law', in the name of a superior undeconstructable justice, will also be used in these other fields.

III. WALTER BENJAMIN'S CRITIQUE OF THE FORCE OF LAW: A SOURCE FOR DERRIDA?

The second part of 'Force of Law: The Mystical Foundation of Authority'[71] consists of a close-reading of, and comment on, Walter Benjamin's 'Critique of the Force of Law' (*'Zur Kritik der Gewalt'*), published in 1921, one year after Adolf Hitler and his Nazi party began their public propaganda activities in Germany. Walter Benjamin (1892-1940) was a prominent member of the Frankfurt School who never concealed his Jewish origin. He developed a Marxist type of messianism, and thereby often made use of apocalyptic images of destruction. The main theme of his 'Critique of the Force of Law' is the latent, if not publicly visible, erosion of the German parliamentary system in the 1920s – an erosion that is most conspicuous in the omnipresence of a repressive police force during the Weimar Republic. When Hitler came to power, the repressive instrument of control that he was going to use to consolidate himself as totalitarian leader was already in place. It is this Nazi-background that formed the occasion for Derrida to read his analysis of Benjamin's text at a Conference on 'Nazism and the Final Solution: Probing the Limits of Representation' (University of California, 1990). In a postscript to this analysis he will also reconstruct what would have been Benjamin's reaction to the culmination of the state's brutal use of force: the extermination of the Jews in the concentration camps – an event of which the latter was unaware, since he committed suicide in Spain in 1940.

71. *Ibid.*, 973-1045.

1. *'Law-Instituting Force' and 'Law-Preserving Force': A Questionable Separation*

Derrida begins his analysis with examining the notion of critique. He finds out that Benjamin did not understand critique as 'criticism' but, in the tradition of Kant's critiques, as a critical examination of the meaning of the term 'force' (*Gewalt*). It is due to this critical examination that Benjamin drew a distinction between: "the founding force, the one that institutes and positions law (*die rechtsetzende Gewalt*, 'law-instituting force') and the force that conserves, the one that maintains, confirms, insures the permanence and enforceability of law (*die rechterhalende Gewalt*: 'law-preserving force')."[72] Benjamin would like to keep this distinction intact, whereas, as we will see, Derrida will set out to blur the distinction, by underlining the continuity between the two types of force. According to Derrida, the force that violently institutes the state and its laws continues to repeat itself in the force that insures the permanence and enforceability of the law. Benjamin, on the contrary, for clarity's sake reflects on them as if they were two separate aspects; in the end, however, he too will have to admit that the appearance on the scene of a repressive police force erodes (or in Derrida's parlance: deconstructs) the neat separation. Even then Benjamin will call this erosion a degeneration, a sort of fall from a state of innocence.

Right from the outset, Derrida observes, Benjamin highlights the state's particular interest in the monopoly of 'force' (*Gewalt*). Indeed, the judicial system of the modern nation state deprives the citizens of the use of violence – vendetta is forbidden. In order to warrant social peace, the state arrogates this 'violence' to itself so as to be able to protect the citizens against attacks on their properties and against infringements on their civil rights. In view of this role it is eager to keep the monopoly of 'force' in its own hands, and not to share it with any body else. True, the system is willing to accept and endure the presence of evil doers (even mafiosi) who break the law; it closes its eyes to these violations, as long as they are perpetrated with the purpose of getting some personal profit. Yet, it feels obligated to forcefully react against those who dare to confront the legal authority of the state as such and the way it issues, in a sovereign manner, decrees to be enforced by law. This bias of self-protection from the side of the state is a curious phenomenon that is worth analyzing; it raises the question of legitimacy: how is this 'monopoly of

---

72. *Ibid.*, 981. I render the notion of *Gewalt* with 'force', even if in Derrida's English text *Gewalt* is translated as 'violence'.

force' to be justified? Again, the answer takes on the form of a tautology: Force is used in the enactment of the law because the law is intrinsically endowed with this force. Force belongs *de jure* to the law. This explains why the law, on closer inspection, "doesn't strive to protect any given just and legal ends (*Rechtszwecke*) but law itself."[73] When challenged by external occasions the law protects in the first place its own authority by the force of law and, if necessary, by martial violence. It declares itself legitimate because it has the power to do so. It uses this performative language, Derrida adds, to avoid further critical questions. It declares itself sacrosanct and expects this declaration to be respected. This is, as we have seen, the 'mystical foundation' of its authority.

The above description deals mainly with the law-preserving force of the judicial system. Yet, this analysis will gradually lead Benjamin to consider the other aspect: the 'law-instituting force', or what in the previous section has been called the violent origin of the law system. In his study of the difference between the 'natural law approach' and the 'positive law approach' Benjamin notices that the advocates of the 'positive law approach' are aware of the historical origin of the laws. The law code that Napoléon Bonaparte, e.g., imposed on France and on the European countries he conquered is not a neutral text; it has a violent origin. Of course, one might expect this violent undertone to ebb in the course of time, so as no longer to influence the law-preserving force. This is what Benjamin thought in the beginning. However, in his reflections on the general strike, he will have to admit that the founding violence of the law-instituting force irrupts again: the general strike is a potential for revolution which threatens the state's hegemony on power, and which, therefore, out of an instinct for its own preservation it must repress, resorting, if necessary, to violence, to the very means by which its own grip on power was initially secured.

In the 1920s general strikes were used as a weapon to force factories to give their employees an equitable pay. For Benjamin, these general strikes are violent actions, and not just a cessation or interruption of work. They had to be negotiated with the state which has a monopoly on force and violence. General strikes are in certain circumstances allowed by the state, but always for a limited period. If not, they could become the beginning of a violent revolution that might topple the 'existing order'. By permitting a general strike under these conditions the state tolerates for a while the existing status quo under which it has to share its monopoly of force with the trade unions. At the same time it realizes that this sharing

73. *Ibid.*, 987.

of force creates a dangerous and destabilizing political situation, although it is the price to be paid for restoring social peace. It is at his moment, Benjamin underlines, that the memory of the founding violence pops up again. Whenever the state leaders have to confront a 'counter-power' (the organized strikers) within the nation, they will subconsciously perhaps call to memory the 'founding violence' with which the state was grounded, even if this grounding act resulted in a more or less ordered parliamentary system. This is the moment where the police force – the 'state security' – will make its appearance in the public sphere, apparently to remind the citizens that those in power occupy their legitimate place thanks to the victory their predecessors once gained through revolutionary violence. The police force is, so to speak, the 'specter' and the spectral reappearance of this violent founding event – of the event of 'law-instituting force'.

Derrida likes to muse about 'specters' and spectral reappearances.[74] He situates them in the 'in between' between presence and absence. For that reason they seem to act like haunting dreams that visit people and make them face up to memories they would much prefer to forget and repress. Nonetheless these haunting memories always return and create a ghostly atmosphere in which one can hardly distinguish between what is real and what is unreal. Applying this notion of spectrality to the police, Derrida, in his comments on Benjamin, comes to the following conclusion. For Benjamin, the police becomes 'spectral' because they blur the demarcation line between 'law-instituting force' and 'law-preserving force'. One would expect policemen to merely enforce the existing laws, and in doing so maintain 'law and order'. "But today," Benjamin exclaims, "the police are no longer content to enforce the law, and thus to conserve it; they invent it, they publish ordinances, they intervene whenever the legal situation isn't clear to guarantee security. These days which is to say nearly all the time." Benjamin finds this situation unacceptable. For him, "the police are ignoble because in their authority 'the separation of the force that founds and the force that conserves is suspended'."[75] In modern times the police behave like lawmakers.

The police are present everywhere in visible form, but at the same time they allude to the absence of the erstwhile demarcation line between the 'law-instituting force' and the 'law-preserving force'. This 'absence' or

74. See his work *Specters of Marx*.
75. W. Benjamin, "Zur Kritik der Gewalt," *Archiv für Sozialwissenschaften und Sozialpolitik* (1921) 286, cited in J. Derrida, "Force of Law," 1007.

'blurring' of the demarcation line makes them take on a ghostly appearance. Whoever encounters them feels that what they represent is false because of the arbitrariness with which they brandish the weapon of the law. This arbitrariness makes them 'dreaded policemen'. As individuals they may be nice persons, but once on duty they become phantom-like figures because they represent a judicial order that has become a ghost. Derrida summarizes: "Let us take the example of the police, this index of a phantom-like force because it mixes foundation with conservation. Well, the police that thus capitalize on force aren't simply the police. They do not simply consist of policemen in uniform, occasionally helmeted, and armed [...] By definition, the police are present or represented everywhere that there is force of law. They are present; sometimes invisible but always effective, wherever the preservation of the social order is at stake." And, he continues: "The police aren't just the police [...] They are there, the faceless figure of an existence (*Dasein*) coextensive with the existence (*Dasein*) of the state (*polis*) [...] They are a threatening force without a 'form'. As such they are ungraspable in every way. In so-called civilized states the specter of its ghostly apparition is all-pervasive."[76]

Derrida highly appreciates Benjamin's analysis. He points out that the blurring of the two orders which Benjamin eventually unearthed indicates that the 'text' itself in which the categories of 'law-instituting force' and 'law-preserving force' function has become fake and deceptive. One could even speak of a 'self-deconstruction' of the text and of the legal system. For him, Benjamin has convincingly demonstrated that, because of this internal contradiction that had crept into it, the legal system as it functioned in the German republic (*Weimarer Republik*) after World War I (1918-1933) was doomed to ruin. The maintenance of 'law and order' was no longer lawful – it could no longer be justified by invoking the impartial motif of the 'conservation of the law', since the rule of violence and arbitrariness had annulled this impartiality. For Benjamin, the system must disintegrate and will have to be replaced with something else. This is also the opinion of Derrida, although he himself has a somewhat different explanation of the re-emergence of the 'foundational' force in the domain of the 'conservation of the law'.

This alternative reading is based on his own philosophy, one that seeks to question every fixed notion of origin. We already know about Derrida's interest in 'archeology': in an 'origin' that is not an 'origin' in the common understanding of that term. For him, the non-historical, immemorial anteriority of *khôra*, the mysterious 'matrix of *différance*',

---

76. "Force of Law," 1009-1011.

can never be associated with a self-presence that in circularity returns to itself. That is the reason why he is able to link this 'matrix of *différance*' to an 'impossible' future that is always still to come. From this background Derrida argues that 'origin' in the common understanding of the term is by definition 'self-referential', on the basis of being 'present to itself'. It is precisely this mechanism that guarantees the iterability of the origin. The self-present origin repeats itself in its quality of selfsame origin, just as in phenomenology the *eidos* or the essence of the phenomenon lends itself to be repeated again and again. True, in its subsequent stages of development the origin may slightly alter itself, but this alteration insures, in the end, the unbroken presence of the selfsame origin.[77] For Derrida, it is this iterability that, right from the outset, accounts for the blurring of the distinction between 'law-instituting force' and 'law-preserving force'. He writes: "What threatens the rigor of the distinction between the two types of force is at bottom the paradox of iterability. Iterability requires the origin to repeat itself originarily, to alter itself so as to have *the value of origin*, that is: to conserve itself. Right away there are police and the police legislate, not content to enforce the law that would have had no force before the police [existed]. This iterability inscribes conservation in the essential structure of foundation."[78]

When Benjamin concluded that the system will have to be replaced with something else, he meant: the democratic system as it functioned in his days. For him, the German democracy was no longer a genuine democracy, since it was infected with the 'spirit' of the police. Consequently the separation of the legislative and executive powers, which is required for the good functioning of a parliamentary democracy, has been seriously eroded. Members of the parliament are no longer free to discuss questions such as the abolition of the death penalty, or the mandatory military service, not to mention the growing military-industrial complexes about which it is even forbidden to ask questions. By banning these topics from the agenda of parliamentary deliberation, the government basically violates the principle of 'accountability to the people' – the people who elected them. This shows, Benjamin exclaims, that there is 'something rotten' in the legal system of the state, if not in the democratic institution itself: "There is not yet any democracy worthy of this name. Democracy remains to come: to engender or to regenerate."[79] It goes

---

77. Derrida gives here a sketch of the Hegelian dialectics, according to which the 'sublated' origin re-emerges again in the final synthesis.
78. J. Derrida, "Force of Law," 1008-1009.
79. *Ibid.*, 1013.

without saying that Derrida welcomes this idea of a democracy to come, for it is close to what he himself stands for: the dream of an 'impossible' democracy to come – in which justice is done to everybody beyond strict legality.

2. Demythologizing Benjamin's Apocalyptic Interruption of History

Derrida is also pleased to observe how Benjamin at a certain moment has recourse to a 'God who is above reason' (above the universal rules to which judges are wont to have recourse). He writes: "This sudden reference to God above reason and above universality, beyond a sort of *Aufklärung* of law, is nothing other than a reference to the irreducible singularity of each situation. And the audacious thought, as necessary as it is perilous, of what I shall here call a sort of justice without 'legality' (*droit*) – this is not one of Benjamin's expressions – is just as much required for the uniqueness of the individual as it is for the people and the language, in short for history."[80]

Derrida is rather selective in rendering Benjamin's reasoning about 'God above reason and above universality'. He mainly picks up the aspect of the uniqueness of persons. For the rest, he is not inclined to ascribe any activity – even a saving activity – to God. This is in marked contrast to Benjamin, who has apparently no problem with the poetic language of the Bible. For Benjamin, God acts (as will become clearer below) by destroying and by building, by slaying and commanding respect for the living. These words also return in Derrida's account of Benjamin, but they are, in fact, citations and not part of his own vocabulary. Let us recall that for Derrida, *khôra* is the immemorial 'place' (or 'non-place') of differentiation and deferral (*différance*), which as such does not give any thing; it only sends negative signals to warn individuals and institutions against any tendency of locking themselves up in endless self-referential loop. This sending of signals happens in an 'anonymous' way; it gives us no clue about the nature of this dark ground of *différance*. Derrida's notion of *khôra* is worlds apart from a personalized God. On the other hand, his selective reading is, to a certain extent, justified, if one considers that Judaic thinking develops an approach to justice in which justice must be done to every particular person. In this sense, the ethical obligation always brings one into a sphere 'above' the 'universality of the law', thus running counter to the universal ethical imperative that has been so much praised in modern thinking. Both Benjamin and Derrida are apparently

80. *Ibid.*, 1023-1024.

sensitive to the Judaic ethos. Let is not forget that both are of Jewish descent and like to fall back – each in their own way – on their Judaic heritage.

As far as Benjamin is concerned, his recourse to God as apocalyptic 'interruption' comes as no surprise. He carefully explains what this 'interruption' consists of, and contrasts it with the Greek notion of 'justice'. If in the Greek tradition the law system is founded on the irruption (or fate) of a divine violence whose endemic force is still echoed in the actual practices of the law with its chastisements and penalties, up to the death penalty, then the Judaic tradition is quite the opposite. Here the divine power stands at the other side of revenge and bloodshed: "instead of founding legality (*droit*), it destroys it; instead of setting limits and boundaries, it annihilates them; instead of luring people into mistakes and [ensuing] expiations, it strikes; and above all, this is the essential point, instead of slaying with bloodshed, it slays and annihilates *without bloodshed.*"[81] In the Greek tradition, justice demands sacrifice – must make victims –, whereas in Judaism the divine power is seen as establishing reconciliation by absorbing penalty and sacrifice into its own being. In all its destructive power the Hebrew God is pro-life: God's 'interrupting' power (*Gewalt*) "may annihilate goods, life, legality (*droit*), the foundation of legality (*droit*), and so on, but it never mounts an attack to destroy the soul of the living. Consequently we have no right to conclude that 'divine violence' leaves the field open for all human crimes. 'Thou shall not kill' remains an absolute imperative."[82] From this it follows that the principle of the most destructive divine 'violence' commands the respect of the living being, beyond legality (*droit*).

Respect for the living being 'beyond legality' is an idea that Derrida, too, holds dear, even if he relegates to the background the voice of the living God who enjoins this respect. This, however, does not prevent him from addressing some critical questions to Benjamin, especially from the viewpoint of the holocaust (the 'Final Solution') that in the meantime took place. In this light he carefully examines what Benjamin understands by the sanctity of life. At bottom it means that "man's non-being would be still more terrible than man's not-yet-being-just, than the not yet attained condition of the just man, purely and simply. In other words, what makes for the worth of man, of his *Dasein* [his 'being there'] and his life, is that he contains the potential, the possibility of

81. *Ibid.*, 1027 [translation modified].
82. *Ibid.*, 1029.

justice, the yet-to-come (*avenir*) of justice, the yet-to-come of his being-just, of his having-to-be-just."[83] The Hebrew God, thus, never obliterates the human potential for justice in spite of his violent destruction of the existent legal order. Yet, for Derrida, this statement is obscured by Benjamin's next analysis: the linkage of a violent revolution-to-come to the divine destructive power the precise outbreak of which necessarily escapes human knowledge. The violent revolution Benjamin has in mind would be the outcome of a decision taken by the sovereign divine power. There can, thus, not be the slightest doubt about its just foundation. But, Benjamin adds, it is not given to us to know the precise moment when this divine decision is going to take place. Our conjectures about the day of God's violent interruption of history may be mistaken: "Less possible and also less urgent for humankind, however, is to decide when unalloyed violence has been realized in a particular case."[84]

Derrida is afraid of the dire consequences of such an apocalyptic messianism. That is the reason why in a postscript he muses about the nature of the violence (*Gewalt*) that lead to the 'Final Solution' (*die Endlösung*): the extermination of the Jews in the gas chambers of the Nazi concentration camps. One would not do justice to the 'Final Solution' by regarding it as the peak of the Greek foundational myth according to which sacrifice – in this scenario the elimination of the Jews – would be required in order to preserve and renew the legal order. In such a scenario the 'Final Solution' solely highlight the particular Enlightenment approach which basically espoused the 'logic' of the Greek foundational myth: in order for an encompassing justice to be established those who are perceived as threatening the legal order must be eliminated. This, however, can hardly have been Benjamin's option, for whom the apocalyptic destruction (the 'Final Solution') is to be located at the other side of Enlightenment thought: in Judaism the destruction flows from the irruption of a divine violence (*Gewalt*) whose ultimate rationale remains unfathomable: "As soon as one leaves this [Enlightenment] order, history begins – and the violence of divine justice – but here we humans cannot measure judgments, which is to say also decidable interpretations."[85] One can only hope that, in this annihilation, the not yet fully disclosed human potential for establishing a just society is preserved; for the divine anger is, after all, believed to bring about reconciliation along paths that are not accessible to human knowledge.

83. *Ibid.*, 1029.
84. *Ibid.*, 1033, citing W. Benjamin, "Zur Kritik der Gewalt," 300.
85. J. Derrida, "Force of Law," 1043.

Derrida, finds this a terrifying option. It may seduce some people to interpret the atrocities of the holocaust as the result of a 'divine inscrutable decision' the good effects of which we are not (yet) able to perceive. Such a seduction is the more real, the more one realizes that what happened in the concentration camps was an 'annihilation without bloodshed': the Jews were gassed and their *not bleeding* bodies cremated. He therefore warns against the danger of apocalyptic imagery and its seductive power. Those who would give in to this seduction should realize the extent to which they make themselves collaborators of the 'Final Solution'. Involuntarily perhaps, Benjamin's ruminations on divine justice may lodge him in the vicinity of Heidegger. For Heidegger, humanity's destiny is inscrutable, an idea which prevented him from protesting against the scandal of the holocaust.

Derrida concludes his meditation on 'Benjamin and the Final Solution' with the statement that for him Benjamin's text is "too messianico-Marxist or too archeo-eschatological."[86] Indeed, he himself links his 'messianic dream' of the 'impossible' to an archaeology that is a-historical, to the *khôra*, or the immemorial past of a place or non-place of *différance* that "remains irreducible to historicization, humanization, anthropo-theologization of revelation [... it remains] the absolute heterogeneity to philosophy, and the Judaeo-Christian history of revelation,"[87] and thus also to the apocalyptic messianism of destruction and rebuilding. Because Derrida's dream of the 'impossible' is founded on a *khôra* that 'gives nothing', but only sends signals of warning and resistance, it escapes the temptation of a Jewish Marxist eschatology that expects the irruption of a new order of justice from a divinely ordained destruction of the previous state of affairs. This is, of course, not to say that Derrida has no affinity at all with Benjamin or with Marx. He rather seeks to rethink what is valuable in them without falling prey to the illusion of an 'objectivist' philosophy of history that is seen as achieving its goals without regard to the particularity of the persons involved. This is the topic of his book *Specters of Marx* that I will analyze in the next chapter. It is in this work, too, that Derrida will bring up his notion of messianicity, as distinct from any type of messianism.

---

86. *Ibid.*, 1045.
87. R. Kearny, "On the Gift," 76.

CHAPTER TEN

DERRIDA'S POLITICAL ETHICS:
FURTHER ELABORATIONS. THE INTERNATIONAL SCENE

In a twofold way, Chapter Nine laid down the foundations of Derrida's political ethics: 1) by sketching Derrida's move beyond phenomenology in his considerations on the 'impossible' gift and 2) by highlighting Derrida's move beyond legality in his exploration of an 'impossible' justice. Both elements will return in Chapter Ten, in which I will bring together three topics on which Derrida takes a stand in international affairs: the international economic order, the question of immigrants, and the pardon sought by certain heads of state for past crimes. The common element that runs through Derrida's examination of the three topics is a search for a new international law and its institutions.

The first part of the chapter will deal with Derrida's appropriation of the legacy of Karl Marx, at a moment when no alternative seemed to exist to the neo-liberal world order. From Marx, Derrida inherits a concern about those who are left behind by the capitalistic system. For them, there is apparently no place in the new 'democratic' order that is being propagated worldwide. From this background, Derrida will plead for a 'New International' whose program is being implemented by those who call themselves the 'antiglobalists'. In this context, Derrida will proclaim his messianic dream of an 'impossible' democracy to come. The second part of the chapter will deal with the questions of hospitality and cosmopolitanism, and with the restrictions imposed upon them by interstate treaties. This again means that only those foreigners are welcome who are expected to fortify the economies of the receiving nations, whereas unwanted immigrants are excluded. To depict the seriousness of this situation, Derrida will give an account of the French immigration laws, and the way in which French intellectuals protested them by urging municipalities to become 'cities of refuge' as these existed in the Abrahamic tradition of 'unconditional' hospitality. The last part of the chapter will reflect on the typically Abrahamic notion of 'unconditional' forgiveness, that is: forgiveness of that which is unforgivable. It will critically examine the extent to which this notion is at least partially operative in recent phenomena such as the South African 'Truth and Reconciliation Commission' – and the extent to which it is not. The same clarification of terms will be undertaken with respect to the forgiveness asked by the Japanese Prime Minister Murayama and the French president Chirac for the 'crimes against humanity' perpetrated by their respective nations, and with respect to the amnesty granted in France after the Second World War.

I. DERRIDA AND THE LEGACY OF MARX

On April 22 and 23, 1993, Derrida delivered two addresses at a conference organized by the 'Center for Ideas and Society' of the University of California, Riverside. The general topic of the conference was 'Whither Marxism?'. This question was accompanied by some urgency. In 1989 the once powerful communist East Bloc had imploded, and in 1992 Francis Fukuyama published his book *The End of History and the Last Man*,[1] in which he celebrated the triumph of capitalism: unrestrained free-market economy combined with pluralistic democracies are presented as the apogee of human history, leaving no place for any other viable alternative. This allows us to understand the conference's choice of the topic: how to rethink Marxism so that it is once again relevant to contemporary social movements. Derrida augmented the texts of his two addresses and published them in a book entitled *Specters of Marx: The State of Debt, the Work of Mourning, and the New International*. In this work he sets the stage for a plethora of ghosts and specters.

1. *Spectrality*

There is first of all the 'specter of communism' that is still hovering around. Already in the *Communist Manifesto*, Marx had characterized the movement as a terrifying specter for all the powers of old Europe: "A spectre is haunting Europe – the spectre of communism. All the powers of old Europe have entered into a holy alliance to exorcise this spectre: Pope and Tsar, Metternich and Guizot, French Radicals and German police-spies."[2] For Derrida, the specter evoked by Marx is not just a specter that surfaced in the past. When referring to this specter, he observes that the specter is a *revenant*: it appears and reappears, haunting people with the prospect that it cannot be repressed once and for all.

---

1. F. Fukuyama, *The End of History and the Last Man* (New York: The Free Press, 1992).
2. Communist Manifesto http://www.marxists.org/archive/marx/works/1848/communist-manifesto/ch01.htm.

So, one may expect it to return in the form "of a communism still to come"[3] – one which new holy alliances will try again to exorcise. This is already a first reply to the detractors of communism and the protagonists of the capitalistic New Order, who like Fukuyama celebrate the death of Marxism.

But, second, there are also the specters in Marx himself – in plural, that is to say: there are the several faces of Marx that continue to haunt both his enemies and his 'allies' (leftist thinkers like Derrida). First comes the ghost of Marx, the prophet, who knew to rally millions of 'wretched' people in order to liberate them from the fetters of an inhumane existence – the Marx who believed in the messianic dream of a realm of justice and brotherhood. That is the specter Derrida both welcomes and fears (because of the 'impossible' injunctions it enjoins). For him, "this messianic remains an *ineffaceable* mark – a mark one neither can nor should efface – of Marx's legacy."[4] Besides this messianic ghost there is also the ghost of Marx, the father of dialectical materialism. This is a ghost to which Derrida would not wish to return. Nor is he inclined to mourn the implosion of the East Bloc, for the Marxism that characterized that region and which had now collapsed was, after all, modeled on Marx's ontology, with its Hegelian understanding of history as a progression through dialectical leaps. Orthodox Marxism holds that, once the revolutionary industrial proletariat has taken possession of the newest technological apparatus, it is destined to change the 'face of the earth'. Derrida is skeptical about this perspective; he wants to exorcise it as a bad spirit, and this for two reasons.

In the wake of Heidegger, Derrida doubts whether the calculating mentality of technology will really be able to inaugurate the era of a 'greater humanization' of the human race. Second, he fears that the exclusive role attributed to the party in planning the revolution and subsequently structuring the 'new society' permanently under its control will suffocate genuine democratic deliberations in the public square. He fears that it will not take long before the 'liberated' proletariat is at the mercy of an utterly totalitarian system. When the axiomatics of the party are given full rein, despotism lurks around the corner. He writes: "Nazi, fascist, or Soviet totalitarianisms – *not one* of these regimes was possible without what

---

3. J. Derrida, *Specters of Marx: The State of Debt, the Work of Mourning, and the New International*, trans. P. Kamuf (New York and London: Routledge, 1994) 37. Originally published as idem, *Spectres de Marx: L'état de la dette, le travail du deuil et la nouvelle internationale* (Paris: Galilée, 1993).

4. *Ibid.*, 28.

could be called the axiomatics of the party. Now, as one can see fore-shadowed, it seems, everywhere in the world today, the structure of the party is becoming not only more and more suspect [...] but also radically unadapted to the new – tele-techno-media – conditions of public space, of political life, of democracy, and of the *new* modes of representation (both parliamentary and non-parliamentary) that they call up."[5] Not only is the one-party system oppressive, it also blocks all sorts of multifaceted innovations in techno-science and human relations.

The prophetic, messianic specter of Marx, which is the driving force behind his revolutionary enterprise, seems to clash with the other ghost that also took possession of Marx: that of the mastermind of a worldwide one-party-led counter-empire that is destined to win the victory over the empire of the capitalistic world order. Derrida admits that his selective reading of Marx's ghosts is entirely his own choice. The reader will already have understood why he made this choice. Insofar as Marx still adheres to modernity's uniform schemas – those which threaten to give rise to a police state in view of maintaining law and order – Derrida would classify him under the rubric of a law maker, one who feels they have to enforce the law on everybody without discrimination. He has already cri-tiqued this attitude in his work 'Force of Law'. On the other hand, inso-far as Marx draws inspiration from his Judaic heritage and continues to dream of a messianism in which justice will be done to everybody – beyond the pitiless enforcement of the law – he can rely on Derrida's whole sympathy.

The listing of ghosts or specters would be incomplete without men-tioning still another type of 'spectrality': that of the commodification of products. In the capitalistic financial system all the fabricated products have become 'commodities' (today we would say: articles of consump-tion). They are wrapped in an atmosphere of money-making and mar-ketability. A table is never just a table, but a use-product offered by the market and speaking the language of the circulation of money and finan-cial transactions that steer the market. The more the use-products speak that language, the more they take on a ghostly appearance that leads the attention away from the real world of their fabrication through human labor. Their ghostly appearance spreads, so to speak, a veil over the – unfair – labor conditions on which the financial world of profit-making thrives. Commenting on Marx's *Capital*, Derrida makes it clear that in the capitalistic enterprise "commodities have business with other commodi-ties, these hardheaded specters have commerce among themselves;

[... that's why] men no longer recognize in [them] the *social* character of their *own* labor. It is as if they were becoming ghosts in their turn. The 'proper' feature of specters, like vampires, is that they are deprived of a specular image, of the true, right specular image. [...] How do you recognize a ghost? By the fact that it does not recognize itself in a mirror. Now that is what happens with the *commerce* of the commodities *among themselves*. These ghosts that are commodities transform human producers into ghosts,"[6] making them forget that the commodities have been produced by laborers who, as social beings, have social relations among themselves. And, Derrida adds, the ghostly disappearance of the importance of just human relations in the labor process is what Marx wanted to exorcise in his analysis of *Capital*.

In this way Derrida has set the stage for a variety of competing ghosts and specters that are present in Marx's legacy. This stage covers, in fact, the whole book and often leaves the readers in disarray: these will have to make out for themselves which ghost they are going to exorcise and which they are going to welcome (in spite of their natural fear of being 'possessed' by the spirit they welcome). At the same time, Derrida's critics have accused him of giving in to the spell of literature. Derrida admits that in *Specters of Marx* the tone is emotional, due to his reference to Hamlet who is haunted by his dead father's spirit. Yet, it is well known that Marx, too, had developed a love for Shakespeare's hauntology. This hauntology has the advantage of presenting a very particular phenomenology that is no longer focused on "a plenitude of a presence to itself, [on a] totality of a presence effectively identical to itself."[7] A Ghost is the visibility of the invisible; the presence of a non-presence, without any focus on the actual now; a ghost has a very particle life-span: it comes and goes: "A ghost never dies, it remains always to come and to come-back."[8]

Although it wavers between a thing and a person, one can address it. One can speak to a ghost especially when realizing that the ghost, in its asymmetry, sees us. This is reminiscent of the invitation ('come') of the unknown stranger in 'On a Newly Arisen Apocalyptic Tone in Philosophy'. There, too the 'come' is addressed to the asymmetry of "an event that cannot be thought under the given category of an event."[9] But the

6. *Ibid.*, 155-156.
7. *Ibid.*, 99.
8. *Ibid.*, 99.
9. J. Derrida, "On a Newly Arisen Apocalyptic Tone in Philosophy," *Raising the Tone of Philosophy*, ed. P. Fenves (Baltimore, MD and London: The Johns Hopkins University Press, 1993) 164. Originally published as idem, *D'un ton apocalyptique adopté naguère en philosophie* (Paris: Galilée, 1983).

hauntology has still another function, when linked to a process of mourning. Here the socially committed person is challenged to decide what s/he
is going to do with the haunting heritage of Marx. For Derrida it is clear:
the debt he owes to Marx is that his practice of deconstruction (and its
yearning for an 'impossible' justice) "would have been impossible and
unthinkable in a pre-Marxist space. Deconstruction has never had any
sense or interest, in my view at least, except as a radicalization [...] in a
certain *spirit of Marxism*."[10]

2. *Criticism of Fukuyama*

As already mentioned, the publication of Fukuyama's book *The End
of History* had been the main occasion for organizing a Conference on
the legacy of Marx. No wonder, thus, that Derrida pays due attention to
this book that in the meantime had become a best-seller. The book proclaims the 'good news' that, in spite of some calamities, such as the horrors of Nazi and Stalinist totalitarianism and the atrocities of Pol Pot, the
world community has embraced at large the ideal of liberal democracy:
"Liberal democracy remains the only coherent aspiration that spans different regions and cultures around the globe. [... Moreover] this move
toward political freedom around the globe, according to Fukuyma, would
have been everywhere accompanied, sometimes followed, sometimes preceded, he writes, by a liberal revolution in economic thought."[11] The
alliance of liberal democracy and the free market is for him the 'good
news' in the last quarter of the 20th century. The reader will already have
observed that Derrida, in his formulation, is rather skeptical about this
'new gospel'. What it presents is, in fact, a Christianized version of
Hegel's philosophy of history. It time and again has recourse to biblical
images, such as the entry in the promised land, and specifies that for the
time being this entry is not yet fully realized, since not all the peoples of
the globe have in actuality already accepted liberal democracy and the
capitalistic free market.

Derrida admits that Christian eschatology lives in a tension between the
'not yet' and the promise of full realization. But, for him, it is dangerous
to use this religious vocabulary in the context of a philosophy of history.
Philosophy has its own language to speak about 'things to come'; more
to the point it was Immanuel Kant who coined the term 'regulative Idea'.
As we will see, however, Derrida finds this 'regulative Idea' still too

10. J. Derrida, *Specters of Marx*, 92.
11. *Ibid.*, 57.

weak to capture what he himself understands by messianic hope. Nonetheless, the notion is helpful to help us perceive where Fukuyama went wrong. A 'regulative Idea' steers our strivings to the attainment of a certain purpose the realization of which is not yet found in empirical reality. This concise definition makes it clear that the 'regulative Idea' which (in the absence of any empirical embodiment) directs our expectation, is not the same thing as that which Fukuyama announces as a reality: the empirical break-through of full-fledged democracies around the globe. In fact, the evangelistic language he uses – 'I bring you the good news' – rhetorically blurs the distinction between regulative Idea and concrete facts. The language of proclamation is, basically, performative language: it apparently brings about what the message announces, namely that the entry in the promised land will of necessity take place, in spite of the fact that some nations have not yet entered it.

This blurring of distinctions turns Fukuyama's discourse into a ghostly rhetoric. That discourse must necessarily oscillate between the affirmation that genuine democracy has already become a fact (at least in major parts of the world) and the proclamation of the 'good news' that liberal democracy will soon be embraced by the peoples and nations who are still living in closed societies with premodern structures. Only on the basis of this oscillation can Fukuyama come up with the slogan of the 'end of history'. In short, "Fukuyama considers this ideal also as an event. Because it would have *already happened*, because the ideal would have presented itself in its form as ideal, this event would have already marked the end of a finite history."[12]

At this juncture Derrida issues a double warning. He, first of all, states that more than ever we stand in need today of the Marxian tradition – of an 'open Marxist tradition, to be sure, and not of Marxist orthodoxy –, since Marxism has a long-standing tradition of examining the contradictions that arise as soon as one dares to take the ideality of a state of affairs (in this case: the ideal democracy) to be a fact that has already taken place in empirical reality. But then, second, even if one would maintain that the European Union or the United States are seriously on the way to becoming full-fledged democracies (in combination with free market economies), a Marxist could not help but ask why there are still so many counter-indications that shatter this dream.

Indeed, can we be so sure that the US and the European Union, in spite of all their rhetoric, are actually behaving as democratic countries? And is the type of democracy they propagate not contaminated by their alliance

12. *Ibid.*, 66.

with free market ideology and its embrace of ruthless competition? Do the
US and the European Union really respect international treaties? Are they
really free from protectionism? And why are they engaged in economic
wars and economic blockades? In pointing a finger of scorn to these
'anomalies' Derrida, moved by indignation, exclaims: "How can one
overlook the economic war that is raging today both between these two
blocs and within the European Community? How can one minimize the
conflicts of the GATT treaty and all that it represents, which the complex
strategies of protectionism recall every day, not to mention the economic
war with Japan and all the contradictions at work within the trade between
the wealthy countries and the rest of the world, the phenomena of pau-
perization and the ferocity of the 'foreign debt?'"[13]

In asking these critical questions Derrida seems to suggest that the
existing Western democracies only hypocritically invite the other nations
to join the 'club', and in doing so they turn out to be very selective. Only
those nations that are willing to accept the self-protective rules and the
ideology of the supremacy of Western democracies are welcomed,
whereas the others are excluded and left at the mercy of further pauper-
ization. The ideal democracy Fukuyama extols is, in fact, not willing to
share its privileges with the entire world-community. That is the reason
why Derrida affirms that what is at stake is the very Idea of democracy.
For him, there are failures and gaps in the existing Western democracies
and not just in the new candidates for such a democracy, as Fukuyama
holds. There is 'something rotten' "in *all* democracies, including the old-
est and most stable of so-called Western democracies."[14]

But at the same time he points out that those who are alert enough to
be worried about these gaps will – instead of covering them up – be able
to start dreaming about a totally new beginning. He writes: "At stake
here is the very concept of democracy as concept of a promise that can
only arise in such a *diastema* (failure, inadequation, disjunction, disad-
justment, being 'out of joint'). That is why we always propose to speak
of a democracy *to come*, not of a *future* democracy in the future present."[15] In plain English: it is only from the bitter awareness of situations
that are 'out of joint' that the messianic hope in a 'democracy to come'
arises. This democracy to come cannot possibly lie in the prolongation
of what we are witnessing now (namely: the growing gap, worldwide,
between the rich and the poor countries) – not even in a prolongation of

13. *Ibid.*, 63.
14. *Ibid.*, 64.
15. *Ibid.*, 64.

step by step revisions that one may observe. The 'democracy to come' will always have to go beyond the actual state of affairs, even of states of affairs that are already on their way to steady readjustment and improvement.

Since the awareness of social deficiencies and the 'birth' of a messianic dream go hand in hand, Derrida lists a whole range of situations that are 'out of joint'. The new situation of unemployment in many Western democracies; the massive exclusion of homeless citizens from participation in democratic processes; the ruthless economic war between the European community, the U.S., and Japan; the concept of 'the free market' that is at odds with the social security system in democratic countries; the scandal of foreign debt which blocks many countries on the road to development; the arms trade; the spread of nuclear weapons which can hardly be stopped in a world where the superpowers fight to preserve their world-hegemony; the inter-ethnic strife as a sad legacy of colonialism; the mafia and the drug cartels that act like phantom-states. But above all he laments the present state of the international law and its institutions: they prove to be dysfunctional because of a long-standing tradition of giving the last word in the interpretation of codes to the countries with the greatest techno-economic and military power.[16]

3. Plea for a 'New International'

Having said this, Derrida turns to one of the key-concepts of the Congress, the 'New International'. This is, of course, an allusion to the 'Communist International' that in earlier days was organized as an alliance of various communist parties. Yet, Derrida wants to go beyond this historical reminiscence, and to define what the program of the 'New International' should look like. For him, "the New International refers to a profound transformation, projected over a long term, of international law, of its concepts, and its field of intervention."[17] It should see to it that the concept of human rights be further diversified (the right to work or economic rights, the right of women and children, and so forth) and that these rights be respected in "the *worldwide* economic and social field, beyond the sovereignty of states and of the phantom-states we mentioned a moment ago."[18] Without mentioning the name 'Globalization' (which was not yet common currency when he gave his talk), it is precisely this

16. See *ibid.*, 81-83.
17. *Ibid.*, 84.
18. *Ibid.*, 84.

phenomenon that Derrida actually had in view: the emergence of a 'world financial and information space' that has gone 'global', working independently of the nation states and dictating how the nation states would be run. Now, it is in this 'worldwide economic and social field' that Derrida wants the basic rights of men, women, and children to be respected. In a sense, one could say, that Derrida already predicted and anticipated the later program of the anti-globalists who in their rallies will protest against sweatshops, the Iraqi-war-for-oil, and child soldiers, to cite just these few examples.

Given the fact that the magnates of great business companies dictate the domestic and international policies of the nation (of the White House e.g.), it is clear for him that the formerly autonomous nation state will no longer be able to stop the ever new waves of shocking dehumanization. These waves are numerous, in spite of the systematic propaganda that emancipatory movements have become redundant. He exclaims: "Never have violence, inequality, exclusion, famine, and thus economic oppression affected as many human beings in the history of the earth and of humanity. Instead of singing the advent of the ideal of liberal democracy and of the capitalist market in the euphoria of the end of history, instead of celebrating the 'end of ideologies' and the end of the great emancipatory discourses, let us never neglect this obvious macroscopic fact, made up of innumerable singular sites of suffering: no degree of progress allows one to ignore that never before, in absolute figures, never have so many men, women, and children been subjugated, starved, or exterminated on the earth."[19]

In order to oppose such a situation a 'world government' or 'super-state' is needed, one that forms a counterpoint to the managers of economic globalization. Yet, such a 'super-state' can hardly see the light of day without pressure from below. It is, thus, imperative that people continue to criticize the existent international law and its institutions for their lack of impartiality in that they are wont to give a preferential treatment to persons and nations with strong financial support. Derrida is well aware of the fact that, with this exhortation, he continues to keep alive the Marxian spirit: "without suspecting the juridical idea in itself, one may still find inspiration in the Marxist 'spirit' to criticize the presumed autonomy of the juridical, and to denounce endlessly the *de facto* take-over of international authorities by powerful nation states, by concentrations of techno-scientific capital and private capital." And he concludes: "A 'New International' is being sought through these crises of international law, it

19. *Ibid.*, 85.

already denounces the limits of a discourse on human rights that will remain inadequate, sometimes hypocritical, and in any case formalistic and inconsistent with itself as long as the law of the market, the 'foreign debt', the inequality of techno-science, the military [...] prevail."[20]

In Derrida's vision, the active members of the 'New International' will no longer be organized like visible trade unions, or party-members: they will live across nations, without national community, without a common belonging to a class or ethnic group, without a contract, without a stable organization, without title or name, even without citizenship. They form, so to speak, a clandestine movement, a 'counter-conjuration' against those who yield power in the globalized world; what cements them together is the "friendship of an alliance without institution."[21] This is, again, a definition of what later was to become the anti-globalist movement. The 'anti-globalists' are not organized along the patterns of classic Marxist movements, with their strong organizational forms. They are rather mushrooming under the pressure of burning societal questions with a worldwide impact. That is the reason why some unapologetic Marxists, like the literary critic Terry Eagleton, have difficulty welcoming Derrida's ideas, which for them are 'a Marxism without Marxism'.

The debate around Derrida's *Specters of Marx* already started with the publication of *Ghostly Demarcations. A Symposium on Jacques Derrida's Specters of Marx* (1999).[22] Some of the objections raised in this book were so serious that Derrida found it necessary to counter them in a short essay *Marx & Sons*.[23] The allegedly 'true Sons of Marx', those who felt themselves proprietorial about Marx, accused Derrida of depoliticizing Marxism. To this Derrida answered by referring to a text in *Specters of Marx*, in which he professed his faith in an existential promise, not to be found in dogmatic Marxism, but capable of generating new forms of action. The text reads as follows: "And a promise must promise to be kept, that is, not to remain 'spiritual' or 'abstract', but to produce events, new effective forms of action, practice, organization, and so forth. To break with the 'party form' or with some form of the State or the International does not mean to give up every form of practical or effective organization. It is exactly the contrary that matters to us here."[24] What he wants to abandon is not effective organization but (a) 'the party form'

20. *Ibid.*, 85.
21. *Ibid.*, 86; 66.
22. *Ghostly Demarcations: A Symposium on Jacques Derrida's Specters of Marx*, ed. M. Spinkler (London: Verso, 1999).
23. J. Derrida, *Marx & Sons* (Paris: Presses universitaires de France, 2002).
24. J. Derrida, *Specters of Marx*, 89. See also J. Derrida, *Marx & Sons*, 25.

of such an organization – a 'party form' which is typical of the 'old' International – as well as (b) the unitary thought form of dogmatic Marxism that steers that partyform organization.

This statement elicited the objection that he no longer regarded the class struggle as the motor for social change. For unapologetic Marxists, social class and class struggle remain the essential features of Marxism. To attenuate these notions would boil down to revisionism, and to opportunist compromises with the powers that be. Again, Derrida was forced to defend himself. He made it clear that he did not want to drop 'the something' called labor class. He rather sought to question the self-evidence with which this notion is used in dogmatic Marxism, as if it were a pure univocal concept that would lend itself to each and every situation. As we already know, Derrida abhors such an eidetic essentialism. Therefore, he pleads for a differentiated approach to the notions of class, and class belonging: "What seemed problematic to me," he writes, "is the principle of identifying the social class with the Idea that such a class is what it is, homogeneous, present and identical to itself [and as such functions] as 'ultimate support'. Yet a certain difference with oneself, a certain heterogeneity of the social force does not seem to me incompatible, *on the contrary*, with the movement of a social struggle."[25] Derrida seeks, thus, to widen a concept that dogmatic Marxism had streamlined, to the point of cutting itself loose from empirical reality.

In the course of the debate Derrida refers to his book *Politics of Friendship* (1997),[26] in which he demonstrated the sterility of fraternities which by definition must introduce exclusions in order to keep intact their so-called purity. This book, he explains, is a critique of genealogies, as well as of the exaltation of like-mindedness – of the idealized couples father-son, brother-brother etc. These genealogies breath a suffocating purism, with no openness at all to the 'impure' and the 'unfamiliar'. So, too, is it with the Marxist concept of social class, and the genealogical link it presupposes. This concept of class creates a strong unity *ad intra*, but also fosters the instinct of banishing the slightest deviation and otherness. However much Marx might have called the industrial proletariat the 'new universal class', the party-form of the Marxist organizations reduces this 'universalism' to something provincial. Hence Derrida's insistence on really universal topics, such as the crises of the international laws that are

---

25. J. Derrida, *Marx & Sons*, 52 [translation mine].

26. J. Derrida, *Politics of Friendship*, trans. G. Collins (London and New York: Verso, 1997). Originally published as idem, *Politiques de l'amitié* (Paris: Galilée, 1994), referred to in idem, *Marx & Sons*, 44.

still patterned after the model of conglomerations of modern nation states. For him, the world community is evolving in a cosmopolitan direction. This new phenomenon challenges one to rethink the location and the impact of the relations of social forces. He writes: "What I am advancing with the New International [...] presupposes so little the suppression of these relations of force and of social domination, but rather: the end of citizenship, national communities, parties and motherland."[27] Whoever studies in the future the tensions and oppositions between social forces worldwide will have to take into account this new, cosmopolitan definition of political engagement.

4. *Derrida's Notion of Messianicity*

For Derrida, those engaged in the 'counter-conjuration' against the capitalistic deformation of modern democracy are, in fact driven by a 'messianic' hope. In various sections of his book he raises this topic; it constitutes, so to speak, the 'backbone' of his late period of philosophizing. Derrida's messianic hope has its roots in the Abrahamic tradition (in Judaism, Christianity, and Islam). Yet, he refuses to call his messianicity a religion, because religions tend to close themselves off from those who do not belong to their flock: the strangers, the non-believers. That is the reason why he prefers to speak of the 'messianic' instead of 'messianism'. For him, messianism is linked to a particular religion, which – even if it has recourse to universal language – tends to tie this 'universal outlook' to a precise cultural setting and to a dogmatic belief system. What he really aspires to is a messianism (the 'messianic' thus) that is detached enough from any socio-cultural background to embrace the whole of humanity in its cultural diversity. For him, the messianic dream is "an a-theological heritage" of Abrahamic messianism; it designates a universal "structure of experience rather than a religion."[28]

1. In *Marx & Sons* Derrida clarifies his a-theological use of the Jewish heritage. For him, this a-theological use is still different from the secular use Karl Marx and Walter Benjamin made of Jewish messianism. Especially for Benjamin, Jewish messianism was a potent metaphor to evoke the breakthrough of totally unexpected new things. So, too, is it for Derrida. He, however, makes it clear that the universal structure of experience he has in view has shed all vestiges of a concrete tradition of revelation. For him, "messianicity has no longer any essential relationship

---

27. J. Derrida, *Marx & Sons*, 54 [translation mine].
28. J. Derrida, *Specters of Marx*, 168.

with what one may associate with messianism: that is to say, at least two things: on the one hand the memory of a particular historical revelation, be it Jewish or Judaeo-Christian, and on the other hand a relatively clear figure of the Messiah."[29] Derrida's messianicity is "a messianicity without messianism."[30] On the other hand, when asking himself the question as to why he is still busy coining and remodeling messianic terms to express his own 'great expectation', he has to admit that a certain acquaintance with Jewish messianism (directly or via Benjamin), must have exerted a decisive influence on his radical notion of messianicity. The question of heritage can apparently not be avoided, even when one opts for an a-theological reception of this heritage.

Derrida had already brought up this difficulty in the 'Villanova Round Table Discussion' of 1994. There he said: "When I insisted in *Specters of Marx* on messianicity, which I distinguished from messianism, I wanted to show that the messianic structure is a universal structure."[31] Having explained the importance of this difference, however, Derrida confesses that he himself is confused about how these relate to each other, and that he sees two possibilities of explaining this relationship. Is it the case, he says, that what he has reconstructed as messianicity is at bottom a basic structure of which the historical messianisms are particular exemplifications? Messianicity would then have to be seen on the same footing as the general structure of revealability Heidegger elaborated in order to shed light on the particular historical revelations and also to gauge their respective credibility. In other words: "[In this view] the religions, say, for instance, the religions of the Book, are but specific examples of this general structure of messianicity. There is the general structure of messianicity, as the structure of experience, and on this groundless ground there have been revelations, a history which one calls Judaism and Christianity, and so on. [...] This is one hypothesis."[32] But besides this hypothesis there is also the other hypothesis, namely, that we would never have known what messianicity is without the specific, irreducible input of the historical religions. He says: "The other hypothesis – and I confess that I hesitate between the two possibilities – is that the events of revelation, the biblical traditions, the Jewish, Christian, and Islamic traditions have been absolute events, irreducible events which have unveiled this messianicity. We would not

29. J. Derrida, *Marx & Sons*, 72-73 [translation mine].
30. *Ibid.*, 71.
31. J. Caputo, "The Villanova Roundtable: A Conversation with Jacques Derrida," in idem, *Deconstruction in a Nutshell* (New York: Fordham University Press, 1997) 22.
32. *Ibid.*, 23.

know what messianicity is without messianism, without these events which were Abraham, Moses, and Jesus Christ, and so on. In that case, singular events would have unveiled or revealed these universal possibilities, and it is only on that condition that we can describe messianicity."[33] On the basis of his hesitation to opt between these two possibilities Derrida concludes that the least he can say is that he is giving his own "reinterpretation of this tradition of the Messiah,"[34] a reinterpretation he framed within a logic of pure excess, beyond any calculated reciprocity in the act of giving.

Let us note in passing that Derrida expressed the same disarray when asking himself how he had first encountered the notion of *khôra*. Here, too, as we have seen in Chapter Nine, he remained undecided. Did the depth and profundity of this notion dawn upon him as a result of his contact with the mystics of a particular religion? Or did he discover the profundity of this notion himself when reflecting on the a-theological and a-historical domain that, on the basis of its immemorial past, must of necessity be located 'before' any historical revelation? There is apparently a parallel between this undecideability and Derrida's hesitation to tell what came first: the particular messianisms of the revealed religions, or the universal structure of messianicity to which these messianisms must be subordinated. Because of the importance of this parallel I quote again the text in which he expresses his hesitancy concerning the 'origin' of his discovery of the notion of *khôra*: "I do not know if this structure [of *khôra*] is really prior to what comes under the name of revealed religion or even of philosophy, or whether it is through philosophy or the revealed religions, the religions of the book, or any other experience of revelation that retrospectively we think what I try to think. I must confess, I cannot make the choice between these two hypotheses."[35] What is clear, however, in both cases is that, compared to the input of religion – the experience of a desert within a desert (Angelus Silesius) and the expectation of a messianicity saving figure – the two Derridaen notions of *khôra* and messianicity open up the perspective in two directions. They introduce (a) a concept of universality-without-exclusion that is not to be found in the religions of the book; and (b) a logic of pure excess that goes beyond any reciprocity in the act of giving, a reciprocity which is always presupposed in the religions of the covenant (God's gift expects a counter-gift).

---

33. *Ibid.*, 23.
34. *Ibid.*, 24.
35. R. Kearny, "On the Gift: A Discussion between Jacques Derrida and Jean-Luc Marion," *God, The Gift and Postmodernism*, ed. J. Caputo and M. Scanlon, 73.

2. These two characteristics – universality and a logic of pure excess – come to the fore in the two major topics Derrida analyses when setting out to give a concrete picture of his messianic dream: democracy and hospitality. His notion of democracy – of 'true democracy' – will no longer be patterned after the ideal of the modern Western nation state. 'True democracy', or the 'rule of the *demos*, the people', ought to be multicultural: without the exclusion of any body, of any race, or any ethnicity. If one realizes this amplification of perspective, one will also grasp why Derrida associates 'democracy' (as it should be) with unconditional respect for, and hospitality to, the neighbor, the 'Other', the stranger – here one perceives the influence of Levinas – and this on a universal scale. For him, the 'messianic', this "waiting without an horizon of the wait"[36] has a universal structure which is accessible to experience. Consequently this universality must always be critically tested: "hospitality is absolute only if its keeps watch over its own universality."[37]

It is this 'universality without any exclusion' that makes unconditional hospitality so difficult and so demanding, but also emotionally uplifting. The kind of hospitality he has in mind is so universal that it does not know in advance who will be the guest to welcome. Because the guest is basically unknowable in advance, Derrida again ushers in the notion of the 'impossible' Idea. True, from time to time he calls the impossible Idea of 'universal hospitality' a regulative Idea in the style of Kant. Yet, at the same time he deviates from this Kantian notion. The regulative Idea, to be sure, arises from the perspective of welcoming the guest, but one that is basically co-structured by the welcoming person him/herself. Such a 'structuring' that originates with the knowing subject already sifts out those to whom one would like to give hospitality. In this way restrictions are built in, such as the requirement of a common citizenship, or a common class-belonging or a common religion. For Derrida, however, that sort of selection blocks the 'universal hospitality to come' and hence also the 'true democracy to come'. The discriminating person seems to be too confident that s/he already knows what universal hospitality is. Because of this presumed knowledge, he/she is no longer engaged in a patient waiting for the unknown 'to come'.

Derrida likes to underline the total surprise of what is going to come. He says: "Even beyond the regulative Idea in its classical form [there is] the Idea, if that is still what it is, of 'democracy to come', its 'Idea' as event of a pledged injunction that orders one to summon the very thing

36. J. Derrida, *Specters of Marx*, 65.
37. *Ibid.*, 168.

that will never present itself in the form of full presence."[38] The 'Idea' will never turn out to be as we imagine it to be, however generous we are. For there will always be the opening of a gap "between an infinite promise" that comes from the impossible Idea and "the always necessarily inadequate forms of what has to be measured against this promise."[39] The infinite promise is, in other words, always untenable. And this for the simple reason that the impossible Idea time and again shatters our own limited images and presentations of what we think hospitality and democracy should be. Confronted with its absolute injunction we must acknowledge that we were mistaken in pretending to know what "infinite respect of the singularity and alterity of the other" really means.[40]

The 'impossible Idea' gives us mainly negative signals (just as the *khôra* does). Yet these negative signals paradoxically keep alive the messianic hope in our hearts. What this messianic hope is all about Derrida describes as follows: "Awaiting without horizon of the wait, awaiting what one does not expect yet or any longer."[41] This awaiting without horizon of the wait refers to the 'democracy to come' – and as part of it: to the 'hospitality to come'. In order to make oneself worthy of the 'impossible' break-through of these 'realities to come', the 'awaiting' person is called upon to put certain basic attitudes into practice, such as: "hospitality without reserve, welcoming salutation accorded in advance to the absolute surprise of the *arrivant* from whom or from which one will not ask anything in return and who or which will not be asked to commit to the domestic contract of any welcoming power (family, State, nation, territory, native soil or blood, language, culture in general, even humanity), *just* opening which renounces any right to property, any right in general."[42]

II. COSMOPOLITANISM: THE RIGHT TO HOSPITALITY

1. *Who and What Is the Stranger?*

In 1996 Derrida conducted a seminar on hospitality. The content of some of the sessions was published a year later. In this published text Derrida mainly explores the situation of the stranger in Greek antiquity: Who

38. *Ibid.*, 65.
39. *Ibid.*, 65.
40. *Ibid.*, 65.
41. *Ibid.*, 65.
42. *Ibid.*, 65.

and what is the stranger? In order to answer this question, Derrida, in a first move, points out that Plato, in his later dialogues, used to stage a scene in which a stranger (*xenos*) played a role in that he questioned the foundations of Greek thought. In the dialogue *Sophist* a stranger is introduced who excuses himself for doubting the pertinence of the old Greek thesis, put forward by Parmenides, that 'being is' and that 'non-being is not'. The stranger, apparently, speaks an alien idiom, different from that of the native citizens; this already earns him the suspicion of being a dissenter, someone who tends to disregard the intellectual achievements of Athens, and who on this account can be compared to a son who murdered his father: the stranger is both a fool and a pervert guilty of patricide. In the dialogue *Politicus* it is again a stranger, received as a guest, who is said to have initiated the frightening discussion about the essential qualities of the statesman, thus avowing his lack of knowledge about the unquestionable truths of the Athenian republic. But there is more to it, Derrida continues: even Socrates, the philosopher who often ironically professed his ignorance, when resorting to his maieutic questioning, is often presented as a stranger: a person who acknowledges his inability to understand the words that are in common usage. This is especially the case in the *Apologia*, in which he confesses to not understanding the juridical terms his opponents use to accuse him of corrupting the youths of Athens with his skeptical philosophy. He informs them that he "does not master the techniques of the court and that therefore he feels like a stranger."[43]

This succinct evocation of what is being associated with the term 'stranger' allows Derrida to focus immediately on what is at stake: The stranger is the one "who has difficulties in speaking the common language, and therefore risks to be bereft of the possibility to defend himself before the legal system of a country that has the power to either welcome or expel him. The stranger is in the first place a stranger to the idiom of the law (*droit*) in which the duty to grant hospitality has been encoded, the right to asylum, its limits, its norms, etc."[44] If the stranger is to apply for hospitality, he must do so in the language of the host country. On the other hand, the conclusion of a pact between the host country and resident strangers was not uncommon in Athens. On the basis of such a pact these strangers were granted certain rights with the imposition of concomitant duties. Socrates alludes to this pact in the *Apologia*

43. J. Derrida and A. Dufourmantelle, *De l'hospitalité* (Paris: Calmann-Lévy, 1997) 21 [translation mine].
44. *Ibid.*, 21 [translation mine].

when he requests that his judges treat him, at least as well as a stranger would be treated, that he at least be accorded the rights that a stranger would be recognized to have. One of these rights was the liberty given to the stranger to speak the foreign language according to his own idiom. For Socrates, this implied the permission to express himself in his usual parlance, which consisted in asking questions of clarification, as he used to do in his dealings with people in the market place. This excursion into Socrates' trial is for Derrida an occasion to examine, with the help of Benveniste's philological studies, the ramifications of such a pact.

Basic to the pact is that it includes the whole family of the resident strangers as well as their descendents. Resident strangers – e.g. the metics (*metoikoi*) from Egypt, Lebanon, Syria, and other Mediterranean countries – were those who, as merchants, along with their families, had been given the right to stay and operate in Athens, while enjoying the legal protection of the city. The metics can be compared to the expatriates of today who earn their living and do business in a foreign country. Derrida points out that in Athens the right to hospitality bestowed on the whole family is not just an extension of the individual right to hospitality of the resident merchant; no, the pact is concluded with the whole clan, that is: with a particular social group that is known by its specific name. But exactly here Derrida sees an aporia emerge: what of those who are not privileged with a famous name – or who have no name at all? "One does not offer hospitality, under these conditions, to an anonymous arrivant, to somebody who does not possess a [famous] name or family name (*patronyme*), or social status. Such a person is not treated as a [resident] stranger, but as one of the many [unwanted] barbarians."[45]

At this juncture Derrida jumps to the practice of modern Europe and quotes in this context Kant's famous text on cosmopolitanism,[46] in which world citizenship is restricted to the ethos of hospitality. Because Derrida dwelled more extensively on this text in a talk delivered in 1997 in Istanbul I will examine the content of this talk in the paragraphs that follow. In *Perpetual Peace*, more precisely in the *Third Definitive Article for a Perpetual Peace*, Kant writes: "Cosmopolitan right shall be limited to conditions of universal hospitality."[47] For Kant, hospitality should, to be sure, be universal, but restricted by conditions. These conditions are stipulated in the treaty concluded between two nations, and as we will see,

45. *Ibid.*, 29 [translation mine].
46. *Ibid.*, 125.
47. J. Derrida, "Hospitality," *Jacques Derrida: Basic Writings*, ed. B. Stocker (London and New York: Routledge, 2007) 243, citing from I. Kant, *Political Writings*, ed. H.S. Riess, transl. H.B. Nisbet (Cambridge: Cambridge University Press, 1991).

this pact is not significantly different from that concluded between the city of Athens and her resident strangers. In the meantime one ought not to forget that 18ᵗʰ century Europe had developed a system of nation states which all had diplomatic relations with each other.

Right from the outset Kant makes it clear that hospitality is a right, not to be confounded with philanthropy. For Derrida, the treatment of hospitality at the level of rights is crucial, since it brackets in its definition sentimental motives that are to be situated in the private sphere. The question of hospitality definitely belongs to the public sphere. It is there that hospitality can be contrasted with its opposite, namely political hostility: "The welcomed guest is a stranger treated as a friend or as an ally, in opposition to the other stranger treated as enemy."[48] This, however, does not mean that hospitality is unconditional. The one who treats the stranger as a friend is also the one who, out of duty, takes the initiative and therefore remains the master in his home. As a matter of fact, in his explanation of the term hospitality, Kant refers to the German word *Wirtbarkeit*. A *Wirt* is like the *patron* of a hotel or of a restaurant. He receives and accommodates the guest but in this quality also determines the rules of the home. Here again Derrida perceives a contradiction, for never does Kant raise the question of an unconditional hospitality in which the host would give up his authority and right to control: "Hospitality is very much by necessity: it is a right, an obligation, a duty, a law, it is the *welcome* of the other stranger as friend but on condition that the host, *the hôte*, the *Wirt*, the one who receives, lodges or gives *asylum* remains the *patron*, the master of the household, on the condition that he keeps the authority of himself in his home [... and that he] thereby affirms the law of hospitality as the law of his household."[49] In other words, the location that is at the receiving end also dictates the rules and the conditions of hospitality; this location can be the household, a hotel, a hospital, a hospice, a family, a city, a nation, and also a language.

This explanation of the term hospitality – in terms of conditional hospitality – allows us to understand Kant's definition of cosmopolitan right: 'Cosmopolitan right shall be limited to conditions of universal hospitality'. Kant introduced the notion of cosmopolitan right when reflecting on the finite entity of the earth which is our common possession: "Since the earth is a globe, they [the human beings] cannot disperse over an infinite area, but must tolerate one's another company."[50] This toleration of one's

48. *Ibid.*, 245.
49. *Ibid.*, 245.
50. *Ibid.*, 246.

other's company does not, however, result in a merger of all the nations. Cosmopolitan right does not coincide with the permanent *right of being a guest* to other communities. Members from other communities cannot claim such a right, since as a distinct entity they cannot expect to be welcomed by other nations as if they were members of the same family. Cosmopolitan right is rather a *right of resort*, that is: of passage. All the members of the human community have a right to travel to other parts of the globe, which is their common possession, and to be welcomed there as passengers by the receiving community. In this light Kant denounces the practice of some coastal dwellers who were in the habit of plundering ships and enslaving stranded seafarers, as well of the habit of some nomads in sacking the villages of other nomadic tribes. Cosmopolitan right basically consists in the assurance that one will not be treated with hostility in passing through someone else's territory.

When Kant wrote down these considerations he was thinking of practical means whereby to warrant perpetual peace. Such a peace can only be reached when the nations, even on remote continents, abandon their tendency to mutual hostility. At the level of modern European nation states this implies not only the furtherance of mutual tolerance in view of a peaceful coexistence, but also the willingness to grant the right of passage and stay to citizens from other nations through interstate treaties: "The foreigner can pass through but cannot stay. He is not given the right of residence. In order for there to be a right of residence it is necessary that there is an accord between States. All of this is placed under – and this is what cosmopolitanism means – an interstate conditionality."[51] At this juncture Derrida cannot help but ask two critical questions: first, what happens with the millions of displaced people today who did not even have the guarantee of citizenship? Are they not falling out of the boat, since their future is not safeguarded by any interstate treaty? Second, the notion of interstate treaty itself seems to cover a whole gamut of applications. After the discoveries of the Americas there were, to be sure, interstate treaties, not between Europeans and the pre-Columbian tribes but between Spain and Portugal about the extension of their colonies: the pre-Columbian inhabitants were regarded as non-existent, as non-human. The same abuse of the right to hospitality and residence happened in various parts of Asia, where the European merchants from Portugal, Great Britain and the Netherlands concluded treatises with the local kings and chiefs to grant them residence in certain enclaves of their territories, but this again as a first step to further colonization: "In East

---

51. *Ibid.*, 263, n. 8.

India foreign troops were brought in under the pretext of merely setting up trading posts. This led to oppression of the natives, incitement of the various Indian states to widespread wars, famine, insurrection, treachery and the whole litany of evils which afflict the human race."[52]

Kant's universal approach is often biased by a reduction of the universal to the outlook and interests of the European nations. Just as the European nations grant (conditional) hospitality to citizens from other nations and remain master in their own household, so too they remain master of their own strategy when concluding treatises of hospitality with their non-European counterparts. During Modernity, European nation states are marked by their tendency to conquer foreign territories overseas. This and similar considerations cause Derrida to be critical of Kant. For him, the basic question is whether Kant, in his political wirings, is really concerned about the destitute stranger who cries out for help? The answer is negative. Illustrative in this respect is the manner in which Kant resolves the difficulty as to whether one is allowed to tell an untruth when the police or a murderer comes and asks whether I am giving hospitality to a certain stranger. This is the case of conscience which Derrida examines in his Paris seminar on hospitality.

For Kant, the answer is clear: in no case is one allowed to tell an untruth, since respect for the truth is the firm rock upon which the integrity of humanity is founded. This is for Kant a 'universal' law that must be respected in any case, in every circumstance: "One must tell the truth in this case, and thus risk to deliver the guest into the hands of death. It is better to break the duty of hospitality than to break the absolute duty of veracity, foundation of [our common] humanity and of human sociability in general."[53] Derrida has problems with Kant's legalistic approach, which reveals the questionable basis upon which the system of conditional hospitality is built: the legal order cannot possibly do justice to each and everybody, not in the least to the stranger. In the Greek and European tradition the stranger has apparently no proper rights. A different voice is heard in the Jewish heritage: here the safety and well-being of the guest/stranger gets priority over all other considerations.

In this respect Derrida mentions the story of Lot as narrated in Genesis, 19: "Lot seems to place the laws of hospitality above all the rest, more in particular above the ethical obligations that tie him to his family and especially to his daughters."[54] Having noticed that Lot received

---

52. *Ibid.*, 247.
53. J. Derrida and A. Dufourmantelle, *De l'hospitalité*, 67 [translation mine].
54. *Ibid.*, 133 [translation mine].

strangers as guests in his home, the male inhabitants of Sodom come and request Lot to deliver the strangers over to them so that they might have sexual intercourse with them. Lot replies that he cannot possibly do so since is he is bound by the law of hospitality which for him is holier than the ethical law of the household. In order, thus, to placate the angry mob he hands over to them his two virgin daughters, so that these may be abused – 'penetrated' – by them instead of the male strangers who enjoy his hospitality.

The law of unconditional hospitality is above the legal stipulations of conditional hospitality. In order to corroborate this thesis Derrida refers to Emmanuel Levinas who advocated that the name or the country of origin of the stranger who appeals for hospitality should not even be asked. Inquiry about the name and the country of origin still smacks of a legalistic approach, whereas true welcoming consists in refraining from asking questions: "Must one not abstain from asking questions [about name and origin], for such questions already announce the so many required conditions that set limits on a hospitality which consequently would be narrowed down to legality and duty?"[55] Such a reticence paves the way for a welcoming of the stranger beyond any economic circularity of calculation – a welcoming that is no longer hampered by the rules of the household, but one which allows oneself to be taken hostage by the stranger. In this reversed perspective "the stranger, the guest one expects, is not only somebody to whom one says 'come', but 'please, enter', enter without lingering, stay with us without hesitation, make haste to enter, 'come in', 'come in me', not only toward me, but in me: occupy me, take your place in me, which at once implies: take my place."[56] 'Take may place': replace me so that I may no longer remain the master in my household.

Derrida perfectly realizes the 'impossible' character of such a welcoming 'hospitality without any further condition'. Yet 'impossible' is not the same as 'unrealizable'. In order for the unconditional hospitality to gradually turn into a concrete reality, its advocates must immerse themselves in the concrete situations that are ruled by legal, conditional hospitality. For it is important for them to experience from within the inadequacies of a legally regulated hospitality. Only on the basis of such an experience will they be able to put pressure on the legislators to amend the existing regulations concerning the admission of strangers. Such a persuasion is imperative right now in the face of the massive influx of

55. *Ibid.*, 119 [translation mine].
56. *Ibid.*, 109 [translation mine].

undesired immigrants in Europe. In these circumstances strategies must be developed to work out "a concrete politics and ethics that would give birth to historical evolutions, effective revolutions, progress, in short to a perfectibility [of the laws]."[57] The burning question of the perfectibility of the laws of immigration will be the treated in more detail in the next section.

2. *The Right to Asylum*

In 1996 Jacques Derrida delivered in Strasburg an address to the 'International Parliament of Writers'. A couple of months earlier this 'parliament' had drafted a charter of hospitality, called 'The Charter for the Cities of Refuge', at a moment when in Paris mass demonstrations were being organized in protest against a law (the Debret Law) that foresaw the massive expulsion of immigrants and people without legal documents (*les sans papiers*). In this address he gives his own comments on the 'charter of hospitality', which he places in a historical context: that of the cities of refuge in the Old Testament and of the places of asylum (mostly churches) in the Middle Ages.

Before delving into history, however, he starts a reflection on the true meaning of cosmopolitanism, knowing that with this topic he would strike a chord with his audience and with his readers, since most of the Frenchmen regard themselves as cosmopolitan citizens, because of the long-standing tradition in France of granting asylum to political refugees – a tradition which recently has dramatically deteriorated. In the word 'cosmopolitanism' Derrida perceives the term 'metropolis' which originally referred to both the city and the state. But, he laments, currently the cities are absorbed in the modern nation state which has subjected them to the state administration. In its previous meeting the 'International Parliament of Writers' had already launched the idea – and concrete strategy – of inviting important cities in the world to reclaim their independence from the state and to transform themselves into 'cities of refuge'. For Derrida, this confederation of 'free cities' that open their gates to strangers, is the beginning of a 'new cosmopolitics', and of a renewal of international law.

Commenting further on the role of these 'free cities', he first of all makes it clear that they must affirm their autonomy within the state in which they are located, and tell the state leaders that they really want to

---

57. *Ibid.*, 131 [translation mine].

be recognized as independent 'cities of refuge', not falling under the control by the national police forces that keep an eye on the immigrants, the deported, the exiles, the stateless and the displaced persons. Derrida underlines the urgency and necessity of this 'exemption', since he does not expect much from the state or the interstate agreements to properly regulate the problem of asylum seekers on their territories. He follows in this Hannah Arendt who already in the mid-1930s had taken to heart the cause of exiles and stateless people, victims of the First World War, in a period of time when no international charters of the right to asylum existed; this issue was not part of the 1924 Charter of the League of Nations, the predecessor of the United Nations. In the meantime the right to asylum has been inscribed in the Geneva Convention (1951), ratified by the United Nations, but this does not mean that all the problems had been resolved. Arendt wrote: "Contrary to the best intentioned humanitarian attempts to obtain new declarations of human rights from international organizations, it should be understood that this idea transcends the *present sphere of international law which still operates in terms of reciprocal agreements and treaties between sovereign states*; and, for the time being, a sphere that is above the nations does not exist. Furthermore, this dilemma would by no means be eliminated by the establishment of a world government."[58] Derrida recognizes that Arendt's concern, first voiced in the 1950's, is no less urgent in his day.

True, the Geneva Convention had forced France to revise a stipulation in the Constitution of 1946 which granted the right to asylum only to persons persecuted because of their action 'in the name of liberty'. In 1954 France extended this definition to cover, in the spirit of the Geneva Convention, "all persons forced into exile 'because their lives and their liberties are found to be under threat by reason of their race, religion, or political opinions'."[59] Nonetheless, the juridical tradition remained restrictive, and applied these criteria only to European citizens. One had to wait till 1967 when in New York a protocol was added to the Geneva Convention declaring that the rule also applied to non-Europeans. But even then the asylum seekers were subjected to harassment and exhaustive cross-examination. For in the last resort their admission depended on the

---

58. H. Arendt, *The Origins of Totalitarianism* (London: George Allen and Unwin Ltd, 1967) 285 cited in J. Derrida, "On Cosmopolitanism," in idem *On Cosmopolitanism and Forgiveness*, trans. M. Dooley and M. Hughes (London and New York, Routledge, 1997) 8. Originally published as idem, *Cosmopolites de tous les pays, encore un effort!* (Paris: Verdier, 1997).

59. J. Derrida, "On Cosmopolitanism," 10-11.

momentary demographico-economic policies of the nation state. When guest workers were needed, the asylum seekers were welcome; if not, they were kept at bay.

This led to opportunistic and even arbitrary implementations of the New York protocol. A distinction began to be made between 'political refugees' and 'economic refugees'. Only those who were able to convince the jurists that a return to their country would endanger their lives because they had been persecuted for racial, religious or political reasons were regarded as 'political refugees' having a claim to asylum. If not they were suspected of having the intention to settle in the country for purely economic reasons, and saw their application rejected. Here again the judicial system employed rigid criteria: the asylum seekers had to prove that their immigration into the new country did not entail any economic gain. But, Derrida exclaims, who is going to make out what economic gain precisely means: a gain compared to what exactly? Even those recognized as political refugees will, economically speaking, generally be better off, because their stay in a country of the European Union will give them better access to labor opportunities than they had in their own countries.

The strictness of the juridical screening is only one aspect of the whole affair. It often takes years before a reasoned juridical response comes, and in the meantime the asylum seekers are regarded as illegal immigrants, 'whose papers are not in order'. They are classified as staying in the country 'without legal documents', and consequently fall under the jurisdiction of the police: the border police in the first instance, but also the police without borders. At this juncture Derrida refers to Walter Benjamin's analysis of the way in which in his days the police controlled anything, not just by applying the law but by actually making the law (see above Chapter Nine). This is what happens now, he says, to the asylum seekers: they are at the mercy of the police who can force them to leave the country. For him, this is one of the most serious problems the 'International Parliament of Writers' should tackle and make public. He writes: "With respect to new police powers (national and international), one is touching here on one of the most serious questions of law that a future elaboration of our charter for the cities of refuge would have to develop and inscribe throughout the course of an interminable struggle: it will be necessary to restrict the legal powers and scope of the police by giving them a purely administrative role under the strict control and regulation of certain political authorities, who will see to it that human rights and a more broadly defined right to asylum are respected."[60]

60. *Ibid.*, 14-15.

This does, of course, not mean that Derrida would contest the right of the police to protect the country against criminals, who are guilty of terrorism, drug-trafficking and mafia practices of all kinds. No, he simply asks that refugees and criminals not be treated interchangeably, and he sees a regrettable development in this direction. He refers to the discussion in the French National Assembly and Senate about the desirability of passing a law (the Toubon-law) designed to treat all hospitality given to strangers 'whose papers are not in order' as an act of terrorism. That law qualifies hospitality granted to unwanted strangers as 'participation in a criminal conspiracy', thus going further than the edict of 1945 that declared that all help to foreigners whose papers are not in order is a 'criminal act'. What earlier was seen as a crime has been upgraded now to 'lending one's support to criminal conspiracy', to terrorism. But, Derrida remarks with indignation that this is in direct contravention of the Schengen accords ratified by France which "permit a conviction of someone for giving help to a foreigner 'without papers' only if it can be proved that this person derived financial profit from such assistance."[61]

These developments make it all the more urgent that cities of refuge be grounded – cities that cultivate the ethos of hospitality, not just by giving the asylum seekers a familiar place of dwelling in the city, but by helping them to develop cordial social contacts with their 'co-citizens'. Having said this, Derrida points however to a danger – that of accommodating the newcomers *and* of subjecting them to the rules of the house, thus adding certain conditions to the unconditional law of hospitality. This tension between unconditional and conditional hospitality is part and parcel of an 'ethic of hospitality' as we have seen in our presentation of Kant's notion of the right to hospitality. On the one hand, unconditional hospitality is not something extraordinary as it coincides with culture itself – the more a culture is welcoming of strangers the more it gives evidence of a high degree of cultural development –; on the other hand, such an unconditional hospitality may, for political reasons, become something less than unconditional: "[T]here is a history of hospitality, an always possible perversion of *the* law of hospitality (which can appear unconditional), and of the laws which come to limit and condition it in its inscription as a law."[62]

Delving back into history Derrida first of all mentions the Hebraic tradition of hospitality. In the book of Numbers it is mentioned that God orders Moses to institute six cities of refuge to give asylum to innocent

61. *Ibid.*, 16.
62. *Ibid.*, 17.

people who are the victims of 'bloody vengeance' for resident aliens and temporary settlers. For further details he hereby refers to a study written by Emmanuel Levinas, 'The Cities of Refuge'.[63] However, here too a restricting clause is inscribed: asylum is being granted, provided the safety or the security of the 'strong city' is guaranteed. In the Middle Ages, too, there were several places of refuge. Each city enjoyed a certain sovereignty and could determine its own laws of hospitality. A city could "order that the borders be open to every one, to every other, to all who might come, without question or without their even having to identify who they are and whence they came."[64] So, too, the churches had a right to grant asylum, called *sanctuary*, whereas kings or lords could allow refugees banned from other cities to be received as guests in their territory.

At the philosophical and theological level a great cosmopolitan tradition started with stoicism and Pauline Christianity. See Ephesians II, 19-20: "And so, therefore, you are no longer foreigners or metics in a foreign land (*xenoi, hospites*), you are fellow-citizens of the Saints, you belong to the House of God." For Derrida, this statement has theologico-political implications, because it radically opts for a world citizenship, for cosmopolitanism. Later on, the cosmopolitan tradition typical of stoicism and Pauline Christianity was resuscitated by Immanuel Kant. In his famous *Third Definite Article for a Perpetual Peace*, which I have already presented above, Kant says: "The law of cosmopolitanism must be restricted to the conditions of universal hospitality."[65] This is, for Derrida, as we have seen, a somewhat enigmatic statement. Indeed, Kant seems at a first glance to extend cosmopolitanism to the law of universal hospitality, which is unconditional, and which is therefore called a 'natural law'. This means that every one, from wherever he or she may be coming, has a right to be received without hostility, since all of us are inhabitants of our common globe. Yet in a second step he builds in a basic condition: although every one has a right to be received as a host, this right is only a 'right of visitation' and not a 'right of residence'. To acquire a right of residence a special permit is needed, depending on the particular treatises among nation states.

Here again, in his plea for the creation of 'cities of refuge', Derrida is not totally happy with the restriction Kant has built into his notion of universal hospitality, because due to this clause we are saddled nowadays

63. E. Levinas, "Les villes-refuges," in idem, *L'au-de-là du verset* (Paris: Minuit, 1982) 51 sqq.

64. J. Derrida, "On Cosmopolitanism," 18.

65. I. Kant, *Perpetual Peace: A Philosophical Essay* (New York and London: Garland Publishing, Inc., 1972) 137-138, cited in J. Derrida, "On Cosmopolitanism," 19.

with the whole problem of 'unwanted asylum seekers' being kept at bay, if not persecuted and harassed by the national police forces. On the other hand, Derrida beliefs that Kant continues to provide us with a deep inspiration, since his starting point is universal hospitality extended to every human person who is living on the face of the earth: the earth being a public domain to which everybody must have access. This makes Derrida conclude that what is needed today – and that to which the new 'cities of refuge' are expected to contribute immensely – is a constant negotiation between what he calls unconditional hospitality (the unconditional right to be received with unrestrained hospitality) and the conditional laws of a right of residence (which Kant elaborated in line with his philosophy of the modern nation state). In Derrida's own wording: what the 'cities of refuge' ought to do is to engage in constant negotiation "between the Law of an unconditional hospitality, offered *a priori* to every other, to all newcomers *whoever they may be* and the conditional laws of a right to hospitality, without which *the* unconditional Law of hospitality would be in danger of remaining a pious and irresponsible desire, without form and without potency, and of even being perverted at any moment."[66]

For Derrida, however, negotiation is not the same thing as cowardly compromise. To negotiate means: to work for the improvement of the law, so that it becomes less repressive and more in conformity with the general principle of unconditionally hosting the stranger. Indeed, insofar as modern thinking lies open to the ideology of the modern nation state, it ought to be revised from the 'postmodern' platform of welcoming the stranger without any discrimination. If modern thinkers boast of being universal in their outlook, they ought to be reminded that their universalism is often thwarted by their location in the modern nation state. This makes us understand why Derrida's criticism of modern political ethics is in the first instance a criticism of this ethics' entanglement in the realpolitik of modern statesmen.

3. *Welcoming the Stranger: Beyond Mere Tolerance*

In the previous chapter I mentioned that Derrida, with his notion of *khôra* (as something more radical than negative theology), wanted to lay down the foundations of a new universal politics, one which would be able to cross the borders, say of European and non-European contexts,

66. J. Derrida, "On Cosmopolitanism," 18.

of Jewish, Christian, and Muslim geographies. Further, on that same occasion he remarked that he was not saying this against Judaism, Christianity, or Islam: he rather hoped that the quintessence of what he was saying could be retranslated into a Jewish discourse, a Christian discourse, and an Islamic discourse, if at least these religions were willing to "integrate the terrible things I am suggesting now."[67] Derrida was suggesting a logic of pure excess which he was afraid the established religions would never be willing to appropriate. Derrida extended, thus, a skeptical invitation to the world religions (the Abrahamic religions in particular) to revise their usual categories and to position themselves more radically – not as fundamentalists, but as advocates of a growing sense of authentic universality. In a word, the world religions must decide where they want to stand in matters of cosmopolitanism and hospitality to the stranger.

This 'skeptical' invitation is certainly not the same as an exhortation to interreligious dialogue (as a means of curbing the religions' natural tendency to cling to their own superiority); it must rather be seen as a plea addressed to them: 'please, try to live up to that universal dimension, provided you have the courage to do so, because it will not be easy'. In saying this Derrida is both open and realistic, for religions are mostly reluctant to explore new domains, even if their respective tradition virtually encourages them to do so.

Whatever the repercussions of this plea may be on a large scale, one surely ought not to exclude that certain people interested in the renewal of the world religions would be willing to learn some lessons from Derrida's cosmopolitanism. I can even imagine that some of them would begin to understand that his logic of pure excess is so rich that it can become a place where religions, in their respective attempts at self-renewal, may effectively meet each other. This interfaith encounter, however, would not be so much at a doctrinal level, but rather at a theologico-political level. I will explain what I mean.

Derrida is, indeed, convinced that politics, even in its secularized form, has theological roots. In his search for a cosmopolitan 'democracy to come' he often laments that the nation state acts as a stumbling block, because it emphasizes so much of its absolute sovereignty, which is in fact a remnant of a theocratic worldview. In his eyes, state sovereignty remains an ambivalent notion. On the one hand, this sovereignty gives the state the right to protect its citizens against external violence, but, on the other hand, it is counterproductive in the furtherance of a worldwide

67. R. Kearny, "On the Gift," 77.

democratic rule in that it also entitles the state to use violence "in controlling its borders, and excluding and repressing non-citizens and so forth" – thus demonstrating the impact of "its theological [theocratic] legacy."[68] Confronted with this theocratic legacy, religions should ask themselves with which power they are going to side: with the theocratic component of the nation state or with the world-wide cosmopolitan ideal that is slowly dawning on the horizon? Are they willing to adjust their theologico-political self preservational instinct (and self-isolation) so as to embark on the promotion of a growing 'world citizenship' across the division of nations, ethnicities and religions?

The formulation of these challenging questions is, of course, mine, although Derrida's ideas form the background against which they arise. The inspiring power of this background particularly comes to the fore in the interview he gave after September 11th. Here he reflects on the value of tolerance (and more so of hospitality, as we will see) in a era of growing intolerance in which Muslims are pitted against Jews and Christians, and vice versa – one ought only to think of the role the Israeli-Palestinian conflict has played in the awful attack on the twin towers in New York. In this reflection he delves into the history of the concept of tolerance and reveals that it has a Christian origin, which also means a theocratic origin that sets limits on openness to the 'other'.

Derrida assesses the notion of tolerance with due nuances. Tolerance, to be sure, is evidently incomparably better than intolerance because of the avoidance of bloodshed. Yet, what makes it deficient is the one-sidedness with which the stronger party agrees to live in a peaceful coexistence with the other, usually weaker party. One ought not, indeed, to forget that historically the practice of tolerance is the result of a compromise after a war situation. In the aftermath of the failure of the Crusades, Christians had to tolerate the presence of non-Christians in their vicinity, whereas after the peace of Westphalia, Catholics tolerated the fact that Protestants wielded power over their territories in a previously undivided Christian Europe. Yet, Derrida critically asks, why should one content oneself with simply tolerating a peaceful coexistence – even if this toleration is heralded now as a Christian virtue? Is that type of tolerance, on closer scrutiny, as 'selfless' as it likes to pretend?

As it turns out, (Christian) tolerance is based on calculation and self-preservation; it has hardly anything to do with the pure gratuity of hospitality that Derrida stands for. When Giovanna Borradori interviewed

---

68. G. Borradori, *Philosophy in a Time of Terror: Dialogues with Jürgen Habermas and Jacques Derrida* (Chicago, IL: The University of Chicago Press, 2003) 124.

Derrida, she asked whether Derrida would agree with the claim that tolerance is a condition of hospitality, to which Derrida vigorously replied: "No, tolerance is actually the opposite of hospitality, or at least its limit. When I think I am being hospitable because I am tolerant, it is because I wish to limit my welcome, to retain power and maintain control over the limits of my 'home', my sovereignty, my 'I can' (my territory, my house, my language, my culture, my religion, and so on)."[69]

Having said this, Derrida admits that, as compared to its Christian origins, the notion of tolerance has in the meantime taken on a slightly modified meaning. He hereby refers to the French president François Mitterand who had at a certain moment ventured to speak of a 'threshold of tolerance' with respect to immigrants. For him, the threshold has been reached "beyond which it is no longer decent to ask a national community to welcome any more foreigners, immigrant workers and the like."[70] In other words, this means that common sense says that there are limits to hospitality; if in these circumstances hospitality is still being granted, it can only be a 'conditional hospitality', one that can still be tolerated because of its limits. Yet, such a conditional hospitality falls short of the 'logic of pure excess', which precisely refuses to impose any condition on the 'coming of the stranger' – a welcoming without reserve that therefore rightly deserves to be called 'unconditional hospitality'.

Derrida likes to call this 'unconditional hospitality' a 'hospitality of *visitation* rather than *invitation*'. For him, a 'conditional hospitality' may still say: "I invite you, I welcome you into *my home*, on the condition that you adapt to the laws and norms of my territory, according to my language, tradition, memory, and so on."[71] Yet, pure, unconditional hospitality goes much further: "It opens or is in advance open to someone who is neither expected nor invited, to whomever arrives as an absolutely foreign *visitor*, as a new *arrival*, nonidentifiable and unforeseeable, in short wholly other [...] The visit might actually be very dangerous, and we must not ignore this fact, but would a hospitality without risk, a hospitality backed by certain assurances, a hospitality protected by an immune system against the wholly other, be true hospitality?"[72]

Derrida concedes that such an excessive unconditional hospitality is practically impossible and can not even become part of any legislation. Nonetheless, he believes that this 'impossible Idea' (which is beyond the

69. G. Borradori, *Philosophy in a Time of Terror*, 127.
70. *Ibid.*, 127-128.
71. *Ibid.*, 128-129.
72. *Ibid.*, 129.

law and beyond ethics) must be kept alive. For without the thought of this pure hospitality we would lack any real perspective allowing us to revise and to correct the existing 'conditional laws of hospitality'. As already mentioned, the immigration policy of most countries continues to make a distinction between 'political immigrants' (those who can prove that they have been persecuted in their home country for racial, religious, or political reasons) and 'economic immigrants' (those who are suspected of having the intention of settling in a country for purely economic reasons). The first category are granted asylum whereas the second are classified as staying in the country 'without legal documents' (*les sans papiers*); they can be expelled from the country at any moment. Yet, Derrida muses, would these people 'without legal documents' not receive a fairer treatment if the thought of 'pure hospitality' would have been kept alive? – the only 'thought' (or unpresentable Idea) which tells us what true hospitality is: "Without at least the thought of this pure and unconditional hospitality, of hospitality *itself*, we would have no concept of hospitality in general and would not even be able to determine any rules for conditional hospitality (with its rituals, its legal status, its norms, its national or international conventions). Without this thought of pure hospitality (a thought that is also, in its own way, an experience) we would not even have the idea of the other, of the alterity of the other, that is: of someone who enters into our lives without having been invited."[73]

For Derrida, these considerations have an unmistakably religious connotation. This becomes evident in the question he asked as to whether 'a hospitality protected by an immune system against the wholly other, could be true hospitality?' In this question resonates something of the 'fear and trembling' that Abraham, in Kierkegaard's reconstruction, experienced when being ordered to kill his only son, Isaac on mount Moriah. In his book *The Gift of Death* (1992) Derrida explores at length Kierkegaard's analysis of this trembling before the 'wholly other', who simply demands the blind obedience of faith to his commands. These commands have nothing in common with the Kantian categorical imperative that only enjoins general ethical obligations. The demands of the 'wholly other' aim at the singular and particular: they address the singular responsible person, urging him/her to face up to a singular, particular situation. This is the predicament of the 'knight of faith', who is forced to transgress the general codes of ethics, so as put his/her own existence in danger.

73. *Ibid.*, 129.

Taking his lead form Levinas' critical remarks on, and daring rein-terpretation of, Kierkegaard's work *Fear and Trembling*,[74] Derrida expands the basic exposure of the 'knight of faith' to the heavenly 'wholly other', so that it in turn may serve as a model and paradigm for one's basic exposure to each and every 'wholly other' (that is: to each and every 'naked face' of the other) within the human community: "If God is completely other, the figure or name of the wholly other, then every other (one) is every (bit) other. *Tout autre est tout autre* [...] It implies that God, as the wholly other, is to be found everywhere there is something of the wholly other."[75] Whereas Kierkegaard mainly focused on the heavenly 'wholly other', Derrida broadens this per-spective to include 'every other one' whom one is obliged to treat, beyond the general rules of ethics, as the 'wholly other'. "[E]very other one, each of the others, is God inasmuch as he or she is, *like* God, wholly other –"[76] a 'wholly other' who, like God, arouses fear and trembling.

True, in *The Gift of Death* no special mention is made of hospitality. Yet the sacrificial gesture of giving up one's home which Derrida regards as the quintessence of true hospitality, surfaces again in the basic expo-sure to each and every 'wholly other', for whom one has to sacrifice that which one regards as one's property, as one's home. Such a sacrifice entails the end of every calculation of gain, the end of an economy that is ruled by the law, and the seemingly sacrosanct obligation to safeguard what is properly one's own. Derrida puts it as follows: "The sacrifice of economy, that without which there is no free responsibility or decision (a decision always takes place beyond calculation), is indeed in this case the sacrifice of the *oikonomia*, namely of the law of the home (*oikos*), of the hearth, of what is one's own or proper, of the private, of the love and affection of one's kin. This is the moment when Abraham gives the sign of absolute sacrifice, namely by putting to death or giving death to his own, putting to death his absolute love for what is dearest, the only son."[77] Abraham, the father of faith, is the one who sacrifices his home. References to the Abrahamic tradition are abundant in Derrida's writ-ings. This was the reason why he invited the Abrahamic religions – Jews, Christians, and Muslims – to initiate their own reflection 'on the terrible

74. E. Levinas, *Noms propres* (Montpellier: Fata Morgana, 1976).
75. J. Derrida, *The Gift of Death*, trans. D. Wills (Chicago, IL and London: The University of Chicago Press, 1995) 77-78. Originally published as idem, "Donner la mort," in idem (ed.), *L'Éthique du don* (Paris: Métaillié-Transition, 1992).
76. J. Derrida, *The Gift of Death*, 87.
77. *Ibid.*, 95.

things I am going to tell'. The above quote makes it clear that Derrida perfectly knows what this Abrahamic tradition is about, be it in matters of 'impossible' hospitality, or in matters of 'impossible' forgiveness. The topic of unconditional forgiveness will be the subject matter of the next section.

III. 'Impossible' Forgiveness

In 1999 Derrida published an essay in the French intellectual journal, *Le monde des débats*, 'On forgiveness'. In the same period of time he prepared a study 'The History of the Lie', published in his book *Without Alibi* (2002), in which he mainly examined the nature of the political lie. Whereas 'On forgiveness' meditates on the 'crimes against humanity' that are brought to International Criminal Courts, but which also inspire heads of the state to ask pardon for the past crimes committed by their country, 'The history of the Lie' shows how difficult it is to make out what a crime against humanity is and what it is not, at least when one listens to the conflicting parties involved. The same historical facts are presented differently depending on which side of the watershed of geopolitical interests one finds oneself. What Israelites today call acts of defense in their national interest – the building of a wall to strategically protect the Israeli territory – is regarded by the Palestinians as a crime. The same is true for the notion of ethnic cleansing. For Israelites, raids on Palestinian militias having links with Hezbollah are a mere question of self-defense, whereas Palestinians decry them as crimes against humanity.

1. *Lies in Politics and the Confession of Crimes against Humanity*

In her book *Truth and Politics* (1972) Hannah Arendt presents politics as a privileged place for lying. She writes: "Lies have always been regarded as necessary and justifiable tools not only of the politician's or the demagogue's but also of the statesman's trade. Why is that so? And what does it mean for the nature and dignity of the political realm, on one side, and the dignity of truth and truthfulness, on the other?"[78] For Arendt, lies as political tools have become a daily occurrence, especially since the rise of the modern nation state. Derrida welcomes this idea,

---

78. H. Arendt, "Truth and Politics," in idem, *Between Past and Future: Eight Exercises in Political Thought* (New York: Vikings, 1972) 3-4, cited in J. Derrida, *Without Alibi*, ed., trans. P. Kamuf (Stanford, CA: Stanford University Press, 2002) 39.

since he himself is in search of a political order that will supersede the self-interest of the modern nation states. With Arendt he acknowledges that, since the advent of modernity, with the exception of Kant, truth and lie (dissimulation of truth) have lost their reference to something absolute: truth begins to be perceived as caught up in historical development; it is subject to change, so that after a while a clear demarcation line between truth and untruth no longer exists. Moreover, the departure from fixed standards of truth is seen as a condition of possibility for progress. This specially applies to the domain of politics. As Arendt puts it, "The [political] liar is an actor by nature; he says what is not so because he wants things to be different from what they are – that is: he wants to change the world."[79]

For Derrida, Arendt is exploring the difficult domain of things that are not true, but also not necessarily false: the world of daydreaming, of creative imagination, of one's dealing with the spectral, and even of self-deception. "The lie to oneself is not [necessarily] 'bad faith',"[80] if one links it to the workings of the unconscious. Such a self-deception, however, turns out to be catastrophic if it is broadcast and magnified by the modern means of communication. This is what happened in totalitarian states – think of Nazi Germany – which develop a real propaganda industry in order to strengthen the citizens' adherence to the ideology of the regime. This may lead to a war between deceiving, if not self-deceiving ideologies, as can be exemplified in the mutual distrust between the United States and the Soviet Union during the Cold War period. In the words of Hannah Arendt: "Politically, the point is that the modern art of self-deception is likely to transform an outside matter into an inside issue, so that an international or inter-group conflict boomerangs onto the scene of domestic politics. The self-deceptions practiced on both sides in the period of the Cold War are too many to enumerate, but obviously they are a case in point."[81] Wavering between self-deception and the will to change the life conditions of the nation, political rhetoric attempts to rally the various strata of citizens around the ideal of the national and/or ethnic unity. The results are an attitude of warfare and the harassing of scapegoats inside the nation, and a "modern manipulation of facts:"[82] The conflicting parties interpret the same empirical facts in a different, antagonistic way, thus fueling the palpable tension that already

79. Hannah Arendt, "Truth and Politics," 250, cited in J. Derrida, *Without Alibi*, 66.
80. J. Derrida, *Without Alibi*, 57.
81. H. Arendt, "Truth and Politics," 255, cited in J. Derrida, *Without Alibi*, 57.
82. J. Derrida, *Without Alibi*, 40.

existed between them. The same manipulation of facts continues after the implosion of the East Bloc: this time in the mode of ethnic strife and ethnic cleansing, as we have witnessed in Bosnia, Chechnya, Israel and Rwanda.

In the meantime, one can witness the advent of a seemingly new epoch in political history. Statesmen in France and Japan solemnly ask forgiveness and pardon for the crimes against humanity perpetrated by their predecessors. Derrida dwells at length on the declaration of remorse made by Prime Minister Murayama on August 15, 1995 on the occasion of the 50th anniversary of the end of the Second World War. In his own name and indirectly in the name of the whole Japanese nation, Murayama asked forgiveness of the Koreans and Chinese for past violence, in the hope that this violence, which still flew from a bygone colonial age, might never repeat itself in the future. Derrida quotes Murayama's letter of declaration: "I regard, in a spirit of humility, these irrefutable facts of history, and express here once again my feelings of deep remorse and state my heartfelt apology. Allow me also to express my feelings of profound mourning for all victims, both at home and abroad, of that history."[83] This apology was followed by concrete measures to re-establish cordial relations with China and Korea. In this apology Derrida sees a sign of progress in history. He writes: "However confused this event may be, and however impure its motivation remains, however calculated and conjunctural the strategy, there is here a progress in the history of humanity and its international laws, of its science and of its conscience."[84]

In France it was president Jacques Chirac who on July 16, 1995, decided to acknowledge the role the French State had played in the persecution of Jews and other victims of the German occupation. He said: "These black hours will stain our history for ever and are an injury to our past and our traditions. Yes, the criminal madness of the occupant was supported ('*secondée*') by the French, by the French State. Fifty-three years ago, on 16 July 1942, 450 policemen and gendarmes, French, under the authority of their leaders, obeyed the demands of the Nazis. That day, in the capital and the Paris region, nearly 10,000 Jewish men, women and children were arrested at home, in the early hours of the morning, and assembled at police stations [...] France, home of the Enlightenment and of the Rights of Man, land of welcome and asylum, France committed that day the irreparable. Breaking its word, it delivered those it protected

83. *Ibid.*, 47.
84. *Ibid.*, 47.

to their executioners."[85] In his analysis of these facts Derrida asks himself the question as to why it took that long before a head of the state
dared to apologize for the 'irreparable' that had occurred in France under
the regime of General Henri Pétain. Pétain had been the head of the
French State, also called the regime of Vichy, from 1940 till 1944. This
French State comprised the territory of France that was not directly under
the control of the Germans: the middle part and the south of France (the
whole westcoast of France up to Paris being occupied by the Germans).
There Pétain ruled in the new provisional capital Vichy, in collaboration
with the Germans. It was also from this city that Pétain ordered the French
police in Paris to register all the Jews and to organize the raids and round-
ups that would lead to their deportation to the concentration camps in
Germany and Poland.

From this background Derrida seeks to understand why General de
Gaulle – who after the defeat of the Germans had restored the French
Republic and become its head of state – refused to apologize for the role
France had played in the extermination of the French Jews. The answer is:
de Gaulle regarded such an apology as an indirect recognition of the legality of the French State under the regime of Pétain which in his eyes was
illegal: "Among former presidents, de Gaulle himself [...] never dreamed
of declaring the culpability of the French State under the Occupation, even
though or perhaps because the culpability of the 'French State' (this was
moreover the official name of France under Vichy, the Republic having
been abolished and renamed *État français*) was in his eyes that of a non-
legitimate if not illegal State."[86] This remained the official position of the
five next presidents, although they put efforts into restoring the unity of the
French people by granting amnesty to those who had collaborated with the
Germans. This leads Derrida to ask: Who has been lying or dissimulating
about the truth: de Gaulle and the five subsequent presidents of the Republic by refusing to admit the culpability of the French nation in the Jewish
question? Or Chirac himself who apparently no longer found it opportune
to go on drawing the distinction between the 'French State' (Pétain's Vichy
regime) and the 'French Republic' (restored under de Gaulle)?

But apparently, Derrida remarks, these intricate questions have
become obsolete on two counts. First there is the new awareness of the
'crimes against humanity', and second, in relation to it: there is the new

85. Allocution de M. Jacques Chirac, président de la République, prononcée lors des
cérémonies commémorant la grande rafle des 16 et 17 juillet 1942 (Paris: Présidence de
la République).
86. J. Derrida, *Without Alibi*, 48.

force that performative declarations have gained when referring to these crimes. In both cases one has to do with a tremendous novelty. Derrida writes: "At issue here is a veracity or a *lie of state* determinable as such, on a stage of international law that did not exist before the Second World War. These hypotheses, in fact, are posed today with reference to juridical concepts such as 'crimes against humanity' that are inventions and thus 'performatives' unknown to humanity before this."[87] These 'performatives' are codified in new juridical concepts: in "contracts, and interstate charters, institutions and courts of justice that are in principle universal and that until now had no place to judge or even register such acts – which moreover were not indentifyable as such."[88] For Derrida, it is this new universality that inaugurates a new historical epoch. The point of reference is article 6 of the statutes of the International Military Tribunal at Nuremberg that was convoked to judge those responsible of the 'crimes against humanity' (read: the extermination of the Jews) during the Nazi regime. Although the judges of the Military Tribunal were on the side of the victors in the war, their notion of 'crimes against humanity' received universal approval because of the extreme atrocities used in the liquidation of the Jewish race. In France the government declared these crimes 'imprescriptible' by a law dated December 26, 1964.

2. *Clarification of Some Basic Notions*

Derrida 's thesis on forgiveness is limpid and succinct: "Yes, there is the unforgivable. Is this not, in truth, the only thing to forgive? The only thing that calls for forgiveness."[89] In 'On Forgiveness' he seeks to explain the shocking notion of 'forgiveness of the unforgivable' by contrasting it with the geopolitics of forgiveness, on the one hand, and the refusal to forgive the unforgivable in the aftermath of the Shoah. With the geopolitics of forgiveness Derrida refers to the recent, worldwide phenomenon of heads of states asking pardon for the atrocities of the past. Above I have given two examples: the Japanese Prime Minister Murayama's expression of remorse for the crimes done to the Chinese and Korean peoples during the Second World War, and President Chirac's apology for the French nation's cruelty against the Jews. In 'On Forgiveness' Derrida adds the case of the 'Truth and Reconciliation Commission' in

87. *Ibid.*, 50.
88. *Ibid.*, 50.
89. J. Derrida, "On Forgiveness," in idem, *Cosmopolitanism and Forgiveness*, 32. Originally published as idem, "Sur le pardon," *Le Monde des débats*, Décembre 1999.

South-Africa, as well as the various gestures of granting amnesty to political enemies in the post-war period. In all these cases he observes a growing awareness of what is at stake in the 'crimes against humanity'. It is from this background that officially pardon is being asked, or that a process of reconciliation is initiated.

As already mentioned, Derrida is convinced that the 'performatives' inspired by the vivid awareness of 'crimes against humanity' mark an advance in civilization. They reveal a worldwide sensitivity for human rights as codified in the *Universal Declaration of Human Rights*; they also point to a 'globalization' of the tradition of forgiveness that is enshrined in the Abrahamic religions, and more particularly in Christianity with its insistence on forgiving one's enemies. He writes: "The globalization of forgiveness resembles an immense scene of confession in progress, thus a virtually Christian convulsion-conversion-confession, a process of Christianization which has no more need for the Christian church."[90] An example in case of this process of Christianization independently of a church is without doubt Murayama's confession of regret in Japan, a non-Christian country.

These laudatory words do, however, not prevent Derrida from being critical of the new phenomenon of publicly asking pardon. One can hardly link it to genuine forgiveness, since in it political considerations are involved. Excuses are proffered in order to repair past damages and to bring about reconciliation among or within the nations. Yet, such a finality takes the edge off the gratuity of forgiveness: "The language of forgiveness, at the service of determined finalities, [is] anything but pure and disinterested. As always in the field of politics."[91] For Derrida, it is clear: just as pure hospitality must move beyond the economy of calculation, so too, pure forgiveness cannot be captured in a political or juridical idiom. By formulating this stance, Derrida already alludes to the notions 'conditional' and 'unconditional' which he used in the context of hospitality and justice. The conditional element here is the framing of the notion of forgiveness in a juridical system, whereas unconditional forgiveness is irreducible to it. He writes: "Forgiveness is often confounded, sometimes in a calculated fashion, with related themes: excuse, regret, amnesty, prescription etc.; so many significations of which certain come under law, a penal law from which [pure] forgiveness must in principle remain heterogeneous and irreducible."[92]

90. *Ibid.*, 31.
91. *Ibid.*, 31.
92. *Ibid.*, 27.

A second domain in which a clarification of terms is needed is the literature around the Shoah, in which this 'crime against humanity' is mostly deemed unforgivable because no or few signs of repentance are shown on the part of the criminals. This is the thesis of Vlamidir Jankélévitch's polemic text *The Imprescriptible*.[93] Derrida disagrees with it. He points out that the Abrahamic tradition speaks of an unconditional forgiveness which only in secondary interpretations is mitigated so as to include repentance as condition for granting forgiveness. Yet, what is essential to this tradition, Derrida maintains, is "a demand for the *unconditional*, gracious, infinite, aneconomic forgiveness granted to the *guilty as guilty*, without counterpart, even to those who do not repent or ask forgiveness."[94] In his reflections on the Shoah, Jankélévitch seems to be insensitive to this essence of the Abrahamic tradition. He does not tire of complaining about the criminals' non-recognition of their fault: that they are guilty of the extermination of the Jews in the concentration camps. For him, this non-recognition is true for the former Nazis in command, but also for Germany as a whole which in the post-war period is only interested in its economic miracle and its strong currency. To attenuate this objection Derrida asks the critical question as to why one should only forgive those who are already on the path to amelioration – those who repent – instead of really aiming at forgiving the *guilty as guilty*. He exclaims: "If I say: 'I forgive you on condition that, asking forgiveness, you would no longer be the same, do I [really] forgive?'"[95]

In order to push the discussion still further Derrida dwells on the argument, also put forward by Jankélévitch, that the Shoah, because of the incomparable amount of suffering and humiliation it imposed on the Jewish people, is basically an inexpiable, irreparable crime. Even if one would consider the possibility of restitution, no punishment or expiatory sacrifice on the part of the guilty would be proportionate to the magnitude of the crime. So, forgiveness does not make sense: "For the inexpiable there is no possible forgiveness according to Jankélévitch, not any forgiveness that would have a meaning, that would make sense." Yet, Derrida retorts: "For the dominant or common axiom of the tradition, finally, and to my eyes the most problematic, is *that forgiveness must have a meaning*."[96] It is precisely because forgiveness has no meaning that it is a gratuitous act beyond any calculation of retribution. Derrida is well aware that he

93. V. Jankélévitch, *L'imprescriptible* (Paris: Seuil, 1986).
94. J. Derrida, "On Forgiveness," 34.
95. *Ibid.*, 38.
96. *Ibid.*, 36.

deviates from current opinions, which – in their tendency to place forgiveness in a juridical framework – associate forgiveness with punishment
or refraining from punishment. He remarks that even Hannah Arendt
regards forgiveness as a correlate to punishment. For her, "people would
be incapable of forgiving what they cannot punish, [just as] they would
be incapable of punishing what reveals itself as unforgivable."[97] For Derrida, such a correlate obscures the gratuitousness of forgiveness, for which
no expiatory retribution is asked.

3. 'Impossible' Forgiveness and Its Impact on the Political and Juridical Order

Pure forgiveness is unconditional and without any regard for retribution. These negative connotations reveal that what is at stake is an 'impossible' forgiveness, a forgiveness that "cannot [and] *must not present itself*
as such [...] without at the same time denying itself, betraying or reaffirming a sovereignty."[98] True forgiveness escapes any juridical or political order, and nonetheless constitutes the firm humus on which reconciliation in the political and juridical order feeds and prospers. Put
differently, pure forgiveness is totally heterogeneous, but is nonetheless
intrinsically tied to the political and juridical order which without it would
loose its vitality. In order to elucidate this complicated relationship, Derrida examines the totally unique genus of pure forgiveness, while also
exploring its connection to political forms of acquittal and amnesty.

Ever since the restoration of the French Republic under General de
Gaulle, the French presidents have at various times decided on amnesties
for the crimes committed under the German Occupation or during the
Algerian war. The rationale of these amnesties is clear: to repair the
national unity that was needed in the time of the Cold War. Yet, to the
extent that political motives prevailed, this act of reconciliation hardly
coincides with forgiveness in its pure form. Political and juridical bodies
"never forgive in the strict sense of the word;"[99] they only acquit and
exonerate (which are precisely judicial terms). This already shows that,
for Derrida, forgiveness is of a completely different genus: it has a different origin, a different source, than amnesty, in spite of possible resem-
blances between them.

97. *Ibid.*, 37.
98. *Ibid.*, 48.
99. *Ibid.*, 45.

An example of the unique genus of pure forgiveness in spite of its apparent similarity to the process of amnesty is the famous 'Truth and Reconciliation Commission' in South-Africa, the primary purpose of which was to restore national unity. Still in prison, Nelson Mandela found it necessary to negotiate the procedures of an amnesty, and this for two reasons: to facilitate the return of the exiles of the African National Congress (ANC), and to avoid murderous actions of vengeance. Part of the procedure was to call to memory the real criminal facts and to 'pardon' the evil-doers, a formula that comes close to the church practice of confession. That is why Desmund Tutu, the Anglican Archbishop who presided over the commission, had no difficulty introducing into the procedure the Christian vocabulary of repentance and forgiveness. Yet, the events themselves made it clear that these two orders must not be confounded. Tutu recounts that one day a black woman, whose husband had been tortured and assassinated by police officers, came to testify before the commission and declared that "A commission or a government cannot forgive. Only I eventually, could do it (and I am not ready to forgive)."[100] From this testimony Derrida deduces two facts: the representatives of the state can judge, but their judgment does not effect forgiveness; second: strictly speaking, only the victims in question (or those legitimately speaking in their name) can forgive, and nobody else. The latter is in line with the Abrahamic tradition, according to which "forgiveness must engage two singularities: the guilty (the 'perpetrator' as they say in South-Africa) and the victim. As soon as a third party intervenes, one can again speak of amnesty, reconciliation, reparation etc., but certainly not of pure forgiveness in the strict sense."[101] Because it is of a different genus, pure forgiveness goes beyond legal reconciliation.

On the other hand, the work of the 'Truth and Reconciliation Commission' – its legal reconciliation – would remain ineffective if its processes did not enable something of the purity of true forgiveness to transpire as a result. This is the point at which the heterogeneous element of 'impossible' forgiveness proves to have an impact on the juridical order, an order which aims primarily and pragmatically at a therapeutic reconciliation. Derrida writes: "Yet, despite all the confusions which reduce forgiveness to amnesty [...] or some political therapy of reconciliation, in short to some historical ecology, it must never be forgotten that all of that refers to an idea of pure and unconditional forgiveness, without which the discourse would not have the least meaning."[102] This

100. *Ibid.*, 43.
101. *Ibid.*, 42.
102. *Ibid.*, 45.

is further illustrated by the fact that the Idea of pure forgiveness can prevent the legal institutions of reconciliation from losing their real edge.
In a disconcerting manner Derrida sets out to show that the Idea of pure
forgiveness, instead of denying the unforgivable, fully acknowledges it.
It is only the awareness of the "unforgivable evil that would make the
question of [true] forgiveness emerge."[103] The bloody conflict between
Bosnians and Serbs cannot be resolved by forcing the parties to bracket
and forget their antagonism. Only the Idea of pure forgiveness, which is
aware of the unforgivable evil, can bring solace and prepare the way for
an elaboration of a legal regulation that would consider the dire wounds
caused by the rivalry.

The question of forgiveness exceeds all institutions and juridical-
political authority, without ceasing to have an impact on them. When in
1964 the French government decided that crimes against humanity were
'imprescriptible' it tried to capture in juridical terms what goes beyond
the authority of the state. Here again Derrida perceives the influence of
the Idea of pure forgiveness on the juridical: "the imprescriptible signals
towards the transcendent order of the unconditional, of forgiveness and
the unforgivable."[104] Let us notice that Derrida in one breath mentions
forgiveness and the unforgivable. For him, as already noted, only the
awareness of the unforgivable (the 'imprescriptible') paradoxically allows
the notion of pure forgiveness to emerge, whereas inversely the Idea of
pure forgiveness sharpens the notion of the unforgivable. In this light
Derrida welcomes the fact that even heads of states, like Pinochet and
Milosovic, are no longer untouchable; they lose their immunity and are
forced to appear before international courts to respond to the accusation
of 'crimes against humanity'. This shows again the extent to which the
notion of the unforgivable has gained worldwide adherence. For Derrida,
this world-wide recognition of the unforgivable – the refusal to grant
impunity to perpetrators of 'crimes against humanity' – marks without
doubt an advance in civilization. A greater advance would still be reached
if broad strata of the world population were to grow in their awareness
of the intrinsic link between pure forgiveness and the full acknowledg-
ment of the unforgivable. Pure forgiveness can only really demonstrate
its authenticity and potency in the face of that which is the truly unforgivable which, nonetheless, it feels it has to forgive.

103. *Ibid.*, 49.
104. *Ibid.*, 53.

GENERAL CONCLUSION

At the end of this study of the political ethics of Lyotard and Derrida
we are able now to account for the correctness of the title of the book.
Indeed, it is not uncommon to hear people ask the skeptical question
'Is there an ethics in the postmodern era?' 'How, for God's sake, can a
real ethical concern be born from life in fragments?' Ethics rather seems
to be the specific prerogative of modernity: "Modernity was, and had to
be," Zygmunt Bauman observes, "the *Age of Ethics* – it would not be
modernity otherwise. Just as the law preceded all order, ethics must pre-
cede all morality. Morality was the *product* of ethics,"[1] and from this
morality depended both a country's technological growth and its advance
in civilization. In the years since the close of World War II, however,
this modern ethics of universal mastery – with its trust in social engi-
neering and the malleability of people – has come under increasing suspicion. Proof of its demise is Lyotard's dictum that today people have lost
the memory of the grand stories – stories capable of molding the hearts
and minds of people because of their rational principles with a universal
impact. Like no other cultural movement in history, modernity boasted
on propounding a universal, encompassing ethics. With modernity's
decline the anxious question arises: which kind of ethics can come in its
place? A regional ethics of the provisional and the fragmentary? Yet,
our intuition and experience seem to tell us that, without some modality
of a universal perspective, no genuine ethics – no genuine political ethics
at least – will ever be able to prosper.

The first topic I will examine in this General Conclusion is the precise
nature of the universality that underlies Lyotard's and Derrida's ethic-
political considerations. As is to be expected, this type of universality
will be greatly different from the homogeneous, standardized universality that characterized the grand narratives of modernity. The second topic
to be examined will be the influence of Jewish thought on the political
ethics of both authors. It will become evident that a new 'universality
without exclusion' presupposes a Hebraic concern for the particular event.
The third topic to be considered are the practical applications that derive

1. Z. Bauman, *Life in Fragments: Essays in Postmodern Morality* (Oxford and Cambridge, MA: Blackwell, 1988) 34.

from both Lyotard's and Derrida's new framework. In this presentation I will treat the contributions of each author separately.

I. A New Kind of Universality

In Part One, I analyzed how Lyotard wrestled with the problem of universality. On the one hand, he developed an instinctive aversion to dominating overall perspectives – in his parlance: speculative phrases – because he feared that they could lead to the imposition of a reign of terror. On the other hand, he felt impelled to revisit the philosophical achievement of Kant, for the double reason that this author championed a universal ethics, but at the same time warned against the pitfall of placing one's hope in deceitful absolutes. For him, Kant is at once the prototype of modern universal ethics, and a critic of speculative transcendental illusions that may undermine this very ethical enterprise. So, when Lyotard goes back to Kant, it is in view of rediscovering a universality that is not, or not yet, infected with the virus of hegemonic mastery in the style of Hegel's absolute idealism, or later of Marx's stringent dialectics of history. It is only in this open space that he feels at home, at the other side of any attempt to "fulfill the phantasm of taking possession of reality [so as] to reinstitute terror."[2]

Even so, as we have seen, Lyotard is on the alert and seeks to eliminate those elements in Kant that Kant's successors might have used or abused in their creation of hegemonic systems: the self-contained substantial subject, with its urge to project an ultimately unified world. In my analysis of Lyotard's reading of the 'unification of the faculties' worked out in Kant's *Critique of Judgment* I called attention to these eliminations. The result is that a heavier accent is placed on diversity and heterogeneity. This comes to the fore in Lyotard's specific understanding of the *sensus communis*. For Lyotard, *sensus communis* "is not common but only *in principle* communicable. There is no assignable community of feeling, no affective consensus in fact. And if we claim to have recourse to one, or *a fortiori* to create one, we are victims of a transcendental illusion and we are encouraging impostures."[3]

Lyotard takes the basic principle of Kant's *Critique of Judgment* seriously, namely that in judgments of taste, which are by definition judgments about the particular, the universal rule is not given in advance, but

---

2. J.-F. Lyotard, *The Postmodern Explained*, trans. D. Barry et al. (Minneapolis, MN and London: University of Minnesota Press, 1992) 16. See Chapter One: I.3.

3. J.-F. Lyotard, "Sensus Communis," *Judging Lyotard*, ed. A. Benjamin (London and New York: Routledge, 1992) 24. See Chapter Three: II.3.

must still be found.[4] Applied to the community of taste this means: when judging singular facts – and singular political facts for that matter – one cannot start from a universal consensus about the value of these singular facts. Rather, this universal perspective is something for which the community of taste is still in search. Such a universal perspective can only dawn upon the community on the basis of authentic feelings, especially those awakened by one's vivid contact with the supersensible. The separate faculties – scientific, ethical, and esthetic – are driven to go to their limits, to the extent of witnessing their collapse before the majestic power of the absolute. At that point of culmination, they experience the sublime feeling of rapture and awe, and precisely this varied experience – varied because it is always singular – prompts them to feel an attunement with one another. So too is it with the separate members of the community of taste. They experience a sense of 'unity', each time a member succeeds in proffering an inspiring example of what it means for her to be attracted by a universal rule beyond her reach, with the result that other members may be inspired to engage in a comparable, singular adventure. Even if one would link this 'unity' to the notion of the universal, this notion turns out to be something unique. The universality and necessity associated with the judgment of taste "are [only] promised; they are promised singularly every time, but are only just promised. There could be no greater misunderstanding of the judgments of taste than to declare them simply universal and necessary."[5]

For Lyotard, and apparently also for Kant, the yardstick of the universal is the supersensible, also more solemnly termed: the unpresentable, and one's vivid contact with it. This contact takes place at the moment at which one feels the inadequacy between one's striving to go to the limit and the majestic power of the limit itself. Or, formulated in terms of the relationship between the creative imagination and the 'thought' or 'Idea' that exceeds the imagination: it takes place at the moment our imagination feels itself inadequate to present the supersensible Idea. The feelings arising from the experience of this inadequacy bear different names. At the level of ethics, "[t]he feeling that our imagination is inadequate (*unangemessen*) to [present] an Idea that is a law for us – this feeling is respect (*Achtung*)."[6] In the realm of the aesthetics of the

4. See I. Kant, *Critique of Judgment*, *Akademie* edition, 179, trans. W. Pluhar (Indianapolis, IN: Hackett Publishing Company, 1987) 18. See Chapter One: I.3.

5. J.-F. Lyotard, *Lessons on the Analytic of the Sublime*, trans. E. Rottenberg (Stanford, CA: Stanford University Press, 1994) 19. See Chapter Three: II.3.

6. J.-F. Lyotard, *Lessons on the Analytic of the Sublime*, 117, citing from I. Kant, *Critique of Judgment*, §27, *Akademie* edition, 257. See Chapter Three: II.4.

sublime a soul-stirring delight is added to this feeling of respect: "The mind (*das Gemüt*) harkens now to the voice of Reason [... The feeling of being] called on or requisitioned by the voice of Reason is an absolute delight."[7] The voice of Reason is a voice that can and must be heard, but whose essence cannot be rendered present in empirical reality. It is by following its call that one experiences respect and delight – feelings that 'signal' the impact of the presence of the unpresentable. As the term itself suggests, Reason is an entity, or better, an accompanying horizon, with a truly universal range. Yet, just as the supersensible Idea, which Kant often specifies as the 'Idea of Reason', only signals its presence in the arousal of sublime feelings, so too the universality contained in, and promised by, Reason makes its presence felt in uplifting feelings of dedication and commitment.

Lyotard adheres to this insight also when replacing Kant's substantial subject and its ideal of compact unity with a thinking/feeling 'self' that lives and evolves in the fluidity of time. The sole and crucial difference is that now he fills in the promised universality inherent in the 'Idea of Reason' not with some homogeneous pattern but with the proliferation of a plurality of irreducible perspectives which all require that they be rigorously respected in their heterogeneity. Even such a 'diminished', temporalized self will be able, in Lyotard's perspective, to sense the elation and the respect Kant associates with the experience of the sublime; it will be able to harbor feelings that bring one into contact with the supersensible, understood now as the mysterious cradle of multiplicity and pluralization. For Lyotard, this turn to multiplicity is a decisive step forward, which "would consist in the fact that it is not only the Idea of a single purpose which would be pointed to in our feeling, but already the Idea that this purpose consists in the formation and free exploration of Ideas in the plural, the Idea that this end is the beginning of the infinity of heterogeneous finalities."[8] This step forward does not, however, imply, a stepping out of the basic Kantian insight that all that can be said about the noble 'Idea of Reason' – finalized now towards the respect for heterogeneity – must prove and 'signal' its reality in the revelatory medium of feelings of awe and delight – the typical feelings of the sublime. Also when honored now as the cradle of pluralization, the 'Idea of Reason', remains and must remain an unpresentable Idea. It can and must be

7. J.-F. Lyotard, *Lessons on the Analytic of the Sublime*, 119-121. See Chapter Three: II.4.

8. J.-F. Lyotard, "The Sign of History," *The Lyotard Reader*, ed. A. Benjamin (Oxford: Blackwell, 1989) 409. See Chaper Three: I.

thought, but its full realization can never be found in empirical reality, although special feelings unmistakably signal its unattainable presence.

This basic Kantian background remains in place in Lyotard's judgment of the signs of progress in history. Whereas Kant tended to interpret collectively shared, disinterested feelings of enthusiasm as a sign that humanity had come a step closer to its ultimate purpose, Lyotard looks at history, especially the history shaped by modern hegemonic planning, in term of historical catastrophes that arouse in him a feeling of deep melancholy. Given his turn to pluralization, this change in perspective is understandable. From the perspective of his new yardstick of a proliferation of heterogeneous perspectives, each ruthlessly obtained victory in history must be seen, not as a 'victory', but rather as the tragic suppression of other possible, heterogeneous perspectives. The spectacle of this suppression is a source of grief, but also the seed of a commemoration that seeks to keep alive the perspective of a final break-through of respect for plurality: "A deep melancholy can be a feeling of the sublime [...] Each sublime feeling testifies to an Idea of reason. Melancholy testifies to an Idea of Reason and to its absence in empirical reality. This is a way to testify to things relegated to oblivion. It is a feeling that can point to the sublime, and thus 'prove', signify, and bear witness to the fact that this Idea is not lost. Grief over politics, provided this feeling is unanimous and not geared towards a particular interest, can be regarded as a historically meaningful sign."[9] It is also this melancholic confrontation with the ruins of what the 'Idea of Reason' seemed to assure that prompts Lyotard to ask the anxious question: 'Is it happening?' 'Could it be that, in the given circumstances, the unpresentable Idea of the release of heterogeneities – of true universality – is drawing near in its quasi-impossible break-through?'[10]

The Kantian emotional background, finally, sheds light on Lyotard's elucidation of the notion of the 'differend', that is: of the special conflict in which the losing party is threatened with being silenced: "I would call a differend the case where a plaintiff is divested of the means to argue and becomes a victim."[11] To be divested of the means to argue not only relates to the incapacity of providing proofs for one's case; it is aggravated by the fact that the wronged party is obliged to conduct her defense in the

---

9. C. Pries, "Das Undarstellbare – Gegen das Vergessen: Ein Gespräch zwischen Jean-François Lyotard und Christine Pries," *Das Erhabene: Zwischen Grenzerfahrung und Grössenwahn*, ed. idem (Weinheim: Acta Humaniora, 1989) 332 [translation mine]. See Chapter Two: III.2.

10. See Chapter Five: III.4.

11. J.-F. Lyotard, *The Differend*, trans. G. Van Den Abbeele (Manchester: University of Manchester Press, 1988) no 12, p. 9. See Chapter Four: II.

idiom – the legal stipulations in the Western tradition of jurisprudence –
of the ruling party, and lacks the means to go beyond this established
structure: "the 'regulation' of the conflict [...] is done in the idiom of one
of the parties while the wrong suffered by the other is not signified in that
idiom."[12] This again is, for the philosopher who has to assess this political fact, a source for speechless grief, and a motive for bearing witness
to the unpresentable Idea of justice and what it properly stands for.

The example of the differend particularly shows the extent to which
Lyotard emotionally sides with the party that is put in the wrong by the
powers to be and on the basis of the self-protective criteria developed by
them. When trying to characterize the type of universality that must have
motivated Lyotard's option, the most apt expression I found for it is 'universality without exclusion':[13] Lyotard is ultimately committed to a 'universality without exclusion'. As long as he encounters on his path people that are victimized through unwarranted exclusion, he cannot help
but raise his voice in protest, and have emotional recourse to the 'unpresentable' Idea which from a Kantian perspective enjoys a universal range.
Yet, while in Kant's days this universality was conceived after the pattern of the Newtonian laws that always act in the selfsame way without
any exception, Lyotard, in the wake of Theodor Adorno's 'philosophizing after Auschwitz', places the accent on the 'exceptions' that regrettably
have infiltrated the notion of universality: by way of tragic segregations
and genocidal eliminations. His longing is that exclusions like these will
no longer be part of the genuine universality to come.

* * *

Let is come now to the examination of Derrida. Does he, in turn, profess his belief in a new universality, and does this new universality bear
the marks of the unpresentable, in the style of Lyotard? In order to answer
this question, I will take my point of departure in the late writings of Derrida, for it is there that he brings up the notions of an 'impossible' justice to come, of an 'impossible' hospitality to be granted etc. – realities
that are all 'unpresentable'. When reading a sentence like "[T]he Idea of
democracy to come [...] will never present itself in the form of full presence,"[14] I initially thought that Derrida was just espousing Lyotard's

---

12. *Ibid.*, no 12, p. 9. See Chapter Four: II.
13. See Chapter Five: III.4.
14. J. Derrida, *Specters of Marx* (New York and London: Routledge, 1994) 65. See
Chapter Ten: I.4.

Kantian inspired notion of the unpresentable Idea; I even developed this line of thought in an article published in 2006.[15] Having delved deeper in Derrida's studies of Husserl, however, I must now modify this view: although Derrida is well acquainted with Kant's outlook on supersensible Ideas, his primary motivation for venturing to speak about 'things that cannot present themselves in the form of full presence' is his critical reading and deconstruction of Husserl. His talk about non-presentable things to come is rooted in his overcoming of phenomenology: the 'impossible' things to come are, for him, the object of an 'aphanology'.

Before engaging in this deconstruction of Husserl I would like to mention first that Derrida is more forthright than Lyotard in using the term 'universal'. As a matter of fact, I had to reconstruct for myself the new kind of universality that Lyotard was employing, or at least presupposing, when treating topics like the differend or in his move beyond Kant's substantial subject and, related to it, beyond Kant's ultimately unified world. With Derrida such a reconstruction is not considered necessary. From the outset he launched the term 'universal' (with special qualifications, to be sure) in order to announce his political ethics. In his discussion with Jean-Luc Marion at a Villanova Conference he unambiguously affirms that what he seeks to lay down with his notion of *khôra*, as an "absolutely universal place" of resistance, is the foundation of "a universal politics" that "crosses the borders of our common context – European, Jewish, Christian, Muslim, and philosophical."[16] The same uncomplicated use of the term 'universal' comes to the fore when Derrida promulgates his new program of messianicity: "When I insisted in *Specters of Marx* on messianicity, which I distinguished from messianism, I wanted to show that the messianic structure is a universal structure."[17]

The forthright use of the 'universal' can easily be explained from the context of the discussion with Marion. In this discussion Derrida attempts to discover a level that is deeper and broader than that of the revealed religions, in particular the Abrahamic religions. When Derrida terms his messianic structure a universal structure, he does so because, for him, the universality-claim and the messianisms of the religions are inevitably

15. See G. De Schrijver, "The Derridean Notion of Hospitality as a Resource for Inter-religious Dialogue," *Louvain Studies* 31 (2006) 88-90.
16. R. Kearny, "On the Gift: A Discussion between Jacques Derrida and Jean-Luc Marion," *God, The Gift and Postmodernism*, ed. J. Caputo and M. Scanlon (Bloomington, IN and Indianapolis, IN: Indiana University Press, 1999) 76. See Chapter Nine: I.2.
17. J. Caputo, "The Villanova Roundtable: A Conversation with Jacques Derrida," in idem, *Deconstruction in a Nutshell* (New York: Fordham University Press, 1997) 22. See Chapter Ten: I.4.

mixed up with the particular ritual and cultural elements of the religion in question. That is the reason why he speaks of "the general structure of messianicity, as the structure of experience,"[18] on which the particular religions are founded.[19] Yet, this general or universal structure is for Derrida also an achievement in its own right. Together with *khôra*, as the absolutely universal place of resistance, the messianic universal structure forms the platform, as we already noted, from which to develop a universal political ethics. The contrast with Lyotard is striking. Whereas Lyotard – from a deep-seated distrust of modernity's hegemonic universalist dreams – only ventures to speak in sordino and with an undertone of melancholy, of a 'universality without exclusion' that is still to come, Derrida acts like a 'young Turk'. Unlike Lyotard, the representative of the old, aging but still influential Occident, Derrida is from his early days a multicultural Arab, French-speaking Jew, who dares to dream about 'impossible' things to come. His political ethics will be characterized by a rhythm of excess that seldom found its literary expression in this way.

Derrida did not, however, reach this insight into the 'impossible things to come' overnight. It is preceded by more than a decade of reflection on Husserl's phenomenology, a reflection that began with his critical examination, as a young scholar, of Husserl's notion of teleology. Already in his doctoral dissertation *The Problem of Genesis in Husserl's Phenomenology* and in his article 'Genesis and Structure in Husserl's Phenomenology' he pointed out that, for Husserl, the notion of genesis has a clear finality, *a telos* that gives a precise future-orientation to the adventure of the *Wesensschau*. Husserl's basic axioms, such as the immediate appearance of the *eidos* to consciousness, as well as the uninterrupted stream of living consciousness, are in fact placed in a structure that is geared towards the attainment of an ever-greater plenitude of manifestation. Yet, Derrida asked, how can things appear to consciousness in the here and now that are not yet actually present? How will Husserl be able to account phenomenologically for the strong future orientation of his system, which moreover he links to the Kantian Idea of completeness and totality? The intuition on which phenomenology is based must be that of a lived experience, but in taking his lead from the Kantian Idea, Husserl apparently disregards the basic principle of phenomenology itself, for the Kantian Idea itself is not accessible to lived experience.

---

18. J. Caputo, "The Villanova Roundtable: A Conversation with Jacques Derrida," 23. See Chapter Ten: I.4.

19. In the Second Part of the General Conclusion I will have to bring in nuances to this statement.

In his *Edmund Husserl's Origin of Geometry: An Introduction* Derrida voices the same verdict. He, first of all, points out that Husserl, when accounting for the transmission-in-history of the originally perceived mathematical idealities, develops an anticipatory structure of intentionality. This anticipatory structure strives towards an infinite approximation to the ultimate goal and ideal of geometry, namely encompassing knowledge. For Derrida, this infinite approximation is itself an ideality, that is: it is thought as an infinite process that has its correlate in the Kantian Idea of Reason. It is this correlate that steers the whole process: "It is the presence for consciousness of an *Idea in the Kantian sense* that at once authorizes and prescribes this idealization of anticipation."[20] Yet, Derrida observes, the Idea in the Kantian sense can never appear in immediacy to consciousness, an aspect that Husserl apparently neglected to examine: "Husserl never made the [Kantian] Idea *itself* the *theme* of a phenomenological description."[21] If he had done so, he would have realized that any such attempt would be doomed to failure. The principle of all principles in phenomenology requires that the thing itself 'in person' must be immediately present to consciousness. Yet, the Kantian Idea is not a thing itself 'in person', or a finite thing: it is a regulative Idea, a horizon within which the thing itself 'in person' appears to consciousness.

From analyses like these Derrida will later conclude that an encompassing view must always be deferred – a basic aspect of his notion of *différance* – and also that that which immediately presents itself to consciousness is always mixed up with non-presence. Full presence to oneself is an illusion. In *Speech and Phenomena* Derrida carefully examined the gradual disappearance of a metaphysics of presence in Husserl's late writings. When studying e.g. Husserl's analysis of the linguistic expression, he remarked that, for Husserl, such an expression is valid whenever it intends an object, and that this intention ought not to be accompanied with the vivid experience of the intuiting person. The sole intentionality, isolated from the object-presenting intuition in the immediacy of consciousness, is enough for the validity of the expression.[22] It is enough to say: this expression intends the object 'stone', without the speaking person having an immediate intuition of what 'stone' means for her. This liberation of the sign from the dogma of intuitionism has far reaching consequences. It, first of all, frees the sign from its subjection to the experiencing subject with her tendency to self-presence and the building

20. J. Derrida, *Edmund Husserl's Origin of Geometry: An Introduction* (Lincoln, NE and London: University of Nebraska Press, 1989) 135. See Chapter Seven: III.3.2.
21. J. Derrida, *Edmund Husserl's Origin of Geometry*, 137. See Chapter Seven: III.3.2.
22. See Chapter Eight: II.3.

of closed systems. Not only has the sign been freed to engage in a free play with other signs ('signifiers') – the Nietzschean aspect[23] –, it is also released to take on unheard of significations to come. As Caputo writes: "[Derrida's] analysis of Husserl is not meant to confine us, negatively, to a hollow and empty play of signifiers [...] but to release the signifying power of the sign, to allow the signifier to head for the future, for the unfilled and unfulfillable coming of something that eye has not seen, nor ear heard."[24] This liberation of the sign, second, leads to a reversal of Husserl's understanding of the Kantian Idea: Whereas for the early Husserl the Kantian Idea suggested an infinite approximation to complete knowledge, the late Husserl saw in it an ideal towards which we are constantly moving: The Kantian Idea is nothing else than a *telos* whose attainment must be endlessly deferred: "That Husserl always thought of infinity as an Idea in the Kantian sense, as the indefiniteness of an '*ad infinitum*', leads one to believe that he never [...] believed in the accomplishment of an 'absolute knowledge';"[25] his notion of temporalization rather points to an incessant postponement of fulfillment, which of necessity includes the infiltration of absence, and 'lack of being'.

The liberation of the sign (the 'signifier') from the grip of the subject that intuits the *eidos* in the immediacy of consciousness and the reversal of the meaning attached to the Kantian Idea – incessant deferral instead of continuous approximation – are the two elements that prepare the way for Derrida's elaboration of an 'aphanology'. According to this aphanology the pure essence or *eidos*, which is seen now as an *eidos* to come, can never appear to consciousness in the form of full presence. This basic insight surfaces in the text we already quoted: 'The Idea of democracy to come will never present itself in the form of full presence'. The incentive to venture down the path of describing things that 'cannot phenomenologically present themselves to consciousness' comes without doubt from Derrida's contact with Levinas. In his *Totality and Infinity* Levinas called attention to the demands arising from the naked face of the other, and remarked that these demands shatter the self-imprisonment of Husserl's cogito and divest it of its phenomenological magic: "Husserl 'sees in the cogito a subjectivity with no support from without,

23. See Chapter Six: III.4.

24. J. Caputo, "Derrida and Marion: Two Husserlian Revolutions," *Religious Experience and the End of Metaphysics*, ed. J. Bloechl (Bloomington, IN and Indianapolis, IN: Indiana University Press, 2001) 120. See Chapter Eight: III.

25. J. Derrida, *Speech and Phenomena: Introduction to the Problem of Signs in Husserl's Phenomenology* (Evanston, IL: Northwestern University Press, 1973) 101. See Chapter Eight: II.3.

constituting the Idea of infinity itself, and providing himself with it as object'. Now, the infinite(-ly other) cannot be an object because it is speech [addressing me], the origin of meaning and the world. Therefore, no phenomenology can account for ethics, speech, and justice."[26]

In *Speech and Phenomena* Derrida has come to appreciate the late Husserl, who through a phenomenological analysis had acknowledged the inalienable alterity of the other ('we are never able to fathom what the other in her alterity thinks and feels'). Nonetheless he assimilates Levinas' insight into the non-phenomenality of the other, adding to it that we are able to show phenomenologically that it is impossible for us to capture the other in terms of full presence,[27] or to foresee what the other is going to enjoin upon us as ethical obligation. With this thesis he subscribes to Levinas's later program, namely "to find within phenomenology the injunction to go beyond phenomenology [...] to go phenomenologically beyond phenomenology."[28]

In an exemplary manner Derrida carries out this task in his analysis of the gift. In the common understanding of the gift three factors come into play: a giver (i) gives something (ii) to somebody (iii). In order, however, to attain the level of pure gift, one would have to forget that there is a giver, so as to avoid any entanglement in the economic logic of retribution, which annuls the gift. According to this logic the giver may derive satisfaction from what she is doing, whereas the receiver may feel obligated to give something in return, be it only gratitude. Yet, the pure gift exceeds any type of economic calculation: "*At the limit, the gift as gift, ought not to appear as gift: either to the donee or to the donor*. It cannot be gift as gift except by not being present as gift."[29] In other words, as soon as the gift "keeps its phenomenality or, if one prefers, its appearance as gift [...] the simple phenomenon of the gift, annuls it as a gift, transforming the apparition into a phantom and the operation into a simulacrum."[30] The same is true for genuine forgiveness: it "cannot, *must not present itself* as such [...] without at the same time denying itself, betraying or reaffirming a sovereignty."[31] That is the reason why Derrida

---

26. *Ibid.*, 106. Quoting from E. Levinas, *Totality and Infinity*. See Chapter Eight: I.1.

27. See Chapter Eight: I.2.

28. R. Kearny, "On the Gift A Discussion between Jacques Derrida and Jean-Luc Marion," 75. See Chapter Nine: I.2.

29. J. Derrida, *Given Time*. 1: *Counterfeit Money* (Chicago, IL and London: The University of Chicago Press, 1992) 14. See Chapter Nine: I.1.

30. J. Derrida, *Given Time*, 14. See Chapter Nine: I.1.

31. J. Derrida, "On Forgiveness," in idem, *Cosmopolitanism and Forgiveness*, 48. See Chapter Ten: III.3.

speaks of an 'impossible' forgiveness, an 'impossible' gift, an 'impossible' hospitality etc., and finally of *the* impossible – qualifications which all point to an excess beyond calculation.

It is precisely this excess that elicits a strong desire in those who feel themselves emotionally uplifted by the purity of a gratuitous gift, or by the selfless gesture of unconditional hospitality. In an effort to account for these feelings Derrida has recourse to the Kantian context of the sublime: "The gift as such cannot be known, but it can be thought of. We can think what we cannot know [...] It is this thinking, this excess, which interests me."[32] This is a clear allusion to the Kantian 'Idea of Reason' which – as we have seen in our analysis of Lyotard – can and must be thought, but which as such cannot be found in empirical reality, although it signals it presence in the sublime feelings of awe and delight felt by those who commit themselves to the truth of this Idea. A similar emotional tone resonates in Derrida's evocation of *the* impossible that awakens one's desire for things not heard of: "If the [excessive] gift is another name of the impossible, we still think it, we name it, we desire it. We intend it. And this *even if* or *because* or *to the extent that we never* encounter it, we never know it, we never verify it, we never experience it in its present existence or in its phenomenon. The gift *itself* – we dare not say the gift *in itself* – will never be confused with the presence of its phenomenon;"[33] it is beyond phenomenality, and therefore intensely desired.

The final question to be asked is: how does all this relate to Derrida's universal politics and to his universal messianic structure of experience? From where does the qualification 'universal' arise in Derrida's considerations about *the* impossible? The answer is simple. Whereas Lyotard evolved in the direction of a 'universality without any exception', Derrida strikes the same sensitive chord with his desire for *the* impossible. The universality he advocates is a 'universality of excess': a universality that goes beyond the limits of calculating reason and defies any self-protective instinct –a universality of pure generosity.

II. THE INFLUENCE OF JEWISH THOUGHT

The publication in which the influence of Jewish thought on Lyotard is the most evident is without doubt his *Heidegger and the "jews"*

32. R. Kearny, "On the Gift," 60. See Chapter Nine: I.2.
33. J. Derrida: *Given Time*, 29. See Chapter Nine: I.1.

(1988). In this work he wrote the 'jews' without capitalization, precisely to underline that, for him, the qualification 'jew' was not to be restricted to ethnic identity or, as in the case also of Derrida,[34] to circumcision. To Lyotard's way of thinking, unconventional philosophers and artists can also be called 'jews': unruly individuals that refuse to let themselves be assimilated into the mainstream Greek-Christian culture. He writes: "'the jews' are within the 'spirit' of the Occident that is so preoccupied with foundational thinking, the entity that resists this spirit."[35] Lyotard was born a Catholic; in his youth, he even thought of entering the Dominican order. So, the influence of Jewish thought on his philosophy only slowly emerged. Lyotard's early writings, such as *Libidinal Economy* (1975) or *Lessons on Paganism* (1977), rather reflected the influence of the Paris milieu of the 1960s and 1970s with its particular interest in Marx, Freud and Nietzsche.

These early works mark a departure from Western foundational thinking in that they stress the importance of polytheism, that is: of the right to multiplicity, plurality and competition in defiance of any constraint by uniform, streamlined thought. This defiance is stressed in *The Postmodern Condition: A Report on Human Knowledge* (1979). There Lyotard resuscitates Nietzsche's agonistics by advocating the use of creative, competing 'moves' in order to destabilize the system and, through this shock, to increase its performativity: "The novelty of an unexpected 'move', with its correlative displacement of a partner or group of partners, can supply the system with that increased performativity it forever demands and consumes."[36] At that moment of his writer's career, Lyotard sees in unrestrained competition the motor for real advance in knowledge production, so much so that I suspected him of giving with his *Postmodern Condition* a legitimization of the liberal free market.

Lyotard's interest in Jewish thought was initiated by his concern about victims in competitive society, and in law courts operating with well-defined schemes of what is right and what is not. Yet, it took him some time to assimilate the 'spirit' of this thought. This assimilation began with his study of Kant's *Critique of Judgment*, and of the notion of the sublime which occupies a central place in it. Especially in his analysis of the notion of enthusiasm, which is a modality of the feeling of the sublime,

34. See J. Derrida, *Circumfession* (Chicago, IL: University of Chicago Press, 1993). Originally published as G. Bennington et J. Derrida, *Circonfession* (Paris: Seuil, 1991).
35. J.-F. Lyotard, *Heidegger and "the jews"* (Minneapolis, MN: University of Minnesota Press, 1990) 22. See Chapter Four: IV.
36. J.-F. Lyotard, *The Postmodern Condition: A Report on Knowledge* (Minneapolis, MN: University of Minnesota Press, 1984) 15. See Chapter One: I.1.

Kant disclosed the Jewish roots of this feeling. In order to counter the objection that contact with the unpresentable/the infinite, because it is beyond visibility, could never arouse feelings of awe and elation, he writes: "Though an exhibition of the infinite can as such never be more than merely negative, it still expands the soul. Perhaps the most sublime passage in the Jewish Law is the commandment: Thou shalt not make unto thee any graven image, or any likeness of anything that is in heaven or on earth, etc. This commandment alone can explain the enthusiasm that the Jewish people in their civilized era felt for their religion when they compared it with that of other peoples [...] It is indeed a mistake to worry that depriving this presentation of whatever could commend it to the senses will result in its carrying with it no more than a cold and life-less approval without any moving force or emotion. It is exactly the other way round. For once the senses no longer see anything before them, while yet the unmistakable and indelible Idea of morality remains, one would sooner need to temper the momentum of an unbounded imagination so as to keep it from rising to enthusiasm, than to seek to support these Ideas with images and childish devices for fear that they would otherwise be powerless."[37]

In *The Differend* Lyotard spends many pages on the tragic side-effects of erroneous interpretations of political enthusiasm. He criticizes Marx's reading of the enthusiasm that Marx witnessed in the agitation of the pro-letariat, and which he captured in the speculative phrase of the dictator-ship of the proletariat under the guidance of the communist vanguard. Yet, in this way the enthusiasm has been divested of its focus on the invisible well-spring and pressed into the logic of a dialectics of history that already posits the very reality of the heretofore only dreamed-of ideal. It would not take long before this political enthusiasm, turned into a grand story of political domination, was to establish its reign of terror. This explains why Lyotard, in his own report on the feeling of the sublime, relates it to a deep melancholy, to a "sadness," to use Kant's words, "that rests on an antipathy involving principles. Such a sadness is sublime because it rests on Ideas; even grief [....] may be included among the *vig-orous* affects, if it has its basis in moral Ideas."[38] When Lyotard reflects on historical catastrophes like Auschwitz, Budapest 1956, Kolyma, etc. he rather experiences an enthusiasm 'e contrario': a sadness that is, in its

---

37. I. Kant, *Critique of Judgment*, Akademie edition, 274, trans. W. Pluhar, 135. See Chapter Two: II.3.

38. I. Kant, *Critique of Judgment*, Akademie edition, 276, trans. W. Pluhar, 137. See Chapter Two: III.2.

own manner, uplifting, because it keeps alive the lure emanating from the Ideas of Reason (*Vernunft*) in circumstances in which their power seems no longer to have an effect on human history.

This melancholic background, however, does not prevent Lyotard from developing a positive outlook on the power of the Ideas of Reason. Especially in his reflections on art and the role of the avant-garde in it, he revisits the Jewish background of the feeling of the sublime at the other side of every pictorial representation. For him, aesthetics or *aisthesis* cannot possibly lead to the sublime feeling, because the latter bears witness to the might of the unpresentable beyond the realm of the senses: "Nothing can lead from *aisthesis* to the hidden feeling, to the sublime pain and joy that are the inimitable deposit left by the unfelt shock of the alliance, unreachable by any artifact, even when it is of pious speech."[39] With this statement Lyotard seeks to describe what non-figurative artists, like the American Jewish painter Barnett Newman, must have felt when they tried to evoke the power of the unpresentable by painting on their canvases a graphic 'now' moment of dazzling interruption: "One cannot present the absolute. But one can present that there is some absolute [...] The current of 'abstract' painting has its source in this requirement for indirect and all but ungraspable allusion to the invisible in the visible."[40]

One would be seriously mistaken, however, if one were to associate this 'allusion of the invisible in the visible' with some form of Greek thought, which – as certainly is the case with Plato – spontaneously prioritizes seeing and contemplation over listening. The above reference to the 'shock of the alliance' already brings this listening, as a major characteristic of the Jewish religion, into focus. The turn to receptivity, 'passivity' and listening is further highlighted in Lyotard's discussion with Thébaut in *Just Gaming*. In this work the question is broached as to the source and origin of moral obligation. Again it is Kant who gives the baffling answer: the moral obligation cannot be deduced from theoretical knowledge; it comes from listening to the unsettling disturbance of the categorical imperative: 'you must': "What seems to me so strong in Kant's position, of course, as well as in Levinas', is that they reject in principle [...] a derivation or [...] a deduction"[41] of the 'you must' from an intellectual construct or from a metaphysical superstructure in the style of Plato. The 'you must' abruptly interrupts the logic of the system

---

39. J.-F. Lyotard, *Heidegger and "the jews"*, 38. See Chapter Four: IV.

40. J.-F. Lyotard, *The Inhuman: Reflections on Time* (Cambridge: Polity Press, 1991) 126. See Chapter Four: V.

41. J.-F. Lyotard and J.-L. Thébaud, *Just Gaming* (Minneapolis, MN: University of Minnesota Press, 1985) 45. See Chapter Four: I.1.

builder. The 'you must' is not even part of what is called an experience, "because experience, by itself, always supposes its description, and thus the privilege granted to the play of the descriptive,"[42] namely that it has an 'author' engaged in describing states of affairs but who, in actuality, does not listen.

To listen to the commanding voice is part of the heteronomy of the covenant, an insight Lyotard owes to Emmanuel Levinas. In *Heidegger and the "jews"* he defines the covenant as an event in which the Jewish people are taken hostage by a nameless voice that enjoins the obligation: 'be just', remember the shock of the covenant: "This simple people is taken hostage by a voice that does not tell them anything, save that it (this voice) is, and that all representation and naming of it are forbidden, and that they, this people, only needs to listen to its tone, to be obedient to a timbre."[43] In order to shed light on the effects of this commanding voice Lyotard has recourse to Freud's notion of the 'unconscious affect' that infiltrates the psychic system in order to destabilize it. This destabilization takes place in two phases: Initially there is a first shock of which one is unaware but which has the power to unsettle the psyche; then come the aftershocks that continue to haunt the soul and which make one realize the deep disorientation one has undergone. The covenant is, in essence, an uninvited reality that invades the whole person. In this context Lyotard speaks of an immemorial past, of a strange experience which one is unable to place in one's ordinary chronologization of time: "Ungraspable by consciousness, this time threatens it. It threatens it permanently [...] In truth, it is not even permanence. It has nothing of the *per-*, of crossing, of passing in it [...]; it merely has *manere, sistere* in it: menace, manence."[44] As a result, the dispossessed person gets the impression of her house being inhabited by an uninvited stranger.

When describing the shock of this dispossession, Lyotard remarks that it always comes too early and too late: The Jews always live in "the too early – too late: a people unprepared for the revelation of the alliance, always too young for it; and as a result, too old, too paralyzed by preoccupations, idolatries, and even studies to achieve the sanctity required by the promise."[45] The shock always comes as a surprise; one is never prepared for it because one's attention is turned to other things, such as the organization of one's life and that of the community. Yet, precisely

42. *Ibid.*, 46. See Chapter Four: I.1.
43. J.-F. Lyotard, *Heidegger and "the jews"*, 21. See Chapter Four: IV.
44. *Ibid.*, 17. See Chapter Four: IV.
45. *Ibid.*, 37. See Chapter Four: IV.

at that moment the shock confronts one with the obligation to remember the alliance and to reflect on how one ought to act accordingly. This reflection has a typically Jewish flavor; and this is the main reason why, for Lyotard, the Nazi-regime sought to eliminate the Jews: "'The jews' do not appear evil, or inept, to take on the challenge of mobilization, because they are the nomadism of thought, not riveted to their roots, but essentially transportable, like books, money, jewels, the violin. But they are evil if they are riveted to their book, to the stupor of a covenant, of an immemorial 'shock' whose affection they try to reserve against all compromise."[46]

The shock of the covenant does not tell the Jews what they have to do in the concrete to be just. It is up to each of them to discern how they are to implement the obligation of the Law. Attention to, and concern for, the particular[47] is what singles them out, as well as a reflection on the consequences of their action. For Lyotard, such a reflection ought also to steer the activities and options of postmodern artists and writers. This is particularly so because these artists and writers are not proceeding according to pre-established rules: having undergone a shock that compels them to return to their 'infancy' – to their state of receptivity and dispossession – they are still, in line with the method of Kant's *Critique of Judgment*, in search of the rules. Only at the end of the day will they be able to fathom which line of thought they had been following: "The postmodern artist or writer [...] is not in principle governed by pre-established rules [...] Such rules and categories are what the work or text is investigating. The artist and the writer therefore work without rules and in order to establish the rules for what *will have been made*. This is why the work and the text can take on the properties of an event; it is also why they would arrive too late for their author, or, what amounts to the same thing, why the work of making them would always begin too soon. *Post-modern* would be understanding according to the paradox of the future (*post*) anterior (*modo*)."[48]

Two further elements illustrate Lyotard's Jewish penchant. In his work *The Differend*, he takes Auschwitz as the prototype of the feeling that is left by a differend. He evokes the anguish and the powerlessness of the survivors of the Holocaust, when they are forced by those who negate the reality of this event, to scientifically prove that gas chambers were indeed used in the concentration camps: "The silence imposed on knowledge

---

46. *Ibid.*, 40. See Chapter Four: IV.
47. See Chapter Five: III.2.
48. J.-F. Lyotard *The Postmodern Explained*, 9. See Chapter Five: I.3.

does not impose the silence of forgetting, it imposes a feeling."[49] In *Heidegger and the "jews"* Lyotard further explores the reason why Heidegger did not protest against the extermination of the Jews. The answer is: a divergence in 'world views'. By paying attention to the temporality of existence – 'thrownness into an existence unto death' – Heidegger, to be sure, 'deconstructed' the substantial (transcendental) subject that, since Descartes, had come to dominate the European philosophical scene. Yet, this dissipative approach to time did not affect Heidegger's notion of place – and of the people having their home in it. This led him to engage in the "sacralization of a territory for this people,"[50] which prepared the ideology of Hitler's National Socialism. For Lyotard, Heidegger reintroduced the Sacred but not the Holy whose presence is felt in one's respect for the Law – in one's feeling of being obligated. Heidegger's thought "hermetically seals his silence on the question of the Holocaust. This silence *is* this nonquestion, this closure and foreclosure: the 'forgetting' that thought is without beginning and unfounded, that it does not have to 'give place' to Being but is owed to a nameless Law."[51] The basic insight that 'thought is without beginning and unfounded' will come back in Derrida's philosophical considerations.

* * *

Derrida is of Jewish descent and upbringing. As an adolescent he sought to free himself from the ritualistic constraints of his religion and avidly began to read emancipated Western authors, such as Rousseau, Gide, and Nietzsche. Especially Nietzsche, and later also Heidegger, will exert a potent influence on the young Derrida: "The authors who appeal to Derrida from the viewpoint of what one might call his *Stimmung* are Nietzsche and Heidegger,"[52] philosophers who can hardly be said to have something in common with Judaism. From the outset Derrida was fascinated by Nietzsche's 'History of an Error: How the True World Finally became a Fable' (published in *Twilight of the Idols*). He shared Nietzsche's sarcastic assault on the true world – the world of the Platonic ideas – that downgraded the import of sensitivity, artistic playfulness, and passions: "attack on the roots of passion means an attack on the roots

---

49. J.-F. Lyotard, *The Differend*, no 93, p. 56. See Chapter Four: III.
50. J.-F. Lyotard, *Heidegger and "the jews"* , 92. See Chapter Four: IV.
51. *Ibid.*, 94. See Chapter Four: IV.
52. J.-M. Salanskis, "La philosophie de Jacques Derrida et la spécificité de la déconstruction au sein des philosophies du *linguistic turn*," *Derrida: la déconstruction*, ed. Ch. Ramon (Paris: Presses universitaires de France, 2005) 42. See Chapter Six.

of life."[53] On the whole, however, Derrida was more interested in Nietzsche's perspectivism than in the latter's vitalism (the vital affirmation of
life). This can be demonstrated in his tenacious endeavor to transpose
Nietzschean insights to the domain of semiotics.

Having repudiated de Saussure prioritization of the signified (the
notional concept) over the signifier (the written word), Derrida began to
distrust the Western concept of a 'philosophy of presence', and to critically assess every type of thought that exalted immediate contact with the
'Idea' (the mentally conceived ideality), while disregarding the input of
the senses and of the interrelated connections in the world of becoming:
"As the face of pure intelligibility it [the signified] refers to an absolute
logos to which it is immediately united."[54] He also showed that this 'philosophy of presence' found its further articulation in the age-old tradition
of the priority of speech over writing. In speech one hears oneself speak:
one has the impression of feeling oneself immediately present to oneself,
as an echo of one's direct contact with the eternally valid truth of the signified. Consequently, writing is regarded as something less; as a falling
out of the paradise of immediate presence: "While the phonetic signifier
[speech] would remain in animate proximity, in the living contact of
mneme or psyche, the graphic signifier [writing], which reproduces it or
imitates it, goes one degree further away, falls outside of life; all life is
distilled out of it and is put to sleep in the type of its double."[55] Yet, that
which pretends to be an eternally valid 'signified' must be dethroned,
deconstructed, and debunked as a hollow phrase, especially in an epoch
in which people have begun to feel at home in the ever changing 'house
of language'.

For Derrida, there is only one way to dethrone the eternally valid 'signified', namely by reducing it to what it simply is: a signifier among
other signifiers; a word or a sign referring to other words or signs, and
obtaining through this web of interrelations its proper meaning. He follows in this the general axiom of semiotics: We ought to look at the sign
as having a meaning determined by its relations with other elements in a
system rather than as a tie with an object in the world. It is this interplay
that Derrida, in a Nietzschean fashion, describes as the 'play' of signifiers.

53. J. Derrida, *Spurs: Nietzsche's Styles* (Chicago, IL and London: University of
Chicago Press,1979) 93. Quoting from Friedrich Nietzsche, *Twilight of the Idols*, trans.
W. Kaufmann. See Chapter Six: II.1.

54. J. Derrida, *Of Grammatology*, trans. G. Spivak (Baltimore, MD and London: The
Johns Hopkins University Press, 1974 [1976]) 13. See Chapter Six: III.2.

55. J. Derrida, *Dissemination*, trans. B. Johnson (Chicago, IL: The University of
Chicago Press, 1981) 110 [translation modified]. See Chapter Six: III.2.

Yet, in doing so he goes a step further than this general axiom, for it is evident for him that only when one dares to dream of the implosion of the transcendental signified will free rein be given to the incessant play of signifiers: "One could call *play* the absence of the transcendental signified as limitlessness of play;"[56] "Writing is a game within language."[57] For Derrida, the erasure of the transcendental 'signified' inaugurates an era of boundless creativity, freed of the constraints of an erstwhile single dominating center of meaning. Finally the glorious day has come when limitless dissemination can be celebrated – when it will be given to people to rejoice in the *perpetuum mobile* of writing: "I define writing," Derrida says, "as the impossibility of a chain arresting itself on a signified that would not relaunch it, so as to have already put itself in the position of the signifying substitution."[58]

To welcome this unsheltered situation of 'dissipation without a center' is, of course, not easy. Derrida feels that some will develop a nostalgia for the lost origin. In the course of their incessant wandering without clear orientation they will yearn for the vanished beacon that formerly steered their lives. He therefore invites his readers to look at this incessant wandering in positive terms. What matters is "[t]he affirmation of a world of signs without fault, without truth, and without origin which is offered to an active interpretation. *This affirmation then determines the noncenter otherwise than as loss of the center.* And it plays without security [...] In absolute chance, affirmation also surrenders itself to *genetic* indetermination, to the *seminal* adventure of a trace."[59] On the other hand, there is still one security left: the wandering will not be brought to a close. Dissemination ('the seminal adventure of a trace') crosses all sorts of borders and limits. There is a dispersal of codified meaning, because every word can be reconnected to all sorts of other words in ever new constellations. This incessant interweaving cannot be arrested by any authoritative source. This is Derrida's new assurance, in the wake of Nietzsche, after the evaporation of the erstwhile reassuring foundation of metaphysics.

Some commentators opine that Derrida with his focus on incessant dispersal developed a worldview that is close to that of the 'wandering Jew'. The 'wandering Jew' has no stable home and is wont to cross al sorts of borders and limits. They even venture that Derrida lapsed into a kind of

56. J. Derrida, *Of Grammatology*, 50. See Chapter Six: II.2.
57. *Ibid.*, 50. See Chapter Six: II.2.
58. J. Derrida, *Positions*, trans. A. Bass (London: Athlone, 1972) 82. See Chapter Six: II.2.
59. J. Derrida, *Writing and Difference*, trans. A. Bass (Chicago, IL: University of Chicago Press, 1978) 292. See Chapter Six: III.4.

Cabbala or heretic Jewish hermeneutics according to which the Tables of
the Covenant had been broken into pieces so that consequently the new
religiosity would consist in a mystical erring from sign to sign, from one
provisional reading of the fragmented Thora to another. In 1984 the
American theologian Mark Taylor wrote a book entitled *Erring: A Postmodern A/theology*[60] that rendered thematic these cabbalistic features in
the early Derrida, whereas Susan Handelman already in 1983 wrote:
"We might say that Derrida and the Jewish heretic hermeneutics do precisely that: forsake God but perpetuate a Thora, Scripture or Law in their
own displaced and ambivalent ways."[61]

    There may be a grain of truth in this cabbalistic reading of the early
Derrida. My contention would be that his revisiting of Judaism (in his
own way, to be sure) rather took place from the moment he launched the
notion 'différance' as a new 'foundation', or better: 'non-foundation' that
ought to come to replace Heidegger's notion of Being. There Derrida
refers to a strange disturbance that is 'more original', and 'older' than
Being. In assessing Heidegger's ontological difference between 'Being'
and the 'beings' (das *Sein und die Seienden*) Derrida remarks that Heidegger, in line with the ontotheology he sought to deconstruct, prioritizes
a transcendental 'Signified' – Being – over the 'signifiers', the 'beings'.
The beings are downgraded to something secondary compared to the
voice of Being that wishes to have its voice heard. For Derrida, this subordination can only be overcome if one erases the classical notion of
Being as the foundation of all things, an erasure that Heidegger partly
achieved by graphically crossing out the word Being: "[T]he sense of
Being is not a transcendental or trans-epochal signified (even if it was
always dissimulated within the epoch) but already, in a truly *unheard of*
sense, a determined signifying trace [...] The ontico-ontological difference and its ground (*Grund*) are not absolutely originary. *Différance* by
itself would be more 'originary'."[62] For Derrida, 'différance' right from
the outset punctures, suspends, and postpones presence, and is therefore
more 'originary' than that which till now has been called the origin and
the ground. This more 'originary' entity can properly speaking not be
termed a ground; it rather challenges every notion of grounding foundation: "It is the domination of beings that *différance* everywhere comes
to solicit, in the sense that *sollicitare*, in old Latin, means: to shake as a

60. M. Taylor, *Erring: A Postmodern A/theology* (Chicago, IL and London: University of Chicago Press, 1984).
    61. See *Displacement, Derrida and After*, ed. M. Krapnick (Bloomington, IN: Indiana
University Press, 1983) 115.
    62. J. Derrida, *Of Grammatology*, 23. See Chapter Six: III.3.

whole, to make tremble in entirety. Therefore, it is the determination of Being as presence or as beingness that is interrogated by the thought of *différance* [...] Not only is there no kingdom of *différance*, but *différance* instigates the subversion of every kingdom. Which makes it obviously threatening and infallibly dreaded by everything within us that desires a kingdom, the past or future presence of a kingdom."[63]

By stressing that *différance* is 'more original' than Being (as supposed ground) Derrida engages in a domain that is both external and anterior to the self-referential concepts of the metaphysics of presence. It is from this exteriority and anteriority that *différance* punctures and subverts the 'kingdom of presence'. Derrida's assimilation of Levinas' *Totality and Infinity* had already sensitized him to the import of an exteriority that explodes every reciprocity. The command issuing from the 'naked face' cannot possibly be captured in a relation of reciprocity; it causes a rupture, and a separation. Pure exteriority challenges the circularity of a thought that is locked up in self-affection.[64] Yet, in order to render a metaphysics of presence forever impossible, a further exploration is needed of the mythical anteriority of spacing and *différance*.

Derrida does this exploration in his study of the notion *khôra*, the mysterious receptacle that Plato introduced in his dialogue *Timaeus* as a way of explaining how eternal ideas were given a material form in the world of becoming. But besides being a fertile womb that gives birth to the entities it receives, *khôra* is also a place, or a 'non place' of disturbance; it issues warnings from an immemorial past and holds out the promise of the 'impossible'. As a dreadful actor in the mythical past it can be compared to what Lacan termed 'the Thing' whose disturbance reaches us from an immemorial past and which does not cease to haunt us in our daily dealings. It is to this dreadful 'Thing' to which Lyotard had recourse in order to evoke the shock of dispossession that the Jews underwent in their encounter with the God of the covenant. When observing these associations – the dreadful 'Thing, disturbance from an immemorial past, shock of dispossession – I am tempted to read Derrida's welcoming of *khôra* as his 'homecoming' to Judaism, a return to that which Lyotard, in his criticism of Heidegger, had called: the awareness "that thought is without beginning and unfounded, that it does not have to 'give place' to Being but is owed to a nameless Law."[65]

---

63. J. Derrida, "Différance," in idem, *Margins of Philosophy*, trans. Alan Bass (Chicago, IL: University of Chicago Press, 1982) 21-22. See Chapter Eight: III.2.

64. See Chapter Eight: I.1.

65. J.-F. Lyotard, *Heidegger and "the jews"*, 94 [translation modified]. See Chapter Four: IV.

This homecoming is confirmed in the way Derrida distances himself from Heidegger's dictum that the 'Ground' of all things – 'Being' in Heidegger's parlance – is the gracious giver of all things. For him, such a statement smacks of Greek thought with its focus on visibility and manifestation, elements that will lead to the elaboration of a philosophy of presence. For Derida, *khôra* is a hidden ground – or better: a hidden place or non-place – that gives birth to things that are not her own. *Khôra* does not give anything to 'beings'; it only reminds them that because they have been conceived in her womb they are marked with the seal of non-identity and non-presence to oneself (with 'spacing' as Derrida says). This is in sharp contrast with Heidegger who holds that Being is there as the entity that gives in abundance: "Radically nonhuman and atheological, one cannot not even say that *khôra* gives place or that *there is* the *khôra*. The *es gibt*, thus translated, too vividly announces or recalls the dispensation of God, of man, or even that of the Being of which certain texts by Heidegger speak (*es gibt das Sein*). *Khôra* is not even that (*ça*), the *es* or *id* of giving, [since it is itself] before all subjectivity. It does not give place as one would give something. [...] It is radically ahistorical, because nothing happens through it and nothing happens to it."[66] Nonetheless it lies 'at the basis' of the dream of 'the impossible things to come' which Derrida will render thematic in his notion of messianicity. *Khôra* is the immemorial past that prepares the break-through of unheard of things to come, in excess to the common notion of human history.

In commenting on testimonies of the German mystic Angelus Silesius Derrida sees a prefiguration of *khôra* in Silesius' 'desert within a desert', as well as in his 'wandering there where nobody can go'.[67] This prompts us to envisage the possibility that Derrida took his inspiration from some type of radical mysticism when referring to *khôra's disturbance*. In part one of the General Conclusion I raised the notion of the messianic; at that moment I failed to mention Derrida's perplexity when confronting the following dilemma: Is it the case, he asked, that what he has reconstructed as messianicity is at bottom a basic structure of which the historical messianisms are particular exemplifications? Or, the other alternative: Is it so that we would never have known what this general structure of messianicity is without the specific, irreducible input of the

---

66. J. Derrida, "How To Avoid Speaking? Denials," *Languages of the Unsayable*, ed. S. Budick and W. Iser (New York: Columbia University, 1989) 37. See Chapter Eight: III.3.
67. See Chapter Nine: I.2.

historical religions? Confronted with this dilemma, Derrida had to admit that he could not decide what to choose.[68] It is a remarkable fact that with respect to the notion of *khôra* he formulated the same dilemma: "I do not know if this structure [of *khôra*] is really prior to what comes under the name of revealed religion or even of philosophy, or whether it is through philosophy or the revealed religions, the religions of the book, or any other experience of revelation that retrospectively we think what I try to think. I must confess, I cannot make the choice between these two hypotheses."[69]

This shows, again, that Derrida's reading (which is *his* reading) of the role of *khôra* in Plato's creation narrative is, unconsciously perhaps, elicited by the atmosphere of dispossession that he must have come to know in the religion of his youth. This religion, as Lyotard has pointed out, is characterized by the focus on listening – listening to the disturbing voice – and not on 'seeing', as is the case in Greek thought. This contrast between listening and seeing comes to the fore in Derrida's discussion with Marion on mystical theology. Both authors take their point of departure in the dissociation of intention and intuition which the late Husserl had introduced. On the basis of this dissociation, Marion believed that an excess of intuition and vision must be possible that exceeds any intending of the same. For him, such an excess of intuition takes place in the crowning element of the mystical theology of Dionysius the Areopagite, the *via eminentiae*, in which the mystic, after a long period of purification, feels transported to an excess of vision that surpasses his strongest expectations. To which Derrida replied: "The excess, the structure, in which I am interested, is not an excess of intuition;"[70] it is an excess that jumps out of the schemas of phenomenology, and plunges into the realm of the 'impossible things to come'. Phenomenology is the realm of seeing; the realm of the 'impossible things to come' is that of listening: one only gets access to it by listening to the admonitions of *khôra*.

In the above pages I have primarily focused on the long process of Derrida's homecoming to Judaism. In his later works this return can be taken for granted. One ought only to look at the explicitly Jewish topics that abound in it: justice done to the individual, the welcoming of the stranger, and the noble gestures of giving and forgiving. The crucial difference will consist in Derrida's radicalization of these notions, a subject I will treat in the next part of this General Conclusion.

68. See Chapter Ten: I.4.
69. R. Kearny, "On the Gift," 73. See Chapter Nine: I.2.
70. *Ibid.*, 71. See Chapter Nine: I.2.

III. PRACTICAL APPLICATIONS

We are able now to examine the practical applications of the respective world views of Lyotard and Derrida. In Lyotard these applications ought to be situated within his enlarged Kantian philosophy whose ultimate aim is to promote the recognition of a multiplicity of perspectives, and thus also of a multiplicity of justices. Although Derrida, too, advocates a multiplicity of perspectives, his line of thought will follow a different path – that of the overcoming of phenomenology – which finally will lead him to elaborate a logic of excess that is grafted upon an aphanology, and which holds out the perspective of 'impossible things to come'.

I will begin with an overview of Lyotard's thought. Within his enlarged Kantian framework one can discern three domains in which he came to formulate practical applications of his general world view: (i) his deliberation on political facts carried out in light of the Idea of 'a republic of reasonable beings'; (ii) his debunking of false universalizations with the help of language pragmatics and the Kantian notion of transcendental illusion; and, (iii) his practice of taking sides with the 'silenced party': his refusal to stifle the differend in order to save the honor of the unpresentable Idea.

(i) *Deliberation in light of the Idea of 'a republic of reasonable beings'*. This is the deliberation Lyotard himself practices. In line with Kant, Lyotard places a strong emphasis on the feeling of being obliged: 'be just'. Yet, and this is typical of Kant's formalism, this felt obligation does not reveal how one is to account for one's ethical decision. In order to justify it, one ought to engage in a reflective judgment, which is by definition in search of its rules. In this search, the golden rule will be helpful that says: 'act in such a way that the maxim of your action can serve as a universal principle'. This rule compels one to reflect on the consequences of one's actions so as to steer one's moral feelings in a certain direction. In Lyotard's case these moral feelings are colored by his commitment to the recognition of a genuine multiplicity – by his concern for liberating people from subordination to just one center of thought and influence.

The practical case to which Lyotard applied the golden rule was the following political reality: in the early 1970s members of the Red Army Fraction (RAF) in Germany had made an incursion into, and destroyed the computer of, the American garrison in Heidelberg, because evidence was found that this computer was used to program the bombing in Hanoi, a bombing that killed thousands of civilians. For Lyotard, the destruction of this computer is justified. He discussed these matters with Jean-Loup Thébaut, who insisted that Lyotard should explain why he was opposed to the use of that computer. Upon this insistence, Lyotard, first of all, referred to his moral feelings. "If you asked me why I am on that side, I think that I would answer that I do not have an answer to the question 'why?' and that this is of the order of ... 'transcendence'. That is: here I feel a prescription to oppose a given thing, and I think that it is a just one. This is where I feel that I am playing the game of the just [...] Yes, I feel obliged with respect to the prescription that Americans should [get] out of Vietnam, or the French out of Algeria." In a further elucidation he, finally, had recourse to the Kantian Idea of the 'republic of reasonable beings': "If I were to be pushed, I would answer that what regulates this feeling of obligation is the Kantian Idea. The Americans in Vietnam, the French in Algeria, were doing something that prohibited that the whole of reasonable beings could continue to exist. In other words, the Viet-namese or the Algerians saw themselves placed in a position where the pragmatics of obligation was forbidden to them. They had the right to rebel."[71]

It is worth analyzing the way in which Lyotard employs the 'golden rule'. In its Kantian formulation it reads as follows: "Act in such a way that (*so dass*, says the German) the maxim of your will may serve as a principle of universal legislation."[72] In his comment on it Lyotard speci-fies: "The famous *so dass* [so that] of the imperative does not say: 'if you want to be this, then do that' [...] The *so dass* marks the properly reflec-tive use of judgment. It says: Do whatever, not on condition that, but *in such a way as* that which you do, the maxim of what you do, can always be valid as, etc. We are not dealing here with a determinant synthesis but with an Idea of human society [... This supersensible Idea] *does not* deter-mine *what* I have to do. It regulates me, but without telling me *what* there is to be done."[73] In his days Kant must have understood this regulation in a different way than Lyotard. Kant disallowed rebellion, which in his eyes was a self-defeating concept: rebellion can never lay the foundation of a rationally organized state, or a rationally organized world community. This disallowance is understandable: it is entirely in line with that which Lyotard eliminated from the Kantian program: the self-contained sub-stantial subject, with its urge to project an ultimately unified world.

Lyotard looks in a different manner at this regulation by the super-sensible Idea. For him, this supersensible Idea holds out the prospect of a pluralization of perspectives on a world scale. So, he has no problem

71. J.-F. Lyotard and J.-L. Thébaud, *Just Gaming*, 70. See Chapter Four: I.2.
72. *Ibid.*, 47. See Chapter Four: I.2.
73. *Ibid.*, 85. See Chapter Four: I.2.

with justifying a rebellion against a unifying center. Apparently his stay in Algeria led him to sympathize with the motives of the population in fighting for their independence from colonial rule: colonization by world powers cannot possibly be in accordance with the demands of justice (with a 'republic of reasonable beings'). It is from this background that Lyotard criticizes the presence of the American armed forces in Vietnam, and finds it legitimate that the RAF destroyed one of the computers that were used in Germany to program the bombing of Hanoi. He openly approves this 'terrorist' act. For him, it is a justified act of rebellion born from the felt obligation to combat the forces that obstruct the Vietnamese people's striving for self-determination, a self-determination that is promised and required by the regulative Idea of a 'republic of reasonable beings'.

(ii) *Debunking of false universalizations*. Lyotard realizes that the grand narratives are also products of a deliberation. Yet, instead of taking the supersensible Idea (the 'republic of reasonable beings') as a regulative norm, they regard this Idea as already fleshed out in history. They take, in other words, this Idea as if it were a realized fact. In doing so they fall prey to that which Kant termed *transcendental illusion*. For Kant, transcendental illusions must be avoided because they cause fanaticism and brutal eliminations. A handy instrument with which to debunk them is language pragmatics. Lyotard employs it in order to neatly separate phrases and regimens of phrases that must not be confused with one another. On this basis, he is able to disclose that whoever falls prey to transcendental illusion "confuses what can be presented as an object for a cognitive phrase and what can be presented as an object for a speculative and/or ethical phrase."[74] This confusion is, e.g., at work in Marx's usage of the term 'proletariat'. Marx coined this term to designate the rebellious workers in many European countries. These rebellious workers are an object for a cognitive phrase, but not for a speculative phrase. Marx, however, tied the object for a cognitive phrase to a speculative universalization; he jumped from this cognitive plane to a universal statement with ostensive power: 'When you look for a new universal class, here it is: the proletariat whose suffering is universal'. The rest of the story is well known: the party vanguard feels it has to steer the destiny of the universal class, in such a way that the empirically existing workers have no other choice than to comply with the dictates of the vanguard. The vanguard issues dictates because it deems its task to be that

---

74. J.-F. Lyotard, "The Sign of History," 399. See Chapter Five: II.

of safeguarding the purity of the speculative phrase and its implementation in real life.

The absorption of the cognitive phrase into the speculative phrase gives rise to totalizing absolutes. These can easily be detected, if one pays attention to their unjustifiable universalizations. The grand ideal they propose can never be deduced from empirical reality – it can not be found in empirical reality –; nonetheless it is, in its ideality, brandished as a slogan to rally people around the same program. Besides the "Marxist narrative of emancipation from exploitation," Lyotard also mentions "the *Aufklärer* narrative of emancipation from ignorance and servitude through knowledge and egalitarianism," and "the capitalist narrative of emancipation from poverty through technoindustrial development."[75] These grand narratives may clash with each other, but "in all of them, the givens arising from events are situated in the course of a history whose end, even if it remains beyond reach, is called universal freedom, the true fulfillment of all humanity."[76] In the face of these new absolutes, centered around the promise and attainment of '*universal* freedom' and the true fulfillment of *all humanity*, Lyotard exclaims: "War on totality. Let us attest to the unpresentable, let us activate the differends and save the honor of the name."[77]

For Lyotard, the confusion of the rules of the cognitive phrase and that of the speculative phrase does not occur at random. It presupposes a collective 'we' that – although it is only particular – arrogates to itself the right to speak in the name of the universal. An example in case of such a leap from the particular to the universal – and, consequently, from the cognitive to the speculative phrase – is the *Declaration of the Rights of Man and of the Citizen* (1789). Here an Assembly of the French nation declares itself entitled to issue a universal declaration of human rights. The enjoyment of civil rights in the new republic after the French Revolution was for the French citizens such a decisive step in the advance of civilization that a French Assembly deemed it necessary to solemnly declare that these rights are universal rights, to be shared by all humans on the globe. But again two entities are lumped together that cannot be equated: the particular, historical French nation and the whole of humanity (which is a speculative Idea). In order to resolve the tension between the two disparate entities, the name of the Supreme Being is invoked: "By soliciting its presence and by imploring its recommendation, the

---

75. J.-F. Lyotard, *The Postmodern Explained*, 25. See Chapter Five: II.

76. *Ibid.*, 25. See Chapter Five: II.

77. *Ibid.*, 16. See Chapter Five: II.

Assembly authorizes itself not only as French but also as human."[78] The fact that a French Assembly invokes the Supreme Being, the source of (modern) 'rationality', clothes these French addressors with the dignity of 'being human', of 'being the universally human': they feel entitled to represent the whole of humanity. Texts like these give us a vivid awareness of the type of universality that Lyotard seeks to discredit: the modern idea of universality whose universalizing logic of the 'speculative phrase' is of necessity also a logic of conquest.

(iii) *The refusal to stifle the differend*. I have already mentioned Lyotard's notion of the differend in the context of the Shoah. The differend is defined as follows: "A case of differend between two parties takes place when the 'regulation' of the conflict that opposes them is done in the idiom of one of the parties while the wrong suffered by the other is not signified in that idiom."[79] The survivors of the Shoah were not able to scientifically prove that the gas chambers in the concentration camps had been effectively used to kill the Jews, because the Germans had destroyed most of the documents that could serve as proof. Lyotard shares their impotence and speechlessness before the injustice done to them, and insists that these feelings should not be stifled. His reaction to the Shoah shows in an exemplary manner his siding with those who are put in the wrong because what they attempt to present as proof is not regarded as valid in the idiom of legalistic jurisprudence.

With this methodology Lyotard struck a chord in activists who speak up for minorities that are threatened in their existence by the Western 'speculative phrase' of conquest. David Carroll puts it as follows: "The *differend* has as its critical-political goal the uncovering of *differends* where they have been repressed or supposedly resolved; it argues for the necessity of listening to the idiom not given its day in court, to the silence imposed on the victims of oppression and injustice. It attacks all mechanisms of repression, all courts, institutions, systems of thought that perpetrate the injustice of universal judgment and thus do not recognize the silence imposed on their victims."[80] What Carroll terms here the injustice of a universal judgment has in fact nothing to do with Kant's reflective judgment. It is a judgment that derives its alleged legitimacy from a set of juridical notions that are part of the Western cognitive system, whereas Lyotard, with Kant, has shown that ethical obligation cannot be

78. J.-F. Lyotard, *The Differend*, Declaration of 1789, 5. See Chapter Five: II.
79. *Ibid.*, no 12, p. 9. See Chapter Four: II.
80. D. Carroll, "Rephrasing the Political with Kant and Lyotard: From Aesthetics to Political Judgment," *Diacritics*, Vol. 14, No 3 (1984) 78. See Chapter Five: III.3.

derived from cognitive constructs. Whoever happens to witness how the procedures of courts also may make victims with their cognitive apparatus, must feel saddened, a sadness which, as a 'sublime' feeling, testifies to the 'unpresentable'.

Examples of the differend can be multiplied. They often relate to the insensitivity Western people have developed in their dealings with other cultures. Westerners take it for granted that their collective 'we' is a universal 'we', a 'we' that is put forth as representing the whole of humanity. Through the manipulation of the language game, Westerners have come to present their norms as universally binding norms. It is time that we admit that such manipulation is deceptive and unfair, that it blocks the break-through of a 'justice of multiplicity'. In his article 'Pagans, Perverts or Primitives?' Bill Readings analyses, in the style of Lyotard, the conflict that Herzog evoked in his film 'Where the Green Ants Dream'. In the film, an Australian mining company and an Aboriginal tribe are locked in a conflict over land. The aborigines are not able to give 'proof', acceptable in Western jurisprudence, for their claim to 'property rights' over the land. The only elements they can adduce as proof are some wooden objects carved with undecipherable markings, but these objects do not make any sense to the Western mind: they cannot be regarded as legal documents. The aborigines are thus silenced. They are not able to express themselves in the Western idiom of jurisprudence and legality; moreover they are separated by a gulf from the mentality of the Western occupants. For them, the land is not just a territory 'on which' they live and which they treat merely as a 'natural resource'. Land is sacred, and the sacredness of the land is, in fact, the basis for the sacredness of the people themselves. This view sharply contrasts with the Western notion of land as a commodity, something that can be successively utilized for many purposes, mining included. It is impossible for them to grasp the abstract notion of space that goes hand in hand with legal possession, which in turn puts the land in the service of industrialization and development.

* * *

Derrida's philosophical background significantly differs from that of Lyotard. Whereas Lyotard's enlarged Kantianism led him to debunk the unjustified universalizations that followed from a confusion of ideality and real life (confusion of the 'ought' and the 'is'), Derrida's critical dialogue with phenomenology sensitized him to the study of concrete items, such as true justice, true democracy, the purity of the gift, of forgiveness, and hospitality. This focus on concrete items is typical of the various schools of phenomenology. One ought only to think of Max Scheler's phenomenological analysis of 'Repentance and Rebirth' or of Merleau-Ponty's phenomenology of bodily existence. This focus also remains in place when Derrida seeks to go beyond phenomenology so as to reach out for 'impossible things to come', which are in each case specified. Sometimes the choice of these topics depended on an invitation to deliver a key-note address at a conference, such as the conference organized by the Cardozo Law School or that on the Legacy of Marx. To the former we owe his reflection on the link between deconstruction and justice; the latter resulted in a reflection on the evacuation of true democracy in the era of globalization. Conspicuous in these reflections is the deconstructive, revolutionary undertone with which Derrida criticizes the European law system and international legal agreements. Other topics, such as the gift, hospitality and forgiveness, are rather of his own choice, and reveal his return to Jewish sources. Given the positive content of these topics, Derrida's treatment of them is less deconstructive, and rather inspired by a yearning for a quasi-unattainable purity. A separate presentation of the more general topics and the typically Jewish ones is therefore in order. Much more than Lyotard, Derrida will corroborate his position with the help of, and in confrontation with, existing studies on the topic in question.

1. *The more general topics.* In his key-note address at the Cardozo Law School, Derrida raised the question as to the possible link between deconstruction and the desire for justice. The answer is: yes, that link exists. Deconstruction questions the self-assurance of the legal order, and speaks up for a justice that is threatened in its existence by the rigid enforcement of the law: true justice is "without economic circularity, without calculation, and without rules, without reason and without rationality. We can recognize in it, indeed, accuse, identify a madness [...] And deconstruction [...] is mad about this kind of justice. Mad about this desire for justice."[81] The statement that the desire for justice, is 'without rules' is reminiscent of Lyotard's insistence on a deliberation that, in line with Kant's reflective judgment, is in search of its rules. Yet, for Derrida, this search for the rules is marked by an urge to decide. Just as for Kierkegaard to whom he refers, the instant of decision – of a just decision – is pure madness; it is always a precipitation in advance of what is

---

81. J. Derrida, "Force of Law: The 'Mystical' Foundation of Authority," *Cardozo Law Review* 11 (1990) 965. See Chapter Nine: II.3.

reasonable, driven by urgency, and "acting in the night of non-knowledge and no rule. Not [in the night] of the absence of rules and knowledge but [in the night] of a reinstitution of rules which by definition is not preceded by any knowledge or by any guarantee as such."[82] This is the agony one experiences when trying to live up to the demands of an 'impossible justice'.

Derrida is rather skeptical about the merits of legal justice. It, first of all, is unable to do justice to each and every single person, because the rule of law is enshrined in universal categories; and second, on close inspection, the legal system tends only to do justice to itself. At this juncture Derrida quotes the saying of Montaigne "Laws keep up their good standing, not because they are just, but because they are laws: that is the mystical foundation of their authority, they have no other."[83] In a further elucidation of this 'mystical foundation' Derrida points to the violent origin of the laws, the modern European laws in particular: they all have been instituted to consolidate one or another of the nation's victories over its adversaries: "Since the origin of authority, the foundation or ground, the position of the law can't by definition rest on anything else but themselves, they are themselves a violence without ground."[84] Derrida borrows the notion of violence from Walter Benjamin's 'Critique of the Force of Law' ('Zur Kritik der Gewalt'). Benjamin drew a distinction between the 'law-instituting force' and the 'law-preserving force'. For him, the former bases its authority on violence, in order to defend and consolidate the achievements of the new regime established through warfare, whereas the latter insures the permanence and enforceability of law, and is thus less marked by the recourse to violence. Derrida, however, questions this neat separation. For him, also the law-preserving law has a violent character. This becomes evident when one watches the behavior of policemen, something which Benjamin eventually did at the end of his research: "One would expect policemen to merely enforce the existing laws, and in doing so maintain 'law and order'. But today the police are no longer content to enforce the law, and thus to conserve it; they invent it, they publish ordinances, they intervene whenever the legal situation isn't clear to guarantee security. These days which is to say nearly all the time."[85]

---

82. *Ibid.*, 968-969. See Chapter Nine: II.3.

83. *Ibid.*, 939, quoting Montaigne, *Essais III, XIII, De l'expérience*, Pleiade, 1203. See Chapter Nine: II.2.

84. J. Derrida, "Force of Law," 943. See Chapter Nine: II.2.

85. W. Benjamin, "Zur Kritik der Gewalt," *Archiv für Sozialwissenschaften und Sozialpolitik* (1921) 286, quoted in J. Derrida, "The Force of Law," 1007. See Chapter Nine: III.1.

In modern times the police behave like lawmakers. In his later considerations about the right to asylum, Derrida will also call attention to the role
of the police in the harassment of unwanted strangers.

In the above considerations Derrida sketched a 'genealogy' of the
authority behind the enactment of the law. He is convinced that such a
deconstructive approach will make a great many readers alert to the clash
between legality and the justice one expects to be done to every single
person. It is this clash that awakens a longing for true justice – of a notion
of justice that no longer functions as a Kantian regulative Idea that opens
a horizon of expectancy, but of an 'impossible' justice to come, radically
beyond the contours of what one would expect to be possible: "It is
because of this structural urgency and precipitation of justice that the latter has no horizon of expectancy (regulative or messianic[86]). But for this
very reason, it may have an *avenir*, a 'to come'." And, he adds: "it is precisely because justice has the pure quality of 'to come' that it will be able
to transform and to recast the juridical and political concepts we inherited from the past."[87] Without the uprooting notion of an excess of justice (excess when compared to legal justice) a transformation of the juridical concepts will not be possible. That is the reason why Derrida insists
on entering a discussion with specialists in jurisprudence, in order to
negotiate with them revisions in the legal system: "We must calculate,
negotiate the relation between the calculable [the legal system] and the
incalculable [the 'impossible' justice to come], and negotiate without
[being in possession of] the sort of rule that still will have to be invented
there where we are cast, there where we find ourselves."[88] Such a discussion will include pressing world-problems, such as the question of
human rights, and other areas of social justice and emancipation. Just as
it took centuries before the Western nations revoked the existing laws on
slavery – a revocation that would not have seen the light of day without
so many activists' commitment to this 'impossible' dream – so, too, it
may take still decades before respect for human rights, in all its aspects,
will be accepted by the world community.

In his key-note address at the conference on Marx's legacy, Derrida
further explores the clash between legality and the desire for an 'impossible justice' on a world scale. Inspired by Marx's prophetic side (and not

86. 'Messianic' is understood here as 'flowing from messianism'. For the distinction
between religious messianism and Derrida's universal notion of messianicity, see Chapter
Ten: I.4.
87. J. Derrida, "Force of Law," 969. See Chapter Nine: II.3.
88. *Ibid.*, 971. See Chapter Nine: II.3.

by the Marx of the unitary thought form that steers that 'partyform' organization) he pleads for the creation of a New International that would
gather people from various social strata and races around the same ideal
– people who will live and act across nations, without national community, without a common belonging to a class or ethnic group, without a
contract, without a stable organization, without title or name, even without citizenship. What will unite them is a 'counter-conjuration' against
those who yield power in the globalized world. Derrida himself sets the
tone of this counter-conjuration. He contests the thesis of Fukuyama's
book *The End of History* according to which no alternative is left to the
triumph of capitalism in its conjunction with liberal democracy. Against
Fukuyama he argues that liberal democracy is indifferent to the rights of
minorities or the plight of people living in dire poverty. Precisely in the
era of globalization the scandal is that "[n]ever have violence, inequality, exclusion, famine, and thus economic oppression affected as many
human beings in the history of the earth and of humanity [...] Never have
so many men, women, and children been subjugated, starved, or exterminated on the earth."[89]

In the face of these injustices Derrida develops his messianic dream of
an 'impossible' democracy to come, one that is no longer ruled by an
international law system and jurisprudence that safeguard the interests
of the rich countries. It is, thus, imperative that one continue to criticize
the existing international law and its institutions for their lack of impartiality in that they are predisposed to give preferential treatment to persons and nations with strong financial support. Derrida does not tire, in
a Marxian spirit, of criticizing "the presumed autonomy of the juridical,
[...] and the *de facto* take-over of international authorities by powerful
nation states, by concentrations of techno-scientific capital and private
capital." And he concludes: "A 'New International' is being sought
through these crises of international law; it already denounces the limits
of a discourse on human rights that will remain inadequate, sometimes
hypocritical, and in any case formalistic and inconsistent with itself as
long as the law of the market, the 'foreign debt', the inequality of techno-
science, the military [...] prevail."[90] Just as in his key-note address at the
Cardozo Law School he insists on a "profound transformation, projected
over a long term, of international law, of its concepts, and its field of
intervention."[91] This profound transformation must go hand in hand with

89. J. Derrida, *Specters of Marx*, 85. See Chapter Ten: I.3.
90. *Ibid.*, 84. See Chapter Ten: I.3.
91. *Ibid.*, 85. See Chapter Ten: I.3.

a further diversification of the human rights, such as the right to work or economic rights, and the rights of women and children, rights to be respected in "the *worldwide* economic and social field, beyond the sovereignty of states."[92]

2. *Typically Jewish topics*. A typically Jewish topic is, without doubt, the notion of the gift with the qualification of pure gratuity Derrida attaches to it: a gift without economic circularity and without profit calculation. In fact, Derrida already had this notion in mind when defining true justice as a justice "without economic circularity, without calculation, and without rules, without reason and without rationality –"[93] a justice at the other side of legal stipulations that mirror the self-interest of the juridical apparatus. His systematic reflection on the gift, however, must be placed in the context of his critical assessment of Marcel Mauss's study, *The Gift: the Form and Reason for Exchange in Archaic Societies* (1950). In this assessment Derrida distanced himself from the schema 'gift, debt, and counter gift' that is in vogue in ancient tribes. For him, "Marcel Mauss's *The Gift* speaks of everything but the gift: It deals with economy, exchange, contract (*do ut des*); it speaks of raising the stakes, sacrifice, gift *and* counter gift – in short, everything that in the thing itself impels the gift *and* the annulment of the gift."[94] It is this confrontation with Mauss that occasioned him to develop an aphanology of the gift: the pure gift cannot phenomenologically appear without annulling its gratuitous character. Yet, as I showed in the second part of this General Conclusion, the overcoming of phenomenology was for Derrida also a homecoming to the Jewish roots of 'listening'. That is the reason why I term Derrida's 'gift of the excess' a typically Jewish topic. Indeed, for Derrida, one's commitment to the 'impossible gift' is "is a matter – desire beyond desire – of responding faithfully but also as rigorously as possible to the injunction or the order of the *gift* ('give')."[95]

Derrida will certainly not deny that the gratuitous gift is also a central topic in the New Testament, although in his discussion with Marion he suspects the Christian notion of the gift of revelation of still being contaminated with the logic of the counter gift: Marion's attempt at giving Christian revelation a phenomenological status points, for him, in that

direction.[96] This discussion shows, again, that Derrida with his aphanology – the pure gift never appears – tries "to find a place where a new discourse and a new politics could be possible,"[97] a discourse and a politics
that will be truly universal. His considerations about giving hospitality to
strangers makes this clear.

Already his treatment of 'democracy to come' in the age of globalization showed Derrida's interest in genuine cosmopolitanism. In order to
define true hospitality he, first of all, examines what Kant has to say about
it. In his *Third Definitive Article for a Perpetual Peace*, Kant writes:
"Cosmopolitan right shall be limited to conditions of universal hospitality."[98] For Kant, hospitality should, to be sure, be universal, but restricted
by conditions. So too, will a cosmopolitan right to visit an alien country
be restricted by conditions that are based on interstate agreements.
At this juncture Derrida asks the question as to how one has to treat stateless people, or immigrants that face the impossibility of obtaining legal
documents: should they simply be denied hospitality? Derrida learned
the pertinence of this question from Hannah Arendt, who already in the
mid-1930s had taken to heart the cause of exiles and stateless people,
victims of the First World War, in a period of time when no international
charters of the right to asylum existed. In her *The Origins of Totalitarianism* Arendt argued that the idea of asylum for illegal immigrants "transcends the *present sphere of international law which still operates in
terms of reciprocal agreements and treaties between sovereign states*."[99]
With his notion of unconditional hospitality, which is as 'impossible' a
reality as the 'impossible' gift, Derrida aims at bringing about "historical evolutions, effective revolutions, progress, in short a perfectibility [of
the laws]."[100]

Inspired by Levinas, who wrote a book about *The Cities of Refuge* in
ancient Israel, Derrida, together with the Parliament of Writers, pleads for
the creation of 'Cities of Refuge' in which strangers are given asylum. In
these cities harassment by the police would no longer be possible. The

96. See Chapter Nine: I.2.
97. R. Kearny, "On the Gift," 76. See Chapter Nine: I.2.
98. J. Derrida, "Hospitality," *Jacques Derrida: Basic Writings*, ed. B. Stocker (London
and New York: Routledge, 2007) 243, quoting from I. Kant, *Political Writings*, ed.
H.S. Riess, trans. H.B. Nisbet (Cambridge: Cambridge University Press, 1991). See Chapter Ten: II.1.
99. Hannah Arendt, *The Origins of Totalitarianism* (London: George Allen and Unwin
Ltd, 1967) 285 quoted in J. Derrida, "On Cosmopolitanism," in idem *On Cosmopolitanism
and Forgiveness*, trans. M. Dooley and M. Hughes (London and New York, Routledge,
1997) 8. See Chapter Ten: II.2.
100. J. Derrida and A. Dufourmantelle, *De l'hospitalité* (Paris: Calmann-Lévy, 1997)
131 [translation mine]. See Chapter Ten: II.1.

charter of the 'Cities of Refuge' would "restrict the legal powers and scope of the police by giving them a purely administrative role under the strict control and regulation of certain political authorities, who will see to it that human rights and a more broadly defined right to asylum are respected."[101] The ethos to be developed in these cities is a welcoming without reserve: "welcoming salutation accorded in advance to the absolute surprise of the *arrivant* from whom or from which one will not ask anything in return and who or which will not be asked to commit to the domestic contract of any welcoming power (family, state, nation, territory, native soil or blood, language, culture in general, even humanity), *just* opening which renounces any right to property, any right in general."[102]

A third typically Jewish topic is Derrida's notion of 'impossible forgiveness'. From the outset he places this notion in the context of an international recognition, in the wake of the Nuremberg Tribunal, of 'crimes against humanity'. Derrida welcomes the fact that a prime minister of Japan and a French president both asked pardon for the crimes their countries committed during the Second World War, and also that an event could take place such as the 'Truth and Reconciliation Commission' in South-Africa. At the same time he warns against a politization of forgiveness: Excuses are proffered in order to bring about reconciliation among or within the nations. Yet, such a finality takes the edge off the gratuity of forgiveness: "The language of forgiveness, at the service of determined finalities, [is] anything but pure and disinterested. As always in the field of politics."[103] For Derrida forgiveness must go beyond calculation: Pure forgiveness is unconditional and without any regard for retribution. That unconditionality is part of the Abrahamic tradition. That is the reason why Derrida repudiates the thesis of Jankélévitch that the atrocities of the Shoah are unforgivable because the Germans do no show any sign of remorse. To this thesis Derrida retorts: "Yes, there is the unforgivable. Is this not, in truth, the only thing to forgive? The only thing that calls for forgiveness."[104] This statement encapsulates the whole of Derrida's thought on forgiveness: for him, true forgiveness instead of denying the unforgivable, fully acknowledges it. It is only the awareness of the "unforgivable evil that would make the question of [true] forgiveness emerge."[105]

* * *

101. J. Derrida, "On Cosmopolitanism," 14-15. See Chapter Ten: II.2.
102. J. Derrida, *Specters of Marx*, 65. See Chapter Ten: I.4.
103. J. Derrida, "On Forgiveness," 31. See Chapter Ten: III.2.
104. *Ibid.*, 32. See Chapter Ten: III.2.
105. *Ibid.*, 49. See Chapter Ten: III.2.

I began this General Conclusion by asking whether a political ethics is still possible in the postmodern setting. When looking back at the various topics around which Derrida and Lyotard elaborated their political ethics, the answer is undeniably: yes, such a political ethics remains possible. These two philosophers are, to be sure, 'postmodern' in their own right: their criticism is primarily directed against Western imperialism and the legal apparatus of jurisprudence that is part of the modern nation state. They also react to this domination in their own respective manner. Lyotard voices a strong protest against the Western grand narratives of conquest, but he also realizes the fragility of this protest. In spite of his strong commitment he seems to reckon with a possible defeat, which in turn will fuel his persuasion that he must go on bearing witness to the Idea – that the Idea of a life of human dignity is not lost. This witnessing may take on the form of a speechless sadness that cries to heaven, but which continues to hope that once a better idiom may be found to convince the stronger party in the differend about the truthfulness of the testimony of the weaker party. Lyotard's political ethics is marked by a reflexivity that is emblematic of the old Occident. Compared to Lyotard, Derrida profiles himself as a cheerful revolutionary, who believes in the perfectibility of the legal system world-wide. For him, there is no need to testify to the lost Idea, so that it may again return and earn recognition. The injunction he receives from the purity of the 'impossible Idea to come' is so powerful that he has no doubt about its final effectiveness. The 'impossible' Ideas of justice, democracy, hospitality and forgiveness are so inspiring, precisely because of their non-appearance in empirical reality, that they are deemed to be able to drastically change the existing state of affairs. Derrida is convinced that without these 'impossible' Ideas, we would not know how to proceed more correctly in matters of justice, hospitality etc. Derrida is a philosopher and activist of radical change, to be carried out on the international scene of a genuine cosmopolitan civilization 'to come'.

INDEX

abolition of slavery, 310
aboriginals, 113, 168-170, 394
Abrahamic tradition
  a-theological reception of, 333-334, 354
  roots of messianic hope, 334-335
  too regional, 298, 335
  unconditional forgiveness, 321, 360, 363, 401
  unconditional hospitality, 321, 350, 355
  see also Derrida's messianicity
absolute
  carries thought to its limits, 85-86
  felt presence of the, 41, 82-83
  human vocation to think the, 82
  totalizing absolutes, 156, 392
Adorno, Theodor
  Auschwitz invalidates Hegel, 44, 370
  metaphysics in its fall, 131, 149
  micrologies, 131
advance in civilization
  apology for crimes against humanity, 357
  forgiving the unforgivable, 364
  heterogeneous pluralization, 58, 66-67, 96, 170
  multiculturalism, 171, 347
  refusal to grant impunity, 364
  search for new idioms, 114, 171
African National Congress, 363
Algerian Front of National Liberation, XXI-XXII, 63, 110
alliance
  abstract painting and, 133, 141, 380
  passivity and listening, 121, 246, 380
  remembering the, 100, 121, 124, 140, 381
  shock of the, 100, 129, 140, 381, 390
  see also covenant
Allison, David, 180, 258
Alsace-Loraine, 159
American Synagogue Architecture Exhibition, 134

Angelus Silesius
  imagery of the desert, 297, 335
  precursor of *khôra*?, 297, 387
anti-globalists, 321, 330-331
aphanology
  in Derrida, XXIX, 371, 375, 399
  of the gift, 282, 284, 375, 399-400
  in Heidegger, 203, 284
  in Levinas, 248, 375
Arendt, Hannah, 77, 345, 355-356, 362, 400
Aristotle
  cosmological time, 213
  Metaphysics, 195
  political judgment, 103
Artaud, Antonin, 219
a-temporal anteriority
  khôra, place of disturbance, 132, 273, 296, 387
  Lacan's 'thing', 132
  spacing, 274
  see also khôra
Attridge, Derek, XXII
Augustin, St., 296
Auschwitz
  denial of gas chambers, 100, 114-116, 142, 381, 393
  feeling left by, 100, 114-117, 381
  scandal of, XXVII, 21, 28, 44, 54, 119-120, 136, 319-320, 378
  see also final solution; Shoah
avant-garde painters
  evocation of the unpresentable, 129, 151, 379
  is it happening?, 131-132, 135, 138, 142, 164, 171
  non-figurative painting, 133, 141
  suspending 'now' (Burke), 129, 132, 142
  see also Newman, Barnett

Baader-Meinhof Gang, 109
Barron, Anne, 168
Bauman, Zygmunt, XXV, 11-12, 365

Bayerische Rundfunk, 219
Beardsworth, Richard, 15, 23, 90-91
beautiful
    death, 100, 117-120
    harmonious feelings, 27
    interplay 'imagination' 'indeterminate concept', 27, 75
    purposiveness without purpose,30
Ben Aknoun, Algeria, XXI
Benjamin, Andrew, 15, 43, 53, 67
Benjamin, Walter
    apocalyptic interruption, 281, 311, 318-320
    beyond legality, 317
    divine violence, 318-319
    final solution, 318-320
    law-instituting and law-preserving force, 312-313, 315
    Marxist messanism, 311, 320
    recourse to God above reason, 317
    repressive police, 312, 314-315, 346, 396
    respect for the living, 318
    Zur Kritik der Gewalt, 281, 300, 311-319, 396
Bennington, Geoffrey, XXII, 143
Benveniste, Émile, 339
Bernet, Rudolf, 222, 235, 242
bio-engineering, 310
Blanchot, Maurice, 194
Bloechl, Jeffrey, 267, 374
Böhme, Hartmut, 35
Boeve, Lieven, 98
Bonaparte, Napoléon, 313
Borradori, Giovanna, 351-353
Bosnia, 357, 364
Braque, Georges, 151
Brito, Emilio, 203
Budapest 1956, 44-45, 58, 67, 378
Budick, Sanford, 275
Burke, Edmund, 31, 35, 101, 130-132, 142, 165

Canadian universities, 4, 15
capitalism
    affinity with the sublime, XXV
    battle for domination, 159, 324
    calculating rationality, XXVI, 69, 159
    consensus theory and, 149

free market, 321-322, 377
great business companies, 330
impact on everything, 63
insensitivity to Ideas, 70, 136, 162
protectionism, 328
space-time contraction and, 70, 135-136
Caputo, John, XXIV, 266-267, 289-291, 308, 334-335, 371-372
Cardoso Law Review, 299
Cardoso Law School, New York, 281, 298, 305, 395
Carroll, David, 106, 111, 167, 393
Cashinahua, 104, 156
categorical imperative
    defies experience, 106, 380
    does not tell: do this, 65, 108, 139, 166, 390
    maxim of my action 'universalizable', 99, 107-108, 139, 390
    not deducible from theory, 103-107, 138, 379
    see also Kantian Idea of freedom; republic of reasonable beings
Cerisy-la-Salle, 183, 222
Cézanne, Paul, 151
Chechnya, 357, 364
Chirac, Jacques, 322, 357-359
Christian revelation, 277-278, 291, 296-298, 335, 399
Christianity, 155, 297, 326, 334-335, 350-352, 354, 360, 363, 371
cities of refuge, 321, 344, 347-349, 400-401
Cold War, 356, 362
Collège international de philosophie, XXIV
colonialism, XX-XXII, 113, 169, 341-342, 357, 390
community of taste
    emotional undertone, 78-79
    Hannah Arendt on, 77-78
    judgment of taste, 31, 78
    no affective consensus, 59, 78, 367
    role of singular models, 59, 62, 367
    sensus communis diversified, 59, 80, 120, 367
    sensus communis signals Idea of Reason, 81-82, 367-368
Constantine, Algeria, XX

BIBLIOTHECA EPHEMERIDUM THEOLOGICARUM LOVANIENSIUM

SERIES III

151. B. DOYLE, *The Apocalypse of Isaiah Metaphorically Speaking.A Study of the Use, Function and Significance of Metaphors in Isaiah 24-27*, 2000. XII-453 p. 75 €

152. T.MERRIGAN & J.HAERS (eds.), *The Myriad Christ.Plurality and the Quest for Unity inContemporary Christology*, 2000.XIV-593 p. 75 €

153. M.SIMON, *Le catéchisme de Jean-Paul II.Genèse et évaluation de son commentaire du Symbole des apôtres*, 2000. XVI-688 p. 75 €

154. J. VERMEYLEN, *La loi du plus fort. Histoire de la rédaction des récits davidiques de 1 Samuel 8 à 1 Rois 2*, 2000. XIII-746 p. 80 €

155. A. WÉNIN (ed.), *Studies in the Book of Genesis. Literature, Redaction and History*, 2001. XXX-643 p. 60 €

156. F. LEDEGANG, *Mysterium Ecclesiae. Images of the Church and its Members in Origen*, 2001. XVII-848 p. 84 €

157. J.S. BOSWELL, F.P. MCHUGH & J. VERSTRAETEN (eds.), *Catholic Social Thought: Twilight of Renaissance*, 2000. XXII-307 p. 60 €

158. A. LINDEMANN (ed.), *The Sayings Source Q and the Historical Jesus*, 2001. XXII-776 p. 60 €

159. C. HEMPEL, A. LANGE & H. LICHTENBERGER (eds.), *The Wisdom Texts from Qumran and the Development of Sapiential Thought*, 2002. XII-502 p. 80 €

160. L. BOEVE & L. LEIJSSEN (eds.), *Sacramental Presence in a Postmodern Context*, 2001. XVI-382 p. 60 €

161. A. DENAUX (ed.), *New Testament Textual Criticism and Exegesis. Festschrift J. Delobel*, 2002. XVIII-391 p. 60 €

162. U. BUSSE, *Das Johannesevangelium. Bildlichkeit, Diskurs und Ritual. Mit einer Bibliographie über den Zeitraum 1986-1998*, 2002. XIII-572 p. 70 €

163. J.-M. AUWERS & H.J. DE JONGE (eds.), *The Biblical Canons*, 2003. LXXXVIII-718 p. 60 €

164. L. PERRONE (ed.), *Origeniana Octava. Origen and the Alexandrian Tradition*, 2003. XXV-X-1406 p. 180 €

165. R. BIERINGER, V. KOPERSKI & B. LATAIRE (eds.), *Resurrection in the New Testament. Festschrift J. Lambrecht*, 2002. XXXI-551 p. 70 €

166. M. LAMBERIGTS & L. KENIS (eds.), *Vatican II and Its Legacy*, 2002. XII-512 p. 65 €

167. P. DIEUDONNÉ, *La Paix clémentine. Défaite et victoire du premier jansénisme français sous le pontificat de Clément IX (1667-1669)*, 2003. XXXIX-302 p. 70 €

168. F. GARCÍA MARTÍNEZ, *Wisdom and Apocalypticism in the Dead Sea Scrolls and in the Biblical Tradition*, 2003. XXXIV-491 p. 60 €

169. D. OGLIARI, *Gratia et Certamen: The Relationship between Grace and Free Will in the Discussion of Augustine with the So-Called Semipelagians*, 2003. LVII-468 p. 75 €

170. G. COOMAN, M. VAN STIPHOUT & B. WAUTERS (eds.), *Zeger-Bernard Van Espen at the Crossroads of Canon Law, History, Theology and Church-State Relations*,2003. XX-530 p. 80 €

171. B. BOURGINE, *L'herméneutique théologique de Karl Barth.Exégèse et dogmatique dans le quatrième volume de la Kirchliche Dogmatik*, 2003. XXII-548 p. 75 €

172. J. HAERS & P. DE MEY (eds.), *Theology and Conversation: Towards a Relational Theology*, 2003. XIII-923 p. 90 €

218. G. Van Belle – J.G. van der Watt – J. Verheyden (eds.), *Miracles and Imagery in Luke and John. Festschrift Ulrich Busse*, 2008. XVIII-287 p.
78 €

219. L. Boeve – M. Lamberigts – M.Wisse (eds.), *Augustine and Postmodern Thought: A New Alliance against Modernity?*, 2009. XVIII-277 p.   80 €

220. T. Victoria, *Un livre de feu dans un siècle de fer: Les lectures de l'Apocalypse dans la littérature française de la Renaissance*, 2009. XXX-609 p.   85 €

221. A.A. den Hollander – W. François (eds.), *Infant Milk or Hardy Nourishment? The Bible for Lay People and Theologians in the Early Modern Period*, 2009. XVIII-488 p.   80 €

222. F.D. Vansina, *Paul Ricœur. Bibliographie primaire et secondaire. Primary and Secundary Bibliography 1935-2008*, Compiled and updated in collaboration with P. Vande Casteele, 2008. XXX-621 p.   80 €

223. G. Van Belle – M. Labahn – P. Maritz (eds.), *Repetitions and Variations in the Fourth Gospel: Style, Text, Interpretation*, 2009. XII-712 p.   85 €

224. H. Ausloos – B. Lemmelijn – M. Vervenne (eds.), *Florilegium Lovaniense: Studies in Septuagint and Textual Criticism in Honour of Florentino García Martínez*, 2008. XVI-564 p.   80 €.

225A-B. E. Brito, *Philosophie moderne et christianisme*, 2010. VIII-1514 p.
130 €.

226. U. Schnelle (ed.), *The Letter to the Romans*, 2009. XVIII-894 p.   85 €.

227. M. Lamberigts – L. Boeve – T. Merrigan in collaboration with D. Claes – M. Wisse (eds.), *Orthodoxy, Process and Product*, 2009. X-416 p.   74 €.

228. G. Heidl – R. Somos (eds.), *Origeniana nona: Origen and the Religious Practice of His Time*, 2009. XIV-752 p.   95 €.

229. D. Marguerat (ed.), *Reception of Paulinism in Acts – Réception du paulinisme dans les Actes des Apôtres*, 2009. VIII-340 p.   74 €.

230. A. Dillen – D. Pollefeyt (eds.), *Children's Voices: Children's Perspectives in Ethics, Theology and Religious Education*, 2010. X-450 p.   72 €.

231. P. Van Hecke – A. Labahn (eds.), *Metaphors in the Psalms*, 2010.
Forthcoming.

232. G. Auld – E. Eynikel (eds.), *For and Against David: Story and History in the Books of Samuel*, 2010.   Forthcoming.

233. C. Vialle, *Une analyse comparée d'Esther TM et LXX: Regard sur deux récits d'une même histoire*, 2010.   Forthcoming.

234. T. Merrigan – F. Glorieux (eds.), *"Godhead Here in Hiding": Incarnation and the History of Human Suffering*, 2010.   Forthcoming.

235. M. Simon, *La vie dans le Christ dans le catéchisme de Jean-Paul II*, 2010.
Forthcoming.

PRINTED ON PERMANENT PAPER • IMPRIME SUR PAPIER PERMANENT • GEDRUKT OP DUURZAAM PAPIER - ISO 9706

N.V. PEETERS S.A., WAROTSTRAAT 50, B-3020 HERENT